Social Deviance

edited by

Erich Goode

State University of New York at Stony Brook

Allyn and Bacon

Boston • London • Toronto • Sydney • Tokyo • Singapore

Executive Editor: *Karen Hanson*
Editorial Assistant: *Jennifer Jacobson*
Cover Administrator: *Suzanne Harbison*
Composition Buyer: *Linda Cox*
Manufacturing Buyer: *Aloka Rathnam*
Marketing Manager: *Joyce Nilsen*
Production Coordinator: *Deborah Brown*
Editorial-Production Service: *P. M. Gordon Associates*

A Simon & Schuster Company
Needham Heights, MA 02194

Library of Congress Cataloging-in-Publication Data

Social Deviance / edited by Erich Goode.
p. cm.
Includes bibliographical references.
ISBN 0–205–16583–4
1. Deviant behavior. I. Goode, Erich.
HM291.S5874 1995
302.5'42—dc20 95–15294
CIP

Printed in the United States of America

10 9 8 7 6 5 4 3 2 1 00 99 98 97 96

Contents

PART IV: Forms of Deviance 217

Preface

Deviance is both a phenomenon in the social world and a subject of study. *Deviance* is simply a departure from a given norm; exactly what or who is considered deviant depends on which norm we are talking about. It is almost certain that ever since humans began living in groups, rules defining acceptable and unacceptable behavior and their characteristics have been laid down and that as soon as these rules were promulgated, they were violated. When this happened, some members of these human collectivities undoubtedly began wondering about what *caused* this deviation from the prescribed norm. Hence, in all likelihood, speculation on what has been regarded as wrongdoing has been going on for many millennia.

Until the past thirty years or so nearly all this speculation was based on the assumption that the cause of the wrongdoing required an explanation. The "Why?" question almost always meant: *Why do they do it?* Either: What is it about these *persons* that causes them to engage in deviance? Or: What *conditions* cause some people to deviate? The rule that defined the deviation was assumed to be valid and was taken as a kind of constant, not in need of an explanation. Ever since travelers have returned home from lands all over the world, we have known that different societies have different rules and norms; that is, we have been aware of cultural *relativism* for hundreds of years. This has not stopped some observers from thinking that their own society's rules are correct and those of other societies are in error.

Thus, most of us who speculate about deviation from social norms do not stop to ask some very fundamental questions—ones even more basic than the "Why do they do it?" question; questions regarding the basis of *the rules themselves.* Some of the questions this orientation asks include: "Why are certain rules laid down in the first place?" "Which rules are laid down?" "Whose rules are they?" "Who has the power to define the norms and their violation?" "Who, and what, is designated as deviant?" "What characteristics are regarded as deviant?" "What happens to someone who is singled out as deviant?" "What is the nature of the punishment that results from a particular definition of wrongdoing?" "How do members of the society keep wrongdoing—and wrongdoers—in line?" This second set of questions is very different from those that take the validity of the rules for granted. These questions look at deviance as a social construct and not a concrete phenomenon in the real world that requires an explanation.

The sociology of deviance, prior to thirty years ago, that focused mainly on the earlier "Why do they do it?" question, has traditionally asked questions such as: Why do some individuals violate society's rules while the rest of us do not? What is *different* about them? Are there "kinds of people" who are especially attracted to deviating from the norms? Or, do certain social conditions encourage some individuals to violate the norms? Is it certain societies, or the circumstances in which some of us live, that encourage deviance? Or, perhaps, are there specific groups or social categories in which deviation is more likely to take place than in others? Why crime, homosexuality, delinquency, alcoholism, drug abuse, rape, mental illness? This approach has been referred to by a variety of terms, including *positivism, objectivism, determinism,* and *essentialism*. A central assumption of this approach is that social reality can be studied in much the same way as the natural world of biology, chemistry, and physics.

The questions that this approach asks are perfectly valid questions, and a great deal of evidence has been generated to suggest possible or likely answers to them. But, again, these questions assume that it is deviation from specific norms that requires an explanation. Why not examine the construction and the application of these norms as well? Do other societies accept or tolerate—or encourage—homosexual behavior? Why does Western society condemn homosexuality? How and why did our particular definition or construction of homosexuality arise? What maintains it? How and when did the American definition of juvenile delinquency arise? What functions or purposes were behind its construction? Do societies everywhere have the same definition of crime? How is murder seen and defined elsewhere? Rape? Robbery? Why are certain psychoactive substances acceptable and legal in this society, while other substances are condemned and against the law? Do these definitions differ elsewhere? Why does our society "panic" over the abuse of certain drugs at certain times, and remain relatively unconcerned during other periods? Does the level of alcohol consumption that is defined as unacceptable vary from one society to another? On the most general level this approach asks, "How do rules arise and how do they function?" It has sometimes been termed as *constructionism*. It does not have the time-honored tradition behind it that the "Why do they do it?" approach has, but constructionism has taken over as the guiding approach of many sociologists of deviance today.

Both questions—"Why do they do it?" and "How do rules arise and how do they function?"—are woven into the fabric of the field. I have taught courses on the sociology of deviance for more than twenty years, and I am convinced that any anthology on the subject has to balance a variety of concerns. In this book I have attempted to provide a balance between the two principal emphases since they are, after all, a balance reflected by the concerns of the field as a whole. Any reading material, and any instructor using a given set of reading materials, must also balance the needs and interests of the students taking the course and what the practitioners of a given field are up to in their research and writing enterprises. In making the selections for this anthology I have attempted to cater to both audiences. (Unlike most book editors in this area, I have occasionally deleted some of the material from included works that would be of more interest to a professional audience than to a student.) I have also provided a balance between classic and contemporary work, and theoretical, conceptual, and empirical, or more substantive, writings. And lastly, I have provided introductions and explanatory materials for each section, thereby providing a balance between the voices of the authors of the selected works and my interpretation of their works.

The manner in which I have organized this anthology is, I am convinced, the most productive way of arranging a deviance course. What could be more basic? Definitions and concepts, theories attempting to explain deviance, theories accounting for condemnation and social control, and types or examples of deviance, or deviant behavior systems: I have found that students understand the subject best when the course is organized in this way. I have also attempted to select materials that are clearly written and that discuss some of the most essential and revealing features of the world of deviance. I put together this anthology because I could not find a selection of readings which, in my estimation, provided these multiple balances. While several worthwhile books of readings remain in print in this field, none gives me quite what I want. Some are organized in a very different fashion, some focus on certain concerns and orientations and ignore others, while others provide little or no interpretation or reprint selections that students find difficult and esoteric. My guess is that a number of other instructors feel the same way. I have learned from, and have enjoyed, putting this anthology together; I sincerely hope that both the student and the instructor will find it enlightening and enjoyable.

A word of caution. As I said above, this anthology represents something of a balance between contemporary and classic writings in the field. This means that some of the selections were published in past decades; the oldest appeared in print well over 50 years ago. Certain stylistic conventions were followed in the past that are unacceptable today. For instance, the generic "he" was widely used until well into the 1970s. (It is still used today by some hide-bound traditionalists.) Today, a feminist would take legitimate offense at reading a "he" in an article or book that presumably was intended to refer to men and women equally. (In fact, the generic "he" focuses attention on males, not on men and women equally.) One of the selections in this anthology refers to grown women as "girls," which is an unacceptable practice today. The word "Negro" was used by Blacks and whites alike to refer to African Americans until the late 1960s; today, this word has an archaic, anachronistic ring. In a selection in this anthology, an author refers to the physically disabled as "cripples." Again, this term is unacceptable—even offensive—today. By reprinting selections from the past, in no way do I endorse the stylistic conventions the authors used. These conventions reflect those that were in common use at the time; hence, they must be read in historical context. It would be inappropriate for me to correct writings from the past for their contemporary correctness, (although I am guilty of doing this when not doing so would impede communication). I sincerely hope that no reader takes offense at stylistic sins that were not regarded as sins at the time they were put on paper. Perhaps that is one lesson the sociology of deviance teaches us.

Erich Goode

Part I

Social Deviance: An Introduction

After studying deviance for some twenty-five years, I remain convinced that it is the most fascinating subject in the field of sociology—and possibly the entire academic curriculum. There is, to begin with, its *inherent* appeal. What could be more fascinating than wrongdoing, rule breaking, skulduggery, malfeasance, scandal, evil deeds of every description? Tune in the six o'clock news or pick up your daily newspaper and read the headlines. What's in the news? Murder, rape, gang violence, armed robbery, drug abuse, child molestation, sexual indiscretion, political corruption.

The House of Representatives passes a gun control bill. A woman sues the President of the United States, claiming that he sexually harassed her. A popular singer pays millions of dollars to the family of a boy who says he was sexually molested by him. A former athlete, actor, and corporate spokesperson is charged with the murder of his former wife and her friend. A 17-year-old boy, sentenced to three years in prison for stealing $20 worth of ice cream bars from a school cafeteria, is granted a new trial. A Harvard psychiatrist argues that his patients' stories of being abducted and medically experimented on by extraterrestrials are literally true. One of the most powerful politicians in Washington is charged with embezzlement and the misuse of public funds. Before she dies, a mother with AIDS searches for a substitute mother for her daughter. Homosexuals are denied the right to march in a religious parade. In a public swimming pool, a group of teenage boys accost a 14-year-old girl and yank off the top of her two-piece bathing suit; laughing, they seek out a new victim. Newly released documents reveal that for thirty years, the Federal Bureau of Investigation had been keeping a file on the radical, civil rights, and supposedly subversive activities and associates of composer and conducter Leonard Bernstein. A Wall Street trader in stocks and bonds is accused of perpetrating a $350 million fraud. A 23-year-old South Carolina woman is charged with murdering her young sons.

These stories make the headlines because they are inherently interesting. Readers and viewers want to know more about them; they sell newspapers, magazines, and air time. The field of the sociology of deviance has received some hard knocks during the past generation: It is too liberal, or conservative, or radical, or middle-of-the-road; or it isn't sufficiently rigorous or theoretical or empirical; or it doesn't carve out a subject area that is conceptually consistent; it is "stagnant" or its practitioners are "dogmatic." Yet, none of its critics argue that it is boring. And it endures. The sociology of deviance remains one of the most fascinating courses in sociology.

I personally find the study of the doings of street people, homosexuals, prostitutes, drug addicts, pornographers, and their ilk fascinating—what Alvin Gouldner once contemptuously referred to as "the cool world" (1968) and what Alexander Liazos, in a similarly dismissive fashion, referred to as the behavior of "nuts, sluts, and deviated preverts" (1972). (I also find the harmful doings of the rich and powerful interesting.) And I find public and political reactions to such disreputable populations and behaviors fascinating as well. Whether these are the most theoretically powerful and most strategic research sites is also an important issue to me. I assume that in the study of such populations and behaviors I will be able to locate and explain general social processes. That is, sociologists of deviance have the same mission in their research that all other sociologists have—not to glorify the small details but to draw out generalizations about how social life works. I sometimes detect that some of the field's critics attack the study of deviant phenomena because they sense that some researchers might derive pleasure from the study of their chosen subject matter. These behaviors and populations are, it must be admitted, by their very nature, of human interest. But simply because our subject matter is interesting does not mean that there is no possibility of using it as a strategic research site. And because we decided to study it, in part, because of that fascination, again, does not mean that we cannot tell other sociologists about the nature of social life generally. What I'm saying is that our motives can be mixed. We can find our subject matter interesting simply because of what it's *about* while at the same time it can be the basis for our understanding of how society as a whole works. We should never get so entangled in the intricate details of deviant behavior or populations that we are unable to tell anyone outside the field about what they say about social life in general.

In short, sociologists of deviance do not examine the wrongdoing of some members of the society, and the efforts of some members of the society to do something about that wrongdoing, solely and exclusively for the intrinsic fascination such behavior has for us. (That motive is probably there anyway.) To me, the sociology of deviance is almost uniquely positioned to yield generalizations of relevance to the entire field. But to grasp this point, we must leave the "cool" world, the world of scandal, violence, crime, and unconventional sex for a moment: The fact is, deviance takes place in *all* areas of life, in any and all social and physical settings—and not just in the world of disreputable people.

Physicians pad insurance claims; executives pad their expense accounts; scientists "cook" or "fudge" their data; students cheat on exams; professors sexually harass students; writers plagiarize from works by other authors; journalists fabricate interviews they never conducted; mechanics charge for unnecessary repairs; contractors purchase and build with cheap, illegal, or unauthorized materials, or don't complete jobs that have been paid for; children steal cookies they've been told not to touch; parents slap children when they know they shouldn't; friends spread malicious gossip about one another; individuals who are in happy marriages are sexually unfaithful to their spouses; and so on.

I'm not saying that we are all deviants, because that would be extremely misleading. Many of us are fairly conformist in nearly all the things we do; some of us break only very minor rules whereas others break society's most serious rules, and do so quite frequently. What I am saying is that deviance is not some exotic, marginal territory where bizarre human creatures sneak and skulk about. Instead, it takes place wherever humans act and interact. *Deviance takes place in everyday life.* And it is one of the major dimensions that determines the structure and dynamics of social life generally.

Does cheating on exams threaten the viability of the educational institution? If it does, what will happen to the society as a whole? If it is widespread, does punishing cheaters lessen or exacerbate that threat? What about tolerating cheating? What impact does that have? What about unethical business practices? Does it fatten the company's profits at the expense of the worker, the customer, the public generally? How much unethical business behavior can the society tolerate before it begins to disintegrate? Alternatively, how much policing of business can go on before both business and the economy as a whole are hobbled, inhibited, undermined? What happens to the quality of life in a neighborhood or community in which crime is widespread, rampant? How much drug use and dealing can take place before the vital, necessary functions of everyday life are undermined or threatened? How much police corruption can take place in a precinct before the residents begin to fear and distrust the very agents who are empowered to uphold the law? These are not dry, abstract, strictly academic questions, but questions that have real-life, blood-and-guts consequences; some societies or communities *have* disintegrated, *are* disintegrating, and following—or not following—rules, or some faction's rules, may have a great deal to do with their demise. In them, society's capacity to nurture and protect its citizens is seriously undermined. Clearly, deviance is at the very center of social structure and social process.

This anthology will reflect the richness and diversity of the sociology of deviance. Its scope will be fairly eclectic, that is, it will incorporate discussions of a wide range of approaches and perspectives. Until the 1960s, deviance was looked at in only one way; researchers in the field asked only one kind of question: What *causes* deviant behavior? What *causes* crime? What *causes* juvenile delinquency? It was assumed that the issue of what exactly this behavior is we're calling deviance, crime, and delinquency is an obvious and settled question. However, in bits and pieces previously, but more systematically since the 1960s, a new sort of question came to be asked: Why rules? Whose rules? Why laws? Why punishment? Why are these particular categories of behavior condemned? Why not those? In short, why social control?

The first endeavor—"What causes deviant behavior?"—has been given a variety of names: positivism, etiology, essentialism, objectivism, realism. It takes the concrete reality of the behavioral category under investigation for granted and inquires into what leads people to engage in it. Whether the causes are biological, psychological, or social and structural, the same logic applies. Either some people have a condition or a personality that makes it likely that they will violate the rules of the society in which they live, or some some situations, contexts, communities, social structures, or societies make it likely that a substantial proportion of the people living in them, again, will violate society's rules. In short, the positivist, etiological, or objectivist enterprise asks: How did people get that way?—that is, how did they get to be the kinds of people who commit deviant actions? (Sagarin, 1975, p. 201). Or, what is it about certain environments that make deviant behavior more likely to take place?

The second endeavor has been referred to as subjectivism or *constructionism*. It asks not why some people break the rules or how some social contexts induce people to break the rules. Instead, constructionism is interested in how those rules—and the categories on which they are based—came about in the first place and how these rules and those categories are applied. This approach asks about how deviance and crime are defined and what people say and do about them. In short: How and why are certain people, behaviors, or conditions *defined* in a disvalued manner? (Sagarin, 1975, p. 201).

The classic sociological approaches, and much current sociological research, adopt an essentialistic, positivistic, or causal perspective. People deviate because the communities in which they live are disorganized; because American society is subject to the strain that comes about from a disjunction between the goals they aspire to and the fact that many cannot attain them; because they belong to groups or subcultures that encourage a violation of the law or society's rules; because they lack self-control (Gottfredson and Hirschi, 1990); because they are faced with opportunities that present them with unguarded property they may make off with (Cohen et al., 1980; Gould, 1969); because the society in which they live is marked by huge discrepancies in the distribution of wealth (Braithwaite, 1979; Braithwaite and Braithwaite, 1980); and so on. There is something of an embarrassment of riches when it comes to sociological explanations of deviant behavior. Yet, none is currently regarded as *the* or even *a* dominant explanation in the field. What we see is a multiplicity of theories, each, to some degree, addressing a somewhat different aspect of deviance. Any well-rounded study of deviance must inevitably include a study of the many approaches that have made a major mark on the field. Two of these approaches—social disorganization theory and anomie theory—suffered a sharp decline in attention from the field in the years following their heyday, but, as we'll see, are in the process of making a comeback. In this anthology, we will be introduced to some of those classic sociological inquiries into the causes of deviant behavior.

The social construction of deviance—the "Why social control?" question—is a more recent endeavor; as I said, this approach was not seriously or systematically undertaken until the 1960s. Functionalism, which was dominant in American sociology generally in the 1940s, 1950s, and early 1960s, made some contributions to the question of why certain rules were generated and enforced, but it rarely asked the question "*Whose* rules?" It wasn't until the labeling theorists came along—aside from two early precursors (Tannenbaum, 1938; Lemert, 1951)—in the 1960s that the questions "Why rules?" and "Whose rules?" assumed central importance in the study of deviance. It is, in any case, a very different endeavor from what the essentialists and the etiologists were doing, that is, asking why rules are broken. The functionalists and the labeling theorists, the Marxists and the conflict theorists, the feminists and the "new" sociologists of social control are all concerned, in one way or another and in varying degrees, with the issue of social control. It is a concern that every student of deviance must appreciate and understand. We will encounter these perspectives in the pages that follow.

These two approaches, the study of the *causes* of deviance on the one hand, and the *definition* and *social control* of deviance on the other, lay out much of the territory of our field; they comprise most of what the sociology of deviance is concerned with. These two concerns are complementary rather than contradictory. Investigating them is an adventure. I invite the student to join me in that adventure.

References

Braithwaite, John. 1979. *Inequality, Crime, and Public Policy*. London: Routledge & Kegan Paul.

Braithwaite, John, and Valerie Braithwaite. 1980. The effect of income inequality and social democracy on homicide. *British Journal of Criminology,* 20 (January): 45–53.

Cohen, Lawrence E., Marcus Felson, and Kenneth C. Land. 1980. Property crime rates in the United States: A macrodynamic analysis. *American Journal of Sociology,* 86 (July): 90–118.

Gottfredson, Michael R., and Travis Hirschi. 1990. *A General Theory of Crime*. Stanford, Calif.: Stanford University Press.

Gould, LeRoy C. 1969. The changing structure of property crime in an affluent society. *Social Forces,* 48 (1): 50–59.

Gouldner, Alvin W. 1968. The sociologists as partisan: Sociology and the welfare state. *The American Sociologist,* 3 (May): 103–116.

Lemert, Edwin M. 1951. *Social Pathology: A Systematic Approach to the Theory of Sociopathic Behavior.* New York: McGraw-Hill.

Liazos, Alexander. 1972. The poverty of the sociology of deviance: Nuts, sluts, and preverts. *Social Problems,* 20 (Summer): 103–120.

Sagarin, Edward. 1975. *Deviants and Deviance: An Introduction to the Study of Disvalued People and Behavior.* New York: Praeger.

Tannenbaum, Frank. 1938. *Crime and the Community*. New York: Ginn.

Chapter 1

Definitions and Basic Concepts

What is the most productive way to define deviance? What makes an action or a condition wrong? Is it because of the characteristics of and the qualities contained within that action or that condition? Or can almost any act or condition be declared wrong, judged as deviance, regardless of its inner characteristics or qualities? To put the matter another way: What's important in deciding what's deviant—the act or condition itself, or how that act or condition is seen and evaluated? As we saw, deviance may be defined either as an essentialistic phenomenon—that is, as a thing with specific, concretely real features that we can identify and locate—or as a constructed phenomenon, that is, as a phenomenon that exists because certain observers or audiences *define* specific actions as wrong.

The essentialistic definition of deviance, or "deviance as objectively given," sees actions as wrong *not* because they violate a given society's or group's norms, rules, or laws, but because they are *objectively* wrong or *absolutely* evil: They violate a law of nature, or science, or the rules of God, or have offended the universe in some way. This approach sees certain intrinsic features in acts of wrongdoing; an act (less often, a condition) is wrong because it *is* a certain way or has certain consequences.

For instance, the fundamentalist Christian and orthodox Catholic view that abortion is murder—an inherent evil in the eyes of God—is a good example of an essentialistic definition of the deviance of one action in particular. It matters not in the slightest that it is condoned or tolerated—or legal—in some societies or quarters or at some periods of human history. To the fundamentalist Christian and orthodox Catholic, abortion is *always* an evil action—by its very nature, the murder of an unborn child—and therefore deviant in nature; it is intrinsically, inherently, absolutely, and *essentialistically* evil. The quality of deviance inheres in the act and not in how people feel about it. Some utopian Marxists believe (or at least, they did in the 1960s and early 1970s) that wrongdoing or deviance is, or should be, defined by the exploitation of one's fellow human beings. In this scheme of things, actions such as racism, sexism, imperialism, oppression, and exploitation are wrong, therefore deviant, and should be discussed as such.

All the many varieties of absolutism can be boiled down to two: those that base their definition of wrongdoing on *evil* (such as fundamentalist Christianity) and those that base their definition on clear-cut *harm* (such as utopian Marxism). To the orthodox Christian, solitary masturbation is wrong not so much because it harms the body as it harms the soul; it is an offense in God's eyes. In contrast, to the utopian Marxist, a landlord who knowingly refuses to remove lead paint from the walls of an apartment, which chips off and is eaten by a child who suffers brain damage as a consequence, is engaged in wrongdoing—deviance—and should be punished. It is wrong specifically because it harms someone—specifically, an innocent child. In both of these cases, it matters not at all that the action in question may not be seen or judged as wrong by certain humans. What counts is that they are wrong *in and of themselves*.

A second type of definition of deviance is subjective rather than objective, relative rather than absolute, constructed rather than essentialistic. What deviance *is* does not depend on the inner, intrinsic, or inherent properties an act (or, less often, a condition) might have—that is, its objective characteristics. Instead, what makes an act deviant is what certain people (or audiences) make of that act—what they think of it and how they react to it. The constructionist definition sees deviance as defined solely and exclusively by the rules, the norms, or the laws of a given society or group and by the nature of the reactions that a given action or condition generates. What makes an action (or a condition) deviant is the actual or potential condemnation that it would attract from observers or "audiences." If the norms, or an "audience," condemn the behavior, it is a form of deviance regardless of its objective harm, the essential qualities it possesses, what we think of it, or what we imagine a "higher authority" (such as God, nature, or medicine) regards it. To the subjectivist, intrinsic harm or evil *does not come into the picture at all*. What counts is how it is judged, what specific, designated audiences think of the act and how they react to it and those who engage in it. If abortion is acceptable in a given society, to the constructionist, it is not deviant. If infanticide is or was accepted or tolerated in certain societies at certain times, that, too, is *not* an example of deviant behavior. If letting your elderly parents die on a frozen ice floe once they are no longer economically productive is the norm in a given society, then in that society, that action is not deviant (though it may be seen as deviant elsewhere). Again, to the constructionist, the *only* factor that defines deviance is how actions (or conditions) are seen and evaluated by the members of a particular society.

Religious fundamentalists such as Jerry Falwell hold the essentialist position. They argue that what should be seen as wrongdoing is absolute rather than spelled out by societal definitions and reactions. Actions are wrong or evil—fundamentalist Christians do not usually use the term *deviance*—insofar as they are *an offense in the eyes of God*. What *makes* an act (conditions are rarely examined as deviance) wrong is an objective fact—God disapproves of it. It matters not in the least whether abortion, pornography, or homosexuality may be tolerated or encouraged in a given society at a given time; the social definition of an act is completely irrelevant to its deviant status. It is its status in the eyes of God that defines it as wrong, and that alone. (Exactly *how* the Christian is supposed to figure out what is offensive to God is a separate matter.) Evil is defined by its essentialistic, indwelling, objective properties; what is evil at one time is evil at all other times; what is evil in one place is evil everywhere. Social definitions have nothing to do with its status as wrongdoing.

This same essentialistic or objectivistic approach is adopted by utopian Marxists, as exemplified by the selection by Alexander Liazos, "Deviance as Exploitation: Beyond Nuts and Sluts." Liazos does not like the fact that sociologists have defined deviance by the norms or public or audience reactions, whether actual or potential. That is too relativistic, he says; it masks the truly ugly nature of some actions. He wishes to redefine deviance to include various harmful wrongs that have traditionally been hidden and condoned by the powers that be: sexism, racism, imperialism, exploitation, oppression, and so on. Liazos believes that, *even though they do not attract condemnation,* certain actions should be studied as deviant behavior anyway. They are deviant, and should be so regarded, because they possess certain inner or inherent characteristics—some objective, essentialistic properties—that mark them off from actions that should not be regarded as deviance. We should look at oppression, exploitation, and so on as deviance *because they are harmful to powerless people.* Even though Liazos's article, from which this selection has been taken, is extremely widely quoted, the field of the sociology of deviance has not followed his path in that it has not shifted to an absolutist or an essentialistic definition of deviance; nor have many sociologists chosen to look at wrongs such as racism and oppression as forms of deviance.

What Liazos's political radicalism and Falwell's fundamentalist Christianity have in common is the view that deviance is not in the eye of the beholder, but resides in some specific, concrete property contained by certain actions themselves. Of course, even though both approaches are absolutistic and essentialistic, the specific actions that each designates as deviant are completely different. Religious fundamentalists would point to homosexuality, abortion, and pornography as deviant, actions that (perhaps except for pornography, because some would say that it exploits women) Marxists would not regard as wrong. In contrast, utopian Marxists would point to imperialism, oppression, exploitation, sexism, and racism—actions and institutions that are not high on religious conservatives' lists of inherent evils. Their lists of deviant actions hardly overlap at all.

A very different approach is offered by the subjective or constructionist approach. Some version of constructionism is the dominant definition in the field of the sociology of deviance. Howard S. Becker, in "Outsiders," offers a classic constructionist discussion of deviance. Deviance is a social creation, Becker says. By that he does not mean that certain "deviant" actions are caused by sociological factors. He means that deviance is generated or created by the rules themselves. No rules, no deviance; it is social groups who create rules—they are not handed down from above. What makes an action deviant is the punishment or condemnation *of* the actor or perpetrator *by* certain observers or "audiences." It is this punishment or condemnation that imparts a specifically deviant character to those actions.

But, as with the objectivistic or essentialistic approach, constructionism offers several varieties. The *normative* definition sees deviance as defined solely and exclusively by a violation of the norms. It assumes an "omniscient," all-seeing, or

"God's eye" or "fly on the wall" observer who witnesses each and every act that takes place in a society and determines, in an impartial fashion, which ones violate the norms and which ones don't. Those that do are automatically instances of deviance. These acts do not have to be seen by real-life audiences or observers, the people who enact them do not have to be seen, caught, heard about, or punished. The behavior in question could have taken place in secret, known only to the actor. (Of course, we are assuming that *we* know that the act violated the norms, otherwise we couldn't categorize it as deviance.) Actual, concrete audience or observer reactions are not necessary for the normative definition. All that is necessary for an act to be regarded sociologically as deviance is that it violates a norm. Public reactions are not necessary. Of course, all normative definitions assume that acts that violate the norms are *likely* to produce punishing, negative reactions, but they are not necessary to the definition. A violation of the norms is all that's necessary for the normative definition of deviance. The normative definition is very comfortable with the concept of "secret" deviance. And with the notion that there exist types or categories or classes of deviance. For instance, regardless of how they may be reacted to in a particular instance, same-sex sexual acts are deviant in American society because such acts tend to be widely condemned. Simply because they are not in a *particular* instance is irrelevant.

The *reactive* definition is also a variety of constructionism. To the reactivist, deviance is defined by how it is concretely seen, defined, reacted to. Both see deviance as a social construct. The difference between reactivism and the normative definition is that the latter argues that deviance exists in the abstract, without being condemned in a particular instance. The reactivist definition, in contrast, insists that what makes an act deviant is that it is actually, concretely, and literally condemned and punished. No condemnation, no deviance. To the reactivist, there is no such thing as "secret deviance." It is a contradiction in terms. How can an act be deviant if it is secret, since what makes actions deviant is the negative reactions they generate? For example, to the reactivist, the "perfect murder," the murder that the killer gets away with, that no one but the killer knows about, does not exist. If a killing has not been observed by others, and the killer not apprehended or punished, *it is not murder at all.* No punishment, no deviance. Deviance is *constituted* or *created* by negative social reactions. An unapprehended rapist is not a rapist at all; a woman may be fully aware that she was raped, but if she does not know who her attacker was, to the reactivist, he is not a rapist. No reaction, no deviance. If someone engages in a dark, secret, unsavory action in a closet and no one finds out about it, it is not deviant at all. The only thing that defines deviance is public reactions. If that is missing, then, to the reactivist, there's no deviance at all.

In the fourth selection that follows, "Deviance, Norms, and Social Reaction," I distinguish between the "objectively given" approach to deviance (which I've also referred to as essentialism or absolutism) and the "subjectively problematic" approach (that is, constructionism or relativism). As I said in the introduction, essentialism (belief in a fixed reality) is not exactly the same thing as absolutism (the view that right and wrong are pregiven). But absolutism is the most *extreme* form of essentialism. Each approach has several varieties. Essentialists can be broken down, at the very least, into the view of deviance as evil and deviance as harm. Seeing deviance as harm does not really challenge the logic of absolutism, it simply refocuses the spotlight of deviance onto a different set of actions.

In this selection, I also try to reconcile the two different but basically constructionist definitions—the normative and the reactivist. In my view, this reconciliation is consistent with Becker's view in *Outsiders* (1963). I suggest that a "soft" reactive definition is the best way to look at deviance. A soft or moderate reactive definition of deviance argues that it is possible to define as deviant actions that would be regarded as wrong in most instances if they were discovered. The reconciliation boils down to recognizing that there is a difference between *societal* and *situational* deviance (Plummer, 1979). Societal deviance is made up of all those actions that represent technical violations of the norms, that can be included in types or categories of widely condemned behaviors, that would be condemned if they were discovered. Such actions may or may not have concretely and literally resulted in condemnation. We know before they are discovered or result in condemnation or punishment, that homosexuality, child abuse, murder, drug dealing, adultery, robbery, and so on violate the norms of this society; we know that such actions are likely to be condemned. Hence, we know in advance that they are forms of deviance—*societal* deviance. But remember: The strict reactive definition argues that no such thing as societal deviance exists, since it is only actions that result in real-life, concrete, or situational apprehension and punishment that are worthy of the name deviance.

Situational deviance is all those actions that result, in specific instances, in actual, concrete condemnation. To the strict or hard reactivist, *all* deviance is situational deviance. The soft or moderate reactivist recognizes the existence of both societal and situational deviance, but recognizes that sociological factors may result in some widely condemned actions not being condemned in specific instances. And the normative definition assumes that all societal deviance will more or less naturally and inevitably result in situational punishment and condemnation; if there are discrepancies, they are not very interesting.

To sum up. It is important to spell out the differences between *absolutist* and *relative, essentialist* and *constructionist* definitions of deviance. The dominant definition of deviance is *relativistic* and *constructionist*. A contrast with at least two absolutist views—fundamentalist Christianity and utopian Marxism—may be instructive. Likewise, among adherents of the relativistic definition of deviance, there are some differences. Two major varieties of relativism are the "normative" and the "reactivist" definitions. I attempt to resolve some of their differences by introducing the "soft" or "moderate" reactivist definition of deviance.

References

Becker, Howard S. 1963. *Outsiders: Studies in the Sociology of Deviance*. New York: Free Press.

Plummer, Kenneth. 1979. Misunderstanding labelling perspectives. In David Downes and Paul Rock (eds.), *Deviant Interpretations*. London: Martin Robertson, pp. 85–121.

Wrongdoing as an Offense in the Eyes of God

JERRY FALWELL, ED DOBSON, and ED HINDSON

Abortion

Life is a miracle. Only God Almighty can create life, and He said, "Thou shalt not kill." Nothing can change the fact that abortion is the murder of human life.... Experts now estimate that between 8 million and 10 million babies have been murdered since January 22, 1973, when the Supreme Court, in a decision known as *Roe v. Wade,* granted women an absolute right to abortion on demand during the first two trimesters of pregnancy—that is, during the first six months of pregnancy. No other major civilized nation in history has ever been willing to permit late abortion except for the gravest of medical reasons.

Human life is precious to God. Christ died upon the cross for every man and woman who has ever lived and who will ever live. In the past, America was known for honoring and protecting the right of a person to live. No one disagrees that the state exists to protect the lives of its citizens. But we are in danger of losing our respect for the sanctity of human life. America has allowed more persons to be killed through abortion than have been eliminated in all our major wars. Only a perverted society would make laws protecting eagles' eggs yet have no protection for precious unborn human life.

Equally ironic, there is a great debate going on today regarding capital punishment. In America, we kill babies and protect criminals, even though the death penalty is definitely a deterrent to crime. The time has now come that we must speak up in defense of the sanctity and dignity of human life.

In reality, life began with God and, since Adam, has simply passed from one life cell to another. From the moment of fertilization any further formulation of the individual is merely a matter of time, growth, and maturation. This is a growth process that continues throughout our entire lives. At three weeks, just twenty-one days after conception, a tiny human being already has eyes, a spinal cord, a nervous system, lungs, and intestines. The heart, which has been beating since the eighteenth day, is pumping a blood supply totally separate from that of the mother. All this occurs before the mother may even be aware of the new life within her body. By the end of the seventh week we see a well-proportioned small-scale baby with fingers, knees, ankles, and toes. Brain waves have been recorded as early as forty-three days. By eleven weeks all organ systems are present and functioning in this new embryonic life....

From *The Fundamentalist Phenomenon: The Resurgence of Conservative Christianity,* eds. Jerry Falwell with Ed Dobson and Ed Hindson (Garden City, N.Y.: A Doubleday-Galilee Original, 1981), pp. 195–205 (with deletions). Reprinted by permission of the senior author.

One of the major arguments of the pro-abortionists is that the unborn child is a fetus, not a person. It should be noted that "fetus" is Latin for "unborn child." Unfortunately, the tendency today is to change traditional terminology and substitute words like "conceptus" for "child." No one wants to use the term "murder" for abortion, so we simply call it "termination of pregnancy." This technique is usually employed to defend the indefensible. It is much easier to refer to the elimination of "P.O.C.s" (products of conception) than to the slicing, poisoning, and flushing away of a million little boys and girls....

Pornography

The pornographic explosion distorts the biblical view of women, perverts American youth, and corrupts the moral fiber of society.... Proliferation of pornography into our society is striking evidence of our decadence. The moral fiber of our nation is so deteriorated that we cannot possibly survive unless there is a complete and drastic turnabout soon. A permissive society that tolerates pornography has the same hedonistic attitude that destroyed ancient civilizations. Pornographers are idolaters who idolize money and will do anything for materialistic gain. They are men who have reprobate minds and who need divine deliverance....

Homosexuality

Less than a decade ago, the word "homosexual" was a word that was disdained by most Americans and represented the nadir of human indecency. It was used as a word of contempt. All of this has changed. What was considered a deviant life-style is now considered by many Americans as an alternative life-style. There is even legislation pending that would legitimize homosexuals as "normal." Today thousands of men and women in America flaunt their sin openly. The entire homosexual movement is an indictment against America and is contributing to its ultimate downfall.

History confirms that when homosexuality reaches epidemic levels in society, that society is in serious crisis and on the verge of collapse. God considers the sin of homosexuality as abominable. He destroyed the cities of Sodom and Gomorrah because of their involvement in this sin. The Old Testament law is clear concerning this issue: "Thou shalt not lie with mankind, as with womankind: it is abomination" (Lev. 18:22). God still abhors the sin of homosexuality. In the New Testament, there are numerous references to it. In Romans 1:26–28, we read: "For this cause God gave them up unto vile affections: for even their women did change the natural use into that which is against nature: And likewise also the men, leaving the natural use of the woman, burned in their lust one toward another...." These people willingly rejected God's revealed truth. Consequently, God "gave them up to uncleanness through the lusts of their own hearts, to dishonor their own bodies between themselves" (Rom. 1:24).

A bill has been introduced in Congress which, if passed, would establish homosexuals in America as a bona fide minority like women, blacks, or Hispanics.... This is a clear indication of the moral decay of our society. Americans began by accepting homosexuality as an alternate life-style, recognizing it as legitimate, and now they are attempting to legalize it....

In light of our opposition to the sin of homosexuality, we must always make it clear that we love people and are genuinely interested in their personal needs. I believe that homosexuals require love and help. We must not allow homosexuality to be presented to our nation as an alternate or acceptable life-style. It will only serve as a corrupting influence upon our next generation and will bring down the wrath of God upon America. I love homosexuals as people for whom Christ died, but I must hate their sin. Jesus Christ offers forgiveness and deliverance from that sin and from all other sins.

Deviance as Exploitation: Beyond Nuts and Sluts[1]

ALEXANDER LIAZOS

I examined 16 textbooks in the field of "deviance," eight of them readers, to determine the state of the field. Theoretically, eight take the labelling-interactionist approach; three more tend to lean to that approach; four others argue for other orientations (anomie, structural-functional, etc.) or, among the readers, have an "eclectic" approach; and one (McCaghy, et al., 1968) is a collection of biographical and other statements by "deviants" themselves, and thus may not be said to have a theoretical approach (although, as we shall see, the selection of the types of statements and "deviants" still implies an orientation and viewpoint). A careful examination of these textbooks revealed a number of ideological biases. These biases became apparent as much from what these books leave unsaid and unexamined, as from what they do say. The field of the sociology of deviance, as exemplified in these books, contains three important theoretical and political biases.

1. All writers, especially those of the labelling school, either state explicitly or imply that one of their main concerns is to *humanize* and *normalize* the "deviant," to show that he is essentially no different from us. But by the very emphasis on the "deviant" and his identity problems and subculture, the opposite effect may have been achieved. The persisting use of the label "deviant" to refer to the people we are considering is an indication of the feeling that these people are indeed different.

2. By the overwhelming emphasis on the "dramatic" nature of the usual types of "deviance"—prostitution, homosexuality, juvenile delinquency, and others—we have neglected to examine other, more serious and harmful forms of "deviance." I refer to *covert institutional violence* (defined and discussed below) which leads to such things as poverty and exploitation, the war in Vietnam, unjust tax laws, racism and sexism, and so on, which cause psychic and material suffering for many Americans, black and white, men and women.

3. Despite explicit statements by these authors of the importance of *power* in the designation of what is "deviant," in their substantive analyses they show a profound unconcern with power and its implications. The really powerful, the upper classes and the power elite, those Gouldner (1968) calls the "top dogs," are left essentially unexamined by these sociologists of deviance.

Always implicit, and frequently explicit, is the aim of the labelling school to humanize and normalize the "deviant." Two statements by Becker and Matza are representative of this sentiment.

From Alexander Liazos, "The Poverty of the Sociology of Deviance: Nuts, Sluts, and Preverts." ©1972 by the Society for the Study of Social Problems. Reprinted from *Social Problems,* vol. 20 (Summer 1972), pp. 103–120 (with deletions), by permission.

> In the course of our work and for who knows what private reasons, we fall into deep sympathy with the people we are studying, so that while the rest of society views them as unfit in one or another respect for the deference ordinarily accorded a fellow citizen, we believe that they are at least as good as anyone else, more sinned against than sinning (Becker, 1967:100–101).

> The growth of the sociological view of deviant phenomena involved, as major phases, the replacement of a correctional stance by an *appreciation* of the deviant subject, the tacit purging of a conception of pathology by a new stress on human *diversity*, and the erosion of a simple distinction between deviant and conventional phenomena, resulting from intimate familiarity of the world as it is, which yielded a more sophisticated view stressing *complexity* (Matza, 1969:10).

For number of reasons, however, the opposite effect may have been achieved; and "deviants" still seem different. I began to suspect this reverse effect from the many essays and papers I read while teaching the "deviance" course. The clearest example is the repeated use of the word "tolerate." Students would write that we must not persecute homosexuals, prostitutes, mental patients, and others, that we must be "tolerant" of them. But one tolerates only those one considers less than equal, morally inferior, and weak; those equal to oneself, one accepts and respects; one does not merely allow them to exist, one does not "tolerate" them.

The repeated assertion that "deviants" are "at least as good as anyone else" may raise doubts that this is in fact the case, or that we believe it. A young woman who grew up in the South in the 1940's and 1950's told Quinn (1954:146): "'You know, I think from the fact that I was told so often that I must treat colored people with consideration, I got the feeling that I could mistreat them if I wanted to.'" Thus with "deviants"; if in fact they are as good as we are, we would not need to remind everyone of this fact; we would take it for granted and proceed from there. But our assertions that "deviants" are not different may raise the very doubts we want to dispel. Moreover, why would we create a separate field of sociology for "deviants" if there were not something different about them? May it be that even we do not believe our statements and protestations?

The continued use of the word "deviant" (and its variants), despite its invidious distinctions and connotations, also belies our explicit statements on the equality of the people under consideration. To be sure, some of the authors express uneasiness over the term. For example, we are told,

> In our use of this term for the purpose of sociological investigation, we emphasize that we do not attach any value judgement, explicitly or implicitly, either to the word "deviance" or to those describing their behavior or beliefs in this book (McCaghy, et al., 1968:v).

Lofland (1969:2, 9–10) expresses even stronger reservations about the use of the term, and sees clearly the sociological, ethical, and political problems raised by its continued use. Yet, the title of his book is *Deviance and Identity*.

Szasz (1970: xxv–xxvi) has urged that we abandon use of the term [deviance]:

> Words have lives of their own. However much sociologists insist that the term "deviant" does not diminish the worth of the person or group so categorized, the implication of inferiority adheres to the word. Indeed, sociologists are not wholly exempt from blame: they describe addicts and homosexuals as deviants, but never Olympic champions or Nobel Prize winners. In fact, the term is rarely applied to people with admired characteristics, such as great wealth, superior skills, or fame—whereas it is often applied to those with despised characteristics, such as poverty, lack of marketable skills, or infamy.
>
> The term "social deviants"... does not make sufficiently explicit—as the terms "scapegoat" or "victim" do—that majorities usually categorize persons or groups as "deviant" in order to set them apart as inferior beings and to justify their social control, oppression, persecution, or even complete destruction.

Terms like victimization, persecution, and oppression are more accurate descriptions of what is really happening. But even Gouldner (1968), in a masterful critique of the labelling school, while describing social conflict, calls civil-rights and anti-war protesters "political deviants." He points out clearly that these protesters are resisting openly, not slyly, conditions they abhor. Gouldner is discussing political struggles; oppression and resistance to oppression; conflicts over values, morals, interests, and power; and victimization. Naming such protesters "deviants," even if *political* deviants, is an indication of the deep penetration within our minds of certain prejudices and orientations.

Given the use of the term, the definition and examples of "deviant" reveal underlying sentiments and views. Therefore, it is important that we redefine drastically the entire field, especially since it is a flourishing one: "Because younger sociologists have found deviance such a fertile and exciting field for their own work, and because students share these feelings, deviance promises to become an even more important area of sociological research and theory in the coming years" (Douglas, 1970a:3).

The lists and discussions of "deviant" acts and persons reveal the writers' biases and sentiments. These are acts which, "like robbery, burglary or rape [are] of a simple and dramatic predatory nature..." (The President's Commission on Law Enforcement and the Administration of Justice, in Dinitz, et al., 1969:105). All 16 texts, without exception, concentrate on actions and persons of a "dramatic predatory nature," on "preverts." This is true of both the labelling and other schools. The following are examples from the latter:

> Ten different types of deviant behavior are considered: juvenile delinquency, adult crime, prison sub-cultures, homosexuality, prostitution, suicide, homicide, alcoholism, drug addiction and mental illness (Rushing, 1969: preface).

> Traditionally, in American sociology the study of deviance has focused on criminals, juvenile delinquents, prostitutes, suicides, the mentally ill, drug users and drug addicts, homosexuals, and political and religious radicals (Lefton, et al., 1968:v).

> Deviant behavior is essentially violation of certain types of group norms; a deviant act is behavior which is proscribed in a certain way. [It must be] in a disapproved direction, and of sufficient degree to exceed the tolerance limit of the community....[such as] delinquency and crime, prostitution, homosexual behavior, drug addiction, alcoholism, mental disorders, suicide, marital and family maladjustment, discrimination against minority groups, and, to a lesser degree, role problems of old age (Clinard, 1968:28).

Finally, we are told that these are some examples of deviance every society must deal with: "...mental illness, violence, theft, and sexual misconduct, as well as...other similarly difficult behavior" (Dinitz, et al.,1968:3).

The list stays unchanged with the authors of the labelling school.

> ...in Part I, "The Deviant Act," I draw rather heavily on certain studies of homicide, embezzlement, "naive" check forgery, suicide and a few other acts...in discussing the assumption of deviant identity (Part II) and the assumption of normal identity (Part III), there is heavy reference to certain studies of paranoia, "mental illness" more generally, and Alcoholics Anonymous and Synanon (Lofland, 1969:34).

> Homicide, suicide, alcoholism, mental illness, prostitution, and homosexuality are among the forms of behavior typically called deviant, and they are among the kinds of behavior that will be analyzed (Lofland, 1969:1). Included among my respondents were political radicals of the far left and the far right, homosexuals, militant blacks, convicts and mental hospital patients, mystics, narcotic addicts, LSD and Marijuana users, illicit drug dealers, delinquent boys, racially mixed couples, hippies, health-food users, and bohemian artists and village eccentrics (Simmons, 1969:10).

Simmons (1969:27, 29, 31) also informs us that in his study of stereotypes of "deviants" held by the public, these are the types he gave to people: homosexuals, beatniks, adulterers, marijuana smokers, political radicals, alcoholics, prostitutes, lesbians, ex-mental patients, atheists, ex-convicts, intellectuals, and gamblers. In Lemert (1967) we find that except for the three introductory (theoretical) chapters, the substantive chapters cover the following topics: alcohol drinking, four; check forgers, three; stuttering, two; and mental illness, two. Matza (1969) offers the following list of "deviants" and their actions that "must be appreciated if one adheres to a naturalistic perspective": paupers, robbers, motorcycle gangs, prostitutes, drug addicts, promiscuous homosexuals, thieving Gypsies, and "free love" Bohemians (1969:16). Finally, Douglas' collection (1970a) covers these forms of "deviance": abortion, nudism, topless barmaids, prostitutes, homosexuals, violence (motorcycle and juvenile gangs), shoplifting, and drugs.

The omissions from these lists are staggering. The covert, institutional forms of "deviance" [discussed below] are nowhere to be found. Reading these authors, one would not know that the most destructive use of violence in the last decade has been the war in Vietnam, in which the U.S. has heaped unprecedented suffering on the people and their land; more bombs have been dropped in Vietnam than in the entire World War II. Moreover, the robbery of the corporate world—through tax breaks, fixed prices, low wages, pollution of the environment, shoddy goods, etc.—is passed over in our fascination with "dramatic and predatory" actions. Therefore, we are told that "while they certainly are of no greater social importance to us than such subjects as banking and accounting [or military violence], subjects such as marijuana use and motorcycle gangs are of far greater interest to most of us. While it is only a coincidence that our scientific interests correspond with the emotional interest in deviants, it is a happy coincidence and, I believe, one that should be encouraged" (Douglas, 1970a:5). And Matza (1969:17), in commenting on the "appreciative sentiments" of the "naturalistic spirit," elaborates on the same theme: "We do not for a moment wish that we could rid ourselves of deviant phenomena. We are intrigued by them. They are an intrinsic, ineradicable, and vital part of human society."

An effort is made to transcend this limited view and substantive concern with dramatic and predatory forms of "deviance." Becker (1964:3) claims that the new (labelling) deviance no longer studies only "delinquents and drug addicts, though these classical kinds of deviance are still kept under observation." It increases its knowledge "of the processes of deviance by studying physicians, people with physical handicaps, the mentally deficient, and others whose doings were formerly not included in the area." The powerful "deviants" are still left untouched, however. This is still true with another aspect of the new deviance. Becker (1964:4) claims that in the labelling perspective "we focus attention on the other people involved in the process. We pay attention to the role of the non-deviant as well as that of the deviant." But we see that it is the ordinary non-deviants and the low-level agents of social control who receive attention, not the powerful ones (Gouldner, 1968).

In fact, the emphasis is more on the *subculture* and *identity* of the "deviants" themselves rather than on their oppressors and persecutors. To be sure, in varying degrees all authors discuss the agents of social control, but the fascination and emphasis are on the "deviant" himself. Studies of prisons and prisoners, for example, focus on prison subcultures and prisoner rehabilitation; there is little or no consideration of the social, political, economic, and power conditions which consign people to prisons. Only now are we beginning to realize that most prisoners are *political prisoners*—that their "criminal" actions (whether against individuals, such as robbery, or conscious political acts against the state) result largely from current social and political conditions, and are not the work of "disturbed" and "psychopathic" personalities. This realization came about largely because of the writings of political prisoners themselves: Malcolm X (1965), Eldridge Cleaver (1968), and George Jackson (1970), among others.

In all these books, notably those of the labelling school, the concern is with the "deviant's" subculture and identity: his problems, motives, fellow victims, etc. The collection of memoirs and apologies of "deviants" in their own words (McCaghy, et al., 1968) covers the lives and identities of "prevert deviants": prostitutes, nudists, abortionists, criminals, drug users, homosexuals, the mentally ill, alcoholics, and suicides. For good measure, some "militant deviants" are thrown in: Black Muslims, the

SDS, and a conscientious objector. But one wonders about other types of "deviants": how do those who perpetrate the covert institutional violence in our society view themselves? Do they have identity problems? How do they justify their actions? How did the robber barons of the late 19th century steal, fix laws, and buy politicians six days of the week and go to church on Sunday? By what process can people speak of body counts and kill ratios with cool objectivity? On these and similar questions, this book (and all others)[2] provides no answers; indeed, the editors seem unaware that such questions should or could be raised.

Becker (1964), Rubington and Weinberg (1968), Matza (1969), and Bell (1971) also focus on the identity and subculture of "prevert deviants." Matza, in discussing the assumption of "deviant identity," uses as examples, and elaborates upon, thieves and marijuana users. In all these books, there are occasional references to and questions about the larger social and political structure, but these are not explored in any depth; and the emphasis remains on the behavior, identity, and rehabilitation of the "deviant" himself. This bias continues in the latest book which, following the fashions of the times, has chapters on hippies and militant protesters (Bell, 1971).

Even the best of these books, Simmons' *Deviants* (1969), is not free of the overwhelming concentration of the "deviant" and his identity. It is the most sympathetic and balanced presentation of the lives of "deviants": their joys, sorrows, and problems with the straight world and fellow victims. Simmons demystifies the processes of becoming "deviant" and overcoming "deviance." He shows, as well as anyone does, that these victims *are* just like us; and the differences they possess and the suffering they endure are imposed upon them. Ultimately, however, Simmons too falls prey to the three biases shown in the work of others: a) the "deviants" he considers are only of the "prevert" type: b) he focuses mostly on the victim and his identity, not on the persecutors; and c) the persecutors he does discuss are of the middle-level variety, the agents of more powerful others and institutions.

Because of these biases, there is an implicit, but very clear, acceptance by these authors of the current definitions of "deviance." It comes about because they concentrate their attention of those who have been *successfully labelled as "deviant,"* and not on those who break laws, fix laws, violate ethical and moral standards, harm individuals and groups, etc., but who either are able to hide their actions, or, when known, can deflect criticism, labelling, and punishment. The following are typical statements which reveal this bias.

"...no act committed by members of occupational groups [such as white-collar crimes], however unethical, should be considered as crime unless it is punishable by the state in some way" (Clinard, 1968:269). Thus, if some people can manipulate laws so that their unethical and destructive acts are not "crimes," we should cater to their power and agree that they are not criminals.

Furthermore, the essence of the labelling school encourages this bias, despite Becker's (1963:14) assertion that "...insofar as a scientist uses 'deviant' to refer to any rule-breaking behavior and takes as his subjects of study only those who have been *labelled* deviant, he will be hampered by the disparities between the two categories." But as the following statements from Becker and others show, this is in fact what the labelling school does do.

Deviance is "created by society... *social groups create deviance by making the rules whose infraction constitutes deviance,* and by applying those rules to particular people and labelling them as outsiders" (Becker, 1963:8–9). Clearly, according to this view, in cases where no group has labelled another, no matter what the other group or individuals have done, there is nothing for the sociologist to study and dissect.

> Rules are not made automatically. Even though a practice may be harmful in an objective sense to the group in which it occurs, the harm needs to be discovered and pointed out. People must be made to feel that something ought to be done about it (Becker, 1963:162).

> What is important for the social analyst is not what people are by his lights or by his standards, but what it is that people construe one another and themselves to be for what reasons and with what consequences (Lofland, 1969:35).

> ...deviance is in the eyes of the beholder. For deviance to become a social fact, somebody must perceive an act, person, situation, or event as a departure from social norms, must categorize that perception, must report the perception to others, must get them to accept this definition of the situation, and must obtain a response that conforms to this definition. Unless all these requirements are met, deviance as a social fact does not come into being (Rubington and Weinberg, 1968:v).

The implication of these statements is that the sociologist accepts current, successful definitions of what is "deviant" as the only ones worthy of his attention. To be sure, he may argue that those labelled "deviant" are not really different from the rest of us, or that there is no act intrinsically "deviant," etc. By concentrating on cases of successful labelling, however, he will not penetrate beneath the surface to look for other forms of "deviance"—undetected stealing, violence, and destruction. When people are not powerful enough to make the "deviant" label stick on others, we overlook these cases. But is it not as much a *social fact,* even though few of us pay much attention to it, that the corporate economy kills and maims more, is more violent, than any violence committed by the poor (the usual subjects of studies of violence)? By what reasoning and necessity is the "violence" of the poor in the ghettoes more worthy of our attention than the military bootcamps which numb recruits from the horrors of killing the "enemy" ("Oriental human beings," as we learned during the Calley trial)? But because these acts are not labelled "deviant," because they are covert, institutional, and normal, their "deviant" qualities are overlooked and they do not become part of the province of the sociology of deviance. Despite their best liberal intentions, these sociologists seem to perpetuate the very notions they think they debunk, and others of which they are unaware.

As a result of the fascination with "nuts, sluts, and preverts," and their identities and subcultures, little attention has been paid to the unethical, illegal, and destructive actions of powerful individuals, groups, and institutions in our society. Because these actions are carried out quietly in the normal course of events, the sociology of deviance does not consider them as part of its subject matter. This bias is rooted in the very conception and definition of the field. It is obvious when one examines the treatment, or, just as often, lack of it, of the issues of violence, crime, and white-collar crime.

Discussions of violence treat only one type: the "dramatic and predatory" violence committed by individuals (usually the poor and minorities) against persons and property. For example, we read, "crimes involving violence, such as criminal homicide, assault, and forcible rape, are concentrated in the slums" (Clinard, 1968:123). Wolfgang, an expert on violence, has developed a whole theory on the "subculture of violence" found among the lower classes (e.g., in Rushing, 1969:233–40). And Douglas (1970a:part 4, on violence) includes readings on street gangs and the Hell's Angels. Thompson (1966), in his book on the Hell's Angels, devotes many pages to an exploration of the Angels' social background. In addition, throughout the book, and especially in his concluding chapter, he places the Angels' violence in the perspective of a violent, raping, and destructive society, which refuses to confront the reality of the Angels by distorting, exaggerating, and romanticizing their actions. But Douglas reprints none of these pages; rather, he offers us the chapter where, during a July 4 weekend, the Angels were restricted by the police within a lakeside area, had a drunken weekend, and became a tourist sideshow and circus.

In short, violence is presented as the exclusive property of the poor in the slums, the minorities, streets gangs, and motorcycle beasts. But if we take the concept *violence* seriously, we see that much of our political and economic system thrives on it. In violence, a person is *violated*—there is harm done to his person, his psyche, his body, his dignity, his ability to govern himself (Garver, in Rose, 1969:6). Seen in this way, a person can be violated in many ways; physical force is only one of them. As the readings in Rose (1969) show, a person can be violated by a system that denies him a decent job, or consigns him to a slum, or causes him brain damage by near-starvation during childhood, or manipulates him through the mass media, and so on endlessly.

Moreover, we must see that *covert institutional violence* is much more destructive than overt individual violence. We must recognize that people's lives are violated by the very normal and everyday workings of institutions. We do not see such events and situations as violent because they are not dramatic and predatory; they do not make for fascinating reading on the lives of preverts; but they kill, maim, and destroy many more lives than do violent individuals.

Here are some examples. Carmichael and Hamilton (1967:4), in distinguishing between *individual* and *institutional* racism, offer examples of each:

> When white terrorists bomb a black church and kill five black children, that is an act of individual racism, widely deplored by most segments of the society. But when in that same city—Birmingham, Alabama—five hundred black babies die each year because of lack of proper food, shelter, and medical facilities, and thousands more are destroyed and maimed physically, emotionally and intellec-

> tually because of conditions of poverty and discrimination in the black community, that is a function of institutional racism.

Surely this is violence; it is caused by the normal, quiet workings of institutions run by respectable members of the community. Many whites also suffer from the institutional workings of a profit-oriented society and economy; poor health, dead-end jobs, slum housing, hunger in rural areas, and so on, are daily realities in their lives. This is surely much worse violence than any committed by the Hell's Angels or street gangs. Only these groups get stigmatized and analyzed by sociologists of deviance, however, while those good people who live in luxurious homes (fixing tax laws for their benefit) off profits derived from an exploitative economic system—they are the pillars of their community.

Violence is committed daily by the government, very often by lack of action. The same system that enriches businessmen farmers with billions of dollars through farm subsidies cannot be bothered to appropriate a few millions to deal with lead poisoning in the slums. Young children

> ...get it by eating the sweet-tasting chips of peeling tenement walls, painted a generation ago with leaded paint.
>
> According to the Department of Health, Education, and Welfare, 400,000 children are poisoned each year, about 30,000 in New York City alone. About 3,200 suffer permanent brain damage, 800 go blind or become so mentally retarded that they require hospitalization for the rest of their lives, and approximately 200 die.
>
> The tragedy is that lead poisoning is totally man-made and totally preventable. It is caused by slum housing. And there are now blood tests that can detect the disease, and medicines to cure it. Only a lack of purpose sentences 200 black children to die each year (Newfield, 1971).[3]

Newfield goes on to report that on May 20, 1971, a Senate-House conference eliminated $5 million from an appropriations budget. In fact, 200 children had been sentenced to death and thousands more to maiming and suffering.

Similar actions of violence are committed daily by the government and corporations; but in these days of misplaced emphasis, ignorance, and manipulation we do not see the destruction inherent in these actions. Instead, we get fascinated, angry, and misled by the violence of the poor and the powerless. We see the violence committed during political rebellions in the ghettoes (called "riots" in order to dismiss them), but all along we ignored the daily violence committed against the ghetto residents by the institutions of the society: schools, hospitals, corporations, the government. Check any of these books on deviance, and see how much of this type of violence is even mentioned, much less explored and described.

It may be argued that some of this violence is (implicitly) recognized in discussions of "white-collar" crime. This is not the case, however. Of the 16 books under consideration, only three pay some attention to white-collar crime (Cohen, 1966; Clinard, 1968; Dinitz, et al., 1969); and of these, only the last covers the issue at some length. Even in these few discussions, however, the focus remains on the *individuals* who commit the actions (on their greediness, lack of morality, etc.), not on the economic and political institutions within which they operate. The selection in Dinitz, et al. (1969: 99–109), from the President's Commission on Law Enforcement and the Administration of Justice, at least three times (pp. 101, 103, 108) argues that white-collar crime is "pervasive," causes "financial burdens" ("probably far greater than those produced by traditional common law theft offenses"), and is generally harmful. At least in these pages, however, there is no investigation of the social, political, and economic conditions which make the pervasiveness, and lenient treatment, of white-collar crime possible.

The bias against examining the structural conditions behind white-collar crime is further revealed in Clinard's suggestions on how to deal with it (in his chapter "The Prevention of Deviant Behavior"). The only recommendation in three pages of discussion (704–7) is to teach everyone more "respect" for the law. This is a purely moralistic device; it pays no attention to the structural aspects of the problem, to the fact that even deeper than white-collar crime is ingrained a whole network of laws, especially tax laws, administrative policies, and institutions which systematically favor a small minority. More generally, discussions on the prevention of "deviance" and crime do not deal with institutional violence, and what we need to do to stop it.

But there is an obvious explanation for this oversight. The people committing serious white-collar crimes and executing the policies of violent institutions are respectable and responsible individuals, not "deviants"; this is the view of the President's Commission on Law Enforcement and the Administration of Justice.

> Significantly, the Antitrust Division does not feel that lengthy prison sentences are ordinarily called for [for white-collar crimes]. It "rarely recommends jail sentences greater than 6 months—recommendations of 30-day imprisonment are most frequent" (Dinitz, et al., 1969:105).

> Persons who have standing and roots in a community, and are prepared for and engaged in legitimate occupations, can be expected to be particularly susceptible to the threat of criminal prosecution. Criminal proceedings and the imposition of sanctions have a much sharper impact upon those who have not been hardened by previous contact with the criminal justice system (in Dinitz, et al., 1969:104).

At the same time, we are told elsewhere by the Commission that white-collar crime is pervasive and widespread; "criminal proceedings and the imposition of sanctions" do not appear to deter it much....

I want to start my concluding comment with two disclaimers.

a) I have tried to provide some balance and perspective in the field of "deviance," and in doing so I have argued against the exclusive emphasis on *nuts, sluts, and preverts* and their identities and subcultures. I do not mean, however, that the usually considered forms of "deviance" are unworthy of our attention. Suicide, prostitution, madness, juvenile delinquency, and others *are* with us; we cannot ignore them. People do suffer when labelled and treated as "deviant" (in *this* sense, "deviants" *are* different from conformists). Rather, I want to draw attention to phenomena which also belong to the field of "deviance."

b) It is because the sociology of deviance, especially the labelling approach, contains important, exciting, and revealing insights, because it tries to humanize the "deviant," and because it is popular, that it is easy to overlook some of the basic ideological biases still pervading the field. For this reason, I have tried to explore and detail some of these biases. At the same time, however, I do not mean to dismiss the contributions of the field as totally negative and useless. In fact, in my teaching I have been using two of the books discussed here, Simmons (1969) and Rubington and Weinberg (1968).

The argument can be summarized briefly. (1) We should not study only, or predominantly, the popular and dramatic forms of "deviance." Indeed, we should banish the concept of "deviance" and speak of oppression, conflict, persecution, and suffering. By focusing on the dramatic forms, as we do now, we perpetuate most people's beliefs and impressions that such "deviance" is the basic cause of many of our troubles, that these people (criminals, drug addicts, political dissenters, and others) are the real "troublemakers"; and, necessarily, we neglect conditions of inequality, powerlessness, institutional violence, and so on, which lie at the bases of our tortured society. (2) Even when we do study the popular forms of "deviance," we do not avoid blaming the victim for his fate; the continued use of the term "deviant" is one clue to this blame. Nor have we succeeded in normalizing him; the focus on the "deviant" himself, on his identity and subculture, has tended to confirm the popular prejudice that he is different.

References

Becker, Howard S. 1963. Outsiders. New York: Free Press.

———. (ed.) 1964. The Other Side. New York: Free Press.

———. 1967. "Whose side are we on?" Social Problems 14:239–247 (reprinted in Douglas, 1970a, 99–111; references to this reprint).

Bell, Robert R. 1971. Social Deviance: A Substantive Analysis. Homewood, Illinois: Dorsey.

Carmichael, Stokeley and Charles V. Hamilton. 1967. Black Power. New York: Random House.

Cleaver, Eldridge. 1968. Soul On Ice. New York: McGraw-Hill.

Clinard, Marshall B. 1968. Sociology of Deviant Behavior. (3rd ed.) New York: Holt, Rinehart, and Winston.

Cohen, Albert K. 1966. Deviance and Control. Englewood Cliffs, N.J.: Prentice-Hall.

Dinitz, Simon, Russell R. Dynes, and Alfred C. Clarke (eds.). 1969. Deviance. New York: Oxford University Press.

Douglass, Jack D. (ed.) 1970a. Observations of Deviance. New York: Random House.

———. (ed.) 1970b. Deviance and Respectability: The Social Construction of Moral Meanings. New York: Basic Books.

Gittlin, Todd and Nanci Hollander. 1970. Uptown: Poor Whites in Chicago. New York: Harper and Row.

Gouldner, Alvin W. 1968. "The sociologist as partisan: Sociology and the welfare state." American Sociologist 3:2, 103–116.

Jackson, George. 1970. Soledad Brother. New York: Bantam Books.

Lefton, Mark, J. K. Skipper, and C. H. McCaghy (eds.). 1968. Approaches to Deviance. New York: Appleton-Century-Crofts.

Lemert, Edwin M. 1967. Human Deviance, Social Problems, and Social Control. Englewood Cliffs, N.J.: Prentice-Hall.

Liazos, Alexander. 1970. Processing for Unfitness: socialization of "emotionally disturbed" lower-class boys into the mass society. Ph.D. dissertation, Brandeis University.

Lofland, John. 1969. Deviance and Identity. Englewood Cliffs, N.J.: Prentice-Hall.

McCaghy, Charles H., J. K. Skipper, and M. Lefton (eds.). 1968. In Their Own Behalf: Voices from the Margin. New York: Appleton-Century-Crofts.

Malcolm X. 1965. The Autobiography of Malcolm X. New York: Grove.

Matza, David. 1969. Becoming Deviant. Englewood Cliffs, N.J.: Prentice-Hall.

Newfield, Jack. 1971. "Let them eat lead." New York Times, June 16, p. 45.

Rose, Thomas (ed.). 1969. Violence in America. New York: Random House.

Rubington, Earl and M. S. Weinberg (eds.). 1968. Deviance: The Interactionist Perspective. New York: Macmillan.

Rushing, William A. (ed.). 1969. Deviant Behavior and Social Processes. Chicago: Rand McNally.

Simmons, J. L. 1969. Deviants. Berkeley, Cal.: Glendessary.

Szasz, Thomas S. 1970. The Manufacture of Madness. New York: Harper and Row.

Thompson, Hunter S. 1966. Hell's Angels. New York: Ballantine.

Notes

1. The subtitle of this paper came from two sources. a) A Yale undergraduate once told me that the deviance course was known among Yale students as "nuts and sluts." b) A former colleague of mine at Quinnipiac College, John Bancroft, often told me that the deviance course was "all about those preverts." When I came to write this paper, I discovered that these descriptions were correct, and concise summaries of my argument. I thank both of them. I also want to thank Gordon Fellman for a very careful reading of the first draft of the manuscript, and for discussing with me the general and specific issues I raise here.

2. With the exception of E. C. Hughes, in Becker (1964).

3. As Gittlin and Hollander (1970) show, the children of poor whites also suffer from lead poisoning.

Outsiders: Studies in the Sociology of Deviance

HOWARD S. BECKER

All social groups make rules and attempt, at some times and under some circumstances, to enforce them. Social rules define situations and the kinds of behavior appropriate to them, specifying some actions as "right" and forbidding others as "wrong." When a rule is enforced, the person who is supposed to have broken it may be seen as a special kind of person, one who cannot be trusted to live by the rules agreed on by the group. He is regarded as an *outsider*.

But the person who is thus labeled an outsider may have a different view of the matter. He may not accept the rule by which he is being judged and may not regard those who judge him as either competent or legitimately entitled to do so. Hence, a second meaning of the term emerges: the rule-breaker may feel his judges are *outsiders*.

In what follows, I will try to clarify the situation and process pointed to by this double-barrelled term: the situations of rule-breaking and rule-enforcement and the processes by which some people come to break rules and others to enforce them.

Some preliminary distinctions are in order. Rules may be of a great many kinds. They may be formally enacted into law, and in this case the police power of the state may be used in enforcing them. In other cases, they represent informal agreements, newly arrived at or encrusted with the sanction of age and tradition; rules of this kind are enforced by informal sanctions of various kinds.

Similarly, whether a rule has the force of law or tradition or is simply the result of consensus, it may be the task of some specialized body, such as the police or the committee on ethics of a professional association, to enforce it; enforcement, on the other hand, may be everyone's job or, at least, the job of everyone in the group to which the rule is meant to apply.

Many rules are not enforced and are not, in any except the most formal sense, the kind of rules with which I am concerned. Blue laws, which remain on the statute books though they have not been enforced for a hundred years, are examples. (It is important to remember, however, that an unenforced law may be reactivated for various reasons and regain all its original force, as recently occurred with respect to the laws governing the opening of commercial establishments on Sunday in Missouri.) Informal rules may similarly die from lack of enforcement. I shall mainly be concerned with what we can call the actual operating rules of groups, those kept alive through attempts at enforcement.

Finally, just how far "outside" one is, in either of the senses I have mentioned, varies from case to case. We think of the person who commits a traffic violation or gets a little too drunk at a party as being, after all, not very different from the rest of us and treat his infraction tolerantly. We regard the thief as less like us and punish him severely. Crimes such as murder, rape, or treason lead us to view the violator as a true outsider.

In the same way, some rule-breakers do not think they have been unjustly judged. The traffic violator usually subscribes to the very rules he has broken. Alcoholics are often ambivalent, sometimes feeling that those who judge them do not understand them and at other times agreeing that compulsive drinking is a bad thing. At the extreme, some deviants (homosexuals and drug addicts are good examples) develop full-blown ideologies explaining why they are right and thy those who disapprove of and punish them are wrong.

Definitions of Deviance

The outsider—the deviant from group rules—has been the subject of much speculation, theorizing, and scientific study. What laymen want to know about deviants is: why do they do it? How can we account for their rule-breaking? What is there about them that leads them to do forbidden things? Scientific research has tried to find answers to these questions. In doing so it has accepted the common-sense premise that there is something inherently deviant (qualitatively distinct) about acts that break (or seem to break) social rules. It has also accepted the common-sense assumption that the deviant act occurs because some characteristic of the person who commits it makes it necessary or inevitable that he should. Scientists do not ordinarily question the label "deviant" when it is applied to particular acts of people but rather take it as given. In so doing, they accept the values of the group making the judgment.

It is easily observable that different groups judge things to be deviant. This should alert us to the possibility that the person making the judgment of deviance, the process by which that judgment is arrived at, and the situation in which it is made may all be intimately involved in the phenomenon of deviance. To the degree that the common-sense view of deviance and the scientific theories that begin with its premises assume that acts that break rules are inherently deviant and thus take for granted the situations and processes of judgment, they may leave out an important variable. If scientists ignore the variable character of the process of judgment, they may by that omission limit the kinds of theories that can be developed and the kind of understanding that can be achieved.[1]

Our first problem, then, is to construct a definition of deviance. Before doing this, let us consider some of the definitions scientists now use, seeing what is left out if we take them as a point of departure for the study of outsiders

The simplest view of deviance is essentially statistical...from the average. When a statistician analyzes the results of an agricultural experiment, he describes the stalk of corn that is exceptionally tall and the stalk that is exceptionally short as deviations from the mean or average. Similarly, one can describe anything that differs from what is most common as a deviation. In this view, to be left-handed or redheaded is deviant, because most people are right-handed and brunette.

So stated, the statistical view seems simple-minded, even trivial. Yet it simplifies the problem by doing away with many questions of value that ordinarily arise in discussions of the nature of deviance. In assessing any particular case, all one need do is calculate the distance of the behavior involved from the average. But it is too simple a solution. Hunting with such a definition, we return with a mixed bag—people who are excessively fat or thin, murderers, redheads, homosexuals, and traffic violators. The mixture contains some ordinarily thought of as deviants and others who have broken no rule at all. The statistical definition of deviance, in short, is too far removed from the concern with rule-breaking which prompts scientific study of outsiders.

A less simple but much more common view of deviance identifies it as something essentially pathological, revealing the presence of a "disease." This view rests, obviously, on a medical analogy. The human organism, when it is working efficiently and experiencing no discomfort, is said to be "healthy." When it does not work efficiently, a disease is present. The organ or function that has become deranged is said to be pathological. Of course, there is little disagreement about what constitutes a healthy state of the organism. But there is much less agreement when one uses the notion of pathology analogically, to describe kinds of behavior that are regarded as deviant. For people do not agree on what constitutes healthy behavior. It is difficult to find a definition that will satisfy even such a select and limited group as psychiatrists; it is impossible to find one that people generally accept as they accept criteria of health for the organism.[2]

Sometimes people mean the analogy more strictly, because they think of deviance as the product of mental disease. The behavior of a homosexual or drug addict is regarded as the symptom of a mental disease just as the diabetic's difficulty in getting bruises to heal is regarded as a symptom of his disease. But mental disease resembles physical disease only in metaphor....[3] The medical metaphor limits what we can see much as the statistical view does. It accepts the lay judgment of something as deviant and, by use of analogy, locates its source within the individual, thus preventing us from seeing the judgment itself as a crucial part of the phenomenon.

Some sociologists also use a model of deviance based essentially on the medical notions of health and disease. They look at a society, or some part of a society, and ask whether there are any processes going on in it that tend to reduce its stability, thus lessening its chance of survival. They label such processes deviant or identify them as symptoms of social disorganization. They discriminate between those features of society which promote stability (and thus are "functional") and those which disrupt stability (and thus are "dysfunctional"). Such a view has the great virtue of pointing to areas of possible trouble in a society of which people may not be aware.[4]

But it is harder in practice than it appears to be in theory to specify what is functional and what dysfunctional for a society or social group. The question of what the purpose or goal (function) of a group is and, consequently, what things will help or hinder the achievement of that purpose, is very often a political question. Factions within the group disagree and maneuver to have their own definition of the group's function accepted. The function of the group or organization, then, is decided in political conflict, not given in the nature of the organization. If this is true, then it is likewise true that the questions of what rules are to be enforced, what behavior regarded as deviant, and which people labeled as outsiders must also be regarded as political.[5] The functional view of deviance, by ignoring the political aspect of the phenomenon, limits our understanding.

Another sociological view is more relativistic. It identifies deviance as the failure to obey group rules. Once we have described the rules a group enforces on its members, we can say with some precision whether or not a person has violated them and is thus, on this view, deviant.

This view is closest to my own, but it fails to give sufficient weight to the ambiguities that arise in deciding which rules are to be taken as the yardstick against which behavior is measured and judged deviant. A society has many groups, each with its own set of rules, and people belong to many groups simultaneously. A person may break the rules of one group by the very act of abiding by the rules of another group. Is he, then deviant? Proponents of this definition may object that while ambiguity may arise with respect to the rules peculiar to one or another group in society, there are some rules that are very generally agreed to by everyone, in which case the difficulty does not arise. This, of course, is a question of fact, to be settled by empirical research. I doubt there are many such areas of consensus and think it wiser to use a definition that allows us to deal with both ambiguous and unambiguous situations.

Deviance and the Responses of Others

The sociological view I have just discussed defines deviance as the infraction of some agreed-upon rule. It then goes on to ask who breaks rules, and to search for the factors in their personalities and life situations that might account for the infractions. This assumes that those who have broken a rule constitute a homogeneous category, because they have committed the same deviant act.

Such an assumption seems to me to ignore the central fact about deviance: it is created by society. I do not mean this in the way it is ordinarily understood, in which the causes of deviance are located in the social situation of the deviant or in "social factors" which prompt his action. I mean, rather, that *social groups create deviance by making the rules whose infraction constitutes deviance,* and by applying those rules to particular people and labeling them as outsiders. From this point of view, deviance is *not* a quality of the act the person commits, but rather a consequence of the application by others of rules and sanctions to an "offender." The deviant is one to whom that label has successfully been applied; deviant behavior is behavior that people so label.[6]

Since deviance is, among other things, a consequence of the responses of others to a person's act, students of deviance cannot assume that they are dealing with a homogeneous category when they study people who have been labeled deviant. That is, they cannot assume that these people have actually committed a deviant act or broken some rule, because the process of labeling may not be infallible; some people may be labeled deviant who in fact have not broken a rule. Furthermore, they cannot assume that the category of those labeled deviant will contain all those who actually have broken a rule, for many offenders may escape apprehension and thus fail to be included in the population of "deviants" they study. Insofar as the category lacks homogeneity and fails to include all the cases that belong in it, one cannot reasonably expect to find common factors of personality or life situation that will account for the supposed deviance.

What, then, do people who have been labeled deviant have in common? At the least, they share the label and the experience of being labeled as outsiders. I will begin my analysis with this basic similarity and view deviance as the product of a transaction that takes place between some social group and one who is viewed by that group as a rule-breaker. I will be less concerned with the personal and social characteristics of deviants than with the process by which they come to be thought of as outsiders and their reactions to that judgment.

Malinowski discovered the usefulness of this view for understanding the nature of deviance many years ago, in his study of the Trobriand Islands....[7] Whether an act is deviant, then, depends on how other people react to it. You can commit clan incest and suffer from no more than gossip as long as no one makes a public accusation; but you will be driven to your death if the accusation is made. The point is that the response of other people has to be regarded as problematic. Just because one has committed an infraction of a rule does not mean that others will respond as though this had happened. (Conversely, just because one has not violated a rule does not mean that he may not be treated, in some circumstances, as though he had.)

The degree to which other people will respond to a given act as deviant varies greatly. Several kinds of variation seem worth noting. First of all, there is variation over time. A person believed to have committed a given "deviant" act may at one time be responded to much more leniently than he would be at some other time. The occurrence of "drives" against various kinds of deviance illustrates this clearly. At various times, enforcement officials may decide to make an all-out attack on some particular kind of deviance, such as gambling, drug addiction, or homosexuality. It is obviously much more dangerous to engage in one of these activities when a drive is on than at any other time. (In a very interesting study of crime news in Colorado newspapers, Davis found that the amount of crime reported in Colorado newspapers showed very little association with actual changes in the amount of crime taking place in Colorado. And, further, that people's estimate of how much increase there had been in crime in Colorado was associated with the increase in the amount of crime news but not with any increase in the amount of crime).[8]

The degree to which an act will be treated as deviant depends also on who commits the act and who feels he has been harmed by it. Rules tend to be applied more to some persons than others. Studies of juvenile delinquency make the point clearly. Boys from middle-class areas do not get as far in the legal process when they are apprehended as do boys from slum areas. The middle-class boy is less likely, when picked up by the police, to be taken to the station; less likely when taken to the station to be booked; and it is extremely unlikely that he will be convicted and sentenced.[9] This variation occurs even though the original infraction of the rule is the same in the two cases. Similarly, the law is differentially applied to Negroes and whites. It is well known that a Negro believed to have attacked a white woman is much more likely to be punished than a white man who commits the same offense; it is only slightly less well known that a Negro who murders another Negro is much less likely to be punished than a white man who commits murder.[10] This, of course, is one of the main points of Sutherland's analysis of white-collar crime: crimes committed by corporations are almost always prosecuted as civil cases, but the same crime committed by an individual is ordinarily treated as a criminal offense.[11]

Some rules are enforced only when they result in certain consequences. The unmarried mother furnishes a clear example. Vincent[12] points out that illicit sexual relations seldom result in severe punishment or social censure for the offenders. If, however, a girl becomes pregnant as a result of such activities the reaction of others is likely to be severe. (The illicit pregnancy is also an interesting example of the differential enforcement of rules on different categories of people. Vincent notes that unmarried fathers escape the severe censure visited on the mother.)

Why repeat these commonplace observations? Because, taken together, they support the proposition that deviance is not a simple quality, present in some kinds of behavior and absent in others. Rather, it is the product of a process which involves responses of other people to the behavior. The same behavior may be an infraction of the rules at one time and not at another; may be an infraction when committed by one person, but not when committed by another; some rules are broken with impunity, others are not. In short, whether a given act is deviant or not depends in part on the nature of the act (that is, whether or not it violates some rule) and in part on what other people do about it.

Some people may object that this is merely a terminological quibble, that one can, after all, define terms any way he wants to and that if some people want to speak of rule-breaking behavior as deviant without reference to the reactions of others they are free to do so. This, of course, is true. Yet it might be worthwhile to refer to such behavior as *rule-breaking behavior* and reserve the term *deviant* for those labeled as deviant by some segment of society. I do not insist that this usage be followed. But it should be clear that insofar as a scientist uses "deviant" to refer to any rule-breaking behavior and takes as his subject of study only those who have been *labeled* deviant, he will be hampered by the disparities between the two categories.

If we take as the object of our attention behavior which comes to be labeled as deviant, we must recognize that we cannot know whether a given act will be categorized as deviant until the response of others has occurred. Deviance is not a quality that lies in behavior itself, but in the interaction between the person who commits an act and those who respond to it.

Whose Rules?

I have been using the term "outsiders" to refer to those people who are judged by others to be deviant and thus to stand outside the circle of "normal" members of the group. But the term contains a second meaning, whose analysis leads to another important set of sociological problems: "outsiders," from the point of view of the person who is labeled deviant, may be the people who make the rules he had been found guilty of breaking.

Social rules are the creation of specific social groups. Modern societies are not simple organizations in which everyone agrees on what the rules are and how they are to be applied in specific situations. They are, instead, highly differentiated along social class lines, ethnic lines, occupational lines, and cultural lines. These groups need not and, in fact, often do not share the same rules. The problems they face in dealing with their environment, the history and traditions they carry with them, all lead to the evolution of different sets of rules. Insofar as the rules of various groups conflict and contradict one another, there will be disagreement about the kind of behavior that is proper in any given situation.

Italian immigrants who went on making wine for themselves and their friends during Prohibition were acting properly by Italian immigrant standards, but were breaking the law of their new country (as, of course, were many of their Old American neighbors). Medical patients who shop around for a doctor may, from the perspective of their own group, be doing what is necessary to protect their health by making sure they get what seems to them the best possible doctor; but, from the perspective of the physician, what they do is wrong because it breaks down the trust the patient ought to put in his physician. The lower-class delinquent who fights for his "turf" is only doing what he considers necessary and right, but teachers, social workers, and police see it differently.

While it may be argued that many or most rules are generally agreed to by all members of a society, empirical research on a given rule generally reveals variation in people's attitudes. Formal rules, enforced by some specially constituted group, may differ from those actually thought appropriate by most people.[13] Factions in a group may disagree on what I have called actual operating rules. Most important for the study of behavior ordinarily labeled deviant, the perspectives of the people who engage in the behavior are likely to be quite different from those of the people who condemn it. In this latter situation, a person may feel that he is being judged according to rules he has had no hand in making and does not accept, rules forced on him by outsiders.

To what extent and under what circumstances do people attempt to force their rules on others who do not subscribe to them? Let us distinguish two cases. In the first, only those who are actually members of the group have any interest in making and enforcing certain rules. If an orthodox Jew disobeys the laws of kashruth only other orthodox Jews will regard this as a transgression; Christians or nonorthodox Jews will not consider this deviance and would have no interest in interfering. In the second case, members of a group consider it important to their welfare that members of certain other groups obey certain rules. Thus, people consider it extremely important that those who practice the healing arts abide by certain rules; this is the reason the state licenses physicians, nurses, and others, and forbids anyone who is not licensed to engage in healing activities.

To the extent that a group tries to impose its rules on other groups in the society, we are presented with a second question: Who can, in fact, force others to accept their rules and what are the causes of their success? This is, of course, a question of political and economic power. [The] political and economic process through which rules are created and enforced [must be considered]. Here it is enough to note that people are in fact always *forcing* their rules on others, applying them more or less against the will and without the consent of those others. By and large, for example, rules are made for young people by their elders. Though the youth of this country exert a powerful influence culturally—the mass media of communication are tailored to their interests, for instance—many important kinds of rules are made for our youth by adults. Rules regarding school attendance and sex behavior are not drawn up with regard to the problems of adolescence. Rather, adolescents find themselves surrounded by rules about these matters which have been made by older and more settled people. It is considered legitimate to do this, for youngsters are considered neither wise enough nor responsible enough to make proper rules for themselves.

In the same way, it is true in many respects that men make the rules for women in our society (though in America this is changing rapidly). Negroes find themselves subject to rules made for them by whites. The foreign-born and those otherwise ethnically peculiar often have their rules made for them by the Protestant Anglo-Saxon minority. The middle class makes rules the lower class must obey—in the schools, the courts, and elsewhere.

Differences in the ability to make rules and apply them to other people are essentially power differentials (either legal or extralegal). Those groups whose social position gives them weapons and power are best able to enforce their rules. Distinctions of age, sex, ethnicity, and class are all related to differences in power, which account for differences in the degree to which groups so distinguished can make rules for others.

In addition to recognizing that deviance is created by the responses of people to particular kinds of behavior, by the labeling of that behavior as deviant, we must also keep in mind that the rules created and maintained by such labeling are not universally agreed to. Instead, they are the object of conflict and disagreement, part of the political process of society.

Notes

1. Cf. Donald R. Cressey, "Criminological Research and the Definition of Crimes," *American Journal of Sociology,* LVI (May, 1951), 546–551.

2. See the discussion in C. Wright Mills, "The Professional Ideology of Social Pathologists," *American Journal of Sociology,* XLIX (September, 1942), 165–180.

3. Thomas Szasz, *The Myth of Mental Illness* (New York: Paul B. Hoeber, Inc., 1961), pp. 44–45; see also Erving Goffman, "The Medical Model and Mental Hospitalization," in *Asylums: Essays on the Social Situation of Mental Patients and Other Inmates* (Garden City: Anchor Books, 1961), pp. 321–386.

4. See Robert K. Merton, "Social Problems and Sociological Theory," in Robert K. Merton and Robert A. Nisbet, editors, *Contemporary Social Problems* (New York: Harcourt, Brace and World, Inc., 1961), pp. 697–737; and Talcott Parsons, *The Social System* (New York: The Free Press of Glencoe, 1951), pp. 249–325.

5. Howard Brotz similarly identifies the question of what phenomena are "functional" or "dysfunctional" as a political one in "Functionalism and Dynamic Analysis," *European Journal of Sociology,* II (1961), 170–179.

6. The most important earlier statements of this view can be found in Frank Tannenbaum, *Crime and the Community* (New York: Ginn, 1938), and E. M. Lemert, *Social Pathology* (New York: McGraw-Hill Book Co., Inc., 1951). A recent article stating a position very similar to mine is John Kitsuse, "Societal Reaction to Deviance: Problems of Theory and Method," *Social Problems,* 9 (Winter, 1962), 247–256.

7. Bronislaw Malinowski, *Crime and Custom in Savage Society* (New York: Humanities Press, 1926), pp. 77–80.

8. F. James Davis, "Crime News in Colorado Newspapers," *American Journal of Sociology,* LVII (January, 1952), 325–330.

9. See Albert K. Cohen and James F. Short, Jr., "Juvenile Delinquency," in Merton and Nisbet, *op. cit.,* p. 87.

10. See Harold Garfinkel, "Research Notes on Inter- and Intra-Racial Homicides," *Social Forces,* 27 (May, 1949), 369–381.

11. Edwin H. Sutherland, "White Collar Criminality," *American Sociological Review,* V (February, 1940), 1–12.

12. Clark Vincent, *Unmarried Mothers* (New York: The Free Press of Glencoe, 1961), pp. 3–5.

13. Arnold M. Rose and Arthur E. Prell, "Does the Punishment Fit the Crime?—A Study in Social Valuation," *American Journal of Sociology,* LXI (November, 1955), 247–259.

Deviance, Norms, and Social Reaction

ERICH GOODE

The basic dimension of deviance as "objectively given" versus "subjectively problematic" addresses the question, "Can deviance exist in the abstract, *as deviance,* in the absence of negative judgments by audiences?" That is, can an act or a trait be regarded by the sociologist as a form of deviance independent of its evaluation by hypothetical or actual observers? This question is answered in different ways by the various sociological approaches studying deviance. It is answered in the affirmative by two theoretical approaches, idealistic utopian Marxists and social pathologists. Theorists adopting both positions believe that they know deviance when they see it, that the status of certain acts and traits with respect to deviance is "objectively given," or an absolute fact. It does not much matter what anyone else thinks about the behavior or the individuals under evaluation; these theorists believe that they are, themselves, the relevant audience. Utopian Marxists argue that acts such as exploitation, oppression, racism, sexism, and imperialism should be regarded as deviant. These actions are wrong *regardless* of how they are evaluated or judged; the evil in these actions is an objective fact, even if this fact is not recognized in a given society. Social pathologists view the conventional, law-abiding society as a kind of healthy organism and deviance as a kind of sickness; deviance eats away at the normal, healthy body, and should be eliminated, much the way a disease is cured. Again, what deviance is is an objective fact that is determined not by the evaluations and judgments of audiences but by consultation with a social pathologist.

The opposite perspective is that *what deviance is* is *not* an objective fact but a matter of judgment *by* specific audiences. Deviance exists when the members of specific societies, or categories within a given society, regard a given action or condition wrong and punishable. Judgments of deviance vary from one society to another, one segment within a society to another, and one historical time period to another. Deviance, in other words, is "relative" rather than absolute, a subjective phenomenon rather than an objective fact. However, there are at least three varieties of relativistic definitions—the normative, the "hard" reactive, and the "soft" reactive definitions of deviance. The principal difference between them is whether a hypothetical act or condition can be regarded as deviance or whether each *actual case* must be encountered, judged, and reacted to before it may properly be regarded as deviance. In other words, can deviance exist in the abstract, as a *type* or *category* or *class* of actions and conditions?

The "normative" definition, while relativistic, is based on the notion that deviance can be determined by an external observer who witnesses or learns about an

From Erich Goode, "Deviance, Norms, and Social Reaction," *Deviant Behavior,* 3 (October–December): 47–53. Adapted by permission of the author and publisher.

TABLE 1.1 Different Approaches to Deviance

Approach	Specific perspective	Basis for deviance
Absolutist (Deviance as "objectively given")	1. Social pathology (orthodox psychoanalysis, conventional morality, etc.)	Immorality and/or "sickness"
	2. Marxist-radical	Exploitation and oppression
Relativistic (Deviance as "subjectively problematic")	1. Normative perspectives (anomie theory, learning theory, etc.)	A formal violation of norms
	2. "Soft" reactive theory (some brands of labeling theory)	Past, present, and/or potential future negative reactions of audiences either experienced or inferred by ego
	3. "Hard" reactive theory (ethno-methodology, some brands of labeling theory, etc.)	Actual, concrete negative reactions by specific audiences

action or condition, compares it with a given society's norms, and notes a discrepancy between the two. The normative definition regards all acts or conditions *that violate a society's norms* as deviance. A given action or condition does not have to be seen or evaluated by a member of that society, nor does the perpetrator or possessor have to be apprehended or punished. All that is necessary to for us to know that something is deviant is that it is in contradiction with a given normative code. The normative definition holds that it is possible to have such a thing as *secret deviance*—acts or conditions that no one but the perpetrator or possessor knows about. Secrecy has nothing to do with its deviant status; secret or not, *any* violation of a normative code constitutes or defines deviance.

Moreover, it is possible to have *classes* or *categories* of deviance. It isn't necessary to observe or learn about *each and every* individual act or condition and determine the deviant status of *each one separately*. If an action or a condition falls into a general *category* of commonly punished actions or conditions, it is deviant (Black and Reiss, 1970). If we know that norms exist in a society condemning sexual intercourse with a member of the same sex, and we encounter or find out about a case of it in real life, we *already* know that it is deviant—even before we determine whether it has *in fact* resulted in punishment for the participants. We can know *in advance* whether an act is deviant by consulting a society's normative code. To be plain about it, to the normative definition, *deviance is a violation of the norms.*

The "hard" reactive definition argues that deviance exists *when and only when* an action or a condition *has actually and concretely* resulted in punishment or condemnation. No condemnation, no deviance. If an action that *seems like* others that have been punished in the past is never detected, *it isn't deviant*. To the "hard" reactive theorist, there's no such thing as "secret" deviance; it's a contradiction in terms. We can't know in advance how an act or a condition will be reacted to; we have to wait and see in each actual instance. To the "hard" reactive sociologists, there's no such thing as the "perfect murder." In fact, we can't know whether a given killing is a murder in the first place until it has been judged as such by a real audience, for instance, a jury (Wilson, 1970; Pollner, 1974). It is the negative reaction that *constitutes* deviance; it is what brings its reality about in the first place.

In the view of many deviance specialists, there are problems with both the normative and the "hard" reactive definitions of deviance. My solution is to adopt the "soft" reactive definition, which I'll discuss momentarily. Here are a few problems with the normative definition.

By calling deviance a simple violation of the norms, we run into a number of theoretical and empirical problems.

problems w/ normative

1. First, we turn the norms, which in reality are concepts, into hard, concrete phenomena, pretending that "the norms" cause behavior in some abstract, unspecified fashion. *A norm* does not cause us to behave in a certain way; we do so because of actual, concrete messages we've learned from childhood (along with a feeling that certain actions are right, good, and proper, fear of sanctions, desire for rewards, and a number of other factors), and what each one of us learns is a bit different.

2. The normative definition also underplays exceptions, assuming that everyone in a given society (except the deviant) agrees with the norms. But in every society, there are social circles, pockets large and small, whose members have a very different notion of right and wrong from the mainstream. Often, behavior enacted in those circles and outside the mainstream is rewarded, not punished. Is it still deviant behavior?

3. The normative definition does not adequately provide for contingencies and extenuating circumstances that alter an audience's judgment of whether an act or an individual is *in fact* actually *regarded* as deviant. Conveying a seriously injured person to a hospital often entails breaking the speed limit; in that case, will a police officer give the speeder a ticket (Gibbs, 1972)? If not, can we still refer to speeding as deviant in general?

4. The normative definition also ignores the distinction between violations of norms that generate no special attention and ones that cause audiences to punish the actor or possessor. As Erikson (1964: 10) says, a bank teller who is a petty "slave to routine," who is more concerned with following the rules than with serving customers, and a bank robber are both violating the norm, but the first "does not ordinarily create any concern in the rest of the community," whereas the second "triggers the whole machinery of social control into vigorous action."

5. The normative definition also disregards the role of the audience in interpreting, modifying, amplifying, discouraging, and in general influencing deviant behavior—that is, it fails to grasp the interactional nature of behavior, the fact that it is enmeshed in a dialog, or give-and-take situation. In other words, the hold "the norms" have on an actor weakens when parties someone is close to and interacting with reward rather than punish their violation. When a minor act of delinquency becomes elaborated into a truly major one, how meaningful is it for us to refer to either as a normative violation?

And yet, we are ensnared in a true dilemma here. On the one hand, we cannot know for sure if a given—albeit widely condemned—act will *actually* be punished, since so many exceptions and contingencies abound. As Kitsuse (1962) demonstrates, when heterosexuals discover that someone they know or are interacting with is a homosexual, they do not necessarily, or even usually, react in a condemnatory, punishing fashion. If homosexuality is so often not reacted to negatively, is it proper to refer to it *in general* as a form of deviance, the hard reactivist sociologist asks?

On the other hand, as Gibbs (1972) points out, we *do* have some idea *in advance* which acts or conditions are *likely* to result in condemnation and punishment; sanctioning is not a random process with respect to social reactions. The sight of a totally naked man walking down the street is, under nearly all circumstances we could hypothesize, *highly likely* to result in negative sanctions for him. To me, this means that some sort of a blend or synthesis of the normative and the hard reactive definitions becomes necessary.

In my view, a "soft" version of the reactive definition handles this dilemma. My understanding of soft reactivism contains the following particulars:

1. Norms do not by themselves cause (or inhibit) behavior. What "the norms" are is a set of inferences constructed by sociologists as a result of adding up and averaging out reactions that they have seen to behavior in many situations and contexts, in the presence of a wide range of audiences. That is, the sociologist should be able to say, regarding a certain act, "To me, this looks very much like an example of behavior I've seen punished just about everywhere. Therefore, I'll call it an instance of deviance. From this, I can infer what the norms are." The normative sociologists have got the whole process backwards: they work from the supposed norms to societal reactions. Soft reactive sociologists do the reverse: they build up an image of what the norms look like as a result of observing societal reactions. Asking respondents what they regard as deviance is a substitute for this, a second-best but sometimes necessary methodology to get around the fact that there is simply a great deal of behavior we cannot observe.

2. No rule is absolute. Not even the most rigid determinist can possibly expect "a correlation coefficient of 1.0" to be necessary to identify group norms. Consequently, the soft reactive theorist must adopt a probabilistic approach to deviance: "individual or group behavior is deviant if it falls within a class of behavior for which there is a probability of negative sanctions subsequent to its detection" (Black and Reiss, 1970:63). If the sociologist is sufficiently empathic, he or she will be able to discern whether the specific audience witnessing or evaluating the behavior in question will judge that it actually belongs to that general class of behavior that has generated punishment for the actors in the past. To the extent that "norm violations" are *not* "reacted against," they are thereby not instances of deviant behavior.

3. Because most behavior that *would* earn the actor punishment is never detected, let alone sanctioned, any reasonable observer is forced to ask the question:

what is the actor's perception of how the audience feels regarding his or her behavior? How does this perception influence the actor's further behavior? His or her self-image? The enactor of deviant behavior must navigate in a sea of imputed negative judgments regarding his or her behavior (see Warren and Johnson, 1972:77, on this point). The actor's putative labeling by audiences cannot be ignored in this process. (The actor's evaluation of his or her behavior is a separate, although important, issue; all actors are also audiences to their own behavior.)

4. The societal reactions do not (necessarily) create the behavior in question de novo or ab ovo. It is true, as Meier asserts, that the police "do not define crime" nor do psychiatrists "generate mental disorders" (in the sense that the behavior in question would not have existed in the absence of the judgments in question), but they are part of the process that renders certain actions deviant in the first place. They impart *to* certain acts their peculiarly deviant ("criminal," "sick," etc.) quality. Although societal reaction does not create the actual behavior we define as homosexuality, it does lend to it a stigmatized status—and influences certain features that would be lacking in the absence of negative labeling. (See the debate on this issue in Whitam, 1977; Goode, 1981; and the rejoinders that follow.)

References

Black, Donald J., and Albert J. Reiss, Jr. 1970. "Police Control of Juveniles." American Sociological Review 35:63–77.

Erikson, Kai T. 1964. "Notes on the Sociology of Deviance." Pp. 9–21 in Howard S. Becker (ed.), The Other Side: Perspectives on Deviance. New York: Free Press.

Gibbs, Jack P. 1972. "Issues in defining deviant behavior." Pp. 39–92 in R. A. Scott and J. D. Douglas (eds.), Theoretical Perspectives on Deviance. New York: Basic Books.

Goode, Erich. 1981. "Comments on the homosexual role." Journal of Sex Research 17 (Feb.): 54–65.

Kitsuse, John I. 1962. "Societal reaction to deviant behavior." Social Problems 9 (Winter): 247–256.

Pollner, Melvin. 1974. "Sociological and common-sense models of the labelling process." Pp. 27–40 in R. Turner (ed.), Ethnomethodology: Selected Readings. Baltimore: Penguin.

Rubington, Earl, and Martin S. Weinberg (eds). 1978. Deviance: The Interactionist Perspective (3rd ed.). New York: Macmillan.

Warren, Carol A. B., and John M. Johnson. 1972. "A critique of labeling theory from the phenomenological perspective." Pp. 69–92 in R. A. Scott and J. D. Douglas (eds.), Theoretical Perspectives on Deviance. New York: Basic Books.

Whitam, Frederick L. 1977. "The homosexual role: A reconsideration." Journal of Sex Research 13 (Feb.): 1–11.

Wilson, Thomas P. 1970. "Normative and interpretive paradigms in sociology." Pp. 57–79 in J. D. Douglas (ed.), Understanding Everyday Life. Chicago: Aldine.

Part II

Theories of Deviant Behavior

Since the dawn of human collectivities, we have wondered about why certain people act in ways, some feel, they shouldn't act. *Why do they do it?* has been the dominant question about wrongdoing. Why is this man violent? Why is that woman strange? Why does the child over there tell so many lies? Why do these people take advantage of others?

The same questions that trouble the man and woman in the street also generate the curiosity of sociologists of deviance and crime. As we've seen, one major approach to the study of deviance is to ask, "Why deviance?" That is, why do some people engage in deviant behavior? Some of these explanations point to differences among individuals; these are called "kinds of people" theories. These individualistic or kinds of people explanations may be genetic or hormonal (wrongdoing is caused by the possession of certain biological traits), psychological (personality characteristics or differences in rewarding or punishing experiences), or even sociological (for instance, people learn that engaging in deviance has positive value as a result of interacting in groups that espouse that value). To answer the question, "Why do they do it?" or "Why deviance?" we study the characteristics or traits of individual people, their experiences, their backgrounds, and so on.

Other explanations point to differences in *social structure;* that is, certain contexts or situations are more likely to encourage violations of the norms: Deviance is more common in certain societies or communities, or under certain circumstances because of the nature of those societies, those communities, those circumstances. Everyone who lives in them is subject to their influence, although, of course, not all who are will necessarily deviate. To answer the question, "Why deviance?" we need to know about the characteristics, not of individuals, but of the larger structures in which these individuals live—the society, the community, the neighborhood, or specific social contexts. For instance, saying that, generally speaking, people will break the law if they know they will escape detection and apprehension is a structural not an individual statement; it has nothing to do with the characteristics of *who* we are looking at—in general, an absence of surveillance and punishment will increase the likelihood of violating the law. To say that people who live in a society in which standards and norms no longer grip the populace—commonly referred to as *anomie*—where everyone is unsure of what is right and wrong, are more likely to violate certain norms is to make a *structural* not an individual statement.

The first and most ancient explanation for deviance and other acts of wrongdoing is demonic possession: "The devil made him do it." "Evil spirits made her do it." Possession by the devil or evil spirits has been the dominant explanation for evil and other untoward behavior for tens of thousands of years. A half-million years ago, Stone Age humans drilled holes into the skulls of individuals who engaged in wrongdoing of some kind—individuals who, today, would probably be recognized as being mentally ill—so that evil spirits could escape. The ancient Hebrews, Egyptians, Babylonians, Assyrians, Greeks, and Romans performed rites of exorcism to cast out demonic beings presumably dwelling in the body and soul of transgressors. In Renaissance Europe, hundreds of thousands of men and women, 85 percent of whom were women, were burned at the stake for "consorting with the devil" and presumably engaging in wicked deeds as a consequence. Even among a fairly well-educated European elite, demonic possession was a dominant explanation for certain kinds of wrongdoing until the early 1600s. In the Salem colony in Massachussetts, an outbreak of witchcraft accusations took place. Unlike its European predecessor, only 350 people were accused, and only 20 were executed; the whole episode was over in a year. Clearly, by the late 1600s, Western society did not have the structural or cultural wherewithal to mount a major offensive against witchcraft. Western society has simply become too secular, too materialistic, too skeptical of accusations of demonic causes for wrongdoing. The mainstream of Western society shifted its explanation for deviance from the spiritual to the material realm. Nonetheless, pockets or subcultures of dissenters, who retain a belief in the validity of demonic possession as an explanation for evil, remain.

In the past 300 years or so the so-called man and woman on the street have held their own theories of deviance and other forms of wrongdoing. In legal commentaries, plays, poems, sagas, songs, and in everyday talk among ordinary members of the society there has been "a prolonged attempt to make sense of the existence of wickedness"; in societies everywhere, individuals "have repeatedly dwelt on the conflict between good and evil." This speculation has been dubbed "shadow criminology" or "proto-criminology" (Downes and Rock, 1982, p. 50). Such speculation tends to be unsystematic, diffuse, and ad hoc—made up for the moment on an act-by-act, crime-by-crime basis. These explanations tend to be commonsensical and usually without empirical foundation. Shadow criminology has always been and remains the most popular form of theorizing about deviance.

Perhaps the first sophisticated and academically respectable perspective or theory of criminal and deviant behavior is the "free will" or classical school of criminology of Cesare Beccaria (1738–1794) and his followers (Vold and Bernard, 1986, pp. 18–34). Rather than being seen as a result of seduction by demonic spirits, or the commonsense forces that rule public speculation, violations of norms, rules, and laws were thought to be caused by *free will*, a rational calculation of pleasure and pain. Individuals choose among a number of alternative courses of action according to the benefits they believe will accrue to them. They avoid activities that will bring them more pain or cost than pleasure; they seek those where the calculus favors the pleasure side of the equation. This model, then, sees people as free, rationalistic, and hedonistic. Actions that bring pleasure to an individual will be enacted and continued; those that are painful will be abandoned. The way to ensure conformity to society's norms and laws, these eighteenth-century thinkers believed, is to apprehend and punish offenders just sufficiently painfully so that they realize that they will lose out in this pain-pleasure calculation.

Some time in the middle of the nineteenth century, coinciding more or less with the publication of Charles Darwin's influential book, *On the Origin of Species* (1859), criminological thinking shifted away from free will to seeing crime as behavior that was to some extent beyond the control, understanding, and rational will of the criminal. Instead, one school believed that criminal and other deviant behaviors were caused by biological defects of one kind or another. Cesare Lombroso (1835–1909), in his book, *Criminal Man* (1876), argued that most crime is committed by primitive evolutionary throwbacks, representatives of an earlier, more primitive form of humanity, as much apelike as human in their makeup. While biological thinking declined in importance after the turn of the nineteenth century, it began to make a comeback in the 1960s, and remains a robust approach to deviance and crime, although in the field of sociology, its influence is fairly small.

"Social pathology" is the name given to the late-nineteenth- to early-twentieth-century perspective that adopted an organic or medical analogy toward deviance and crime. Social pathologists believed that society is very much like an organism and deviance and crime are very much like a disease. To the social pathologist, deviance represented an inability to fit into the normal, healthy social body; it was, by its very nature, pathological. There were two elements that underlay the organic analogy; social pathology was an uneasy alliance or marriage between science (or, in this case, pseudo-science) and conventional moralism. The "science" part was a corruption of evolutionary biology, while the "moralism" part was an evaluation of certain behaviors as "bad" and others as "good." Social pathology viewed progressive evolution as an inevitability. It accepted the view of society as evolving slowly, steadily, and progressively toward a better and better state. Certain elements or forces derailed society's progress. Two in particular were discussed. Some individuals—deviants—were seen as unable or unwilling to adjust to conventional, mainstream society's laws, standards, values, and norms. The cause? A failure of socialization was theorized to be the most basic cause of deviance and crime. Some people can't contribute their fair share to the community. Or they are so contrary and selfish they won't do so. Though evolution was seen as an inevitability, social pathologists thought that progressive elements in the society would hasten that process by working to motivate individuals to fit into the conventional social structure. In addition to individual pathologies, there are structural pathologies. Some institutions move at slower or faster rates than others. This is the process that is referred to as "cultural lag." Some people may be bewildered by the contradictions they face; they can't keep up with the complexities that modern life presents them. (For a discussion of the social pathology perspective, see Mills, 1943, 1963, pp. 525–552; Davis, 1980, pp. 31–55; Rubington and Weinberg, 1977, pp. 17–24). Social pathology had its heyday roughly between 1880 and 1920; by the end of World War I, students and researchers of deviance, crime, and delinquency recognized that society was not really very much like an organism and deviance was not really very much like a disease, and seeing them that way was not very productive. Consequently, they moved on to other approaches.

The 1920s saw the emergence of a distinctly different approach to the study of deviance and crime: social disorganization. This approach is so important in the development of the field, and remains important in its own right as an approach that is still used today, that I devote an entire chapter, Chapter 2, to social disorganization theory.

Anomie or strain theory developed out of an insight by Robert K. Merton in 1938: In American society, deviance is the product of the disjunction between the norms and values of the society, which teach us to want and expect material success, and its economic structure, which restricts the access of most of us to that selfsame material success. As with social disorganization, although anomie theory declined in importance after its heyday in the 1950s and early 1960s, it made a comeback in the 1980s; it remains an important approach in the study of deviance to this day. Hence, anomie theory deserves its own chapter, Chapter 3.

In the third edition of Edwin Sutherland's textbook on criminology (1939), a theory of crime was presented; this theory emphasized that crime (and by extension, deviance and delinquency as well) is learned in ordinary social interaction with intimates. Learning theory, like social disorganization and anomie theory, remains a central explanation of deviance and crime, and, like those theories, deserves its own chapter; two versions of learning theory are presented in Chapter 4.

These three causal theories do not exhaust all sociological explanations of deviant behavior; far from it. Some theories emphasize opportunities to commit deviance and crime (Cohen et al., 1980; Gould, 1969). Others see an explanation of deviance as commonsensical and obvious—breaking the rules is fun and it gets us what we want; instead, what requires an explanation is conventional, rule-abiding behavior. And what explains following the rules are our bonds to conventional society (Hirschi, 1969). Still other theories emphasize that criminals (and by extension, this certainly includes many enactors of deviance) lack the self-control that governs the rest of us (Gottfredson and Hirschi, 1990). Some of these theories are specialized; they do not attempt to explain deviance in general. Some are addressed mainly or exclusively to property crime; some address crime but not necessarily certain forms of deviance. Still, in one way or another, they all focus on one or another form of rule breaking. At this point, there is no master theory that is both widely adopted and seems to explain all, or nearly all, forms of deviance. Consequently, it is necessary to be fairly eclectic or broad in our approach to theories of deviance. Given the wide variety of deviant behaviors, this makes a great deal of sense. It is entirely possible that there is no consistent, overarching behavioral entity that we refer to as deviance.

Perhaps what makes deviance a social phenomenon is the way it is conceptualized, seen, reacted to, and dealt with.

Theories of deviant behavior are legion, and no anthology can possibly hope to cover them all. What I have done is to present the three theories that, as measured by how often they are cited and referred to in the field, are the most important causal approaches in the study of deviance. Their development and reception tell us a great deal about the field; it is to social disorganization, anomie theory, and learning theory that we must now turn our attention.

References

Cohen, Lawrence E., Marcus Felson, and Kenneth C. Land. 1980. Property crime rates in the United States: A macrodynamic analysis, 1947–1977. *American Journal of Sociology,* 86 (July): 90–118.

Davis, Nanette J. 1980. *Sociological Constructions of Deviance: Perspectives and Issues in the Field* (2nd ed.). Dubuque, Iowa: William C. Brown.

Downes, David, and Paul Rock. 1982. *Understanding Deviance: A Guide to the Sociology of Crime and Rule Breaking.* Oxford, England: Clarendon Press.

Gottfredson, Michael R., and Travis Hirschi. 1990. *A General Theory of Crime.* Stanford, Calif.: Stanford University Press.

Gould, LeRoy C. 1969. The changing structure of property crime in an affluent society. *Social Forces,* 48 (1): 50–59.

Hirschi, Travis. 1969. *Causes of Delinquency.* Berkeley: University of California Press.

Mills, C. Wright. 1943. The professional ideology of social pathologists. *American Journal of Sociology,* 49 (September): 165–180.

Mills, C. Wright. 1963. *Power, Politics, and People: The Collected Essays of C. Wright Mills* (ed. Irving Louis Horowitz). New York: Bantam Books.

Rubington, Earl, and Martin S. Weinberg (eds.). 1977. *The Study of Social Problems: Five Perspectives.* New York: Oxford University Press.

Sutherland, Edwin H. 1939. *Principles of Criminology* (3rd ed.). Philadelphia: Lippincott.

Vold, George B., and Thomas J. Bernard. 1986. *Theoretical Criminology* (3rd ed.). New York: Oxford University Press.

Chapter 2

Social Disorganization

Just after World War I, a school of thought emerged out of the research that was conducted in the city of Chicago by professors and graduate students at the University of Chicago. In fact, Chicago sociology became practically coterminous with the sociology of Chicago. The social disorganization school is often referred to as the "Chicago school" for these reasons. This school is associated with some of sociology's most noteworthy American founders, including W. I. Thomas, Robert Park, Ernest Burgess, and Clifford Shaw. The Chicago school also trained the very first generation of African-American sociologists, an illustrious group of sociologists that included Horace Cayton, St. Clair Drake, and E. Franklin Frazier, who was the first, and for a couple of generations, remained the only, Black president of the American Sociological Association.

The Chicago school shifted its primary emphasis from individual pathology and individual problems of adjustment, which were social pathology's emphases, to seeing the social structure as the source of the problem. The principal culprit was social change. Neighborhoods became overwhelmed by social change. Change brought about instability and disruption, not gradual, evolutional transitions that were supposed to move the society in a positive direction. Along with this disruption and conflict, various forms of deviance and crime emerged. Disorganization theorists adopted the *ecological* approach to human behavior. In biology, change involves a competition between and among biological species. In social life, change involves competition between and among different social groups and categories. In biology, a territory in which a certain species grows is invaded by a new and competing species. The two or more species compete for dominance in a territory. The weaker species loses out. Its representatives die out, move on to a new and less desirable territory, and must make adjustments and accommodations to defeat and migration. At some point, a new equilibrium or assimilation is reached, a new symbiotic order that reflects the hold the dominant species has gained in the territory.

In a parallel way, human groups, too, compete for dominance in a territory. There are winners and losers. The losers experience a breakdown in normative structure. Social control breaks down and deviance increases. The losing population experiences social disorganization. The parallel between biological species and social groups is not a perfect one, of course. For one thing, in human neighborhoods, it is often the so-called invading group that is the *less* powerful group, the group that experiences a great deal of social disorganization, whereas the group that leaves is the more powerful group, the group that relocates in a newer neighborhood, one that they define as more desirable. Yet, in this process, presumably, it is the group that leaves whose members experience relatively little social disorganization. Still, if we see the school as emphasizing competition between and among social categories, and see *ecology* as central—that is, geographical and social location as determining or influencing deviance through the mechanism of social disorganization—we can grasp its most important points. Certain neighborhoods or communities are disorganized. Community controls have broken down. Many of their residents are adrift, isolated, unattached, unentangled, and unencumbered by social control. Simply by living in a specific neighborhood in the city, residents are free, or are pressured to engage in, deviant and criminal actions. They are freed from the scrutiny and control of conventional society. In a nutshell: *Social change produces community disorganization, which causes personal disorganization, which, in turn, causes deviant behavior.*

As a consequence, deviance varies systematically by physical and geographical location. Where somebody is located residentially determines the likelihood that that person will commit deviant and criminal behavior. The structural characteristics of a neighborhood determine its crime rate, the likelihood that its residents will be mentally ill, that its juvenile residents will engage in delinquency and get into trouble with the law, and so on. Deviance is absent in some neighborhoods and common, even routine, in others. Residents live in neighborhoods that are in transition, in which many people live who have been torn from their roots, from traditional structures. These are areas in which the population is geographically and socially unstable, moves a great deal, and is made up of diverse social, economic, and racial groups or categories; relatively few homeowners; neighborhoods with many immigrants or migrants; many single, unmarried, unattached males; absent fathers; in a high proportion of community households, many members per household, some of them unrelated; residents who live next to one another, or in the same neighborhood, who don't know one another, and who don't care about one another. These are indicators or measures or manifestations of social disorganization.

The social disorganization school made a number of contributions to sociology generally and to the study of deviance specifically. One is empirical. It was a combination of two approaches: the objective and the subjective, the quantitative and the qualitative. The approach that attempts to measure objectively external factors and conditions, such as the crime rate, the divorce rate, ratios of foreign-born, percentages of home ownership, and so on. And the approach that focuses on the subjective side of social life, that attempts to explore the meaning of social life as experienced by subjects and informants themselves. In short, it was both social-scientific and ethnographic at the same time.

In other words, as I see it, one of the major contributions of the social disorganization school was empirical. It said to sociologists of deviance: Get up out of your armchairs, stop theorizing from your offices, your ivory towers, get out into the streets, find out what deviance is really like. Get close, nose to nose, face to face. Study the social world close up, with no illusions.

The second contribution the so-called Chicago school made was *empathic*—putting yourself in the deviant's shoes. It "asks us to imagine that deviants are people like ourselves" (Pfohl, 1994, p. 209). Why? Because they are the products not of pathology, a defective biological makeup, or possession by a wicked demon, but by the rather accidental, fortuitous contingency of their geographical or spatial location "in the natural location of a changing society" (p. 299). In short, deviants have been "disproportionately exposed to the disruptive forces of rapid social change" (p. 209). If the rest of us were to be exposed to the same forces, we might very well have ended up doing or being the same thing.

But social disorganization theory has sustained substantial criticism over the decades; after the 1940s, it fell out of favor with deviance researchers. In the late 1980s and early 1990s, it made something of a comeback, and a number of sociologists are once again working within the social disorganization framework (Skogan, 1990; Bursik and Grasmick, 1993). However, it will never regain the undisputed status as the premier and most influential approach in deviance research it held between 1920 and 1940.

The first problem that much of the field has seen with the social disorganization approach is that it was not always careful in the operationalization of some of its central concepts. Why is this particular concept defined in this particular way? Does it make theoretical or empirical sense? Why, for instance, is a large number of persons per household a measure or indicator of disorganization? In many Asian immigrant households newly arrived in the United States, a large number of family members—some cousins or even more distantly related—live in the same dwelling unit. Yet, the members of these households have low rates of crime and other forms of deviance. Why is a high proportion of unmarried men a sign or measure of disorganization? Is a college dormitory a disorganized institution because there are a lot of single men living in it? Do educated professional lesbians live "disorganized" lives because they do not have males living with them? If a neighborhood had many such households, would it automatically be disorganized? Today, in most suburban neighborhoods (such as the one I live in) most residents simply do not know one another. Except for perhaps a half-dozen families, I know no one in my neighborhood, and yet, its crime rate is relatively low. How do we explain this? While it is one thing to point out statistical regularities, it is quite another to use statistical relationships as conceptual categories, as fundamental definitions of our basic explanatory factors. Too often, the social disorganization theorists expressed their biases in their definitions and concepts.

Second—and this is related to the first problem—the Chicago theorists failed to recognize that they identified a certain kind of community organization rather than the *absence* of community organization. If neighborhood patterns departed from it, the community was seen as disorganized. But what they failed to recognize was that there are different forms of social and community organization. Differences in organization may be confused with the presence of disorganization (Pfohl, 1994, p. 210). The way of life of other social categories was often interpreted as "disorganized" when seen through the lens of their own white, middle-class perspective. For instance, while I suspect that, statistically speaking, for a child growing up, it's advantageous to have a positive, functioning, intact, complete parental set, this is far from necessary, and in a substantial proportion of the cases, there are departures from this pattern. In the case of the African-American family, female-headed households represented an organized adaptation to the removal or disappearance of black males, from slavery on. William Whyte (1943) showed that the Italian slum of the 1930s had its own version of social organization, even though it was different from the organization the Chicago school envisioned as adaptive. In short, different *kinds* of organization cannot be equated with social disorganization.

Third, there was something of a middle-class bias in the thinking of the social disorganization school. Many socially disapproved activities are committed as frequently, or more so, by the affluent, middle-class members of the society. Deviance is not an exclusively or even mainly a lower-class phenomenon. Members of the Chicago school studied street crime, mental illness, drug addiction, delinquency, alcoholism, street prostitution—"disreputable" or so-called nuts and sluts deviance and crimes. There probably is a statistical or probabilistic connection between socioeconomic status and the commission of these deviant behaviors, but it is far from an absolute relationship. There are many, many middle-class drug addicts, many affluent mentally ill people, many well-to-do alcoholics, and so on. It's a relationship with a lot of exceptions. In addition, in many ways, middle-class and upper-middle-class individuals have ways of insulating or protecting themselves from surveillance and observation by agencies of social control. The particular *expressions* of middle-class deviance are often less visible. Middle-class call girls are less visible than lower- or working-class street prostitutes. Middle-class alcoholics have friends and associates who shield them from observation and control and are less likely to get into trouble than working- and lower-class skid row alcoholics. Physician narcotic addicts learn how to use drugs with a minimum of risk, while lower- and working-class street junkies or crack heads don't and can't.

So the first two problems with the correlation between socioeconomic and deviance are these: First, we have to deal with the theoretical problems posed by the exceptions, and second, there is the problem raised by the assumption that the sociologist's observation of a phenomenon is precisely the same as the frequency of its occurrence.

There is another problem with the relationship between deviance and socioeconomic status: Many forms of deviance are ignored by this approach; they simply don't fit in with the theory. There are many forms of "organized respectable deviance" (Pfohl, 1994, p. 211). Examples include embezzlement, false and illegal advertising, illegal pollution, the abuse of government power, corporate price fixing, and so on. The people who engage in such behavior do not live in disorganized neighborhoods. They live, for the most part, in affluent or at least middle-class urban neighborhoods or in the comfortable suburbs. Disorganization theory can't handle such forms of deviance. The theory considers deviance of disreputable rather than "respectable" individuals.

Another major flaw in social disorganization theory is that the theory does not deal with the problems that social stratification causes in people's lives—and which, in turn, can influence their likelihood of engaging in deviance and crime. The Chicago school approach assumed that what they were seeing in transitional neighborhoods was the impact of social disorganization. But it happens that the neighborhoods that undergo the most dramatic change were also the *poorest* neighborhoods. "Slums are the product of an unequal distribution of material resources.... Neglected is the possibility that people [may] deviate because social stratification has robbed them of human resources and a sense of dignity" (Pfohl, 1994, p. 212). It is entirely possible that poor people "may experience higher rates of what the society...defines as deviant, not because they lack organized normative constraints, but because they are frustrated, angry, or seeking escape from the oppression of a stratified social existence" (p. 212). Disorganization may very well be a "historical by-product of social domination by the powerful" (p. 212). Social disorganization theory did not grasp the essentially political character of deviance, that is, its close connection to stratification and the allocation of society's resources. Instead, it saw deviance as an inevitable by-product of a more or less natural process.

For some of these reasons, social disorganization theory declined in importance during the 1940s. It is also possible that it lost influence as a result of the decline of the University of Chicago as the overwhelmingly dominant sociology department in the country and the emergence in post–World War II America of a relatively quiet period, a period with less explosive, less obvious social change, smoother urbanization patterns, suburbanization rather than urbanization, and an extremely low rate of immigration. In other words, one of the factors that may have reduced the influence of social disorganization theory was the decline of some of the forces and factors that originally made social pathology irrelevant and brought social disorganization to center stage as an explanation for deviance and crime. As I said, today, the approach is far from dead. In fact, it has made something of a comeback in the past five to ten years or so. But it is not the overwhelmingly dominant approach the way it was in the 1920s, 1930s, and early 1940s. It did make a contribution to the study of deviance, but by the end of the Second World War, it was time to move on to other perspectives.

Robert Faris and Warren Dunham present a classic discussion of the social disorganization approach to deviance and crime in "Natural Areas of the City." Social disorganization theory saw cities as a set of concentric circles, much like an archery target, with the most disorganized and high-deviance areas toward the center and the least disorganized and lowest-deviance areas as being located toward the outer fringes, near the suburbs. In highly disorganized areas, social control has broken down and residents drift into "unconventionality and into dissipations of various kinds." Rodney Stark offers a more contemporary version of social disorganization theory in "Deviant Places: A Theory of the Ecology of Crime." Thirty propositions, employing factors ranging from social density to the visibility of offenses, help explain why deviance and crime are more common in some locations than in others.

References

Bursik, Robert J., Jr., and Harold G. Grasmick. 1993. *Neighborhoods and Crime: The Dimensions of Effective Community Control*. New York: Lexington Books.

Pfohl, Stephen. 1994. *Images of Deviance and Social Control: A Sociological History* (2nd ed.). New York: McGraw-Hill.

Skogan, Wesley G. 1990. *Disorder and Decline: Crime and the Spiral of Decay in American Neighborhoods*. New York: Free Press.

Natural Areas of the City

ROBERT E. L. FARIS and H. WARREN DUNHAM

A relationship between urbanism and social disorganization has long been recognized and demonstrated. Crude rural-urban comparisons of rates of dependency, crime, divorce and desertion, suicide, and vice have shown these problems to be more severe in the cities, especially the large rapidly expanding industrial cities. But as the study of urban sociology advanced, even more striking comparisons between the different sections of a city were discovered. Some parts were found to be as stable and peaceful as any well-organized rural neighborhood while other parts were found to be in the extreme stages of social disorganization. Extreme disorganization is confined to certain areas and is not characteristic of all sections of the city.

Out of the interaction of social and economic forces that cause city growth a pattern is formed in these large expanding American cities which is the same for all the cities, with local variations due to topographical and other differences. This pattern is not planned or intended, and to a certain extent resists control by planning. The understanding of this order is necessary to the understanding of the social disorganization that characterizes urban life.

The Natural Areas Depicted as Circular Zones

The most striking characteristics of this urban pattern, as described by Professor Burgess,[1] may be represented by a system of concentric zones, shown in Figure 2.1. Zone I, at the center, is the central business district. The space is occupied by stores, business offices, places of amusement, light industry, and other business establishments. There are few residents in this area, except for transients inhabiting the large hotels, and the homeless men of the "hobohemia" section which is usually located on the fringe of the business district.

Zone II is called the zone in transition. This designation refers to the fact that the expanding industrial region encroaches on the inner edge. Land values are high because of the expectation of sale for industrial purposes, and since residential buildings are not expected to occupy the land permanently, they are not kept in an improved state. Therefore, residential buildings are in a deteriorated state and rents are low. These slums are inhabited largely by unskilled laborers and their families. All the settlements of foreign populations as well as the rooming-house areas are located in this zone.

Zone III, the zone of workingmen's homes, is inhabited by a somewhat more stable population with a higher percentage of skilled laborers and fewer foreign-born and unskilled. It is intermediate in many respects between the slum areas and

From Robert E. L. Faris and Warren Dunham, *Mental Disorders in Urban Areas* (Chicago: University of Chicago Press, 1965), pp. 1–10, 19–21. © The University of Chicago Press. Reprinted by permission of the publisher.

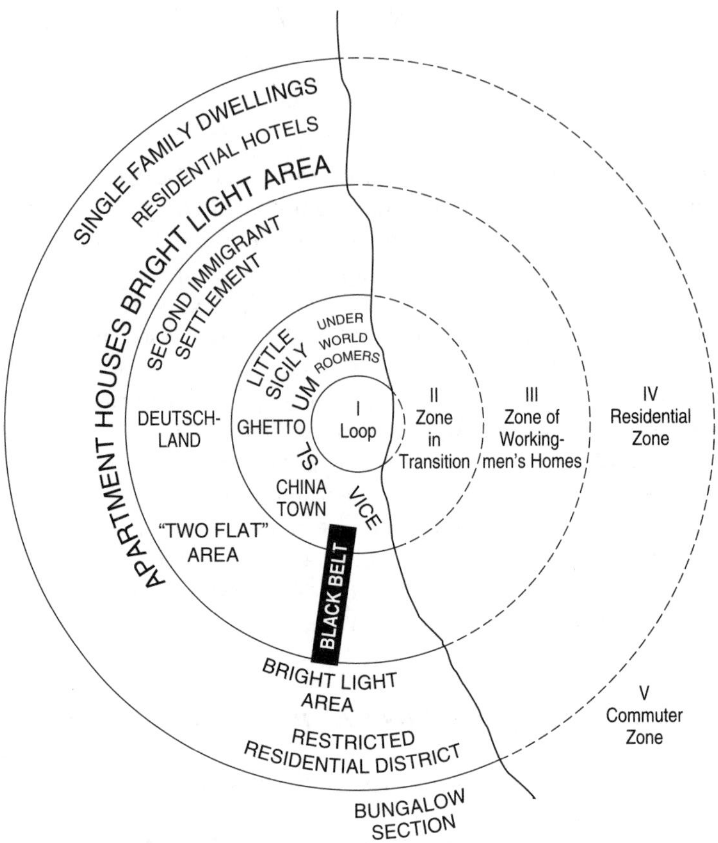

Figure 2.1 Natural Areas and Urban Zones

From R. E. Park and E. W. Burgess, *The City* (Chicago: University of Chicago Press, 1925). © The University of Chicago Press. Reprinted by permission of the publisher.

the residential areas. In it is located the... or second immigrant settlement colonies, representing the second generation of those families who have migrated from Zone II.

Zones IV and V, the apartment-house and commuters' zones, are inhabited principally by upper-middle-class families. A high percentage own their homes and reside for long periods at the same address. In these areas stability is the rule and social disorganization exceptional or absent.

The characteristics of the populations in these zones appear to be produced by the nature of the life within the zones rather than the reverse. This is shown by the striking fact that the zones retain all their characteristics as different populations flow through them. The large part of the population migration into the city consists of the influx of unskilled labor into the second zone, the zone in transition. These new arrivals displace the populations already there, forcing them to move farther out into the next zone. In general, the flow of population in the city is of this character, from the inner zones toward the outer ones. Each zone, however, retains its characteristics whether its inhabitants be native-born white, foreign-born, or Negro. Also each racial or national group changes its character as it moves from one zone to the next.

Within this system of zones, there is further sifting and sorting of economic and social institutions and of populations. In the competition for land values at the center of the city, each type of business finds the place in which it can survive. The finding of the place is not infrequently by trial and error, those locating the wrong place failing. There emerge from this competition financial sections, retail department store sections, theater sections, sections for physicians' and dentists' offices, for specialized shops, for light industry, for warehouses, etc.

Similarly, there are specialized regions for homeless men, for rooming-houses, for apartment hotels, and for single homes. The location of each of these is determined ecologically and the characteristics also result from the interaction of unplanned forces. They maintain their characteristics in spite of the flow of various racial and national groups through them and invariably impress their effects on each of these groups. These have been called "natural areas" by Professor Park,[2] because they result from the interactions of natural forces and are not the result of human intentions.

Fortunately, the city of Chicago has been studied somewhat more intensively than most cities of its size. Certain of these areas are significant in relation to social disorganization. It is possible to define and describe these areas with certain kinds of objective data. The major divisions of the city can be seen [on a map]. Extending outward from the central business district are the principal industrial and railroad properties. The rooming-house sections extend along three arms radiating from the center to the north, west, and south. The slum areas are roughly defined by the regions containing over 50 per cent foreign-born and native-born of foreign parentage and over 50 per cent Negro. Beyond these areas is the residential section. In the Lake Calumet section at the southeastern corner of the city is another industrial region inhabited by a foreign-born population.

Too small to be shown on [a] map are the areas of homeless men—the "hobohemia" areas.[3] These are located on three main radial streets and are just outside the central business district. Their inhabitants are the most unstable in the city. The mobility and anonymity of their existence produce a lack of sociability and in many cases deterioration of the personality. Although spending their time in the most crowded parts of the city, these homeless men are actually extremely isolated. For the most part they represent persons unable to obtain an economic foothold in society, and so they maintain themselves by occasional labor, by petty thievery, by begging, and by receiving charity. As they have no opportunity for normal married life, their sexual activities are limited to relations with the lowest type of prostitutes and to homosexuals. The rate of venereal infection is high among these men. Chronic alcoholism is also a common characteristic of the members of this group. Their lives are without goal or plan, and they drift aimlessly and alone, always farther from the conventional and normal ways of living.

Another area of importance is the rooming-house area. This is usually located along main arteries of transportation and a little farther from the center of the city. In Chicago there are several rooming-house sections, the three largest consisting of arms radiating to the north, west, and south, just beyond the hobohemia areas, each extending for something over two miles in length and from a half-mile to over a mile in width. The populations of these areas are principally young, unmarried white-collar workers, who are employed in the central business district during the day and live in low-priced rented rooms within walking distance or a short ride from their work.[4] Within the area the population is constantly shifting, turning over entirely about once each four months. Anonymity and isolation also characterize the social relations in this area; no one knows his neighbors and no one cares what they might think or say. Consequently the social control of primary group relations is absent, and the result is a breakdown of standards of personal behavior and a drifting into unconventionality and into dissipations and excesses of various sorts. The rates of venereal diseases and of alcoholism are high in this area, and the suicide rate is higher than for any other area of the city.[5]

The foreign-born slum areas occupy a large zone surrounding the central business and industrial area. Within this zone there are a number of segregated ethnic communities, such as the Italian, Polish, Jewish, Russian, and Mexican districts. The newly arrived immigrants of any nationality settle in these communities with their fellow-countrymen. In these groups the language, customs, and many institutions of their former culture are at least partly preserved. In some of the most successfully isolated of these, such as the Russian-Jewish "ghetto," the Old-World cultures are preserved almost intact. Where this is the case, there may be a very successful social control and little social disorganization, especially in the first generation. But as soon as the isolation of these first-settlement communities begins to break down, the disorganization is severe. Extreme poverty is the rule; high rates of juvenile delinquency, family disorganization, and alcoholism reflect the various stresses in the lives of these populations.

Two distinct types of disorganizing factors can be seen in the foreign-born slum areas. The first is the isolation of the older generation, the foreign-born who speak English with difficulty or not at all and who are never quite able to become assimilated to the point of establishing intimate friendships with anyone other than their native countrymen. Within the segregated ethnic communities these persons are well adapted to their surroundings, but as soon as they move away or are deserted by their neighbors, they suffer from social isolation.[6] The second type of disorganizing factor operates among the members of the second and third generations. The very high delinquency rate among the second-generation children has been shown by Shaw.[7] This disorganization can be shown to develop from the nature of the child's social situation. Also growing out of the peculiar social situation of the second generation is the mental conflict of the person who is in process of transition between two cultures—the culture of his ancestors and the culture of the new world in which he lives. As he attends American schools and plays with children of other than his own nationality, the child soon finds himself separated from the world of his parents. He loses respect for their customs and traditions and in many cases becomes ashamed of his own nationality, while at the same time he often fails to gain complete acceptance into the American group of his own generation. This is particularly true if he is distinguished by color or by features which betray his racial or national origin.

This person is then a "man without a culture," for though he participates to some extent in two cultures, he rejects the one and is not entirely accepted by the other.[8]

The Negro areas are, in general, similar in character to the foreign-born slum areas. The principal Negro district in Chicago extends for several miles southward from the business district. Two smaller Negro districts are located on the Near West Side, as well as one on the Near North Side. In the larger area on the South Side, the social disorganization is extreme only at the part nearest the business district.[9] In the parts farther to the south live the Negroes who have resided longer in the city and who have become more successful economically. These communities have much the same character as the nearby apartment-house areas inhabited by native-born whites.

For some miles along the Lake Front in Chicago a long strip of apartment-hotel districts has grown up. These districts occupy a very pleasant and favorable location and attract residents who are able to pay high rentals. The rates of various indices of social disorganization are in general low in these sections.

The outlying residential districts of middle-class and upper-middle-class native-born white population live in apartments, two-flat homes, and single homes. In these districts, and especially the single home areas in which there is a large percentage of homes owned by the inhabitants, the population is stable and there is little or no social disorganization in comparison with those areas near the center of the city.

Not only are such statistical facts as population composition, literacy, dependency rates, and disease rates known to vary greatly in the different sections of the city, but also mental life and behavior. In one of the most conclusive of these studies, the study of juvenile delinquency by Clifford R. Shaw and his associates,[10] sufficient control was obtained to establish with reasonable certainty that the high rates of delinquency were products not of the biological inferiority of the population stocks that inhabit the slum areas, nor of any racial or national peculiarity, but rather of the nature of the social life in the areas themselves. The delinquency rates remained constantly high in certain urban areas which were inhabited by as many as six different national groups in succession. Each nationality suffered from the same disorganization in these areas and each nationality alike improved after moving away from the deteriorated areas.

As has been shown, the natural areas which have been defined above can be identified by the use of certain mathematical indices for different types of social phenomena. Such indices as the percentage of foreign-born, the percentage of homes owned, the sex ratio, the median rentals paid, the density of population, the rate of mobility, the educational rate, the percentage of rooming-houses and hotels, and the percentage of condemned buildings, roughly tend to identify these areas and to differentiate between them. These indices might be regarded as ones which measure the extent of social disorganization between the different communities and the natural areas of the city. Other types of objective data, representing such social problems as juvenile delinquency, illegitimacy, suicide, crime, and family disorganization, might be considered as indices representing effects or results of certain types of social processes As in the research of Clifford Shaw which has been described above, the rates for these different social problems tend to fit rather closely into the ecological structure of the city as described by Park, Burgess, and others. In other words, in all of these social problems there is the concentration of high rates close to the center of the city, with the rates declining in magnitude as one travels in any direction toward the city's periphery. Shaw's study of juvenile delinquency gives one of the most complete pictures of this pattern. The other studies, in general, show the same pattern with certain variations which develop because of the location of certain ethnic groups in certain parts of the city.

The problem of mental disorder has been for the first time approached by the utilizing of this ecological technique. It is the attempt to examine the spatial character of the relations between persons who have different kinds of mental breakdowns. While this type of approach is used in this study, the authors wish to emphasize that they regard it as having definite limitations in understanding the entire problem of mental disorder. It can be looked upon as a purely cultural approach and as such does not tend to conflict with any understanding of this problem which may come from biological, physiological, or psychological approaches. However, in the light of these previous studies of social problems utilizing this method it does seem particularly desirable to study the distribution of the different types of mental disorders.

Notes

1. R. E. Park and E. W Burgess, *The City* (Chicago: University of Chicago Press, 1925).
2. R. E. Park, "Sociology," in *Research in the Social Sciences,* ed. Wilson Gee (New York: Macmillan Co., 1929), pp. 28–29.
3. Nels Anderson, *The Hobo* (Chicago: University of Chicago Press, 1923).
4. H. W. Zorbaugh, *The Gold Coast and the Slum* (Chicago: University of Chicago Press, 1929).
5. R. S. Cavan, *Suicide* (Chicago: University of Chicago Press, 1928).
6. Louis Wirth, *The Ghetto* (Chicago: University of Chicago Press, 1928).
7. C. R. Shaw et al., *Delinquency Areas* (Chicago: University of Chicago Press, 1929).
8. Everett Stonequist, *The Marginal Man* (New York: Charles Scribner's Sons, 1937).
9. E. Franklin Frazier, *The Negro Family in Chicago* (Chicago: University of Chicago Press, 1932).
10. C. R. Shaw and H. D. McKay, *Report on the Causes of Crime,* National Commission on Law Observance and Enforcement (Washington, D.C.: U.S. Government Printing Office, 1931).

Deviant Places: A Theory of the Ecology of Crime

RODNEY STARK

It is well known that high rates of crime and deviance can persist in specific neighborhoods despite repeated, complete turnovers in the composition of their populations. That this occurs suggests that more than "kinds of people" explanations are needed to account for the ecological concentration of deviance—that we also need to develop "kinds of places" explanations. This essay attempts to codify more than a century of ecological research on crime and deviance into an integrated set of 30 propositions and offers these as a first approximation of a theory of deviant places.

Norman Hayner, a stalwart of the old Chicago school of human ecology, noted that in the area of Seattle having by far the highest delinquency rate in 1934, "half the children are Italian." In vivid language, Hayner described the social and cultural shortcomings of these residents: "largely illiterate, unskilled workers of Sicilian origin. Fiestas, wine-drinking, raising of goats and gardens...are characteristic traits." He also noted that the businesses in this neighborhood were run down and on the wane and that "a number of dilapidated vacant business buildings and frame apartment houses dot the main street," while the area has "the smallest percentage of home-owners and the greatest aggregation of dilapidated dwellings and run-down tenements in the city" (Hayner, 1942:361–363). Today this district, which makes up the neighborhood surrounding Garfield High School, remains the prime delinquency area. But there are virtually no Italians living there. Instead, this neighborhood is the heart of the Seattle black community.

Thus we come to the point. How is it that neighborhoods can remain the site of high crime and deviance rates *despite a complete turnover in their populations?* If the Garfield district was tough *because* Italians lived there, why did it stay tough after they left? Indeed, why didn't the neighborhoods the Italians departed to become tough? Questions such as these force the perception that the composition of neighborhoods, in terms of characteristics of their populations, cannot provide an adequate explanation of variations in deviance rates. Instead, *there must be something about places as such* that sustains crime.[1]

This paper attempts to fashion an integrated set of propositions to summarize and extend our understanding of ecological sources of deviant behavior. In so doing, the aim is to revive a *sociology* of deviance as an alternative to the social psychological approaches that have dominated for 30 years. That is, the focus is on traits of places and groups rather than on traits of individuals. Indeed, I shall attempt to show that by adopting survey research as the *preferred* method of research, social

From Rodney Stark, "Deviant Places: A Theory of the Ecology of Crime," *Criminology*, vol. 25, no. 4 (1987), pp. 893–909.

scientists lost touch with significant aspects of crime and delinquency. Poor neighborhoods disappeared to be replaced by individual kids with various levels of family income, but no detectable environment at all. Moreover, the phenomena themselves became bloodless, sterile, and almost harmless, for questionnaire studies cannot tap homicide, rape, assault, armed robbery, or even significant burglary and fraud—too few people are involved in these activities to turn up in significant numbers in feasible samples, assuming that such people turn up in samples at all. So delinquency, for example, which once had meant offenses serious enough for court referrals, soon meant taking $2 out of mom's purse, having "banged up something that did not belong to you," and having a fist fight. This transformation soon led repeatedly to the "discovery" that poverty is unrelated to delinquency (Tittle, Villemez, and Smith, 1978).

Yet, through it all, social scientists somehow still knew better than to stroll the streets at night in certain parts of town or even to park there. And despite the fact that countless surveys showed that kids from upper- and lower-income families scored the same on delinquency batteries, even social scientists knew that the parts of town that scared them were not upper-income neighborhoods. In fact, when the literature was examined with sufficient finesse, it was clear that class *does* matter—that serious offenses are very disproportionately committed by a virtual under class (Hindelang, Hirschi, and Weis, 1981).

So, against this backdrop, let us reconsider the human ecology approach to deviance. To begin, there are five aspects of urban neighborhoods which characterize high deviance areas of cities. To my knowledge, no member of the Chicago school ever listed this particular set, but these concepts permeate their whole literature starting with Park, Burgess, and McKenzie's classic, *The City* (1925). And they are especially prominent in the empirical work of the Chicago school (Faris and Dunham, 1939; Shaw and McKay, 1942). Indeed, most of these factors were prominent in the work of 19th-century moral statisticians such as the Englishmen Mayhew and Buchanan, who were doing ecological sociology decades before any member of the Chicago school was born. These essential factors are (1) density; (2) poverty; (3) mixed use; (4) transience; and (5) dilapidation.

Each of the five will be used in specific propositions. However, in addition to these characteristics of places, the theory also will incorporate some specific *impacts* of the five on the moral order as *people respond to them*. Four responses will be assessed: (1) moral cynicism among residents; (2) increased opportunities for crime and deviance; (3) increased motivation to deviate; and (4) diminished social control.

Finally, the theory will sketch how these responses further *amplify* the volume of deviance through the following consequences: (1) by attracting deviant and crime-prone people and deviant and criminal activities to a neighborhood; (2) by driving out the least deviant; and (3) by further reductions in social control.

The remainder of the paper weaves these elements into a set of integrated propositions, clarifying and documenting each as it proceeds Citations will not be limited to recent work, or even to that of the old Chicago school, but will include samples of the massive 19th-century literature produced by the moral statisticians. The aim is to help contemporary students of crime and deviance rediscover the past and to note the power and realism of its methods, data, and analysis. In Mayhew's (1851) immense volumes, for example, he combines lengthy, first-person narratives of professional criminals with a blizzard of superb statistics on crime and deviance.

Before stating any propositions, one should note the relationship between this essay and ongoing theoretical work, especially my deductive theory of religion (Stark and Bainbridge, 1987). A major impediment to the growth of more formal and fully deductive theories in the social sciences is that usually one lacks the space necessary to work out the links between an initial set of axioms and definitions and the relevant set of propositions (statements deduced from the axioms and definitions). In consequence, it is not shown that the propositions outlined here follow logically from my axiomatic system, but they can be derived. For those interested in these matters, one can refer to the more complete formulation of control theory that was derived in *A Theory of Religion* (Stark and Bainbridge, 1987) to explain the conditions under which people are recruited by deviant religious movements. In any event, logical steps from one proposition to another will be clear in what follows, but the set as a whole must be left without obvious axiomatic ancestry.

Proposition 1: *The greater the density of a neighborhood, the more association between those most and least predisposed to deviance.*

At issue here is not simply that there will be a higher proportion of deviance-prone persons in dense neighborhoods (although, as will be shown, that is true, too), rather it is proposed that there is a higher average level of interpersonal interactions in such neighborhoods and that individual traits will have less influence on patterns of contact. Consider kids. In low-density neighborhoods—wealthy suburbs, for example—some active effort is required for one 12-year-old to see another (a ride from a parent often is required). In these settings, kids and their parents can easily limit contact with bullies and those in disrepute. Not so in dense urban neighborhoods—the "bad" kids often live in the same building as the "good" ones, hang out close by, dominate the nearby playground, and are nearly unavoidable. Hence, peer groups in dense neighborhoods will tend to be inclusive, and all young people living there will face maximum peer pressure to deviate—as differential association theorists have stressed for so long.

Proposition 2: *The greater the density of a neighborhood, the higher the level of moral cynicism.*

Moral cynicism is the belief that people are much worse than they pretend to be. Indeed, Goffman's use of the dramaturgical model in his social psychology was rooted in the fact that we require ourselves and others to keep up appearances in public. We all, to varying degrees, have secrets, the public airing of which we would find undesirable. So long as our front-stage performances are credible and creditable, and we shield our backstage actions, we serve as good role models (Goffman, 1959, 1963). The trouble is that in dense neighborhoods it is much harder to keep up appearances—whatever morally discreditable information exists about us is likely to leak.

Survey data suggest that upper-income couples may be about as likely as lower-income couples to have physical fights (Stark and McEvoy, 1970). Whether that is true, it surely is the case that upper-income couples are much less likely to be *overheard* by the neighbors when they have such a fight. In dense neighborhoods, where people live in crowded, thin-walled apartments, the neighbors do hear. In these areas teenage peers, for example, will be much more likely to know embarrassing things about one another's parents. This will color their perceptions about what is normal, and their respect for the conventional moral standards will be reduced. Put another way, people in dense neighborhoods will serve as inferior role models for one another—the same people would *appear* to be more respectable in less dense neighborhoods.

Proposition 3: *To the extent that neighborhoods are dense and poor, homes will be crowded.*

The proposition is obvious, but serves as a necessary step to the next propositions on the effects of crowding, which draw heavily on the fine paper by Gove, Hughes, and Galle (1979).

Proposition 4: *Where homes are more crowded, there will be a greater tendency to congregate outside the home in places and circumstances that raise levels of temptation and opportunity to deviate.*

Gove and his associates reported that crowded homes caused family members, especially teenagers, to stay away. Since crowded homes will also tend to be located in mixed-use neighborhoods (see Proposition 9), when people stay away from home they will tend to congregate in places conducive to deviance (stores, pool halls, street corners, cafes, taverns, and the like).

Proposition 5: *Where homes are more crowded, there will be lower levels of supervision of children.*

This follows from the fact that children from crowded homes tend to stay out of the home and that their parents are glad to let them. Moreover, Gove and his associates found strong empirical support for the link between crowding and less supervision of children.

Proposition 6: *Reduced levels of child supervision will result in poor school achievement, with a consequent reduction in stakes in conformity and an increase in deviant behavior.*

This is one of the most cited and strongly verified causal chains in the literature on delinquency (Thrasher, 1927; Toby and Toby, 1961; Hirschi, 1969; Gold, 1970; Hindelang, 1973). Indeed, Hirschi and Hindelang (1977:583) claim that the "school variables" are among the most powerful predictors of delinquency to be found in survey studies: "Their significance for delinquency is nowhere in dispute and is, in fact, one of the oldest and most consistent findings of delinquency research."

Here Toby's (1957) vital concept of "stakes in conformity" enters the propositions. Stakes in conformity are those things that people risk losing by being detected in deviant actions. These may be things we already possess as well as things we can reasonably count on gaining in the future. An important aspect of the school variables is their potential for future rewards, rewards that may be sacrificed by deviance, but only for those whose school performance is promising.

Proposition 7: *Where homes are more crowded, there will be higher levels of conflict within families weakening attachment and thereby stakes in conformity.*

Gove and his associates found a strong link between crowding and family conflict, confirming Frazier's (1932:636) observations:

> So far as children are concerned, the house becomes a veritable prison for them. There is no way of knowing how many conflicts in Negro families are set off by the irritations caused by overcrowding people, who come home after a day of frustration and fatigue, to dingy and unhealthy living quarters.

Here we also recognize that stakes in conformity are not merely material. Indeed, given the effort humans will expend to protect them, our attachments to others are among the most potent stakes in conformity We risk our closest and most intimate relationships by behavior that violates what others expect of us. People lacking such relationships, of course, do not risk their loss.

Proposition 8: *Where homes are crowded, members will be much less able to shield discreditable acts and information from one another, further increasing moral cynicism.*

As neighborhood density causes people to be less satisfactory role models for the neighbors, density in the home causes moral cynicism. Crowding makes privacy more difficult. Kids will observe or overhear parental fights, sexual relations, and the like. This is precisely what Buchanan noted about the dense and crowded London slums in 1846 (in Levin and Lindesmith, 1937:15):

> In the densely crowded lanes and alleys of these areas, wretched tenements are found containing in every cellar and on every floor, men and women, children both male and female, all huddled together, sometimes with strangers, and too frequently standing in very doubtful consanguinity to each other. In these abodes decency and shame have fled; depravity reigns in all its horrors.

Granted that conditions have changed since then and that dense, poor, crowded areas in the center cities of North America are not nearly so wretched. But the essential point linking "decency" and "shame" to lack of privacy retains its force.

Proposition 9: *Poor, dense neighborhoods tend to be mixed-use neighborhoods.*

Mixed use refers to urban areas where residential and commercial land use coexist, where homes, apartments, retail shops, and even light industry are mixed together. Since much of the residential property in such areas is rental, typically there is much less resistance to commercial use (landlords often welcome it because of the prospects of increased land values). Moreover, the poorest, most dense urban neighborhoods often are adjacent to the commercial sections of cities, forming what the Chicago school called the "zone of transition" to note the progressive encroachments of commercial uses into a previously residential area. Shaw and McKay (1942:20) describe the process as follows:

> As the city grows, the areas of commerce and light industry near the center encroach upon areas used for residential purposes. The dwellings in such areas, often already undesirable because of age, are allowed to deteriorate when such

> invasion threatens or actually occurs, as further investment in them is unprofitable. These residences are permitted to yield whatever return can be secured in their dilapidated condition, often in total disregard for the housing laws....

Shaw and McKay were proponents of the outmoded concentric zonal model of cities, hence their assumption that encroachment radiates from the city center. No matter, the important point is that the process of encroachment occurs whatever the underlying shape of cities.

Proposition 10: *Mixed use increases familiarity with and easy access to places offering the opportunity for deviance.*

A colleague told me he first shoplifted at age eight, but that he had been "casing the joint for four years." This particular "joint" was the small grocery store at the corner of the block where he lived, so he didn't even have to cross a street to get there. In contrast, consider kids in many suburbs. If they wanted to take up shoplifting they would have to ask mom or dad for a ride. In purely residential neighborhoods there simply are far fewer conventional opportunities (such as shops) for deviant behavior.

Proposition 11: *Mixed-use neighborhoods offer increased opportunity for congregating outside the home in places conducive to deviance.*

It isn't just stores to steal from that the suburbs lack, they also don't abound in places of potential moral marginality where people can congregate. But in dense, poor, mixed-use neighborhoods, when people leave the house they have all sorts of places to go, including the street corner. A frequent activity in such neighborhoods is leaning. A bunch of guys will lean against the front of the corner store, the side of the pool hall, or up against the barber shop. In contrast, out in the suburbs young guys don't gather to lean against one another's houses, and since there is nowhere else for them to lean, whatever deviant leanings they might have go unexpressed. By the same token, in the suburbs, come winter, there is no close, *public* place to congregate indoors.

Thus, we can more easily appreciate some fixtures of the crime and delinquency research literature. When people, especially young males, congregate and have nothing special to do, the incidence of their deviance is increased greatly (Hirschi, 1969). Most delinquency, and a lot of crime, is a social rather than a solitary act (Erickson, 1971).

Proposition 12: *Poor, dense, mixed-use neighborhoods have high transience rates.*

This aspect of the urban scene has long attracted sociological attention. Thus, McKenzie wrote in 1926 (p. 145): "Slums are the most mobile...sections of a city. Their inhabitants come and go in continuous succession."

Proposition 13: *Transience weakens extra-familial attachments.*

This is self-evident. The greater the amount of local population turnover, the more difficult it will be for individuals or families to form and retain attachments.

Proposition 14: *Transience weakens voluntary organizations, thereby directly reducing both informal and formal sources of social control* (see Proposition 25).

Recent studies of population turnover and church membership rates strongly sustain the conclusion that such membership is dependent upon attachments, and hence suffers where transience rates reduce attachments (Wuthnow and Christiano,

1979; Stark, Doyle, and Rushing, 1983; Welch, 1983; Stark and Bainbridge, 1985). In similar fashion, organizations such as PTA or even fraternal organizations must suffer where transience is high. Where these organizations are weak, there will be reduced community resources to launch local, self-help efforts to confront problems such as truancy or burglary. Moreover, neighborhoods deficient in voluntary organizations also will be less able to influence how external forces such as police, zoning boards, and the like act vis-à-vis the community, a point often made by Park (1952) in his discussions of natural areas and by more recent urban sociologists (Suttles, 1972; Lee, Oropesa, Metch, and Guest, 1984; Guest, 1984).

In their important recent study, Simcha-Fagan and Schwartz (1986) found that the association between transience and delinquency disappeared under controls for organizational participation. This is not an example of spuriousness, but of what Lazarsfeld called "interpretation" (Lazarsfeld, Pasanella, and Rosenberg, 1972). Transience *causes* low levels of participation, which in turn *cause* an increased rate of delinquency. That is, participation is an *intervening variable* or *linking mechanism* between transience and delinquency. When an intervening variable is controlled, the association between X and Y is reduced or vanishes.

Proposition 15: *Transience reduces levels of community surveillance.*

In areas abounding in newcomers, it will be difficult to know when someone doesn't live in a building he or she is entering. In stable neighborhoods, on the other hand, strangers are easily noticed and remembered.

Proposition 16: *Dense, poor, mixed-use, transient neighborhoods will also tend to be dilapidated.*

This is evident to anyone who visits these parts of cities. Housing is old and not maintained. Often these neighborhoods are very dirty and littered as a result of density, the predominance of renters, inferior public services, and a demoralized population (see Proposition 22).

Proposition 17: *Dilapidation is a social stigma for residents.*

It hardly takes a real estate tour of a city to recognize that neighborhoods not only reflect the status of their residents, but confer status upon them. In Chicago, for example, strangers draw favorable inferences about someone who claims to reside in Forest Glen, Beverly, or Norwood Park. But they will be leery of those who admit to living on the Near South Side. Granted, knowledge of other aspects of communities enters into these differential reactions, but simply driving through a neighborhood such as the South Bronx is vivid evidence that very few people would actually *want* to live there. During my days as a newspaper reporter, I discovered that to move just a block North, from West Oakland to Berkeley, greatly increased social assessments of individuals. This was underscored by the frequent number of times people told me they lived in Berkeley although the phone book showed them with an Oakland address. As Goffman (1963) discussed at length, stigmatized people will try to pass when they can.

Proposition 18: *High rates of neighborhood deviance are a social stigma for residents.*

Beyond dilapidation, neighborhoods abounding in crime and deviance stigmatize the moral standing of all residents. To discover that you are interacting with a person through whose neighborhood you would not drive is apt to influence the subsequent interaction in noticeable ways. Here is a person who lives where homicide, rape, and assault are common, where drug dealers are easy to find, where prostitutes stroll the sidewalks waving to passing cars, where people sell TVs, VCRs, cameras, and other such items out of the trunks of their cars. In this sense, place of residence can be a dirty, discreditable secret.

Proposition 19: *Living in stigmatized neighborhoods causes a reduction in an individual's stake in conformity.*

This is simply to note that people living in slums will see themselves as having less to risk by being detected in acts of deviance. Moreover, as suggested below in Propositions 25–28, the risks of being detected also are lower in stigmatized neighborhoods.

Proposition 20: *The more successful and potentially best role models will flee stigmatized neighborhoods whenever possible.*

Goffman (1963) has noted that in the case of physical stigmas, people will exhaust efforts to correct or at least minimize them—from plastic surgery to years of therapy. Presumably it is easier for persons to correct a stigma attached to their neighborhood than one attached to their bodies. Since moving is widely perceived as easy, the stigma of living in particular neighborhoods is magnified. Indeed, as we see below, some people do live in such places because of their involvement in crime and deviance. But, even in the most disorderly neighborhoods, *most* residents observe the laws and norms. Usually they continue to live there simply because they can't afford better. Hence, as people become able to afford to escape, they do. The result is a process of selection whereby the worst role models predominate.

Proposition 21: *More successful and conventional people will resist moving into a stigmatized neighborhood.*

The same factors that *pull* the more successful and conventional out of stigmatized neighborhoods *push* against the probability that conventional people will move into these neighborhoods. This means that only less successful and less conventional people *will* move there.

Proposition 22: *Stigmatized neighborhoods will tend to be overpopulated by the most demoralized kinds of people.*

This does not mean the poor or even those engaged in crime or delinquency. The concern is with persons unable to function in reasonably adequate ways. For here will congregate the mentally ill (especially since the closure of mental hospitals), the chronic alcoholics, the retarded, and others with limited capacities to cope (Faris and Dunham, 1939; Jones, 1934).

Proposition 23: *The larger the relative number of demoralized residents, the greater the number of available "victims."*

As mixed use provides targets of opportunity by placing commercial firms within easy reach of neighborhood residents, the demoralized serve as human targets of opportunity. Many muggers begin simply by searching the pockets of drunks passed out in doorways and alleys near their residence.

Proposition 24: *The larger the relative number of demoralized residents, the lower will be residents' perception of chances for success, and hence they will have lower perceived stakes in conformity.*

Bag ladies on the corner, drunks sitting on the curbs, and schizophrenics muttering in the doorways are not advertisements for the American Dream. Rather, they testify that people in this part of town are losers, going nowhere in the system.

Proposition 25: *Stigmatized neighborhoods will suffer from more lenient law enforcement.*

This is one of those things that "everyone knows," but for which there is no firm evidence. However, evidence may not be needed, given the many obvious reasons why the police would let things pass in these neighborhoods that they would act on in better neighborhoods. First, the police tend to be reactive, to act upon complaints rather than seek out violations. People in stigmatized neighborhoods complain less often. Moreover, people in these neighborhoods frequently are much less willing to testify when the police do act—and the police soon lose interest in futile efforts to find evidence. In addition, it is primarily vice that the police tolerate in these neighborhoods, and the police tend to accept the premise that vice will exist *somewhere.* Therefore, they tend to condone vice in neighborhoods from which they do not receive effective pressures to act against it (see Proposition 14). They may even believe that by having vice limited to a specific area they are better able to regulate it. Finally, the police frequently come to share the outside community's view of stigmatized neighborhoods—as filled with morally disreputable people, who deserve what they get.

Proposition 26: *More lenient law enforcement increases moral cynicism.*

Where people see the laws being violated with apparent impunity, they will tend to lose their respect for conventional moral standards.

Proposition 27: *More lenient law enforcement increases the incidence of crime and deviance.*

This is a simple application of deterrence theory. Where the probabilities of being arrested and prosecuted for a crime are lower, the incidence of such crimes will be higher (Gibbs, 1975).

Proposition 28: *More lenient law enforcement draws people to a neighborhood on the basis of their involvement in crime and deviance.*

Reckless (1926:165) noted that areas of the city with "wholesome family and neighborhood life" will not tolerate "vice," but that "the decaying neighborhoods have very little resistance to the invasions of vice." Thus, stigmatized neighborhoods become the "soft spot" for drugs, prostitution, gambling, and the like. These are activities that require public awareness of where to find them, for they depend on customers rather than victims. Vice can function only where it is condoned, at least to some degree. In this manner, McKenzie (1926:146) wrote, the slum "becomes the hiding-place for many services that are forbidden by the mores but which cater to the wishes of residents scattered throughout the community."

Proposition 29: *When people are drawn to a neighborhood on the basis of their participation in crime and deviance, the visibility of such activities and the opportunity to engage in them increases.*

It has already been noted that vice must be relatively visible to outsiders in order to exist. Hence, to residents, it will be obvious. Even children not only will know *about* whores, pimps, drug dealers, and the like, they will *recognize* them. Back in

1840, Allison wrote of the plight of poor rural families migrating to rapidly growing English cities (p. 76):

> The extravagant price of lodgings compels them to take refuge in one of the crowded districts of the town, in the midst of thousands in similar necessitous circumstances with themselves. Under the same roof they probably find a nest of prostitutes, in the next door a den of thieves. In the room which they occupy they hear incessantly the revel of intoxication or are compelled to witness the riot of licentiousness.

In fact, Allison suggested that the higher social classes owed their "exemption from atrocious crime" primarily to the fact that they were not confronted by the temptations and seductions to vice that assail the poor. For it is the "impossibility of concealing the attractions of vice from the younger part of the poor in the great cities which exposes them to so many causes of demoralization."

Proposition 30: *The higher the visibility of crime and deviance, the more it will appear to others that these activities are safe and rewarding.*

There is nothing like having a bunch of pimps and bookies flashing big wads of money and driving expensive cars to convince people in a neighborhood that crime pays. If young girls ask the hookers on the corner why they are doing it, they will reply with tales of expensive clothes and jewelry. Hence, in some neighborhoods, deviants serve as role models that encourage residents to become "street wise." This is a form of "wisdom" about the relative costs and benefits of crime that increases the likelihood that a person will spend time in jail. The extensive recent literature on perceptions of risk and deterrence is pertinent here (Anderson, 1979; Jenson, Erickson, and Gibbs, 1978; Parker and Grasmick, 1979).

Conclusion

A common criticism of the ecological approach to deviance has been that although many people live in bad slums, most do not become delinquents, criminals, alcoholics, or addicts. Of course not. For one thing, as Gans (1962), Suttles (1968), and others have recognized, bonds among human beings can endure amazing levels of stress and thus continue to sustain commitment to the moral order even in the slums. Indeed, the larger culture seems able to instill high levels of aspiration in people even in the worst ecological settings. However, the fact that most slum residents aren't criminals is beside the point to claims by human ecologists that aspects of neighborhood structure can sustain high rates of crime and deviance. Such propositions do not imply that residence in such a neighborhood is either a necessary or a sufficient condition for deviant behavior. There is conformity in the slums and deviance in affluent suburbs. All the ecological propositions imply is a substantial correlation between variations in neighborhood character and variations in crime and deviance rates. What an ecological theory of crime is meant to achieve is an explanation of why crime and deviance are so heavily concentrated in certain areas, and to pose this explanation in terms that do not depend entirely (or even primarily) on *compositional* effects—that is, on answers in terms of "kinds of people."

To say that neighborhoods are high in crime because their residents are poor suggests that controls for poverty would expose the spuriousness of the ecological effects. In contrast, the ecological theory would predict that the deviant behavior of the poor would vary as their ecology varied. For example, the theory would predict less deviance in poor families in situations where their neighborhood is less dense and more heterogeneous in terms of income, where their homes are less crowded and dilapidated, where the neighborhood is more fully residential, where the police are not permissive of vice, and where there is no undue concentration of the demoralized.

As reaffirmed in the last paragraphs of this essay, the aim here is not to dismiss "kinds of people" or compositional factors, but to restore the theoretical power that was lost when the field abandoned human ecology. As a demonstration of what can be regained, let us examine briefly the most serious and painful issue confronting contemporary American criminology—black crime.

It is important to recognize that, for all the pseudo–biological trappings of the Chicago school (especially in Park's work), their primary motivation was to refute "kinds of people" explanations of slum deviance based on Social Darwinism. They regarded it as their major achievement to have demonstrated that the real cause of slum deviance was social disorganization, not inferior genetic quality (Faris, 1967).

Today Social Darwinism has faded into insignificance, but the questions it addressed remain—especially with the decline of human ecology. For example, like the public at large, when American social scientists talk about poor central city neighborhoods, they mainly mean black neighborhoods. And, since they are not comfortable with racist explanations, social scientists have been almost unwilling to discuss the question of why black crime rates are so high. Nearly everybody knows that in and of itself, poverty offers only a modest part of the answer. So, what else can safely be said about blacks that can add to the explanation? Not much, *if* one's taste is for answers based on characteristics of persons. A lot, if one turns to ecology.

Briefly, my answer is that high black crime rates are, in large measure, the result of *where* they live.

For several years there has been comment on the strange fact that racial patterns in arrest and imprisonment seem far more equitable in the South than in the North and West. For example, the ratio of black prison inmates per 100,000 to white prison inmates per 100,000 reveals that South Carolina is the most equitable state (with a ratio of 3.2 blacks to 1 white), closely followed by Tennessee, Georgia, North Carolina, Mississippi, and Alabama, while Minnesota (22 blacks to 1 white) is the least equitable, followed by Nebraska, Wisconsin, and Iowa. Black/white arrest ratios, calculated the same way, also show greater equity in the South while Minnesota, Utah, Missouri, Illinois, and Nebraska appear to be least equitable (Stark, 1986). It would be absurd to attribute these variations to racism. Although the South has changed immensely, it is not credible that cops and courts in Minnesota are far more prejudiced than those in South Carolina.

But what *is* true about the circumstance of Southern blacks is that they have a much more normal ecological distribution than do blacks outside the South. For example, only 9% of blacks in South Carolina and 14% in Mississippi live in the central core of cities larger than 100,000, but 80% of blacks in Minnesota live in large center cities and 85% of blacks in Nebraska live in the heart of Omaha. What this means is that large proportions of Southern blacks live in suburbs, small towns, and rural areas where they benefit from factors conducive to low crime rates. Conversely, blacks outside the South are heavily concentrated in precisely the kinds of places explored in this essay—areas where the probabilities of *anyone* committing a crime are high. Indeed, a measure of black center city concentration is correlated .49 with the black/white arrest ratio and accounts for much of the variation between the South and the rest of the nation (Stark, 1986).

"Kinds of people" explanations could not easily have led to this finding, although one might have conceived of "center city resident" as an individual trait. Even so, it is hard to see how such an individual trait would lead to explanations of why place of residence mattered. Surely it is more efficient and pertinent to see dilapidation, for example, as a trait of a building rather than as a trait of those who live in the building.

Is there any reason why social scientists must cling to individual traits as the *only* variables that count? Do I hear the phrase "ecological fallacy"? What fallacy? It turns out that examples of this dreaded problem are very hard to find and usually turn out to be transparent examples of spuriousness—a problem to which *all* forms of nonexperimental research are vulnerable (Gove and Hughes, 1980; Stark, 1986; Lieberson, 1985).

Finally, it is not being suggested that we stop seeking and formulating "kinds of people" explanations. Age and sex, for example, have powerful effects on deviant behavior that are not rooted in ecology (Gove, 1985). What is suggested is that, although males will exceed females in terms of rates of crime and delinquency in all neighborhoods, males in certain neighborhoods will have much higher rates than will males in some other neighborhoods, and female behavior will fluctuate by neighborhood too. Or, to return to the insights on which sociology was founded, social structures are real and cannot be reduced to purely psychological phenomena. Thus, for example, we can be sure that an adult, human male will behave somewhat differently if he is in an all-male group than if he is the only male in a group—and no sex change surgery is required to produce this variation.

References

Allison, Archibald. 1840. The Principles of Population and the Connection With Human Happiness. Edinburgh: Blackwood.

Anderson, L. S. 1979. The deterrent effect of criminal sanctions: Reviewing the evidence. In Paul J. Brantingham and Jack M. Kress (eds.), Structure, Law and Power. Beverly Hills: Sage.

Bursik, Robert J., Jr., and Jim Webb. 1982. Community change and patterns of delinquency. American Journal of Sociology 88:24–42.

Erickson, Maynard L. 1971. The group context of delinquent behavior. Social Problems 19: 114–129.

Faris, Robert E. L. 1967. Chicago Sociology, 1920–1932. San Francisco: Chandler.

Faris, Robert E. L. and Warren Dunham. 1939. Mental Disorder in Urban Areas. Chicago: University of Chicago Press.

Frazier, E. Franklin. 1932. The Negro in the United States. New York: Macmillan.

Gans, Herbert J. 1962. The Urban Villagers. New York: Free Press.

Gibbs, Jack P. 1975. Crime, Punishment, and Deterrence. New York: Elsevier.

Goffman, Erving. 1959. Presentation of Self in Everyday Life. New York: Doubleday.

———. 1963. Stigma. Englewood Cliffs, NJ: Prentice-Hall.

Gold, Martin. 1970. Delinquent Behavior in an American City. Belmont, CA: Brooks/Cole.

Gove, Walter R. 1985. The effect of age and gender on deviant behavior: A biopsychological perspective. In Alice Rossi (ed.), Gender and the Life Course. New York: Aldine.

Gove, Walter R. and Michael L. Hughes. 1980. Reexamining the ecological fallacy: A study in which aggregate data are critical in investigating the pathological effects of living alone. Social Forces 58:1,157–1,177.

Gove, Walter R., Michael L. Hughes, and Omer R. Galle. 1979. Overcrowding in the home. American Sociological Review 44: 59–80.

Guest, Avery M. 1984. Robert Park and the natural area: A sentimental review. Sociology and Social Research 68:1–21.

Hayner, Norman S. 1942. Five cities of the Pacific Northwest. In Clifford Shaw and Henry McKay (eds.), Juvenile Delinquency and Urban Areas. Chicago: University of Chicago Press.

Hindelang, Michael J. 1973. Causes of delinquency: A partial replication and extension. Social Problems 20:471–478.

Hindelang, Michael J., Travis Hirschi, and Joseph G. Weis. 1981. Measuring Delinquency. Beverly Hills: Sage.

Hirschi, Travis. 1969. Causes of Delinquency. Berkeley: University of California Press.

Hirschi, Travis and Michael J. Hindelang. 1977. Intelligence and delinquency: A revisionist view. American Sociological Review 42:571–587.

Jensen, Gary F., Maynard L. Erickson, and Jack Gibbs. 1978. Perceived risk of punishment and self-reported delinquency. Social Forces 57:57–58.

Jones, D. Caradog. 1934. The Social Survey of Merseyside, Vol. III. Liverpool: University Press of Liverpool.

Lazarsfeld, Paul F., Ann K. Pasanella, and Morris Rosenberg. 1972. Continuities in the Language of Social Research. New York: Free Press.

Lee, Barrett A., Ralph S. Oropesa, Barbara J. Metch, and Avery M. Guest. 1984. Testing the decline-of-community thesis: Neighborhood organizations in Seattle, 1929 and 1979. American Journal of Sociology 89:1,161–1,188.

Levin, Yale and Alfred Lindesmith. 1937. English Ecology and Criminology of the Past Century. Journal of Criminal Law and Criminology 27:801–816.

Lieberson, Stanley. 1985. Making It Count: The Impoverishment of Social Research and Theory. Berkeley: University of California Press.

Mayhew, Henry. 1851. London Labor and the London Poor. London: Griffin.

McKenzie, Roderick. 1926. The scope of human ecology. Publications of the American Sociological Society 20:141–154.

Minor, W. William and Joseph Harry. 1982. Deterrent and experimental effects in perceptual deterrence research. Journal of Research in Crime and Delinquency 18:190–203.

Park, Robert E. 1952. Human Communities: The City and Human Ecology. New York: The Free Press.

Park, Robert E., Ernest W. Burgess, and Roderick McKenzie. 1925. The City. Chicago: University of Chicago Press.

Parker, J. and Harold G. Grasmick. 1979. Linking actual and perceived certainty of punishment: An exploratory study of an untested proposition in deterrence theory. Criminology 17:366–379.

Reckless, Walter C. 1926. Publications of the American Sociological Society 20:164–176.

Shaw, Clifford R. and Henry D. McKay. 1942. Juvenile Delinquency and Urban Areas. Chicago: University of Chicago Press.

Simcha-Fagan, Ora and Joseph E. Schwartz. 1986. Neighborhood and delinquency: An assessment of contextual effects. Criminology 24: 667–699.

Stark, Rodney. 1986. Crime and Deviance in North America: ShowCase. Seattle: Cognitive Development Company.

Stark, Rodney and William Sims Bainbridge. 1985. The Future of Religion. Berkeley: University of California Press.

———. 1987. A Theory of Religion. Bern and New York: Lang.

Stark, Rodney, Daniel P. Doyle, and Jesse Lynn Rushing. 1983. Beyond Durkheim: Religion and suicide. Journal for the Scientific Study of Religion 22:120–131.

Stark, Rodney and James McEvoy. 1970. Middle class violence. Psychology Today 4:52–54, 110–112

Suttles, Gerald. 1968. The Social Order of the Slum. Chicago: University of Chicago Press.

———. 1972. The Social Construction of Communities. Chicago: University of Chicago Press.

Thrasher, Frederick M. 1927. The Gang. Chicago: University of Chicago Press.

Tittle, Charles R., Wayne J. Villemez, and Douglas A. Smith. 1978. The myth of social class and criminality: An empirical assessment of the empirical evidence. American Sociological Review 43:643–656.

Toby, Jackson. 1957. Social disorganization and stake in conformity: Complementary factors in the predatory behavior of hoodlums. Journal of Criminal Law, Criminology and Police Science 48:12–17.

Toby, Jackson and Marcia L. Toby. 1961. Law School Status as a Predisposing Factor in Subcultural Delinquency. New Brunswick: Rutgers University Press.

Welch, Kevin. 1983. Community development and metropolitan religious commitment: A test of two competing models. Journal for the Scientific Study of Religion 22:167–181.

Wuthnow, Robert and Kevin Christiano. 1979. The effects of residential migration on church attendance. In Robert Wuthnow (ed.), The Religious Dimension. New York: Academic Press.

Note

1. This is *not* to claim that neighborhoods do not change in terms of their levels of crime and deviance. Of course they do, even in Chicago (Bursik and Webb, 1982). It also is clear that such changes in deviance levels often are accompanied by changes in the kinds of people who live there. The so-called gentrification of a former slum area would be expected to reduce crime and deviance there as the decline of a once nicer neighborhood into a slum would be expected to increase it. However, such changes involve much more than changes in the composition of the population. Great physical changes are involved too, and my argument is that these have effects of their own.

Chapter 3

Anomie or Strain Theory

Emile Durkheim (1856–1917) is considered one of the founding figures of the field of sociology. Just before the turn of the nineteenth century, Durkheim published an extremely influential book titled *Suicide* (1897/1951). In that book, he wrote that during periods of disruptions of the traditional social order, a state of *anomie* or normlessness prevails, where the norms no longer grip the members of a society. For Durkheim, when periods of anomie prevail, the populace is no longer guided by culturally approved appetites. Unlimited greed is the rule. Human desire runs rampant. People no longer have any guidelines for what is permissible and what is not, what is possible and what is not. Their lust for anything and everything is unleashed. According to Durkheim, a state of anomie causes or contributes to a particular kind of deviance—suicide or, to be more specific, anomic suicide.

Robert K. Merton adapted this insight to his own theory, in one of the most influential articles ever published in sociology, "Social Structure and Anomie" (1938). Although Merton's conception of the genesis of anomie was different—indeed, his very conception of anomie was different—he retained the view that anomie was instrumental in unleashing greedy behavior, behavior that was directed at attaining goals that, under normal circumstances, would not be desired or sought. Behind both Durkheim's and Merton's conception of anomie was a loud and vehement voice clamoring "I want! I want! I want!" For Durkheim, what unleashed this voice was a disruption of the traditional social order.

In contrast, for Merton, what unleashed or generated anomie was a disparity, gap, or disjunction between cultural goals that all the members of specific societies are encouraged to achieve and the social and economic structure that permits only some members of the society to achieve those goals while others languish in frustrated, unfulfilled ambition. We live in a *malintegrated* society, one in which one aspect (the widespread expectation of success) is out of whack with another (the inability of large numbers to succeed). Merton's theory hinges on economic inequality: It is mainstream culture, which teaches us to value, want, need, and expect material success, plus a limited economic structure, that produces strain. Strain, in turn, demands adaptation. And various adaptations to that strain represent different forms of deviance. Though goal blockage does not necessarily lead to crime, it is a condition that makes certain kinds of deviance and crime more likely. Notice the main point of Merton's theory of deviance: It is that *conventional, mainstream values*—the routine workings of traditional institutions—and not marginal groups or pathological conditions, that cause deviance. In Merton's scheme of things, it is we who have caused deviance, our normal, everyday, conventional desires and expectations.

Some observers (Pfohl, 1994, p. 262) have argued that Merton's theory is, to a significant degree, a product of his background. His parents were poor immigrants from Eastern Europe, and he grew up in a poor, slum neighborhood in Philadelphia. He received a scholarship to Temple University, got good grades, and received a fellowship to Harvard; after completing his Ph.D., in the depth of the Depression, Merton managed to land one of the very few jobs that was available in academic sociology at that time, at Tulane University, in New Orleans. Within just a few short years, as a 30-year-old, he became a full professor and the chairman of its sociology department. In 1940, he was offered a job at Columbia. Eventually, he became the most eminent sociologist in the country, and, for a time, in the world. Stephen Pfohl argues that Merton's experience of mobility—from the slums of Philadelphia to college at Temple to graduate school at Harvard to, when he wrote the article, a professorship at Tulane—helps explain his conceptualization and formulation of anomie theory. Merton never assumed, as some academics with a middle-class background do, that the attainment of the middle-class goal of material success is automatic. He never forgot the fact that he managed to achieve certain material goals, while many of the friends and neighbors he left behind in his old neighborhood did not. He tried to understand what would happen to them, given the fact that they desired many material things they would never achieve. In spite of his success, he never forgot about the fact that frustrated ambition motivated a great deal of unconventional and deviant behavior.

It must be emphasized that, though Merton is and never was a political radical, there is a critical aspect to his theory, at the very least an *implicit* criticism of the society. This is why three Marxists in the 1970s—Taylor, Walton, and Young—refer to Merton as a "cautious rebel" (1973, pp. 101–104). On the one hand, he stands outside the system and coolly analyzes the disjunction between goals and means. On the other hand, if what Merton says is true, for us to reduce the level of crime in this country we would have to radically restructure its system of stratification. It is *inequality* that causes crime—and equality that can reduce crime. Merton himself never made this mental or theoretical leap, though it is implicit in his work.

As Pfohl says, disorganization theory, which was developed before Merton's anomie theory was formulated, attempted to *depoliticize* deviance (1994, pp. 211–212). In contrast, Merton's approach has distinct political implications for stratification and its consequences, though, again, he did not pursue them. If social disorganization resulted from a "natural," almost evolutionary process, there wasn't much we could do about it. If that is so, deviance and crime are normal or natural by-products of an inevitable movement of a neighborhood from one condition to another. Merton suggested that this was not the case. Anomie is not natural or inevitable. It results from frustrated ambition—from the fact that American society teaches its members to want and expect certain things but does not provide opportunities to achieve them. If the achievement structure of the society were to change, if the attainment of material goals were more widespread, the crime rate would decline sharply. Change access to achievement (or the valuation of material success) and you change the crime rate; this seems to be the implication of anomie or strain theory.

Merton has a rather grandiose conception of anomie theory. By that I mean he sees it as playing a major rather than a limited or partial role in the origin of deviant behavior. At one point, he does, it is true, state that anomie theory "is designed to account for some, not all deviant behavior" (1957, p. 178). And in yet another place, he says: "It is only when [goals and means are disjunctive that] deviant behavior ensues on a large scale" (p. 146). A number of commentators (myself included) have challenged the theory on the basis that the theory is irrelevant for—it simply doesn't address or explain—many, in all likelihood, most, forms of deviance: homosexuality, much, possibly most, recreational drug use, mental illness, alcoholism, obesity, pornography, rape, child molestation, and so on. And consider white-collar crime: Successful, affluent executives who have attained culturally approved goals are seeking further goals through disapproved means. If success is evaluated subjectively by the individual, Merton does not explore the possibility. In the eyes of many observers, anomie theory cannot be regarded as a general theory of deviance. Though Merton is often vague as to which behaviors the theory accounts for and which it does not (Clinard, 1964, p. 19), he clearly believes that rates of deviance vary by degrees of anomie. And here, many sociologists find serious fault with the theory.

That, in any case, is the theory, and one criticism of it. It's a simple yet elegant theory, and some sociologists regard it as distinctly sociological. And it has had a tremendous influence on the thinking of the field of deviance. It's been attacked, dismissed, amended, built upon, modified, and defended. For more than a decade and a half after it was first devised in 1938, it had relatively little impact. In 1955, Albert K. Cohen published his influential book, *Delinquent Boys* (1955), which was based on Merton's anomie theory. That discussion seemed to touch off widespread interest in Merton's theory. During the second half of the 1950s and throughout much of the 1960s, anomie theory was the most often used approach in the study of deviance. Then, during the 1970s and early 1980s, anomie theory went into an eclipse. But beginning some time in the 1980s, the theory made a comeback; today (as we see in the Messner and Rosenfeld selection), it is being revived. As we saw with social disorganization, some sociological theories do not die, they are recycled.

Anomie theory received two major modifications in 1955 and 1960; they are what I would call "friendly" criticisms. The first came from Albert Cohen (1955) and the second from Cloward and Ohlin (1960). Both discussions focused exclusively on lower-class gang delinquency. Cohen argued that lower-class boys suffer not so much from the frustration that comes from not being able to acquire material goods but from the frustration that comes from being at the bottom of the heap—*status* frustration rather than *economic* frustration. And he argues that their particular "adaptation" is non-utilitarian rather than utilitarian; it does not serve a material but a symbolic goal. The way they satisfy their status strivings is by being "bad"—by destroying things and expressing contempt for middle-class values, not by attempting to achieve success. But in Cohen's theory, the basic logic of Merton's anomie theory remains intact. With one exception: Cohen argues that Merton's theory is *structural* in its explanation of the origin of strain, but it is not interactional in its explanation of the mechanism by which strain is translated into deviant or criminal behavior. Merton's theory is *atomistic* in this regard, Cohen argues. Given strain, what then? How does each individual come to hit upon a deviant solution to this strain? Merton conceives of individuals arriving at deviant solutions on their own. What Cohen argues is necessary is for individuals in contexts or structures that breed strain to get together, interact, express this frustration, and collectively generate a solution to the problem of strain. Nowhere does Merton explain the mechanism by which individual frustration is communicated to others and is translated into collective action. In Cohen's eyes, this is a major flaw in the theory.

In their book, *Delinquency and Opportunity* (1960), Richard Cloward and Lloyd Ohlin also offer a "friendly" criticism in that they, too, see the necessity for collective solutions generated by structurally generated problems. They see neighborhood structures as generating specific types of solutions. Without these structures, it is difficult to see, they argue, just what sorts of solutions or adaptations, deviant or otherwise, individuals would hit upon to alleviate their problem of strain. This structural mechanism is missing in Merton's theory. Merton's theory is structural in seeing the *causes* of deviance but individualistic in seeing how people who are subject to strain work out their own deviant "solutions" or "adaptations." Cloward and Ohlin also believe that Merton is naive in assuming that deviant adaptations are readily available to all. Just as conventional goals are attainable—or not attainable—differentially and structurally, likewise, unconventional or illegitimate goals are differentially and structurally attainable or not attainable. Merton should not have assumed that illegitimate opportunities were attainable for all. Both are problematic, both require an explanation. But Cloward and Ohlin, likewise, retain the basic framework of anomie/strain thinking. Neither theoretical addendum challenges the basic integrity or logic of the theory.

Some observers believe we can separate Merton's classic formulation, so-called classic strain or anomie theory, from more current or modern or contemporary versions. Merton's theory has been reformulated, rewritten, adapted, "corrected." One modern version broadens the notion of goals to encompass any and all goals, and broadens the factors that facilitate or retard the attainment of these goals far beyond Merton's original focus on social class. In a sense, the theory has been depoliticized. The stratificational link has been removed, and the theory has been totally transformed. We're all pursuing goals that may not be attainable, not just goals of economic success, either. We all have to deal with the strain or frustration that results from blocked aspirations. Person X wants to be popular with the opposite sex, and can't because he's ugly or has bad breath. Person Y wants to become a race car driver and go around a track at 200 miles per hour, but can't because he has slow reflexes and poor coordination. Person Z wants to paint beautiful landscapes, but can't because she has no talent. And so on. What do these people do? Some people believe that by broadening Merton's original focus to include any and all goals, the vigor and strength of the theory have been drained out of it; it has acquired a focus that is altogether too amorphous (Messner and Rosenfeld, 1994). Still, it is important to recognize that, in spite of its eclipse until recent years, the anomie or strain perspective is still used as a theoretical focus in the study of deviance, and will probably continue to guide some researchers in their effort to understand wrongdoing. At the same time, it must also be recognized that anomie theory will never retain the dominance it held in the study of deviance in the 1950s and 1960s. Today, it is simply one of a number of viable perspectives in the field.

Messner and Rosenfeld extend Merton's anomie scheme as well as trace the development of this important sociological concept in the study of deviance. They argue that the United States is "a society organized for crime." Our conventional norms and institutions generate, encourage, in a sense, cause, deviant behavior, or at least certain forms of it. The pressure to achieve extends into corporate and violent realms. Crime is not the product of personal or structural pathologies or poverty, discrimination, or poor law enforcement. Rather, Messner and Rosenfeld argue, crime derives in significant measure from the routine pursuit of the American Dream. Moreover, they say (and this is a theme Merton did not explore in any detail), the strain that results from frustrated desire is structurally distributed, that is, the motivation to commit deviance is distributed according to one's position in society. Children of the upper-middle classes are more likely to succeed and thus, less likely to deviate. (Although those who do *not* succeed will almost certainly suffer from anomie and will be motivated to violate certain norms as a consequence.) In contrast, the children of lower- and working-class parents are less likely to achieve the American Dream and hence will be more likely to seek success through the type of "adaptation" Merton referred to as "innovation," that is, they will seek success through illegitimate means, such as theft, drug dealing, and prostitution. Some of the criticisms leveled at Merton's original article are still relevant to Messner and Rosenfeld's renovations, but the theory remains an original, innovative, and insightful approach to deviance.

References

Clinard, Marshall B. 1964. The theoretical implications of anomie and deviant behavior. In Marshall B. Clinard (ed.), *Anomie and Deviant Behavior: A Discussion and Critique*. New York: Free Press, pp. 1–56.

Cloward, Richard, and Lloyd E. Ohlin. *Delinquency and Opportunity: A Theory of Gang Delinquency*. New York: Free Press.

Cohen, Albert K. 1955. *Delinquent Boys: The Subculture of the Gang*. New York: Free Press.

Durkheim, Emile. 1897/1951. *Suicide* (trans. John A. Spaulding and George Simpson, ed. George Simpson). New York: Free Press.

Merton, Robert K. 1938. Social structure and anomie. *American Sociological Review,* 3 (October): 672–682.

Merton, Robert K. 1957. *Social Theory and Social Structure* (rev. and enlarged ed.). New York: Free Press.

Messner, Steven F., and Richard Rosenfeld. 1994. *Crime and the American Dream*. Belmont, Calif.: Wadsworth.

Pfohl, Stephen. 1994. *Images of Deviance and Social Control* (2nd ed.). New York: McGraw-Hill.

Taylor, Ian, Paul Walton, and Jock Young. 1973. *The New Criminology: For a Social Theory of Deviance*. London: Routledge & Kegan Paul.

Social Structure and Anomie

ROBERT K. MERTON

There persists a notable tendency in sociological theory to attribute the malfunctioning of social structure primarily to those of man's imperious biological drives which are not adequately restrained by social control. In this view, the social order is solely a device for "impulse management" and the "social processing" of tensions. These impulses which break through social control, be it noted, are held to be biologically derived. Nonconformity is assumed to be rooted in original nature.[1] Conformity is by implication the result of a utilitarian calculus or unreasoned conditioning. This point of view, whatever its other deficiencies, clearly begs one question. It provides no basis for determining the nonbiological conditions which induce deviations from prescribed patterns of conduct. In this paper, it will be suggested that certain phases of social structure generate the circumstances in which infringement of social codes constitutes a "normal response."[2]

The conceptual scheme to be outlined is designed to provide a coherent, systematic approach to the study of sociocultural sources of deviate behavior. Our primary aim lies in discovering how some social structures *exert a definite pressure* upon certain persons in the society to engage in nonconformist rather than conformist conduct. The many ramifications of the scheme cannot all be discussed; the problems mentioned outnumber those explicitly treated.

Among the elements of social and cultural structure, two are important for our purposes. These are analytically separable although they merge imperceptibly in concrete situations. The first consists of culturally defined goals, purposes, and interests. It comprises a frame of aspirational reference. These goals are more or less integrated and involve varying degrees of prestige and sentiment. They constitute a basic, but not the exclusive, component of what Linton aptly has called "designs for group living." Some of these cultural aspirations are related to the original drives of man, but they are not determined by them. The second phase of the social structure defines, regulates, and controls the acceptable modes of achieving these goals. Every social group invariably couples its scale of desired ends with moral or institutional regulation of permissible and required procedures for attaining these ends. These regulatory norms and moral imperatives do not necessarily coincide with technical or efficiency norms. Many procedures which from the standpoint of *particular individuals* would be most efficient in securing desired values, e.g., illicit oil-stock schemes, theft, fraud, are ruled out of the institutional area of permitted conduct. The choice of expedients is limited by the institutional norms.

To say that these two elements, culture goals and institutional norms, operate jointly is not to say that the ranges of alternative behaviors and aims bear some constant relation to one another. The emphasis upon certain goals may vary indepen-

From Robert K. Merton, "Social Structure and Anomie," *American Sociological Review,* vol. 3 (October 1938), pp. 672–682.

dently of the degree of emphasis upon institutional means. There may develop a disproportionate, at times, a virtually exclusive, stress upon the value of specific goals, involving relatively slight concern with the institutionally appropriate modes of attaining these goals. The limiting case in this direction is reached when the range of alternative procedures is limited only by technical rather than institutional considerations. Any and all devices which promise attainment of the all important goals would be permitted in this hypothetical polar case.[3] This constitutes one type of cultural malintegration. A second polar type is found in groups where activities originally conceived as instrumental are transmitted into ends in themselves. The original purposes are forgotten and ritualistic adherence to institutionally prescribed conduct becomes virtually obsessive.[4] Stability is largely ensured while change is flouted. The range of alternative behaviors is severely limited. There develops a tradition-bound, sacred society characterized by neophobia. The occupational psychosis of the bureaucrat may be cited as a case in point. Finally, there are the intermediate types of groups where a balance between culture goals and institutional means is maintained. These are the significantly integrated and relatively stable, though changing, groups.

An effective equilibrium between the two phases of the social structure is maintained as long as satisfactions accrue to individuals who conform to both constraints, viz., satisfactions from the achievement of the goals and satisfactions emerging directly from the institutionally canalized modes of striving to attain these ends. Success, in such equilibrated cases, is twofold. Success is reckoned in terms of the product and in terms of the process, in terms of the outcome and in terms of activities. Continuing satisfactions must derive from sheer *participation* in a competitive order as well as from eclipsing one's competitors if the order itself is to be sustained. The occasional sacrifices involved in institutionalized conduct must be compensated by socialized rewards. The distribution of statuses and roles through competition must be so organized that positive incentives for conformity to roles and adherence to status obligations are provided *for every position* within the distributive order. Aberrant conduct, therefore, may be viewed as a symptom of dissociation between culturally defined aspirations and socially structured means.

Of the types of groups which result from the independent variation of the two phases of the social structure, we shall be primarily concerned with the first, namely, that involving a disproportionate accent on goals. This statement must be recast in a proper perspective. In no group is there an absence of regulatory codes governing conduct, yet groups do vary in the degree to which these folkways, mores, and institutional controls are effectively integrated with the more diffuse goals which are part of the culture matrix. Emotional convictions may cluster about the complex of socially acclaimed ends, meanwhile shifting their support from the culturally defined implementation of these ends. As we shall see, certain aspects of the social structure may generate countermores and antisocial behavior precisely because of differential emphases on goals and regulations. In the extreme case, the latter may be so vitiated by the goal-emphasis that the range of behavior is limited only by considerations of technical expediency. The sole significant question then becomes, which available means is most efficient in netting the socially approved value?[5] The technically most feasible procedure, whether legitimate or not, is preferred to the institutionally prescribed conduct. As this process continues, the integration of the society becomes tenuous and anomie ensues.

Thus, in competitive athletics, when the aim of victory is shorn of its institutional trappings, and success in contests becomes construed as "winning the game" rather than "winning through circumscribed modes of activity," a premium is implicitly set upon the use of illegitimate but technically efficient means. The star of the opposing football team is surreptitiously slugged; the wrestler furtively incapacitates his opponent through ingenious but illicit techniques; university alumni covertly subsidize "students" whose talents are largely confined to the athletic field. The emphasis on the goal has so attenuated the satisfaction deriving from sheer participation in the competitive activity that these satisfactions are virtually confined to a successful outcome. Through the same process, tension generated by the desire to win in a poker game is relieved by successfully dealing oneself four aces, or, when the cult of success has become completely dominant, by sagaciously shuffling the cards in a game of solitaire. The faint twinge of uneasiness in the last instance and the surreptitious nature of public delicts indicate clearly that the institutional rules of the game *are known* to those who evade them, but that the emotional supports of these rules are largely vitiated by cultural exaggeration of the success-goal.[6] They are microcosmic images of the social macrocosm.

Of course, this process is not restricted to the realm of sport. The process whereby exaltation of the end generates a *literal demoralization,* i.e., a deinstitutionalization, of the means is one which characterizes many[7] groups in which the two phases of the social structure are not highly integrated. The extreme emphasis upon the accumulation of wealth as a symbol of success[8] in our own society militates against the completely effective control of institutionally regulated modes of acquiring a fortune.[9] Fraud, corruption, vice, crime, in short, the entire catalogue of proscribed behavior, becomes increasingly common when the emphasis on the *culturally induced* success-goal becomes divorced from a coordinated institutional emphasis. This observation is of crucial theoretical importance in examining the doctrine that antisocial behavior most frequently derives from biological drives breaking through the restraints imposed by society. The difference is one between a strictly utilitarian interpretation which conceives man's ends as random and an analysis which finds these ends deriving from the basic values of the culture.[10]

Our analysis can scarcely stop at this juncture. We must turn to other aspects of the social structure if we are to deal with the social genesis of the varying rates and types of deviate behavior characteristic of different societies. Thus far, we have sketched three ideal types of social orders constituted by distinctive patterns of relations between culture ends and means. Turning from these types of *culture patterning,* we find five logically possible, alternative modes of adjustment or adaptation *by individuals* within the culture-bearing society or group.[11] These are schematically presented in the following table, where (+) signifies "acceptance," (−) signifies "elimination," and (±) signifies "rejection and substitution of new goals and standards."

	Culture Goals	Institutionalized Means
I. Conformity	+	+
II. Innovation	+	−
III. Ritualism	−	+
IV. Retreatism	−	−
V. Rebellion[12]	±	±

Our discussion of the relation between these alternative responses and other phases of the social structure must be prefaced by the observation that persons may shift from one alternative to another as they engage in different social activities. These categories refer to role adjustments in specific situations, not to personality in toto. To treat the development of this process in various spheres of conduct would introduce a complexity unmanageable within the confines of this paper. For this reason, we shall be concerned primarily with economic activity in the broad sense, "the production, exchange, distribution, and consumption of goods and services" in our competitive society, wherein wealth has taken on a highly symbolic cast. Our task is to search out some of the factors which exert pressure upon individuals to engage in certain of these logically possible alternative responses. This choice, as we shall see, is far from random.

In every society, Adaptation I (conformity to both culture goals and means) is the most common and widely diffused. Were this not so, the stability and continuity of the society could not be maintained. The mesh of expectancies which constitutes every social order is sustained by the modal behavior of its members falling within the first category. Conventional role behavior oriented toward the basic values of the group is the rule rather than the exception. It is this fact alone which permits us to speak of a human aggregate as comprising a group or society.

Conversely, Adaptation IV (rejection of goals and means) is the least common. Persons who "adjust" (or maladjust) in this fashion are, strictly speaking, *in* the society but not *of* it. Sociologically, these constitute the true "aliens." Not sharing the common frame of orientation, they can be included within the societal population merely in a fictional sense. In this category are *some* of the activities of psychotics, psychoneurotics, chronic autists, pariahs, outcasts, vagrants, vagabonds, tramps, chronic drunkards, and drug addicts.[13] These have relinquished, in certain spheres of activity, the culturally defined goals, involving complete aim-inhibition in the polar case, and their adjustments are not in accord with institutional norms. This is not to say that in some cases the source of their behavioral adjustments is not in part the very social structure which they have in effect repudiated nor that their very existence within a social area does not constitute a problem for the socialized population.

This mode of "adjustment" occurs, as far as structural sources are concerned, when both the culture goals and institutionalized procedures have been assimilated thoroughly by the individual and imbued with affect and high positive value, but where those institutionalized procedures which promise a measure of successful attainment of the goals are not available to the individual. In such instances, there results a twofold mental conflict insofar as the moral obligation for adopting institutional means conflicts with the pressure to resort to illegitimate means (which may attain the goal) and inasmuch as the individual is shut off from means which are both legitimate *and* effective. The competitive order is maintained, but the frustrated and handicapped individual who cannot cope with this order drops out. Defeatism, quietism, and resignation are manifested in escape mechanisms which ultimately lead the individual to "escape" from the requirements of the society. It is an expedient which arises from continued failure to attain the goal by legitimate measures and from an inability to adopt the illegitimate route because of internalized prohibitions and institutionalized compulsives, *during which process the supreme value of the success-goal has as yet not been renounced.* The conflict is resolved by eliminating *both* precipitating elements, the goals and means. The escape is complete, the conflict is eliminated, and the individual is asocialized.

Be it noted that where frustration derives from the inaccessibility of effective institutional means for attaining economic or any other type of highly valued "success," that Adaptations II, III, and V (innovation, ritualism, and rebellion) are also possible. The result will be determined by the particular personality, and thus, the *particular* cultural background, involved. Inadequate socialization will result in the innovation response, whereby the conflict and frustration are eliminated by relinquishing the institutional means and retaining the success-aspiration; an extreme assimilation of institutional demands will lead to ritualism, wherein the goal is dropped as beyond one's reach but conformity to the mores persists; and rebellion occurs when emancipation from the reigning standards, due to frustration or to marginalist perspectives, leads to the attempt to introduce a "new social order."

Our major concern is with the illegitimacy adjustment. This involves the use of conventionally proscribed but frequently effective means of attaining at least the simulacrum of culturally defined success—wealth, power, and the like. As we have seen, this adjustment occurs when the individual has assimilated the cultural emphasis on success without equally internalizing the morally prescribed norms governing means for its attainment. The question arises, Which phases of our social structure predispose toward this mode of adjustment? We may examine a concrete instance, effectively analyzed by Lohman,[14] which provides a clue to the answer. Lohman has shown that specialized areas of vice in the near north side of Chicago constitute a "normal" response to a situation where the cultural emphasis upon pecuniary success has been absorbed, but where there is little access to conventional and legitimate means for attaining such success. The conventional occupational opportunities of persons in this area are almost completely limited to manual labor. Given our cultural stigmatization of manual labor, and its correlate, the prestige of white collar work, it is clear that the result is a strain toward innovational practices. The limitation of opportunity to unskilled labor and the resultant low income cannot compete *in terms of conventional standards of achievement* with the high income from organized vice.

For our purposes, this situation involves two important features. First, such antisocial behavior is in a sense "called forth" by certain conventional values of the culture *and* by the class structure involving differential access to the approved opportunities for legitimate, prestige-bearing pursuits of the culture goals. The lack of high integration between the means-and-end elements of the cultural pattern and the particular class structure combine to favor a heightened frequency of antisocial conduct in such groups. The second consideration is of equal significance. Recourse to the first of the alternative responses, legitimate effort, is limited by the fact that actual advance toward desired success-symbols through conventional channels is, despite our persisting open-class ideology,[15] relatively rare and difficult for those handicapped by little formal education and few economic resources. The dominant pressure of group standards of success is, therefore, on the gradual attenuation of legitimate, but by and large ineffective, strivings and the increasing use of illegitimate, but more or less effective, expedients of vice and crime. The cultural demands made on persons in this situation are incompatible. On the one hand, they are asked to orient their conduct toward the prospect of accumulating wealth, and on the other, they are largely denied effective opportunities to do so institutionally. The consequences of such structural inconsistency are psychopathological personality, and/or antisocial conduct, and/or revolutionary activities. The equilibrium between culturally designated means and ends becomes highly unstable with the progressive emphasis on attaining the prestige-laden ends by any means whatsoever. Within this context, Capone represents the triumph of amoral intelligence over morally prescribed "failure," when the channels of vertical mobility are closed or narrowed[16] *in a society which places a high premium on economic affluence and social ascent for all its members.*[17]

The last qualification is of primary importance. It suggests that other phases of the social structure besides the extreme emphasis on pecuniary success must be considered if we are to understand the social sources of antisocial behavior. A high frequency of deviate behavior is not generated simply by "lack of opportunity" or by this exaggerated pecuniary emphasis. A comparatively rigidified class structure, a feudalistic or caste order, may limit such opportunities far beyond the point which obtains in our society today. It is only when a system of cultural values extols, virtually above all else, certain *common* symbols of success *for the population at large* while its social structure rigorously restricts or completely eliminates access to approved modes of acquiring these symbols *for a considerable part of the same population* that antisocial behavior ensues on a considerable scale. In other words, our egalitarian ideology denies by implication the existence of noncompeting groups and individuals in the pursuit of pecuniary success. The same body of success-symbols is held to be desirable for all. These goals are held to *transcend class lines,* not to be bounded by them, yet the actual social organization is such that there exist class differentials in the accessibility of these *common* success-symbols. Frustration and thwarted aspiration lead to the search for avenues of escape from a culturally induced intolerable situation; or unrelieved ambition may eventuate in illicit attempts to acquire the dominant values.[18] The American stress on pecuniary success and ambitiousness for all thus invites exaggerated anxieties, hostilities, neuroses, and antisocial behavior.

This theoretical analysis may go far toward explaining the varying correlations between crime and poverty.[19] Poverty is not an isolated variable. It is one in a complex of interdependent social and cultural variables. When viewed in such a context, it represents quite different states of affairs. Poverty as such, and consequent limitation of opportunity, are not sufficient to induce a conspicuously high rate of criminal behavior. Even the often mentioned "poverty in the midst of plenty" will not necessarily lead to this result. Only insofar as poverty and associated disadvantages in competition for the culture values approved for *all* members of the society are linked with the assimilation of a cultural emphasis on monetary accumulation as a symbol of success in antisocial conduct a "normal" outcome. Thus, poverty is less highly correlated with crime in southeastern Europe than in the United States. The possibilities of vertical mobility in these European areas would seem to be fewer than in this country, so that neither poverty per se nor its association with limited opportunity is sufficient to account for the varying correlations. It is only when the full configuration is considered, poverty, limited opportunity, and a commonly shared system of success symbols, that we can explain the higher association between poverty and crime in our society than in others where rigidified class structure is coupled with *differential class symbols of achievement.*

In societies such as our own, then, the pressure of prestige-bearing success tends to eliminate the effective social constraint over means employed to this end. "The-end-justifies-the-means" doctrine becomes a guiding tenet for action when the cultural structure unduly exalts the end and the social organization unduly limits possible recourse to approved means. Otherwise put, this notion and associated behavior reflect a lack of cultural coordination. In international relations, the effects of this lack of integration are notoriously apparent. An emphasis upon national power is not readily coordinated with an inept organization of legitimate, i.e., internationally defined and accepted, means for attaining this goal. The result is a tendency toward the abrogation of international law, treaties become scraps of paper, "undeclared warfare" serves as a technical evasion, the bombing of civilian populations is rationalized,[20] just as the same societal situation induces the same sway of illegitimacy among individuals.

The social order we have described necessarily produces this "strain toward dissolution." The pressure of such an order is upon outdoing one's competitors. The choice of means within the ambit of institutional control will persist as long as the sentiments supporting a competitive system, i.e., deriving from the possibility of outranking competitors and hence enjoying the favorable response of others, are distributed throughout the entire system of activities and are not confined merely to the final result. A stable social structure demands a balanced distribution of affect among its various segments. When there occurs a shift of emphasis from the satisfactions deriving from competition itself to almost exclusive concern with successful competition, the resultant stress leads to the breakdown of the regulatory structure.[21] With the resulting attenuation of the institutional imperatives, there occurs an approximation of the situation erroneously held by utilitarians to be typical of society generally wherein calculations of advantage and fear of punishment are the sole regulating agencies. In such situations, as Hobbes observed, force and fraud come to constitute the sole virtues in view of their relative efficiency in attaining goals—which were for him, of course, not culturally derived.

It should be apparent that the foregoing discussion is not pitched on a moralistic plane. Whatever the sentiments of the writer or reader concerning the ethical desirability of coordinating the means-and-goals phases of the social structure, one must agree that lack of such coordination leads to anomie. Insofar as one of the most general functions of social organization is to provide a basis for calculability and regularity of behavior, it is increasingly limited in effectiveness as these elements of the structure become dissociated. At the extreme, predictability virtually disappears, and what may be properly termed cultural chaos or anomie intervenes.

This statement, being brief, is also incomplete. It has not included an exhaustive treatment of the various structural elements which predispose toward one rather than another of the alternative responses open to individuals; it has neglected, but not denied the relevance of, the factors determining the specific incidence of these responses; it has not enumerated the various concrete responses which are constituted by combinations of specific values of the analytical variables; it has omitted, or included only by implication, any consideration of the social functions performed by illicit responses; it has not tested the full explanatory power of the analytical scheme by examining a large number of group variations in the frequency of deviate and conformist behavior; it has not adequately dealt with rebellious conduct which seeks to refashion the social framework radically; it has not examined the relevance of cultural conflict for an analysis of culture-goal and institutional-means malintegration. It is suggested that these and related problems may be profitably analyzed by this scheme.

Notes

1. E.g., Ernest Jones, *Social Aspects of Psychoanalysis,* 28, London, 1924. If the Freudian notion is a variety of the "original sin" dogma, then the interpretation advanced in this paper may be called the doctrine of "socially derived sin."

2. "Normal" in the sense of a culturally oriented, if not approved, response. This statement does not deny the relevance of biological and personality differences which may be significantly involved in the *incidence* of deviate conduct. Our focus of interest is the social and cultural matrix; hence we abstract from other factors. It is in this sense, I take it, that James S. Plant speaks of the "normal reaction of normal people to abnormal conditions." See his *Personality and the Cultural Pattern,* 248, New York, 1937.

3. Contemporary American culture has been said to tend in this direction. See André Siegfried, *America Comes of Age,* 26–37, New York, 1927. The alleged extreme(?) emphasis on the goals of monetary success and material prosperity leads to dominant concern with technological and social instruments designed to produce the desired result, inasmuch as institutional controls become of secondary importance. In such a situation, innovation flourishes as the *range of means* employed is broadened. In a sense, then, there occurs the paradoxical emergence of "materialists" from an "idealistic" orientation. Cf. Durkheim's analysis of the cultural conditions which predispose toward crime and innovation, both of which are aimed toward efficiency, not moral norms. Durkheim was one of the first to see that "contrairement aux idées courantes le criminel n'apparait plus comme un etre radicalemente insociable, comme une sorte d'element parasitaire, de corps etranger et inassimilable,

introduit au sein de la societe; c'est un agent regulier de la vie sociale" (Contrary to common thinking, the criminal no longer appears as a totally unsociable human being, as a sort of parasite, alien and unassimilable, introduced in the midst of society; he is a regular member of social life). See *Les Regles de la Methode Sociologique,* 86–89, Paris, 1927.

4. Such ritualism may be associated with a mythology which rationalizes these actions so that they appear to retain their status as means, but the dominant pressure is in the direction of strict ritualistic conformity, irrespective of such rationalizations. In this sense, ritual has proceeded farthest when such rationalizations are not even called forth.

5. In this connection, one may see the relevance of Elton Mayo's paraphrase of the title of Tawney's well-known book. "Actually the problem *is not that of the sickness of an acquisitive society; it is that of the acquisitiveness of a sick society." Human Problems of an Industrial Civilization,* 153, New York, 1933. Mayo deals with the process through which wealth comes to be a symbol of social achievement. He sees this as arising from a state of anomie. We are considering the unintegrated monetary-success goal as an element in producing anomie. A complete analysis would involve both phases of this system of interdependent variables.

6. It is unlikely that interiorized norms are completely eliminated. Whatever residuum persists will induce personality tensions and conflict. The process involves a certain degree of ambivalence. A manifest rejection of the institutional norms is coupled with some latent retention of their emotional correlates. "Guilt feelings," "sense of sin," "pangs of conscience" are obvious manifestations of this unrelieved tension; symbolic adherence to the nominally repudiated values or rationalizations constitutes a more subtle variety of tensional release.

7. "Many," and not all, unintegrated groups, for the reason already mentioned. In groups where the primary emphasis shifts to institutional means, i.e., when the range of alternatives is very limited, the outcome is a type of ritualism rather than anomie.

8. Money has several peculiarities which render it particularly apt to become a symbol of prestige divorced from institutional controls. As Simmel emphasized, money is highly abstract and impersonal. However acquired, through fraud or institutionally, it can be used to purchase the same goods and services. The anonymity of metropolitan culture, in conjunction with this peculiarity of money, permits wealth, the sources of which may be unknown to the community in which the plutocrat lives, to serve as a symbol of status.

9. The emphasis upon wealth as a success-symbol is possibly reflected in the use of the term "fortune" to refer to a stock of accumulated wealth. This meaning becomes common in the late sixteenth century (Spenser and Shakespeare). A similar usage of the Latin *fortuna* comes into prominence during the first century B.C. Both these periods were marked by the rise to prestige and power of the "bourgeoisie."

10. See Kingsley Davis, "Mental Hygiene and the Class Structure," *Psychiatry,* 1928, I, esp. 62–63; Talcott Parsons, *The Structure of Social Action,* 59–60, New York, 1937.

11. This is a level intermediate between the two planes distinguished by Edward Sapir, namely, culture patterns and personal habit systems. See his "Contribution of Psychiatry to an Understanding of Behavior in Society," *American Journal of Sociology,* 1937, 42:862–70.

12. This fifth alternative is on a plane clearly different from that of the others. It represents a *transitional* response which seeks to *institutionalize* new procedures oriented toward revamped cultural goals shared by the members of the society. It thus involves efforts to *change* the existing structure rather than to perform accommodative actions *within* this structure, and introduces additional problems with which we are not at the moment concerned.

13. Obviously, this is an elliptical statement. These individuals may maintain some orientation to the values of their particular differentiated groupings within the larger society or, in part, of the conventional society itself. Insofar as they do so, their conduct cannot be classified in the "passive rejection" category (IV). Nels Anderson's description of the behavior and attitudes of the bum, for example, can readily be recast in terms of our analytical scheme. See *The Hobo,* 93–98, et passim, Chicago, 1923.

14. Joseph D. Lohman, "The Participant Observer in Community Studies," *American Sociological Review,* 1937, 2:890–98.

15. The shifting historical role of this ideology is a profitable subject for exploration. The "office-boy-to-president" stereotype was once in approximate accord with the facts. Such vertical mobility was probably more common then than now, when the class structure is more rigid. (See the following note.) The ideology largely persists, however, possibly because it still performs a useful function for maintaining the status quo. For insofar as it is accepted by the "masses," it constitutes a useful sop for those who might rebel against the entire structure, were this consoling hope removed. This ideology now serves to lessen the probability of Adaptation V. In short, the role of this notion has changed from that of an approximately valid empirical theorem to that of an ideology, in Mannheim's sense.

16. There is a growing body of evidence, though none of it is clearly conclusive, to the effect that our class structure is becoming rigidified and that vertical mobility is declining. Taussig and Joslyn found that American business leaders are being *increasingly* recruited from the upper ranks of our society. The Lynds have also found a "diminished chance to get ahead" for the working classes in Middletown. Manifestly, these objective changes are not alone significant; the individual's subjective evaluation of the situation is a major determinant of the response. The extent to which this change in opportunity for social mobility has been recognized by the least advantaged classes is still conjectural, although the Lynds present some suggestive materials. The writer suggests that a case in point is the increasing frequency of cartoons which observe in a tragi-comic vein that "my old man says everybody can't be President. He says if ya can get three days a week steady on W. P. A. work ya ain't doin' so bad either." See F. W. Taussig and C. S. Joslyn, *American Business Leaders,* New York, 1932; R. S. and H. M. Lynd, *Middletown in Transition,* 67 ff., chap. 12, New York, 1937.

17. The role of the Negro in this respect is of considerable theoretical interest. Certain elements of the Negro population have assimilated the dominant caste's values of pecuniary success and social advancement, but they also recognize that social ascent is at present restricted to their own caste almost exclusively. The pressures upon the Negro which would otherwise derive from the structural inconsistencies we have noticed are hence not identical with those upon lower class whites. See Kingsley Davis, op. cit., 63; John Dollard, *Caste and Class in a Southern Town,* 66 ff., New Haven, 1936; Donald Young, *American Minority People,* 581, New York, 1932.

18. The psychical coordinates of these processes have been partly established by the experimental evidence concerning *Anspruchsniveaus* and levels of performance. See Kurt Lewin, *Vorsatz, Willie und Bedurfnis,* Berlin, 1926; N. F. Hoppe, "Erfolg und Misserfolg," *Psycholische Forschung,* 1930, 14:1–63; Jerome D. Frank, "Individual Differences in Certain Aspects of the Level of Aspiration," *American Journal of Psychology,* 1935, 47:119–28.

19. Standard criminology texts summarize the data in this field. Our scheme of analysis may serve to resolve some of the theoretical contradictions which P. A. Sorokin indicates. For example, "not everywhere nor always do the poor show a greater proportion of crime...many poorer countries have had less crime than the richer countries....The [economic] improvement in the second half of the nineteenth century, and the beginning of the twentieth, has not been followed by a decrease of crime." See his *Contemporary Sociological Theories,* 560–61, New York, 1928. The crucial point is, however, that poverty has varying social significance in different social structures, as we shall see. Hence, one would not expect a linear correlation between crime and poverty.

20. See M. W. Royse, *Aerial Bombardment and the International Regulation of War,* New York, 1928.

21. Since our primary concern is with the sociocultural aspects of this problem, the psychological correlates have been only implicitly considered. See Karen Horney, *The Neurotic Personality of Our Time,* New York, 1937, for a psychological discussion of this process.

A Society Organized for Crime

STEVEN F. MESSNER and RICHARD ROSENFELD

The Virtues and Vices of the American Dream

...We locate the sources of crime in the very same values and behaviors that are conventionally viewed as part of the American success story. From this vantage point, high rates of crime in the United States are not the "sick" outcome of individual pathologies, such as defective personalities or aberrant biological structures. Neither are they the "evil" consequence of individual moral failings, such as greed. Nor does the American crime problem simply reflect universally condemned social conditions, such as poverty and discrimination, or ineffective law enforcement or lax punishment of criminals. Rather, crime in America derives, in significant measure, from highly prized cultural and social conditions.

...The American Dream itself and the normal social conditions engendered by it are deeply implicated in the problem of crime. In our use of the term *the American Dream,* we refer to a broad cultural ethos that entails a commitment to the goal of material success, to be pursued by everyone in society, under conditions of open, individual competition. The American Dream has both an evaluative and a cognitive dimension associated with it. People are socialized to accept the *desirability* of pursuing the goal of material success under the specified conditions, and they are encouraged to *believe* that the chances of realizing the Dream are sufficiently high to justify a continued commitment to this cultural goal. These beliefs and commitments in many respects define what it means to be an enculturated member of our society. The ethos refers quite literally to the *American* dream....

The Dark Side of the American Dream

The strong and persistent appeal of the American Dream has without question been highly beneficial for our society. The commitments associated with this cultural ethos have provided the motivational dynamic for economic expansion, extraordinary technological innovation, and high rates of social mobility. But there is a paradoxical quality to the American Dream. The very features that are responsible for the impressive accomplishments of American society have less desirable consequences as well. The American Dream is a double-edged sword, contributing to both the best and the worst elements of the American character and society. In the words of sociologist Robert K. Merton, "...a cardinal American virtue, 'ambition,' promotes a cardinal American vice, 'deviant behavior'" (Merton, 1968). The cultural emphasis on achievement, which promotes productivity and innovation, also generates pressures to succeed at any cost. The glorification of individual competition, which fosters ambition and mobility, drives people apart and weakens the collective sense of community. Finally, the preoccupation with monetary rewards, which undergirds economic demand in a market economy, severely restricts the kinds of achievements to which people are motivated to aspire....

Universalism and Economic Inequality. Another feature of the American Dream that has paradoxical implications is its *universalism*. All Americans, regardless of social origins or social location, are encouraged to embrace the tenets of the dominant cultural ethos. The cultural imperative to succeed, or at least to keep on trying to succeed, respects no social boundaries. This universalism of goals is in many respects a matter of pride for Americans. It reflects an underlying democratic ethos and a belief in a common entitlement for everyone in society. Yet this universal application of goals of monetary success inevitably creates serious dilemmas for large numbers of individuals in a social structure characterized by appreciable economic inequality. Because the culture precludes the possibility of noncompeting groups, and because it does not assign high priority to goals other than that of monetary success, the status of being economically "unequal" is readily equated with being "unsuccessful" and, by extension, "unworthy."

It might thus seem reasonable to expect that the universalism inherent in the American Dream is naturally conducive to egalitarian social structures. Accordingly, the current level of inequality in the United States might be viewed as something of an aberration, a temporary mismatch between culture and social structure—a betrayal of the American Dream....

We suggest that the persistent economic inequality in the United States is best understood not as a departure from fundamental cultural orientations but rather as an expression of them. Despite the universalistic component of the American Dream, the basic logic of this cultural ethos actually *presupposes* high levels of inequality. A competitive allocation of monetary rewards requires both winners and losers; and "winning" and "losing" have meaning only when rewards are distributed unequally. In addition, the motivation to endure the competitive struggle is not maintained easily if the monetary difference between winning and losing is inconsequential. In short, there is a fundamental tension built into the very fabric of the American Dream. This ethos provides the cultural foundation for a high level of economic inequality; yet a high level of inequality relegates large segments of the population to the role of "failure" as defined by the standards of the very same cultural ethos.

The American Dream thus has a dark side that must be considered in any serious effort to uncover the social sources of crime. It encourages an exaggerated emphasis on monetary achievements while devaluing alternative criteria of success; it promotes a preoccupation with the realization of goals while deemphasizing the importance of the ways in which these goals are pursued; and it helps create and sustain social structures with limited capacities to restrain the cultural pressures to disregard legal restraints.

The general idea that crime is produced by many of the same features of American society that also contribute to its successes is not new. This notion, which can be termed the "criminogenic hypothesis," was part of the critical social problems literature that emerged in the United States during the 1960s.... The intellectual roots of our orientation are to be found not in contemporary critiques of American society but in the classical sociological analyses of Emile Durkheim and Robert K. Merton, specifically in their analyses of social deviance and "anomie."

The Rise, Fall, and Revival of the Anomie Perspective

Core Ideas, Assumptions, and Propositions

The French sociologist Emile Durkheim, a founding figure in sociology, directed attention in the late nineteenth century to the critical role of social factors in explaining human behavior. He also introduced the term *anomie* to refer to a weakening of the normative order in society, and he explored in some detail the consequences of anomie for suicide, a form of deviant behavior that typically is explained with reference to psychological factors (Durkheim, 1893/1964; 1897/1966).

Our analysis is grounded in the variant of anomie theory associated with the work of the American sociologist Robert K. Merton. Merton combines strategic ideas from Durkheim with insights borrowed from Karl Marx, another founding figure in the social sciences, to produce a provocative and compelling account of the social forces underlying deviant behavior in American society. Although we go beyond Merton's thesis in several important respects, we nevertheless borrow liberally from his arguments and from the anomie research program in sociology and criminology.

Most important, we accept Merton's underlying premise that motivations for crime do not result simply from the flaws, failures, or free choices of individuals. A complete explanation of crime ultimately must consider the sociocultural environments in which people are located. Similar to motivations and desires that promote conformity to norms, deviant and criminal motivations cannot be predicted solely on the basis of assumptions about the "native drives" of the human species. They must be explained, instead, with reference to the particular cultural settings in which people conduct their daily lives. The cultural conditioning of human motivations and desires has been expressed very nicely by Schopenhauer: "We want what we will, but we don't will what we want."

We also find considerable merit in the observation, basic to both Merton's and Marx's sociological analysis, that strains, tensions, and contradictions are built into concrete forms of social organization. These internal contradictions ultimately provide the impetus for change, and they help to account for the dynamic aspects of collective social life. Undesirable forms of behavior, such as crime, may thus be inevitable features of the normal workings of the social system, just as are more desirable forms of behavior. Crime does not have to be understood as the product of mysterious or bizarre forces; it can be viewed as an ordinary and predictable response to prevailing sociocultural conditions.

Merton argued that the United States is a prime example of a social system characterized by internal strain and contradictions. Specifically, Merton observed that there is an exaggerated emphasis on the goal of monetary success in American society coupled with a weak emphasis on the importance of using the socially acceptable means for achieving this goal. This is a normal feature of American culture—as we suggested earlier, it is an integral part of the American Dream. In addition, there is socially structured inequality in the access to the legitimate means for attaining success. The result of these cultural and structural conditions is a pronounced strain toward anomie, that is, a tendency for social norms to lose their regulatory force. Merton implied that this anomic quality of life is responsible for the high rates of crime and deviance characteristic of the United States. He also proposed that similar sociocultural processes account for the social distribution of crime. The pressures toward anomie, according to Merton, are socially structured. They become progressively more intense at lower levels of the social class hierarchy, because obstacles to the use of the legitimate means for success are greater in the lower classes.

The "Golden Age" of Anomie Theory

Merton's version of anomie theory was introduced to the scholarly community in an article entitled "Social Structure and Anomie," originally published in the *American Sociological Review* in 1938. This article had little immediate impact on the fields of criminology and the sociology of deviance. As one commentator, Stephen Pfohl, has observed, the "essay sat dormant for about fifteen years after its first publication" (1985, p. 226). Then in the 1950s, anomie theory began to capture the imagination of influential theorists and researchers. Ambiguities in the original statement of the theory were identified and remedies proposed. Prominent sociologists and criminologists integrated aspects of anomie theory with other criminological ideas to construct explanations of crime and deviance that were both more comprehensive and more precise than Merton's original formulation. The most noteworthy of these efforts were Albert Cohen's *Delinquent Boys* and Richard Cloward's and Lloyd Ohlin's *Delinquency and Opportunity* (Cohen, 1955; Cloward and Ohlin, 1960).

Cohen extended Merton's theory to explain how delinquent subcultures emerged from reactions by working-class youth to the middle-class success norms of school. Cloward and Ohlin joined Merton's theory with the "differential association" perspective on crime developed by Edwin Sutherland to explain how different forms of criminal and deviant activity, including the activities commonly associated with urban youth gangs, resulted from the failure of lower-class youth to achieve economic success in both the legitimate and the illegitimate "opportunity structures" of the contemporary city. The general import of these extensions of Merton's theory was a highlighting of the ways in which basic structural conditions can generate subcultures conducive to criminal motivations, thereby explaining the social distribution of crime within a society. Merton himself further advanced the anomie research program by responding to early criticisms of his original theoretical statement and offering expanded and revised versions of the theory in a series of subsequent publications in 1959, 1964, and 1968.

In addition to a growing interest in the theoretical structure of Merton's argument, a large number of empirical studies informed by anomie theory appeared in the late 1950s and throughout the 1960s. Concerted efforts were made to apply the theory to a wide range of deviant behaviors, including crime, delinquency, drug addiction, mental illness, and alcoholism. Researchers interested in macro-level analysis proposed objective indicators of anomie to explain aggregate crime rates, while those interested in individual-level analysis developed social psychological scales of the subjective experience of confronting an "anomic" environment.

The overall influence of the anomie perspective on the sociological study of deviance during the middle years of the twentieth century is difficult to overstate. In the 1992 edition of his widely used criminology textbook, Don Gibbons proclaims that the body of ideas associated with the anomie perspective has served as "the most influential formulation on the sociology of deviance over the past fifty years, as attested to by the copious citations in sociological textbooks" (1992). Jonathan Turner offers a similar assessment in his text on sociological theory, suggesting that there is probably no single sociological essay published in this century that has prompted as much research and theoretical commentary as Merton's "Social Structure and Anomie" (1978). In addition, the impact of anomie theory has not been limited to the academic community. Major policy initiatives such as the Mobilization for Youth Program in the 1960s and the War on Poverty more generally were heavily indebted to the general ideas associated with the anomie perspective.

Decline and Revival

Interest in anomie theory, however, dropped markedly in the 1970s and 1980s. Researchers were less likely to draw on the anomie perspective for theoretical guidance, as reflected in the declining number of citations to Merton's work beginning in the early 1970s. In addition, several highly respected scholars directed harsh criticisms at the anomie perspective. In an influential monograph on juvenile delinquency published in 1978, Ruth Kornhauser dismissed the utility of "strain theory," the label given to anomie theory by criminological theorists in the 1970s, on both theoretical and empirical grounds. She argued that the theory suffers from grievous logical flaws and that its central empirical claims (for example, that the discrepancy between aspirations and achievements is a cause of delinquency) lack support in the research literature. Kornhauser concluded her review of the perspective with the blunt advice to colleagues to turn their attention elsewhere in efforts to explain crime and delinquency (1978).

Anomie theory came under fire from a number of theoretical positions in the 1970s and '80s, but it would be a mistake to attribute its declining stature during that time to any definitive disconfirmation of its principal claims or to the emergence of a clearly superior alternative. Theoretical dominance in sociology and criminology reflects not only the intrinsic merits of perspectives but also broader social and political conditions. As the liberal consensus that characterized the postwar era in the United States weakened in the late 1970s; as the welfare state and antipoverty programs came under political fire during the early years of the Reagan administration; as the social movements that provided the political pressure for social welfare policies disappeared; and, most important, as crime rates continued to climb—the necessary social supports for a theory universally regarded as advocating liberal social reform as a way to reduce crime largely withered away.

The anomie perspective appears, however, to be enjoying a resurgence of interest in criminology. This is reflected in critical reviews of the earlier critiques, original empirical research applying the perspective, and efforts to elaborate the general theory. Perhaps part of the reason for the renewed interest in anomie theory is the return of an intellectual climate more receptive to its principal premises and claims. Given the growing awareness of vexing contemporary social problems—such as homelessness, the urban underclass, persistent economic stagnation accompanied by glaring social inequalities, and urban decay in general—explanations of social behavior cast in terms of fundamental characteristics of society, rather than individual deficiencies, are likely once again to "make sense" to many criminologists.

But, regardless of the extent to which anomie theory is in tune with the general intellectual climate, we maintain that this theoretical perspective warrants renewed attention in its own right. The diagnosis of the crime problem advanced by Merton in the 1930s remains highly relevant to contemporary conditions. The most valuable and insightful feature of the anomie perspective, in our view, is that it treats as problematic those enduring cultural and social conditions that liberals and conservatives alike view as potential solutions for crime, such as economic growth, a renewed "competitiveness," and greater equality of opportunity—in short, a renewed commitment to the American Dream.

Unfinished Business

The anomie perspective as developed by Merton and his followers does not, however, provide a fully comprehensive, sociological explanation of crime in America. The most glaring limitation of Merton's analysis is that it focuses exclusively on one aspect of social structure—inequality in access to the legitimate means for success. As a consequence, it stops short of an explication of the ways in which specific features of the broader *institutional structure* of society—beyond the stratification system—interrelate to generate the anomic pressures that are held to be responsible for crime.

Anomie theory is thus best regarded as a work in progress. In the words of Albert Cohen, an influential proponent of the anomie perspective: "Merton has laid the groundwork for an explanation of deviance [and crime] on the sociological level, but the task, for the most part, still lies ahead" (1985).

References

Cloward, Richard, and Lloyd E. Ohlin. 1960. *Delinquency and Opportunity: A Theory of Delinquent Gangs.* New York: Free Press.

Cohen, Albert K. 1955. *Delinquent Boys: The Culture of the Gang.* New York: Free Press.

Cohen, Albert K. 1985. The assumption that crime is a product of environments: Sociological approaches. In Robert E. Meier (ed.), *Theoretical Methods in Criminology.* Newbury Park, Calif.: Sage, pp. 223–243.

Durkheim, Emile. 1893/1964. *The Division of Labor in Society.* New York: Free Press.

Durkheim, Emile. 1897/1966. *Suicide: A Study in Sociology.* New York: Free Press.

Gibbons, Don C. 1992. *Society, Crime, and Criminal Behavior* (6th ed.). Englewood Cliffs, N.J.: Prentice-Hall.

Kornhauser, Ruth R. 1978. *Social Sources of Delinquency: An Appraisal of Analytic Methods.* Chicago: University of Chicago Press.

Merton, Robert K. 1938. Social structure and anomie. *American Sociological Review,* 3 (October): 672–682.

Merton, Robert K. 1964. "Anomie, anomia, and social interaction." In Marshall B. Clinard (ed.), *Anomie and Deviant Behavior.* New York: Free Press, pp. 213–242.

Merton, Robert K. 1968. *Social Theory and Social Structure* (rev. and enlarged ed.). New York: Free Press.

Pfohl, Stephen J. 1985. *Images of Deviance and Social Control: A Sociological History.* New York: McGraw-Hill.

Turner, Jonathan H. 1978. *The Structure of Sociological Theory* (rev. ed.). Homewood, Ill.: Dorsey Press.

Chapter 4

Social Learning: Differential Association and Cultural Transmission

As its name implies, "learning theory" argues that deviant, criminal, and delinquent behaviors are learned, much as the other components of a culture are learned. There are two principal versions of learning theory: Edwin Sutherland's theory of differential association and Walter Miller's cultural transmission theory. Both stress the central role played by learning in causing deviant behavior. Deviance is a form of learned behavior, both argue. But it is not learned from the general society, from the mainstream culture, the society as a whole, learning theory argues; in contrast with anomie theory, the broader culture discourages—it does not encourage—deviance and crime. We do not interact with members of "the society" generally as a broad, vague entity. We interact with certain specific people who have certain specific attitudes and values with respect to conformity and deviance. Some members of the society endorse deviance over conventionality, criminal over law-abiding values. It is in these "pockets" of unconventionality that values endorsing deviant behavior are learned; they are the breeding grounds of deviant behavior and crime. It is because of a stronger exposure to these unconventional values in comparison with more conventional, mainstream values that someone engages in deviance and crime.

Edwin Sutherland (1883–1950) was a sociologist who wrote an extremely influential textbook on crime. Its first edition, titled *Criminology,* was published in 1924; in its third edition (1939) Sutherland introduced his theory of differential association. The book went through ten editions, the last of which was published in 1978; the last four editions were edited and written by one of Sutherland's students, Donald Cressey. For Sutherland, these "pockets" of unconventionality may be found *anywhere* two or more people interact with and learn values from one another. It could be a group of adolescent friends hanging out on a street corner, a delinquent gang, a high school clique or friendship network, a college fraternity, a friendship network among bank employees, a network of "druggies" on a college campus, an organized criminal gang network, a particular crowd that hangs out in a local bar, and so on. Any intimate social scene or circle or group could be the locus of differential association and socialization to criminal values—including a two-person group. Someone could learn criminal values from a best friend or a lover; a choir or altar boy could learn deviant values and engage in deviant behavior as a result of contact with an unconventional priest; an employer, if the relationship is close enough, could teach an employee deviant values, which, in turn, could result in that person engaging in deviant behavior. For Sutherland, *priority* (how early in one's life the interaction takes place), *intensity* (how intimate the relationship is), *frequency* (how often during a given time period interaction takes place), and *duration* (how long the relationship lasts) determine the likelihood that someone in contact with a social circle or person who holds deviant values could be socialized to hold them himself or herself (Sutherland, 1947; Sutherland and Cressey, 1978, pp. 79–83).

In short: *Crime is learned in interaction with others in intimate interpersonal groupings.* Individuals who associate differentially (hence the name, the theory of differential association) with others who espouse criminal values are likely to engage in criminal behavior themselves. Sutherland is interested specifically in criminal behavior, or what he refers to as "violations of law." The content of what is learned in these "pockets" of unconventionality is "definitions favorable to violations of law." More specifically, Sutherland argues, a person becomes criminal or delinquent "because of an excess of definitions favorable to violation of law over definitions unfavorable to violation of law" (1978, p. 81). In other words, it is the ratio of norms that says it is acceptable to engage in crime to norms that say it is wrong; when that ratio tips in a positive direction, criminal behavior becomes likely. Sutherland's theory does not apply solely and exclusively to violations of law; presumably, it can be extended to include deviance generally (Akers, 1985).

Sutherland's perspective is extremely broad and, some say, far too vague to be capable of empirical test. Walter Miller's version of learning theory is more specific and focused. It is focused with respect to the agent of socialization, and focused with respect to the particular *type* of deviance it examines. As for the latter, it concentrates on juvenile delinquency, not deviance generally. As for the former, the agents of deviant socialization, Miller argues that delinquent values are learned in a limited number of social groupings: the family, the community and neighborhood, and peer networks—in other words, in class-based gatherings, those with a measure of generational continuity. Delinquent values are passed down from generation to generation. It is Miller's contention that delinquent values are learned as a consequence of lower-class membership. Simply by being a socialized member of the lower class in this society, one automatically learns values that encourage breaking the law. By being a conforming member of lower-class subculture, one is encouraged to engage in crime and delinquency.

Such values as the desire for excitement or "action"; belief in fate rather than individual responsibility; the need to be tough and not back down in a confrontation; the need to be "smart," that is, to con or dupe or outwit others; the need for independence and autonomy and yet, experiencing control over one's action as an oppressive yet constant fixture in one's life; all make it almost inevitable that members of the lower class, primarily young males, will run afoul of the law. Some of these values (which Miller refers to as "focal concerns") will not necessarily be positively valued under any and all circumstances or situations, but will be honored specifically under certain conditions, as an alternative to the humiliation that conformity would entail. For instance, even in the lower class, it is better to stay out of trouble than get into it, but if that means backing down in a confrontation and hence undermining one's manhood, then trouble is preferable to no trouble (Miller, 1958).

The basic assumption of learning theory—that deviance is learned—is widely accepted in the field. There is hardly a sociologist of deviance alive who does not believe that learning is at least part of the reason that some people engage in deviance. Is it possible to imagine that engaging in deviance is completely independent of culture, subculture, and other learning mechanisms? Hardly anyone rejects the idea that *some aspects* or some processes of deviance and social control are learned. But the questions, *what aspects, which processes?* have to be answered. Does learning cause deviant behavior or simply accompany it?

My feeling is, the theory that deviant behavior is learned is far too ambitious; it overexplains. Learning theory is not a general theory of deviance at all. Some forms of deviance are indeed learned by differentially interacting with others one is close to. But people do not simply fall into social circles at random. They are drawn to groups of peers in part because they already share certain values and activities in common with the members of those groups. Teenage recreational drug use provides an example. Individuals differentially interact with and are thereby differentially socialized by certain social circles, but they are also differentially recruited into certain social circles as well. As to which of these two processes—differential socialization or differential recruitment—is more powerful depends on the type of deviance in question. Moreover, if one falls into a social circle with whom one strongly disagrees concerning basic values, attitudes, and norms, typically one will drift away from that circle to one that is more compatible rather than be converted to those values, attitudes, and norms. For instance, homosexuality is certainly not "caused" by differential exposure to homosexual values. However, *in becoming involved in homosexual circles,* one is highly likely to learn homosexual values. But these values do not cause one to become a homosexual or engage in homosexuality; one is attracted to circles of homosexuals in part because one *already* shares certain aspects of homosexual values and behavior. One has allowed oneself to be recruited into the homosexual subculture. The homosexual subculture did not cause one's homosexuality, one's homosexuality caused one to be socialized into homosexual values. Sutherland's theory leaves out of the picture what we want to know most of all: What causes some of us to be drawn to social circles or associations whose members espouse certain values or engage in certain behaviors?

In the words of Erdwin Pfuhl and Stuart Henry, some individuals have a "biographical affinity" for certain kinds of deviance. This affinity may encourage them to engage in deviance. But it does not cause them to do so or determine deviance. In the final analysis, deviance remains a choice, an act of human will, a decision one makes within the context of certain background and structural factors that operate. People learn that certain behaviors are possible, even permissible in certain contexts, and they learn that others believe them to be desirable or valued, but this learning process does not make that person want to do something, or, finally, to do it. Only the acting, thinking, feeling individual does that. And in understanding this process, we need to understand what goes on inside the individual's mind, to empathize with his or her emotions (Pfuhl and Henry, 1993, pp. 55–57).

One major problem with Walter Miller's theory, like Sutherland's, can be simply put: It is overly deterministic; if what Miller says is true, then why don't all lower-class boys become delinquents? Some do; some don't. To say that lower-class boys are *more likely* to engage in delinquent acts than middle-class boys is not a satisfying answer because the theory is based on the idea that lower-class boys learn delinquent values and behaviors the same way they learn conventional values and behaviors, like eating with a fork, brushing their teeth, and speaking the English language. But the fact is, they all do these things, but not all are delinquent. If it is true, as Miller says, that lower-class culture is a "generating milieu" of gang delinquency, and contrary to the theory some lower-class boys become delinquent and some don't, then clearly, some other factors have to be at work, and they require elaboration. Even if we were to grant that lower-class youth are more likely to engage in delinquent behaviors generally (which not all sociologists do), this would still not explain why a fairly low proportion of lower-class youth are involved in serious violations of the law. In short, Miller's theory, like Sutherland's, overexplains. It also *under*explains in that there are many forms of deviance, crime, and delinquency it does not deal with at all. If a straightforward learning process explains lower- and working-class delinquency, then how do we explain middle-class delinquency? Or forms of deviance, delinquency, and crime that are not found disproportionately at the bottom rungs of the socioeconomic ladder, such as homosexuality, computer crime, and weekend recreational marijuana use?

In addition, both Sutherland's and Miller's theories leave labeling out of the picture; labeling is especially crucial when we focus on social class as a cause of delinquency, deviance, and crime, as Miller does centrally and as Sutherland does secondarily (Sutherland and Cressey, 1978, pp. 229–237). While it may be true that lower-class members of the society are more likely to engage in possibly most actions that are regarded as deviant and criminal, it is also true that higher-status individuals are more likely to successfully insulate themselves from a variety of deviance labeling processes. We'll look at this mechanism in Part III. Suffice it to say at this point that the relationship between an action that would be judged as deviant and the process by which a person actually is judged as a deviant is problematic and far from straightforward. It is a relationship in which neither major advocate of learning theory, Sutherland or Miller, seemed especially interested.

In short, our two versions of learning theory are extremely limited and partial explanations of deviance, crime, and delinquency. Sutherland's theory at least claims to be broader and more powerful than it in fact actually is. Learning applies under certain circumstances to certain deviant behaviors and certain deviance-making processes, but not most others. (And keep in mind, it does not apply to deviant conditions at all.) For most purposes, learning is a process that many deviants experience in becoming deviant, but it is not a general explanation for the behavior in question. Nonetheless, learning is a process that must be examined in any serious, systematic look at deviance. It deserves our attention.

References

Akers, Ronald L. 1985. *Deviant Behavior: A Social Learning Approach* (3rd ed.). Belmont, Calif.: Wadsworth.

Miller, Walter B. Lower class culture as a generating milieu of gang delinquency. *Journal of Social Issues,* 14 (3): 5–19.

Pfuhl, Erdwin H., and Stuart Henry. 1993. *The Deviance Process* (3rd ed.). New York: Aldine de Gruyter.

Sutherland, Edwin H. 1947. *Principles of Criminology* (4th ed.). Philadelphia: J. B. Lippincott.

Sutherland, Edwin H., and Donald R. Cressey. 1978. *Criminology* (10th ed.). Philadelphia: J. B. Lippincott.

Differential Association

EDWIN H. SUTHERLAND

Two Types of Explanations of Criminal Behavior

Scientific explanations of criminal behavior may be stated either in terms of the processes which are operating at the moment of the occurrence of crime or in terms of the processes operating in the earlier history of the criminal. In the first case, the explanation may be called "mechanistic," "situational," or "dynamic"; in the second, "historical" or "developmental." Both types of explanation are desirable. The mechanistic type of explanation has been favored by physical and biological scientists, and it probably could be the more efficient type of explanation of criminal behavior. As Gibbons said:

> In many cases, criminality may be a response to nothing more temporal than the provocations and attractions bound up in the immediate circumstances. It may be that, in some kinds of lawbreaking, understanding of the behavior may require detailed attention to the concatenation of events immediately preceding it. Little or nothing may be added to this understanding from a close scrutiny of the early development of the person.[1]

However, criminological explanations of the mechanistic type have thus far been notably unsuccessful, perhaps largely because they have been formulated in connection with an attempt to isolate personal and social pathologies among criminals. Work from this point of view has, at least, resulted in the conclusion that the immediate determinants of criminal behavior lie in the person-situation complex.

The objective situation is important to criminality largely to the extent that it provides an opportunity for a criminal act. A thief may steal from a fruit stand when the owner is not in sight but refrain when the owner is in sight; a bank burglar may attack a bank which is poorly protected but refrain from attacking a well-protected bank. A corporation which manufactures automobiles seldom violates the pure food and drug laws, but a meat-packing corporation might violate these laws with great frequency. But in another sense, a psychological or sociological sense, the situation is not exclusive of the person, for the situation which is important is the situation as defined by the person who is involved. That is, some persons define a situation in which a fruit-stand owner is out of sight as a "crime-committing" situation, while others do not so define it. Furthermore, the events in the person-situation complex at the time a crime occurs cannot be separated from the prior life experiences of the

From Edwin H. Sutherland and Donald R. Cressey, *Criminology,* 10th ed. (Philadelphia: J. B. Lippincott, 1978), pp. 79–83. The text was written by Sutherland and published in the third edition of *Principles of Criminology* in 1947; this version remains essentially unchanged. Reprinted by permission of the publisher.

criminal. This means that the situation is defined by the person in terms of the inclinations and abilities which he or she has acquired. For example, while a person could define a situation in such a manner that criminal behavior would be the inevitable result, past experiences would, for the most part, determine the way in which he or she defined the situation. An explanation of criminal behavior made in terms of these past experiences is a historical or developmental explanation.

The following paragraphs state such a developmental theory of criminal behavior on the assumption that a criminal act occurs when a situation appropriate for it, as defined by the person, is present. The theory should be regarded as tentative, and it should be tested by...factual information and theories which are applicable.

Developmental Explanation of Criminal Behavior

The following statements refer to the process by which a particular person comes to engage in criminal behavior:

1. *Criminal behavior is learned.* Negatively, this means that criminal behavior is not inherited, as such; also, the person who is not already trained in crime does not invent criminal behavior, just as a person does not make mechanical inventions unless he has had training in mechanics.

2. *Criminal behavior is learned in interaction with other persons in a process of communication.* This communication is verbal in many respects but includes also "the communication of gestures."

3. *The principal part of the learning of criminal behavior occurs within intimate personal groups.* Negatively, this means that the impersonal agencies of communication, such as movies and newspapers, play a relatively unimportant part in the genesis of criminal behavior.

4. *When criminal behavior is learned, the learning includes (a) techniques of committing the crime, which are sometimes very complicated, sometimes very simple; (b) the specific direction of motives, drives, rationalizations, and attitudes.*

5. *The specific direction of motives and drives is learned from definitions of the legal codes as favorable or unfavorable.* In some societies an individual is surrounded by persons who invariably define the legal codes as rules to be observed, while in others he is surrounded by persons whose definitions are favorable to the violation of the legal codes. In our American society these definitions are almost always mixed, with the consequence that we have culture conflict in relation to the legal codes.

6. *A person becomes delinquent because of an excess of definitions favorable to violation of law over definitions unfavorable to violation of law.* This is the principle of differential association. It refers to both criminal and anticriminal associations and has to do with counteracting forces. When persons become criminal, they do so because of contacts with criminal patterns and also because of isolation from anticriminal patterns. Any person inevitably assimilates the surrounding culture unless other patterns are in conflict; a southerner does not pronounce *r* because other southerners do not pronounce *r*. Negatively, this proposition of differential association means that associations which are neutral so far as crime is concerned have little or no effect on the genesis of criminal behavior. Much of the experience of a person is neutral in this sense, for instance, learning to brush one's teeth. This behavior has no negative or positive effect on criminal behavior except as it may be related to associations which are concerned with the legal codes. This neutral behavior is important especially as an occupier of the time of a child so that he or she is not in contact with criminal behavior during the time the child is so engaged in the neutral behavior.

7. *Differential associations may vary in frequency, duration, priority, and intensity.* This means that associations with criminal behavior and also associations with anticriminal behavior vary in those respects. Frequency and duration as modalities of associations are obvious and need no explanation. Priority is assumed to be important in the sense that lawful behavior developed in early childhood may persist throughout life, and also that delinquent behavior developed in early childhood may persist throughout life. This tendency, however, has not been adequately demonstrated, and priority seems to be important principally through its selective influence. Intensity is not precisely defined, but it has to do with such things as the prestige of the source of a criminal or anticriminal pattern and with emotional reactions related to the associations. In a precise description of the criminal behavior of a person, these modalities would be rated in quantitative form and a mathematical ratio would be reached. A formula in this sense has not been developed, and the development of such a formula would be extremely difficult.

8. *The process of learning criminal behavior by association with criminal and anticriminal patterns involves all of the mechanisms that are involved in any other learning.* Negatively, this means that the learning of criminal behavior is not restricted to the process of imitation. A person who is seduced, for instance, learns criminal behavior by association, but this process would not ordinarily be described as imitation.

9. *While criminal behavior is an expression of general needs and values, it is not explained by those general needs and values, since noncriminal behavior is an expression of the same needs and values.* Thieves generally steal in order to secure money, but likewise honest laborers work in order to secure money. The attempts by many scholars to explain criminal behavior by general drives and values, such as the happiness principle, striving for social status, the money motive, or frustration, have been, and must continue to be, futile, since they explain lawful behavior as completely as they explain criminal behavior. They are similar to respiration, which is necessary for any behavior, but which does not differentiate criminal from noncriminal behavior.

It is not necessary, at this level of explanation, to explain why persons have the associations they have; this certainly involves a complex of many things. In an area where the delinquency rate is high, a boy who is sociable, gregarious, active, and athletic is very likely to come in contact with the other boys in the neighborhood, learn delinquent behavior patterns from them, and become a criminal; in the same neighborhood the psychopathic boy who is isolated, introverted, and inert may remain at home, not become acquainted with the other boys in the neighborhood, and not become delinquent. In another situation, the sociable, athletic, aggressive boy may become a member of a scout troop and not become involved in delinquent behavior. The person's associations are determined in a general context of social organization. A child is ordinarily reared in a family; the place of residence of the family is determined largely by family income; and the delinquency rate is in many respects related to the rental value of the houses. Many other aspects of social organization affect the associations of a person.

The preceding explanation of criminal behavior purports to explain the criminal and noncriminal behavior of individual persons. As indicated earlier, it is possible to state sociological theories of criminal behavior which explain the criminality of a community, nation, or other group. The problem, when thus stated, is to account for variations in crime rates, which involve a comparison of the crime rates of various groups or the crime rates of a particular group at different times. The explanation of a crime rate must be consistent with the explanation of the criminal behavior of the person, since the crime rate is a summary statement of the number of persons in the group who commit crimes and the frequency with which they commit crimes. One of the best explanations of crime rates from this point of view is that a high crime rate is due to social disorganization. The term *social disorganization* is not entirely satisfactory, and it seems preferable to substitute for it the term *differential social organization*. The postulate on which this theory is based, regardless of the name, is that crime is rooted in the social organization and is an expression of that social organization. A group may be organized for criminal behavior or organized against criminal behavior. Most communities are organized for both criminal and anticriminal behavior, and, in that sense the crime rate is an expression of the differential group organization. Differential group organization as an explanation of variations in crime rates is consistent with the differential association theory of the processes by which persons become criminals.

Note

1. Don C. Gibbons, "Observations on the Study of Crime Causation," *American Journal of Sociology,* 77:262–278, 1971.

Lower Class Culture as a Generating Milieu of Gang Delinquency

WALTER B. MILLER

Focal Concerns of Lower Class Culture

There is a substantial segment of present-day American society whose way of life, values, and characteristic patterns of behavior are the product of a distinctive cultural system which may be termed "lower class." Evidence indicates that this cultural system is becoming increasingly distinctive, and that the size of the group which shares this tradition is increasing. The lower class way of life, in common with that of all distinctive cultural groups, is characterized by a set of focal concerns—areas or issues which command widespread and persistent attention and a high degree of emotional involvement. The specific concerns cited here, while by no means confined to the American lower classes, constitute a distinctive *patterning* of concerns which differs significantly, both in rank order and weighting, from that of American middle class culture. Table 4.1 presents a highly schematic and simplified listing of six of the major concerns of lower class culture. Each is conceived as a "dimension" within which a fairly wide and varied range of alternative behavior patterns may be followed by different individuals under different situations. They are listed roughly in order of the degree of *explicit* attention accorded each and, in this sense, represent a weighted ranking of concerns. The "perceived alternatives" represent polar positions which define certain parameters within each dimension. As will be explained in more detail, it is necessary in relating the influence of these "concerns" to the motivation of delinquent behavior to specify *which* of its aspects is oriented to, whether orientation is *overt* or *covert, positive* (conforming to or seeking the aspect) or *negative* (rejecting or seeking to avoid the aspect).

The concept "focal concern" is used here in preference to the concept "value" for several interrelated reasons: (1) It is more readily derivable from direct field observation. (2) It is descriptively neutral—permitting independent consideration of positive and negative valences as varying under different conditions, whereas "value" carries a built-in positive valence. (3) It makes possible more refined analysis of subcultural differences, since it reflects actual behavior, whereas "value" tends to wash out intracultural differences since it is colored by notions of the "official" ideal.

Trouble

Concern over "trouble" is a dominant feature of lower class culture. The concept has various shades of meaning; "trouble" in one of its aspects represents a situation or a kind of behavior which results in unwelcome or complicating involvement with

From Walter B. Miller, "Lower Class Culture as a Generating Milieu of Gang Delinquency," *Journal of Social Issues,* vol. 14, no. 3 (1958), pp. 5–19 (with deletions). Reprinted by permission of the publisher.

TABLE 4.1 Focal Concerns of Lower Class Culture

Area	Perceived alternatives (state, quality, condition)	
1. Trouble:	law-abiding behavior	law-violating behavior
2. Toughness:	physical prowess, skill; "masculinity"; fearlessness, bravery, daring	weakness, ineptitude; effeminacy; timidity, cowardice, caution
3. Smartness:	ability to outsmart, dupe, "con"; gaining money by "wits"; shrewdness, adroitness in repartee	gullibility, "con-ability"; gaining money by hard work; slowness, dull-wittedness, verbal maladroitness
4. Excitement:	thrill; risk, danger; change, activity	boredom; "deadness," safeness; sameness, passivity
5. Fate:	favored by fortune, being "lucky"	ill-omened, being "unlucky"
6. Autonomy:	freedom from external constraint; freedom from superordinate authority; independence	presence of external constraint; presence of strong authority; dependency, being "cared for"

official authorities or agencies of middle class society. "Getting into trouble" and "staying out of trouble" represent major issues for male and female, adults and children. For men, "trouble" frequently involves fighting or sexual adventures while drinking; for women, sexual involvement with disadvantageous consequences. Expressed desire to avoid behavior which violates moral or legal norms is often based less on an explicit commitment to "official" moral or legal standards than on a desire to avoid "getting into trouble," e.g., the complicating consequences of the action.

The dominant concern over "trouble" involves a distinction of critical importance for the lower class community—that between "law-abiding" and "non-law-abiding" behavior. There is a high degree of sensitivity as to where each person stands in relation to these two classes of activity. Whereas in the middle class community a major dimension for evaluating a person's status is "achievement" and its external symbols, in the lower class personal status is very frequently gauged along the law-abiding–non-law-abiding dimension. A mother will evaluate the suitability of her daughter's boyfriend less on the basis of his achievement potential than on the basis of his innate "trouble" potential. This sensitive awareness of the opposition of "trouble-producing" and "non-trouble-producing" behavior represents both a major basis for deriving status distinctions and an internalized conflict potential for the individual.

As in the case of other focal concerns, which of two perceived alternatives—"law-abiding" or "non-law-abiding"—is valued varies according to the individual and the circumstances; in many instances there is an overt commitment to the "law-abiding" alternative, but a covert commitment to the "non-law-abiding." In certain situations, "getting into trouble" is overtly recognized as prestige-conferring; for example, membership in certain adult and adolescent primary groupings ("gangs") is contingent on having demonstrated an explicit commitment to the law-violating alternative. It is most important to note that the choice between "law-abiding" and "non-law-abiding" behavior is still a choice *within* lower class culture; the distinction between the policeman and the criminal, the outlaw and the sheriff, involves primarily this one dimension; in other respects they have a high community of interests. Not infrequently brothers raised in an identical cultural milieu will become police and criminals respectively....

Toughness

The concept of "toughness" in lower class culture represents a compound combination of qualities or states. Among its most important components are physical prowess, evidenced both by demonstrated possession of strength and endurance and by athletic skill; "masculinity," symbolized by a distinctive complex of acts and avoidances (bodily tattooing, absence of sentimentality, non-concern with "art," "literature," conceptualization of women as conquest objects, etc.); and bravery in the face of physical threat. The model for the "tough guy"—hard, fearless, undemonstrative, skilled in physical combat—is represented by the movie gangster of the thirties, the "private eye," and the movie cowboy.

The genesis of the intense concern over "toughness" in lower class culture is probably related to the fact that a significant proportion of lower class males are reared in a predominantly female household and lack a consistently present male figure with whom to identify and from whom to learn essential components of a "male" role. Since women serve as a primary object of identification during pre-adolescent years, the almost obsessive lower class concern with "masculinity" probably resembles a type of compulsive reaction-formation. A concern over homosexuality runs like a persistent thread through lower class culture. This is manifested by the institutionalized practice of baiting "queers," often accompanied by violent physical attacks, an expressed contempt for "softness" or frills, and the use of the local term for "homosexual" as a generalized pejorative epithet (e.g., higher class individuals or upwardly mobile peers are frequently characterized as "fags" or "queers"). The distinction between "overt" and "covert" orientation to aspects of an area of concern is especially important in regard to "toughness." A positive overt evaluation of behavior defined as "effeminate" would be out of the question for a lower class male; however, built into lower class culture is a range of devices which permit men to adopt behaviors and concerns which in other cultural milieux fall within the province of women, and at the same time to be defined as "tough" and manly. For example, lower class men can be professional short-order cooks in a diner and still be regarded as "tough." The highly intimate circumstances of the street corner gang involve the recurrent expression of strongly affectionate feelings towards other men. Such expressions, however, are disguised as their opposite, taking the form of ostensibly aggressive verbal and physical interaction (kidding, "ranking," roughhousing, etc.).

Smartness

"Smartness," as conceptualized in lower class culture, involves the capacity to outsmart, outfox, outwit, dupe, "take," "con" another or others and the concomitant capacity to avoid being outwitted, "taken," or duped oneself. In its essence, smartness involves the capacity to achieve a valued entity—material goods, personal status—through a maximum use of mental agility and a minimum use of physical effort. This capacity has an extremely long tradition in lower class culture and is highly valued. Lower class culture can be characterized as "non-intellectual" only if intellectualism is defined specifically in terms of control over a particular body of formally learned knowledge involving "culture" (art, literature, "good" music, etc.), a generalized perspective on the past and present conditions of our own and other societies, and other areas of knowledge imparted by formal educational institutions. This particular type of mental attainment is, in general, overtly disvalued and frequently associated with effeminacy; "smartness" in the lower class sense, however, is highly valued.

The lower class child learns and practices the use of this skill in the street corner situation. Individuals continually practice duping and outwitting one another through recurrent card games and other forms of gambling, mutual exchanges of insults, and "testing" for mutual "con-ability." Those who demonstrate competence in this skill are accorded considerable prestige. Leadership roles in the corner group are frequently allocated according to demonstrated capacity in the two areas of "smartness" and "toughness"; the ideal leader combines both, but the "smart" leader is often accorded more prestige than the "tough" one—reflecting a general lower class respect for "brains" in the "smartness" sense.

The model of the "smart" person is represented in popular media by the card shark, the professional gambler, the "con" artist, the promoter. A conceptual distinction is made between two kinds of people: "suckers," easy marks, "lushes," dupes, who work for their money and are legitimate targets of exploitation; and sharp operators, the "brainy" ones, who live by their wits and "getting" from the suckers by mental adroitness.

Involved in the syndrome of capacities related to "smartness" is a dominant emphasis in lower class culture on ingenious aggressive repartee. This skill, learned and practiced in the context of the corner group, ranges in form from the widely prevalent semi-ritualized teasing, kidding, razzing, "ranking," so characteristic of male peer group interaction, to the highly ritualized type of mutual insult interchange known as "the dirty dozens," "the dozens," "playing house," and other terms. This highly patterned cultural form is practiced on its most advanced level in adult male Negro society, but less polished variants are found throughout lower class culture—practiced, for example, by white children, male and female, as young as four or five. In essence, "doin' the dozens" involves two antagonists who vie with each other in the exchange of increasingly inflammatory insults, with incestuous and perverted sexual relations with the mother a dominant theme. In this form of insult interchange, as well as on other less ritualized occasions for joking, semi-serious, and serious mutual invective, a very high premium is placed on ingenuity, hair-trigger responsiveness, inventiveness, and the acute exercise of mental faculties.

Excitement

For many lower class individuals the rhythm of life fluctuates between periods of relatively routine or repetitive activity and sought situations of great emotional stimulation. Many of the most characteristic features of lower class life are related to the search for excitement or "thrill." Involved here are the highly prevalent use of alcohol by both sexes and the widespread use of gambling of all kinds—playing the numbers, betting on horse races, dice, cards. The quest for excitement finds what is perhaps its most vivid expression in the highly patterned practice of the recurrent "night on the town." This practice, designated by various terms in different areas ("honky-tonkin'"; "goin' out on the town"; "bar hoppin'"), involves a patterned set of activities in which alcohol, music, and sexual adventuring are major components. A group or individual sets out to "make the rounds" of various bars or night clubs. Drinking continues progressively throughout the evening. Men seek to "pick up" women, and women play the risky game of entertaining sexual advances. Fights between men involving women, gambling, and claims of physical prowess, in various combinations, are frequent consequences of a night of making the rounds. The explosive potential of this type of adventuring with sex and aggression, frequently leading to "trouble," is semi-explicitly sought by the individual. Since there is always a good likelihood that being out on the town will eventuate in fights, etc., the practice involves elements of sought risk and desired danger.

Counterbalancing the "flirting with danger" aspect of the "excitement" concern is the prevalence in lower class culture of other well-established patterns of activity which involve long periods of relative inaction or passivity. The term "hanging out" in lower class culture refers to extended periods of standing around, often with peer mates, doing what is defined as "nothing," "shooting the breeze," etc. A definite periodicity exists in the pattern of activity relating to the two aspects of the "excitement" dimension. For many lower class individuals the venture into the high risk world of alcohol, sex, and fighting occurs regularly once a week, with interim periods devoted to accommodating to possible consequences of these periods, along with recurrent resolves not to become so involved again.

Fate

Related to the quest for excitement is the concern with fate, fortune, or luck. Here also a distinction is made between two states—being "lucky" or "in luck" and being unlucky or jinxed. Many lower class individuals feel that their lives are subject to a set of forces over which they have relatively little control. These are not directly equated with the supernatural forces of formally organized religion, but relate more to a concept of "destiny," or man as a pawn of magical powers. Not infrequently this often implicit worldview is associated with a conception of the ultimate futility of directed effort towards a goal: if the cards are right, or the dice good to you, or if your lucky number comes up, things will go your way; if luck is against you, it's not worth trying. The concept of performing semi-magical rituals so that one's "luck will change" is prevalent; one hopes as a result to move from the state of being "unlucky" to that of being "lucky." The element of fantasy plays an important part in this area. Related to and complementing the notion that "only suckers work" (Smartness) is the idea that once things start going your way, relatively independent of your own effort, all good things will come to you. Achieving great material rewards (big cars, big houses, a roll of cash to flash in a fancy night club), valued in lower class as well as in other parts of American culture, is a recurrent theme in lower class fantasy and folk lore....

The prevalence in the lower class community of many forms of gambling, mentioned in connection with the "excitement" dimension, is also relevant here. Through cards and pool which involve skill, and thus both "toughness" and "smartness"; or through race horse betting, involving "smartness"; or through playing the numbers, involving predominantly "luck," one may make a big killing with a minimum of directed and persistent effort within conventional occupational channels. Gambling in its many forms illustrates the fact that many of the persistent features of lower class culture are multi-functional—serving a range of desired ends at the same time. Describing some of the incentives behind gambling has involved mention of all of the focal concerns cited so far—Toughness, Smartness, and Excitement, in addition to Fate.

Autonomy

The extent and nature of control over the behavior of the individual—an important concern in most cultures—has a special significance and is distinctively patterned in lower class culture. The discrepancy between what is overtly valued and what is covertly sought is particularly striking in this area. On the overt level there is a strong and frequently expressed resentment of the idea of external control, restrictions on behavior, and unjust or coercive authority. "No one's gonna push *me* around," or "I'm gonna tell him he can take the job and shove it..." are commonly expressed sentiments. Similar explicit attitudes are maintained to systems of behavior-restricting rules, insofar as these are perceived as representing the injunctions and bearing the sanctions of superordinate authority. In addition, in lower class culture a close conceptual connection is made between "authority" and "nurturance." To be restrictively or firmly controlled is to be cared for. Thus the overtly negative evaluation of superordinate authority frequently extends as well to nurturance, care, or protection. The desire for personal independence is often expressed in such terms as "I don't need *nobody* to take care of me. I can take care of myself!" Actual patterns of behavior, however, reveal a marked discrepancy between expressed sentiment and what is covertly valued. Many lower class people appear to seek out highly restrictive social environments wherein stringent external controls are maintained over their behavior. Such institutions as the armed forces, the mental hospital, the disciplinary school, the prison or correctional institution, provide environments which incorporate a strict and detailed set of rules, defining and limiting behavior and enforced by an authority system which controls and applies coercive sanctions for deviance from these rules. While under the jurisdiction of such systems, the lower class person generally expresses to his peers continual resentment of the coercive, unjust, and arbitrary exercise of authority. Having been released, or having escaped from these milieux, however, he will often act in such a way as to insure recommitment, or choose recommitment voluntarily after a temporary period of "freedom."...

Focal Concerns of the Lower Class Adolescent Street Corner Group

The one-sex peer group is a highly prevalent and significant structural form in the lower class community. There is a strong probability that the prevalence and stability of this type of unit is directly related to the prevalence of a stabilized type of lower class child-rearing unit—the "female-based" household. This is a nuclear kin unit in which a male parent is either absent from the household, present only sporadically, or, when present, only minimally or inconsistently involved in the support and rearing of children. This unit usually consists of one or more females of childbearing age and their offspring. The females are frequently related to one another by blood or marriage ties, and the unit often includes two or more generations of women, e.g., the mother and/or aunt of the principal childbearing female.

The nature of social groupings in the lower class community may be clarified if we make the assumption that it is the *one-sex peer unit* rather than the two-parent family unit which represents the most significant relational unit for both sexes in lower class communities. Lower class society may be pictured as comprising a set of age-graded one-sex groups which constitute the major psychic focus and reference group for those over twelve or thirteen. Men and women of mating age leave these groups periodically to form temporary marital alliances, but these lack stability, and after varying periods of "trying out" the two-sex family arrangement, they gravitate back to the more "comfortable" one-sex grouping, whose members exert strong pressure on the individual *not* to disrupt the group by adopting a two-sex household pattern of life. Membership in a stable and solidary peer unit is vital to the lower class individual precisely to the extent to which a range of essential functions—psychological, educational, and others—is not provided by the "family" unit.

The adolescent street corner group represents the adolescent variant of this lower class structural form. What has been called the "delinquent gang" is one subtype of this form, defined on the basis of frequency of participation in law-violating activity; this subtype should not be considered a legitimate unit of study per se, but rather as one particular variant of the adolescent street corner group. The "hanging" peer group is a unit of particular importance for the adolescent male. In many cases it is the most stable and solidary primary group he has ever belonged to; for boys reared in female-based households the corner group provides the first real opportunity to learn essential aspects of the male role in the context of peers facing similar problems of sex-role identification....

Lower Class Culture and the Motivation of Delinquent Behavior

The customary set of activities of the adolescent street corner group includes activities which are in violation of laws and ordinances of the legal code. Most of these center around assault and theft of various types (the gang fight; auto theft; assault on an individual; petty pilfering and shoplifting; "mugging"; pocketbook theft).

Members of street corner gangs are well aware of the law-violating nature of these acts; they are not psychopaths, or physically or mentally "defective"; in fact, since the corner group supports and enforces a rigorous set of standards which demand a high degree of fitness and personal competence, it tends to recruit from the most "able" members of the community.

Why, then, is the commission of crimes a customary feature of gang activity? The most general answer is that the commission of crimes by members of adolescent street corner groups is motivated primarily by the attempt to achieve ends, states, or conditions which are valued and to avoid those that are disvalued within their most meaningful cultural milieu, through those culturally available avenues which appear as the most feasible means of attaining those ends.

The operation of these influences is well illustrated by the gang fight—a prevalent and characteristic type of corner group delinquency. This type of activity comprises a highly stylized and culturally patterned set of sequences. Although details vary under different circumstances, the following events are generally included. A member or several members of group A "trespass" on the claimed territory of group B. While there they commit an act or acts which group B defines as a violation of their rightful privileges, an affront to their honor, or a challenge to their "rep." Frequently this act involves advances to a girl associated with group B; it may occur at a dance or party; sometimes the mere act of "trespass" is seen as deliberate provocation. Members of group B then assault members of group A, if they are caught while still in B's territory. Assaulted members of group A return to their "home" territory and recount to members of their group details of the incident, stressing the insufficient nature of the provocation ("I just *looked* at her! Hardly even said anything!") and the unfair circumstances of the assault ("About *twenty* guys jumped just the *two* of us!"). The highly colored account is acutely inflammatory; group A, perceiving its honor violated and its "rep" threatened, feels obligated to retaliate in force. Sessions of detailed planning now occur; allies are recruited if the size of group A and its potential allies appears to necessitate larger numbers; strategy is plotted, and messengers dispatched. Since the prospect of a gang fight is frightening to even the "toughest" group members, a constant rehearsal of the provocative incident or incidents and declamations of the essentially evil nature of the opponents accompany the planning process to bolster possibly weakening motivation to fight. The excursion into "enemy" territory sometimes results in a full scale fight; more often group B cannot be found, or the police appear and stop the fight, "tipped off" by an anonymous informant. When this occurs, group members express disgust and disappointment; secretly there is much relief; their honor has been avenged without incurring injury; often the anonymous tipster is a member of one of the involved groups.

The basic elements of this type of delinquency are sufficiently stabilized and recurrent as to constitute an essentially ritualized pattern, resembling both in structure and expressed motives for action classic forms such as the European "duel," the American Indian tribal war, and the Celtic clan feud. Although the arousing and "acting out" of individual aggressive emotions are inevitably involved in the gang fight, neither its form nor motivational dynamics can be adequately handled within a predominantly personality-focused frame of reference.

It would be possible to develop in considerable detail the processes by which the commission of a range of illegal acts is either explicitly supported by, implicitly demanded by, or not materially inhibited by factors relating to the focal concerns of lower class culture. In place of such a development, the following three statements condense in general terms the operation of these processes:

1. Following cultural practices which comprise essential elements of the total life pattern of lower class culture automatically violates certain legal norms.

2. In instances where alternate avenues to similar objectives are available, the non-law-abiding avenue frequently provides a relatively greater and more immediate return for a relatively smaller investment of energy.

3. The "demanded" response to certain situations recurrently engendered within lower class culture involves the commission of illegal acts.

The primary thesis of this paper is that the dominant component of the motivation of "delinquent" behavior engaged in by members of lower class corner groups involves a positive effort to achieve states, conditions, or qualities valued within the actor's most significant cultural milieu.... A large body of systematically interrelated attitudes, practices, behaviors, and values characteristic of lower class culture are designed to support and maintain the basic features of the lower class way of life. In areas where these differ from features of middle class culture, action oriented to the achievement and maintenance of the lower class system may violate norms of middle class culture and be perceived as deliberately non-conforming or malicious by an observer strongly cathected to middle class norms. This does not mean, however, that violation of the middle class norm is the dominant component of motivation; it is a by-product of action primarily oriented to the lower class system. The standards of lower class culture cannot be seen merely as a reverse function of middle class culture—as middle class standards "turned upside down"; lower class culture is a distinctive tradition many centuries old with an integrity of its own.

From the viewpoint of the acting individual, functioning within a field of well-structured cultural forces, the relative impact of "conforming" and "rejective" elements in the motivation of gang delinquency is weighted preponderantly on the conforming side. Rejective or rebellious elements are inevitably involved, but their influence during the actual commission of delinquent acts is relatively small compared to the influence of pressures to achieve what is valued by the actor's most immediate reference groups. Expressed awareness by the actor of the element of rebellion often represents only that aspect of motivation of which he is explicitly conscious; the deepest and most compelling components of motivation—adherence to highly meaningful group standards of Toughness, Smartness, Excitement, etc.—are often unconsciously patterned. No cultural pattern as well established as the practice of illegal acts by members of lower class corner groups could persist if buttressed primarily by negative, hostile, or rejective motives; its principal motivational support, as in the case of any persisting cultural tradition, derives from a positive effort to achieve what is valued within that tradition, and to conform to its explicit and implicit norms.

Part III

Theories of Social Control: An Introduction

In this part of the book, we switch gears rather drastically. All the perspectives or approaches we've looked at so far are etiological in focus, that is, their interest is on the cause or causes of deviance as a form of behavior. Why do they do it? is their lodestar question. What factors or conditions make deviant behavior more likely? Etiological or causal theories are concerned with the occurrence, enactment, rate, or distribution of deviant behavior.

Of course, we've only looked at the specifically *sociological* theories of deviant behavior. Some others lie outside sociology's scope: for instance, biological (hormonal, genetic, physiological, and so on) and psychological (behaviorist, personality, psychiatric, psychoanalytic, and so on) theories. But still, whether individual or structural, whether biological, psychological, or sociological, these theories are all focused on the same basic question: *Why deviant behavior?* Why do some individuals commit it more than others? What conditions do certain persons have that cause them to commit deviance? Why is it more common in some communities or societies than in others? Why are members of certain social categories more likely to engage in it than others? What social conditions do certain persons live in or have in their background that cause them to commit deviant behavior? What situations or contexts (such as freedom from surveillance and punishment) generate higher rates of deviance than others?

All etiological or causal theories see deviance as a type of *action*. All, in one way or another—each in its own way, and to varying degrees—accept the essentialist or objectivist or positivist assumption. All see deviance as a specific, identifiable "thing" that social scientists can lay their hands on. All, or a substantial proportion of, actions that are referred to as "deviance" possess enough inner, inherent, or intrinsic properties in common to give them a term that applies to all equally. All these actions are seen as part of an entity, a syndrome, an umbrella phenomenon whose representatives or cases or examples can be grouped together in the same category because all instances of it are similar in some objectivistic, inherent respect. These instances possess more or less clear-cut, identifiable traits that attract some individuals, causing them to engage in it.

Picture these two different concerns in a particular case. In 1992, a Wisconsin man, Jeffrey Dahmer, was convicted of a series of horrific killings. The essentialist, concerned with etiology, would focus on *why such behavior takes place*—both in general and in this particular case. Mass murder would be taken as *a type of action with a common thread* that demands an explanation. Whether biological, psychological, or sociological, etiological theories agree that mass murder is an identifiable phenomenon in need of an explanation.

In contrast, the constructionist would focus on *what is made* of the Jeffrey Dahmer case: the arrest, the media coverage, the trial, the punishment and incarceration, the public reaction, and commentary—what part Jeffrey Dahmer played in American society's mass psyche or collective consciousness. These are very different enterprises, although both concern themselves with deviant behavior. In Part III, we will look at the constructionist enterprise—what is made of deviance, how the society reacts to behavior and conditions defined as deviance, what the society does about deviance, how persons labeled as deviants are treated and dealt with. The French philosopher Michel Foucault referred to the latter enterprise as "discourse."

Now, not all public reactions and commentary make up the enterprise of social control. *Social control* is everything that is designed to induce members of a society to conform to the norms. This could include a slap in the face, social isolation, a sharp rebuke, a gentle reminder, or arrest, incarceration, even execution. But broad as social control is, *social constructions* of deviance are far broader, far more encompassing than social control alone. Social constructions include any and all conceptions of and reactions to deviance, whether they may be referred to as social control or not. Still, social control of deviance is one major type—*the* major type—of all the many possible social constructions of deviance, and it is of central importance in any study on the subject.

An aside for a moment: Notice that, except for the biological framework, we can't very well ask questions about how certain involuntarily acquired physical characteristics come into existence. (With the possible exception of obesity, which is widely thought to be caused, at least *in part,* behaviorally, that is, because certain people eat too much and are too inactive.) You can't very well account for the existence or occurrence of traits like ugliness or blindness or shortness and so on with a sociological explanation of its causality. When it comes to physical characteristics, "all etiological theories appear inadequate" (Sagarin, 1975, p. 201). Yes, the researcher can study correlations or statistical relationships between social factors or characteristics and physical traits such as blindness or extreme shortness. And yes, some of the "causes" of these physical traits are unquestionably indirectly related to these social factors. But, for the most part, they are caused by a variety or hodgepodge of factors and variables, many of them physical or biological in origin. As a consequence, the etiological or essentialistic approach has shunned physical traits as deviance and has focused almost exclusively on deviant *behavior.* In contrast, the constructionist approach focuses on both behavior *and* conditions. Clearly, both behavior and physical traits fall under the jurisdiction of constructionism. Regardless of what causes blindness, in a given society, blindness and the blind are thought about, written about, and reacted to in a certain way; regardless of what causes obesity, the obese are treated in a certain way in a given society. In this sense, the constructionist approach is far broader in its scope.

This distinction between deviance as a type of *action* by the essentialists and deviance as seen as a label or *reaction* by the constructionists forces us to address the question: What exactly are these people *doing* when they engage in actions we refer to as deviance? Are they engaged in an action that belongs, naturally and inevitably, in a given category? Are categories simply yet another social construct, artificially and socially created for certain reasons or purposes? Notice that all of the practitioners of the "Why deviance?" approach agree that rules and laws designating what's deviant and criminal vary somewhat. Only a few etiological sociologists are "hard" or "strict" essentialists in that they believe that social categories (like "crime," "deviance," "homosexuality," and "drug use") possess identical natural, universal indwelling traits. They agree that something is deviant only to the extent that norms exist condemning and punishing perpetrators. All these approaches, to my knowledge, are at least minimally relativistic. Still, they agree that there is *some* common core shared by all cases designated as deviant and criminal, above and beyond their social designation. To the extent that that is so, then the etiological enterprise is on firm ground. But if the social labels of "crime," "deviance," "homosexuality," and "drug use" point to cases *with no common thread whatsoever* aside from the label, then searching for causes must be regarded as somewhat suspect.

I believe that there *is* some common core to certain forms of deviance and certain crimes (though not, I think, for deviance in general and possibly not even for crime in general). Still, I do not question the etiological enterprise. There may be enough concrete features that some forms of deviance and crime have in common for us to come up with one or several valid explanations for why they occur. It's a question of emphasis. There may be both cultural relativity and, in addition, some common core to what's deviant and crime. The constructionist enterprise does not so much contradict the essentialist program as complement it.

The constructionist enterprise, then, represents a different approach from the etiological or essentialistic program. Constructionists ask about rules and judgments of deviance and how laws are made and enforced. To the constructionist, deviance and crime are seen not so much as a type of *action* as a type of *infraction*. Here, we have to look at how judgments of deviance come into being, that is, rule making and rule enforcement. In this endeavor, we do not assume that certain behaviors are identifiable things in the world. Instead, we turn our gaze to the process by which certain judgments come to be made. We make the assumption that an explanation of rules and their enforcement is problematic. By problematic I mean, social control does not happen automatically, it requires an explanation.

Most commonsense views of deviance do not see rules and laws as problematic; to the hypothetical man and woman on the street, it is obvious why rules and laws are devised—because deviance and crime are often harmful to the society. Societies devise these rules and laws for their own protection. If there were no rules, no laws, no punishments for wrongdoing, every society would collapse into a condition described by the English social philosopher Thomas Hobbes (1588–1679): chaos, anarchy, and a vicious state of war of all against all in which the weak would perish and only the strong would survive.

If it were true that all forms of behavior we identify as deviant indeed had specific, readily identifiable traits in common and one of those traits was that they inflict clear-cut harm on the society in some way, then our need to explain rules against them would be little more than common sense. It would be immediately obvious that rules are devised to protect the society in which these behaviors occurred. Of course rules against deviant behavior—why not? Who needs an explanation? Every human society has to protect itself against harm. Otherwise none would survive. An explanation for why deviance and crime exist isn't necessary, common sense tells us; it's too obvious to bother with. In this case, is common sense right? Does the society set up the machinery of control (to quote Kai Erikson) "in order to protect itself against the harmful effects of deviation in much the same way that an organism mobilizes its resources to combat an invasion of germs"? (Erikson, 1964, p. 12). That's not especially interesting, is it? Basically, the question isn't very challenging. It's intuitively obvious. We assume that societies would marshal some form of social control to combat harmful behavior, behavior that would threaten the society's viability or its very existence. Otherwise it would perish.

That's the assumption we have to examine more closely.

According to George Herbert Mead, Emile Durkheim, and Kai Erikson, "it is by no means clear that all" (and here, I'd substitute, *most*) "acts considered deviant in a culture are in fact (or even in principle) harmful to group life" (Erikson, 1964, p. 12). If this is true—if it is true that most actions deemed deviant do little or no direct harm to the society or its members—we would need to know how a community or society decides that the enactor of "what forms of conduct should be singled out" for punishment, condemnation, hostility, censure. In short, *why social control?* Why are some actions punished and not others; why are some actors, some enactors of deviant behavior, punished and not others? Why is the same action punished in one society but not another, why at one time but not another? In short, once we've severed the inherent or intrinsic or automatic connection between deviance and harm, we are free to wonder about the origin, nature, and dynamics of social control.

Clearly, the constructionists do not agree that all, even most, instances of what's referred to as deviance have this quality of harmfulness in common. That societies everywhere need to protect themselves against inherently, intrinsically damaging behavior by setting rules to discourage it. They all agree that we need an explanation of or an account for rules and their enforcement. That the existence of these rules is problematic; it requires an explanation. And it is that explanation that they wish to supply. So, instead of asking "Why deviance?" they ask "Why rules?" "Why condemnation?" "Why punishment?" "Why laws?" "Why the enforcement of laws?"—a very different emphasis from that which investigates the causes of deviant behavior.

Some of the approaches I've categorized in Part III have some of both emphases, that is, they are both etiological and concerned with rules and their enforcement, but they are more concerned with the latter than the former. Marxism asks both "Why rules?" and "Why deviance?"; so does feminism. At the same time, the emphasis of all the perspectives in this part of the anthology—functionalism, labeling theory, conflict theory and Marxism, feminism, and the "new" sociology of social control—are more constructionist than etiological in their approach to deviance. So, let's look at the flip side of deviance now: social control as problematic. How do rules come into being? How are they enforced? And against whom? These are the sorts of questions that attract us when we examine social control as problematic.

One last point. The preceding discussion should have made this point clear, but just in case it did not: The "social control" approach to deviance is *not* concerned with the proper method of "controlling" deviants or criminals. Sociologists who write about social control are not *agents* of social control, nor is their work focused on questions of how physicians, psychiatrists, mental hospitals, the police, the courts, jails and prisons can best "control" crime and criminals, homosexuality and homosexuals, drug addiction and drug addicts, the mental illness and the mentally ill, rape and rapists, and so on. Social control theorists are not in the business of offering suggestions for treatment, therapy, punishment—or any other form of "control." Their job is both broader and, in a sense, more critical; it is to understand how deviance "discourse" came into being and how it works. To show that social control *is a social product,* and not simply a rational technology that dropped from the skies, with no social roots whatsoever. Sociologists who study social control aim to understand its *what, how,* and *why;* in so doing, far from working hand-in-glove with agents of social control, they stand a bit outside the enterprise and offer a critique of it. If anything, their efforts are almost exactly the *opposite* of those of agents of social control. Their aim is to show what a social, a human—and *fallible*—enterprise social control is.

Reference

Erikson, Kai T. 1964. Notes on the sociology of deviance. In Howard S. Becker (ed.), *The Other Side: Perspectives on Deviance.* New York: Free Press, pp. 9–21.

Sagarin, Edward. 1975. *Deviants and Deviance: An Introduction to Disvalued People and Behavior.* New York: Praeger.

Chapter 5

Functionalism

Although Kai Erikson's classic and often-cited article, "Notes on the Sociology of Deviance" (1962, 1964, 1966, pp. 3–29), is typically seen as a prime example of labeling theory, in fact, in it, he does an extremely elegant job of summing up the functionalist paradigm. The functionalist approach to deviance, as with functionalism generally, takes as its central, guiding question: *How is social order possible?* This leads to a number of related questions: How do societies survive? How can societies be organized as to maximize their chance of survival? What do societies do to eliminate or reduce the likelihood of harmful, threatening practices, customs, or institutions? What do they do to encourage beneficial practices and institutions?

Functionalism's analysis of deviance falls into three broad points; the first two are fairly commonsensical while the third is counterintuitive, or contrary to common sense.

Functionalism's first point concerning deviance is that certain actions are dysfunctional or harmful; they threaten or undermine a society's chances of survival. Thus, in order to survive, societies need to discourage this harmful or threatening behavior.

Its second point is that, by punishing the deviant for that harmful behavior, society draws its "moral boundaries," sets an example for others, and discourages such behavior, thereby increasing its chances for survival. In other words, punishing the deviant is "functional" or beneficial.

Functionalism's third, and not nearly so obvious point on deviance, is that, in controlled amounts, certain *types* of deviance may be beneficial or functional for the survival of the society. They exist, and have continued throughout recorded time, because they serve a function for the society, because they help the society to adapt to the challenges of survival.

Functionalism starts with the assumption that certain behaviors are *dysfunctional* or intrinsically harmful to the society as a whole. Such behaviors tear at the social fabric. They make the society a dangerous, problematic place in which to live. They reduce a society's likelihood of survival. Consequently, rules must be set up to condemn and discourage such behavior so it cannot inflict harm on the society. The society must protect itself from harmful behavior. That's why we have rules; that's why we have punishment. That's why we have *deviance,* that is to say, that's why rules are set up to condemn perpetrators of certain actions: Such condemnation reduces the incidence of such harmful behavior.

For instance, Kingsley Davis (1949, pp. 401–404) argues that incest is a form of behavior that, if permitted to flourish, would undermine the very foundation of the society, threatening the viability and stability of the society. The incest taboo is one of the very few cultural universals that exists, Davis states; why? Why have societies practically everywhere and at all times punished sex and marriage between close family members? It is not to prevent genetic inbreeding, Davis argues, since many societies are ignorant of the connection between sex and procreation, and yet they outlaw incestual relations. And it is not instinctual, he says, since humans possess no full-fledged instincts. Incest is taboo practically everywhere, argues Davis, because relationships and lines of authority within the family must be clear and unambiguous; if a father were also the lover of his daughter, for instance, his role with her *as* a father would be undermined, he may be a rival against his own son for the affection of his daughter, and his husbandly relationship with his wife—who, in this hypothetical scenario, is the mother of his lover—would be undermined and corrupted. Rivalry and confused status lines would produce a level of conflict that no family system could sustain. The very basis of reproduction on which all societies depend for continuity would be threatened. The incest taboo is "absolutely indispensable" to the functioning of the family and the very survival of the society (p. 404). Since incest is "dysfunctional," it must be prohibited; and the prohibition, as well as attendant punishments of violations, successfully keep the incidence of incest down to tolerable levels.

Another fairly conventional, traditional, or commonsense argument within the functionalist paradigm is the closely related view that *punishing* the deviant is positively functional for the society. This is what Erikson means by his statement (1964, p. 14): "Morality and immorality meet at the public scaffold." It is in the punishment of deviants that conventional members of the society do what Ben-Yehuda refers to as drawing and redrawing the moral boundaries of the society (1985). The punishment of deviants also reminds wavering or seducible members of the society what happens to someone who strays from the straight and narrow path. In the words of Talcott Parsons, punishment is "a ritual expression of the sentiments which uphold the institutionalized values which the criminal has violated. This ritual expression serves to consolidate those sentiments and above all to strengthen them in that part of the population which has positive but latent motivations to the deviance being punished" (1951, p. 310). In a phrase, the punishment of deviance is positively functional for the society as a whole because it keeps the level of certain harmful behaviors to a minimum.

These two points—that some forms of deviance are harmful, and preventing them by punishing perpetrators is positively functional for the society—represent only two of functionalism's lines of thought concerning deviance. These "protectionist" arguments are functionalism's most obvious and commonsense points; they constitute what may be referred to as functionalism's "minor" mode. As David Matza says, overwhelmingly, the functionalists did not emphasize the "dysfunctions" or harmful effects of deviance and the positive impact of punishing norm violators, but the functions, or positive consequences, of deviance (Matza, 1969, p. 55). Above all, the functionalists wished to be (in their time) interesting, original, daring, radical, even shocking.

Thus, functionalism's "major"—and counterintuitive—mode is this: In controlled amounts, certain kinds of deviant behavior, though they may be condemned, may actually be beneficial or positively functional for the society, or for a social group in a given society. Societies or groups do not want to "stamp out" deviance, because deviance is a resource for human collectives. If the deviant were to be cast out, the society would be less cohesive, less stable, less smoothly functioning. The deviant is *good* for the society or the group. Some deviant behaviors contribute to the functioning of the collective (Dentler and Erikson, 1959). Persistence is the key here: Why do certain behaviors, such as prostitution, persist for thousands of years? They must make a positive contribution, otherwise they wouldn't have been around for all that time. Persistence, then, is a clue to functionality. Deviance shores up and draws society's moral boundaries (Ben-Yehuda, 1985). Certain forms of deviance—which do not threaten society's core or central values or society's viability—in controlled amounts, can offer certain functions to the society's stability, cohesion, and functioning.

For instance, Robert K. Merton argues that bossism and the urban political machine, although hopelessly corrupt, nepotistic, and routinely implicated in criminal behavior, offers a variety of assistance that cannot be obtained by any other social institution (1957, pp. 72–82). Daniel Bell argues that, while organized crime is engaged in illegal activity that may harm the society in some ways, it offers an unusual "ladder of success" to the talented, enterprising members of certain ethnic groups who might cause trouble in more harmful ways (1961). Willard Waller and E. R. Hawkins (1936) argued that crime is an industry exactly like every other industry: It earns a profit, it employs workers, it contributes to the economy. Far from *subtracting* its profits from a nation's economy—which sees crime as *costing* the society money—these profits should be *added* to it. If these criminal endeavors were to be wiped out overnight, the society would be plunged into the kind of economic depression that would follow the collapse of legal industries such as the steel, automobile, and electrical appliance industries. In a sense, then, crime is beneficial or "functional" for the society. And Lewis Coser (1956) argued that even certain kinds of social conflict may contribute to a society's maintenance, cohesion, and survival.

What "functions"—positive or negative—an institution or custom has depend on which segments of the society we are examining. Does an institution or custom have an impact on the society as a whole, taken as a unified entity? Or does it have different sorts of consequences for different segments of the society—for instance, rich versus poor, men versus women, Blacks versus whites, and so on? Functionalists of deviance seem to be arguing that we can refer to functions for the society as a whole, that we do not need to refer to different functions for different groups or categories. For instance, Kingsley Davis's often-cited article (written with Wilbert Moore), "Some

Principles of Stratification" (1945), argued that social stratification is positively functional for the society, taken as a wholistic entity. Social stratification maximizes cohesion, stability, ensures the protection of the social order. This position has been critiqued countless times on the grounds that the "society" as a whole is a fiction; it doesn't exist. What *does* exist is a hierarchy of strata or classes with different—even contrary—interests. Stratification is fine for the upper classes; they benefit from it. But, at the same time, it may be oppressive and exploitative for members of the lower or working strata or classes. It doesn't have a single, specific impact on the society as a whole; in fact, it has a different impact on variously located segments of or classes within the society. An identity of interests for the society as a whole cannot be assumed, as the functionalist theory of stratification seems to have done (Gouldner, 1970).

A similar argument can be launched against Kingsley Davis's classic article, "The Sociology of Prostitution" (1937). Following the points I just made, functionalists would argue that the persistence of prostitution throughout human history and around the world indicates that it is functional for the society: "Enabling a small number of women to take care of the needs of a large number of men, it is the most convenient sexual outlet for an army, and for the legions of strangers, perverts, and physically repulsive in our midst. It performs a function, apparently, which no other institution fully performs" (p. 755). Prostitution permits a sexual outlet that is not disruptive. Unlike having sex with the wives and relatives of friends, and unmarried girlfriends and mistresses, Davis argues, sex with a prostitute has a minimal negative impact on traditional social relations and institutions. Ironically, then, prostitution protects and sustains the conventional, traditional family and makes the society more stable; this deviant institution is "functional" for the society.

But for what or for whom is prostitution functional? Davis argues that it is functional for the society as a whole. But is it? Is it functional for the patriarchal family, therefore maintaining a system of dominance of men over women, keeping women in an inferior position? Is it possible that the institution of prostitution, which maintains the practice but stigmatizes the prostitute, is dysfunctional—not positively functional—for women generally and prostitutes specifically? Although some functional analyses did focus on an institution or custom's consequences for specific segments of the society (Merton, 1957, pp. 25–30, 38–46), as a general rule, in their concrete analyses, functionalists focused on the impact of institutions and behavior on the society as a whole. Later approaches, which were critical of functionalism, saw much more diversity and heterogeneity in the impact of a given institution or practice. A given institution or custom may be beneficial for one category at the expense of the interests of another. Too often, functionalism seemed to be justifying the status quo (Gouldner, 1970). Davis's argument on the functions of prostitution, which is based on a society-wide identity of interests, does not hold up under close scrutiny; it is based on a mistaken commonality in the various interests of the many factions in a society and, more specifically, on the inevitability of the patriarchal family. As Downes and Rock say, as soon as the question "functional for whom?" is raised, "the bottom falls out of the functionalist case" (p. 107).

Functionalism was never a dominant approach in the study of deviance. As a general theory of how society works, functionalism was the dominant approach in sociology from the 1940s to the early 1960s; after sustained criticism from more progressive, pluralistic, and radical approaches (for instance, Gouldner, 1970), functionalism went into a sharp decline after the 1960s. During the 1980s, an approach whose practitioners refer to themselves as "neofunctionalists" emerged (Alexander, 1985), indicating something of a revival of the functionalist approach. Still, today, the functionalist approach is in disrepute among most sociologists (Downes and Rock, 1988, p. 88).

In spite of its limitations, functionalism did make at least two contributions to the study of deviance. One is that it purged the automatic implication of pathology from the phenomenon of deviance (Matza, 1969, pp. 31–37, 53–62, 73–80). Prior to the functionalists, most observers assumed that deviance was "bad" for the society, that it was caused by "evil" (or undesirable) factors and mechanisms, and that it had "evil" (or harmful) consequences. Functionalists argued that this was not necessarily the case, that deviance can be generated by causes most of us see as good, and may have consequences most of us see in positive terms. Functionalism was the first perspective historically to argue that deviance is not necessarily a result of an undesirable or abnormal condition and that it does not always produce negative consequences. Deviance is, in fact, part and parcel of the normal functioning of any society.

And the second contribution of functionalism to the study of deviance was to shift the focus in the field away from an exclusive concern with why some people engage in deviant behavior, or why certain societal conditions encouraged certain forms of deviance or deviance in general, to a concern with why and how rules are made and enforced. In other words, *why social control?* Why is social control focused on the specific behaviors it condemns? Why are other behaviors less harshly punished? Why do certain behaviors persist in spite of social control? These concerns expanded the field of the sociology of deviance and prepared the way for later, mainly social control–oriented approaches, notably, labeling theory, conflict theory, and feminism. As Downes and Rock tell us, there is a hidden but perfectly vigorous functionalism "still lurking" in much of the sociology of deviance (p. 110).

Ben-Yehuda presents a functionalist analysis of the Renaissance witch craze. Accusing certain members in the society of witchcraft was a sign that the "old order" of medieval Europe was crumbling; scapegoats had to be designated as the enemy to unify what was an increasingly disunited society. It was in the societies in which medieval Catholicism was most strongly challenged by Protestantism, secularism, humanism, and unorthodox sects that the witch craze was most virulent; in the societies in which Catholicism was most traditional, secure, and unchallenged, witch trials and burning witches at the stake were far less common. In short, the Renaissance witch craze served a function for a waning medieval society: It drew the moral boundaries of the society sharply, in no uncertain terms. The fact that the forces of change swept away the old order shows that functions need not be a permanent, ahistorical fixture; they depend on the nature and character of the society we're looking at. The positive functions of the Renaissance witch craze were not sufficient to maintain European society as it had existed, more or less, for a thousand years. At times, functions may be overwhelmed by social change.

One last point is in order here. Sociologists have not usually thought of functionalism as a member of those schools of thought that are concerned with social control. This is because its answer to the "Why social control?" question implies inevitability. All the other perspectives we'll be looking at in this section of the anthology—labeling theory or interactionism, Marxism, conflict theory, feminism, the "new" sociology of social control—see social control as *problematic*. By that I mean they see it as an institution that not only requires an explanation but that *could have been different* had social conditions been otherwise. In other words, these other theories argue that the particular form of social control that exists is not an institution that, somehow, dropped from the skies; instead, it was brought into being and maintained in part because it serves the interests of certain powerful segments of the society. Functionalism differs from this perspective and sees social control as an almost automatic mechanism that emerges, somehow, to serve the interests *of the society as a whole*. These two aspects of functionalism—its assumption of the automaticity of social control and its view that social control serves the society as a whole—mark the theory off sharply and dramatically from the other theories of social control. At the same time, its concern is not the cause of deviance but why rules are set up and enforced; hence, it belongs—uneasily—in the company of the other theories.

References

Alexander, Jeffrey (ed.). 1985. *Neofunctionalism*. Newbury Park, Calif.: Sage.

Bell, Daniel. 1961. Crime as an American way of life: A queer ladder of social mobility. In *The End of Ideology: On the Exhaustion of Political Ideas in the Fifties* (rev. ed.). New York: Free Press.

Ben-Yehuda, Nachman. 1985. *Deviance and Moral Boundaries*. Chicago: University of Chicago Press.

Coser, Lewis. 1956. *The Functions of Social Conflict*. New York: Free Press.

Davis, Kingsley. 1937. The sociology of prostitution. *American Sociological Review,* 2 (October): 744–755.

———. 1949. *Human Behavior*. New York: Macmillan.

Davis, Kingsley, and Wilbert E. Moore. 1945. Some principles of stratification. *American Sociological Review,* 10 (April): 242–249.

Dentler, Robert A., and Kai T. Erikson. 1959. The functions of deviance in groups. *Social Problems,* 7 (Fall): 98–107.

Downes, David, and Paul Rock. 1988. *Understanding Deviance: A Guide to the Sociology of Crime and Rule Breaking* (2nd ed.). Oxford, England: Oxford University Press.

Erikson, Kai T. 1962. Notes on the sociology of deviance. *Social Problems,* 9 (Spring): 307–314.

Erikson, Kai T. 1964. Notes on the sociology of deviance. In Howard S. Becker (ed.), *The Other Side: Perspectives on Deviance*. New York: Free Press, pp. 9–21.

Erikson, Kai T. 1966. *Wayward Puritans: A Study in the Sociology of Deviance*. New York: John Wiley & Sons.

Gouldner, Alvin W. 1970. *The Coming Crisis of American Sociology*. New York: Basic Books.

Matza, David. 1969. *Becoming Deviant*. Englewood Cliffs, N.J.: Prentice-Hall.

Merton, Robert K. 1957. *Social Theory and Social Structure* (rev. ed.). New York: Free Press.

Parsons, Talcott. 1951. *The Social System*. New York: Free Press.

Waller, Willard W., and E. R. Hawkins. 1936. Critical notes on the cost of crime. *Journal of Criminal Law and Criminology,* 26 (January): 679–694.

The Functions of Social Deviance

KAI T. ERIKSON

It is common practice in sociology to picture deviant behavior as an alien element in society. Deviance is considered a vagrant form of human activity which has somehow broken away from the more orderly currents of social life and needs to be controlled. And since it is generally understood that this sort of aberration could only occur if something were wrong within the organization of society itself, deviant behavior is described almost as if it were leakage from machinery in poor condition: it is an incidental result of disorder and anomie, a symptom of internal breakdown.

The purpose of the following remarks will be to review this conventional outlook and to argue that it provides too narrow a framework for many kinds of sociological research. Deviation, we will suggest, recalling Durkheim's classic statement on the subject, can often be understood as a normal product of stable institutions, an important resource which is guarded and preserved by forces found in all human organizations.[1] . . .

In recent years, sociological theory has become more and more concerned with the concept "social system"—an organization of society's component parts into a form which sustains internal equilibrium, resists change, and is boundary maintaining. In its most abstract form, the "system" concept describes a highly complex network of relations, but the scheme is generally used by sociologists to draw attention to those forces in the social order which promote a high level of uniformity among human actors and a high degree of symmetry within human institutions. The main organizational drift of a system, then, is seen as centripetal: it acts to draw the behavior of actors toward those centers in social space where the core values of the group are figuratively located, bringing them within range of basic norms. Any conduct which is neither attracted toward this nerve center by the rewards of conformity nor compelled toward it by other social pressures is considered "out of control," which is to say, deviant.

This basic model has provided the theme for most contemporary thinking about deviation, and as a result little attention has been given to the notion that systems operate to maintain boundaries. To say that a system maintains boundaries is to say that it controls the fluctuation of its constituent parts so that the whole retains a defined range of activity, a unique pattern of constancy and stability, within the larger environment. Because the range of human behavior is potentially so wide, social groups maintain boundaries in the sense that they try to limit the flow of behavior within their domain so that it circulates within a defined cultural territory. Boundaries, then, are an important point of reference for persons participating in any system. A people may define its boundaries by referring to a geographical location, a set of honored traditions, a particular religious or political viewpoint, an occupational specialty, a common language, or just some local way of doing things; but in any case, members of the group have some idea about the contours of the niche they occupy in social space. They know where the group begins and ends as a special entity; they know what kinds of experience "belong" within these precincts and what kinds do not.

For all its apparent abstractness, a social system is organized around the movements of persons joined together in regular social relations. The only material found in a system for marking boundaries, then, is the behavior of its participants; and the kinds of behavior which best perform this function are often deviant, since they represent the most extreme variety of conduct to be found within the experience of the group. In this sense, transactions taking place between deviant persons on the one side and agencies of control on the other are boundary maintaining mechanisms. They mark the outside limits of the area within which the norm has jurisdiction, and in this way assert how much diversity and variability can be contained within the system before it begins to lose its distinct structure, its cultural integrity.

A social norm is rarely expressed as a firm rule or official code. It is an abstract synthesis of the many separate times a community has stated its sentiments on a given kind of issue. Thus the norm has a history much like that of an article of common law: it is an accumulation of decisions made by the community over a long period of time which gradually gathers enough moral eminence to serve as a precedent for future decisions. And like an article of common law, the norm retains its validity only if it is regularly used as a basis for judgment. Each time the group censures some act of deviation, then, it sharpens the authority of the violated norm and declares again where the boundaries of the group are located.

It is important to notice that these transactions between deviant persons and agents of control have always attracted a good deal of attention in this and other cultures. In our own past, both the trial and punishment of deviant offenders took place in the public market and gave the crowd a chance to participate in a direct, active way. Today we no longer parade deviants in the town square or expose them to the carnival atmosphere of Tyburn, but it is interesting to note that the "reform" which brought about this change in penal policy coincided almost precisely with the development of newspapers as media of public information. Perhaps this is no more than an accident of history, but it is nevertheless true that newspapers (and now radio and television) offer their readers the same kind of entertainment once supplied by public hangings or the use of stocks and pillories. An enormous amount of modern "news" is devoted to reports about deviant behavior and its punishment: indeed the largest circulation newspaper in the United States prints very little else. Yet how do we explain what makes these items "newsworthy" or why they command the great attention they do? Perhaps they satisfy a number of psychological perversities among the mass audience, as commentators sometimes point out, but at the same time they constitute our main source of information about the normative contours of society. In a figurative sense, at least, morality and immorality meet at the public scaffold, and it is during this meeting that the community declares where the line between them should be drawn.

People who gather together into communities need to be able to describe and anticipate those areas of experience which lie outside the immediate compass of the group—the unseen dangers which in any culture and in any age seem to threaten its security. Traditional folklore depicting demons, devils, witches and evil spirits, may be one way to give form to these otherwise formless dangers, but the visible deviant is another kind of reminder. As a trespasser against the group norms, he represents those forces which lie outside the group's boundaries: he informs us, as it were, what evil looks like, what shapes the devil can assume. And in doing so, he shows us the difference between the inside of the group and the outside. It may well be that without this ongoing drama at the outer edges of group space, the community would have no inner sense of identity and cohesion, no sense of the contrasts which set it off as a special place in the larger world.

Thus deviance cannot be dismissed simply as behavior which *disrupts* stability in society, but may itself be, in controlled quantities, an important condition for *preserving* stability.

This raises a delicate theoretical issue. If we grant that deviant forms of behavior are often beneficial to society in general, can we then assume that societies are organized in such a way as to promote this resource? Can we assume, in other words, that forces operate within the social order to recruit deviant actors and commit them to deviant forms of activity? Sociology has not yet developed a conceptual language in which this sort of question can be discussed with any ease, but one observation can be made which gives the question an interesting perspective—namely, that deviant activities often seem to derive support from the very agencies designed to suppress them. Indeed, the institutions devised by society for discouraging deviant behavior are often so poorly equipped for that task that we might well ask why this is considered their "real" function at all.

It is by now a thoroughly familiar argument that many of the institutions built to inhibit deviation actually operate in such a way as to perpetuate it. For one thing, prisons, hospitals, and similar agencies of control provide aid and shelter to large numbers of deviant persons, sometimes enhancing their survival chances in the world as a whole. But beyond this, such institutions gather marginal people into tightly segregated groups, give them an opportunity to teach one another the skills and attitudes of a deviant career, and often provoke them into employing these skills by reinforcing their sense of alienation from the rest of society. It should be pointed out, furthermore, that this process is found not only in the institutions which actually confine the deviant, but throughout the general community as well.

The community's decision to bring deviant sanctions against an individual is not a simple act of censure. It is a sharp rite of transition, at once moving him out of his normal position in society and transferring him into a distinct deviant role. The ceremonies which accomplish this change of status, ordinarily, have three related phases. They provide a formal *confrontation* between the deviant suspect and representatives of his community (as in the criminal trial or psychiatric case conference); they announce some *judgment* about the nature of his deviancy (a verdict or diagnosis, for example); and they perform an act of social *placement*, assigning him to a special role (like that of prisoner or patient) which redefines his position in society. These ceremonies tend to be events of wide public interest and usually take place in a dramatic, ritualized setting. Perhaps the most obvious example of a commitment ceremony is the criminal trial, with its elaborate formality and ritual pageantry, but more modest equivalents can be found everywhere that procedures are set up to judge whether someone is deviant or not.

Now an important feature of these ceremonies in our own culture is that they are almost irreversible. Most provisional roles conferred by society—like those of the student or conscripted soldier, for example—include some kind of terminal ceremony to mark the individual's movement back out of the role once its temporary advantages have been exhausted. But the roles allotted to the deviant seldom make allowance for this type of passage. He is ushered into the deviant position by a decisive and often dramatic ceremony, yet is retired from it with hardly a word of public notice. And as a result, the deviant often returns home with no proper license to resume a normal life in the community. Nothing has happened to cancel out the stigmas imposed upon him by earlier commitment ceremonies; from a formal point of view, the original verdict or diagnosis is still in effect. It should not be surprising, then, that the members of the community seem reluctant to accept the returning deviant on an entirely equal footing. In a very real sense, they do not know who he is.

A circularity is thus set into motion which has all the earmarks of a "self-fulfilling prophesy," to use Merton's fine phrase. On the one hand, it seems obvious that the community's reluctance to accept the deviant back helps reduce whatever chance he might otherwise have for a successful readjustment. Yet on the other hand, everyday experience seems to show that this reluctance is entirely reasonable, for it is a well-known and highly publicized fact that large numbers of ex-convicts return to criminal activity and that many discharged mental patients suffer later breakdowns. The common assumption that deviants are not often cured or reformed, then, may be based on a faulty premise, but this assumption is stated so frequently and with such conviction that it often creates the facts which later "prove" it to be correct. If the returning deviant has to face the community's apprehensions often enough, it is understandable that he too may begin to wonder whether he has graduated from the deviant role—and respond to the uncertainty by resuming deviant activity. In some respects, this may be the only way for the individual and his community to agree as to what kind of person he really is, for it often happens that the community is only able to perceive his "true colors" when he lapses momentarily into some form of deviant performance.

Moreover, this prophesy is found in the official policies of even the most advanced agencies of control. Police departments could not operate with any real effectiveness if they did not regard ex-convicts as an almost permanent population of offenders, a pool from which to draw suspects; and psychiatric hospitals could not do a responsible job in the community if they were not alert to the fact that ex-patients are highly susceptible to relapse. Thus the prophesy gains currency at many levels within the social order, not only in the poorly informed opinions of the community at large, but in the best informed theories of most control agencies as well.

In one form or another, this problem has been known in Western culture for many hundreds of years, and the single fact that this is so becomes a highly significant one for sociology. If the culture has supported a steady flow of deviant behavior throughout long periods of historical evolution, then the rules which apply to any form of functionalist thinking would suggest that strong forces must be at work to keep this flow intact—and this because it contributes in some important way to the survival of the system as a whole. This may not be reason enough to assert that deviant behavior is "functional," in any of the many senses of that term, but it should make us wary of the assumption that human communities are organized in such a way as to prevent deviance from occurring.

This in turn might suggest that our present models of society, with their emphasis on the harmony and equilibrium of social life, do a one-sided job of representing the situation. Perhaps two different and often competing currents are found in any well-functioning system: those forces which promote a high over-all degree of conformity among its members, and those forces which encourage some degree of diversity so that actors can be deployed throughout social space to patrol the system's boundaries. These different gravitational pulls in the social system set up a constant tension of opposites, outlining the area within which human life, with all its contradiction and variety, takes place....

These brief remarks are no more than a prelude to further thinking and research, and in the remaining paragraphs we will try to indicate some of the directions this line of reasoning might take.

In the first place, this paper has indirectly addressed itself to one of the oldest problems in sociology. It is all very well for an investigator to conclude that something called a "system" has certain "requirements" in respect to its participants, but the major problem for research is to ask how these needs are imposed upon the people who eventually satisfy them. Ordinarily, the fact that deviant behavior is not evenly distributed throughout the social structure is explained by declaring that something called "anomie" or "disorganization" prevails at certain sensitive points. Deviance leaks out through defects in the social structure; it occurs when the system *fails* to impose its needs on human actors. But if we consider the possibility that even the best organized collectivity needs to produce occasional episodes of deviation for the sake of its own stability, we are engaged in quite another order of inquiry. Perhaps the coherence of some social groupings is maintained only when a few juvenile offenders are enlisted to balance the conformity of an adult majority; perhaps communities can retain a sense of their own territorial identity only if they keep up an ongoing dialogue with deviants who mark and publicize the outer limits of group space; perhaps some families can remain intact only if one of its members becomes a visible deviant to serve as a focus for the rest. If these suppositions prove useful, we should try to learn how a social system appoints certain of its members to deviant roles and how it encourages them to spend a period of service testing the group's boundaries. This is not to suggest that a system necessarily creates the crises which impel people into deviant activity but that it deploys these resources in a patterned, organized way.

In the second place, it is evident that cultures vary in the way they regulate deviant traffic moving back and forth from their outer boundaries. We might begin with the observation, for example, that many features of the traffic pattern in our own culture seem to have a marked Puritan cast: a defined portion of the population, largely drawn from young adult groups and from the lower economic classes, is stabilized in deviant roles and often expected to remain there indefinitely. The logic which prevails in many of our formal agencies of control and in the public attitudes which sustain them sometimes seems to echo earlier Puritan theories about predestination, reprobation, and the nature of sin. Be this as it may, different traffic patterns are found in other parts of the world which offer an interesting contrast. There are societies in which deviance is considered a natural mode of behavior for the young, a pursuit which they are expected to abandon once they move through defined ceremonies into adulthood. There are societies which give license to large groups of people to engage in deviant behavior during certain seasons or on certain days of the year. And there are societies which form special groups whose stated business is to act in ways contrary to the normal expectations of the culture. Each of these patterns regulates deviant traffic differently, yet each of them provides some institutional means for a person to give up a deviant career without any kind of permanent stigma. In either of these cases, the person's momentary commitment to deviant styles of behavior is easily reversed—when the group promotes him to manhood, declares a period of festival to be over, or permits him to give up the insignia which marked his membership in a band of "contraries." Perhaps the most interesting problem here from the point of view of pure research is to see whether these various patterns are functionally equivalent in any meaningful way. Perhaps the most interesting problem for those of us who lean over into the applied areas of the field, however, is to ask whether we have anything to learn from those cultures which permit re-entry into normal social life for persons who have spent a period of time in the deviant ranks and no longer have any special need to remain there.

Note

1. Emile Durkheim, *The Rules of Sociological Method* (translated by S. A. Solovay and J. H. Meuller), New York: The Free Press of Glencoe, 1958.

The European Witchcraze

NACHMAN BEN-YEHUDA

From the early decades of the fifteenth century until 1650, continental Europeans executed between two and five hundred thousand witches (according to conservative estimates), more than 85 percent of whom were women....

The riddle of the European witchcraze is closely linked to specific changes in societal boundaries in different realms that took place between the fourteenth and seventeenth centuries. Thus, I suggest that medieval society was crumbling as new social, political, economic, scientific, and religious forms came into being. The boundaries of the old order were changing in a very significant way along more than one dimension. These changes brought about innovative institutional arrangements in all social spheres. As a result, new and positive reactions to the changes became possible, since old traditions, and limitations were broken (e.g., in the areas of art and science). However, there was also an extreme negative reaction, a ferocious witch-hunt aimed at restoring the old societal boundaries....

Timing: Why Did the Witch-Hunts Begin?

The witchcraft myth was largely created by the Dominican friars....Until the thirteenth century, the Catholic Church's official policy regarding witchcraft was summarized in the *Canon episcopi,* which regarded beliefs in witchcraft as mere illusions. The Inquisition, an ecclesiastical court answerable only to itself, was founded in the thirteenth century in order to combat deliberate, continued, and public denial of the Church's doctrine, primarily by the Cathari and, to a much lesser extent, by the Waldenses. Thus, the Inquisition's primary objective was to single out and reconvert heretics (see Lea 1901, vols. 1, 2; Madaule 1967; Sumption 1978; Nelson 1971; Wakefield and Evans 1969)....

By the end of the thirteenth century,... the two major heretic factions—the Cathari and Waldensians—were in essence eliminated, while other groups were either too small or more easily controlled. In order to justify the existence of the Inquisition's machinery, the Inquisitors began to search for new apostates.

[They] demanded, from the thirteenth century on, that their authority be expanded to include witches they claimed to have found in the Pyrenees and the Alps....

The professional concerns of the Inquisitors explain why they began to take interest in the witches as early as the thirteenth century. But the transformation of this interest into an elaborate demonological theology did not take place until the

From Nachman Ben-Yehuda, *Deviance and Moral Boundaries: Witchcraft, the Occult, Science Fiction, Deviant Sciences and Scientists* (Chicago: University of Chicago Press, 1985), pp. 23–70 (with deletions).

fifteenth century, and only at that time did the general public begin to share the interest of the Inquisitors in witches. What were the conditions of these two fateful developments? The answer to this question requires a broad perspective on the social, institutional, intellectual, and emotional changes that prepared the ground for these and other developments that began in the thirteenth century and reached their culmination between the fifteenth and the seventeenth centuries. During this period, the medieval social order underwent a series of significant changes, which completely altered the dominant European outlook.

According to Pirenne (1937), the growth of cities and of an industrial form of production started in the Low Countries and in England in the twelfth century, and from there reached down the Rhine in the thirteenth century, reaching a peak in the fourteenth (Nicolas 1976). Among the changes of this economic expansion were a significant increase in population size, perfection of the monetary system, and the mapping of new lands. The expansion of commerce was not limited only to central Europe; ore-mining began in Poland (Molenda 1976) and Mediterranean trade flourished at the same time (Ashtor 1957, 1976; Abulafia 1981)....

This economic development brought with it increased trade, expanded urban industry, standardization, exports, division of labor, and specialization (Bernard 1972; Griggs 1980; Thrupp 1972; Le Goff 1972, 1980, pp. 43–52). By the end of the thirteenth century, "the development of industry and commerce had completely transformed the appearance and indeed the very existence of society.... Continental Europe was covered with towns from which the activity of the new middle class radiated in all directions...the circulation of money was perfected...new forms of credit came into use" (Pirenne 1937, pp. 189–90). All this was only the beginning of a process that peaked in the period we call the Renaissance. These centuries proved not only a turning point in commerce (Bogucka 1980; Lane 1932) but also in geographical discoveries and their utilization (Postan and Rich 1952; Pounds 1979). "The exploration and exploitation of non-European areas by Europeans during the fifteenth and sixteenth centuries form one of the greatest phenomena of the Renaissance" (Penrose 1962, p. vii), no doubt forcing "a re-evaluation of the idea of Europe as a model Christian society" (Rattansi 1972, p. 7).

These extreme and relatively rapid changes made deep inroads in the hierarchic structure of feudal society sanctioned and legitimized by the Catholic Church. In the medieval tradition, the moral boundaries of society were clearly defined. Christendom was ruled spiritually by Rome and structured in a uniformly conceived hierarchic feudal order, firmly embedded in the finite cosmic order ruled by God. This order was threatened by the Jews and Moslems, but their faiths were in many ways related to the Christian tradition and the relationship to them was clearly defined: they had to be converted and saved, and if recalcitrant, fought and suppressed. But the changes we have described above were not so easily categorized. The late medieval order was threatened by the rise of an urban society that did not fit into the feudal hierarchy, by the increased contact with non-Christian people who did not fit the conversion-conflict model, and by the resultant autonomy of economic and political transactions from theological guidance. Indeed, this was all part of what Brown (1969) describes as the disengagement of the sacred from the profane.

The stress and confusion created by these circumstances were further aggravated by external catastrophes, especially the devastating epidemics of plague and cholera that decimated the population of Europe and lasted throughout the fourteenth century. Even the physical climate underwent severe changes in those fateful centuries, "affecting . . . central and eastern Europe . . . by changes in temperature. . . . The coldest time began in the thirteenth century with the onset of the Little Ice Age which, with exceptions of occasional periods of warmth, lasted until well into the eighteenth century" (J. C. Russell 1972, pp. 51–52; see also Lamb 1982; Ladurie 1971; Robock 1979). To add to the confusion and distress, in 1456 Halley's comet was clearly visible in the sky. The appearance of the comet was often interpreted as a bad omen and created much anxiety, fear, and unrest. . . .

Stress and confusion, however, were only one aspect of these developments (Holmes 1975). There was confusion about the moral boundaries of society and the cognitive map of the world; frequently there was fear of impending doom. But there was also an opening up of new possibilities, a rise of standards of living in the wake of the great catastrophes of the fourteenth century. Those who survived the epidemics inherited the wealth of the deceased, and even those who had to maintain themselves by their work could obtain far better wages than before because of the shortage of manpower.

Thus the fifteenth century was a time of great enterprise, bold thought, innovation, as well as one of deep confusion and anomie, a feeling that society had lost its norms and boundaries and that the uncontrollable forces of change were destroying all order and moral tradition. . . . The witchcraze was a negative reaction to this emerging culture in the sense that its purpose was to counteract and prevent change and to reestablish traditional social–moral boundaries and religious authority.

. . . By persecuting witches, society, led by the Church, attempted to redefine its boundaries. This was one of the numerous instances in which deviance served the social functions of emphasizing and creating moral boundaries and enhancing solidarity. In fact, this was fictitious deviance, created for those purposes.

Until the Renaissance, the Catholic Church was at its peak of power. All problems were treated as theological or theosophical, and there were no serious threats to its authority and its well-defined norms. This is the reason that during the so-called Dark Ages, we have hardly any record of a witchcraze. As the results of the differentiation process became visible in the fifteenth century, and a sharp decline in the Church's authority was noticeable, it "began to need an opponent whom it could divinely hate" in order to affirm old standards (Williams 1959, p. 37). The differentiation of the societal community vibrated the structure of the medieval order and directly threatened the Church's authority and legitimacy. For a highly rigid system, one can hardly imagine a greater danger. Thus, the major "social stress" was the differentiation process itself.

It is obvious why the church "needed" an opponent. But it needed a very special type of deviant-opponent to redefine its legitimacy. The opponent had to be widely perceived as a threat to society itself and to the Christian world view. What could do this better than witchcraft? This helps us understand why only the most rapidly developing countries where the Church was weakest experienced a virulent witchcraze. Where the Church was strong hardly any witchcraze worth mentioning occurred, even in rapidly developing societies such as the Italian city states. Although this was not the first time that the Church had been threatened, this development, culminating in the Reformation, was the first time that it had to cope with a large-scale challenge to its very existence and legitimacy (Elton 1963).

Nevertheless, Protestants persecuted witches with almost the same zeal as the Catholics, despite many objective differences between them. Protestantism might have been a result of the differentiation process, but this is not to say that Protestants were capable of either mastering or steering the process itself. Both Protestants and Catholics felt threatened by the process and by each other. "The Reformation shattered the unity of Christendom, and religious conflicts... the Wars of Religion... destroyed the illusion of the perfect Christian societies" (Rattansi 1972, p. 7).

This interpretation makes plausible the choice of such a strange and esoteric phenomenon as witchcraft for elaboration into a myth in the early modern era. Dominican theory portrayed witchcraft and witches as the negative mirror-image of the "true faith." As Clark (1980) points out, in a social world generally characterized by dualism, the Dominican theory made much sense. It was possible to attribute all the undesirable phenomena associated with the anomie of the age to the conspiracy of Satan and the witches against Christianity. By associating everything negative, bad, and vicious with witchcraft, the ideal components of the true faith were highlighted. In his *Daemonologie* (1597), King James gave this idea direct expression: "Since the Devil is the verie contrarie opposite to God, there can be no better way to know God, than by the contrarie." In this sense, the witchcraze could be called a "collective search for identity" (Klapp 1969), and the authors of the *Malleus maleficarum* were what Becker (1963, pp. 42–163) called "moral entrepreneurs" taking part in what Gusfield (1967) termed "moral crusade," striving to restore the integrity of the old religious–moral community. Witches were the only deviants who could be construed as attacking the very core of the social system.

This explains, not only why a number of theologians and intellectuals found in demonology a satisfactory diagnosis of the moral ills of their time, but why this abstruse theory became so readily accepted by the masses. "The individual was confronted with an enormously wider range of competing beliefs in almost every area of social and intellectual concern, while conformity-inducing pressures of a mainly ecclesiastical sort were weakened or discredited" (Rattansi 1972, pp. 7–8). The existential crisis of individuals—expressed in terms of anomie, alienation, strangeness, powerlessness, and anxiety—created a fertile soil in which the Dominican solution could flourish.

What could better explain the strain felt by the individual than the idea that he was part of a cataclysmic struggle between the "sons of light" and the "sons of darkness?" His acceptance of this particular explanation was further guaranteed by the fact that he could help the sons of light to trap the sons of darkness—the despised witches—and thus play a real role in ending the cosmic struggle in a way that would bring salvation nearer. Thus the differentiation process threatened, not only the macroinstitutional level, but also the microlevel—each individual's cognitive map. In such a case, a redefinition of moral boundaries and a restructuring of cognitive maps would be more than welcome: For this reason the witchcraze won such extensive popular support....

The existence of widespread strain due to the inadequacy of traditional concepts, especially in the religious-moral sphere, has [now] been documented. However, it is also possible to show that much of this tension was focused on women, which explains why witches—usually female ones—could become such effective symbols in a new ideology....

Toward the end of the thirteenth century, many families moved from the rural areas to towns, changing their economic outlook and shifting from producing and exchanging goods to a purely cash economy. This shift had a number of consequences: (1) the family could hardly afford to support ill, unemployed, or unproductive members; (2) it changed from a property-holding, working unit to a consuming unit; (3) as a result of the great number of peasants coming to town, the worker's real wages remained very low, and any fluctuation in business caused severe survival problems. This situation understandably produced considerable insecurity among the new city-dwellers (Cohn 1961; Helleiner 1967); consequently, male employees in large-scale enterprises (textiles, flour mills, mining) subsisted close to the starvation level and could not afford marriage. Moreover, guild members who had not reached master status were forbidden by the guild to marry.... These factors created very strong pressures upon women to enter the job market, either to support their families, if they had any, or to support themselves, if they were alone....

During the fourteenth century, Europe experienced severe demographical changes that bore directly on the concentration on women as victims of witch-hunts. In particular, the Black Death (1347–51) had devastating and far-reaching effects. Although the major epidemic abated in 1350, the disease reappeared intermittently in various localities until the end of the century. The mortality rate was particularly high in cities because of the density of population and the absence of hygienic conditions.... The effect of the plague on the population was... devastating. "Two thirds or three quarters or five sixths of the inhabitants of Europe fell victim to the pest" (Lea 1901, 2:378–79). It can be assumed with a fair degree of certainty that between thirty and fifty percent of the population was annihilated by this disaster (Bridbury 1973; Cipolla 1974; Griggs 1980, p. 54; Langer 1964; J. C. Russell 1972; Usher 1956; Ziegler 1971)....

After the major plagues had passed, the peasant and wage-laborer survivors found themselves in a highly favorable and advantageous position. As a direct result of the shortage in manpower (Spengler 1968, p. 433), their real income was tremendously increased, food supplies improved, and job security magnified. In addition, many survivors had inherited large amounts of wealth from their deceased relatives (Langer 1964). Chojnacki (1974) notes in particular that women enjoyed increased economic success and wealth and that "their determination to keep control of their enlarged wealth also increased" (p. 198). Thus he documents the fact that following the end of the plague, women became increasingly active in the economy and gained much economic power.

Under such favorable conditions, one might expect an increase in the population size, but this did not occur (Nelson 1971; Spengler 1968; Deevey 1960; Helleiner

1957).... The fact that the population did not increase and the birth rate decreased in the second half of the fourteenth century was due to the massive use of contraception and infanticide (Helleiner 1967, p. 71). Why these techniques were used can be easily understood.

Because part of the population was—quite suddenly—exposed to a high standard of living because of an increase in real income, these people did not want to undermine their new prosperity by raising large families. Furthermore, the economic, monetary, commercial, and urban revolutions that accompanied the Renaissance and Reformation probably also gave a powerful stimulus to the rise of individualism and egoism. Those who married took care to limit the number of their offspring, while those who did not marry made efforts to prevent pregnancy (Spengler 1968, pp. 436–37, 440). The Church bitterly complained of the widespread use of *coitus interruptus,* by married and single persons alike, as a means of preventing pregnancy (Himes 1936; Noonan 1965; Wrigley 1969, p. 124). Although historical research on infanticide is still itself in its infancy and cannot yet provide us with reliable numbers concerning the actual scope of the phenomenon in the twelfth through fifteenth centuries, a growing number of scholars have suggested that the rate and scope increased sharply and significantly during the period under question....

It is quite clear that the fifteenth and sixteenth centuries brought with them one of the most severe demographic changes Europe had ever experienced (Midelfort 1972, pp. 184–86; Noonan 1968; J. C. Russell 1972; Spengler 1968; Wrigley 1969): "...(1) a high age of marriage and (2) a high proportion of people [who] never marry at all" ([Hajnal] 1965, p. 101; see also Spengler 1968, p. 1433, and Wrigley 1969, p. 90)...."More single men married late because they could not 'afford' to marry younger" ([Hajnal] 1965, pp. 117, 132, 133).... The origin of this marriage pattern lies "somewhere about the sixteenth century [and] became quite widespread... in the general population... in the seventeenth century" (ibid., p. 134; see also J. C. Russell 1972, p. 60). Litchfield (1966) gives us additional figures that exemplify changes in the family structure and functions. He reports that the age of marriage for males rose to twenty-five and more. He also indicates that among the upper middle class in Florence in the sixteenth century, larger dowries were required for marriage. This both delayed marriages and motivated more of the ruling classes in Catholic countries to send their daughters to convents, which required smaller dowries (pp. 202–3). The rise of Beguins reflected new arrangements concerning marriage and the status of women in the fifteenth and sixteenth centuries. The parallel development in Protestant countries was an increased number of spinsters. Midelfort reports similar facts, and he adds that in some places, the age of marriage for women rose to twenty-three and even twenty-seven. He also reports that the proportion of those remaining single rose from five to fifteen or even twenty percent (1972, p. 184). Wrigley notes that "between two fifths and three fifths of the women of childbearing age 15–44 were unmarried" (1969, P. 90).

...The significance of a high proportion of unmarrieds is tremendous in a society that attaches a stigma to being single. In particular, the appearance of a large number of unmarried women produced serious problems, and it is probably no coincidence that a significant number of the witches were either widows or spinsters (at least when the persecutions started). Later on, however, married women and young girls were persecuted as well (Midelfort 1972).

It is evident from all this that, beginning in the twelfth century and throughout the entire period with which we are concerned, the social role of women was in constant flux. Urban industrial life compelled them to step outside their traditional roles. Women entered a market characterized by lack of manpower. Their assumption of "male" employment, particularly in cities, where the job market was tighter, produced a virulent misogyny (Bainton 1971, pp. 9–14; Kelso 1956; Midelfort 1972, p. 183). Two centuries earlier women could not get married because men could not afford marriage; in the fifteenth century, they were unable to marry because of men's reluctance to marry.

There were other deep changes in women's social roles as sexual partners and mothers. As we have seen, there was widespread use of contraception and infanticide, which the church strongly and fiercely denounced as most evil. Trexler notes that "child-killing has been regarded almost exclusively as a female crime, the result of women's inherent tendency to lechery, passion, and lack of responsibility.... Infanticide was... the most common social crime imputed to... witches... by the demonologists" (1973, pp. 98, 103; also see Lea 1957, vol. 1; Murray 1918; Sprenger and Kramer 1968). Furthermore, Piers (1978) notes that as large waves of immigrants came into the newly established towns, many of them extremely poor, women had no choice but to sell themselves. Many times, they also followed armed forces who traveled throughout Europe fighting numerous wars. Because of the low pay, prostitutes had to have masses of customers. They thus became bearers of various venereal diseases. Even the higher-status job of a servant meant that a woman was at the disposal of her master's (or his friends') sexual appetite. Piers points out that the servant's unquestioning sexual availability was, many a time, the only thing that stood between her and plain starvation. All these conditions obviously created countless cases of pregnancy, which many times ended in infanticide.

But infanticide was not only a result of the fact that many children were born out of wedlock. Many rich women either could not breast-feed their offspring or did not want to. Consequently, wet nurses were sought. There are indications that many wet nurses were poor women who hired themselves after their infants either died naturally or more often, were killed (Piers 1978). Trexler suggests that it is quite possible that in many cases, becoming a wet nurse was a planned course of action. It was a safe, comfortable living. No wonder, then, that midwives were among the chief suspects of witchcraft (Forbes 1966; Heinsohn and Steiger 1982). The Dominicans suspected—and probably rightly so—that midwives were experts in birth control and no doubt helped and cooperated in infanticide....

Under the chaotic circumstances described above—large numbers of unmarried men and women, sexual license, sinful contraception, infanticide—the relationship between the sexes must frequently have been one of mutual exploitation fraught with deep feelings of guilt and resentment. Because of the powerlessness of women under secular and religious law, and their inferior status, it was convenient to project on them all the resentment and guilt. The ideology of the witch-hunt made use of these emotions. It made it possible for men who indulged in sex that proved unhealthy for them to accuse women of taking away their generative powers. Those who were party to contraception through *coitus interruptus* could project their guilt on women for stealing their seed. The fantasies about the unlimited sexual powers and depravity of women might have been a reflection of the fear engendered by the large number of unmarried women not subject to the authority of fathers or husbands, as, according to prevailing standards, they ought to have been.

It is thus clear why women were the principal victims of witch-hunts. The witchcraze paralleled profound changes in women's roles and in the structure of the family. The tensions reflected in the images of demonology must have been very widespread among men, who presumably in large numbers took advantage of the prevailing sexual freedom. Among married women, who probably did not or could not indulge in illicit sex, there must have been strong feelings against "bad women" who might have "bewitched" their husbands and sons. Therefore, the female witch, using sex to corrupt the world, was a "suasive image" of great power in an ideology that aimed to rid the world of Satan's power, of all the effects of social change, and to restore its moral boundaries.

Timing: Termination of the Witchcraze

...In their most devastating form, the witch-hunts lasted until the seventeenth century, or to be more accurate, till the end of the Thirty Years' War in the Peace of Westphalia (1648)....

The coincidence of the termination of the worst of the craze with the close of the Thirty Years' War is not just chance. The Peace of Westphalia gave official recognition and legitimacy to religious pluralism and symbolically ended the struggle to redefine the moral system of Europe. The stresses, insecurity, and instability experienced by persons living in war-stricken areas provided fuel to the burning furnace of the final phase of the witchcraze. But once stability was achieved and religious pluralism accepted, the witch-hunts weakened, finally disappearing altogether.

It is thus evident that by the seventeenth century, new cognitive maps and new institutional arrangements had emerged. There was a demarcation between science, magic, and religion, recognition of autonomy of government and economy in England, and settlement of secular and spiritual relationships elsewhere in a way that recognized supremacy of the political sphere. A new social order had visibly and triumphantly been created. The age of "reason" was at hand within its model of the "rational man." It was the era of emerging nation states, where man's loyalty was to his state and not to the Church. This was part of a more general secularization of society. When the differentiation process came so far, the basis for the witchcraze was, in fact, eliminated. The reasons for its beginning and duration ceased to exist. A new definition of societal borders was taking shape, the societal community was already fractured, and the witch-hunt had no purpose whatsoever....

Chapter 6

Labeling Theory: The Interactionist Approach

Labeling theory was the first approach to focus specifically on deviance that emphasized social control. (Functionalism's approach was far broader than deviance alone.) While the earlier etiological or causal approaches (social pathology, social disorganization, learning theory, anomie theory) asked the question, why deviant and criminal behavior? labeling theory turned the question around and asked: *Why social control?* Why do certain behaviors generate punishment? Why are certain persons punished? How and why does social control arise, how and why is it exercised, against what behaviors and what enactors (or supposed enactors)? Labeling theorists expanded the scope of the study of deviance, enlarged its territory of inquiry. Not only was it now possible to investigate social control in a more systematic way, but in so doing, labeling theory also made it possible to investigate two areas of inquiry that were not possible with the more traditional etiological or causal theories: first, deviant conditions or states of being (being handicapped, ugly, fat, short, and so on), and second, persons who did *not* engage in the deviant behavior of which they are accused, but are punished nonetheless (the "falsely accused"). The territory of the sociological study of deviance was vastly expanded by the innovations of the labeling approach.

Although some parallels existed, the approach proposed by the labeling theory was very different from that adopted by functionalism. Perhaps the most obvious difference between the two approaches is that while functionalism is almost exclusively a *macro* approach (focusing on the broad, institutional, or societal level), the interactionist perspective is predominantly (though not exclusively) a *micro* approach, that is, it is more likely to focus on the interpersonal, face-to-face level of analysis. The functionalist approach asks for the functions or consequences of a certain institution or practice *for the society as a whole* (or, less commonly, for designated segments of the society), while the labeling theorist is more likely to ask what consequences labeling has *on persons so designated.* And third, labeling theory is focused more or less exclusively on deviance, while functionalism's interest is far broader; it reaches into the functions of any and all practices and social institutions.

Howard Becker, undoubtedly the most influential of the labeling theorists, doesn't like the term "labeling theory" (1973, p. 178). "Labeling" is only one aspect to the perspective, not the whole thing, and perhaps not necessarily even the most important aspect. Second, says Becker, the approach he and the other "labeling" theorists put forth wasn't even a theory, that is, it wasn't an attempt at explaining the question of etiology or why certain individuals, or individuals in certain social contexts, are more likely to deviate (pp. 178–179). So, both the "labeling" and the "theory" parts of the name are invalid and misleading, Becker says. It is better to call the approach "interactionism" or "the interactionist approach" (p. 183). Unfortunately, we are stuck with the term, labeling theory. It's popular, it's handy, it's catchy, and so, most people in the field refer to the approach as labeling theory. Consequently, that is the term I will use throughout this book to refer to what Becker means by interactionism in the study of deviance.

In many ways, labeling theory has been a "sociological straw man" (Petrunik 1980). (Today, we'd use the nonsexist term, "straw person.") That is, most of the critiques of this approach have been based on a simplified, stereotypical, even imaginary version of the theory rather than a theory based on what its advocates actually proposed. There is a virtual industry of commentary on the approach. It's possible that, for no other approach (with the possible exception of anomie theory) has there been as great a discrepancy or disproportion between the total volume of the writings of the original theory and the total volume of commentary on and criticism of the theory. The reason may be that it is possible to read the texts of labeling theory and discern a "strong" and a "weak" version of what it says. It is possible that the critics are taking the strong version as what the theory says and the defenders are taking the weak version as what it says. Some critics will say they are not distorting what the approach says because, they will say, it is possible to read labeling theorists' work and—look! Here's the proof! Here's what it says! To document their case, they point to a passage that seems to back up their assertion.

So, let's look at these two versions of labeling theory: the strong and the weak versions. This discussion can be broken down into distinct and separate dimensions, each dimension with a strong and a weak version. In each case it is the weak version that is more common among labeling theorists; in each case it is the strong version that is associated with the theory in the minds of its critics. In each case the theory is criticized for saying something its practitioners don't quite say.

The first dimension is the question of defining what's deviant in the first place. How is deviance defined? What makes a given action deviant? To begin with, we have the strong version. It is this: *Reactions to behavior constitute deviance.* This is the so-called "hard" or "strict" reactivist definition we looked at in Chapter 1. To this approach, there is no such thing as secret deviance. If a given action hasn't been punished or condemned, it's not deviant. Period, end of story. This view is held by John Kitsuse, a labeling theorist (1962, 1964). Kitsuse believes that if an individual actor is not observed and condemned for a given action, that act is not an instance of deviance. No condemnation, no deviance. An unpunished murder (the so-called perfect murder) *cannot be referred to as murder at all.* An act that *would be* regarded as strange, aberrant, worthy of condemnation if it were observed is not deviant unless and until it is observed and results in punishment for the perpetrator. To the strict, hard, or strong reactivist, "secret deviance" is a contradiction in terms; it simply does not exist.

The "weak" version, which is held, at least in places, by Becker, Kai Erikson, Edwin Lemert, and Erving Goffman, is that there *can* be such a thing as secret deviance. In the absence of labeling, we do have deviance, at least in some respects, because we have the phenomenon of "potentially discreditable" traits or persons or behavior. Becker (1973, p. 181) refers to acts that are "potentially deviant" ("likely to be defined as deviant when discovered"). Erikson refers to a "class of episodes" that is labeled as deviant, indicating that each individual act need not be literally and concretely labeled to be referred to as deviant (1964, p. 11), that *types of actions* can be so designated. Goffman distinguishes between individuals who are already *discredited,* that is, stigmatized or labeled, and those who possess "undisclosed discrediting information," that is, who are "potentially deviant" (1961, pp. 41–42). As we'll see shortly, Lemert distinguishes between "primary deviation"—enacting behavior that would result in punishment if it were discovered, and "secondary deviation," or using one's publicly acknowledged deviant role as a basis of relating to others. In short, of the major labeling theorists, all but Kitsuse adopt the weak definition of deviance. Deviance, they say, can exist in secret; it does not have to be discovered and result in punishment to qualify as deviance. Deviant behavior is behavior that is likely to result in condemnation and punishment if it were discovered. All too often, it is the strong version that has been identified as labeling theory's definition of deviance, while it is the softer or weak version that is most widely accepted among labelists.

A second dimension of labeling theory that marks the strong version off from the weak version is the issue of *contingency,* or what determines who or what gets labeled. The strong version would be that labels are applied randomly with respect to behavior. It doesn't much matter *what* you do, labels are applied so randomly with respect to behavior that the only thing that counts is *contingency.* The crucial factor here is *not* whether someone has engaged in potentially condemnable behavior but incidental, seemingly accidental features, such as race, socioeconomic status, sex, appearance, and so on. In *Asylums,* Goffman made a statement about mental illness that seems to say that contingency counts more than someone's behavior or mental condition. He said: "Insofar as there are more mentally ill persons outside mental hospitals than inside them, one could say that mental patients suffer not from mental illness but from contingency" (1961, p. 135). Said one critic, Ronald Akers, one almost gets the impression that people go about their business, then—wham!—bad society applies a deviant or discrediting label on them, out of the blue, independent of what they've done (1985, p. 31). Following up on the strong version of contingency in labeling, some would argue that because contingency is the *only* factor that determines labeling, the rich and powerful can get away with being labeled while it is always the poor and weak who get punished. Labeling is random as far as behavior is concerned; it is more or less entirely determined by status and power and not at all (or only secondarily) by what one does. As far as I know, labeling theorists have not argued the hard line on contingency, although it can be found in Chambliss's article on the "Saints" and the "Roughnecks" (1973).

The weak version of the labeling process and the role of contingencies is that, yes, there is some relationship between what one does and the characteristics one possesses on the one hand, and the outcome of the labeling process on the other. Individuals who get labeled are *more likely* to have engaged in behavior widely regarded as deviant and possess traits that are widely disvalued, but this is not always the case. Contingencies certainly modify this relationship. Many individuals who are known to have engaged in deviant behavior, or who are known to possess deviant traits, are not themselves condemned as deviants. Enough individuals fit this characterization for us to regard contingency as an interesting factor in modifying the labeling process, enough individuals to take this as an interesting process worthy of study. Not all boys who break the law are regarded as juvenile delinquents. Not all persons who should be diagnosed by psychiatrists as mentally disordered are diagnosed by psychiatrists and labeled informally as crazy. Almost certainly, boys who commit crimes are more likely to be labeled as delinquents. Almost certainly, the mentally ill are more likely to be diagnosed and labeled as such. What we want to know is, how does this process work? What factors mitigate the labeling process? How and why does contingency operate? To my way of thinking, these questions are truer to the heart of labeling concerns than the hard line on contingency. To me, the strong version of contingency is an inaccurate portrayal of labeling theory. Again, one can locate one or another passage to defend this portrayal, but the bulk of labeling writings support the weaker version. It's the version that I hold in my own thinking and, I think, that most labelists hold as well. Not only do I not believe that labelists support the strong version, in addition, it is not an accurate description of empirical reality. The weak version is both accurate as a depiction of what labeling theorists said and accurate as a depiction of what's going on in the real or empirical world.

And the third dimension we must examine to understand the labeling approach to deviance is the issue of the impact or the effects of labeling. As with the other two points, there is a strong and a weak version on this issue as well. The strong version is that: Labeling, punishment, condemnation, and stigma always and inevitably result in strengthening the deviant's commitment to deviance, strengthening the individual's commitment to a deviant identity, and strengthening his or her ties to the deviant community. The punishment of deviance always results in a social rejection of the deviant, followed by an inability of the deviant to reenter the conventional community, a searching about by the deviant for a community that will accept him or her, that will validate and valorize his or her behavior and identity, finding that deviant community and mingling, associating, and interacting with like-minded and like-acting individuals, individuals who have also been rejected, and being further socialized into a deviant way of life, thereby resulting in an intensification of a commitment to deviant behavior, a deviant role, and a deviant identity.

This version can indeed be found in the work of Frank Tannenbaum, who wrote about juvenile delinquency in his book, *Crime and the Community,* which was published in 1938. I'd refer to Tannenbaum as a precursor of labeling theory rather than one of the original labeling theorists.

The weak version of the effects or impact of labeling is this: Labeling and punishment often but do not always or necessarily produce an intensification of a deviant identity or to further deviant behavior. This is the approach that we see in Lemert's discussion; he argues that punishing deviance often has the result of stamping it out rather than intensifying it. This happened, Lemert says, with polygyny (one husband, more than one wife) among the Mormons in Utah, and it has happened in numerous instances in the history of political radicalism in Europe. In these cases, social control produces a decline, not a rise, in the deviant behavior that was punished (1951, p. 63). Becker also says that punishing deviance often results in less deviance, not always or necessarily more. For instance, he argues, punishing marijuana smoking often results in the user giving up the grass (1963, p. 59). Becker says: "Obviously, everyone caught in one deviant act and labeled a deviant does not move inevitably toward greater deviance.... The prophecies do not always confirm themselves, the mechanisms do not always work" (p. 36). Thus, I'd say the caricature (the strong version) that is often drawn by critics of deviance is inaccurate. Labelists have emphasized the ironic deviance-strengthening consequence of labeling. And the field has picked up on that aspect, because it is more interesting, more original, more daring, than the weaker version. But again, it is not the whole story in the labelists' writings, nor is it the whole story in real life. Once again, the weak version—while less interesting, less original, and less daring—is more accurate as a depiction of what labelists wrote.

It is very easy, as some have done, to simplify and vulgarize what labeling theory says. Properly understood, the approach says that labeling is a *factor* in the drama of deviance; it is not the whole story. Labeling is not omnipotent or all-powerful, and it is not omniscient, or all-knowing; it is not omnipresent, or present everywhere at all times; it is not monolithic, entirely consistent in its impact; and it does not cover deviants evenly, like a coat of paint. It is simply an ingredient in the stew. It is likely that most of the time, individuals who break the rules escape detection. (Of course, this varies from one deviant act to another and from one deviant actor to another.) It is even likely that, much of the time, when rule breakers are detected by persons who see their behavior as a violation, enactors are not punished or condemned. There is, as John Kitsuse says (1962, 1964), a great deal of variation in reactions to deviance—just as there is a great deal of predictability as well (Gibbs 1972). And the factors that are predicted to influence the labeling process don't always operate in the predicted direction.

The labelists emphasize that what they've pointed to is a tendency, not an absolute rule. Labelists say, the higher the status, influence, and resources of the rule breaker, the greater the likelihood that he or she will escape negative sanction. Does this always happen? Of course not! For most behaviors, does it usually happen?

Almost certainly! We must be careful to make comparative and relative—not absolute—statements. Every single case can't possibly prove a point. Is the labeling process solely a function of contingencies? Does negative labeling have nothing to do with what one does and solely and exclusively to do with who one is? Of course not! Are status and power a factor in the labeling process? Of course they are, although other factors operate as well. So, the careful student of labeling theory must not make glib, superficial, and simplistic statements about what the perspective supposedly says.

I have reprinted three classic selections from the labeling literature. Frank Tannenbaum's *Crime and the Community* (1938) was the first systematic statement of the labeling position. In it, Tannenbaum made two points: First, the labeling process ("the dramatization of evil") can have a dramatic impact both on the community at large and the person so labeled; and second, however deviance labeling occurs, it can have the "self-fulfilling prophecy" effect of strengthening a commitment to a deviant identity and escalating deviant behavior. These insights had a substantial impact on the later labeling approach (Becker 1963, p. 9); still, most contemporary observers consider Tannenbaum's arguments, however original they were for their time, exaggerated and a bit one-sided.

Edwin Lemert, who began writing about deviant phenomena about a dozen years later than Tannenbaum (1951), argued that locating the *cause* of deviant behavior is not a useful exercise. In fact, deviance is a "polygenetic" phenomenon: It has a variety of causes. What's important is the *impact of deviance labeling*. Lemert made the all-important distinction between "primary" and "secondary" deviation. Primary deviation is the simple violation of norms, the simple enactment of formally deviant behavior or the possession of formally deviant characteristics. By itself, primary deviation is of no sociological significance unless and until it results in condemnation and punishment of its enactor or possessor. What is important is the process by which it becomes a basis for disassociating its enactor or possessor from the rest of the society, and what consequences that has for the person and for the society. When the person labeled as a deviant comes to use the label as a basis for acting different, he or she has become a secondary deviant. A secondary deviant has incorporated a deviant role into his or her own identity; this may result in further deviant behavior and an entrenchment into the deviant role, although a variety of processes may mitigate this process. Once again, Lemert's pinpointing the processes of labeling and deviant adaptations was influential in later labelists' thinking.

Howard Becker's discussion of the "sequential model" of deviance highlighted labeling theory's central concerns and focused on its differences with the more traditional etiological approaches. Labeling matters, Becker emphasized; it is not a secondary issue in the study of deviance, it is absolutely central. Labeling is central to the deviant "career," Becker insisted, that is, in following up on deviant impulses and continuing to enact deviant behavior. Once again, Becker insisted, "branding" someone as a deviant may reinforce the very behavior the punishment is supposedly designed to extinguish. Labeling may deny the deviant reentry into the conventional community, thereby making the "illegitimate" alternatives viable, attractive, and possibly the only option available. Like Lemert, Becker emphasized that this process is not inevitable; often, social control is effective in that it eliminates the deviant behavior it condemns and punishes. Still, the "self-fulfilling process" is interesting enough to merit close investigation, Becker insists. With the appearance of Becker's most important publication, *Outsiders* (1963) and a companion anthology published a year later, *The Other Side* (1964), which contained a number of parallel articles by his colleagues, contemporaries, and fellow labelists, the principal components of labeling theory were in place. By the early 1960s, for the sociological study of deviance, a new theory was born.

References

Akers, Ronald L. 1985. *Deviant Behavior: A Social Learning Approach* (3rd ed.). Belmont, Calif.: Wadsworth.

Becker, Howard S. 1963. *Outsiders: Studies in the Sociology of Deviance*. New York: Free Press.

Becker, Howard S. (ed.). 1964. *The Other Side: Perspectives on Deviance*. New York: Free Press.

Becker, Howard S. 1973. Labelling theory reconsidered. In *Outsiders: Studies in the Sociology of Deviance* (rev. ed.). New York: Free Press, pp. 177–208.

Chambliss, William J. 1973. The saints and the roughnecks. *Society,* 11 (December): 24–31.

Erikson, Kai T. 1962. Notes on the sociology of deviance. *Social Problems,* 9 (Spring): 307–314.

Erikson, Kai T. 1964. Notes on the sociology of deviance. In Howard S. Becker (ed.), *The Other Side: Perspectives on Deviance*. New York: Free Press, pp. 9–21.

Gibbs, Jack P. 1972. Issues in defining deviant behavior. In Robert A. Scott and Jack D. Douglas (eds.), *Theoretical Perspectives on Deviance*. New York: Basic Books, pp. 39–68.

Goffman, Erving. 1961. *Asylums*. New York: Doubleday-Anchor.

Kitsuse, John I. 1962. Societal reactions to deviant behavior: Problems of theory and method. *Social Problems,* 9 (Winter): 247–257.

Kitsuse, John I. 1964. Societal reactions to deviant behavior: Problems of theory and method. In Howard S. Becker (ed.), *The Other Side: Perspectives on Deviance*. New York: Free Press, pp. 87–102.

Lemert, Edwin M. 1951. *Social Pathology: A Systematic Approach to the Theory of Sociopathic Behavior*. New York: McGraw-Hill.

Petrunik, Michael. 1980. The rise and fall of 'labelling theory': The construction and destruction of a sociological strawman. *Canadian Journal of Sociology,* 5 (3): 213–233.

Tannenbaum, Frank. 1938. *Crime and the Community*. New York: Ginn.

Delinquency: The Self-Fulfilling Prophecy and the Dramatization of Evil

FRANK TANNENBAUM

In the conflict between the young delinquent and the community there develop two opposing definitions of the situation. In the beginning the definition of the situation by the young delinquent may be in the form of play, adventure, excitement, interest, mischief, fun. Breaking windows, annoying people, running around porches, climbing over roofs, stealing from pushcarts, playing truant—all are items of play, adventure, excitement. To the community, however, these activities may and often do take on the form of a nuisance, evil, delinquency, with the demand for control, admonition, chastisement, punishment, police court, truant school. This conflict over the situation is one that arises out of a divergence of values. As the problem develops, the situation gradually becomes redefined. The attitude of the community hardens definitely into a demand for suppression. There is a gradual shift from the definition of the specific acts as evil to a definition of the individual as evil, so that all his acts come to be looked upon with suspicion. In the process of identification his companions, hang-outs, play, speech, income, all his conduct, the personality itself, become subject to scrutiny and question. From the community's point of view, the individual who used to do bad and mischievous things has now become a bad and unredeemable human being. From the individual's point of view there has taken place a similar change. He has gone slowly from a sense of grievance and injustice, of being unduly mistreated and punished, to a recognition that the definition of him as a human being is different from that of other boys in his neighborhood, his school, street, community. This recognition on his part becomes a process of self-identification and integration with the group which shares his activities. It becomes, in part, a process of rationalization; in part, a simple response to a specialized type of stimulus. The young delinquent becomes bad because he is defined as bad and because he is not believed if he is good. There is a persistent demand for consistency in character. The community cannot deal with people whom it cannot define. Reputation is this sort of public definition. Once it is established, then unconsciously all agencies combine to maintain this definition even when they apparently and consciously attempt to deny their own implicit judgment.

Early in his career, then, the incipient professional criminal develops an attitude of antagonism to the regulated orderly life that he is required to lead. This attitude is hardened and crystallized by opposition. The conflict becomes a clash of wills. And experience too often has proved that threats, punishments, beatings, commitments to institutions, abuse and defamation of one sort or another, are of no avail. Punishment breaks down against the child's stubbornness. What has happened is

From Frank Tannenbaum, "Delinquency: The Self-Fulfilling Prophecy and the Dramatization of Evil." In *Crime and the Community* (Ginn and Company, 1938), pp. 17–21.

that the child has been defined as an "incorrigible" both by his contacts and by himself, and an attempt at a direct breaking down of will generally fails.

The child meets the situation in the only way he can, by defiance and escape—physical escape if possible, or emotional escape by derision, anger, contempt, hatred, disgust, tantrums, destructiveness, and physical violence. The response of the child is just as intelligent and intelligible as that of the schools, of the authorities. They have taken a simple problem, the lack of fitness of an institution to a particular child's needs, and have made a moral issue out of it with values outside the child's ken. It takes on the form of war between two wills, and the longer the war lasts, the more certainly does the child become incorrigible. The child will not yield because he cannot yield—his nature requires other channels for pleasant growth; the school system or society will not yield because it does not see the issues involved as between the incompatibility of an institution and a child's needs, sometimes physical needs, and will instead attempt to twist the child's nature to the institution with that consequent distortion of the child which makes an unsocial career inevitable. The verbalization of the conflict in terms of evil, delinquency, incorrigibility, badness, arrest, force, punishment, stupidity, lack of intelligence, truancy, criminality, gives the innocent divergence of the child from the straight road a meaning that it did not have in the beginning and makes its continuance in these same terms by so much the more inevitable.

The only important fact, when the issue arises of the boy's inability to acquire the specific habits which organized institutions attempt to impose upon him, is that this conflict becomes the occasion for him to acquire another series of habits, interests, and attitudes as a substitute. These habits become as effective in motivating and guiding conduct as would have been those which the orderly routine social institutions attempted to impose had they been acquired.

This conflict gives the gang its hold, because the gang provides escape, security, pleasure, and peace. The gang also gives room for the motor activity which plays a large role in a child's life. The attempt to break up the gang by force merely strengthens it. The arrest of the children has consequences undreamed of, for several reasons.

First, only some of the children are caught though all may be equally guilty. There is a great deal more delinquency practiced and committed by the young groups than comes to the attention of the police. The boy arrested, therefore, is singled out in specialized treatment. This boy, no more guilty than the other members of his group, discovers a world of which he knew little. His arrest suddenly precipitates a series of institutions, attitudes, and experiences which the other children do not share. For this boy there suddenly appear the police, the patrol wagon, the police station, the other delinquents and criminals found in the police lock-ups, the court with all its agencies such as bailiffs, clerks, bondsmen, lawyers, probation officers. There are bars, cells, handcuffs, criminals. He is questioned, examined, tested, investigated. His history is gone into, his family is brought into court. Witnesses make their appearance. The boy, no different from the rest of his gang, suddenly becomes the center of a major drama in which all sorts of unexpected characters play important roles. And what is it all about? about the accustomed things his gang has done and has been doing for a long time. In this entirely new world he is made conscious of himself as a different human being than he was before his arrest. He becomes classified as a thief, perhaps, and the entire world about him has suddenly become a different place for him and will remain different for the rest of his life.

The first dramatization of the "evil" which separates the child out of his group for specialized treatment plays a greater role in making the criminal than perhaps any other experience. It cannot be too often emphasized that for the child the whole situation has become different. He now lives in a different world. He has been tagged. A new and hitherto non-existent environment has been precipitated out for him.

The process of making the criminal, therefore, is a process of tagging, defining, identifying, segregating, describing, emphasizing, making conscious and self-conscious; it becomes a way of stimulating, suggesting, emphasizing, and evoking the very traits that are complained of. If the theory of relation of response to stimulus has any meaning, the entire process of dealing with the young delinquent is mischievous in so far as it identifies him to himself or to the environment as a delinquent person.

The person becomes the thing he is described as being. Nor does it seem to matter whether the valuation is made by those who would punish or by those who would reform. In either case the emphasis is upon the conduct that is disapproved of. The parents or the policeman, the older brother or the court, the probation officer or the juvenile institution, in so far as they rest upon the thing complained of, rest upon a false ground. Their very enthusiasm defeats their aim. The harder they work to reform the evil, the greater the evil grows under their hands. The persistent suggestion, with whatever good intentions, works mischief, because it leads to bringing out the bad behavior that it would suppress. The way out is through a refusal to dramatize the evil. The less said about it the better. The more said about something else, still better....

The dramatization of the evil therefore tends to precipitate the conflict situation which was first created through some innocent maladjustment. The child's isolation forces him into companionship with other children similarly defined, and the gang becomes his means of escape, his security. The life of the gang gives it special mores, and the attack by the community upon these mores merely overemphasizes the conflict already in existence, and makes it the source of a new series of experiences that lead directly to a criminal career.

In dealing with the delinquent, the criminal, therefore, the important thing to remember is that we are dealing with a human being who is responding normally to the demands, stimuli, approval, expectancy, of the group with whom he is associated. We are dealing not with an individual but with a group....

That group may be a small gang, a gang of children just growing up, a gang of young "toughs" of nineteen or twenty, or a gang of older criminals of thirty. If we are not dealing with a gang we may be dealing with a family. And if we are not dealing with either of these especially we may be dealing with a community. In practice all these factors—the family, the gang, and the community—may be important in the development and the maintenance of that attitude towards the world which makes a criminal career a normal, an accepted and approved way of life.

Direct attack upon the individual in these circumstances is a dubious undertaking. By the time the individual has become a criminal his habits have been so shaped that we have a fairly integrated character whose whole career is in tune with the peculiar bit of the environment for which he has developed the behavior and habits that cause him to be apprehended. In theory isolation from that group ought to provide occasion for change in the individual's habit structure. It might, if the individual were transplanted to a group whose values and activities had the approval of the wider community, and in which the newcomer might hope to gain full acceptance eventually. But until now isolation has meant the grouping in close confinement of persons whose strongest common bond has been their socially disapproved delinquent conduct. Thus the attack cannot be made without reference to group life.

The attack must be on the whole group; for only by changing its attitudes and ideals, interests and habits, can the stimuli which it exerts upon the individual be changed. Punishment as retribution has failed to reform, that is, to change character. If the individual can be made aware of a different set of values for which he may receive approval, then we may be on the road to a change in his character. But such a change of values involves a change in stimuli, which means that the criminal's social world must be changed before he can be changed.

Primary and Secondary Deviation

EDWIN M. LEMERT

There has been an embarrassingly large number of theories, often without any relationship to a general theory, advanced to account for various specific pathologies in human behavior. For certain types of pathology, such as alcoholism, crime, or stuttering, there are almost as many theories as there are writers on these subjects. This has been occasioned in no small way by the preoccupation with the origins of pathological behavior and by the fallacy of confusing *original* causes with *effective* causes. All such theories have elements of truth, and the divergent viewpoints they contain can be reconciled with the general theory here if it is granted that original causes or antecedents of deviant behaviors are many and diversified. This holds especially for the psychological processes leading to similar pathological behavior, but it also holds for the situational concomitants of the initial aberrant conduct. A person may come to use excessive alcohol not only for a wide variety of subjective reasons but also because of diversified situational influences, such as the death of a loved one, business failure, or participating in some sort of organized group activity calling for heavy drinking of liquor. Whatever the original reasons for violating the norms of the community, they are important only for certain research purposes, such as assessing the extent of the "social problem" at a given time or determining the requirements for a rational program of social control. From a narrower sociological viewpoint the deviations are not significant until they are organized subjectively and transformed into active roles and become the social criteria for assigning status. The deviant individuals must react symbolically to their own behavior aberrations and fix them in their sociopsychological patterns. The deviations remain primary deviations or symptomatic and situational as long as they are rationalized or otherwise dealt with as functions of a socially acceptable role. Under such conditions normal and pathological behaviors remain strange and somewhat tensional bedfellows in the same person. Undeniably a vast amount of such segmental and partially integrated pathological behavior exists in our society and has impressed many writers in the field of social pathology.

Just how far and for how long a person may go in dissociating his sociopathic tendencies so that they are merely troublesome adjuncts of normally conceived roles is not known. Perhaps it depends upon the number of alternative definitions of the same overt behavior that he can develop; perhaps certain physiological factors (limits) are also involved. However, if the deviant acts are repetitive and have a high visibility, and if there is a severe societal reaction, which, through a process of identification is incorporated as part of the "me" of the individual, the probability is greatly increased that the integration of existing roles will be disrupted and that

From Edwin M. Lemert, "Primary and Secondary Deviation." In *Social Pathology: A Systematic Approach to the Theory of Sociopathic Behavior* (New York: McGraw-Hill, 1951), pp. 75–78.

reorganization based upon a new role or roles will occur. (The "me" in this context is simply the subjective aspect of the societal reaction.) Reorganization may be the adoption of another normal role in which the tendencies previously defined as "pathological" are given a more acceptable social expression. The other general possibility is the assumption of a deviant role, if such exists; or, more rarely, the person may organize an aberrant sect or group in which he creates a special role of his own. *When a person begins to employ his deviant behavior or a role based upon it as a means of defense, attack, or adjustment to the overt and covert problems created by the consequent societal reaction to him, his deviation is secondary.* Objective evidences of this change will be found in the symbolic appurtenances of the new role, in clothes, speech, posture, and mannerisms, which in some cases heighten social visibility, and which in some cases serve as symbolic cues to professionalization.

It is seldom that one deviant act will provoke a sufficiently strong societal reaction to bring about secondary deviation, unless in the process of introjection the individual imputes or projects meanings into the social situation which are not present. In this case anticipatory fears are involved. For example, in a culture where a child is taught sharp distinctions between "good" women and "bad" women, a single act of questionable morality might conceivably have a profound meaning for the girl so indulging. However, in the absence of reactions by the person's family, neighbors, or the larger community, reinforcing the tentative "bad-girl" self-definition, it is questionable whether a transition to secondary deviation would take place. It is also doubtful whether a temporary exposure to a severe punitive reaction by the community will lead a person to identify himself with a pathological role, unless, as we have said, the experience is highly traumatic. Most frequently there is a progressive reciprocal relationship between the deviation of the individual and the societal reaction, with a compounding of the societal reaction out of the minute accretions in the deviant behavior, until a point is reached where ingrouping and outgrouping between society and the deviant is manifest. At this point a stigmatizing of the deviant occurs in the form of name calling, labeling, or stereotyping.

The sequence of interaction leading to secondary deviation is roughly as follows: (1) primary deviation; (2) social penalties; (3) further primary deviation; (4) stronger penalties and rejections; (5) further deviation, perhaps with hostilities and resentment beginning to focus upon those doing the penalizing; (6) crisis reached in the tolerance quotient, expressed in formal action by the community stigmatizing of the deviant; (7) strengthening of the deviant conduct as a reaction to the stigmatizing and penalties; (8) ultimate acceptance of deviant social status and efforts at adjustment on the basis of the associated role.

As an illustration of this sequence the behavior of an errant schoolboy can be cited. For one reason or another, let us say excessive energy, the schoolboy engages in a classroom prank. He is penalized for it by the teacher. Later, due to clumsiness, he creates another disturbance and again he is reprimanded. Then, as sometimes happens, the boy is blamed for something he did not do. When the teacher uses the tag "bad boy" or "mischief maker" or other invidious terms, hostility and resentment are excited in the boy, and he may feel that he is blocked in playing the role expected of him. Thereafter, there may be a strong temptation to assume his role in the class as defined by the teacher, particularly when he discovers that there are rewards as well as penalties deriving from such a role. There is, of course, no implication here that such boys go on to become delinquents or criminals, for the mischief-maker role may later become integrated with or retrospectively rationalized as part of a role more acceptable to school authorities. If such a boy continues this unacceptable role and becomes delinquent, the process must be accounted for in the light of the general theory.... There must be a spreading corroboration of a sociopathic self-conception and societal reinforcement at each step in the process.

The most significant personality changes are manifest when societal definitions and their subjective counterpart become generalized. When this happens, the range of major role choices becomes narrowed to one general class. This was very obvious in the case of a young girl who was the daughter of a paroled convict and who was attending a small Middle Western college. She continually argued with herself and with the author, in whom she had confided, that in reality she belonged on the "other side of the railroad tracks" and that her life could be enormously simplified by acquiescing in this verdict and living accordingly. While in her case there was a tendency to dramatize her conflicts, nevertheless there was enough societal reinforcement of her self-conception by the treatment she received in her relationship with her father and on dates with college boys to lend it a painful reality. Once these boys took her home to the shoddy dwelling in a slum area where she lived with her father, who was often in a drunken condition, they abruptly stopped seeing her again or else became sexually presumptive.

Deviant Behavior

HOWARD S. BECKER

It is not my purpose here to argue that only acts which are regarded as deviant by others are "really" deviant. But it must be recognized that this is an important dimension, one which needs to be taken into account in any analysis of deviant behavior. By combining this dimension with another—whether or not an act conforms to a particular rule—we can construct the following set of categories for the discrimination of different kinds of deviance.

Two of these types require very little explanation. *Conforming* behavior is simply that which obeys the rule and which others perceive as obeying the rule. At the other extreme, the *pure deviant* type of behavior is that which both disobeys the rule and is perceived as doing so.[1]

Types of Deviant Behavior

	Obedient Behavior	*Rule-breaking Behavior*
Perceived as deviant	Falsely accused	Pure deviant
Not perceived as deviant	Conforming	Secret deviant

The two other possibilities are of more interest. The *falsely accused* situation is what criminals often refer to as a "bum rap." The person is seen by others as having committed an improper action, although in fact he has not done so. False accusations undoubtedly occur even in courts of law, where the person is protected by rules of due process and evidence. They probably occur much more frequently in nonlegal settings where procedural safeguards are not available.

An even more interesting kind of case is found at the other extreme of *secret deviance*. Here an improper act is committed, yet no one notices it or reacts to it as a violation of the rules. As in the case of false accusation, no one really knows how much of this phenomenon exists, but I am convinced the amount is very sizable, much more so than we are apt to think. One brief observation convinces me this is the case. Most people probably think of fetishism (and sado-masochistic fetishism in particular) as a rare and exotic perversion. I had occasion several years ago, however, to examine the catalog of a dealer in pornographic pictures designed exclusively for devotees of this specialty. The catalog contained no pictures of nudes, no pictures of any version of the sex act. Instead, it contained page after page of pictures of girls in straitjackets, girls wearing boots with six-inch heels, girls holding whips, girls in handcuffs, and girls spanking one another. Each page served as a sample of as many as 120 pictures stocked by the dealer. A quick calculation revealed that the catalog advertised for immediate sale somewhere between fifteen and twenty thousand different photographs. The catalog itself was expensively printed and this fact, taken together with the number of photographs for sale, indicated clearly that the dealer did a land-office business and had a very sizable clientele. Yet one does not run across sado-masochistic fetishists every day. Obviously, they are able to keep the fact of their perversion secret ("All orders mailed in a plain envelope").

Similar observations have been made by students of homosexuality, who note that many homosexuals are able to keep their deviance secret from their nondeviant associates. And many users of narcotic drugs, as we shall see later, are able to hide their addiction from the nonusers they associate with.

The four theoretical types of deviance, which we created by cross-classifying kinds of behavior and the responses they evoke, distinguish between phenomena that differ in important respects but are ordinarily considered to be similar. If we ignore the differences we may commit the fallacy of trying to explain several different kinds of things in the same way, and ignore the possibility that they may require different explanations. A boy who is innocently hanging around the fringes of a delinquent group may be arrested with them some night on suspicion. He will show up in the official statistics as a delinquent just as surely as those who have actually been involved in wrongdoing, and social scientists who try to develop theories to explain delinquency will attempt to account for his presence in the official records in the same way they try to account for the presence of the others. But the cases are different; the same explanation will not do for both.

Simultaneous and Sequential Models of Deviance

The discrimination of types of deviance may help us understand how deviant behavior originates. It will do so by enabling us to develop a sequential model of deviance, a model that allows for change through time. But before discussing the model itself, let us consider the differences between a sequential model and a simultaneous model in the development of individual behavior.

First of all, let us note that almost all research in deviance deals with the kind of question that arises from viewing it as pathological. That is, research attempts to discover the "etiology" of the "disease." It attempts to discover the causes of unwanted behavior.

This search is typically undertaken with the tools of multivariate analysis. The techniques and tools used in social research invariably contain a theoretical as well as a methodological commitment, and such is the case here. Multivariate analysis assumes (even though its users may in fact know better) that all the factors which operate to produce the phenomenon under study operate simultaneously. It seeks to discover which variable or what combination of variables will best "predict" the behavior one is studying. Thus, a study of juvenile delinquency may attempt to discover whether it is the intelligence quotient, the area in which a child lives, whether or not he comes from a broken home, or a combination of these factors that accounts for his being delinquent.

But, in fact, all causes do not operate at the same time, and we need a model which takes into account the fact that patterns of behavior *develop* in orderly sequence. In accounting for an individual's use of marihuana, as we shall see later, we must deal with a sequence of steps, of changes in the individual's behavior and perspectives, in order to understand the phenomenon. Each step requires explanation, and what may operate as a cause at one step in the sequence may be of negligible importance at another step. We need, for example, one kind of explanation of how a person comes to be in a situation where marihuana is easily available to him, and another kind of explanation of why, given the fact of its availability, he is willing to experiment with it in the first place. And we need still another explanation of why, having experimented with it, he continues to use it. In a sense, each explanation constitutes a necessary cause of the behavior. That is, no one could become a confirmed marihuana user without going through each step. He must have the drug available, experiment with it, and continue to use it. The explanation of each step is thus part of the explanation of the resulting behavior.

Yet the variables which account for each step may not, taken separately, distinguish between users and nonusers. The variable which disposes a person to take a particular step may not operate because he has not yet reached the stage in the process where it is possible to take that step. Let us suppose, for example, that one of the steps in the formation of an habitual pattern of drug use—willingness to experiment with use of the drug—is really the result of a variable of personality or personal orientation such as alienation from conventional norms. The variable of personal alienation, however, will only produce drug use in people who are in a position to experiment because they participate in groups in which drugs are available; alienated people who do not have drugs available to them cannot begin experimentation and thus cannot become users, no matter how alienated they are. Thus alienation might be a necessary cause of drug use, but distinguish between users and nonusers only at a particular stage in the process.

A useful conception in developing sequential models of various kinds of deviant behavior is that of *career.* Originally developed in studies of occupations, the concept refers to the sequence of movements from one position to another in an occupational system made by any individual who works in that system. Furthermore, it includes the notion of "career contingency," those factors on which mobility from one position to another depends. Career contingencies include both objective facts of social structure and changes in the perspectives, motivations, and desires of the individual. Ordinarily, in the study of occupations, we use the concept to distinguish between those who have a "successful" career (in whatever terms success is defined within the occupation) and those who do not. It can also be used to distinguish several varieties of career outcomes, ignoring the question of "success."

The model can easily be transformed for use in the study of deviant careers. In so transforming it, we should not confine our interest to those who follow a career that leads them into ever-increasing deviance, to those who ultimately take on an extremely deviant identity and way of life. We should also consider those who have a more fleeting contact with deviance, whose careers lead them away from it into conventional ways of life. Thus, for example, studies of delinquents who fail to become adult criminals might teach us even more than studies of delinquents who progress in crime.

[Here] I will consider the possibilities inherent in the career approach to deviance.

Deviant Careers

The first step in most deviant careers is the commission of a nonconforming act, an act that breaks some particular set of rules. How are we to account for the first step?

People usually think of deviant acts as motivated. They believe that the person who commits a deviant act, even for the first time (and perhaps especially for the first time), does so purposely. His purpose may or may not be entirely conscious, but there is a motive force behind it. We shall turn to the consideration of cases of intentional nonconformity in a moment, but first I must point out that many nonconforming acts are committed by people who have no intention of doing so; these clearly require a different explanation.

Unintended acts of deviance can probably be accounted for relatively simply. They imply an ignorance of the existence of the rule, or of the fact that it was applicable in this case, or to this particular person. But it is necessary to account for the lack of awareness. How does it happen that the person does not know his act is improper? Persons deeply involved in a particular subculture (such as a religious or ethnic subculture) may simply be unaware that everyone does not act "that way" and thereby commit an impropriety. There may, in fact, be structured areas of ignorance of particular rules. Mary Haas has pointed out the interesting case of interlingual word taboos.[2] Words which are perfectly proper in one language have a "dirty" meaning in another. So the person, innocently using a word common in his own language, finds that he has shocked and horrified his listeners who come from a different culture.

In analyzing cases of intended nonconformity, people usually ask about motivation: why does the person want to do the deviant thing he does? The question assumes that the basic difference between deviants and those who conform lies in the character of their motivation. Many theories have been propounded to explain why some people have deviant motivations and others do not. Psychological theories find the cause of deviant motivations and acts in the individual's early experiences, which produce unconscious needs that must be satisfied if the individual is to maintain his equilibrium. Sociological theories look for socially structured sources of "strain" in the society, social positions which have conflicting demands placed upon them such that the individual seeks an illegitimate way of solving the problems his position presents him with. (Merton's famous theory of anomie fits into this category.)[3]

But the assumption on which these approaches are based may be entirely false. There is no reason to assume that only those who finally commit a deviant act actually have the impulse to do so. It is much more likely that most people experience deviant impulses frequently. At least in fantasy, people are much more deviant than they appear. Instead of asking why deviants want to do things that are disapproved of, we might better ask why conventional people do not follow through on the deviant impulses they have.

Something of an answer to this question may be found in the process of commitment through which the "normal" person becomes progressively involved in conventional institutions and behavior. In speaking of commitment, I refer to the process through which several kinds of interests become bound up with carrying out certain lines of behavior to which they seem formally extraneous. What happens is that the individual, as a consequence of actions he has taken in the past or the operation of various institutional routines, finds he must adhere to certain lines of behavior, because many other activities than the one he is immediately engaged in will be adversely affected if he does not. The middle-class youth must not quit school, because his occupational future depends on receiving a certain amount of schooling. The conventional person must not indulge his interests in narcotics, for example, because much more than the pursuit of immediate pleasure is involved; his job, his family, and his reputation in his neighborhood may seem to him to depend on his continuing to avoid temptation.

In fact, the normal development of people in our society (and probably in any society) can be seen as a series of progressively increasing commitments to conventional norms and institutions. The "normal" person, when he discovers a deviant impulse in himself, is able to check that impulse by thinking of the manifold consequences acting on it would produce for him. He has staked too much on continuing to be normal to allow himself to be swayed by unconventional impulses.

This suggests that in looking at cases of intended nonconformity we must ask how the person manages to avoid the impact of conventional commitments. He may do so in one of two ways. First of all, in the course of growing up the person may somehow have avoided entangling alliances with conventional society. He may, thus, be free to follow his impulses. The person who does not have a reputation to maintain or a conventional job he must keep may follow his impulses. He has nothing staked on continuing to appear conventional.

However, most people remain sensitive to conventional codes of conduct and must deal with their sensitivities in order to engage in a deviant act for the first time. Sykes and Matza have suggested that delinquents actually feel strong impulses to be law-abiding, and deal with them by techniques of neutralization: "justifications for deviance that are seen as valid by the delinquent but not by the legal system or society at large." They distinguish a number of techniques for neutralizing the force of law-abiding values.

> In so far as the delinquent can define himself as lacking responsibility for his deviant actions, the disapproval of self or others is sharply reduced in effectiveness as a restraining influence....The delinquent approaches a "billiard ball" conception of himself in which he sees himself as helplessly propelled into new situations.... By learning to view himself as more acted upon than acting, the

delinquent prepares the way for deviance from the dominant normative system without the necessity of a frontal assault on the norms themselves....

A second major technique of neutralization centers on the injury or harm involved in the delinquent act.... For the delinquent...wrongfulness may turn on the question of whether or not anyone has clearly been hurt by his deviance, and this matter is open to a variety of interpretations.... Auto theft may be viewed as "borrowing," and gang fighting may be seen as a private quarrel, an agreed upon duel between two willing parties, and thus of no concern to the community at large....

The moral indignation of self and others may be neutralized by an insistence that the injury is not wrong in light of the circumstances. The injury, it may be claimed, is not really an injury; rather, it is a form of rightful retaliation or punishment.... Assaults on homosexuals or suspected homosexuals, attacks on members of minority groups who are said to have gotten "out of place," vandalism as revenge on an unfair teacher or school official, thefts from a "crooked" store owner—all may be hurts inflicted on a transgressor, in the eyes of the delinquent....

A fourth technique of neutralization would appear to involve a condemnation of the condemners.... His condemners, he may claim, are hypocrites, deviants in disguise, or impelled by personal spite.... By attacking others, the wrongfulness of his own behavior is more easily repressed or lost to view....

Internal and external social controls may be neutralized by sacrificing the demands of the larger society for the demands of the smaller social groups to which the delinquent belongs such as the sibling pair, the gang, or the friendship clique.... The most important point is that deviation from certain norms may occur not because the norms are rejected but because other norms, held to be more pressing or involving a higher loyalty, are accorded precedence.[4]...

One of the mechanisms that leads from casual experimentation to a more sustained pattern of deviant activity is the development of deviant motives and interests.... Many kinds of deviant activity spring from motives which are socially learned. Before engaging in the activity on a more or less regular basis, the person has no notion of the pleasures to be derived from it; he learns these in the course of interaction with more experienced deviants. He learns to be aware of new kinds of experiences and to think of them as pleasurable. What may well have been a random impulse to try something new becomes a settled taste for something already known and experienced. The vocabularies in which deviant motivations are phrased reveal that their users acquire them in interaction with other deviants. The individual *learns,* in short, to participate in a subculture organized around the particular deviant activity.

Deviant motivations have a social character even when most of the activity is carried on in a private, secret, and solitary fashion. In such cases, various media of communication may take the place of face-to-face interaction in inducting the individual into the culture. The pornographic pictures I mentioned earlier were described to prospective buyers in a stylized language. Ordinary words were used in a technical shorthand designed to whet specific tastes. The word "bondage," for instance, was used repeatedly to refer to pictures of women restrained in handcuffs or straitjackets. One does not acquire a taste for "bondage photos" without having learned what they are and how they may be enjoyed.

One of the most crucial steps in the process of building a stable pattern of deviant behavior is likely to be the experience of being caught and publicly labeled as a deviant. Whether a person takes this step or not depends not so much on what he does as on what other people do, on whether or not they enforce the rule he has violated. Although I will consider the circumstances under which enforcement takes place in some detail later, two notes are in order here. First of all, even though no one else discovers the nonconformity or enforces the rules against it, the individual who has committed the impropriety may himself act as enforcer. He may brand himself as deviant because of what he has done and punish himself in one way or another for his behavior. This is not always or necessarily the case, but may occur. Second, there may be cases like those described by psychoanalysts in which the individual really wants to get caught and perpetrates his deviant act in such a way that it is almost sure he will be.

In any case, being caught and branded as deviant has important consequences for one's further social participation and self-image. The most important consequence is a drastic change in the individual's public identity. Committing the improper act and being publicly caught at it place him in a new status. He has been revealed as a different kind of person from the kind he was supposed to be. He is labeled a "fairy," "dope fiend," "nut," or "lunatic," and treated accordingly.

In analyzing the consequences of assuming a deviant identity let us make use of Hughes' distinction between master and auxiliary status traits.[5] Hughes notes that most statuses have one key trait which serves to distinguish those who belong from those who do not. Thus the doctor, whatever else he may be, is a person who has a certificate stating that he has fulfilled certain requirements and is licensed to practice medicine; this is the master trait. As Hughes points out, in our society a doctor is also informally expected to have a number of auxiliary traits: most people expect him to be upper middle class, white, male, and Protestant. When he is not there is a sense that he has in some way failed to fill the bill....

Hughes deals with this phenomenon in regard to statuses that are well thought of, desired and desirable (noting that one may have the formal qualifications for entry into a status but be denied full entry because of lack of the proper auxiliary traits), but the same process occurs in the case of deviant statuses. Possession of one deviant trait may have a generalized symbolic value, so that people automatically assume that its bearer possesses other undesirable traits allegedly associated with it.

To be labeled a criminal one need only commit a single criminal offense, and this is all the term formally refers to. Yet the word carries a number of connotations specifying auxiliary traits characteristic of anyone bearing the label. A man who has been convicted of housebreaking and thereby labeled a criminal is presumed to be a person likely to break into other houses; the police, in rounding up known offenders for investigation after a crime has been committed, operate on this premise. Further, he is considered likely to commit other kinds of crimes as well, because he has shown himself to be a person without "respect for the law." Thus, apprehension for one deviant act exposes a person to the likelihood that he will be regarded as deviant or undesirable in other respects.

There is one other element in Hughes' analysis we can borrow with profit: the distinctions between master and subordinate statuses.[6] Some statuses, in our society as in others, override all other statuses and have a certain priority.... The status of deviant (depending on the kind of deviance) is this kind of master status. One receives the status as a result of breaking a rule, and the identification proves to be more important than most others. One will be identified as a deviant first, before other identifications are made. The question is raised: "What kind of person would break such an important rule?" And the answer is given: "One who is different from the rest of us, who cannot or will not act as a moral human being and therefore might break other important rules." The deviant identification becomes the controlling one.

Treating a person as though he were generally rather than specifically deviant produces a self-fulfilling prophecy. It sets in motion several mechanisms which conspire to shape the person in the image people have of him. In the first place, one tends to be cut off, after being identified as deviant, from participation in more conventional groups, even though the specific consequences of the particular deviant activity might never of themselves have caused the isolation had there not also been public knowledge and reaction to it. For example, being a homosexual may not affect one's ability to do office work, but to be known as a homosexual in an office may make it impossible to continue working there. Similarly, though the effects of opiate drugs may not impair one's working ability, to be known as an addict will probably lead to losing one's job. In such cases, the individual finds it difficult to conform to other rules which he had no intention or desire to break, and perforce finds himself deviant in these areas as well. The homosexual who is deprived of a "respectable" job by the discovery of his deviance may drift into unconventional, marginal occupations where it does not make so much difference. The drug addict finds himself forced into other illegitimate kinds of activity, such as robbery and theft, by the refusal of respectable employers to have him around.

When the deviant is caught, he is treated in accordance with the popular diagnosis of why he is that way, and the treatment itself may likewise produce increasing deviance. The drug addict, popularly considered to be a weak-willed individual who cannot forego the indecent pleasures afforded him by opiates, is treated repressively. He is forbidden to use drugs. Since he cannot get drugs legally, he must get them illegally. This forces the market underground and pushes the price of drugs up far beyond the current legitimate market price into a bracket that few can afford on an ordinary salary. Hence the treatment of the addict's deviance places him in a position where it will probably be necessary to resort to deceit and crime in order to support his habit. The behavior is a consequence of the public reaction to the deviance rather than a consequence of the inherent qualities of the deviant act.

Put more generally, the point is that the treatment of deviants denies them the ordinary means of carrying on the routines of everyday life open to most people. Because of this denial, the deviant must of necessity develop illegitimate routines.

The influence of public reaction may be direct, as in the instances considered above, or indirect, a consequence of the integrated character of the society in which the deviant lives.

Societies are integrated in the sense that social arrangements in one sphere of activity mesh with other activities in other spheres in particular ways and depend on the existence of these other arrangements. Certain kinds of work lives presuppose a certain kind of family life, as we shall see when we consider the case of the dance musician.

Many varieties of deviance create difficulties by failing to mesh with expectations in other areas of life. Homosexuality is a case in point. Homosexuals have difficulty in any area of social activity in which the assumption of normal sexual interests and propensities for marriage is made without question. In stable work organizations such as large business or industrial organizations there are often points at which the man who would be successful should marry; not to do so will make it difficult for him to do the things that are necessary for success in the organization and will thus thwart his ambitions. The necessity of marrying often creates difficult enough problems for the normal male, and places the homosexual in an almost impossible position. Similarly, in some male work groups where heterosexual prowess is required to retain esteem in the group, the homosexual has obvious difficulties. Failure to meet the expectations of others may force the individual to attempt deviant ways of achieving results automatic for the normal person.

Obviously, everyone caught in one deviant act and labeled deviant does not move inevitably toward greater deviance in the way the preceding remarks might suggest. The prophecies do not always confirm themselves, the mechanisms do not always work. What factors tend to slow down or halt the movement toward increasing deviance? Under what circumstances do they come into play?

One suggestion as to how the person may be immunized against increasing deviance is found in a recent study of juvenile delinquents who "hustle" homosexuals.[7] These boys act as homosexual prostitutes to confirmed adult homosexuals. Yet they do not themselves become homosexual. Several things account for their failure to continue this kind of sexual deviancy. First, they are protected from police action by the fact that they are minors. If they are apprehended in a homosexual act, they will be treated as exploited children, although in fact they are the exploiters; the law makes the adult guilty. Second, they look on the homosexual acts they engage in simply as a means of making money that is safer and quicker than robbery or similar activities. Third, the standards of their peer group, while permitting homosexual prostitution, allow only one kind of activity, and forbid them to get any special pleasure out of it or to permit any expressions of endearment from the adult with whom they have relations. Infractions of these rules, or other deviations from normal heterosexual activity, are severely punished by the boy's fellows.

Apprehension may not lead to increasing deviance if the situation in which the individual is apprehended for the first time occurs at a point where he can still choose between alternate lines of action. Faced, for the first time, with the possible ultimate and drastic consequences of what he is doing, he may decide that he does not want to take the deviant road, and turn back. If he makes the right choice, he will be welcomed back into the conventional community; but if he makes the wrong move, he will be rejected and start a cycle of increasing deviance.

Ray has shown, in the case of drug addicts, how difficult it can be to reverse the deviant cycle.[8] He points out that drug addicts frequently attempt to cure themselves and that the motivation underlying their attempts is an effort to show nonaddicts whose opinions they respect that they are really not as bad as they are thought to be. On breaking their habit successfully, they find, to their dismay, that people still treat them as though they were addicts (on the premise, apparently, of "once a junkie, always a junkie").

A final step in the career of a deviant is movement into an organized deviant group. When a person makes a definite move into an organized group—or when he realizes and accepts the fact that he has already done so—it has a powerful impact on his conception of himself. A drug addict once told me that the moment she felt she was really "hooked" was when she realized she no longer had any friends who were not drug addicts.

Members of organized deviant groups of course have one thing in common: their deviance. It gives them a sense of common fate, of being in the same boat. From a sense of common fate, from having to face the same problems, grows a deviant subculture: a set of perspectives and understandings about what the world is like and how to deal with it, and a set of routine activities based on those perspectives. Membership in such a group solidifies a deviant identity.

Moving into an organized deviant group has several consequences for the career of the deviant. First of all, deviant groups tend, more than deviant individuals, to be pushed into rationalizing their position. At an extreme, they develop a very complicated historical, legal, and psychological justification for their deviant activity. The homosexual community is a good case. Magazines and books by homosexuals and for homosexuals include historical articles about famous homosexuals in history. They contain articles on the biology and physiology of sex, designed to show that homosexuality is a "normal" sexual response. They contain legal articles, pleading for civil liberties for homosexuals. Taken together, this material provides a working philosophy for the active homosexual, explaining to him why he is the way he is, that other people have also been that way, and why it is all right for him to be that way.

Most deviant groups have a self-justifying rationale (or "ideology"), although seldom is it as well worked out as that of the homosexual. While such rationales do operate, as pointed out earlier, to neutralize the conventional attitudes that deviants may still find in themselves toward their own behavior, they also perform another function. They furnish the individual with reasons that appear sound for continuing the line of activity he has begun. A person who quiets his own doubts by adopting the rationale moves into a more principled and consistent kind of deviance than was possible for him before adopting it.

The second thing that happens when one moves into a deviant group is that he learns how to carry on his deviant activity with a minimum of trouble. All the problems he faces in evading enforcement of the rule he is breaking have been faced before by others. Solutions have been worked out. Thus, the young thief meets older thieves who, more experienced than he is, explain to him how to get rid of stolen merchandise without running the risk of being caught. Every deviant group has a great stock of lore on such subjects and the new recruit learns it quickly.

Thus, the deviant who enters an organized and institutionalized deviant group is more likely than ever before to continue in his ways. He has learned, on the one hand, how to avoid trouble and, on the other hand, a rationale for continuing....

Notes

1. It should be remembered that this classification must always be used from the perspective of a given set of rules; it does not take into account the complexities that appear when there is more than one set of rules available for use by the same people in defining the same act. Furthermore, the classification has reference to types of behavior rather than types of people, to acts rather than personalities. The same person's behavior can obviously be conforming in some activities, deviant in others.

2. Mary R. Haas, "Interlingual Word Taboos," *American Anthropologist,* 53 (July–September, 1951), 338–344.

3. Robert K. Merton, *Social Theory and Social Structure* (New York: The Free Press of Glencoe, 1957), 131–194.

4. Gresham M. Sykes and David Matza, "Techniques of Neutralization: A Theory of Delinquency," *American Sociological Review,* 22 (December, 1957) 667–669.

5. Everett C. Hughes, "Dilemmas and Contradictions of Status," *American Journal of Sociology,* L (March, 1945), 353–359.

6. *Ibid.*

7. Albert J. Reiss, Jr., "The Social Integration of Queers and Peers," *Social Problems,* 9 (Fall, 1961), 102–120.

8. Marsh Ray, "The Cycle of Abstinence and Relapse Among Heroin Addicts," *Social Problems,* 9 (Fall, 1961), 132–140.

Chapter 7

Conflict Theory and Marxist Criminology

There are many varieties of conflict theory; one of them is Marxism. At the same time, Marxism has a number of features that are unique to itself and set it off from conflict theory in general. Thus, it is usually referred to as a completely separate perspective rather than a variety of conflict theory. Conflict theory, as distinct from Marxism, is often referred to as "pluralistic," or "interest group," or sometimes "liberal" conflict theory. Although the two approaches cannot be equated, they do nonetheless share several features in common.

Karl Marx (1818–1883) was a German philosopher and sociologist who wrote about the flaws and imminent downfall of industrial capitalism. At one time, he was the most influential author of all time; today, however, among most intellectuals, the majority of his ideas are considered discredited. Marx developed a perspective, referred to as Marxism, that focused on class struggle as the key to all human history. In industrial capitalism, the classes that are in conflict are the capitalist class or the *bourgeoisie,* that is, the class whose members control the significant resources, money-making property, or *capital,* and the working class or the *proletariat*. The bourgeoisie not only own and control the means of production, they also dictate the content of all of the other institutions of the society; thus, in capitalist society, the dominant institutions are bourgeois art, bourgeois law, a bourgeois system of justice, a bourgeois system of education, a bourgeois mass media, the bourgeois state, and so on. In each case, these institutions both support and reflect the rule and interests of the capitalist elite; in each case, they represent ideological underpinning for the status quo. It is the *job* or *function* of these bourgeois institutions to consolidate the power of the powerful and to maintain its rule. But since that rule is based on exploitation and oppression, it is fatally flawed; eventually, those who are exploited and oppressed will rise up and destroy capitalism and usher in a new economic system—socialism. The fact that nothing like this has in fact taken place—indeed, that many societies once regarded as socialist are now readopting a capitalist economic system—has dimmed Marxism's luster and appeal for many intellectuals.

Marx and his coauthor, Friedrich Engels (1820–1895), did not write a great deal specifically about crime and deviance. Much of what has been referred to as "Marxist criminology" has been pieced together by their many followers from their more general approach and from their few writings on the subject. The Marxist theory of deviance and crime would make two principal points.

First, as we saw, the bourgeoisie controls the dominant social institutions; this includes the media, which, in turn, influence public opinion; the legislature and the legislative process, which determine the criminal law; and the criminal justice system, including the police, the courts, and the jails and prisons. These institutions, again, reflect and uphold the rule and the interests of the capitalist class. The media support bourgeois interests by focusing on, and creating folk enemies—or deviants—out of street criminals, perpetrators of sensationalistic, or "underworld," or "prevert" kinds of crimes and, in turn, ignoring the "real" crimes of the rich and the powerful—corporate crimes, war crimes, oppression, exploitation, racism, sexism, and so on. (We encountered this argument in the piece in the first chapter by Alexander Liazos, whose original article was entitled "Nuts, Sluts, and Preverts: The Poverty of the Sociology of Deviance.") The law and the criminal justice system support bourgeois interests by criminalizing and punishing the powerless street criminal and ignoring the truly harmful corporate and white-collar criminal. Thus, the first point a Marxist approach to deviance and crime would make is that *social control reflects and consolidates the rule of the powerful.* The social control apparatus is designed, and functions, to protect and maintain the interests of the capitalist class.

The second point a Marxist criminologist would make is a bit afield of the subject of social control; in fact, it fits squarely within the focus of Part III, "Theories of Deviant Behavior." It is that *capitalist society is criminogenic.* Capitalism is a ruthless, exploitative system. At its foundation is an economy that depends on a high rate of unemployment, which in turn means that many poor, out-of-work people have no alternative but to commit crime to survive. It is based on a dog-eat-dog ethic, which in turn promotes a business climate, and business practices, which depend on exposing workers to dangerous working conditions, polluting the environment, selling unsafe products, cutting corners, forming monopolies, driving real competitors out of business, making blatantly untrue advertising claims, and so on. Even the general cultural climate of capitalism is based on ruthlessness, promoting a culture of crime and violence, thereby inducing extraordinarily high rates of rape, murder, assault, and robbery. Moreover, the Marxist would say, the fact that capitalism generates a large, poor, powerless underclass whose members lack many basic human amenities, makes it necessary for many of them to engage in criminal behavior for their sheer survival. Marxism's answer to the question *what causes crime?* is: It is *capitalism* that causes crime.

Conflict theory shares many points in common with Marxism, but differs on a number of points as well. Both reject functionalism's view of society as a coherent entity with common interests. Both, for instance, would most emphatically reject

Kingsley Davis and Wilbert Moore's theory that stratification is good for the society as a whole, a discussion we encountered in Chapter 5 on functionalism. Both would reject the view that the institution of prostitution is functional for the society as a whole; in analyzing prostitution, both would search for interests and functions among the more powerful groups or segments of the society. Both see different segments of the society as competing, conflicting, and antagonistic; both see the allocation of society's resources as a "zero sum game"—that is, what one group gets is at the expense of another. Both examine the crucial role of dominance or *hegemony* in definitions of deviance and crime. Practitioners of both are more likely to be interested in social control or *reactions to* deviance and crime than in etiology, or their *causes*. (Although, as we saw, Marxists are also interested in the question of what causes crime; to them, the culprit is the capitalist system.) Both see social control—including the content and the enforcement of the criminal law—as the outcome of a power struggle among categories or segments or groups in the society. Both reject the view that laws are an expression or a reflection of the social consciousness of a society. For instance, both would reject the validity of Emile Durkheim's concept of the collective consciousness or the collective conscience. And both reject the view that laws are written and passed so that society as a whole will be protected from harm. Both see the law mainly as a means of forcing one more powerful group's beliefs and way of life onto the rest of the society. Both argue that laws are passed and enforced mainly because they uphold the ideology or material interests of certain relatively powerful sectors of the society.

This is a long list of similarities. But non-Marxist conflict theory and Marxism part company on a number of crucial points.

The key difference between them is the economic dimension. As we saw, Marxism holds that the principal split in capitalist society is between the capitalist or property-owning class, the bourgeoisie, and the class of workers, or the proletariat. "Property" refers to anything that can turn a profit—what Marx refers to as "the means of production." All conflicts of any consequence are between capitalists and the workers; all other conflicts are secondary in importance. And all interests can be reduced to economic interests. Conflicts centering around sex or gender, race, ethnicity, religion, region, culture, and so on—all are either *reflections* of class conflicts or *subordinate* to class conflicts. Laws are passed and enforced to control workers and maximize profits and power for the elite, that is, the capitalist class; behavior is condemned and "deviantized" to the extent that it threatens the power and profits of the capitalist class. Everything of any importance revolves around the economic dimension. To Marx, the "locomotive" of history and all social change is the class struggle.

As we saw, Marxism has suffered a drastic decline in influence over the past generation or so. From today's perspective, the Marxist approach seems overly deterministic, one-dimensional, and intentional. It seems to assume that capitalism is—or capitalists are—engaged in purposive, rationalistic behavior at all times in producing deviants, channeling certain problem populations into deviant statuses, dealing with the overproduction of deviance in an effective, instrumental fashion. Today, we know that matters are not that simple. The capitalist class itself is divided on key issues, coordination is not such a simple matter, even the powerful lose out in a number of struggles, a variety of groups and coalitions wield power on certain issues to block the interests or wishes of the capitalist class, both the powerful and the less powerful often act in ways that are contrary to their class or economic interests, many factors or forces act on everyone in influencing what we do, and some of them are utterly irrelevant to the economic dimension. From the perspective of today, Marxism seems more a literary metaphor than a theory that explains real-life behavior. In any case, it influenced a whole generation of deviance theorists, and it may make a comeback in the future.

Non-Marxist conflict theory (or pluralistic conflict theory) is far more complex and far less deterministic in its orientation. And it does argue that the economic dimension is simply one among a range or variety of factors or forces influencing the world of deviance labeling and criminal legislation and enforcement. Other factors also play a decisive role; they cannot be reduced to or subsumed under the economic dimension. Again, by itself, race, sex or gender, religion, region, culture, and so on all influence who or what is regarded as deviant and criminal in a given society at a given time. Can anyone seriously believe that hostility toward homosexuality and homosexuals—which, in Western society, has roots that go back to ancient Israel, over 3,000 years ago, long before the appearance of capitalism—is an issue of class interests, the profits and power of the economic elite? That the recent panic over drug abuse is *primarily* a struggle between the bourgeoisie and the proletariat? That the recent attempt to define cigarette smoking as deviant and criminal is *simply* an expression of dominant class interests? Conflict theory looks at a much wider range of influences, dimensions, factors, and forces in the drama of deviance defining and criminalization. And it examines the manner in which power is in fact wielded in a large industrial society—through compromise, coalitions, alliances, both victories and defeats for the powerful, irrational or quasi-rational actions, grassroots activism, stops and starts, stalemates, and so on. It is far from the one-dimension, overly intentional, strictly deterministic enterprise that traditional or orthodox Marxists make it out to be.

The Marxist approach to deviance and crime, like labeling theory, reversed the traditional question raised by etiology—why deviance?—and focused more on the issue of social control. Marxism shared with functionalism its concern for the functions of institutions and practices. Unlike functionalism, however, Marxism argued that what is beneficial for one class (the bourgeoisie, the capitalist class, the very rich) might very well be harmful for another (the proletariat, the workers, the poor).

In the 1970s, Marxism was a viable approach to the study of deviance and crime. It was an approach that some researchers or scholars adopted, put on like a suit of armor. It was their approach to the study of deviance and crime. Just about every aspect of every phenomenon was looked at through this perspective. It was a way of looking at deviance. It billed itself as a kind of "Big Bang" theory through which everything could be explained. The theory colored and shaped everything these criminologists saw. It was like a filter through which all reality passed. It was an all-embracing perspective. These researchers and scholars saw themselves *as Marxists;* it was how they viewed the world. Of course, there are still scholars and researchers who retain this totalistic perspective. But today, it is less likely to be the case than a generation ago. Class struggle, the central idea in Marxism, is still important for some things. And certainly social class is a fundamental feature of human existence in capitalist society. The nature of capitalism does shape some aspects of the world of deviance. One need not go to foolish lengths, as some Marxist scholars did in the past, to argue that economic factors are crucial. So I'd suggest that Marxism, like most other perspectives, can be seen as a tool kit of interesting, powerful, and productive concepts and even propositions. One can take the approach piecemeal rather than as an all-embracing perspective. This is not how Marxists of the past worked. And, no doubt, this is not how many orthodox, dogmatic, true-blue Marxists would want the approach to be used today. But I suspect that this is how it will be used, increasingly, in the future. Because it just doesn't *work* as a totalistic, all-embracing approach to deviance and crime. It's too confining; it doesn't address a lot of important issues. And, if we do draw propositions out of it, it is too often simply wrong in its predictions.

Certainly, for instance, we can see that rape is common in many precapitalist societies; in some of them, it is even more common than it is in capitalist societies. Thus, rape cannot be seen as the product of capitalism, as some Marxists a generation ago claimed. Certainly we can see that most victims of crime are the poor and the weak rather than the rich and the powerful, and that it is foolish to see crime as a kind of primitive rebellion against capitalism. All law in capitalist society is not contrary to the interests of the people, as some Marxists foolishly proclaimed in the 1970s—no matter how we define interests, no matter how we define "the people," and no matter how we define law. It just isn't true, and, I submit, if anyone wanted to investigate the question, we could demonstrate that it isn't the case with fairly solid evidence. As more conventional criminologists have pointed out, it is the weak and the powerless who are most likely to be victimized by street crime, a category of crime that Marxists once insisted that we pay a great deal *less* attention to. So, it might be worthwhile to pick the bones of Marxism and come out with interesting propositions piecemeal—use it as a tool kit rather than a lens or filter through which to view everything that takes place in the world.

While it is true that some fairly traditional Marxists are still doing research and writing, they are fewer in number, they are no longer regarded as the—or even a—cutting edge of the field; it is a great deal less fashionable today to be a Marxist than it was a generation ago. It just isn't where it's at anymore in the field of criminology and the sociology of deviance. The Marxist approach had too many holes; most of its practitioners saw this and moved on to other approaches and concerns. Its place has been taken, to some extent, by feminism and by the "new" sociology of social control, which we'll look at in the next section.

Steven Spitzer outlines the Marxist theory of deviance. Usually, Marxist analysis begins with a discussion of what the author sees as the deficiencies in the traditional or even bourgeois (that is, non-Marxist) approaches. Spitzer believes that events in capitalist society work from the top down, that is, the capitalist society is dominated and controlled by the capitalist elite, whose interests determine how deviants are defined and treated. Spitzer's theory addresses both social control and etiology, because he believes that the powerless "underclass" behaves as it does as a consequence of the control of society's resources by the powerful class. The apparatus of social control distinguishes between "social junk," or relatively harmless but burdensome deviants, who must be treated and processed, and who drain off society's resources (such as the mentally ill), and social dynamite, such as street criminals, who pose a threat to the capitalist order and must be incarcerated and, under extreme circumstances, executed.

Sheley summarizes the main points of the conflict theory of law and crime. He shows that the definition of what a crime is, is subject to definition, revision, compromise, and negotiation. The law can be regarded as an "instrument of power" rather than as a means of protecting the society from clear-cut harm. Law enforcement, too, in part, reflects the need of the powerful segments of the society to protect their interests. Still, interests are pursued by all segments of the society and which one wins out in a given struggle is far from a foregone conclusion. Capitalist society is organized into multiple interest groups, which cut across class lines. And often, interests are symbolic and ideological rather than exclusively economic. Conflict theory offers a much broader, more realistic, and more convincing approach to the enactment and enforcement of criminal law than Marxism. Still, both have their proponents in the field, and both have much to offer the student of deviance.

Toward a Marxian Theory of Deviance [1]

STEVEN SPITZER

This paper considers the prospects for the development of a Marxian interpretation of deviance and control. The weaknesses of conventional perspectives are identified and an approach is suggested which applies the insights of Marxian theory to an investigation of deviance production in modern society. This process is explored with special attention to the capitalist mode of production, the system of class control in capitalist societies, the genesis and maintenance of "problem populations," the channeling of these populations into deviant statuses, and the distinctive character of deviant groups. The emergence of monopoly and state capitalism is examined in an attempt to understand the dynamics of structural change, deviance production and social control. The overproduction of deviance in advanced capitalist societies and attempts at the "solution" of this problem are also discussed.

Within the last decade American sociologists have become increasingly reflective in their approach to deviance and social problems. They have come to recognize that interpretations of deviance are often ideological in their assumptions and implications, and that sociologists are frequently guilty of "providing the facts which make oppression more efficient and the theory which makes it legitimate to a larger constituency" (Becker and Horowitz, 1972: 48). To combat this tendency students of deviance have invested more and more energy in the search for a critical theory. This search has focused on three major problems: (1) the definition of deviance, (2) the etiology of deviance, and (3) the etiology of control.

Traditional Theories and Their Problems

Traditional theories approached the explanation of deviance with little equivocation about the phenomenon to be explained. Prior to the 1960s the subject matter of deviance theory was taken for granted and few were disturbed by its preoccupation with "dramatic and predatory" forms of social behavior (Liazos, 1972). Only in recent years have sociologists started to question the consequences of singling out "nuts," "sluts," "perverts," "lames," "crooks," "junkies," and "juicers" for special attention. Instead of adopting conventional wisdom about *who* and *what* is deviant, investigators have gradually made the definitional problem central to the sociological enterprise. They have begun to appreciate the consequences of studying the powerless (rather

From Steven Spitzer, "Toward a Marxian Theory of Deviance." © 1975 by the Society for the Study of Social Problems. Reprinted from *Social Problems,* vol. 22 (June 1975), pp. 641–651, by permission.

than the powerful)—both in terms of the relationship between *knowledge of* and *control over* a group, and the support for the "hierarchy of credibility" (Becker, 1967) that such a focus provides. Sociologists have discovered the significance of the definitional process in their own, as well as society's response to deviance, and this discovery has raised doubts about the direction and purpose of the field.

Even when the definitional issue can be resolved critics are faced with a second and equally troublesome problem. Traditional theories of deviance are essentially *non-structural* and *ahistorical* in their mode of analysis. By restricting investigation to factors which are manipulable within existing structural arrangements these theories embrace a "correctional perspective" (Matza, 1969) and divert attention from the impact of the political economy as a whole. From this point of view deviance is *in* but not *of* our contemporary social order. Theories that locate the source of deviance in factors as diverse as personality structure, family systems, cultural transmission, social disorganization and differential opportunity share a common flaw—they attempt to understand deviance apart from historically specific forms of political and economic organization. Because traditional theories proceed without any sense of historical development, deviance is normally viewed as an episodic and transitory phenomenon rather than an outgrowth of long-term structural change. Sensitive sociologists have come to realize that critical theory must establish, rather than obscure, the relationship between deviance, social structure and social change.

A final problem in the search for a critical theory of deviance is the absence of a coherent theory of control. More than ever before critics have come to argue that deviance cannot be understood apart from the dynamics of control. Earlier theories devoted scant attention to the control process precisely because control was interpreted as a natural response to behavior generally assumed to be problematic. Since theories of deviance viewed control as a desideratum, no theory of control was required. But as sociologists began to question conventional images of deviance they revised their impressions of social control. Rather than assuming that societal reaction was necessarily defensive and benign, skeptics announced that controls could actually cause deviance. The problem was no longer simply to explain the independent sources of deviance and control, but to understand the reciprocal relationship between the two.

In elevating control to the position of an independent variable a more critical orientation has evolved. Yet this orientation has created a number of problems of its own. If deviance is simply a *status,* representing the outcome of a series of control procedures, should our theory of deviance be reduced to a theory of control? In what sense, if any, is deviance an achieved rather than an ascribed status? How do we account for the historical and structural sources of deviance apart from those shaping the development of formal controls?

Toward a Theory of Deviance Production

A critical theory must be able to account for both *deviance* and *deviants.* It must be sensitive to the process through which deviance is subjectively constructed and deviants are objectively handled, as well as the structural bases of the behavior and characteristics which come to official attention. It should neither beg the explanation of deviant behavior and characteristics by depicting the deviant as a helpless victim of oppression, nor fail to realize that his identification as deviant, the dimensions of his threat, and the priorities of the control system are a part of a broader social conflict. While acknowledging the fact that deviance is a *status* imputed to groups who share certain structural characteristics (e.g. powerlessness) we must not forget that these groups are defined by more than these characteristics alone.[2] We must not only ask why specific members of the underclass are selected for official processing, but also why they behave as they do. Deviant statuses, no matter how coercively applied, are in some sense achieved and we must understand this achievement in the context of political-economic conflict. We need to understand why capitalism produces both patterns of activity and types of people that are defined and managed as deviant.

In order to construct a general theory of deviance and control it is useful to conceive of a process of deviance production which can be understood in relationship to the development of class society. *Deviance production involves all aspects of the process through which populations are structurally generated, as well as shaped, channeled into, and manipulated within social categories defined as deviant.* This process includes the development of and changes in: (1) deviant definitions, (2) problem populations, and (3) control systems.

Most fundamentally, deviance production involves the development of and changes in deviant categories and images. A critical theory must examine where these images and definitions come from, what they reflect about the structure of and priorities in specific class societies, and how they are related to class conflict. If we are to explain, for example, how mental retardation becomes deviance and the feeble-minded deviant we need to examine the structural characteristics, economic and political dimensions of the society in which these definitions and images emerged. In the case of American society we must understand how certain correlates of capitalist development (proletarianization and nuclearization of the family) weakened traditional methods of assimilating these groups, how others (the emergence of scientific and meritocratic ideologies) sanctioned intellectual stratification and differential handling, and how still others (the attraction of unskilled labor and population concentrations) heightened concern over the "threat" that these groups were assumed to represent. In other words, the form and content of deviance definition must be assessed in terms of its relationship to both structural and ideological change.

A second aspect of deviance production is the development of and changes in problem behaviors and problem populations. If we assume that class societies are based on fundamental conflicts between groups, and that harmony is achieved through the dominance of a specific class, it makes sense to argue that deviants are culled from groups who create specific problems for those who rule. Although these groups may victimize or burden those outside of the dominant class, their problematic quality ultimately resides in their challenge to the basis and form of class rule. Because problem populations are not always "handled," they provide candidates for, but are in no sense equivalent to, official deviants. A sophisticated critical theory must investigate where these groups come from, why their behaviors and characteristics are problematic, and how they are transformed in a developing political economy. We must consider, for instance, why Chinese laborers in 19th century California and Chicanos in the Southwest during the 1930s became the object of official concern, and why drug laws evolved to address the "problems" that these groups came to represent (Helmer and Vietorisz, 1973; Musto, 1973).

The changing character of problem populations is related to deviance production in much the same way that variations in material resources affect manufacturing. Changes in the quantity and quality of raw materials influence the scope and priorities of production, but the characteristics of the final product depend as much on the methods of production as the source material. These methods comprise the third element in deviance production—the development and operation of the control system. The theory must explain why a system of control emerges under specific conditions and account for its size, focus and working assumptions. The effectiveness of the system in confronting problem populations and its internal structure must be understood in order to interpret changes in the form and content of control. Thus, in studying the production of the "mentally ill" we must not only consider why deviance has been "therapeutized," but also how this development reflects the subtleties of class control. Under capitalism, for example, formal control of the mad and the birth of the asylum may be examined as a response to the growing demands for order, responsibility and restraint (cf. Foucault, 1965).

The Production of Deviance in Capitalist Society

The concept of deviance production offers a starting point for the analysis of both deviance and control. But for such a construct to serve as a critical tool it must be grounded in an historical and structural investigation of society. For Marx, the crucial unit of analysis is the mode of production that dominates a given historical period. If we are to have a Marxian theory of deviance, therefore, deviance production must be understood in relationship to specific forms of socio-economic organization. In our society, productive activity is organized capitalistically and it is ultimately defined by "the process that transforms on the one hand, the social means of subsistence and of production into capital, on the other hand the immediate producers into wage labourers" (Marx, 1967:714).

There are two features of the capitalist mode of production important for purposes of this discussion. First, as a mode of production it forms the foundation or infrastructure of our society. This means that the starting point of our analysis must be an understanding of the economic organization of capitalist societies and the impact of that organization on all aspects of social life. But the capitalist mode of production is an important starting point in another sense. It contains contradictions which reflect the internal tendencies of capitalism. These contradictions are important because they explain the changing character of the capitalist system and the nature of its impact on social, political and intellectual activity. The formulation of a Marxist perspective on deviance requires the interpretation of the process through which the contradictions of capitalism are expressed. In particular, the theory must illustrate the relationship between specific contradictions, the problems of capitalist development and the production of a deviant class.

The superstructure of society emerges from and reflects the ongoing development of economic forces (the infrastructure). In class societies this superstructure preserves the hegemony of the ruling class through a system of class controls. These controls, which are institutionalized in the family, church, private associations, media, schools and the state, provide a mechanism for coping with the contradictions and achieving the aims of capitalist development.

Among the most important functions served by the superstructure in capitalist societies is the regulation and management of problem populations. Because deviance processing is only one of the methods available for social control, these groups supply raw material for deviance production, but are by no means synonymous with deviant populations. Problem populations tend to share a number of social characteristics, but most important among these is the fact that their behavior, personal qualities and/or position threaten the *social relations of production* in capitalist societies. In other words, populations become generally eligible for management as deviant when they disturb, hinder or call into question any of the following:

1. Capitalist modes of appropriating the product of human labor (e.g. when the poor "steal" from the rich)

2. The social conditions under which capitalist production takes place (e.g. those who refuse or are unable to perform wage labor)

3. Patterns of distribution and consumption in capitalist society (e.g. those who use drugs for escape and transcendence rather than sociability and adjustment)

4. The process of socialization for productive and non-productive roles (e.g. youth who refuse to be schooled or those who deny the validity of "family life")[3]

5. The ideology which supports the functioning of capitalist society (e.g. proponents of alternative forms of social organization)

Although problem populations are defined in terms of the threat and costs that they present to the social relations of production in capitalist societies, these populations are far from isomorphic with a revolutionary class. It is certainly true that some members of the problem population may under specific circumstances possess revolutionary potential. But this potential can only be realized if the problematic group is located in a position of functional indispensability within the capitalist system. Historically, capitalist societies have been quite successful in transforming those who are problematic and indispensable (the protorevolutionary class) into groups who are either problematic and dispensable (candidates for deviance processing), or indispensable but not problematic (supporters of the capitalist order). On the other hand, simply because a group is manageable does not mean that it ceases to be a problem for the capitalist class. Even though dispensable problem populations cannot overturn the capitalist system, they can represent a significant impediment to its maintenance and growth. It is in this sense that they become eligible for management as deviants.

Problem populations are created in two ways—either directly through the expression of fundamental contradictions in the capitalist mode of production or indirectly through disturbances in the system of class rule. An example of the first process is found in Marx's analysis of the "relative surplus-population."

Writing on the "General Law of Capitalist Accumulation" Marx explains how increased social redundance is inherent in the development of the capitalist mode of production:

> With the extension of the scale of production, and the mass of the labourers set in motion, with the greater breadth and fullness of all sources of wealth, there is also an extension of the scale on which greater attraction of labourers by capital is accompanied by their greater repulsion.... The labouring population therefore produces, along with the accumulation of capital produced by it, the means by which itself is made relatively superfluous,...and it does this to an always increasing extent (Marx, 1967:631).

In its most limited sense the production of a relative surplus-population involves the creation of a class which is economically redundant. But insofar as the conditions of economic existence determine social existence, this process helps explain the emergence of groups who become both threatening and vulnerable at the same time. The marginal status of these populations reduces their stake in the maintenance of the system while their powerlessness and dispensability render them increasingly susceptible to the mechanisms of official control.

The paradox surrounding the production of the relative surplus-population is that this population is both useful and menacing to the accumulation of capital. Marx describes how the relative surplus-population "forms a disposable industrial army, that belongs to capital quite as absolutely as if the latter had bred it at its own cost," and how this army, "creates, for the changing needs of the self-expansion of capital, a mass of human material always ready for exploitation" (Marx, 1967:632).

On the other hand, it is apparent that an excessive increase in what Marx called the "lowest sediment" of the relative surplus-population, might seriously impair the growth of capital. The social expenses and threat to social harmony created by a large and economically stagnant surplus-population could jeopardize the preconditions for accumulation by undermining the ideology of equality so essential to the legitimation of production relations in bourgeois democracies, diverting revenues away from capital investment toward control and support operations, and providing a basis for political organization of the dispossessed.[4] To the extent that the relative surplus-population confronts the capitalist class as a threat to the social relations of production it reflects an important contradiction in modern capitalist societies: a surplus-population is a necessary product of and condition for the accumulation of wealth on a capitalist basis, but is also creates a form of social expense which must be neutralized or controlled if production relations and conditions for increased accumulation are to remain unimpaired.

Problem populations are also generated through contradictions which develop in the system of class rule. The institutions which make up the superstructure of capitalist society originate and are maintained to guarantee the interests of the capitalist class. Yet these institutions necessarily reproduce, rather than resolve, the contradictions of the capitalist order. In a dialectical fashion, arrangements which arise in order to buttress capitalism are transformed into their opposite—structures for the cultivation of internal threats. An instructive example of this process is found in the emergence and transformation of educational institutions in the United States.

The introduction of mass education in the United States can be traced to the developing needs of corporate capitalism (cf. Karier, 1973; Cohen and Lazerson, 1972; Bowles and Gintis, 1972; Spring, 1972). Compulsory education provided a means of training, testing and sorting, and assimilating wage-laborers, as well as withholding certain populations from the labor market. The system was also intended to preserve the values of bourgeois society and operate as an "inexpensive form of police" (Spring, 1973:31). However, as Gintis (1973) and Bowles (1973) have suggested, the internal contradictions of schooling can lead to effects opposite of those intended. For the poor, early schooling can make explicit the oppressiveness and alienating character of capitalist institutions, while higher education can instill critical abilities which lead students to "bite the hand that feeds them." In both cases educational institutions create troublesome populations (i.e. drop outs and student radicals) and contribute to the very problems they were designed to solve.

After understanding how and why specific groups become generally bothersome in capitalist society, it is necessary to investigate the conditions under which these groups are transformed into proper objects for social control. In other words, we must ask what distinguishes the generally problematic from the specifically deviant. The rate at which problem populations are converted into deviants will reflect the relationship between these populations and the control system. This rate is likely to be influenced by the:

(1) *Extensiveness and Intensity of State Controls.* Deviance processing (as opposed to other control measures) is more likely to occur when problem management is monopolized by the state. As state controls are applied more generally the proportion of official deviants will increase.

(2) *Size and Level of Threat Presented by the Problem Population.* The larger and more threatening the problem population, the greater the likelihood that this population will have to be controlled through deviance processing rather than other methods. As the threat created by these populations exceeds the capacities of informal restraints, their management requires a broadening of the reaction system and an increasing centralization and coordination of control activities.

(3) *Level of Organization of the Problem Population.* When and if problem populations are able to organize and develop limited amounts of political power, deviance processing becomes increasingly less effective as a tool for social control. The attribution of deviant status is most likely to occur when a group is relatively impotent and atomized.

(4) *Effectiveness of Control Structures Organized through Civil Society.* The greater the effectiveness of the organs of civil society (i.e. the family, church, media, schools, sports) in solving the problems of class control, the less the likelihood that deviance processing (a more explicitly political process) will be employed.

(5) *Availability and Effectiveness of Alternative Types of Official Processing.* In some cases the state will be able effectively to incorporate certain segments of the problem population into specially created "pro-social" roles. In the modern era, for example, conscription and public works projects (Piven and Cloward, 1971) helped neutralize the problems posed by troublesome populations without creating new or expanding old deviant categories.

(6) *Availability and Effectiveness of Parallel Control Structures.* In many instances the state can transfer its costs of deviance production by supporting or at least tolerating the activities of independent control networks which operate in its interests. For example, when the state is denied or is reluctant to assert a monopoly over the use of force it is frequently willing to encourage vigilante organizations and private police in the suppression of problem populations. Similarly, the state is often benefited by the policies and practices of organized crime, insofar as these activities help pacify, contain and enforce order among potentially disruptive groups (Schelling, 1967).

(7) *Utility of Problem Populations.* While problem populations are defined in terms of their threat and costs to capitalist relations of production, they are not threatening in every respect. They can be supportive economically (as part of a surplus labor pool or dual labor market), politically (as evidence of the need for state intervention) and ideologically (as scapegoats for rising discontent). In other words, under certain conditions capitalist societies derive benefits from maintaining a number of visible and uncontrolled "troublemakers" in their midst. Such populations are distinguished by the fact that while they remain generally bothersome, the costs that they inflict are most immediately absorbed by other members of the problem population. Policies evolve, not so much to eliminate or actively suppress these groups, but to deflect their threat away from targets which are sacred to the capitalist class. Victimization is permitted and even encouraged, as long as the victims are members of an expendable class.

Two more or less discrete groupings are established through the operations of official control. These groups are a product of different operating assumptions and administrative orientations toward the deviant population. On the one hand, there is *social junk* which, from the point of view of the dominant class, is a costly yet relatively harmless burden to society. The discreditability of social junk resides in the failure, inability or refusal of this group to participate in the roles supportive of capitalist society. Social junk is most likely to come to official attention when informal resources have been exhausted or when the magnitude of the problem becomes significant enough to create a basis for "public concern." Since the threat presented by social junk is passive, growing out of its inability to compete and its withdrawal from the prevailing social order, controls are usually designed to regulate and contain rather than eliminate and suppress the problem. Clear-cut examples of social junk in modern capitalist societies might include the officially administered aged, handicapped, mentally ill and mentally retarded.

In contrast to social junk, there is a category that can be roughly described as *social dynamite*. The essential quality of deviance managed as social dynamite is its potential actively to call into question established relationships, especially relations of production and domination. Generally, therefore, social dynamite tends to be more youthful, alienated and politically volatile than social junk. The control of social dynamite is usually premised on an assumption that the problem is acute in nature, requiring a rapid and focused expenditure of control resources. This is in contrast to the handling of social junk frequently based on a belief that the problem is chronic and best controlled through broad reactive, rather than intensive and selective measures. Correspondingly, social dynamite is normally processed through the legal system with its capacity for active intervention, while social junk is frequently (but not always)[5] administered by the agencies and agents of the therapeutic and welfare state.

Many varieties of deviant populations are alternatively or simultaneously dealt with as either social junk and/or social dynamite. The welfare poor, homosexuals, alcoholics and "problem children" are among the categories reflecting the equivocal nature of the control process and its dependence on the political, economic and ideological priorities of deviance production. The changing nature of these priorities and their implications for the future may be best understood by examining some of the tendencies of modern capitalist systems.

Monopoly Capital and Deviance Production

Marx viewed capitalism as a system constantly transforming itself. He explained these changes in terms of certain tendencies and contradictions immanent within the capitalist mode of production. One of the most important processes identified by Marx was the tendency for the organic composition of capital to rise. Simply stated, capitalism requires increased productivity to survive, and increased productivity is only made possible by raising the ratio of machines (dead labor) to men (living labor). This tendency is self-reinforcing since, "the further machine production advances, the higher becomes the organic composition of capital needed for an entrepreneur to secure the average profit" (Mandel, 1968:163). This phenomenon helps us explain the course of capitalist development over the last century and the rise of monopoly capital (Baran and Sweezy, 1966).

For the purposes of this analysis there are at least two important consequences of this process. First, the growth of constant capital (machines and raw material) in the production process leads to an expansion in the overall size of the relative surplus-population. The reasons for this are obvious. The increasingly technological character of production removes more and more laborers from productive activity for longer periods of time. Thus, modern capitalist societies have been required progressively to reduce the number of productive years in a worker's life, defining both young and old as economically superfluous. Especially affected are the unskilled who become more and more expendable as capital expands.

In addition to affecting the general size of the relative surplus-population, the rise of the organic composition of capital leads to an increase in the relative stagnancy of that population. In Marx's original analysis he distinguished between forms of superfluous population that were floating and stagnant. The floating population consists of workers who are "sometimes repelled, sometimes attracted again in greater masses, the number of those employed increasing on the whole, although in a constantly decreasing proportion to the scale of production" (1967:641). From the point of view of capitalist accumulation the floating population offers the greatest economic flexibility and the fewest problems of social control because they are most effectively tied to capital by the "natural laws of production." Unfortunately (for the capitalists at least), these groups come to comprise a smaller and smaller proportion of the relative surplus-population. The increasing specialization of productive activity raises the cost of reproducing labor and heightens the demand for highly skilled and "internally controlled" forms of wage labor (Gorz, 1970). The process through which unskilled workers are alternatively absorbed and expelled from the labor force is thereby impaired, and the relative surplus-population comes to be made up of increasing numbers of persons who are more or less permanently redundant. The boundaries between the "useful" and the "useless" are more clearly delineated, while standards for social disqualification are more liberally defined.

With the growth of monopoly capital, therefore, the relative surplus-population begins to take on the character of a population which is more and more absolute. At the same time, the market becomes a less reliable means of disciplining these populations and the "invisible hand" is more frequently replaced by the "visible fist." The implications for deviance production are twofold: (1) problem populations become gradually more problematic—both in terms of their size and their insensitivity to economic controls, and (2) the resources of the state need to be applied in greater proportion to protect capitalist relations of production and insure the accumulation of capital.

State Capitalism and New Forms of Control

The major problems faced by monopoly capitalism are surplus population and surplus production. Attempts to solve these problems have led to the creation of the welfare/warfare state (Baran and Sweezy, 1966; Marcuse, 1964; O'Connor, 1973; Gross, 1970). The warfare state attacks the problem of overconsumption by providing "wasteful" consumption and protection for the expansion of foreign markets. The welfare state helps absorb and deflect social expenses engendered by a redundant domestic population. Accordingly, the economic development of capitalist societies has come to depend increasingly on the support of the state.

The emergence of state capitalism and the growing interpenetration of the political and economic spheres have had a number of implications for the organization and administration of class rule. The most important effect of these trends is that control functions are increasingly transferred from the organs of civil society to the organs of political society (the state). As the maintenance of social harmony becomes more difficult and the contradictions of civil society intensify, the state is forced to take a more direct and extensive role in the management of problem populations.

This is especially true to the extent that the primary socializing institutions in capitalist societies (e.g. the family and the church) can no longer be counted on to produce obedient and "productive" citizens.

Growing state intervention, especially intervention in the process of socialization, is likely to produce an emphasis on general-preventive (integrative), rather than selective-reactive (segregative) controls. Instead of waiting for troublemakers to surface and managing them through segregative techniques, the state is likely to focus more and more on generally applied incentives and assimilative controls. This shift is consistent with the growth of state capitalism because, on the one hand, it provides mechanisms and policies to nip disruptive influences "in the bud," and, on the other, it paves the way toward a more rational exploitation of human capital. Regarding the latter point, it is clear that effective social engineering depends more on social investment and anticipatory planning than coercive control, and societies may more profitably manage populations by viewing them as human capital, than as human waste. An investment orientation has long been popular in state socialist societies (Rimlinger, 1961, 1966), and its value, not surprisingly, has been increasingly acknowledged by many capitalist states.[6]

In addition to the advantages of integrative controls, segregative measures are likely to fall into disfavor for a more immediate reason—they are relatively costly to formulate and apply. Because of its fiscal problems the state must search for means of economizing control operations without jeopardizing capitalist expansion. Segregative handling, especially institutionalization, has been useful in manipulating and providing a receptacle for social junk and social dynamite. Nonetheless, the per capita cost of this type of management is typically quite high. Because of its continuing reliance on segregative controls the state is faced with a growing crisis—the overproduction of deviance. The magnitude of the problem and the inherent weaknesses of available approaches tend to limit the alternatives, but among those which are likely to be favored in the future are:

(1) *Normalization*. Perhaps the most expedient response to the overproduction of deviance is the normalization of populations traditionally managed as deviant. Normalization occurs when deviance processing is reduced in scope without supplying specific alternatives, and certain segments of the problem population are "swept under the rug." To be successful this strategy requires the creation of invisible deviants who can be easily absorbed into society and disappear from view.

A current example of this approach is found in the decarceration movement which has reduced the number of inmates in prisons (BOP, 1972) and mental hospitals (NIMH, 1970) over the last fifteen years. By curtailing commitments and increasing turn-over rates the state is able to limit the scale and increase the efficiency of institutionalization. If, however, direct release is likely to focus too much attention on the shortcomings of the state a number of intermediate solutions can be adopted. These include subsidies for private control arrangements (e.g. foster homes, old age homes) and decentralized control facilities (e.g. community treatment centers, halfway houses). In both cases, the fiscal burden of the state is reduced while the dangers of complete normalization are avoided.

(2) *Conversion*. To a certain extent the expenses generated by problem and deviant populations can be offset by encouraging their direct participation in the pro-

cess of control. Potential troublemakers can be recruited as policemen, social workers and attendants, while confirmed deviants can be "rehabilitated" by becoming counselors, psychiatric aides and parole officers. In other words, if a large number of the controlled can be converted into a first line of defense, threats to the system of class rule can be transformed into resources for its support.[7]

(3) *Containment.* One means of responding to threatening populations without individualized manipulation is through a policy of containment or compartmentalization. This policy involves the geographic segregation of large populations and the use of formal and informal sanctions to circumscribe the challenges that they present. Instead of classifying and handling problem populations in terms of the specific expenses that they create, these groups are loosely administered as a homogeneous class who can be ignored or managed passively as long as they remain in their place.

Strategies of containment have always flourished where social segregation exists, but they have become especially favored in modern capitalist societies. One reason for this is their compatibility with patterns of residential segregation, ghettoization, and internal colonialism (Blauner, 1969).

(4) *Support of Criminal Enterprise.* Another way the overproduction of deviance may be eased is by granting greater power and influence to organized crime. Although predatory criminal enterprise is assumed to stand in opposition to the goals of the state and the capitalist class, it performs valuable and unique functions in the service of class rule (McIntosh, 1973). By creating a parallel opportunity structure, organized crime provides a means of support for groups who might otherwise become a burden on the state. The activities of organized crime are also important in the pacification of problem populations. Organized crime provides goods and services which ease the hardships and deflect the energies of the underclass. In this role the "crime industry" performs a cooling-out function and offers a control resource which might otherwise not exist. Moreover, insofar as criminal enterprise attempts to reduce uncertainty and risk in its operations, it aids the state in the maintenance of public order. This is particularly true to the extent that the rationalization of criminal activity reduces the collateral costs (i.e. violence) associated with predatory crime (Schelling, 1967).

Conclusion

A Marxian theory of deviance and control must overcome the weaknesses of both conventional interpretations and narrow critical models. It must offer a means of studying deviance which fully exploits the critical potential of Marxist scholarship. More than "demystifying" the analysis of deviance, such a theory must suggest directions and offer insights which can be utilized in the direct construction of critical theory. Although the discussion has been informed by concepts and evidence drawn from a range of Marxist studies, it has been more of a sensitizing essay than a substantive analysis. The further development of the theory must await the accumulation of evidence to refine our understanding of the relationships and tendencies explored. When this evidence is developed the contributions of Marxist thought can be more meaningfully applied to an understanding of deviance, class conflict and social control.

References

Baran, Paul, and Paul M. Sweezy. 1966. Monopoly Capital. New York; Monthly Review Press.

Becker, Howard S. 1967. "Whose side are we on?" Social Problems 14 (Winter): 239–247.

Becker, Howard S., and Irving Louis Horowitz. 1972. "Radical politics and sociological research: observations on methodology and ideology." American Journal of Sociology 78 (July): 48–66.

Blauner, Robert. 1969. "Internal colonialism and ghetto revolt." Social Problems 16 (Spring): 393–408.

Bowles, Samuel. 1973. "Contradictions in United States higher education." Pp. 165–199 in James H. Weaver (ed.), Modern Political Economy: Radical Versus Orthodox Approaches. Boston: Allyn and Bacon.

Bowles, Samuel, and Herbert Gintis. 1972. "I.Q. in the U.S. class structure." Social Policy 3 (November/December): 65–96.

Bureau of Prisons. 1972. National Prisoner Statistics. Prisoners in State and Federal Institutions for Adult Felons. Washington, D.C.: Bureau of Prisons.

Cohen, David K., and Marvin Lazerson. 1972. "Education and the corporate order." Socialist Revolution (March/April): 48–72.

Foucault, Michel. 1965. Madness and Civilization. New York: Random House.

Frankford, Evelyn, and Ann Snitow. 1972. "The trap of domesticity: notes on the family." Socialist Revolution (July/August): 83–94.

Gintis, Herbert. 1973. "Alienation and power." Pp. 431–465 in James H. Weaver (ed.), Modern Political Economy: Radical Versus Orthodox Approaches. Boston: Allyn and Bacon.

Gorz, Andre. 1970. "Capitalist relations of production and the socially necessary labor force." Pp. 155–171 in Arthur Lothstein (ed.), All We Are Saying... New York: G. P. Putnam.

Gross, Bertram M. 1970. "Friendly fascism: a model for America." Social Policy (November/December): 44–52.

Helmer, John, and Thomas Vietorisz. 1973. "Drug use, the labor market and class conflict." Paper presented at Annual Meeting of the American Sociological Association.

Karier, Clarence J. 1973. "Business values and the educational state." Pp. 6–29 in Clarence J. Karier, Paul Violas, and Joel Spring (eds.), Roots of Crisis: American Education in the Twentieth Century. Chicago: Rand McNally.

Liazos, Alexander. 1972. "The poverty of the sociology of deviance: nuts, sluts and preverts." Social Problems 20 (Summer): 103–120.

Mandel, Ernest. 1968. Marxist Economic Theory (Volume I). New York: Monthly Review Press.

Marcuse, Herbert. 1964. One-Dimensional Man. Boston: Beacon Press.

Marx, Karl. 1964. Class Struggles in France 1848–1850. New York: International Publishers.

———. 1967. Capital (Volume I). New York: International Publishers.

Matza, David. 1969. Becoming Deviant. Englewood Cliffs: Prentice-Hall.

McIntosh, Mary. 1973. "The growth of racketeering." Economy and Society (February): 35–69.

Morris, Norval, and Gordon Hawkins. 1969. The Honest Politician's Guide to Crime Control. Chicago: University of Chicago Press.

Musto, David F. 1973. The American Disease: Origins of Narcotic Control. New Haven: Yale University Press.

National Institute of Mental Health. 1970. Trends in Resident Patients—State and County Mental Hospitals, 1950–1968. Biometry Branch, Office of Program Planning and Evaluation. Rockville, Maryland: National Institute of Mental Health.

O'Connor, James. 1973. The Fiscal Crisis of the State. New York: St. Martin's Press.

Piven, Frances, and Richard A. Cloward. 1971. Regulating the Poor: The Functions of Public Welfare. New York: Random House.

Rimlinger, Gaston V. 1961. "Social security, incentives, and controls in the U.S. and U.S.S.R."

Comparison Studies in Society and History 4(November): 104–124.

———. 1966. "Welfare policy and economic development: a comparative historical perspective." Journal of Economic History (December): 556–571.

Schelling, Thomas. 1967. "Economics and criminal enterprise." Public Interest (Spring): 61–78.

Secombe, Wally. 1973. "The housewife and her labour under capitalism." New Left Review (January–February): 3–24.

Spring, Joel. 1972. Education and the Rise of the Corporate State. Boston: Beacon Press.

———. 1973. "Education as a form of social control." Pp. 30–39 in Clarence J. Karier, Paul Violas, and Joel Spring (eds.), Roots of Crisis: American Education in the Twentieth Century. Chicago: Rand McNally.

Turk, Austin T. 1969. Criminality and Legal Order. Chicago: Rand McNally.

Zaretsky, Eli. 1973. "Capitalism, the family and personal life: parts 1 & 2." Socialist Revolution (January–April/May–June): 69–126, 19–70.

Notes

1. Revised version of a paper presented at the American Sociological Association meetings, August, 1975. I would like to thank Cecile Sue Coren and Andrew T. Scull for their criticisms and suggestions.

2. For example, Turk (1969) defines deviance primarily in terms of the social position and relative power of various social groups.

3. To the extent that a group (e.g. homosexuals) blatantly and systematically challenges the validity of the bourgeois family it is likely to become part of the problem population. The family is essential to capitalist society as a unit for consumption, socialization and the reproduction of the socially necessary labor force (cf. Frankford and Snitow, 1972; Secombe, 1973; Zaretsky, 1973).

4. O'Connor (1973) discusses this problem in terms of the crisis faced by the capitalist state in maintaining conditions for profitable accumulation and social harmony.

5. It has been estimated, for instance, that 1/3 of all arrests in America are for the offense of public drunkenness. Most of these apparently involve "sick" and destitute "skid row alcoholics" (Morris and Hawkins, 1969).

6. Despite the general tendencies of state capitalism, its internal ideological contradictions may actually frustrate the adoption of an investment approach. For example, in discussing social welfare policy Rimlinger (1966:571) concludes that "in a country like the United States, which has a strong individualistic heritage, the idea is still alive that any kind of social protection has adverse productivity effects. A country like the Soviet Union, with a centrally planned economy and a collectivist ideology, is likely to make an earlier and more deliberate use of health and welfare programs for purposes of influencing productivity and developing manpower."

7. In his analysis of the lumpenproletariat Marx (1964) clearly recognized how the underclass could be manipulated as a "bribed tool of reactionary intrigue."

A Conflict Theory of Criminal Law

JOSEPH F. SHELEY

Although not all conflict models are alike, three themes cut across all models: (1) the relativity of criminal definitions, (2) the role of control of major social institutions in maintaining interests, and (3) the definition of law (legislation and enforcement) as an instrument of power.

Criminal Definitions as Relative

Basically, the conflict perspective argues that no act or individual is intrinsically moral or immoral, criminal or noncriminal. If a criminal label is attached to an act or person, there is an underlying reason—such definitions serve some interests within society. If these labels are tied to interests, then they are subject to change as interests change. Thus, every definition of an act as immoral, deviant, or criminal (or the converse) must be viewed as tentative, always subject to redefinition.

Prime examples of the definition-redefinition process are seen in our perpetually changing attitudes, laws, and law enforcement patterns concerning "vices." Several states, for example, have decriminalized certain sexual acts between consenting adults. At one time, possession of marijuana was legal in this country; currently, it is not, though the debate over whether it should be continues. Abortion, once illegal, has been granted a status of legality that is challenged constantly. Gambling once was illegal in Atlantic City, New Jersey; it is now legal. Prostitution is legal in certain counties in Nevada, but outlawed elsewhere in the state as well as in all other states. Being the customer of a prostitute likewise is legal in some states but not in others. For all of these acts, we may wonder which definition reflects their "true" quality or nature: evil (illegal) or good (legal). In practice, we must treat current meanings as "truth," for they are the meanings employed in a court of law. From a conflict perspective, however, we soon realize that nothing is inherently sacred or sacrilegious—all definitions are subject to change.

Some may argue that the emphasis of the conflict perspective on the relativity of moral and legal definitions is demonstrated easily with respect to vices, about which there is little societal consensus, but may not apply so easily to acts that seem uniformly defined by most people over time. For example, cannot murder be called intrinsically wrong if nearly everyone considers it to be and has done so for a very long time?

From Joseph F. Sheley, "A Conflict Theory of Criminal Law." In *Criminology: A Contemporary Handbook* (Belmont, Calif.: Wadsworth Publishing Company, 1991), pp. 21–39 (with deletions).

The conflict theorist likely will counter that universal acceptance of a criminal definition, even over a long period of time, may be mere coincidence. Whether or not universally accepted, a criminal definition almost certainly has its origins in the protection of some power group's interests. And the definition certainly need not be permanent. Radical structural changes such as those created by a severe famine or cultural changes like those fomented in Nazi Germany in the 1930s could cause changes in the value placed on human life. Further, the conflict theorist might argue that definitions of homicide currently are being negotiated. Continual legislative and courtroom debates over the legal status of abortion and euthanasia are, at heart, debates about the limits of acceptable life-taking versus criminal homicide. The same holds true for the fight over capital punishment. Finally, history suggests that a revolutionary political assassin's status as hero or murderer depends on the success of the revolution, not on the intrinsic value of the act of assassination.

Control of Institutions

Conflict theorists argue that there are three basic means of maintaining and enhancing interests in a society: force, compromise, and dominance of social institutions. Force is the least desirable, for it calls attention directly to interest preservation and basically dares others to summon enough counterforce to alter the power structure. Compromise is preferred, because all parties involved somehow benefit; yet, compromise still carries liabilities. The granting of concessions indicates the absence of absolute power in the hands of any one interest group. It points up the weaknesses of certain parties and encourages others to organize further to exploit those weaknesses.

The strongest mechanism for gaining or holding power is dominance of social institutions. Control of such institutions as the law, religion, education, government, economics, and science means control of the world views of members of society, especially regarding questions of interests and power. With respect to the problem of crime and criminals, control of legal institutions means that more powerful groups gain legal support for their interests by outlawing behavior and attitudes that threaten them or by focusing attention away from their own wrongdoings. Control of other institutions, such as religion and education, is used to promote the interests of the more powerful by shaping the opinions of the less powerful concerning the legitimacy of the economic, political, and legal status quo. For example, we note, without arguing its validity, that the religious belief that rewards in the afterlife await those who suffer in this life serves to discourage this life's less powerful from more aggressively seeking the earthly rewards now in the hands of the more powerful. Similarly, an examination of textbooks used in most of our public and private elementary and secondary schools indicates how rarely serious questions are raised concerning the unequal distribution of wealth and power in this society. It should be noted that control of such institutions often exceeds mere instrumental use of them. Instead, the powerful, who control world views, also have their own world views shaped by these same institutions. Their efforts to shape law reflect not only perceptions of interests but a whole value set that labels such interests inherently right and necessary to the health of the collectivity.

Law as an Instrument of Power

Whereas consensus theorists view law as an institution expressing common societal values and controlled by the majority in society, conflict theorists view law as an instrument of control or, in Turk's (1976) words, "a weapon in social conflict." Whoever owns the law owns power. Those who own it fight to keep it; those who want it fight to get it. Indeed, Turk argues, rather than simply reducing conflict, law also produces it by virtue of its status as a resource to be won by some combatants and lost by others. This point is illustrated by the importance given to nominations of Supreme Court justices. Presidents attempt to fill court vacancies with persons sympathetic to their views—that is, with persons more likely to decide cases in a manner protecting the interests of a given president and the parties that president represents.

The value of law as an instrument of power should be quite evident. Most obviously, control of the legal order represents the ability to use specified agents of force to protect one's interests. Beyond this, Turk notes that decisions concerning economic power are made and enforced through law; that is, control of the legislature represents control of the process that determines in part the distribution of economic rewards through such vehicles as tax laws. Further, control of the legal process means control of the organization of governmental decisions in general—decisions concerning the structure of public education, for example. Control of the law aids in determining much of culture; law legitimizes "right" views of the world and delegitimizes "wrong" views. Finally, Turk points out that the attention commanded by the workings of law (police, trials, and so forth) serves to divert attention from more deeply rooted problems of power distribution and interest maintenance. In sum, as Quinney (1970:13) suggests, laws that forbid particular behaviors and make others mandatory are passed by legislators who have gained office through the backing of various interest groups. The ability to have one's interests translated into public policy is a primary indicator of power.

If law is an instrument sought after and employed by powerful interest groups to enhance their position in society, and if criminal law forbids certain acts, we can reasonably define *crime* as acts perceived by those in power as direct or indirect threats to their interests. Conflict theorists note that most of our current criminal law derives directly from English common law. Jeffrey (1957) argues that acts such as murder, theft, and robbery, once considered dispute problems to be settled within or between families, became crimes against the state (wrongs against society) when Henry II, king of England, attempted to centralize his power in a politically divided country by declaring them wrongs against the crown. Hall (1952) has traced theft laws in their present form to their origin in the change from a feudal economy to a capitalist-mercantile economy. As a new economic class of traders and industrialists developed, the need to protect their business interests grew.... The conflict theorists' point is that our definitions of crime have their roots less in general beliefs about right and wrong than in perceived threats to groups with the power to legislate their interests.

Control of Law Enforcement

Law enforcement patterns as well as legislation reflect the attempts of the more powerful to protect their interests. Yeager (1987) notes the tendency of the U.S. Environmental Protection Agency to focus on smaller rather than larger firms when enforcing its regulations.... Likewise, Pontell et al. (1982) note the manner in which the structure of the medical profession thwarts efforts to police physicians' fraud and abuse.

Turning to the issue of street crime, Jacobs (1979:914) writes:

> The more there are inequalities in the distribution of economic power and economic resources, the more one can expect that the social control apparatus of the state will conform to the preferences of monied elites. In this society, the major institution responsible for the coercive maintenance of stability and order is the police.

Jacobs argues that the greater the economic differences in a community, the more likely poorer community members are to attempt forcefully to alter the inequality. Thus, economic elites utilize the police for protection and as a general stabilizer within a community. Jacobs's analysis of police strength in metropolitan areas appears to support his thesis: Law enforcement personnel are more numerous in metropolitan areas where economic inequality is most pronounced.

In the same vein, Liska et al. (1981) report that following civil disorders in the South in the 1950s, 1960s, and early 1970s, whites in cities with larger percentages of nonwhite residents and less residential segregation perceived chances of crime victimization to be greater whether or not actual crime rates changed. Hence, the more powerful whites demanded and received greater police protection....To the extent that black population and political mobilization increased in cities in the late 1960s and early 1970s, cities' expenditures on police services increased—regardless of their crime rates. The authors conclude that police expenditures are a resource that is mobilized when minority groups appear to threaten the political and economic position of more dominant groups. They therefore echo Silver's (1967) characterization of the police as a mechanism designed to control "dangerous classes" in a way that protects wealthier classes, but does so in a manner not directly orchestrated by the wealthy. That is, police protect the wealthy while appearing to protect the poor as well—all under a "war on crime" umbrella....Though essentially agreeing with Marxian theorists that legislation and law enforcement have their roots in group conflict, another cadre of conflict theorists offers a broader explanation of the legal process. *Pluralist theorists* argue that the legal process is not controlled by one specific interest group, but emerges from or is shaped by the conflicting interests of a multiplicity of groups, all seeking something different from a given legal issue. The object of conflict is not always economic interest; it may also reflect status concerns and moral and ideological commitments. Hence, much of what occurs in legal conflicts is symbolic rather than purely instrumental.

Pluralist theories have their roots in historical studies of the process by which issues are contested and resolved rather than in identification of specific key parties involved in conflict (a theme pursued by Marxian theorists). Although pluralists recognize the unequal distribution of wealth and power in this society and its importance in the negotiation of conflict, they do not accord it the degree of significance that Marxian theorists do. Like Marxian theorists, pluralists consider conflict ongoing and ever-changing as new groups vie for power and as groups in power err through oversight, misdefinition of the situation, and miscalculation of policy effects. Like the Marxian approach, the pluralist approach stresses the importance of gaining and preserving power through control of the world view of groups whose explicit or implicit support is required. Pluralists also vary in the degree to which they believe the state has become an autonomous, interested party in the conflict process rather than simply a sought-after resource.

Multiple Interest Groups

Pluralists view society as composed partly of groups with varying awareness of their interests, and who organize to differing degrees to maintain and enhance these interests, and partly of groups unaware of their interests and, therefore, unorganized. Although more organized groups vary in their power to benefit themselves, none is so well organized that it enjoys total freedom to promote its interests. Power relationships and, therefore, the positions of interest groups in the power structure continually are subject to threat of change as groups increase or decrease in awareness and organizational might. New groups constantly are becoming conscious of and organizing around their interests and are posing threats to the traditional power structure (the women's movement is a recent clear case in point). All powerful groups require the support of other powerful groups above and below them in the power hierarchy. Further, no group can afford to arouse direct opposition from the unorganized; failure to placate this latter group may lead to discontent, which in turn breeds awareness of interests and leads to organized threats to the status quo. This same unorganized group also provides a pool of potential support for the various organized and organizing groups....

State Agents

No law exists in a vacuum. Every law represents the intersection of interests of many groups, some cutting across socioeconomic classes. Among interested parties, many pluralists argue, are groups (or agencies) within the state. Legislators themselves have career interests in the legislation they initiate. The creation of laws necessitates the creation of law enforcers (regulatory bureaus, prosecutor's offices, police departments, and so on). Once formed, law enforcement agencies themselves become interest groups whose existence may be threatened by other groups' attempts to decriminalize the behaviors they police, or strengthened through their own attempts to expand the realm of activities they monitor and the procedural powers needed for monitoring. Hence, law enforcement lobbies and public relations divisions attempt to sway legislators and public opinion to preserve or strengthen laws against such activities as drug use, prostitution, homosexuality, and gambling.

Ideological Interests

Pluralists note that the multiplicity of groups involved in a given legislative conflict often indicates a variety of *types* of interest in a given issue. The most obvious of these are economic concerns: Certain groups may stand to lose or to gain economically if a given law is enacted. For example, the passage of antipollution laws clearly threatens some corporate economic interests. Laws allowing attorneys to advertise and set their own fee schedules threaten the economic interests of certain established law firms, but enhance the economic interests of other law firms as well as the general public.

Ideological concerns also influence law, in that laws often express political and moral values. The antipollution laws mentioned above may reflect the political ideologies of groups who believe corporations should be held accountable for the condition of the environment that they in part shape. Laws governing freedom to protest politically obviously are political in nature. The abortion issue now contested in the political arena is largely a moral issue.

Related to the ideology question is the issue of status in the legal process. Certain groups obtain sufficient power to define in large part the character of our culture (the degree to which it is a religious or a secular culture, for example). Some are able to maintain that powerful status, while others lose it and new groups gain it. Thus, the passage of a given law may reflect the rising or falling sociopolitical fortunes of these various groups. The study by Zurcher et al. (1971) of antipornography campaigns, for example, indicates that those opposing pornography are fighting for a change in lifestyle or social climate, that is, for the power to define the cultural character of their particular region. The outcome of such a campaign is, therefore, a comment on the sociopolitical status of these crusaders.

Of course, in line with the pluralist's view of intersecting types of interests, it must be pointed out that the economic interests of producers and sellers of pornography also are at stake in such campaigns. Similarly, those strongly opposed to censorship have an ideological interest in the issue. Local politicians—district attorneys, legislators, and so on—may also be party to an antipornography campaign in order to better their election interests. Finally, we should note that status interests at stake in legislation need not involve large groups of persons or status within the larger society. Pfohl (1977), for example, traces modern child abuse laws to the attempt of pediatric radiologists, a low-status specialty group in medicine, to carve out their own sphere of influence within medicine. Rather than working in an area of specialization supplementary to that of the pediatrician, pediatric radiologists now can enhance their status by becoming partners with pediatricians and psychiatrists in the fight against an important illness syndrome.

Symbolism

The ideological and status interests behind some laws call attention to an important issue in most pluralist theories: *symbolic interests*. Often, the surface issue that is contested is less important to the parties involved than is some underlying, broader issue. Underlying issues cannot always be contested directly in legislatures and courts, because they may be too vague to state in legal terms. Instead, some more specific issue, perhaps only loosely tied to the underlying conflict, often becomes symbolic of the contest, mapping out an arena where it can be fought. At times, the groups involved are concerned only with legislation. They care not whether a law can be or is enforced (though the enforcement issue eventually may become symbolic as well); but only that their view of social, moral, or economic order be given the sacred stamp of the law.

Galliher and Cross (1983) provide an excellent illustration of the symbolic theme in their analysis of Nevada's penalty for possession of marijuana. The state's residents feel the need to convince the outside world, and perhaps themselves, that theirs is not a lawless and immoral world despite the fact that it permits casino gambling, prostitution, and "quicky" marriages and divorces. Further, the state wishes to show the federal government that it can control unwanted consequences of its liberal laws, such as the intrusion of organized crime. Nevada's tough marijuana law addresses both needs. Nevada is the only state in which first-offense possession of even the smallest quantity of the drug constitutes a felony punishable by up to six years in prison. Yet, Galliher and Cross point out that the law seldom is enforced. They argue that its presence on the books signifies less a desire to stamp out marijuana than a symbolic statement to the outside world concerning Nevada's lawfulness and moral character.

Influencing Legal Outcomes

Within the pluralist model of the creation of law, the goal of any given group seeking to maintain or enhance its interests is to influence legislators to write laws and law enforcers to administer laws as the interest group sees fit. Because legislators and law enforcement officials are political beings whose jobs depend on a satisfied constituency, an interest group's immediate aim is to bring constituency pressure to bear upon the officeholder to the extent necessary to accomplish the desired outcome. Thus, an interest group must sway a public that is indifferent or hostile to a position to accept that position as valid and to pressure its political representatives to legitimate it.

Social identity clearly plays a key role in swaying public opinion. Discredited individuals and groups find it difficult to gain a sympathetic ear, whereas prominent and "legitimate" persons (for example, scientific experts and religious leaders) more easily capture an audience. Those attempting to reverse a criminal stigma—that is, to alter the public's definition of a given practice, such as marijuana use or prostitution—find the task extremely difficult, for they appear to have a self-serving interest in changing the public's mind.

Assuming equal social respectability among interested parties in a contest to influence the legal process, the decisive factor is the propaganda effort. Quality of organization and resources utilized in capturing media attention and in directing public sentiment to lawmakers and law enforcers are extremely telling variables. Interest groups attempt to employ symbols of the problem at hand—definitions and pictures of the problem and the people implicated in it that easily capture the public imagination. Thus, stereotypes are promoted (of the drug user, the rapist, the psychopath, the pornographer, and so forth) that fit the general public conception of evil and danger. Edelman (1977:14) argues that the ability to create a "personified" danger—that is, to put a face to the problem even if that face is in reality only a mask—"marshals public support for controls over a much larger number of ambiguous cases symbolically condensed into the threatening stereotype."

Vocabularies also are created that subtly (and at times not so subtly) seek to influence the public (Edelman, 1977:26). For example, proabortion groups choose to characterize themselves as "prochoice," while antiabortion groups label themselves "prolife." Homosexuals present themselves as "gay," while their opponents call them "perverts" (Spector and Kitsuse, 1977:13–16). Such tactics accomplish more than simply gaining a public forum for an issue; they transform the issue into a "good versus evil" contest that allows the public more easily to take a stand.

The result of the propaganda activity of groups contesting an issue often is public indignation about a fiction that has emerged from the competitive propaganda process. For the interest groups, the creation is symbolic; for the public, it is real. Gusfield (1981) offers an illustration in his study of "drinking-driving" laws, or laws governing driving under the influence of alcohol. So effective were the "anti-drunk-driver" campaigns by interested parties that the public now equates the image of "drinking driver" with that of "killer." Gusfield argues that this conception is at odds with reality, at least as it is measured by the types of cases brought before the courts, most of which are treated leniently. Gentry (1988) makes the same point in her discussion of the issue of abducted children as a social problem. So skillful were interested parties in framing this issue that the public came to view the "problem" as one of over 50,000 abductions annually of children by strangers. In fact, what evidence exists indicates that kidnappings by strangers total fewer than 100 per year....

Conclusion

In sum, the conflict perspective seems to address more aggressively and more convincingly the issue of the workings of the legal process than does the consensus mode. Despite criticisms..., the conflict perspective's basic argument cannot be ignored: Laws do not simply appear miraculously on our law books and do not reflect "society's" values. Instead, the acts and people we call "criminal" and our concern with crime at any given time reflect the activity of groups in this society seeking legal support for economic, ideological, and status interests. Sometimes, only a few groups are involved in the struggle for legal support; other times, many groups compete. The issue contested in a legal struggle may be explicit and instrumental, or it may be symbolic of some greater conflict. The ebb and flow of law reflects the ebb and flow of interest groups, and laws emerging from this process must be viewed as tentative and negotiable. The key issue for conflict theorists, then, concerns the political strength of the major economic interests in this society: Do they stand alone, or do they share power with other, relatively weaker groups?

References

Edelman, M. 1977. *Political Language*. New York: Academic Press.

Galliher, J. F., and J. R. Cross. 1983. *Moral Legislation Without Morality*. New Brunswick, N.J.: Rutgers University Press.

Gentry, C. 1988. The social construction of abducted children as a social problem. *Sociological Inquiry* 58:413–425.

Gusfield, J. 1981. *The Culture of Public Problems*. Chicago: University of Chicago Press.

Hall, J. 1952. *Theft, Law and Society*. 2nd ed. Indianapolis, Ind.: Bobbs-Merrill.

Jacobs, D. 1979. Inequality and police strength: Conflict theory and coercive control in metropolitan areas. *American Sociological Review* 44:913–925.

Jeffrey, C. R. 1957. The development of crime in early English society. *Journal of Criminology, Law, Criminology, and Police Science* 47:647–666.

Liska, A., J. Laurence, and M. Benson. 1981. Perspectives on the legal order: The capacity for social control. *American Journal of Sociology* 87:413–426.

Pfohl, S. 1977. The 'discovery' of child abuse. *Social Problems* 24:310–324.

Pontell, H. N., P. D. Jesilow, and G. Geis. 1982. Policing physicians: Practitioner fraud and abuse in a government medical program. *Social Problems* 30:117–125.

Quinney, R. 1970. *The Social Reality of Crime*. Boston: Little, Brown.

Silver, A. 1967. The demand for law and order in civil society: A review of some themes in the history of urban crime, police and riots. In *The Police*, D. Bordua (ed.). New York: Wiley.

Spector, M., and J. I. Kitsuse. 1975. *Constructing Social Problems*. Menlo Park, Calif.: Cummings.

Turk, A. 1976. Law as a weapon in social conflict. *Social Problems* 23:276–291.

Yeager, P. C. 1987. Structural bias in regulatory law enforcement: The case of the U.S. Environmental Protection Agency. *Social Problems* 34:330–344.

Zurcher, L. A., R. George, R. G. Cushing, et al. 1971. The anti-pornography campaign: A symbolic crusade. *Social Problems* 19:217–238.

Chapter 8

Feminism and the New Sociology of Social Control

Much of the way intellectuals and social scientists have viewed the world until the past generation, roughly the past twenty-five years or so, is through an *androcentric* perspective, that is, a male-centered approach. Until fairly recently, men were seen as the center of the universe. Perhaps the most remarkable intellectual change that has taken place in the past generation or so has been an assault against this biased view of reality. Much of the intellectual discourse that has taken place over that period has addressed this crucial point: Men are *not* the center of the universe; women are more than half the human race, and what women do is no less important than what men do; pretending that men are the center of the universe has warped and distorted our vision of reality; women are oppressed by a perpetuation of this archaic androcentric view of the world. In the past, feminists say, there has been a systematic effort to misrepresent women's role in society and keep women relatively powerless and marginal.

In a like fashion, the field of the sociology of deviance and crime, until the past generation, has been marked by the same androcentric bias that has put males into the center of the picture. This does not mean that every single man has produced work that adopted an androcentric approach. Millman (1975) points to the work of Erving Goffman (1961, 1963) as being contrary to that tendency—a man who adopted an approach to deviance that put women as coparticipants with men in the center of the picture. Nor does it mean that every female criminologist in the past has developed, or will or can be expected to develop, a feminist view of deviance and crime. For instance, Millman (1975) argues that Mary Owen Cameron's book (1964) on shoplifting is lacking in the compassion and empathy necessary to the emergence of a feminist approach to deviance and crime.

Thus, as Millman points out, one need not go to extremes to recognize the basic fact that women, taken as a whole, are going to generate a sociology of deviance and crime that is likely to be a bit different from that which has been developed in the past by a previously male-dominated field. Likewise, an androcentric approach may or may not be wrong in every specific detail, but it is consistently biased. In the words of Simone de Beauvoir (1953), traditionally, men have been the *subject,* women have been looked at as "the other." In the study of deviance and crime, men's crime is crime in general; women's crime is specific and unique to women. What would the picture look like if men were no longer center stage, the point of reference, the filter through which all reality is viewed? What would the world look like if men had to share the stage with women? What would a feminist sociology of deviance and crime look like?

It is almost inconceivable that there will ever be *a* feminist criminology or *a* feminist sociology of deviance (Daly and Chesney-Lind, 1988). Instead, what is extremely likely is that previously androcentric approaches will be revised in light of critiques from several distinct and somewhat different, more or less feminist approaches. The hegemony or dominance of androcentrism will decline for Western intellectual discourse generally, for sociology more specifically, and even more specifically for the sociology of deviance and crime, as a result of this challenge from feminism. This is certainly one of the twentieth-century's most profound cultural and intellectual contributions to the future: the decline of androcentrism and the rise of a more female-centered, and therefore more balanced, approach to the study of society.

Although there are many feminisms, and not simply one, perhaps the central assumption on which all feminisms can agree is that "women experience subordination on the basis of their sex" (Gelsthorpe and Morris, 1988, p. 224). And if three points could be distilled from a feminist orientation to deviance and crime, it would be these.

First, in the past, and even to a certain degree today, women have represented a minor theme in writings on deviance. They have been studied less, appeared less often as subjects of attention, remained marginal, secondary, almost invisible. The study of women and deviance suffers from "a problem of omission"; women have been "largely overlooked in the literature" (Millman, 1975, p. 265). As Heidensohn has pointed out (1968), yes, it is true that women commit deviance and crime less often than men, but not to the degree that would be indicated by their virtual exclusion from the literature.

Second, the substantially smaller literature that has looked at women's deviance reflects "a male-biased view" (Millman, 1975, p. 265). Not only was the deviance of women less often studied, but when it was it was nearly always highly *specialized* deviance. For instance, in a chapter entitled "The Criminality of Women," which appeared in a textbook that was eventually published in multiple editions, Walter Reckless (1950, p. 116) argued that the criminal behavior of women should not be considered "in the same order of phenomena as crime in general," meaning the criminal behavior of men. The three, specialized, forms of female deviance that have been examined to some extent by the field have been shoplifting, mental illness, and prostitution.

And third, until recently, the role of women as *victims* of crime and deviance has been underplayed. This is especially the case with respect to rape, domestic assault, and sexual harassment. It was not until the 1970s, when feminist scholarship and research began a systematic examination of the ways women are brutalized and exploited by men, that deviant and criminal activities such as rape (Brownmiller, 1975), wife battering (Martin, 1976), and sexual harassment (MacKinnon, 1979) found a significant place in the literature on deviance, and crime and the suffering inflicted on women at the hands of men were given significant attention. (In fact, some feminists even argued that these practices were so traditional, entrenched, and unpunished that they do not deserve to be referred to as *deviant* behavior at all!) In short, women victims of crime have been "hidden from history" (Summers, 1981).

A generation ago, the feminist approach to deviance and crime did not exist; the perspective is young and still in the process of development. Incomplete as the approach is, it shows great promise to enrich and inform the discipline. No field that treats the behavior of less than half the population as if it were behavior in general can claim to be adequate or valid. The fields of criminology and the sociology of deviance have a long way to go before they fully incorporate the insights of feminism into the way they look at their subject matter. At the same time, feminism may have a more revolutionary impact on the field than that of any of any other perspective we've examined. Feminism forces us to think about sex biases and how they distort our views of deviance, crime, the law, and the criminal justice system. These biases are deep and pervasive. Confronting and overcoming them makes us better sociologists, criminologists, and students of deviants, and perhaps more capable of changing society for the better (Goode, 1994, p. 131).

As with Marxism, the feminist approach to deviance and crime has a second mode as well, a causal or etiological mode. The forms of crime that entail violence against women, feminists argue, are a product of patriarchal society; they maintain a system in which women are repressed and kept in their place. According to this line of reasoning, crimes such as wife beating, sexual harassment, and rape serve a political function for the system as a whole and not merely for the individual men who perpetrate them. Rape and other violent crimes against women represent dominance and control by men over women; they ensure that demands for sexual equality are undermined and silenced (Brownmiller, 1975; Messerschmidt, 1986, pp. 43–44). Such claims are extremely difficult to document; it is not even clear what manner of evidence could be presented that would demonstrate such an argument. Nonetheless, some feminists argue that criminal behavior, like definitions of crime and deviance, supports and maintains the existing system of patriarchy. What causes a particular form of deviance—violence against women—feminists ask. *Patriarchy* causes violence against women.

The approach that focuses *least* on etiology, or the causes of deviance, and *most* on social control itself is called *the new sociology of social control.* (Any approach that refers to itself as a "new" anything is doomed to failure in nomenclature; with the passage of enough time, nothing seems new anymore.) The new sociology of social control takes as its inspiration the writings of the French philosopher Michel Foucault (1926–1984). In his most influential work, *Discipline and Punish* (1979), Foucault argued that modern society, in casting aside brutal measures to punish offenders such as torture and public execution, adopted techniques of social control that were ultimately even more effective and repressive. In ancient and medieval society, only the offender's body was punished; in modern society, the offender's mind and soul are invaded, tampered with, altered, suffused, and infected with society's mechanisms of social control. For Foucault, the model or paradigmatic mechanism of modern social control is the prison designed by Jeremy Bentham (1748–1832)—a design that was never built, it must be said—that was called the *panopticon*. In Bentham's panopticon, a small number of guards could monitor a large number of prisoners. To Foucault, the panoptic principle had become generalized to the society as a whole. We live in a society that is bent on observing and controlling its citizens in a wide range of contexts. In a sense, modern society has become one gigantic, monstrous panopticon.

A group of sociologists and other social scientists and philosophers have taken these ideas as their point of departure in their investigation of deviance and social control. As I said, they have been referred to as "the new sociologists of social control" (Scull, 1988, pp. 685–688). Their central points are these.

First, social control should not be treated as a given; it is a phenomenon that must be explained. Social control does not arise from the "need" of a society to protect itself from the danger posed by normative violations, as the functionalists argued; it does not arise "naturally" through some inevitable, invisible forces. Rather, social control results from the conscious efforts of "definable organizations, groups, and classes" (Scull, 1988, p. 686). Punishment is a political tactic practiced by the powerful in their exercise of control over individuals, groups, and categories who make trouble for them.

Second, social control tends to be coercive, repressive, and far from benign; its job is to restrain troublesome populations. The purpose of psychiatry is not to heal but to control; the purpose of the welfare system is not to provide a safety net for the poor but to control; the purpose of education is not to teach but to control; the purpose of the mass media is not to inform but to control; and so on.

Third, social control is coterminous with state or statelike control. A number of organizations, agencies, or institutions are now performing the function of social control on behalf of or in the service of the state. These include social welfare organizations, psychiatrists and psychiatric agencies, professional organizations, hospitals, clinics, mental health organizations, and so on. It is the contention of our new sociologists of social control or "contrologists" that state control has been assumed by civil society; activities and functions that were once performed by the state have been taken over by these seemingly autonomous, often private, organizations, agencies, and institutions. Troublesome populations can now be controlled on a wide range of fronts by a wide range of agencies. Essentially the same clients are circulated and recirculated among them. "The original compact methods of discipline are... being broken up and made more flexible as they circulate into the new 'regional outposts' of the control network" (Cohen, 1985, p. 111).

Fourth and last, the social control apparatus is unified and coherent. The subsystems "fit together" into interrelated, functionally equivalent parts. The phenomenon of interlocking agencies and institutions working to control troublesome populations is referred to as *transcarceration* (Lowman et al., 1987). Foucault argued that the punitive approach has been transferred "from the penal institution to the entire social body" (1979, p. 298). Controlologists point to a "peno-juridical, mental health, welfare and tutelage complex" in which "power structures can be examined only by appreciating cross-institutional arrangements and dynamics" (Lowman et al., 1987, p. 9; Goode, 1994, pp. 134–136).

Not all observers agree that controlology or the new sociology of social control is an adequate or completely valid perspective toward deviance and crime. Its failure to take *informal* social control into account and its corresponding exclusive focus on formal or state and statelike control, must be regarded as a curiously narrow focus. In fact, if informal social control were to be considered, controlologists would have to admit that social control is a great deal more *decentralized* and *democratic* than they care to admit. And the view that the formal social control apparatus captures and processes the overwhelming majority of norm violators is actually quite erroneous; most persons who violate both the informal norms and the criminal law escape detection and are ignored by the social control apparatus. Instead of a systematic, unrelenting system of formal social control—the panoptic principle Foucault thought dominated modern society—what we see is one that is fitful, erratic, and often impotent, one that fails to detect, capture, or punish most deviants. Moreover, to claim that institutions such as the welfare system function exclusively or primarily for the purpose of social control is misleading. Actually, welfare recipients do complain about too much bureaucratic control in their lives, to be sure, but they also complain that not enough resources are expended by the state to assist them as much as they'd like. Welfare workers see themselves not as substitutes for the police but as overwhelmed functionaries who simply cannot deal with the massive problems their clients face. And lastly, controlologists have not seriously or systematically considered what a *realistic* system of social control would look like. It is much easier to criticize than to suggest workable alternatives (Goode, 1994, pp. 136–138).

In "She Did It All for Love," Marcia Millman explains why, traditionally, the sociology of deviance has been a male-centered or androcentric field and what remedies are necessary to correct this bias. Sociologists of deviance have tended to ascribe activism and heroism to their male subjects and ascribe to the women in their lives a passive, restraining role. The forms of deviance in which women deviants participate, in this male-centered sociological world, are far narrower—and far less exciting—than those in which men participate. And in these male-centered descriptions, empathy is reserved for the male subjects, but not the women in them. And victimization and suffering tend to be underplayed in the work of male sociologists but notably present in research by women. Erving Goffman, Millman says, is a rare exception to this rule.

Perhaps the most prominent new sociologist of social control is Stanley Cohen; in "Visions of Social Control," he introduces the perspective to us. What does society do when faced with "people it regards as deviant," he asks. The number of statelike institutions and organizations designed to deal with the deviant is truly staggering, Cohen points out. Far from seeing social control as benevolent, necessary, and a reasonable reaction to harmful behavior, Cohen sees its more repressive and self-serving side. The "deviancy control system" is "something like" a gigantic fishing net, Cohen claims, with fisherfolk (agents of social control) catching and processing fish (the deviants). Cohen is interested in this net and how it functions.

References

Beauvoir, Simone de. 1953. *The Second Sex* (trans. and ed. H. M. Parshley). New York: Alfred Knopf.

Brownmiller, Susan. 1975. *Against Our Will: Men, Women, and Rape*. New York: Simon & Schuster.

Cameron, Mary Owen. 1964. *The Booster and the Snitch*. New York: Free Press.

Cohen, Stanley. 1985. *Visions of Social Control*. London: Polity Press.

Daly, Kathleen, and Meda Chesney-Lind. 1988. Feminism and criminology. *Justice Quarterly,* 5 (December): 497–538.

Foucault, Michel. 1979. *Discipline and Punish* (trans. Alan Sheridan). New York: Vintage Books.

Gelsthorpe, Loraine, and Allison Morris. 1988. Feminism and criminology in Britain. *British Journal of Criminology,* 28 (Spring): 223–240.

Goode, Erich. 1994. *Deviant Behavior.* 4th ed. Englewood Cliffs, N.J.: Prentice-Hall.

Heidensohn, Frances. 1968. The deviance of women: A critique and an enquiry. *British Journal of Sociology,* 12 (2):160–175.

Lowman, John, Robert J. Menzies, and T. S. Palys (eds.). 1987. *Transcarceration: Essays in the Sociology of Social Control*. Gower, England: Aldershot.

MacKinnon, Catherine A. 1979. *Sexual Harassment of Working Women*. New Haven, Conn.: Yale University Press.

Martin, Del. 1976. *Battered Wives*. San Francisco: Glide Publications.

Messerschmidt, James W. 1986. *Capitalism, Patriarchy, and Crime*. Totowa, N.J.: Rowman & Littlefield.

Millman, Marcia. 1975. She did it all for love: A feminist view of the sociology of deviance. In Marcia Millman and Rosabeth Moss Kanter (eds.), *Another Voice: Feminist Perspectives on Social Life and Social Science*. Garden City, N.Y.: Doubleday-Anchor, pp. 251–279.

Reckless, Walter C. 1950. *The Crime Problem*. New York: Appleton-Century-Crofts.

Scull, Andrew. 1988. Deviance and social control. In Neil J. Smelser (ed.), *Handbook of Sociology*. Newbury Park, Calif.: Sage, pp. 667–693.

Summers, Anne. 1981. Hidden from history: Women victims of crime. In Satyanshu K. Mukherjee and Jocelynne A. Scutt (eds.), *Women and Crime*. North Sydney: George Allen & Unwin Australia, pp. 22–30.

Visions of Social Control

STANLEY COHEN

Social control [is] the organized ways in which society responds to behaviour and people it regards as deviant, problematic, worrying, threatening, troublesome or undesirable in some way or another. This response appears under many terms: punishment, deterrence, treatment, prevention, segregation, justice, rehabilitation, reform or social defence. It is accompanied by many ideas and emotions: hatred, revenge, retaliation, disgust, compassion, salvation, benevolence or admiration. The behaviour in question is classified under many headings: crime, delinquency, deviance, immorality, perversity, wickedness, deficiency or sickness. The people to whom the response is directed, are seen variously as monsters, fools, villains, sufferers, rebels or victims. And those who respond (by doing something or by just studying the subject—jobs which are too often confused) are known as judges, policemen, social workers, psychiatrists, psychologists, criminologists or sociologists of deviance....

My aim here is neither to provide a comprehensive textbook-like study of this field nor to argue for a single thesis, explanatory framework, theory, model, political line or personal grievance. I have simply selected what I take to be some key trends in recent Western social control patterns, and used them as a base from which to speculate on issues of wider social concern. Rather than being either descriptive or prescriptive—both fine sociological enterprises—my bias is theoretical and critical....

The term 'social control' has lately become something of a Mickey Mouse concept. In sociology textbooks, it appears as a neutral term to cover all social processes to induce conformity ranging from infant socialization through to public execution. In radical theory and rhetoric, it has become a negative term to cover not just the obviously coercive apparatus of the state, but also the putative hidden element in all state-sponsored social policy, whether called health, education or welfare. Historians and political scientists restrict the concept to the repression of political opposition, while sociologists, psychologists and anthropologists invariably talk in broader and non-political terms. In everyday language, that concept has no resonant or clear meaning at all.

All this creates some terrible muddles. Historians and sociologists are locked in a protracted debate about whether the history of prisons, mental hospitals and the juvenile court can meaningfully be studied in the same framework as the history of the factory and the control of working class resistance to the state. Analysts of social policy spend time in deciding whether this or that measure by the state is 'really' social control. The question is asked, whether teachers in schools, warders in prisons, psychiatrists in clinics, social workers in welfare agencies, parents in families,

From Stanley Cohen, *Visions of Social Control* (Cambridge, England: Polity Press, 1985), pp. 1–8, 40–43 (with deletions). Reprinted by permission of the publisher.

policemen on the streets, and even bosses in the factories are all, after all, busy doing the 'same' thing.

The answer to these fascinating questions is, no doubt, that 'it depends'—it depends on our image of social control and on the purposes of any definition. My own purpose is to classify, assess and criticize some current changes (proposed or actual) and to comment on other similar exercises. This purpose will be served less well by any essentialist definition than simply by mapping out those 'social control matters' which [I] cover.

My interest is in planned and programmed responses to expected and realized deviance rather than in the general institutions of society which produce conformity. I will use the term 'social control', then, to cover matters considerably narrower and more specific than the general sociological/anthropological terrain of all those social processes and methods through which society ensures that its members conform to expectations. These normally include internalization, socialization, education, peer-group pressure, public opinion and the like, as well as the operations of specialized formal agencies such as the police, the law and all other state powers. But I am interested in something a little wider and more general than the restricted criminological terrain of the formal legal-correctional apparatus for,the control of official crime and delinquency. My focus is those organized responses to crime, delinquency and allied forms of deviant and/or socially problematic behaviour which are actually conceived of as such, whether in the reactive sense (after the putative act has taken place or the actor been identified) or in the proactive sense (to prevent the act). These responses may be sponsored directly by the state or by more autonomous professional agents in, say, social work and psychiatry. Their goals might be as specific as individual punishment and treatment or as diffuse as 'crime prevention,' 'public safety' and 'community mental health.'

I will talk about 'deviance' but my material comes mainly from crime control and, moreover, from ordinary 'bread and butter' adult crime and juvenile delinquency rather than such important types as organized, political, white-collar and state crime. Parallel issues arise in the control of drug abuse, mental illness and sexual deviance and where these are particularly relevant, I will draw on this literature. Another way of restricting my scope is to concentrate on certain societies, notably 'liberal capitalist' states such as the USA, Canada, Britain and other Western European countries. These have social control systems embedded in more or less highly developed commitments to 'welfare' and more or less sophisticated ideologies about 'treatment'. These are also the same societies in which these commitments and ideologies have been the object of so much scepticism over the past decade or so.

It is just these shifts in strategy and beliefs that interest me. [I am less interested in providing a description of the social control apparatus as it stands than in monitoring and predicting] their implications for the future: a sociological seismograph to detect fissures, cracks, quakes, tremors and false alarms. The textbook notion of 'correctional change' draws attention to movements of this sort:

> (1) A transformation of the arrangements employed to deal with convicted offenders (for example, the establishment of the penitentiary system); (2) a change in the severity of punishment dispensed to offenders (for example, an increase

in the average length of time offenders spend in confinement); (3) a change in either the numbers or the proportion of convicted offenders dealt with by various components of the correctional system (for example, an increase in prison population or assignment of an increasing number of convicted offenders to pre-trial diversion programmes); and (4) a change in the prevailing ideologies employed to 'explain' or make sense of offenders and their involvement in criminality.[1]

But this is a list of operational changes—shifts that are often too minor and ephemeral to be of much concern to the non-specialist. I am interested in more dramatic and profound movements, the genuine master shifts against those massively entrenched patterns of organized social control associated with the birth of the modern state: attacks on prisons and mental hospitals, the development of alternative forms of community control, attempts to bypass the whole criminal justice system, scepticism about professional competence; disenchantment with the rehabilitative ideal, the development of new forms of intervention and the ideologies which justify them. I will keep returning to the profoundly ambiguous and contradictory nature of these changes.

There are other control patterns, both of change and stability, that also deserve attention: in the form, content and administration of the criminal law; in the nature of civil law and other forms of regulation or conflict resolution; in the organization and techniques of policing. But these subjects I mention not at all or only in passing. I focus less on detection, apprehension or judicial procedure, than on 'deployment,' that is, the institutional tracks into which populations about to be or already defined as deviant are directed. It is here, particularly in the iconography of prison against community, that visions, claims and changes have been most dramatic. In brief, [I am interested in] punishment and classification. Now is the time for the obligatory self-serving section about how irrelevant, misguided or plain foolish the existing literature on the subject turns out to be.

In truth, the standard literature on social control probably *is* a little more irrelevant, misguided and foolish than it might be in most other areas of sociology. The academic, sociology-of-knowledge reasons for this, lie in the already well-chartered argument about the severance of criminology and the sociology of deviance from the mainstream of sociological concerns. This was not always so. In the classical nineteenth-century tradition of social thought, the concept of social control was near the centre of the enterprise. The great problem of social order was how to achieve a degree of organization and regulation consistent with certain moral and political principles (for example, 'democracy' or 'civil rights') and without an excessive degree of purely coercive control.

In twentieth-century, largely American, sociology this organic connection between social control and a contemplation of the state, became weaker and weaker. The concept lost its political thrust, becoming less structural and more social-psychological. That is, it became more concerned with the 'processes' (a key term) by which the individual was induced into becoming a more-or-less willing participant in the social order. The individual was seen as an actor who learnt scripts and internalized rules and roles or else was pulled or pushed back into shape by something vaguely called 'official' or 'formal' control. This was a reactive, 'trampoline' model of social control. Usually things went pretty smoothly ('consensus'), but every now and then the play broke down, the actors departed from the script and the director was challenged. Then social control was needed to get things back into order.

The social and sociological crises of the sixties were to change all this. Oppression, repression and suppression now became the normal properties of society. Consensus was either non-existent or else precariously maintained by awesome and cunningly disguised systems of social control. The individual could barely breathe, let alone 'internalize'. The struggle was to survive in the belly of that monster, the state. And those old 'deviants'—the nuts, sluts and perverts of criminology and social pathology textbooks—could emerge from their dark closets into the sociological daylight. They were now to be awarded leading roles in the rewritten drama of social reality, as exemplars (first victims and underdogs, then rebels and heroes) of the struggle against social control.

Slowly too, the 'new' sociologists of deviance then, a few years later, the 'new' criminologists came out. Leaving the deviants huddled in their closets with their custodians and healers, these intellectuals proclaimed their independence from 'correctional' interests. Their project was to distance themselves from the machine—not to make it more effective, nor even to humanize it, but to question and demystify its very moral legitimacy. Labelling theorists and their later, rather tougher successors (Marxist or radical criminologists) pushed the notion of social control towards the centre of the stage. It was not just a reactive, reparative mechanism produced when other methods failed, but an active, ever present, almost mystical force which gave crime and deviance their very shapes. Control leads to deviance, was the catechism, not deviance to control. And law and other systems of control were intimately linked with the whole business of maintaining social order, discipline and regulation.

Further, along with these largely academic developments in sociology, wider social movements, whose effects and ideologies I will examine closely, started registering these same changes. The very agents of social control themselves—the professionals who operated the machine—began to scrutinize their own roles. Successive waves of anti-psychiatrists, radical social workers, demedicalizers, deschoolers and delegalizers began to nourish and draw nourishment from those more academic reappraisals of social control. With varying degrees of commitment, credibility and success, they lent their support to movements dedicated to changing, reforming or (amazingly) even abolishing the very agencies and institutions in which they worked.

All these moves—whether within general sociology, specialized subfields such as criminology, or the control apparatus itself—contributed towards a massive theoretical and political reordering of the subject. But (as with the alleged master changes in the apparatus itself) these cognitive shifts have turned out to be much less clear than they seem at first sight. Many have been false alarms or tremors which have registered only slightly in the worlds of theory and practice. What this means—and here comes the criticism of the literature—is that the sociology of social control remains a lot more retarded than these academic rumblings would lead us to expect.

Thus, despite the enterprise of radical demystification, the study of social control shows a wide gap between our private sense of what is going on around us and our professional writings about the social world. This private terrain is inhabited by premonitions of *Nineteen Eighty-Four, Clockwork Orange* and *Brave New World,* by fears about new technologies of mind control, by dark thoughts about the increasing intrusion of the state into family and private lives, by a general unease that more of our actions and thoughts are under surveillance and subject to record and manipulation. Social control has become Kafka-land, a paranoid landscape in which things are done to us, without our knowing when, why or by whom, or even that they are being done. We live inside Burroughs' 'soft machine', an existence all the more perplexing because those who control us seem to have the most benevolent of intentions. Indeed we ourselves appear as the controllers as well as the controlled. Suspending all critical judgement, we accept readily—almost with masochistic pleasure—the notion that *Nineteen Eighty-Four* has literally arrived.

The professional literature, however, reveals little of such nightmares and science fiction projections. Textbooks—those depositories of a discipline's folk wisdom—still use an older and blander language of social control: how norms are internalized, how consensus is achieved, how social control evolves from pre-industrial to industrial societies. Marxist theories, to be sure, confront the concept in a more critical way. But seldom in these powerful and baroque abstractions about the 'ideological' and 'repressive' state apparatus do we get much sense of what is happening in the apparatus. We learn little about those 'transactions' and 'encroachments' going on in Kafka's 'offices.'

For this sense of what the social control apparatus is actually getting up to, the specialized literature is surprisingly unhelpful. Take, for example, the realm where the most formidable and irreversible of all master shifts is alleged to be taking place—the replacement of the closed segregated institution by some form of 'open' community control. Most criminological studies here are of a uniformly low level....

There are, of course, major exceptions to this dull collection. Most notably, there are the various recent schools of revisionist history about the origins of eighteenth- and nineteenth-century control institutions and systems.... It includes Rothman's pioneering history of the origins of the asylum in early nineteenth-century America and, from quite a different intellectual tradition, Foucault's extraordinary 'archaeology' of deviancy control systems.[2] We have here at last a vocabulary with which to comprehend more recent changes. Already, such work has been extended into the contemporary scene, for example in Scull's writings on 'decarceration'[3] and those of Foucault's followers on the 'policing of families' and the 'advanced, psychiatric society.'[4] Less penetrating theoretically, but equally compelling polemically, are the various formulations about the 'therapeutic state,' 'psychiatric despotism,' the 'psychological society,' and 'mind control.'[5] Note, though, that this work, and other allied, but more ambitious social critiques, tend curiously to concentrate on psychiatry—the form of intervention least visible as social control and (arguably) the least appropriate to conceive simply as social control.

The more obvious, everyday forms of control—police, prisons, courts—have been much less frequently chosen for this type of sophisticated theoretical scrutiny. They are no doubt less glamorous and romantic subjects for the social critic. There is much more fun (and theoretical mileage) in studying fashions in psychoanalytical theory, nude encounter groups, primal screaming and sensitivity training, than in peering down the corridors of a juvenile correctional institution. There are, of course, useful statistics and good ethnographies of these more mundane control agencies—police departments, juvenile courts, prisons, crime prevention programmes—but these studies tend to be fragmented and abstracted. They need locating in historical space (How did they get there?), in physical space (the city, the neighbourhood) and, above all, in social space (the network of other institutions such as school and family, broader patterns of welfare and social services, bureaucratic and professional interests).

Imagine a complete cultural dummy—the Martian anthropologist or the historian of centuries to come—picking up a textbook on community corrections, a directory of community agencies, an evaluation study, an annual report. How would he or she make sense of this whole frenzied business, this *mélange* of words?

There are those agencies, places, ideas, services, organizations, and arrangements which all sound a little alike, but surely must be different:

- pre-trial diversion and post-trial diversion;
- all sorts of 'releases'—pre-trial, weekend, partial, supervised, semi-supervised, work and study;
- pre-sentence investigation units and post-adjudication investigation units;
- community-based residential facilities and community residential centres;
- all sorts of 'homes'—community, foster, small group, large group or just group;
- all sorts of 'houses'—half-way, quarter-way and three-quarter-way;
- forestry camps, wilderness and outward-bound projects;
- many kinds of 'centres'—attendance, day, training, community, drop-in, walk-in and store-front;
- hostels, shelters and boarding schools;
- weekend detention, semi-detention and semi-freedom;
- youth service bureaux and something called 'intermediate treatment';
- community services orders, reparation projects and reconciliation schemes;
- citizen-alert programmes, hot-line listening posts, community radio watches and citizen block watches;
- hundreds of tests, scales, diagnostic and screening devices ... and much, much, more.

All these words at least give us a clue about what is happening. But what of:

GUIDE (Girls Unit for Intensive Daytime Education);

TARGET (Treatment for Adolescents Requiring Guidance and Educational Training);

ARD (Accelerated Rehabilitative Dispositions);

PACE (Public Action in Correctional Effort);

RODEO (Reduction of Delinquency through Economic Opportunity);

PREP (Preparation Through Responsive Educational Programs);

PICA (Programming Interpersonal Curricula for Adolescents);

CPI (Critical Period Intervention);

CREST (Clinical Regional Support Team);

VISTO (Volunteers in Service to Offenders); not to mention

READY (Reaching Effectively Acting Out Delinquent Youths);

START (Short Term Adolescent Residential Training); and

STAY (Short Term Aid to Youth).

Then who are all those busy *people* and what might they be doing? Therapists, correctional counsellors, group workers, social workers, psychologists, testers, psychiatrists, systems analysts, trackers, probation officers, parole officers, arbitrators and dispute-mediation experts? And the para-professionals, semi-professionals, volunteers and co-counsellors? And clinical supervisors, field-work supervisors, researchers, consultants, liaison staff, diagnostic staff, screening staff and evaluation staff? And what are these parents, teachers, friends, professors, graduate students and neighbours doing in the system and why are they called 'community crime control resources'? To find our way through all this, let us begin with an over-elaborate, somewhat arch and even, occasionally, quite misleading metaphor.

Imagine that the entrance to the deviancy control system is something like a gigantic fishing net. Strange and complex in its appearance and movements, the net is cast by an army of different fishermen and fisherwomen working all day and even into the night according to more or less known rules and routines, subject to more or less authority and control from above, knowing more or less what the other is doing. Society is the ocean—vast, troubled and full of uncharted currents, rocks and other hazards. Deviants are the fish.

But unlike real fish, and this is where the metaphor already starts to break down, deviants are not caught, sorted out, cleaned, packed, purchased, cooked and eaten. The system which receives the freshly caught deviants has some other aims in mind. After the sorting-out stage, the deviants are in fact kept alive (freeze-dried) and processed (shall we say punished, treated, corrected?) in all sorts of quite extraordinary ways. Then those who are 'ready' are thrown back in the sea (leaving behind only the few who die or who are put to death in the system). Back in the ocean (often with tags and labels which they may find quite difficult to shake off), the returned fish might swim around in a free state for the rest of their lives. Or, more frequently, they might be swept up into the net again. This might happen over and over. Some wretched creatures spend their whole lives being endlessly cycled and recycled, caught, processed and thrown back

Our interest is in the operation of this net and the parent recycling industry which controls it: the whole process, system, machine, apparatus or, as Foucault prefers, the 'capillary network' or 'carceral archipelago'. The whole business can be studied in a number of quite different ways. The fishermen themselves, their production-line colleagues and their managers profess to be interested in only one matter: how to make the whole process *work better*. They want to be sure, they say, that they are catching 'enough' fish and the 'right' fish (whatever those words might mean); that they are processing them in the 'best' way (that the same fish should not keep coming back?); that the whole operation is being carried out as cheaply and (perhaps) as humanely as possible. Other observers, though, especially those given the privileged positions of intellectuals, might want to ask some altogether different questions.

First, there are matters of *quantity:* size, capacity, scope, reach, density, intensity. Just how wide are the nets being cast? Over a period of time, do they get extended to new sites, or is there a contraction—waters which are no longer fished? Do changes in one part of the industry affect the capacity of another part? And just how strong is the mesh or how large are its holes, how intensive is the recycling process? Are there trends in turnover? For example, are the same fish being processed quicker or more new ones being caught?

Second, there are questions about *identity.* Just how clearly can the net and the rest of the apparatus be seen? Is it always visible as a net? Or is it sometimes masked, disguised or camouflaged? Who is operating it? How sure are we about what exactly is being done in all the component parts of the machine?

Third, there is the *ripple* problem. What effect does all this activity—casting the nets, pulling them in, processing the fish—have on the rest of the sea? Do other non-fish objects inadvertently get caught up in the net? Are other patterns disturbed: coral formations, tides, mineral deposits?

Time to switch metaphors to something less elaborate, but more abstract. The deviancy control system occupies a space in any society—both a real space (buildings, technology, staff, clients)—and a social space (ideas, influences, effects). Of any physical object in a space, we may ask questions of *size and density* (how much space is being taken up?); *identity and visibility* (what does the object look like and where are its boundaries?); and *penetration* (how might the object—by magnetism, gravitational pull, radiation or whatever—affect its surrounding space?). These are the three sets of problems which [I wish to] address. Whether or not visions of fishing nets and objects in space help very much, my task is to describe the new patterns of crime control established over the last decades. Again, [I wish my focus to] be on the ideal of community control.

Notes

1. Neal Shover, *A Sociology of American Corrections,* Homewood, Ill.: Jersey Press, 1979, p. 36.

2. Michel Foucault, *Discipline and Punish: The Birth of the Prison* (trans. Alan Sheridan), New York: Vintage Books, 1979.

3. Andrew T. Scull, *Decarceration: Community Treatment and the Deviant—A Radical View,* Englewood Cliffs, N.J.: Prentice-Hall.

4. Jacques Donzelot, *The Policing of Families,* New York: Pantheon, 1979; Robert Castel et al., *The Psychiatric Society,* New York: Columbia University Press, 1981.

5. Nicholas Kittrie, *The Right to Be Different,* Baltimore: Johns Hopkins University Press; Thomas Szasz, *The Manufacture of Madness,* New York: Dell, 1970; Martin L. Gross, *The Psychiatric Society,* New York: Simon & Schuster, 1978; Peter Schrag, *Mind Control,* London: Marion Boyers, 1980.

She Did It All for Love: A Feminist View of the Sociology of Deviance

MARCIA MILLMAN

Social deviance is one of the most important subjects of literary fiction, television, drama, and news coverage. Consequently, we are continuously exposed to speculation about deviance and to stereotypes of both deviant and conventional behavior. Interestingly enough, our sociological stereotypes of deviance closely resemble those that appear in popular culture. A look at certain prototypes of deviant and conventional men and women in the popular media may, therefore, illuminate and introduce our examination of how sociology has approached this subject.

As several literary critics have noted, there is a growing tendency for American and European fiction writers to portray their male heroes as social deviants and their female characters as the natural enemies of these exciting men. Furthermore, in their enmity with men, women are often equated in literature with the stupid, relentless, bourgeois society that ultimately crushes whatever is original and spirited about these modern heroes. Diana Trilling, for example, has argued that our literature reflects our fundamental belief that being gifted (and male) entitles one to a kind of moral independence and the right to excuse one's own behavior by constructing *ad hoc* moral justifications. Women, on the other hand, are usually portrayed in literature and the media as dumbly law-abiding....

The belief is that it is only men who take a serious stand against society and its conventions (at a time when such a stand may have admirable qualities of heroic bravery, individuality, and/or loyalty to one's oppressed group). If women occasionally become socially deviant, their deviance is understood as only secondary, and politically uninspired. It is derivative of their acting like women: falling in love (with a deviant man), being a little too out of control of their emotions (becoming mentally ill), using their sexuality exploitatively but not that differently from other women (becoming a prostitute), or exhibiting some other neurotic weakness or impulsiveness common to women (as becoming a shoplifter).

Our first task, then, will be to examine how, as sociologists and members of this culture, we have come to associate women either with the dullest, most oppressive aspects of society, or else, to view their deviance in narrowly sex-stereotyped (and unappealing) terms, yet to see in our male deviants the expression of creativity and a courage to stand up to society's hypocrisies.

But there is a more difficult question to consider, apart from the issue of how stereotypes of conventional and deviant men and women differ. This other question concerns how our basic understanding and conceptions of deviance and social control have been limited by a systematically male-biased perspective of the world and its activities. There are at least two very important areas of social reality that are frequently overlooked in a male-oriented sociology of deviance. The importance of these subjects becomes obvious in a feminist perspective.

One area concerns the importance of the unofficial, informal, face-to-face, interpersonal regulation in which we routinely engage one another. This subject deserves as much attention as the one that has dominated our work on deviance: that is, the "official" categories (crime, mental illness), and the social control of persons in these categories in official locations (jails, mental hospitals).

The second underinvestigated subject involves somewhat unfashionable topics (because they make one sound moralistic, or at least conventional). This subject has to do with injury, suffering, and other actual, felt consequences of deviance and social control. Here I would include not only the experiences of the "deviant" and the agents of the state, but also those of the victims, family members, and innocent bystanders who have curiously vanished from sociological view. In many ways, the sociology of deviance has transformed itself (as I shall demonstrate) from a tragic vision of the world in which clearly distinguishable representatives of good and evil are driven to their terrible fates into a comic vision of the world in which no one is ever hurt and our acts have no serious consequences.

The argument to be made in this chapter, then, can be summarized in the following way: (1) Sociologists, like others, like to focus on what is exciting. (2) Men, doing most of the research, often found their male deviants to be the most interesting or exciting subjects in the area of deviance (and sometimes the male deviants were attractive because they were contemptuous of society's hypocrisies in ways that middle-class sociologists could not be). Even when such matters did not span the entire subject area, the male deviants were the primary focus of the data, to the exclusion of other features. (3) Because of general public stereotypes that encouraged such a focus and because of their difficulties in identifying with women, male sociologists either overlooked the fact that women could be deviant, or else described female deviants and their deviance in less interesting ways. (4) More importantly, certain topics have been underinvestigated in the study of deviance: particularly everyday deviance and control in interpersonal behavior, and everyday accommodation and suffering with regard to deviance. (5) Finally, men may leave these subjects out of consideration because they are less fun and more uncomfortable to deal with, but women are more likely to notice these subjects in their research because they have to attend to them in their own lives (just as they have to attend to the drudgery and dirty work of cleaning up after other people—whether it be with diapers, bedpans, or typing).

Although an awareness of suffering, accommodation, and interpersonal control in everyday life can be linked with a female view of the world (by virtue of women's present subordinate position, as I mean to show), a sensitivity to these matters has not been restricted to women. In fact, it is a male sociologist, Erving Goffman, who has provided much conceptual material for these aspects of a female social reality. Yet it is not surprising that it is primarily women sociologists who are developing these aspects of his work....

Daniel Bell's essay "Crime as an American Way of Life" (1960) is one of the best-known functionalist explanations of deviance (in functionalist theory the existence and persistence of deviant activity is analyzed in terms of its contribution to the ongoing social order). Bell argued convincingly that organized crime in America served several "useful" purposes: for example, it provided Italian immigrants and their children a ladder of social and political mobility (otherwise closed to them) that would bring them into respectable middle-class life styles. One of the striking aspects of Bell's essay is that he portrays the racketeers and leaders of organized crime as not only loyal and helpful to their ethnic group, but also as brilliant, witty, and personally appealing characters....

Another example of how sociologists may identify with their deviant subjects (and highlight the subjects' attractive features) can be drawn from Howard Becker's study *Outsiders* (1963), of marijuana smokers and jazz musicians; Becker's study is considered to be one of the most important works emerging from the currently popular "labeling" school of deviance. (The labeling school, or "interactionist" perspective, argues that deviance is not in any intrinsic qualities of actors or behavior, but rather occurs when an action gets labeled as deviant; consequently, sociologists of this persuasion study the interactions surrounding the labeling of deviance and the official caretakers and caretaking institutions: police, judges, psychiatrists and prisons, courts and mental hospitals.) No special perceptiveness is required to recognize the identification between Becker and his subjects, for Becker tells us that he did his research while working as a jazz musician himself. Just as Trilling described the modern literary hero as beyond the moral imperatives of ordinary persons because of his unusual talent or sensitivity, so does Becker tell us (sympathetically) that jazz musicians consider themselves to be more sensitive, gifted, and even sexier than ordinary men: "The musician thus sees himself as a creative artist who should be free from outside control, a person different from and better than those outsiders he calls squares..." (1963:91). Becker describes how the wives of jazz musicians try to force their husbands to give up the work they love in favor of conventional jobs....

I don't wish to say that sociologists should be criticized for their identifications and sympathies with their subjects (although these tend to create problems of omission, as I shall show later). On the contrary, studies like Bell's and Becker's are excellent partly because they do succeed in presenting an interior view of their subjects' lives. My point is rather that it is only male deviants who have been studied with such empathy and appreciation. We might also note that the underworlds and subcultures that Becker and Bell describe apparently consist of men only, and women appear in these worlds, and hence in these studies, only in degraded and unpleasant positions.

Since there haven't been many sociologists who take note of women as deviants, women have largely been ignored in the literature or else abandoned to a few deviant categories (mental illness, prostitution, shoplifting) hard to glamorize (with the potential exception of prostitution) the way male deviant occupations are glamorized. It is difficult to imagine mentally ill women running together in gangs and having a lot of fun (though some might disagree), but, then again, in real life, juvenile delinquents probably don't have all that much fun either. A glance through any textbook or collection of articles demonstrates that in many areas of deviance that might just as logically talk about women as about men (for example, alcoholism or drug addiction), the writer has usually either studied only men or spoken as if his subjects were all male. Since prostitution is the only "female" recognized area of deviance that has the potential for presenting portraits of its subjects as exciting and fascinating as most "male" deviant occupations, we may usefully look at important or representative examples of sociological studies of prostitution, bearing in mind the male counterparts we have just reviewed.

Perhaps the best-known sociological analysis of prostitution is Kingsley Davis's functionalist argument (1966) that prostitution is allowed to endure because it actually protects conventional institutions such as marriage. As Matza observed (1969), one of the contributions of functionalist theory to the study of deviance was the insight that there is much surprising "overlap" between deviant and conventional behavior (for example, in his essay that we considered earlier, Daniel Bell compared organized crime to organized business in America). Since prostitution is an occupation, the most obvious point of "overlap" with conventional life should have been on the basis of similarities with conventional occupations. But the tendency for sexual stereotyping was so strong that sociologists like Davis showed the overlap of prostitution with conventional life not through occupational similarities but only through sexual behavior. Davis (1966:349) pointed out that conventional wives, like prostitutes, traded sexual favors for economic support, and Edwin Lemert (1951:238) later extended the comparison to other conventional women whom he claimed used sexuality for economic purposes: the "shopgirls who have sex relations in return for a dinner and a show from their dates obviously are employing sex as a means to certain material goals."...

Since Bell's and Davis's essays are among the best known of functionalist studies of deviance, it is interesting to compare their respective portraits of the deviant subjects. We observed earlier that Bell presents his "criminals" as likable, brilliant, interesting men. This is partly due to the fact that Bell selects some of the more colorful and outstanding characters of the underworld and quotes from their own words about their activities. In contrast, Davis never singles out specific prostitutes (although undoubtedly in the history of prostitution there must have been many interesting and appealing characters) in his analysis, and he certainly never quotes any prostitutes. His essay is only about prostitution (and not prostitutes), while Bell manages to interest us in the racketeer and gambler as well as in organized crime. Female deviants cannot appear as interesting, complicated, or even comprehensible when they are merely assigned to anonymous and passive membership in a category.

But how have prostitutes fared in more contemporary studies? There is no study of prostitution from the "labeling" tradition of equal importance to Becker's study of jazz musicians. But some attention has been paid to prostitutes by sociologists with this orientation. One of the aspects of deviance that has been focused upon by labeling theorists is the world of the deviant subculture. The attention to subculture is related to an effort to return to the old Chicago school's commitment to present the subject's own view of the world and to demonstrate that deviants are not isolated figures but have friends, associates, and social worlds with their rules and regulations like anyone else. It is all the more noteworthy that even when a male sociologist from this persuasion sets out to study prostitute subcultures, the sexual stereotype of women as competitive and unable to create group culture and solidarity apparently outweighs the investigator's ability to discover group life. One recent study of apprenticeship and ideology among prostitutes, for example (Bryan, 1965, 1966), claims that prostitutes' relationships and feelings about one another are characterized by competitiveness, exploitation, distrust, disloyalty, suspiciousness, and lack of group culture. Prostitutes are described as trusting their pimps more than one another. While other (male) deviant subcultures are seen to have strong group solidarity, the world of prostitutes has always been portrayed in the contrary manner (Lemert, 1951:275; Reckless, 1950). But if we consider certain realities about their situation—that they live and work together and depend upon one another to a great extent—we may suspect that it is the stereotype of women as mutually competitive and unable to recognize group interests that renders the male sociologist blind to what must be a complex, integrated female culture among prostitutes. It is probably more difficult for men to notice and understand female group culture when they see it than it is for women to observe male group life. Subordinate groups are generally better practiced in knowing and studying those in power than the other way around. But for whatever reason, it is a curious fact that unlike studies of male deviance, with their emphasis on fraternal bonding and high group commitment, sociologists tend to overlook subcultures of women, deviant or conventional.

Finally, we should note that whereas women appear only in the nagging, unpleasant edges of Becker's world of jazz musicians, in Bryan's study of prostitutes, the pimps not only get considerable attention, but also a large share of the quotations (almost as many as the prostitutes themselves). Indeed, Bryan regards the pimp as an authority on prostitution and uses the pimp's quotations as evidence rather than further material to consider; so in a supposedly empathetic study of prostitutes, the pimps are treated as more intelligent, observant, and trustworthy than the subjects of the study themselves! Howard Becker certainly never asked the wives of jazz musicians what *they* thought about their husbands' occupations, much less quoted them as authorities on the subject.

One major sociological study of prostitution does manage to avoid many of the mistakes of others, precisely because the author depended upon autobiographical accounts from his subjects. Because of his effort to present an interior view of the subject's life, W. I. Thomas's study (1924) was in many ways much less sexually stereotyped than more contemporary works. One of its most impressive achievements was Thomas's ability (missing in many later generations of sociologists, as I shall argue) to describe the pain and suffering that accompanied the lot of the prostitute while simultaneously portraying his subjects as resourceful, intelligent women who coped with the difficulties of their lives as best they could. Like subsequent generations of sociologists, he was aware of the fact that there were many similarities between these "unadjusted" women and conventional women, and he came to this insight some forty years before the labeling theorists made it one of their fundamental principles. For example, Thomas noted that it is difficult to draw a line on the basis of sexual behavior alone between those women one would call prostitutes and those one wouldn't. He also observed that prostitution is not usually a fixed status but rather a transitory activity, which most girls relinquish upon getting married (1924:120), another kind of observation that contemporary sociologists like to make....

Most studies that rely on the "official" statistics of law-enforcement or other governmental agencies tend to describe their subjects in much the same way as these same agencies would, and large sample studies of prostitution are no different in this regard. Perhaps the most famous study of this type was the report *Five Hundred Delinquent Women* written by Sheldon and Eleanor Glueck (1954), which is based on the official case records of 500 women in a state reformatory. The general disposition of this study can be described best by considering a few representative quotations from the Gluecks' summary of major findings:

> The women are themselves on the whole a sorry lot. Burdened with feeblemindedness, psychopathic personality, and marked emotional instability, a large proportion of them found it difficult to survive by legitimate means.
>
> This swarm of defective, diseased, antisocial misfits, then, comprises the human material which a reformatory and a parole system are required by society to transform into wholesome, decent, law-abiding citizens! [1954:299–303]

Apart from the Gluecks' inventory there has been historically little attention paid to female criminality. In a traditional textbook on crime widely used in the fifties, Walter Reckless (1950) devoted a special chapter to "The Criminality of Women" in which he argued that the criminality of women must never be considered "in the same order of phenomena as crime in general" (male being general). In an explanation oddly reminiscent of the old disclaimers for omitting discussions of female sexuality, Reckless claimed that "although crime as a behavior problem or a social problem is complicated and, not easily understood or controlled, the criminality of women is even more complicated and less understood and not subject to easy control" (1950:116). But Reckless does attempt to deal with the problem, and his analysis is so loaded with stereotypes about women, some tired and familiar and others so unusual and entertaining, that a few of them merit our attention:

> ...it appears that practically all the observers agree that women offenders, much more than men offenders, use deceit and indirection in the commission of their offenses. [1950:122]
>
> Observers unanimously agree that poisoning is the principal method of killing used by women.... As a shopper and a housewife, a woman can readily purchase insecticides and rat poisons. And in her role as preparer of food and nurse to the sick, it is easy for her to administer poison. [1950:121]
>
> ...With regard to the offense of aggravated assault, one particular specific female pattern has been the throwing of sulphuric acid into the face of the victim, who was most usually the unfaithful lover. [1950:122]
>
> ...A woman is also prone to make false accusations of a sexual nature. She either fantasizes that she has been attacked or claims that she has been attacked when she has really cooperated. [1950:123]

In reviewing how a male-biased orientation has shaped the sociological study of deviance, then, it is easy to demonstrate that women have either been largely overlooked in the literature (partly because of a general belief that women are very conventional) or else regarded as deviant in only sex-stereotyped (and less appealing than male counterpart) ways. The stereotypes have limited both the *forms* of female deviance that have been recognized (those related to sex or emotion, as in prostitution and mental illness) and the way that sociologists have characterized female deviant behavioral *styles* (being passive, uncritical, unlikely to recognize group interests or have solidarity with other deviant women). But there is an even more serious problem that follows from a male-biased view of deviance, and this is a problem of omission. Certain aspects of social reality involving deviance and conformity are systematically ignored: These have to do with ordinary, chronic, everyday suffering and with the extent to which conventional lives are continually and closely governed by interpersonal regulations about right and wrong. The importance of these subjects becomes more obvious in a feminist perspective, and it is to these questions that we should now turn our attention....

By regarding deviance as a role (which the actor may be managing successfully or not), the interactionist ("labeling," "underdog") sociologists frequently fail to notice that the suffering is real and not make-believe. Thus we may be amused by Mary Owen Cameron's description (1964) of an arrested shoplifter who, not regarding herself as a criminal, tries to reject the role and pleads with the police officer to "make it go away" or asks him, "Will my husband have to know about this?" But in our amusement at an inappropriate response, we ignore the real pain involved in this situation, and consequently we don't entirely comprehend this woman's experience. And this is hardly excusable in a study that is supposed to represent the reasoning and experiences of the deviant actor.

Another example of how suffering gets overlooked when we focus upon certain humorous elements of the dramaturgical aspects of deviance and conventionality can be drawn from Donald Ball's "Ethnography of an Abortion Clinic" (written before abortions were legalized). Ball describes how clinic practitioners try to neutralize the deviant context by enhancing parallels with conventional medical settings. We may smile at the senior practitioner who makes an "elaborate display" of putting on surgical gloves only to contaminate himself by writing up the client's medical history before performing the abortion. But in thinking about the relationships between legal and illegal practitioners, we almost forget that there is a third party involved—the unfortunate client, who might not find the unsterile conditions all that funny. Ball never really looks at the clinic from the point of view of the client, but rather only at the calculations of the practitioners.

Ball's neglect of the client reminds us of the mysterious disappearance of the third party (victims) in sociological research on deviance—an oversight all the more curious since labeling theorists are the first to tell us that the apprehension and designation of deviants are typically arbitrary and capricious matters. That the labeling of deviants is so inconsistent an affair means, of course, that out in the world everyone is breaking rules all the time, and we all have to cope with this reality. Furthermore, some people even break rules which create serious disturbances in other people's lives. When sociologists turned the tables on the "other side," they forgot that there is frequently a third side: like the criminal courts and laws, sociologists deal primarily with the relationship between the state and the accused, and sometimes forget the actual victim....

The labeling theorists do occasionally talk about those who have to bear the brunt of deviance under the rubric of "accommodation to deviance." But the phenomenon is given little attention in their depiction of social reality, considering the enormous importance that accommodation plays in people's daily lives. For example, the readings on "interactionist" (or "labeling") views of deviance assembled by Earl Rubington and Martin S. Weinberg (1973) devote only three of fifty-two articles to "accommodation" to deviance, and all the articles about accommodation concern how wives and families cope with deviance (mental illness, alcoholism) in a family member (usually the husband). For, naturally, the people who most frequently have to put up with the consequences of deviance are the powerless—the poor, and very often, wives and children; and these are the very people with whom sociologists find it difficult to identify....

Aside from the fact that suffering is a real and protracted though neglected aspect of deviance, there is also the fact that the importance of deviance and social control cannot be confined to our standard catalogue of official possibilities: it is something we struggle with constantly in our interpersonal lives—at work, at home, with our friends, and in the streets. The brilliance of Erving Goffman's work is partly due to the fact that no matter how far he strays into the underworlds of spies, conmen, and mental patients, he always brings the analysis back home to the daily interactions of ordinary citizens. Like Freud, he studies the exaggerated cases in order to understand the usual. Goffman begins his analysis of stigmatization by examining the experiences of the blind and the crippled, but finishes by reminding us that we are all, at times, stigmatized: that the normal and stigmatized are not persons but perspectives (1963:138). Now, there are problems with such leaps, for as I argued earlier, concentrating on the role elements tends to make us forget that there is a real difference between being bald and being paraplegic, or between being a mental patient and an awkward guest. We may forget that some persons and some groups suffer much more than others. But Goffman's method is justified because it shocks us into finally paying serious attention to something we would rather overlook: that we engage every day in extraordinarily powerful, consequential, and often painful interpersonal negotiations about what is or is not acceptable and about what our respective places are in a world that provides us with less guidance and certainty about such matters....

There is more to be said about the study of interpersonal regulation, because in still other ways it provides a view of the world that is usually omitted by the limitations of a male-biased imagination. Goffman's writing has been described as "deadpan" and "fish-eyed," but there are few sociological works that capture so well the subjective experience of the person being studied (including the suffering) or that can evoke as much emotional response in the reader. And Goffman's work is important in a feminist perspective because he writes about what the world looks like and feels like to the person who is pushed around and taken advantage of. Although he always considers the interaction from both above and below, from the point of view of the conman as well as the mark, the psychiatrist as well as the patient, the predator as well as the prey, in the end it is always the victim who has the loudest voice in Goffman's work, and it is usually with the victim that the female reader identifies.

For Goffman's assorted victims all represent important aspects of the woman's subordinate position, and women are well acquainted with the maneuvers of his characters as they struggle to cope with a world full of injury. From the mark who can be relied upon not to "squawk" because she wants, at least, to save face after losing everything else (1952), to the terrified teen-age girl who pulls up the blanket and silently pretends to be asleep while the housebreaker creeps into her bed (1971), Goffman's characters parade before us like familiar figures from a woman's nightmares. This is not to say that men, too, cannot or do not identify with the stigmatized or depersonalized. But Goffman's work has a special meaning for readers (women more often than men) who understand the power of interpersonal regulation. The work of Goffman and those (primarily female) sociologists who have been influenced by him provide an extremely promising approach to exploring the complicated relationships between subordinates and superordinates, outsiders and insiders, conventionals and deviants, and women and men as they cope every day with life's smaller ambiguities as well as its larger crises. It is work of this sort that restores many of the elements that have been missing from a one-sided view of the social world.

References

Ball, Donald W. 1967. An abortion clinic ethnography. *Social Problems,* 14 (3):293–301.

Becker, Howard S. 1963. *Outsiders: Studies in the Sociology of Deviance.* New York: Free Press.

Becker, Howard S. (ed.). 1964. *The Other Side: Perspectives on Deviance.* New York: Free Press.

Bell, Daniel. 1960. Crime as an American way of life: A queer ladder of social mobility. In *The End of Ideology.* New York: Free Press.

Bryan, James H. 1965. Apprenticeships in prostitution. *Social Problems,* 12 (3):287–297.

Bryan, James H. 1966. Occupational ideologies and individual attitudes of call girls. *Social Problems,* 13 (4):441–450.

Cameron, Mary Owen. 1964. *The Booster and the Snitch.* New York: Free Press.

Davis, Kingsley. 1966. Sexual behavior. In Robert K. Merton and Robert Nisbet (eds.), *Contemporary Social Problems.* New York: Harcourt, Brace & World.

Glueck, Sheldon, and Eleanor T. Glueck. 1954. *Five Hundred Delinquent Women.* New York: Alfred Knopf.

Goffman, Erving. 1952. On cooling the mark out. *Psychiatry,* 15 (4):451–463.

Goffman, Erving. 1963. *Stigma.* Englewood Cliffs, N.J.: Prentice-Hall/Spectrum.

Goffman, Erving. 1971. *Relations in Public.* New York: Basic Books.

Lemert, Edwin M. 1951. *Social Pathology.* New York: McGraw-Hill.

Matza, David. 1969. *Becoming Deviant.* Englewood Cliffs, N.J.: Prentice-Hall.

Reckless, Walter C. 1950. *The Crime Problem.* New York: Appleton-Century-Crofts.

Rubington, Earl, and Martin S. Weinberg (eds.). 1973. *Deviance: The Interactionist Perspective* (2nd ed.). New York: Macmillan.

Thomas, William I. 1924. *The Unadjusted Girl.* Boston: Little, Brown.

Part IV

Forms of Deviance

All specific forms or examples of deviance can be looked at from the two approaches highlighted in Parts II and III. If a specific form of deviance is a concretely real, essentialistic phenomenon, then a clear and obvious question revolves around etiology: What causes it? Or, more colloquially, *why do they do it?* What factors or variables are associated with its occurrence, incidence, its frequency, its increase and decrease? The theories discussed in Part II help to explain etiology: Community instability and disorganization stimulate a high rate of crime and deviance; a state of society-wide anomie or social strain generates deviant or nonconforming behavior; people learn values and norms that encourage deviance. Other explanations are possible, of course, but all causal theories agree that deviance is a clearly identifiable "thing" in the world that we can identify and lay our hands on, whose origin demands an explanation. Essentialists assume that all reasonable and well-informed observers can agree on a definition of each form or instance or type of deviance—what it is in the world—that defining mental illness, homosexuality, drug use, rape, pornography, and so on, is neither especially problematic nor very interesting.

The etiologist's quest is closely tied into the view that deviance is a concretely real phenomenon. As a thing in the world, forms of deviance are also likely to have concretely real consequences as well; in other words, *etiology presupposes essentialism.* An etiologist does not necessarily look at the consequences of deviance, but an essentialist does. If, for instance, crime is a concretely real thing in the world, it has consequences; how much does crime cost the society? How much is stolen from the public pocket? How many people are harmed by it? What impact does it have for the communities in which it takes place? Which harms the society more—crime or disease? Causes and consequences are two aspects of the essentialist's package.

On the other hand, if deviance is not a clearly identifiable thing in the world but instead is a creation of the social construction process, then we have to ask a variety of very different questions and seek perspectives that address entirely different issues. Why this particular construction rather than a different one? How did this categorization of behavior or traits come to be created and legitimated rather than a different one? Why is this behavior or condition condemned while that one is tolerated or encouraged? Why are laws passed and enforced and against what behaviors? Who initiates the construction process? For what reasons? In the interests of what segments of the society? How do the members of socially condemned categories live and deal with that condemnation? Do they accept the legitimacy of their stigma or do they generate a counterdefinition of who they are and what they do? In short, what is the discourse surrounding deviance?

As we've seen, central to the constructionist's perspective is the assumption of a certain measure of independence between objective harm and the creation of deviant categories. That is, constructionists assume—and believe that evidence supports the view—that certain conditions or behaviors are not condemned *solely* because they harm the society or the members of the society in which they take place. Many relatively benign activities are condemned as deviant, while many extremely harmful acts are praised and encouraged. In addition, when the constructionist looks at changes over time in condemnation and punishment, here, too, the assumption of independence holds: Acts can be condemned more at one time without an increase in incidence or damage, and condemned less at another time without a corresponding decrease. Something else aside from harm is at work here, the constructionist argues, and that "something else" is the principal focus of the constructionist research program. In short, the process of condemnation and punishment contains a strong streak of "irrationality." However, to a constructionist, this process may be quite rational, that is, it may uphold a certain ideology, protect certain interests, create a category of social "demons" who draw attention away from society's "real" problems, maintain the prestige of certain groups or strata, and so on. In short, condemnation and punishment may serve a specific purpose or function for identifiable parties, segments, strata, or classes.

Each type or instance or deviance can be examined both from the etiological or the constructionist perspective. An etiologist would ask, why are drugs and alcohol used and abused? Who uses or abuses psychoactive or mind-altering substances and why? What marks drug users and abusers off from abstainers, experimenters, and light or occasional users? Do some societies encourage drug use and abuse more than others? Is use/abuse greater during some historical periods than others? If so, why?

In contrast, the constructionist would ask, why is the use or abuse of certain psychoactive substances condemned, while the use, even the abuse of others is tolerated? The consumption of tobacco cigarettes kills more Americans, indeed, more people all over the world, than all other drugs combined; why is tobacco legal and nondeviant, while the use, for instance, of marijuana, a far less harmful substance, is illegal and deviant in most places? Contrarily, who's behind the move to criminalize and "deviantize" cigarette smoking? Will it work? Why is smoking condemned more today than a generation ago? Why more in the United States than anywhere else? Why does American society experience drug "panics" or "scares" from time to time? Are they based on real increases in drug abuse and harm, or is their reality constructed out of whole cloth? Who profits from them?

The same parallel sets of questions can be raised for all of the other forms of deviance. The etiologist asks, what is the cause of homosexuality? The constructionist asks, how and why is homosexuality constructed as a category in a certain way? Why is it condemned? Why, where, and in what way are homosexuals persecuted?

The etiologist asks, why pornography? Likewise, the essentialist asks, what consequences does pornography have—for instance, does it cause men to inflict violence on women? Instead, the constructionist asks, how does the society *define* pornography? Is it tolerated, or are consumers condemned? Is its distribution legal or illegal? What consequences is it thought to have? Are movements afoot to change its legal status?

Rape, too, has both its etiological (and essentialistic) and its constructionist side. The etiologist asks: What causes rape? How common is it? Which men rape and why? What social and cultural conditions encourage rape? In which societies is rape common? In which ones is it relatively rare? The constructionist asks: How does the society define and view rape? What is the legal fate of rapists? How do rapists define and justify their own behavior? What role does rape and fear of rape play in a society's consciousness? In women's lives? In men's?

In principle, physical characteristics, too, have this dual aspect; however, sociologists almost never ask etiological questions about involuntarily acquired undesirable physical characteristics. This is because they rarely have a sociological origin. (They may have sociological correlates, but not direct causes.) Instead, traits such as blindness, physical disability, extreme shortness, and so on, are typically caused by accidental, physical, genetic, and physiological factors—in short, a causal or etiological hodgepodge without a center or a focus. Consequently, the sociologist is at a loss to explain them. In contrast, it is the constructionist who directs questions to physical traits. How do the sighted treat the blind? What stereotypes dominate and rule their interactions with them? Why is obesity considered a sign of beauty and power in one society and unsightly and repulsive in another? What provisions does the society have for protecting the rights of the disabled to have access to public facilities? How are the extremely short, the extremely ugly, the physically disfigured treated by so-called normals in this society? Does this treatment vary from one society to another, from one time period to another?

Mental disorder is presumed to have causes that can be explained. The etiologist asks, is mental illness caused by genetic or biochemical factors? Or is it social in origin? Who goes crazy, and why? In contrast, the constructionist asks about the image of the mentally ill. Do definitions of mental illness vary from one society to another? What treatments are prescribed for mental illness; who profits from these treatment modalities? What is the mental illness treatment enterprise or empire like? Why are alternative modalities not instituted?

And last, white-collar crime can be looked at both as a reality with a distinct cause or set of causes and as a certain definition or construction created at a certain time and place by certain parties for a certain purpose. What causes white-collar or corporate crime? What conditions encourage it, what conditions discourage it? Instead, the constructionist asks: How do the public and the law *conceptualize* and *define* white-collar crime? How does the white-collar criminal define his or her own behavior? Why are laws attempting to control white-collar crime so lax and fitfully applied? Why are penalties for crimes that have a serious impact so light? Who profits from a certain legal definition of white-collar crime? Why is the public so indifferent about white-collar crime and so fearful of street crime?

In the selections that follow, I will attempt to raise both the etiological (and essentialistic) questions and the constructionist ones. However, there may be a bit more emphasis on the constructionist's side, since that is where my interests mainly lie. At the same time, I am aware of the fact that deviant categories are not fabricated out of whole cloth, that there are limits to constructionism, and that there are concrete, real-world referents in the world of deviance that cannot be ignored. Consequently, in the sections that follow, both approaches will be relevant although not necessarily equally important.

Chapter 9

Alcoholism and Drug Abuse

The essentialist approach assumes that categories such as drugs, drug abuse, alcohol, and alcoholism encompass clearly delineated realms and that the entities within them make up phenomena with characteristics that clearly set them apart from different categories—for instance, that all substances we refer to as drugs can be clearly distinguished from all substances we don't call drugs. That drugs share essential traits that are entirely lacking in substances that are not referred to as drugs; that they are or do things that nondrugs aren't or don't. Essentialism assumes that alcoholics can be unambiguously distinguished from people who are not referred to as alcoholics. Given the essential reality of drugs, drug abuse, alcohol, and alcoholism, this approach continues, the next step is to explain them. Again, some classic etiological questions would include: Who uses drugs and why? Who abuses drugs and why? Why do some of us become alcoholics while others do not? The etiological or causal quest is a major aspect of sociological studies that deal with the use of psychoactive substances.

The constructionist is also interested in drugs, but adopts a very different perspective. How are drugs defined? Why are some psychoactive or mind-altering substances considered drugs (such as cocaine and heroin) and others—no less potent in their power to influence the human mind—are considered something else again, such as an "acceptable beverage," a "mild pick-me-up," or the source of a "bad but tolerable habit" (alcohol, coffee, and tobacco, for example)? Why is the possession and sale of some psychoactive substances illegal while that of others is perfectly legal to anyone above a certain age? How do the mass media treat stories on the use, abuse, and sale of certain classes of drugs? Why do drug stories in the media cluster in certain years and drop off in others? Why are drug wars waged by certain presidential administrations? What function do they serve? Why do drug scares or panics arise at certain times and places? Who profits from them? What is the public's image of drugs? Where does this image come from?

One task of some constructionists is *debunking,* that is, to demonstrate that drug scares have no solid foundation, that fear of and hostility toward drug dealers and users are misplaced, a product of a mixture of Puritanism and self-serving motives on the part of politicians, elites, the media, and various interest groups. Drug scares, in one form or another, have been taking place in the United States for some two centuries. Craig Reinarman explains how drug scares are constructed; there are, he says, seven ingredients to drug scares: a kernel of truth, media exaggeration, politico-moral entrepreneurs, professional interest groups, a historical context of conflict, an attempt to link drug use to a "dangerous class," and scapegoating.

I agree that the fear of or concern over drug use and abuse is constructed; I believe that constructionism is the most powerful and interesting way that sociologists have of looking at drug abuse. *All* social problems are constructed, *all* designations of deviance are constructs, *all* fears and concerns are plucked out of a vast array of possible conditions or threats to be fearful and concerned about. Why fear and concern about this threat rather than that one? Is it because this one, objectively and concretely speaking, is more dangerous? Or, again, are other factors at work? It is hard to support the view that drug abuse was the most harmful threat that faced the country in the late 1980s. At least a dozen factors or threats caused more death and disease than the consumption of illegal drugs. So why was drug abuse designated as the country's number one problem facing the country in September 1989 *by nearly two-thirds of the population* (Goode, 1993, p. 50)? It's hard to imagine that drug abuse was seen as threatening to so many people simply because they had taken an objective assessment of the problem and reached a conclusion based solely on the evidence.

On the other hand, in my view, the rise in fear and concern over drug abuse in the late 1980s did not come about at a time when the threat from drug abuse was declining, as some observers have claimed. In fact, as I argue, although surveys do show a decline in casual, recreational use of illegal drugs throughout the 1980s, the heavy or chronic abuse of drugs actually increased during this period. Moreover, the concrete indicators of abuse, such as drug overdoses, both lethal and nonlethal, increased as well. To argue, as some have done, therefore, that the fear of or scare over drug abuse in the late 1980s was fabricated practically out of whole cloth is entirely misleading. Though this fear may not have been *caused* by this increase in concrete damage, it did not come about when drug abuse was declining in objective seriousness either (Goode, 1990; Goode and Ben-Yehuda, 1994, pp. 205–223). In short, though the drug crisis or panic was a constructed phenomenon, it was constructed out of a variety of materials, including the dead bodies of drug abusers.

Marsh Ray, in a classic discussion, shows how social definitions, expectations, and interaction work to encourage the recovering addict to return to heroin addiction. Ray's addicts are off drugs altogether, at least for a time, so it is not the physiological action of heroin that causes them to return. What is it? Ray locates the way in which recovering addicts are treated by their friends, associates, and peers, both addicts and nonaddicts, which, in turn, validates their addict self-image as a crucial causal mechanism in this process. It is difficult for the abstainer to sustain a nonaddict image and hence, to abstain from heroin. Only by establishing a meaningful nonaddict identity in both the addict and nonaddict worlds is the recovering addict able to abstain successfully.

References

Goode, Erich. 1990. The American drug panic of the 1980s: Constructionism or objective threat? *International Journal of the Addictions,* 25 (9):1083–1098.

Goode, Erich. 1993. *Drugs in American Society* (4th ed.). New York: McGraw-Hill.

Goode, Erich, and Nachman Ben-Yehuda. 1994. *Moral Panics: The Social Construction of Deviance.* Cambridge, Mass. and Oxford, England: Blackwell.

The Social Construction of Drug Scares

CRAIG REINARMAN

Drug "wars," anti-drug crusades, and other periods of marked public concern about drugs are never merely reactions to the various troubles people can have with drugs. These drug scares are recurring cultural and political phenomena *in their own right* and must, therefore, be understood sociologically on their own terms. It is important to understand why people ingest drugs and why some of them develop problems that have something to do with having ingested them. But the premise of this chapter is that it is equally important to understand patterns of acute societal concern about drug use and drug problems. This seems especially so for U.S. society, which has had *recurring* anti-drug crusades and a *history* of repressive anti-drug laws.

Many well-intentioned drug policy reform efforts in the U.S. have come face to face with staid and stubborn sentiments against consciousness-altering substances. The repeated failures of such reform efforts cannot be explained solely in terms of ill-informed or manipulative leaders. Something deeper is involved, something woven into the very fabric of American culture, something which explains why claims that some drug is the cause of much of what is wrong with the world are *believed* so often by so many. The origins and nature of the *appeal* of anti-drug claims must be confronted if we are ever to understand how "drug problems" are constructed in the U.S. such that more enlightened and effective drug policies have been so difficult to achieve.

[Here], I take a step in this direction. First, I summarize briefly some of the major periods of anti-drug sentiment in the U.S. Second, I draw from them the basic ingredients of which drug scares and drug laws are made. Third, I offer a beginning interpretation of these scares and laws based on those broad features of American culture that make *self-control* continuously problematic.

Drug Scares and Drug Laws

What I have called drug scares (Reinarman and Levine, 1989a) have been a recurring feature of U.S. society for 200 years. They are relatively autonomous from whatever drug-related problems exist or are said to exist.[1] I call them "scares" because, like Red Scares, they are a form of moral panic ideologically constructed so as to construe one or another chemical bogeyman, à la "communists," as the core cause of a wide array of pre-existing public problems.

From Craig Reinarman, "The Social Construction of Drug Scares." In Patricia A. Adler and Peter Adler, eds., *Constructions of Deviance: Social Power, Context, and Interaction* (Belmont, Calif.: Wadsworth Publishing Company, 1994), pp. 92–104. © Craig Reinarman, Department of Sociology, University of California, Santa Cruz.

The first and most significant drug scare was over drink. Temperance movement leaders constructed this scare beginning in the late 18th and early 19th century. It reached its formal end with the passage of Prohibition in 1919.[2] As Gusfield showed in his classic book *Symbolic Crusade* (1963), there was far more to the battle against booze than long-standing drinking problems. Temperance crusaders tended to be native born, middle-class, nonurban Protestants who felt threatened by the working-class, Catholic immigrants who were filling up America's cities during industrialization.[3] The latter were what Gusfield termed "unrepentant deviants" in that they continued their long-standing drinking practices despite middle-class W.A.S.P. norms against them. The battle over booze was the terrain on which was fought a cornucopia of cultural conflicts, particularly over whose morality would be the dominant morality in America.

In the course of this century-long struggle, the often wild claims of Temperance leaders appealed to millions of middle-class people seeking explanations for the pressing social and economic problems of industrializing America. Many corporate supporters of Prohibition threw their financial and ideological weight behind the Anti-Saloon League and other Temperance and Prohibitionist groups because they felt that traditional working-class drinking practices interfered with the new rhythms of the factory, and thus with productivity and profits (Rumbarger, 1989). To the Temperance crusaders' fear of the bar room as a breeding ground of all sorts of tragic immorality, Prohibitionists added the idea of the saloon as an alien, subversive place where unionists organized and where leftists and anarchists found recruits (Levine, 1984).

This convergence of claims and interests rendered alcohol a scapegoat for most of the nation's poverty, crime, moral degeneracy, "broken" families, illegitimacy, unemployment, and personal and business failure—problems whose sources lay in broader economic and political forces. This scare climaxed in the first two decades of this century, a tumultuous period rife with class, racial, cultural, and political conflict brought on by the wrenching changes of industrialization, immigration, and urbanization (Levine, 1984; Levine and Reinarman, 1991).

America's first real drug law was San Francisco's anti-opium den ordinance of 1875. The context of the campaign for this law shared many features with the context of the Temperance movement. Opiates had long been widely and legally available without a prescription in hundreds of medicines (Brecher, 1972; Musto, 1973; Courtwright, 1982; cf. Baumohl, 1992), so neither opiate use nor addiction was really the issue. This campaign focused almost exclusively on what was called the "Mongolian vice" of opium *smoking* by Chinese immigrants (and white "fellow travelers") in dens (Baumohl, 1992). Chinese immigrants came to California as "coolie" labor to build the railroad and dig the gold mines. A small minority of them brought along the practice of smoking opium—a practice originally brought to China by British and American traders in the 19th century. When the railroad was completed and the gold dried up, a decade-long depression ensued. In a tight labor market, Chinese immigrants were a target. The white Workingman's Party fomented racial hatred of the low-wage "coolies" with whom they now had to compete for work. The first law against opium smoking was only one of many laws enacted to harass and control Chinese workers (Morgan, 1978).

By calling attention to this broader political-economic context I do not wish to slight the specifics of the local political-economic context. In addition to the Workingman's Party, downtown businessmen formed merchant associations and urban families formed improvement associations, both of which fought for more than two decades to reduce the impact of San Francisco's vice districts on the order and health of the central business district and on family neighborhoods (Baumohl, 1992).

In this sense, the anti-opium den ordinance was not the clear and direct result of a sudden drug scare alone. The law was passed against a specific form of drug use engaged in by a disreputable group that had come to be seen as threatening in lean economic times. But it passed easily because this new threat was understood against the broader historical backdrop of long-standing local concerns about various vices as threats to public health, public morals, and public order. Moreover, the focus of attention were dens where it was suspected that whites came into intimate contact with "filthy, idolatrous" Chinese (see Baumohl, 1992). Some local law enforcement leaders, for example, complained that Chinese men were using this vice to seduce white women into sexual slavery (Morgan, 1978). Whatever the hazards of opium smoking, its initial criminalization in San Francisco had to do with both a general context of recession, class conflict, and racism, and with specific local interests in the control of vice and the prevention of miscegenation.

A nationwide scare focusing on opiates and cocaine began in the early 20th century. These drugs had been widely used for years, but were first criminalized when the addict population began to shift from predominantly white, middle-class, middle-aged women to young, working-class males, African-Americans in particular. This scare led to the Harrison Narcotics Act of 1914, the first federal anti-drug law (see Duster, 1970).

Many different moral entrepreneurs guided its passage over a six-year campaign: State Department diplomats seeking a drug treaty as a means of expanding trade with China, trade which they felt was crucial for pulling the economy out of recession; the medical and pharmaceutical professions whose interests were threatened by self-medication with unregulated proprietary tonics, many of which contained cocaine or opiates; reformers seeking to control what they saw as the deviance of immigrants and Southern Blacks who were migrating off the farms; and a pliant press which routinely linked drug use with prostitutes, criminals, transient workers (e.g., the Wobblies), and African-Americans (Musto, 1973). In order to gain the support of Southern Congressmen for a new federal law that might infringe on "states' rights," State Department officials and other crusaders repeatedly spread unsubstantiated suspicions, repeated in the press, that, e.g., cocaine induced African-American men to rape white women (Musto, 1973:6–10, 67). In short, there was more to this drug scare, too, than mere drug problems.

In the Great Depression, Harry Anslinger of the Federal Narcotics Bureau pushed Congress for a federal law against marijuana. He claimed it was a "killer weed" and he spread stories to the press suggesting that it induced violence—especially among Mexican-Americans. Although there was no evidence that marijuana was widely used, much less that it had any untoward effects, his crusade resulted in its criminalization in 1937—and not incidentally a turnaround in his Bureau's fiscal fortunes (Dickson, 1968). In this case, a new drug law was put in place by a militant moral-bureaucratic entrepreneur who played on racial fears and manipulated a press willing to repeat even his most absurd claims in a context of class conflict during the Depression (Becker, 1963). While there was not a marked scare at the time, Anslinger's claims were never contested in Congress because they played upon racial fears and widely held Victorian values against taking drugs solely for pleasure.

In the drug scare of the 1960s, political and moral leaders somehow reconceptualized this same "killer weed" as the "drop out drug" that was leading America's youth to rebellion and ruin (Himmelstein, 1983). Bio-medical scientists also published uncontrolled, retrospective studies of very small numbers of cases suggesting that, in addition to poisoning the minds and morals of youth, LSD produced broken chromosomes and thus genetic damage (Cohen et al., 1967). These studies were soon shown to be seriously misleading if not meaningless (Tjio et al., 1969), but not before the press, politicians, the medical profession, and the National Institute of Mental Health used them to promote a scare (Weil, 1972:44–46).

I suggest that the reason even supposedly hard-headed scientists were drawn into such propaganda was that dominant groups felt the country was at war—and not merely with Vietnam. In this scare, there was not so much a "dangerous class" or threatening racial group as multi-faceted political and cultural conflict, particularly between generations, which gave rise to the perception that middle-class youth who rejected conventional values were a dangerous threat.[4] This scare resulted in the Comprehensive Drug Abuse Control Act of 1970, which criminalized more forms of drug use and subjected users to harsher penalties.

Most recently we have seen the crack scare, which began in earnest *not* when the prevalence of cocaine use quadrupled in the late 1970s, nor even when thousands of users began to smoke it in the more potent and dangerous form of freebase. Indeed, when this scare was launched, crack was unknown outside of a few neighborhoods in a handful of major cities (Reinarman and Levine, 1989a) and the prevalence of illicit drug use had been dropping for several years (National Institute on Drug Use, 1990). Rather, this most recent scare began in 1986 when freebase cocaine was renamed crack (or "rock") and sold in pre-cooked, inexpensive units on ghetto streetcorners (Reinarman and Levine, 1989b). Once politicians and the media linked this new form of cocaine use to the inner-city, minority poor, a new drug scare was under way and the solution became more prison cells rather than more treatment slots.

The same sorts of wild claims and Draconian policy proposals of Temperance and Prohibition leaders re-surfaced in the crack scare. Politicians have so outdone each other in getting "tough on drugs" that each year since crack came on the scene in 1986 they have passed more repressive laws providing billions more for law enforcement, longer sentences, and more drug offenses punishable by death. One result is that the U.S. now has more people in prison than any industrialized nation in the world—about half of them for drug offenses, the majority of whom are racial minorities.

In each of these periods more repressive drug laws were passed on the grounds that they would reduce drug use and drug problems. I have found no evidence that any scare actually accomplished those ends, but they did greatly expand the quantity and quality of social control, particularly over subordinate groups perceived as dangerous or threatening. Reading across these historical episodes one can abstract a recipe for drug scares and repressive drug laws that contains the following *seven ingredients:*

1. A Kernel of Truth Humans have ingested fermented beverages at least since human civilization moved from hunting and gathering to primitive agriculture thousands of years ago (Levine, forthcoming). The pharmacopia has expanded exponentially since then. So, in virtually all cultures and historical epochs, there has been sufficient ingestion of consciousness-altering chemicals to provide some basis for some people to claim that it is a problem.

2. Media Magnification In each of the episodes I have summarized and many others, the mass media has engaged in what I call the *routinization of caricature*—rhetorically re-crafting worst cases into typical cases and the episodic into the epidemic. The media dramatize drug problems, as they do other problems, in the course of their routine news-generating and sales-promoting procedures (see Brecher, 1972:321–34; Reinarman and Duskin, 1992; and Molotch and Lester, 1974).

3. Politico-Moral Entrepreneurs I have added the prefix "politico" to Becker's (1963) seminal concept of moral entrepreneur in order to emphasize the fact that the most prominent and powerful moral entrepreneurs in drug scares are often political elites. Otherwise, I employ the term just as he intended: to denote the *enterprise,* the work, of those who create (or enforce) a rule against what they see as a social evil.[5]

In the history of drug problems in the U.S., these entrepreneurs call attention to drug using behavior and define it as a threat about which "something must be done." They also serve as the media's primary source of sound bites on the dangers of this or that drug. In all the scares I have noted, these entrepreneurs had interests of their own (often financial) which had little to do with drugs. Political elites typically find drugs a functional demon in that (like "outside agitators") drugs allow them to deflect attention from other, more systemic sources of public problems for which they would otherwise have to take some responsibility. Unlike almost every other political issue, however, to be "tough on drugs" in American political culture allows a leader to take a firm stand without risking votes or campaign contributions.

4. Professional Interest Groups In each drug scare and during the passage of each drug law, various professional interests contended over what Gusfield (1981:10–15) calls the "ownership" of drug problems—"the ability to create and influence the public definition of a problem" (1981:10), and thus to define what should be done about it. These groups have included industrialists, churches, the American Medical Association, the American Pharmaceutical Association, various law enforcement agencies, scientists, and most recently the treatment industry and groups of those former addicts converted to disease ideology.[6] These groups claim for themselves, by virtue of their specialized forms of knowledge, the legitimacy and authority to name what is wrong and to prescribe the solution, usually garnering resources as a result.

5. Historical Context of Conflict This trinity of the media, moral entrepreneurs, and professional interests typically interacts in such a way as to inflate the extant "kernel of truth" about drug use. But this interaction does not by itself give rise to drug scares or drug laws without underlying conflicts which make drugs into functional villains. Although Temperance crusaders persuaded millions to pledge abstinence, they campaigned for years without achieving alcohol control laws. However, in the tumultuous period leading up to Prohibition, there were revolutions in Russia and Mexico, World War I, massive immigration and impoverishment, and socialist, anarchist, and labor movements, to say nothing of increases in routine problems such as crime. I submit that all this conflict made for a level of cultural anxiety that provided fertile ideological soil for Prohibition. In each of the other scares, similar conflicts—economic, political, cultural, class, racial, or a combination—provided a context in which claims makers could viably construe certain classes of drug users as a threat.

6. Linking a Form of Drug Use to a "Dangerous Class" Drug scares are never about drugs per se, because drugs are inanimate objects without social consequence until they are ingested by humans. Rather, drug scares are about the use of a drug by particular groups of people who are, typically, *already* perceived by powerful groups as some kind of threat (see Duster, 1970; Himmelstein, 1978). It was not so much alcohol problems per se that most animated the drive for Prohibition but the behavior and morality of what dominant groups saw as the "dangerous class" of urban, immigrant, Catholic, working-class drinkers (Gusfield, 1963; Rumbarger, 1989). It was *Chinese* opium smoking dens, not the more widespread use of other opiates, that prompted California's first drug law in the 1870s. It was only when smokable cocaine found its way to the African-American and Latino underclass that it made headlines and prompted calls for a drug war. In each case, politico-moral entrepreneurs were able to construct a "drug problem" by linking a substance to a group of users perceived by the powerful as disreputable, dangerous, or otherwise threatening.

7. Scapegoating a Drug for a Wide Array of Public Problems The final ingredient is scapegoating, i.e., blaming a drug or its alleged effects on a group of its users for a variety of pre-existing social ills that are typically only indirectly associated with it. Scapegoating may be the most crucial element because it gives great explanatory power and thus broader resonance to claims about the horrors of drugs (particularly in the conflictual historical contexts in which drug scares tend to occur).

Scapegoating was abundant in each of the cases noted above. To listen to Temperance crusaders, for example, one might have believed that without alcohol use, America would be a land of infinite economic progress with no poverty, crime, mental illness, or even sex outside marriage. To listen to leaders of organized medicine and the government in the 1960s, one might have surmised that without marijuana and LSD there would have been neither conflict between youth and their parents nor opposition to the Vietnam War. And to believe politicians and the media in the past six years is to believe that without the scourge of crack the inner cities and the so-called underclass would, if not disappear, at least be far less scarred by poverty, violence, and crime. There is no historical evidence supporting any of this.

In short, drugs are richly functional scapegoats. They provide elites with fig leaves to place over unsightly social ills that are endemic to the social system over which they preside. And they provide the public with a restricted aperture of attribution in which only a chemical bogeyman or the lone deviants who ingest it are seen as the cause of a cornucopia of complex problems.

Toward a Culturally Specific Theory of Drug Scares

Various forms of drug use have been and are widespread in almost all societies comparable to ours. A few of them have experienced limited drug scares, usually around alcohol decades ago. However, drug scares have been *far* less common in other societies, and never as virulent as they have been in the U.S. (Brecher, 1972; Levine, 1992; MacAndrew and Edgerton, 1969). There has never been a time or place in human history without drunkenness, for example, but in *most* times and places drunkenness has not been nearly as problematic as it has been in the U.S. since the late 18th century (Levine, forthcoming). Moreover, in comparable industrial democracies, drug laws are generally less repressive. Why then do claims about the horrors of this or that consciousness-altering chemical have such unusual power in American culture?

Drug scares and other periods of acute public concern about drug use are not just discrete, unrelated episodes. There is a historical pattern in the U.S. that cannot be understood in terms of the moral values and perceptions of individual anti-drug crusaders alone. I have suggested that these crusaders have benefitted in various ways from their crusades. For example, making claims about how a drug is damaging society can help elites increase the social control of groups perceived as threatening (Duster, 1970), establish one class's moral code as dominant (Gusfield, 1963), bolster a bureaucracy's sagging fiscal fortunes (Dickson, 1968), or mobilize voter support (Reinarman and Levine, 1989a,b). However, the recurring character of pharmaco-phobia in U.S. history suggests that there is something about our *culture* which makes citizens more vulnerable to anti-drug crusaders' attempts to demonize drugs. Thus, an answer to the question of America's unusual vulnerability to drug scares must address why the scapegoating of consciousness-altering substances regularly *resonates* with or appeals to substantial portions of the population.

There are three basic parts to my answer. The first is that claims about the evils of drugs are especially viable in American culture in part because they provide a welcome *vocabulary of attribution* (cf. Mills, 1940). Armed with "DRUGS" as a generic scapegoat, citizens gain the cognitive satisfaction of having a folk devil on which to blame a range of bizarre behaviors or other conditions they find troubling but difficult to explain in other terms. This much may be true of a number of other societies, but I hypothesize that this is particularly so in the U.S. because in our political culture individualistic explanations for problems are so much more common than social explanations.

Second, claims about the evils of drugs provide an especially serviceable vocabulary of attribution in the U.S. in part because our society developed from a *temper-*

ance culture (Levine, 1992). American society was forged in the fires of ascetic Protestantism and industrial capitalism, both of which demand *self-control*. U.S. society has long been characterized as the land of the individual "self-made man." In such a land, self-control has had extraordinary importance. For the middle-class Protestants who settled, defined, and still dominate the U.S., self-control was both central to religious world views and a characterological necessity for economic survival and success in the capitalist market (Weber, 1930 [1985]). With Levine (1992), I hypothesize that in a culture in which self-control is inordinately important, drug-induced altered states of consciousness are especially likely to be experienced as "loss of control," and thus to be inordinately feared.[7]

Drunkenness and other forms of drug use have, of course, been present everywhere in the industrialized world. But temperance cultures tend to arise only when industrial capitalism unfolds upon a cultural terrain deeply imbued with the Protestant ethic.[8] This means that only the U.S., England, Canada, and parts of Scandinavia have Temperance cultures, the U.S. being the most extreme case.

It may be objected that the influence of such a Temperance culture was strongest in the 19th and early 20th century and that its grip on the American *zeitgeist* has been loosened by the forces of modernity and now, many say, postmodernity. The third part of my answer, however, is that on the foundation of a Temperance culture, advanced capitalism has built a *postmodern, mass consumption culture* that exacerbates the problem of self-control in new ways.

Early in the 20th century, Henry Ford pioneered the idea that by raising wages he could simultaneously quell worker protest and increase market demand for mass-produced goods. This mass consumption strategy became central to modern American society and one of the reasons for our economic success (Marcuse, 1964; Aronowitz, 1973; Ewen, 1976; Bell, 1978). Our economy is now so fundamentally predicated upon mass consumption that theorists as diverse as Daniel Bell and Herbert Marcuse have observed that we live in a mass consumption culture. Bell (1978), for example, notes that while the Protestant work ethic and deferred gratification may still hold sway in the workplace, Madison Avenue, the media, and malls have inculcated a new indulgence ethic in the leisure sphere in which pleasure-seeking and immediate gratification reign.

Thus, our economy and society have come to depend upon the constant cultivation of new "needs," the production of new desires. Not only the hardware of social life such as food, clothing, and shelter but also the software of the self—excitement, entertainment, even eroticism—have become mass consumption commodities. This means that our society offers an increasing number of incentives for indulgence—more ways to lose self-control—and a decreasing number of countervailing reasons for retaining it.

In short, drug scares continue to occur in American society in part because people must constantly manage the contradiction between a Temperance culture that insists on self-control and a mass consumption culture which renders self-control continuously problematic. In addition to helping explain the recurrence of drug scares, I think this contradiction helps account for why in the last dozen years millions of Americans have joined 12-Step groups, more than 100 of which have nothing whatsoever to do with ingesting a drug (Reinarman, forthcoming). "Addiction," or the generalized loss of self-control, has become the meta-metaphor for a staggering array of human troubles. And, of course, we also seem to have a staggering array of politicians and other moral entrepreneurs who take advantage of such cultural contradictions to blame new chemical bogeymen for our society's ills.

Notes

1. In this regard, for example, Robin Room wisely observes "that we are living at a historic moment when the rate of (alcohol) dependence as a cognitive and existential experience is rising, although the rate of alcohol consumption and of heavy drinking is falling." He draws from this a more general hypothesis about "long waves" of drinking and societal reactions to them: "[I]n periods of increased questioning of drinking and heavy drinking, the trends in the two forms of dependence, psychological and physical, will tend to run in opposite directions. Conversely, in periods of a "wettening" of sentiments, with the curve of alcohol consumption beginning to rise, we may expect the rate of physical dependence ... to rise while the rate of dependence as a cognitive experience falls" (1991:154).

2. I say "formal end" because Temperance ideology is not merely alive and well in the War on Drugs but is being applied to all manner of human troubles in the burgeoning 12-Step Movement (Reinarman, forthcoming).

3. From Jim Baumohl I have learned that while the Temperance movement attracted most of its supporters from these groups, it also found supporters among many others (e.g., labor, the Irish, Catholics, former drunkards, women), each of which had its own reading of and folded its own agenda into the movement.

4. This historical sketch of drug scares is obviously not exhaustive. Readers interested in other scares should see, e.g., Brecher's encyclopedic work *Licit and Illicit Drugs* (1972), especially the chapter on glue sniffing, which illustrates how the media actually created a new drug problem by writing hysterical stories about it. There was also a PCP scare in the 1970s in which law enforcement officials claimed that the growing use of this horse tranquilizer was a severe threat because it made users so violent and gave them such super-human strength that stun guns were necessary. This, too, turned out to be unfounded and the "angel dust" scare was short-lived (see Feldman et al., 1979). The best analysis of how new drugs themselves can lead to panic reactions among users is Becker (1967).

5. Becker wisely warns against the "one-sided view" that sees such crusaders as merely imposing their morality on others. Moral entrepreneurs, he notes, do operate "with an absolute ethic," are "fervent and righteous," and will use "any means" necessary to "do away with" what they see as "totally evil." However, they also "typically believe that their mission is a holy one," that if people do what they want it "will be good for them." Thus, as in the case of abolitionists, the crusades of moral entrepreneurs often "have strong humanitarian overtones" (1963:147–8). This is no less true for those whose moral enterprise promotes drug scares. My analysis, however, concerns the character and consequences of their efforts, not their motives.

6. As Gusfield notes, such ownership sometimes shifts over time, e.g., with alcohol problems, from religion to criminal law to medical science. With other drug problems, the shift in ownership has been away from medical science toward criminal law. The most insightful treatment of the medicalization of alcohol/drug problems is Peele (1989).

7. See Baumohl's (1990) important and erudite analysis of how the human will was valorized in the therapeutic temperance thought of 19th-century inebriate homes.

8. The third central feature of Temperance cultures identified by Levine (1992), which I will not dwell on, is predominance of spirits drinking, i.e., more concentrated alcohol than wine or beer and thus greater likelihood of drunkenness.

References

Aronowitz, Stanley, *False Promises: The Shaping of American Working Class Consciousness* (New York: McGraw-Hill, 1973).

Baumohl, Jim, "Inebriate Institutions in North America, 1840–1920," *British Journal of Addiction* 85:1187–1204 (1990).

Baumohl, Jim, "The 'Dope Fiend's Paradise' Revisited: Notes from Research in Progress on Drug Law Enforcement in San Francisco, 1875–1915," *Drinking and Drug Practices Surveyor* 24:3–12 (1992).

Becker, Howard S., *Outsiders: Studies in the Sociology of Deviance* (Glencoe, IL: Free Press, 1963).

Becker, Howard S., "History, Culture, and Subjective Experience: An Exploration of the Social Bases of Drug-Induced Experiences," *Journal of Health and Social Behavior* 8:162–176 (1967).

Bell, Daniel, *The Cultural Contradictions of Capitalism* (New York: Basic Books, 1978).

Brecher, Edward M., *Licit and Illicit Drugs* (Boston: Little Brown, 1972).

Cohen, M. M., K. Hirshorn, and W. A. Frosch, "In Vivo and in Vitro Chromosomal Damage Induced by LSD-25," *New England Journal of Medicine* 227:1043 (1967).

Courtwright, David, *Dark Paradise: Opiate Addiction in America Before 1940* (Cambridge, MA: Harvard University Press, 1982).

Dickson, Donald, "Bureaucracy and Morality," *Social Problems* 16:143–156 (1968).

Duster, Troy, *The Legislation of Morality: Law, Drugs, and Moral Judgement* (New York: Free Press, 1970).

Ewen, Stuart, *Captains of Consciousness: Advertising and the Social Roots of Consumer Culture* (New York: McGraw-Hill, 1976).

Feldman, Harvey W., Michael H. Agar, and George M. Beschner, *Angel Dust* (Lexington, MA: Lexington Books, 1979).

Gusfield, Joseph R., *Symbolic Crusade: Status Politics and the American Temperance Movement* (Urbana: University of Illinois Press, 1963).

Gusfield, Joseph R., *The Culture of Public Problems: Drinking-Driving and the Symbolic Order* (Chicago: University of Chicago Press, 1981).

Himmelstein, Jerome, "Drug Politics Theory," *Journal of Drug Issues* 8 (1978).

Himmelstein, Jerome, *The Strange Career of Marihuana* (Westport, CT: Greenwood Press, 1983).

Levine, Harry Gene, "The Alcohol Problem in America: From Temperance to Alcoholism," *British Journal of Addiction* 84:109–119 (1984).

Levine, Harry Gene, "Temperance Cultures: Concern About Alcohol Problems in Nordic and English-Speaking Cultures," in G. Edwards et al., Eds., *The Nature of Alcohol and Drug Related Problems* (New York: Oxford University Press, 1992).

Levine, Harry Gene, *Drunkenness and Civilization* (New York: Basic Books, forthcoming).

Levine, Harry Gene, and Craig Reinarman, "From Prohibition to Regulation: Lessons from Alcohol Policy for Drug Policy," *Milbank Quarterly* 69:461–494 (1991).

MacAndrew, Craig, and Robert Edgerton, *Drunken Comportment* (Chicago: Aldine, 1969).

Marcuse, Herbert, *One-Dimensional Man: Studies in the Ideology of Advanced Industrial Society* (Boston: Beacon Press, 1964).

Mills, C. Wright, "Situated Actions and Vocabularies of Motive," *American Sociological Review* 5:904–913 (1940).

Molotch, Harvey, and Marilyn Lester, "News as Purposive Behavior: On the Strategic Uses of Routine Events, Accidents, and Scandals," *American Sociological Review* 39:101–112 (1974).

Morgan, Patricia, "The Legislation of Drug Law: Economic Crisis and Social Control," *Journal of Drug Issues* 8:53–62 (1978).

Musto, David, *The American Disease: Origins of Narcotic Control* (New Haven, CT: Yale University Press, 1973).

National Institute on Drug Abuse, *National Household Survey on Drug Abuse: Main Findings 1990* (Washington, DC: U.S. Department of Health and Human Services, 1990).

Peele, Stanton, *The Diseasing of America: Addiction Treatment Out of Control* (Lexington, MA: Lexington Books, 1989).

Reinarman, Craig, "The 12-Step Movement and Advanced Capitalist Culture: Notes on the Politics of Self-Control in Postmodernity," in B. Epstein, R. Flacks, and M. Darnovsky, Eds., *Contemporary Social Movements and Cultural Politics* (Philadelphia: Temple University Press, 1995).

Reinarman, Craig, and Ceres Duskin, "Dominant Ideology and Drugs in the Media," *International Journal on Drug Policy* 3:6–15 (1992).

Reinarman, Craig, and Harry Gene Levine, "Crack in Context: Politics and Media in the Making of a Drug Scare," *Contemporary Drug Problems* 16:535–577 (1989a).

Reinarman, Craig, and Harry Gene Levine, "The Crack Attack: Politics and Media in America's Latest Drug Scare," pp. 115–137 in Joel Best, Ed., *Images of Issues: Typifying Contemporary Social Problems* (New York: Aldine de Gruyter, 1989b).

Room, Robin G. W., "Cultural Changes in Drinking and Trends in Alcohol Problems Indicators: Recent U.S. Experience," pp. 149–162 in Walter B. Clark and Michael E. Hilton, Eds., *Alcohol in America: Drinking Practices and Problems* (Albany: State University of New York Press, 1991).

Rumbarger, John J., *Profits, Power, and Prohibition: Alcohol Reform and the Industrializing of America. 1800–1930* (Albany: State University of New York Press, 1989).

Tijo, J. H., W. N. Pahnke, and A. A. Kurland, "LSD and Chromosomes: A Controlled Experiment," *Journal of the American Medical Association* 210:849 (1969).

Weber, Max, *The Protestant Ethic and the Spirit of Capitalism* (London: Unwin, 1985 [1930]).

Weil, Andrew, *The Natural Mind* (Boston: Houghton Mifflin, 1972).

The Cycle of Abstinence and Relapse Among Heroin Addicts

MARSH B. RAY

Those who study persons addicted to opium and its derivatives are confronted by the following paradox: A cure from physiological dependence on opiates may be secured within a relatively short period, and carefully controlled studies indicate that use of these drugs does not cause psychosis, organic intellectual deterioration, or any permanent impairment of intellectual function. But, despite these facts, addicts display a high rate of recidivism. On the other hand, while the rate of recidivism is high, addicts continually and repeatedly seek cure. It is difficult to obtain definitive data concerning the number of cures the addict takes, but various studies of institutional admissions indicate that it is relatively high, and there are many attempts at home cure that go unrecorded.

This paper reports on a study of abstinence and relapse in which attention is focused on the way the addict or abstainer orders and makes meaningful the objects of this experience, including himself as an object, during the critical periods of cure and of relapse and the related sense of identity or of social isolation the addict feels as he interacts with significant others. It is especially concerned with describing and analyzing the characteristic ways the addict or abstainer defines the social situations he encounters during these periods and responds to the status dilemmas he experiences in them.

Secondary Status Characteristics of Addicts

The social world of addiction contains a loose system of organizational and cultural elements, including a special language or argot, certain artifacts, a commodity market and pricing system, a system of stratification, and ethical codes. The addict's commitment to these values gives him a status and an identity. In addition to these direct links to the world of addiction, becoming an addict means that one assumes a number of secondary status characteristics in accordance with the definitions the society has of this activity. Some of these are set forth in federal and local laws and statutes, others are defined by the stereotypic thinking of members of the larger society about the causes and consequences of drug use.

The addict's incarceration in correctional institutions has specific meanings which he finds reflected in the attitudes adopted toward him by members of non-addict society and by his fellow addicts. Additionally, as his habit grows and the de-

From Marsh B. Ray, "The Cycle of Abstinence and Relapse Among Heroin Addicts." Reprinted with the permission of The Free Press, a division of Simon & Schuster from *The Other Side: Perspectives on Deviance* by Howard S. Becker, pp. 163–177 (with deletions). Copyright ©1964 by The Free Press.

mands for drugs get beyond any legitimate means of supply, his own activities in satisfying his increased craving give him direct experiential evidence of the criminal aspects of self. These meanings of self as a criminal become internalized as he begins to apply criminal argot to his activities and institutional experiences. Thus shoplifting becomes "boosting," the correctional settings become "joints," and the guards in such institutions become "screws."

The popular notion that the addict is somehow psychologically inadequate is supported by many authorities in the field. In addition, support and definition are supplied by the very nature of the institution in which drug addicts are usually treated and have a large part of their experience since even the names of these institutions fix this definition of addiction. For example, one of the out-patient clinics for the treatment of addicts in Chicago was located at Illinois Neuropsychiatric Institute, and the connotations of Bellevue Hospital in New York City, another treatment center for addicts, are socially well established. Then, too, the composition of the staff in treatment centers contributes substantially to the image of the addict as mentally ill, for the personnel are primarily psychiatrists, psychologists, and psychiatric social workers. How such a definition of self was brought forcefully home to one addict is illustrated in the following quotation:

> When I got down to the hospital, I was interviewed by different doctors and one of them told me, "You now have one mark against you as crazy for having been down here." I hadn't known it was crazy house. You know regular people [non-addicts] think this too.

Finally, as the addict's habit grows and almost all of his thoughts and efforts are directed toward supplying himself with drugs, he becomes careless about his personal appearance and cleanliness. Consequently non-addicts think of him as a "bum" and, because he persists in his use of drugs, conclude that he lacks "will power," is perhaps "degenerate," and is likely to contaminate others.

The addict is aware that he is judged in terms of these various secondary social definitions, and while he may attempt to reject them, it is difficult if not impossible to do so when much of his interpersonal and institutional experience serves to ratify these definitions. They assume importance because they are the medium of exchange in social transactions with the addict and non-addict world in which the addict identifies himself as an object and judges himself in relation to addict and non-addict values. Such experiences are socially disjunctive and become the basis for motivated acts....

The Addict Self in Transition

The addict who has successfully completed withdrawal is no longer faced with the need to take drugs in order to avert the disaster of withdrawal sickness, and now enters a period which might best be characterized as a "running struggle" with his problems of social identity. He could not have taken such a drastic step had he not developed some series of expectations concerning the nature of his future relationships with social others. His anticipations concerning these situations may or may not be realistic; what matters is that he has them and that the imagery he holds regarding himself and his potentialities is a strong motivating force in his continued abstinence. Above all, he appears to desire ratification by significant others of his newly developing identity, and in his interactions during an episode of abstinence he expects to secure it.

In the early phases of an episode of cure, the abstainer manifests considerable ambivalence about where he stands in addict and non-addict groups, and in discussions of addiction and addicts, he may indicate his ambivalence through his alternate use of the pronouns "we" and "they" and thus his alternate membership in addict and non-addict society. He may also indicate his ambivalence through other nuances of language and choice of words. Later, during a successful episode of abstinence, the ex-addict indicates his non-membership in the addict group through categorizations that place addicts clearly in the third person, and he places his own addiction and matters pertaining to it in the past tense. For example, he is likely to preface a remark with the phrase "When I was an addict...." But of equal or greater importance is the fact that the ex-addict who is successful in remaining abstinent relates to new groups of people, participates in their experience, and to some extent begins to evaluate the conduct of his former associates (and perhaps his own when he was an addict) in terms of the values of the new group.

> I see the guys around now quite often and sometimes we talk for a while but I don't feel that I am anything like them any more and I always leave before they "make up" [take drugs]. I tell them, "You know what you are doing but if you keep on you'll just go to jail like I did." I don't feel that they are wrong to be using but just that I'm luckier than they are because I have goals. It's funny, I used to call them "squares" for not using and now they call me "square" for not using. They think that they are "hip" and they are always talking about the old days. That makes me realize how far I've come. But it makes me want to keep away from them, too, because they always use the same old vocabulary—talking about "squares" and being "hip."

Thus, while some abstainers do not deny the right of others to use drugs if they choose, they clearly indicate that addiction is no longer a personally meaningful area of social experience for them. In the above illustration the abstainer is using this experience as something of a "sounding board" for his newly developed identity. Of particular note is the considerable loss of meaning in the old symbols through which he previously ordered his experience and his concern with one of the inevitable consequences of drug use. This is a common experience for those who have maintained abstinence for any length of time.

During the later stages of the formation of an abstainer identity, the ex-addict begins to perceive a difference in his relations with significant others, particularly with members of his family. Undoubtedly their attitudes, in turn, undergo modification and change as a result of his apparent continued abstinence, and they arrive at this judgment by observing his cleanliness and attention to personal neatness, his steady employment, and his re-subscription to other values of non-addict society. The ex-addict is very much aware of these attitudinal differences and uses them further to bolster his conception of himself as an abstainer.

> Lots of times I don't even feel like I ever took dope. I feel released not to be dependent on it. I think how nice it is to be natural without having to rely on dope to make me feel good. See, when I was a "junkie" I lost a lot of respect. My father woudn't talk to me and I was filthy. I have to build up that respect again. I do a lot of things with my family now and my father talks to me again. It's like at parties that my relatives give, now they are always running up to me and giving me a drink and showing me a lot of attention. Before they wouldn't even talk to me. See, I used to feel lonely because my life was dependent on stuff and I felt different from regular people. See, "junkies" and regular people are two different things. I used to feel that I was out of place with my relatives when I was on junk. I didn't want to walk with them on the street and do things with them. Now I do things with them all the time like go to the show and joke with them and I go to church with my uncle. I just kept saying to myself that "junkies" are not my people. My relatives don't say things behind my back now and I am gaining their respect slow but sure.

In this illustration there may be observed a budding sense of social insight characteristic of abstainers in this period of their development. Another characteristic feature is the recognition that subscription to non-addict values must be grounded in action—in playing the role of non-addict in participation with non-addicts and thus sharing in their values and perspectives.

The Process of Relapse

The tendency toward relapse develops out of the meanings of the abstainer's experience in social situations when he develops an image of himself as socially different from non-addicts, and relapse occurs when he redefines himself as an addict. When his social expectations and the expectations of others with whom he interacts are not met, social stress develops and he is required to re-examine the meaningfulness of his experience in non-addict society and in so doing question his identity as an abstainer. This type of experience promotes a mental realignment with addict values and standards and may be observed in the abstainer's thoughts about himself in covert social situations, in his direct interpersonal relations with active addicts, and in his experience with representatives of non-addict society. It is in these various settings that his developing sense of self as an abstainer is put to the test.

Experiences with other addicts that promote relapse. Re-addiction most frequently occurs during the period immediately following the physical withdrawal of the drug—the period described earlier as a time of "running struggle" with identity problems for the ex-addict. It is at this point, when the old values and old meanings he experienced as an addict are still immediate and the new ordering of his experience without narcotics is not well established, that the ex-addict seems most vulnerable to relapse. Sometimes the experiences that provoke the questioning of identity that precedes relapse occur within the confines of the very institution where the addict has gone to seek cure. The social expectations of other addicts in the hospital are of vital importance in creating an atmosphere in which identification with the values of non-addict society is difficult to maintain.

> [The last time we talked you said that you would like to tell me about your experiences in the hospital. What were they like?]
>
> Well, during the first time I was at the hospital most of the fellows seemed to hate [to give] the "square" impression, not hate it exactly but refuse to admit [to] it. My own feelings were that everyone should have been a little different in expressing themselves that I would like to accept the extreme opposite. But I felt that I would have disagreements about this with the fellow inmates. They thought I was a very queer or peculiar person that constantly showed disagreement about the problem as they saw it. I never did reach an understanding with them about the problem.

But addicts do not always relapse on first contact with members of the old group. In fact, there is nothing to indicate that addicts relapse only as a result of association. Instead, contacts may go on for some time during which the ex-addict carries on much private self-debate, feeling at one point that he is socially closer to addicts and at another that his real interest lies in future new identities on which he has decided. Typically he may also call to mind the reason he undertook cure in the first place and question the rationality of relapsing. An interesting example of the dilemma and ambivalence experienced under these circumstances and the partial acceding to social pressures from the addict group by applying the definitions of that group to one's own conduct is the experiences of another addict.

> [He had entered the hospital "with the key" and after completing withdrawal he stayed at the hospital for three weeks before voluntarily signing out, although the required period of treatment for a medical discharge at the time was four and one-half months.]
>
> This one kid who was a friend of mine came to me one night and said, "Let's get out of here." So I went and checked out too. Then I got to thinking, "I don't want to go home yet—I'm still sick—and what did I come down here for anyway." So I went up and got my papers back from the officer and tore them up. Then I found this kid and told him that I was staying and he said, "Oh we knew you weren't going to do it—we knew you'd chicken out." Then I went back and put my papers through again. I felt they were trying to "put me down."
>
> When we got out I could have had a shot right away because one of these guys when we got to town said he knew a croaker [physician] who would fix us up, but I didn't go with them. I didn't care what they thought because I got to figuring that I had went this far and I might as well stay off.

> When I got home I stayed off for two months but my mother was hollering at me all the time and there was this one family in the neighborhood that was always "chopping me up." I wanted to tell this woman off because she talked all right to my face but behind my back she said things like she was afraid I would turn her son on because I was hanging around with him. She would tell these things to my mother. I never turned anybody on! She didn't know that but I wanted to tell her. Finally I just got disgusted because nobody wanted to believe me and I went back on.

The experiences of this addict provide an interesting denial of the notion that addicts relapse because of association *per se* and support the thesis that relapse is a function of the kind of object ex-addicts make of themselves in the situations they face.

Relations with non-addicts as a prelude to relapse. While the ex-addict's interaction with addict groups is often a source of experiences which cause him to question the value to him of an abstainer identity, experiences with non-addict groups also play a vital role. In most instances the addict has established a status for himself in the eyes of non-addicts who may be acquainted with his case—members of his family, social workers, law enforcement officers, physicians, and so forth. Through gestures, vocal and otherwise, these non-addicts make indications to the ex-addict concerning his membership and right to participation in their group, for example, the right to be believed when he attempts to indicate to the non-addict world that he believes in and subscribes to its values. In his contacts with non-addicts, the former addict is particularly sensitive to their cues.

During the early phases of an episode of abstinence the abstainer enters various situations with quite definite expectations concerning how he should be defined and treated. He indicates his desire for ratification of his new status in many ways, and finds it socially difficult when he sees in the conduct of others toward him a reference to his old identity as an addict. He is not unaware of these doubts about his identity.

> My relatives were always saying things to me like "Have you really quit using that drug now?" and things like that. And I knew that they were doing a lot of talking behind my back because when I came around they would stop talking but I overheard them. It used to burn my ass.

On the other hand, the non-addicts with whom he has experience during this period have their own expectations concerning the abstainer's probable conduct. Based in part on the stereotypic thinking of non-addict society concerning addiction, in part on unfortunate previous experiences, they may exhibit some skepticism concerning the "cure" and express doubt about the abstainer's prognosis.

The Social Psychological Meaning of Relapse

On an immediate concrete level, relapse requires that the individual reorient himself to the market conditions surrounding the sale of illicit drugs. He must re-establish his sources of supply and, if he has been abstinent for very long, he may have to learn about new fads and fashions in drug use. He may learn, for example, that dolophin is more readily available than heroin at the moment of his return to drug use, that it requires less in the way of preparation, that it calls for such and such amount to safely secure a certain effect, what the effects will be, and so on.

But the ex-addict's re-entrance into the social world of addiction has much deeper meanings. It places demands and restraints upon his interactions and the meaningfulness of his experience. It requires a recommitment to the norms of addiction and limits the degree to which he may relate to non-addict groups in terms of the latter's values and standards. It demands participation in the old ways of organizing conduct and experience and, as a consequence, the readoption of the secondary status characteristics of addiction. He again shows a lack of concern about his personal appearance and grooming. Illicit activities are again engaged in to get money for drugs, and as a result the possibility of more firmly establishing the criminal aspect of his identity becomes a reality.

The social consequence of these experiences and activities is the re-establishment of the sense of social isolation from the non-addict group and a recaptured sense of the meaningfulness of experience in the social world of addiction. It is through these familiar meanings and the reapplication of the symbolic meanings of the addict world to his own conduct that identity and status as an addict are reaffirmed. The ex-addict who relapses is thus likely to comment, "I feel like one of the guys again," or as Street has put it, "It was like coming home."

While repeated relapse on the addict's part may more firmly convince him that "once a junkie, always a junkie" is no myth but instead a valid comment on his way of life, every relapse has within it the genesis of another attempt at cure. From his however brief or lengthy excursions into the world of non-addiction, the relapsed addict carries back with him an image of himself as one who has done the impossible—one who has actually experienced a period when it was unnecessary to take drugs to avoid the dreaded withdrawal sickness. But these are not his only recollections. He recalls, too, his identification of himself as an abstainer, no matter how tentatively or imperfectly this may have been accomplished. He thinks over his experiences in situations while he occupied the status of abstainer and speculates about the possible other outcomes of these situations had he acted differently.

> [Originally from Chicago, he experienced the only voluntary period of abstinence in a long career of addiction while living with his wife in Kansas City, Missouri. After an argument with his wife, during which she reminded him of his previous addiction and its consequences for her, he left her and retuned to Chicago, where he immediately relapsed. After three weeks he was using about $12 worth of morphine daily.] He reports on his thoughts at the time as follows:
>
> Now and then I'm given to rational thinking or reasoning and somehow I had a premonition that should I remain in Chicago much longer, shoplifting and doing the various criminal acts I did to get money for drugs, plus the criminal act of just using the drug, I would soon be in jail or perhaps something worse, for in truth one's life is at stake each day when he uses drugs. I reflected on the life I had known in Kansas City with Rose in contrast to the one I had returned

to. I didn't know what Rose thought had become of me. I thought that more than likely she was angry and thoroughly disgusted and glad that I was gone. However, I wanted to return but first thought it best to call and see what her feelings were.

[At his wife's urging he returned to Kansas City and undertook a "cold turkey" cure in their home. He remained abstinent for a considerable period but subsequently relapsed again when he returned to Chicago.]

Reflections of the above kind provide the relapsed addict with a rich body of material for self-recrimination and he again evaluates his own conduct in terms of what he believes are the larger society's attitudes toward addicts and addiction. It is then that he may again speculate about his own potential for meaningful experiences and relationships in a non-addict world and thus set into motion a new attempt at cure.

Summary

Addiction to narcotic drugs in our society commits the participant in this activity to a status and identity that has complex secondary characteristics. These develop through shared roles and common interpersonal and institutional experience, and as a consequence addicts develop perspectives about themselves and about non-addict values. They evaluate social situations, and in turn are evaluated by the other participants in these situations, in these terms, often with the result that the value of the addict's identity relative to the social world of addiction is brought into question. When this happens the identification of oneself as an addict, committed to the values and statuses of the addict group, is contrasted with new or remembered identities and relationships, resulting in a commitment to cure with its implications of intense physical suffering. In the period following physical withdrawal from heroin, the addict attempts to enact a new social reality which coincides with his desired self-image as an abstainer, and he seeks ratification of his new identity from others in the situations he faces.

But the abstainer's social expectations during a period when he is off drugs are frequently not gratified. Here again, socially disjunctive experiences bring about a questioning of the value of an abstainer identity and promote reflections in which addict and non-addict identities and relationships are compared. The abstainer's realignment of his values with those of the world of addiction results in the redefinition of self as an addict and has as a consequence the actions necessary to relapse. But it should be noted that the seeds of a new attempt at abstinence are sown, once addiction has been re-established, in the self-recriminations engaged in upon remembrance of a successful period of abstinence.

Chapter 10

Homosexuality

Any sociological discussion of homosexuality must inevitably address the issue of whether essentialism or constructionism more adequately describes or accounts for homosexuality and heterosexuality. Is homosexuality a condition? McIntosh asks. Or is it a label, a social construct, a term that has been applied at certain times and places to certain individuals? And are these two approaches contradictory or mutually exclusive, or do they complement each other? Does one have to be right and the other wrong, or are they simply asking altogether different questions? Is homosexuality like diabetes or cancer or left-handedness or being a certain height? That is, is it a condition or state or characteristic, an intrinsic, or indwelling essentialistic trait about which all observers can agree? Or is it (as McIntosh asks) like being a "committee chairman" or Seventh Day Adventist—that is, is what is most crucial about it having a specific status conferred upon one, acquiring a certain identity, and adhering to a specific *role,* with certain rights, duties, and obligations attached thereto?

When most people think about a sociological as opposed to a psychological or biological approach to homosexuality, they tend to think that it is a study of the social—as opposed to the biological or psychological—factors or forces or variables that cause one to "become" a homosexual. In this view, homosexuality is still a pregiven entity, a condition that is "caused" by certain experiences in life. That is, an essentialistic characteristic or quality can be inborn or a product of socialization, or a combination of both (Stein, 1990, p. 330). But, in addition to seeking out possible social causes for homosexuality, the sociological approach also attempts to understand the conferral and role-playing process as well, the public image, the condemnation or acceptance of the behavior or the individuals labeled a certain way—in short, *the social construction of homosexuality.* Even if homosexuality were caused solely and exclusively by biological factors, the sociologist is still interested in how homosexuality is viewed, judged, and treated by the members of a given society—by the *discourse* that surrounds homosexuality. For the sociologist of deviance, two central questions are: Why do sexual behavior and orientation become the basis for dividing humans up into distinct categories—homosexual and heterosexual? and,

Why is homosexuality a basis for condemnation in Western society? These are constructionist questions and until the past generation or so have rarely been asked.

Seeing homosexuality as an inborn condition, as McIntosh says, contributes to its condemnation, to the social control of homosexuals and homosexuality: It keeps individuals who are designated one way or the other separate from one another. Interestingly, says McIntosh, many homosexuals actually welcome the essentialistic view of homosexuality as a condition; they welcome this separation of homosexuality and heterosexuality into two separate worlds. For one thing—and this is a recent development—as a number of homosexual spokespersons, activists, and militants have argued, if homosexuality and heterosexuality *are* inborn conditions, this has two implications: First, one can't (or at least one shouldn't) condemn people for a condition they were born with. (It should be pointed out that this hasn't helped possessors of most undesirable involuntarily acquired conditions, such as being physically handicapped; they still face humiliation, social isolation, and condescension.) Consequently, the condemnation of homosexuals for being homosexual is improper; homosexuals did not choose to become gay; hence, no one has the right to condemn them for this fact. Perhaps equally as important, since it is an inborn condition, some say, homosexual teachers, clergy, and other adult figures or potential role models or, for that matter, child molesters or seducers of adolescents, can't induce otherwise heterosexually inclined young people to become homosexuals as a result of their contact or experiences. You are what you are born with and that is a fixed state or condition; no amount of inducement can derail that basic drive. However, whether inborn or not, homosexuality remains a condemned status in the United States.

In the United States, there is a fairly narrow range of permissible sexual behaviors compared with many societies of the world (broader than some, narrower than others). Many societies of the world have a permissible "place" for homosexual behavior. In one survey of the societies of the world, described in the Human Relations Area File, two-thirds of the societies on which there are data permit at least some members of the society to engage in at least some homosexual acts without condemnation (Ford and Beach, 1951). In a few societies, homosexual behavior at a certain stage of life is not only tolerated and encouraged but it is also *demanded* (almost always only of the men, and usually in warrior societies): One would be a deviant, even an outcast, if one refused to engage in homosexual acts (Herdt, 1987). In McIntosh's terms, in most of these societies, homosexual behavior is permitted, but most do not have homosexuality as we in the West know and conceive it.

In our society, there is an extremely serious and vigorous effort to *essentialize* sexuality. By that I mean to label someone as a homosexual as judged or indicated by one's behavior or other outward indicators. Most members of Anglo-American society are fairly quick to essentialize on the basis of a single episode of homosexual behavior, one homosexual act. Imagine a mother or a father seeing a son (for instance) engaging in fellating another young man. Chances are, they would quickly and readily assign him to the category of homosexuality on the basis of that one act. Ask yourself, what would it take to assign someone to one or another deviant categories: alcoholic, drug addict, mentally ill person, and so on? How many episodes of heavy drinking or drug use or irrational, bizarre behavior would it take before someone is thought of as an alcoholic, a drug addict, a mentally ill person? My guess is, this process would operate more quickly and on the basis of less evidence for homosexuality than would be the case for most deviant categories.

McIntosh argues that in our society, more than in most, we tend to dichotomize homosexuality and heterosexuality. These categories tend to be seen as mutually exclusive. One must belong to one category or the other. If one is in one category, one cannot possibly be a member of the other. Often, as McIntosh says, one reads an argument that makes the claim that a given individual can't possibly be a homosexual because he or she had sex with a member of the opposite sex. It is assumed that if one is a homosexual, one automatically cannot be sexually interested in members of the opposite sex. The more sophisticated of us may grant extenuating circumstances, such as prison, adolescence, or depression, to play a role in a particular event, but for the most part someone with a continuing interest in *both* sexes is a puzzlement. In other societies, this was not the case; for instance, in ancient Greece, men who preferred sex with males typically continued to have sex with women, were married, and had families. Back then, homosexual interest did not preclude heterosexual activity. It is a mistake, McIntosh concludes, to assume that the qualities presumed to characterize homosexuality in this society also hold for other societies as well.

In "Homosexuality: An Introduction," Goode and Troiden spell out some of the principal points that any observer of attempting to understand homosexuality as a form of deviance must attend to. Homosexuality is a constructed phenomenon, we say; it is partly a matter of definition: who is defined as a homosexual and even what homosexuality is in the first place is, to a degree, arbitrary and culture-bound. Homosexuality may be seen as being made up of a number of theoretically distinct and separate (though in concrete reality, statistically related) dimensions. An understanding of each of these dimensions is crucial to an understanding of homosexuality; no single dimension defines anyone definitively and for all time *as* a homosexual. For the purposes of this book, *stigma* plays a central role in the lives of homosexuals. In Western society generally, and in the United States specifically, homosexuality is a form of deviance; its deviant status is, in fact, one of the most interesting features of homosexuality. Religious fundamentalists denounce it as an offense in the eyes of God, psychiatrists pathologize it, nearly half the states in the United States criminalize it, and most Americans consider it morally wrong and avoid social contact with homosexuals. Since the early 1980s, of course, the AIDS epidemic has drastically transformed homosexual life; for many Americans, the fact that AIDS is endemic among homosexuals has brought a certain measure of compassion, while for others, it has stimulated little but contempt and condemnation. To understand homosexuality, it is necessary to understand the dynamics of deviant behavior.

References

Ford, Clelland S., and Frank A. Beach. 1951. *Patterns of Sexual Behavior.* New York: Harper & Row.

Herdt, Gilbert. 1987. *The Sambia: Ritual and Gender in New Guinea.* New York: Holt, Reinhart & Winston.

Stein, Edward (ed.). 1990. *Forms of Desire: Sexual Orientation and the Constructionist Controversy.* New York: Garland Publishing.

Male Homosexuality: An Introduction

ERICH GOODE and RICHARD R. TROIDEN

Like any other area of human life, homosexuality is in large part a matter of definition. Put plainly and simply, there is no possible definition of who is a homosexual, or even what is homosexual behavior, that will satisfy everyone. It is more fruitful to examine different *dimensions* of homosexuality—dimensions which are often, but not necessarily, found together. Past observers have attempted to attach a precise label to specific people and specific acts, thinking that they could be unambiguously classified as *either* homosexual *or* heterosexual. Anna Freud—Sigmund Freud's illustrious daughter—wrote that the ultimate criterion of sexual orientation was the sex of one's masturbatory fantasies. While this might be one of a number of useful criteria, we would like to suggest something quite different.

First: that there is no such thing as a "homosexual."

And second: that there is no such thing, strictly speaking, as "homosexual behavior."

By these statements I do not mean that homosexuals and homosexuality do not exist.

Merely that who and what fall into these categories is arbitrary, not absolute, fixed, or final.

That such categorizing depends on selecting specific criteria for defining people and their behavior.

That these criteria cannot be justified scientifically—they can only be justified according to what one or another observer considers important.

That the nature of one's sexual commitment changes over time, sometimes drastically.

That there are many dimensions of homosexuality; most people will be classified as "homosexual" according to some of them, but not according to others.

And lastly: that homosexuality is a matter of *degree*. There is a *spectrum* from complete homosexuality, through mixed homosexuality, to complete heterosexuality. The two polar types are rare; most of us fall in between them.

Let's look at a few examples to show what we mean.

A young man is unhappily married, and has intercourse with his wife only two or three times a month. But several times a week he visits public urinals knowing that other men will be there who will fellate, or "blow" him. He also masturbates regularly, but always fantasizes intercourse with women when he does. He has no friends who consider themselves homosexuals, is not part of a homosexual subculture, and does not think of himself as a homosexual. While most of his behavior would be technically classified as homosexual in nature, by no other criteria can he

From Erich Goode and Richard R. Troiden, eds., *Sexual Deviance and Sexual Deviants* (New York: William Morrow, 1974), pp. 149–160.

be considered a homosexual. Perhaps in time he will have an extramarital heterosexual affair. Perhaps he and his wife will eventually divorce. But right now, his *identity* is heterosexual, his *subcultural involvement* is heterosexual, his *masturbatory fantasies* are heterosexual—but his *behavior* is predominantly homosexual. Is he a homosexual? That depends on how you want to define it.

An adolescent boy is thought by his peers to be effeminate—a "pansy," a "fruit." The boy thinks that he is, perhaps, a homosexual. He begins to frequent homosexual bars. He is sexually excited by pictures, and even the thought, of handsome, muscular men. Yet, he has not, as yet, engaged in sexual behavior with another man; he has, however, had intercourse with two girls with whom he maintains a close emotional friendship. Is this boy a homosexual? Again, the only accurate answer that could possibly be given to this question is: it depends on what you mean. He is in some senses, but not in others.

A man has been in prison for several years. Prior to his imprisonment, he had intercourse only with women. As a prisoner, he is engaged in a long-term liaison with a younger man. Our man is the "active" partner—that is, he is fellated by the other man, and he inserts his penis into the other man's anus in intercourse. He does not assume the "passive" part in intercourse, ever. Our man thinks of his behavior as masculine—and of the behavior of the other man as feminine. The other man agrees. Among fellow inmates, our man is considered supremely masculine, not by any means a homosexual. Now, his behavior is technically homosexual in the sense that it involves organ contact with a member of the same sex. But it isn't homosexual in the sense that it isn't *regarded* as homosexual by anyone in the social group in which it takes place. The behavior of the "passive" partner in this alliance, the man who is the object of sexual contact, *is* thought to be homosexual. Those of us outside the prison community would think of *both* as homosexual. Prisoners wouldn't agree. Which is it? Is our man engaging in "homosexual behavior" or not? Again, it's a question of perspective, not a solid, indisputable fact.

Alfred Kinsey, in his *Sexual Behavior in the Human Male,* first published in 1948, took a giant step in this area by looking upon sexual orientation as a *continuum*. He devised a "heterosexual-homosexual rating scale," which classified men from 0 to 6 in their degree of being one or the other. This scale was based on: (1) "physical contacts which result in erotic arousal or orgasm," and (2) "psychic response." The 0s were exclusively heterosexual, and 6s were exclusively homosexual, and the 1s through 5s were, in varying degrees, in between. Commenting on the scale, Kinsey wrote:

> Males do not represent two discrete populations, heterosexual and homosexual. The world is not to be divided into sheep and goats. Not all things are black nor all things white. It is a fundamental of taxonomy that nature rarely deals with discrete categories. Only the human mind invents categories and tries to force facts into pigeon-holes. The living world is a continuum in each and every one of its aspects. The sooner we learn this concerning human sexual behavior the sooner we shall reach a sound understanding of the realities of sex.

One of the most often cited statistics in the social science literature is from Kinsey's research: over one-third, or 37 percent, of all American males have at least one homosexual episode which results in orgasm from the onset of adolescence to old age. In addition, about 60 percent of all preadolescent boys engage in some sort of homosexual activity. About 6 percent of the total of all of Kinsey's subjects' orgasms were derived from homosexual contact. About four males in one hundred could be regarded as exclusively homosexual—they had never had any sexual contact with women, and were not aroused by them. About 50 percent of the sample were exclusively heterosexual: they had never had any sexual contact at all with another man, and had never been aroused by one. Clearly, *most* men with some homosexual contact had had very little of it; most of it was adolescent experimentation, it took place very infrequently, and was discontinued fairly soon after its inception. Only about one man in eight (13 percent) had engaged in more homosexual contact than heterosexual—that is, were 3s, 4s, 5s, and 6s on Kinsey's rating scale.

Although Kinsey's research and analysis represented a considerable advance over the literature prior to 1948, today we realize that the situation is even more complex than his scheme allows. To begin with, Kinsey did not consider *self-identity* as a crucial dimension of homosexuality. How a man defines his own gender preference has an enormous impact on his behavior, his sense of ease with his life, his social relations with others, what he thinks, how he feels, his experiences both internal and external. This is not to say that a man who *doesn't think* he is a homosexual, but who is in all other respects, *therefore isn't a homosexual.* All it means is that this particular dimension is lacking in his makeup. *In the sense of self-identity,* he isn't a homosexual; in other respects, he may be. If we fail to consider this dimension, our analysis is necessarily shallow and incomplete.

A second crucial dimension any careful observer of the sexual scene must consider is *subcultural involvement.* This means association with others who are homosexuals—who consider themselves as such, and who practice homosexual behavior. Subcultural involvement refers to one's immersion in a specific social "scene." Like any category of humanity, homosexuals do not form a tightly knit group—but they are a kind of group nonetheless, a "quasi group," or a "near group." Think of any social category: policemen, the very rich, marijuana smokers, bird watchers, people with red hair, Quakers, residents of Chicago. Some of these categories will form the basis for group cohesion; others will not. In speaking of a group or a subculture, we mean that: (a) its members interact with one another more frequently and more intimately than they do with members of other social categories; (b) its members' way of life, and their beliefs, are somewhat different from members of other social categories; (c) its members think of themselves as belonging to a specific group, and they are so defined by those who do not share this trait. In these three senses, then, homosexuals do form a subculture, or group. *But not all men who practice homosexual behavior are involved in the subculture.* In fact, men are *differentially* involved, some almost to the complete exclusion of "straight" people, others absolutely not at all. The degree to which a given man who practices homosexual behavior is involved in and with the homosexual subculture determines many crucial facets of his life, both sexual and nonsexual. To ignore this dimension would be suicidal.

A third crucial dimension of homosexuality often lacking in past analyses is the subjective *meaning* which both participants and nonparticipants attach to behavior, people, and roles people play. By "subjective meaning," I mean simply *whether or not homosexuality is considered part of what's going on*. This isn't dictated by the formal properties of what people are or do; it grows out of certain definitions and judgments which vary from place to place, from time to time. Recall the prisoner we discussed a few pages back: what he did was not considered "homosexuality" by him, by his partner, or by his fellow prisoners. The same goes for our married man who engages in transitory, easily available same-sex oral-genital contact in public lavatories. If these two men were asked, "Have you ever engaged in homosexual behavior?", each would probably answer in the negative. Many young men "hustle" homosexuals for money. They allow themselves to be fellated, but they never reciprocate. They do this only if they are paid, and they maintain a rigid emotional barrier between themselves and the men who fellate them. To break any of these rules would threaten their masculinity, and invite being defined as a homosexual. But within the boundaries of what they do, they do not see their behavior as homosexual. Most have girl friends and eventually drift out of hustling to get married.

In short, technically homosexual behavior—that is, genital contact to the point of orgasm—does not necessarily entail the *subjective meaning* of homosexuality for all involved. We may not all agree on what we see as "homosexual behavior"; conceptions as to what constitutes homosexuality follow different rules. And each perspective has to be examined separately, in its own right.

In order to make our investigation complete, it is necessary to look at *sexual preferences*. Now, it is never the case that everything is equal. No one is faced with the alternative of two sexual partners who are exactly the same except for gender. So we have to visualize gender preference as hypothetical rather than real. We all encounter many people during the course of our day, some of them men, and some women. How does it come to pass that we end up in bed with a member of one or the other sex? Is it because of *availability?* Men in prisons do not choose the gender of their partners; it is forced on them by circumstance. If they had the power of choice, many, perhaps most, would have intercourse with women, not men. It is relatively easy to find willing male sex partners in an urban center after a few minutes of "cruising" in the right place; talking women into bed is generally much more difficult. Many men *prefer* the sexual company of women, but don't want to be subject to the "hassle" it would entail. They end up having sex with men because men are far more readily available. On the other hand, many men prefer to abstain from sex altogether than have intercourse with other men. So we have a spectrum along the dimension of same-sex preference: from the *preferential* homosexual, the man who, in the face of almost unlimited options available, consistently chooses men over women; through the *situational* homosexual, who engages in same-sex intercourse only where women are not to be found, or where men are far more readily available than women; on over to the *confirmed heterosexual,* who prefers no sex to sex with men. Certainly sexual preferences—especially taking existing social context into account—comprises an absolutely crucial dimension of sexuality.

Also, *romantic preferences,* or the potential for becoming *emotionally* involved with men or women, should be considered in any definitional scheme. The ability to fall in love with someone of the same sex affectionately and sensually must be counted as one out of a number of ways of determining sexual orientation. Some men can be said to be *homoemotional.*

Likewise, the ability to be *turned on* physically is important: whether or not one becomes sexually *aroused* by men or by women has to be taken into account in constructing a complete picture of homosexuality. Men who are *homoerotic* are homosexual along this particular dimension. We agree with Anna Freud in this respect: the gender of the object of one's masturbatory fantasies, which fuel sexual excitement, is basic in deciding whether one is homosexual or heterosexual. But again, it is only one dimension out of a number of important dimensions.

And lastly, the public definition of one's sexual role and preference cannot be ignored when understanding the phenomenon of sexual orientation. This does not mean that if anyone else thinks you are a homosexual, therefore you are. But it does mean that being *labeled* as a homosexual will make a great deal of difference to your sexual life, and to your life in general, in a large number of ways. The secret homosexual and the overt homosexual do not lead the same sorts of lives; likewise, the man who is falsely thought to be a homosexual by everyone in a community will not lead the same sort of life as the one who is correctly assumed to be "straight." By itself, the public labeling of our gender preference will have an impact on many other things we consider important. At the very least, it is crucial in influencing one's self-identity and definition. It is not, however, the whole story by itself.

Perhaps the main point to emerge out of this discussion is that *no single dimension of homosexuality alone determines a man's sexual orientation.* A man may be "a homosexual" in a number of *different* ways. And secondly: *these dimensions are not necessarily found together in the same person.* In other words, a given man may be a homosexual in one way, but not in another. Although these dimensions are *often* found together, and are generally correlated with one another, it doesn't *always* happen. We have to examine various *combinations* of characteristics, and the kind of consequences these combinations have for people's lives, both sexual and nonsexual. Too often, one or another of these dimensions has been ignored in the past, or one dimension has been reduced or absorbed into another, or has been thought absolutely and unequivocally to cause the other. Thinking this way is to think in simplified stereotypes. The real world is much more complex.

As with any other area of human sexuality, particularly sexual deviance, the debate on homosexuality can become rancorous and even hostile. We might have supposed that, after centuries of writings on homosexual behavior, some sort of consensus about its nature would be emerging. This appears not to be the case. Perhaps still the most vigorously contested question is whether or not homosexuality is *normal* or *abnormal,* an alternative life-style or a manifestation of psychic pathology, a viable form of behavior or a mental illness. On one side, taking the "pathology" position, are many—perhaps, even now, most—psychiatrists, other physicians, such as endocrinologists, some psychologists, and, of course, most of the public. On the other, we have younger psychiatrists, some other physicians, and most behavioral scientists—anthropologists, psychologists and sociologists principally. The second faction would hold to the "alternative life-style" notion.

Even the most rigid of the sexual pathologists makes a distinction between *exclusive,* or "obligatory," homosexuality (sometimes called *"true"* homosexuality), and episodic, temporary, or *situational* homosexuality. However, exactly where the line is drawn between these two groups isn't altogether clear. Irving Bieber, perhaps the foremost spokesman for the pathology position, and an author of the influential book *Homosexuality: A Psychoanalytic Study,* whose views are as exemplary of the pathology position as anyone's, stated: "An isolated homosexual experience doesn't define a man as homosexual; *but if he has one such experience every year, he would have to be considered homosexual*" (my emphasis; the quote is from the *Playboy* panel on homosexuality, published in April, 1971). This means that a heterosexually active male, *1* percent of whose experiences are homosexual, 99 percent of which are heterosexual, would be considered homosexual at least according to this view.

Writings on homosexuals have tended to focus more or less entirely on the man (or woman—although actually, far, far less has been written on the Lesbian than on the male homosexual) who chooses to remain a homosexual in the face of heterosexual options. A more or less equal desire for both sexes, usually referred to as bisexuality, or "ambisexuality," is not admitted as a possibility by most orthodox psychiatrists. They see the two categories as mutually exclusive.

The first premise of the pathologists is that obligatory homosexuality is the manifestation of a psychosexual *disorder,* equivalent to a disease. They do not say merely that *many* homosexuals are neurotic, or that homosexuals are *more likely* to be sick than heterosexuals. They say that exclusive homosexuality is *always* and *by definition* a sign of disordered sexuality.

Irving Bieber put it this way, in a debate with another psychiatrist before the American Psychiatric Association:

> The central question is: Is homosexuality a normal sexual variant, that develops like left-handedness does in some people, or does it represent some kind of disturbance in sexual development? There is no question in my mind: Every male homosexual goes through an initial stage of heterosexual development, and in all homosexuals, there has been a disturbance of normal heterosexual development, as a result of fears which produce anxieties and inhibitions of sexual function. His sexual adaptation is a substitutive adaptation.

Bieber goes on to make a medical, or pathology, analogy: *"What you have in a homosexual adult is a person whose heterosexual function is crippled like the legs of a polio victim."* While denying that homosexuality *is* a mental illness, Bieber claims that it is the *manifestation of a psychiatric disorder.* (Some may feel that the distinction is one of form rather than of substance.) In an interview with *Playboy,* as part of a panel of experts on homosexuality, Bieber states: "Heterosexuality is part of normal biosocial development, while homosexuality is *always* the result of a disordered sexual development.... It is not normal for a man to make love to a man. It doesn't disorder sexual development for two men to make love to each other. It is merely evidence that their sexuality is already disordered.... I should like to underscore the point that it isn't easy to sidetrack a male from a heterosexual destiny. It takes a lot of trauma...."

Pathologists reject the idea that homosexuality is culturally defined, that it is acceptable in one place and "deviant" in another only because of the historical accident of culture. Homosexuality, Bieber says, "is maladaptive because it is based on fears that are not realistic, and not because of cultural unacceptability. It would be no less abnormal if it were culturally accepted." Homosexuality, according to this view, "is a type of heterosexual inadequacy." It "is *never* unrelated to fears and inhibitions associated with heterosexuality." It is totally incorrect "that normalcy can only be culturally defined and that homosexuality would not be pathological in a society that accepted it." This implies "that if our society accepted it, homosexuals wouldn't suffer any more psychological problems than heterosexuals. During the Victorian era, frigidity was regarded as normal. Can we therefore assume that frigidity created no psychological problems for a woman or for her husband because it was culturally defined as normal? I think not." (This interview appears in the April, 1971, issue of *Playboy*.)

We believe these views to be archaic. They are refuted by the available evidence.

First: the assumption as to the inherent desirability of heterosexuality is merely, solely, and exclusively *a value judgment,* couched in the form of a pseudoscientific medical fact. It is a judgment which anyone is free to accept or reject, according to one's personal feelings and taste.

Second: while pathologists decree that homosexuality represents a kind of inadequate or disordered heterosexual functioning, they never consider the opposite—that heterosexuality represents an inadequate or disordered *homosexual* functioning. Male homosexuality is no more a fear or a hatred of women than heterosexuality is a hatred or a fear of men. If obligatory male homosexuals exclude half the available population from their sexual scope—that is, all women—then obligatory male heterosexuals do likewise: they refuse to consider sex with any and all males. And the faithfully married couple represents the most restrictive of all forms of sexual behavior—aside from celibacy. The least restrictive sexual pattern would be displayed by the bisexual—or better yet, the "polymorphous pansexual," the man or woman who is willing to entertain the notion of sex with anyone, or even anything.

In fact, we could make a third point by taking this argument a step further: men and women who are self-designated homosexuals as a general rule *have had far more heterosexual contact* than heterosexuals have had homosexual contact. The overwhelming majority of homosexuals have at the very least given heterosexuality a try; relatively few heterosexuals, at least after adolescence, have experimented with homosexuality. We might, therefore, see heterosexuality as "compulsive," and homosexuality as freely chosen!

Fourth: there is no evidence whatsoever that there is anything like a "heterosexual destiny." Many sexual pathologists will say that sexual instincts do not necessarily dictate gender sexual choice, but they invoke a "male-female design..., anatomically determined," the result of an inexorable "evolutionary development." Homosexuals "are unable to form a healthy sexual identity in accordance with their anatomical and biological capacities," to quote Dr. Charles Socarides, another outspoken proponent of the pathology viewpoint. But exactly what this all means in precise terms can never be determined. At one time, to be sure, it was in the interest of human survival to reproduce. Certainly heterosexual intercourse was adaptive in an evolutionary sense. Now, of course, the opposite is true: it is in the best interests of humans to maintain the population, rather than to increase it. The anatomic equipment of men and women certainly *permits* heterosexual intercourse—but it does not dictate it. Likewise, the anatomical equipment of men permits homosexual behavior: hands, the mouth, and the anus are as capable of sexual stimulation and satisfaction as is the vagina. And the same may be said of the anatomical equipment of women. Male and female homosexuality is as anatomically "rational" as is heterosexuality.

Fifth: just how the personalities of homosexuals are "disordered" is not altogether clear. Psychologist Evelyn Hooker subjected a number of homosexuals and matched heterosexual controls to personality tests, and then asked a panel of psychiatrists and clinical psychologists to pick out which were which on the basis of their test scores. The panel did not do any better than guessing—indicating either that the tests couldn't tap whatever personality differences these two groups supposedly displayed, or that there were no such differences. Of course, it is always possible to declare *by fiat* that adequate heterosexual functioning is a necessary definition of mental health. Then homosexuality is by definition a sign of a disordered sexuality. But statements which are true by definition don't help us understand the world at all, since literally anything may be declared to be true by defining it that way.

Sixth: if homosexuals actually are sick, and if homosexuality actually is a manifestation of a psychosexual disorder, *psychiatrists would be the last of all researchers to know it.* In order to bolster up their expertise in this area, psychotherapists claim that their patients represent a cross section of all homosexuals, that whatever ailments they complain of are characteristic of homosexuals in general. But some thought renders this claim invalid. It is only homosexuals suffering from psychic distress who seek help of psychiatrists in the first place. What about those who are happy, well adjusted, satisfied with their lives? Why should they seek psychotherapy? The fact is, they wouldn't. And psychiatrists would not know of such people, of how typical they might be, or how atypical their own patients. And their theories do not take this simple fact into account. They reason solely and exclusively from their own patients. Imagine if a psychiatrist tried to claim that all shoe salesmen suffer from neurosis. When pressed for evidence, the reply is: "Because all of my patients who are shoe salesmen suffer from neurosis!" Of course; that's why they see a psychiatrist in the first place! Absurd as this whimsical example is, it corresponds exactly to the quality of evidence that has been presented when the personalities of homosexuals are described. Psychiatric descriptions and explanations of homosexuality are almost without exception based on this fundamental methodological fallacy.

For nearly all heterosexuals, the inherent superiority of heterosexuality is unquestioned, taken for granted. Psychiatric theories and evaluations are little more than a formalization of these popular prejudices. Most of us do not stop and consider just how ingrained these prejudices are.

When the issue of a male homosexual teaching adolescent boys is considered, most heterosexuals will raise the question of whether he will seduce his students. The fact that this possibility holds equally for male heterosexual teachers of adolescent girls rarely enters the minds of most heterosexuals.

Lesbian mothers are often asked if they "brainwash" their daughters to become Lesbians. The fact is that heterosexuals are engaged in an almost daily, nonconscious campaign to "brainwash" their children to become heterosexuals.

When the question of repealing the laws against homosexuality is debated, a cry often goes up that this will open the doors to homosexual assaults upon young boys. Consider this diatribe published in the *Humbard Christian Report* in 1972 (not 1872), quoted by John W. Petras in *Sexuality in Society:*

> Here in Youngstown, we are shocked by a terrible crime against a young boy by a sex pervert which resulted in the boy's murder, yet our lawmakers passed a bill legalizing this crime...! What insanity! This is giving a green light to more and worse sex crimes. This is bringing out into the open what the law and moral standards have always condemned.... This bill, if it passes the Senate, will open a Pandora's box of crime and filth unparalleled in the history of the United States.

Why one case of homosexual violence should be any more typical of homosexuality in general than one case of a heterosexual rape-murder is of heterosexuality in general is not clear. But the fact that this equation is taken seriously by many heterosexuals emphasizes that the same sort of logic does not apply to the two forms of behavior.

The conceptions and theories which have been used in the past have served to stigmatize homosexuals and to rationalize the superiority of heterosexuality. It is time, we believe, to look at homosexuality from a fresh perspective.

The Homosexual Role

MARY McINTOSH

Recent advances in the sociology of deviant behavior have not yet affected the study of homosexuality, which is still commonly seen as a condition characterizing certain persons in the way that birthplace or deformity might characterize them. The limitations of this view can best be understood if we examine some of its implications. In the first place, if homosexuality is a condition, then people either have it or do not have it. Many scientists and ordinary people assume that there are two kinds of people in the world: homosexuals and heterosexuals. Some of them recognize that homosexual feelings and behavior are not confined to the persons they would like to call "homosexuals" and that some of these persons do not actually engage in homosexual behavior. This should pose a crucial problem; but they evade the crux by retaining their assumption and puzzling over the question of how to tell whether someone is "really" homosexual or not. Lay people too will discuss whether a certain person is "queer" in much the same way as they might question whether a certain pain indicated cancer. And in much the same way they will often turn to scientists or to medical men for a surer diagnosis. The scientists, for their part, feel it incumbent on them to seek criteria for diagnosis.

Thus one psychiatrist, discussing the definition of homosexuality, has written:

> ...I do not diagnose patients as homosexual unless they have engaged in overt homosexual behavior. Those who also engage in heterosexual activity are diagnosed as bisexual. An isolated experience may not warrant the diagnosis, but repetetive (sic) homosexual behavior in adulthood, whether sporadic or continuous, designates a homosexual.[1]

Along with many other writers, he introduces the notion of a third type of person, the "bisexual," to handle the fact that behavior patterns cannot be conveniently dichotomized into heterosexual and homosexual. But this does not solve the conceptual problem, since bisexuality too is seen as a condition (unless as a passing response to unusual situations such as confinement in a one-sex prison). In any case there is no extended discussion of bisexuality; the topic is usually given a brief mention in order to clear the ground for the consideration of "true homosexuality."

To cover the cases where the symptoms of behavior or of felt attractions do not match the diagnosis, other writers have referred to an adolescent homosexual phase or have used such terms as "latent homosexual" or "pseudo homosexual." Indeed one of the earliest studies of the subject, by Krafft-Ebing, was concerned with making a distinction between the "invert" who is congenitally homosexual and others who, although they behave in the same way, are not true inverts.[2]

From Mary McIntosh, "The Homosexual Role," ©1968 by the Society for the Study of Social Problems. Reprinted from *Social Problems*, vol. 16 (Fall 1968), pp. 182–192 (with deletions) by permission.

A second result of the conceptualization of homosexuality as a condition is that the major research task has been seen as the study of its etiology. There has been much debate as to whether the condition is innate or acquired. The first step in such research has commonly been to find a sample of "homosexuals" in the same way that a medical researcher might find a sample of diabetics if he wanted to study that disease. Yet, after a long history of such studies, the results are sadly inconclusive and the answer is still as much a matter of opinion as it was when Havelock Ellis published *Sexual Inversion*[3] seventy years ago. The failure of research to answer the question has not been due to lack of scientific rigor or to any inadequacy of the available evidence; it results rather from the fact that the wrong question has been asked. One might as well try to trace the etiology of "committee-chairmanship" or "Seventh-Day Adventism" as of "homosexuality."

The vantage-point of comparative sociology enables us to see that the conception of homosexuality as a condition is, in itself, a possible object of study. This conception and the behavior it supports operate as a form of social control in a society in which homosexuality is condemned. Furthermore, the uncritical acceptance of the conception by social scientists can be traced to their concern with homosexuality as a social problem. They have tended to accept the popular definition of what the problem is and they have been implicated in the process of social control.

The practice of the social labeling of persons as deviant operates in two ways as a mechanism of social control.[4] In the first place it helps to provide a clear-cut, publicized, and recognizable threshold between permissible and impermissible behavior. This means that people cannot so easily drift into deviant behavior. Their first moves in a deviant direction immediately raise the question of a total move into a deviant role with all the sanctions that this is likely to elicit. Secondly, the labeling serves to segregate the deviants from others and this means that their deviant practices and their self-justifications for these practices are contained within a relatively narrow group. The creation of a specialized, despised, and punished role of homosexual keeps the bulk of society pure in rather the same way that the similar treatment of some kinds of criminals helps keep the rest of society law-abiding.

However, the disadvantage of this practice as a technique of social control is that there may be a tendency for people to become fixed in their deviance once they have become labeled. This, too, is a process that has become well-recognized in discussions of other forms of deviant behavior such as juvenile delinquency and drug taking and, indeed, of other kinds of social labeling such as streaming in schools and racial distinctions. One might expect social categorizations of this sort to be to some extent self-fulfilling prophecies: if the culture defines people as falling into distinct types—black and white, criminal and non-criminal, homosexual and normal—then these types will tend to become polarized, highly differentiated from each other.... [In another place I] shall discuss whether this is so in the case of homosexuals and "normals" in the United States today.

It is interesting to notice that homosexuals themselves welcome and support the notion that homosexuality is a condition. For just as the rigid categorization deters people from drifting into deviancy, so it appears to foreclose on the possibility of drifting back into normality and thus removes the element of anxious choice. It appears to justify the deviant behavior of the homosexual as being appropriate for him as a member of the homosexual category. The deviancy can thus be seen as legitimate for him and he can continue in it without rejecting the norms of the society.[5]

The way in which people become labeled as homosexual can now be seen as an important social process connected with mechanisms of social control. It is important, therefore, that sociologists should examine this process objectively and not lend themselves to participation in it, particularly since, as we have seen, psychologists and psychiatrists on the whole have not retained their objectivity but become involved as diagnostic agents in the process of social labeling.[6]

It is proposed that the homosexual should be seen as playing a social role rather than as having a condition. The role of "homosexual," however, does not simply describe a sexual behavior pattern. If it did, the idea of a role would be no more useful than that of a condition. For the purpose of introducing the term "role" is to enable us to handle the fact that behavior in this sphere does not match popular beliefs: that sexual patterns cannot be dichotomized in the way that the social roles of homosexual and heterosexual can.

It may seem rather odd to distinguish in this way between role and behavior, but if we accept a definition of role in terms of expectations (which may or may not be fulfilled), then the distinction is both legitimate and useful. In modern societies where a separate homosexual role is recognized, the expectation, on behalf of those who play the role and of others, is that a homosexual will be exclusively or very predominantly homosexual in his feelings and behavior. In addition, there are other expectations that frequently exist, especially on the part of nonhomosexuals, but affecting the self-conception of anyone who sees himself as homosexual. These are: the expectation that he will be effeminate in manner, personality, or preferred sexual activity; the expectation that sexuality will play a part of some kind in all his relations with other men; and the expectation that he will be attracted to boys and very young men and probably willing to seduce them. The existence of a social expectation, of course, commonly helps to produce its own fulfillment. But the question of how far it is fulfilled is a matter for empirical investigation rather than *a priori* pronouncement. Some of the empirical evidence about the chief expectation—that homosexuality precludes heterosexuality—in relation to the homosexual role in America is examined in the final section of this paper.[7]

In order to clarify the nature of the role and demonstrate that it exists only in certain societies, we shall present the cross-cultural and historical evidence available. This raises awkward problems of method because the material has hitherto usually been collected and analyzed in terms of culturally specific modern western conceptions.

The Homosexual Role in Various Societies

To study homosexuality in the past or in other societies we usually have to rely on secondary evidence rather than on direct observation. The reliability and the validity of such evidence are open to question because what the original observers reported may have been distorted by their disapproval of homosexuality and by their definition of it, which may be different from the one we wish to adopt.

For example, Marc Daniel tries to refute accusations of homosexuality against Pope Julian II by producing four arguments: the Pope had many enemies who might wish to blacken his name; he and his supposed lover, Alidosi, both had mistresses; neither of them was at all effeminate; and the Pope had other men friends about whom no similar accusations were made.[8] In other words Daniel is trying to fit an early sixteenth century Pope to the modern conception of the homosexual as effeminate, exclusively homosexual, and sexual in relation to all men. The fact that he does not fit is, of course, no evidence, as Daniel would have it, that his relationship with Alidosi was not a sexual one.

Anthropologists too can fall into this trap. Marvin Opler, summarizing anthropological evidence on the subject, says,

> Actually, no society, save perhaps Ancient Greece, pre-Meiji Japan, certain top echelons in Nazi Germany, and the scattered examples of such special status groups as the berdaches, Nata slaves, and one category of Chuckchee shamans, has lent sanction in any real sense to homosexuality.[9]

Yet he goes on to discuss societies in which there are reports of sanctioned adolescent and other occasional "experimentation." Of the Cubeo of the North West Amazon, for instance, he says, "*true* homosexuality among the Cubeo is rare if not absent," giving as evidence the fact that no males with persistent homosexual patterns are reported.[10]

Allowing for such weaknesses, the Human Relations Area Files are the best single source of comparative information. Their evidence on homosexuality has been summarized by Ford and Beach,[11] who identify two broad types of accepted patterns: the institutionalized homosexual role and the liaison between men or boys who are otherwise heterosexual.

The recognition of a distinct role of *berdache* or transvestite is, they say, "the commonest form of institutionalized homosexuality." This form shows a marked similarity to that in our own society, though in some ways it is even more extreme. The Mohave Indians of California and Arizona, for example,[12] recognized both an *alyhā*, a male transvestite who took the role of the woman in sexual intercourse, and a *hwamē*, a female homosexual who took the role of the male. People were believed to be born as *alyhā* or *hwamē*, hints of their future proclivities occurring in their mothers' dreams during pregnancy. If a young boy began to behave like a girl and take an interest in women's things instead of men's, there was an initiation ceremony in which he would become an *alyhā*. After that he would dress and act like a woman, would be referred to as "she" and could take "husbands."

But the Mohave pattern differs from ours in that although the *alyhā* was considered regrettable and amusing, he was not condemned and was given public recognition. The attitude was that "he was an *alyhā*, he could not help it." But the "husband" of an *alyhā* was an ordinary man who happened to have chosen an *alybā*, perhaps because they were good housekeepers or because they were believed to be "lucky in love," and he would be the butt of endless teasing and joking.

This radical distinction between the feminine passive homosexual and his masculine active partner is one which is not made very much in our own society,[13] but which is very important in the Middle East. There, however, neither is thought of as being a "born" homosexual, although the passive partner, who demeans himself by his feminine submission, is despised and ridiculed, while the active one is not. In most of ancient Middle East, including among the Jews until the return from the Babylonian exile, there were male temple prostitutes.[14] Thus even cultures that recognize a separate homosexual role may not define it in the same way as our culture does.

Many other societies accept or approve of homosexual liaisons as part of a variegated sexual pattern. Usually these are confined to a particular stage in the individual's life. Among the Aranda of Central Australia, for instance, there are long-standing relationships of several years' duration, between unmarried men and young boys, starting at the age of ten to twelve.[15] This is rather similar to the well-known situation in classical Greece, but there, of course, the older man could have a wife as well. Sometimes, however, as among the Siwans of North Africa,[16] all men and boys can and are expected to engage in homosexual activities, apparently at every stage of life. In all of these societies there may be much homosexual behavior, but there are no "homosexuals."

The Development of the Homosexual Role in England

The problem of method is even more acute in dealing with historical material than with anthropological, for history is usually concerned with "great events" rather than with recurrent patterns. There are some records of attempts to curb sodomy among minor churchmen during the medieval period,[17] which seem to indicate that it was common. At least they suggest that laymen feared on behalf of their sons that it was common. The term "catamite" meaning "boy kept for immoral purposes," was first used in 1593, again suggesting that this practice was common then. But most of the historical references to homosexuality relate either to great men or to great scandals. However, over the last seventy years or so various scholars have tried to trace the history of sex,[18] and it is possible to glean a good deal from what they have found and also from what they have failed to establish.

Their studies of English history before the seventeenth century consist usually of inconclusive speculation as to whether certain men, such as Edward II, Christopher Marlowe, William Shakespeare, were or were not homosexual. Yet the disputes are inconclusive not because of lack of evidence but because none of these men fits the modern stereotype of the homosexual.

It is not until the end of the seventeenth century that other kinds of information become available and it is possible to move from speculations about individuals to descriptions of homosexual life. At this period references to homosexuals as a type and to a rudimentary homosexual subculture, mainly in London, begin to appear. But the earliest descriptions of homosexuals do not coincide exactly with the modern conception. There is much more stress on effeminacy and in particular in transvestism, to such an extent that there seems to be no distinction at first between transvestism and homosexuality.[19] The terms emerging at this period to describe homosexuals—Molly, Nancy-boy, Madge-cull—emphasize effeminacy. In contrast the modern terms—like fag, queer, gay, bent—do not have this implication.[20]

By the end of the seventeenth century, homosexual transvestites were a distinct enough group to be able to form their own clubs in London.[21] Edward Ward's *History of the London Clubs,* published in 1709, describes one called "The Mollies' Club" which met "in a certain tavern in the City" for "parties and regular gatherings." The members "adopt(ed) all the small vanities natural to the feminine sex to such an extent that they try to speak, walk, chatter, shriek and scold as women do, aping them as well in other respects." The other respects apparently included the enactment of marriages and child-birth. The club was discovered and broken up by agents of the Reform Society.[22] There were a number of similar scandals during the course of the eighteenth century as various homosexual coteries were exposed.

A writer in 1729 describes the widespread homosexual life of the period:

> They also have their Walks and Appointments, to meet and pick up one another, and their particular Houses of Resort to go to, because they dare not trust themselves in an open Tavern. About twenty of these sort of Houses have been discovered, besides the Nocturnal Assemblies of great numbers of the like vile Persons, what they call the *Markets,* which are the Royal Exchange, Lincoln's Inn, Bog Houses, the south side of St. James's Park, the Piazzas in Covent Garden, St. Clement's Churchyard, etc.
>
> It would be a pretty scene to behold them in their clubs and cabals, how they assume the air and affect the name of Madam or Miss, Betty or Molly, with a chuck under the chin, and "Oh, you bold pullet, I'll break your eggs," and then frisk and walk away.[23]

The notion of exclusive homosexuality became well-established during this period. When "two Englishmen, Leith and Drew, were accused of paederasty.... The evidence given by the plaintiffs was, as was generally the case in these trials, very imperfect. On the other hand the defendants denied the accusation, and produced witnesses to prove their predilection for women. They were in consequence acquitted."[24] This could only have been an effective argument in a society that perceived homosexual behavior as incompatible with heterosexual tastes.

During the nineteenth century there are further reports of raided clubs and homosexual brothels. However, by this time the element of transvestism had diminished in importance. Even the male prostitutes are described as being of masculine build and there is more stress upon sexual license and less upon dressing up and play-acting.

Thus a distinct, separate, specialized role of "homosexual" emerged in England at the end of the seventeenth century and the conception of homosexuality as a condition which characterizes certain individuals and not others is now firmly established in our society. The term role is, of course, a form of shorthand. It refers not only to a cultural conception or set of ideas but also to a complex of institutional arrangements which depend upon and reinforce these ideas. These arrangements include all the forms of heterosexual activity, courtship, and marriage as well as the labeling processes—gossip, ridicule, psychiatric diagnosis, criminal conviction—and the groups and networks of the homosexual subculture. For simplicity we shall simply say that a specialized role exists....

Conclusion

This paper has dealt with only one small aspect of the sociology of homosexuality. It is, nevertheless, a fundamental one. For it is not until he sees homosexuals as a social category, rather than a medical or psychiatric one, that the sociologist can begin to ask the right questions about the specific content of the homosexual role and about the organization and functions of homosexual groups. All that has been done here is to indicate that the role does not exist in many societies, that it only emerged in England towards the end of the seventeenth century, and that, although the existence of the role in modern America appears to have some effect on the distribution of homosexual behavior, such behavior is far from being monopolized by persons who play the role of homosexual.

Notes

1. Irving Bieber, "Clinical Aspects of Male Homosexuality," in Judd Marmor, editor, *Sexual Inversion,* New York: Basic Books, 1965, p. 248; this is but one example among many.

2. R. von Krafft-Ebing, *Psychopathia Sexualis,* 1889.

3. Later published in H. Ellis, *Studies in the Psychology of Sex,* Vol. 2, New York: Random House, 1936.

4. This is a grossly simplified account. Edwin Lemert provides a far more subtle and detailed analysis in *Social Pathology,* New York: McGraw-Hill, 1951, ch. 4, "Sociopathic Individuation."

5. For discussion of situations in which deviants can lay claim to legitimacy, see Talcott Parsons, *The Social System,* New York: Free Press, 1951, pp. 292–293.

6. The position taken here is similar to that of Erving Goffman in his discussion of becoming a mental patient; *Asylums,* Garden City, N.Y.: Doubleday-Anchor, 1961, pp. 128–146.

7. For evidence that many self-confessed homosexuals in England are not effeminate and many are not interested in boys, see Michael Schofield, *Sociological Aspects of Homosexuality,* London: Longmans, 1965.

8. Marc Daniel, "Essai de méthodologie pour l'étude des aspects homosexuels de l'histoire," *Arcadie,* 133 (January, 1965), pp. 31–37.

9. Marvin Opler, "Anthropological and Cross-Cultural Aspects of Homosexuality," in Marmor, editor, *op. cit.,* p. 174.

10. *Ibid.,* p. 117.

11. C. S. Ford and F. A. Beach, *Patterns of Sexual Behavior,* New York: Harper, 1951, ch. 7.

12. George Devereux, "Institutionalized Homosexuality of the Mohave Indians," *Human Biology,* Vol. 9, 1937, pp. 498–527; reprinted in Hendrik M. Ruitenbeek, editor, *The Problem of Homosexuality in Modern Society,* New York: Dutton, 1963.

13. The lack of cultural distinction is reflected in behavior; Gordon Westwood found that only a

small proportion of his sample of British homosexuals engaged in anal intercourse and many of these had been both active and passive and did not have a clear preference. See *A Minority,* London: Longmans, 1960, pp. 127–134.

14. Gordan Rattray Taylor, "Historical and Mythological Aspects of Homosexuality," in Marmor, *op. cit.;* Fernando Henriques, *Prostitution and Society,* Vol. 1, London: MacGibbon and Kee, 1962, pp. 341–343.

15. Ford and Beach, *op cit.,* p. 132.

16. *Ibid.,* pp. 131–132.

17. Geoffrey May, *Social Control of Sex Expression,* London: Allen and Unwin, 1930, pp. 65 and 101.

18. Especially Havelock Ellis, *Sexual Inversion,* London: Wilson and Macmillan, 1897; Iwan Bloch (E. Dühren, pseud.), *Sexual Life in England Past and Present,* English translation, London: Francis Aldor, 1938; German edition, Charlottenberg, Berlin, 1901–03; Gordon Rattray Taylor, *Sex in History,* London: Thames and Hudson, 1953; Noel I. Garde, *Jonathan to Gide: The Homosexual in History,* New York: Vantage, 1964.

19. Dr. Evelyn Hooker has suggested that in a period when homosexual grouping and a homosexual subculture have not yet become institutionalized, homosexuals are likely to behave in a more distinctive and conspicuous manner because other means of making contact are not available. This is confirmed by the fact that lesbians are more conspicuous than male homosexuals in our society, but does not seem to fit the 17th century, where groups are already described as "clubs."

20. However, "fairy" and "pansy," the commonest slang terms used by non-homosexuals, have the same meaning of effeminate as the earlier terms.

21. Bloch, *op. cit.,* p. 328, gives several examples, but attributes their emergence to the fact that "the number of homosexuals increased."

22. Quoted in *ibid.,* pp. 328–329.

23. Anon, *Hell upon Earth: or the Town in an Uproar,* London, 1729, quoted by G. R. Taylor in Marmor, editor, *op cit.,* p. 142.

24. Bloch, *op. cit.,* p. 334.

Chapter 11

Pornography

Even though the white-hot intensity of the controversy has died down a bit in the past decade, the nature of pornography remains one of the more vigorously contested issues today. One segment or wing of the feminist movement claims that pornography possesses an inner or essentialistic reality; what pornography *is,* is material that depicts violence against women. Women are exploited, abused, brutalized, and harmed in pornographic material; that is specifically what many men find appealing in it. Moreover, this depiction of violence against women, which is *itself* a form of violence, stimulates violence against women in everyday life. Eliminate porn, and violence against women will decline (Dworkin, 1981; Lederer, 1982; Russell, 1993; MacKinnon, 1993). This approach is captured in the slogan, "Pornography is the theory, rape is the practice."

On the other side of the fence we find a different group of feminists, some civil libertarians, anticensorship liberals, a few free-market or laissez-faire conservatives, and literary figures, who argue that pornography is a bogus issue. The evidence does not support the contention that porn causes violence against women, they say; the elimination of porn will have no impact whatsoever on violence against women. Japan is a country with high rates of violent, sado-masochistic pornography; its rates of violence against women are at or near the bottom in the industrialized world. In countries torn by civil violence, rape against women civilians is common, even routine; generally, this takes place in the total absence of exposure to pornography. Outlaw or censor pornography and, ironically, some of the materials that antiporn feminists support—such as material supporting women's right to abortion, that arguing for the rights of homosexuals, medical treatises, even antiporn tracts themselves—will be confiscated (Ellis et al., 1988; Segal and McIntosh, 1992; Heins, 1993; Gibson and Gibson, 1993). Nothing supports the constructionist's argument more than the legal definition of antipornographic materials as pornography.

The constructionist approach to pornography may be stated clearly and simply: What pornography *is,* is defined by different audiences. Instead of seeking some essentialistic quality inherent in certain materials, it is more productive to see pornography as being defined by different audiences. Some material may be pornographic to one audience, or according to a given criterion or definition, but not to other audiences or according to different criteria or definitions. Constructionism would focus not only on what audiences *say* about specific material but also what they *do* about it: whether, how, and why they use it, what they do to restrict access to it or whether they tolerate its distribution, whether they support or oppose politicians who attempt to criminalize its distribution, how they react to someone who is known to use it, and so on.

Constructionism would devise, at the very least, the following definitions of pornography. In each, a particular definition is manifested by a set of actions that spells out that definition.

First, there is the *functional* definition. I do not mean functional in the same sense as the theoretical perspective or approach—functionalism—that spells out the contributions that a given institution, practice, or custom has for the functioning of the society. We looked at this approach in Chapter 5. By functional I mean what function or purpose does pornography serve in the lives of users and consumers? Functionally speaking, pornography is defined by a particular behavior, that is, how it is used. Pornography is any and all material consumed for the purpose of sexual excitation. It is the construction by the consumers of pornography that determines what is pornography—their use of it and the responses it generates in them.

Second, there is the *labeling* definition: works or material that segments of the public define as pornographic, that, it is believed excites lustful thoughts, is sexually vulgar, offensive, shameful, and disgusting. This definition looks at pornography from the point of view of the—mainly disapproving—public.

And, third, there is the *genre* definition: works that are created primarily for the purpose of arousing the lust of an audience of consumers (mainly male). This definition is a commercial construct; according to this definition, pornography is material that follows a distinct formula, or one of a set of formulas, according to what will arouse the pornography-consuming public and thus result in a profit for the distributor. The genre definition takes the point of view of the creators and producers of pornographic works, who in turn are trying to figure out what most turns an audience on, what an audience is most desirous of purchasing.

Clearly, then, according to the constructionist definition, something may be pornographic in one sense but not another, and something may be pornographic to certain audiences but not others.

The constructionist would point to the astounding *variation* in the content of materials that have been designated as pornographic over the centuries. Proof of the constructionist's argument is that materials that were designated as pornographic at one time and place are regarded as being devoid of pornographic content at other times and places. Before the early 1950s—that is to say, in the pre-*Playboy* era—adolescent boys would use pictures that appeared in the *National Geographic* of naked native women as a masturbatory aid. Today, my guess is, such pictures are hardly ever used in this fashion, since so much more arousing materials are available. By our functional constructionist definition, these pictures *were* pornographic before the 1950s, and are *not* pornographic now. In past decades, a number of literary works now legally accepted as nonpornographic—John Cleland's *Memoirs of a Woman of Pleasure* (1749), D. H. Lawrence's *Lady Chatterly's Lover* (1928), and Henry Miller's *Tropic of Cancer* (1934) and *Tropic of Capricorn* (1939) provide examples—were deemed pornographic and therefore legally obscene at one time. In 1814, a painting of a nude woman, titled *Venus,* by Diego Velasquez, was declared by a Spanish Inquisitor General as "obscene." In 1914, while hanging in the National Gallery in London, this work was slashed by a feminist demonstrator because she regarded it as obscene (Troutman, 1965, p. 42). Today, hardly anyone would render this judgment. The point is, social constructions of pornography change over time and vary from one locale to another.

In contrast, the essentialist definition holds that a specific quality or characteristic inherent in material of a certain sort is what defines pornography. Definitions of pornography may vary, but what makes material pornographic is what it contains, not how it is defined. What pornography is, is material of a certain sort; there is a "common core" of pornographic content *even if we are to grant the constructionist's argument.* Functional, labeling, and genre definitions of pornography are all based on qualities or characteristics that certain material possesses. Male or female audiences do not generally react sexually to material that is devoid of sexual content; audiences do not define material as obscene that is utterly lacking in sexual content; producers and distributors do not sell material to the public as pornography that is devoid of sexual content. There is something there—an essentialistic quality—that is generating a reaction, a label, a construction of material as pornography. The likelihood that a blank sheet of paper, a set of mathematical equations, pictures of trees, blue skies, and fields of wheat will be regarded—or socially constructed—as pornographic is very close to nil. (At the same time, consider the fact that Susan Griffin, 1981, regards the work of the German painter Franz Marc, whose principal subject was horses, as pornographic, indicating that, by itself, essential content does not classify something as pornography.) Clearly, what is regarded as pornography typically *does* contain some inner, essentialistic trait, quality, or characteristic, the essentialist would say. Certainly the presence of sexual explicitness has a great deal to do with the fact that certain material will be regarded as pornographic; certainly the ratio of explicit sex to everything else, likewise, contributes to this definition or social construction; and certainly the use or exploitation of women for sexual purposes depicted in certain material contributes to the fact that it is likely to be seen as pornographic. These are qualities that the material possesses; they are essentialistic qualities, not matters of definition. To the extent that material possesses them, it is pornographic; to the extent that it lacks them, it is not.

To the essentialist, pornography is a more or less identifiable phenomenon in the concrete world; it is not especially difficult to know it when we see it. (Of course, it is important to know, essentialists do differ on their definition of pornography!) Pornography contains a number of objective properties that nearly all, or at least all well-informed, right-thinking audiences or parties, can agree *make* a given set of materials pornographic. Once we know what pornography is, the essentialist's job becomes clear: What's important is to find out the *impact* pornography has on its consumers. Unquestionably the central and most pressing issue regarding pornography is whether exposure to it causes men (for the overwhelming majority of pornography's consumers are made up of men) to inflict violence on women. Does the consumption of pornography stimulate men to rape, assault, or otherwise harm women?

How would we answer this question? What evidence could we generate or gather to test the proposition that pornography does or does not cause men to harm women? This is an extremely tricky and difficult empirical question; the evidence is not easy to come by. We can't follow men around, first to determine whether they have consumed pornography, then to determine whether they have inflicted violence on women. Asking them won't yield very meaningful answers. Arrest figures for violent crimes don't help much, since the majority of violent acts don't result in arrest; besides, how would we correlate these arrest rates with pornography consumption, given that we don't have it on a man-for-man basis?

Some researchers have looked at the rates of the consumption of certain pornographic magazines and the rates of rape arrests on a *state-by-state* basis; the reasoning is that if states with high consumption rates of pornography are also the states with high arrest rates for rape, perhaps the correlation indicates a causal relationship as well. Two researchers did indeed find such a correlation: High pornography consumption states tended also to be high rape states (Baron and Straus, 1987, 1989). However, a later examination found that if cities and their suburbs (standard statistical metropolitan areas) are used as the basis for comparison instead of states, the correlation disappears completely (Gentry, 1991). In fact, there is *no* statistical relationship at all between the gross, overall consumption of pornography and arrest rates for rape.

Some social psychologists prefer a different research methodology to test the relationship between the consumption of pornography and violence against women. They expose one group of a sample of males to pornographic materials and another group to nonpornographic materials, then determine whether there is a difference between these two groups with respect to their likelihood of engaging in certain types of aggressive behavior against women. (Obviously, determining if they inflict clear-cut acts of violence on women would be a morally *unacceptable* research method; no psychologist or sociologist would conduct such a study.) One type of action that has been used as a measure of aggression against women is the likelihood of pressing a button that supposedly delivers an electric shock to a woman in a nearby room or booth. (Of course, no shock is in fact actually delivered, it just appears that way to the experimental subject.)

As a general rule, exposure to sexually explicit materials *depicting violence against women* is correlated with inflicting aggressive acts against women in an experimental situation. It is also correlated with believing various rape myths (that women yearn to be raped, for instance), and with sympathy for rapists and a lack of sympathy for rape victims. In contrast, exposure to sexually explicit materials *devoid of violence against women* is either not correlated at all, or has a weak and inconsistent relationship, with such aggressive acts (Donnerstein et al., 1987). Of course, it is an open question as to what sort of carryover there is from these experimentally induced behaviors and attitudes into real-life behaviors and attitudes. Again, empirical research does not lend a great deal of support to the view that exposure to nonviolent sexually explicit material causes violence against women. However, as we saw, some evidence does suggest that violent pornography may cause—at least in an experimental situation—some forms of aggression against women and induce some antifemale attitudinal changes. It is entirely possible that antipornography feminists are obsessed with the wrong enemy; it is unlikely that outlawing and even eliminating sexually explicit materials will significantly reduce violence against women, including rape (Gentry, 1991, p. 285). It is possible that the pornography debate is symbolic of something other than violence against women; indeed, it is likely that the socially *constructed* nature of the pornography debate is far more important than its essentialistic reality.

Gloria Steinem and Ellen Willis offer two contrasting views of pornography. Steinem argues that porn represents a readily identifiable "thing" in the world, clearly distinct from superficially similar phenomena, such as erotica. Willis tells us that identifying this pornography thing isn't quite as simple a task as it appears; one person's porn is another person's erotica. Michael Kimmel offers an informative summary of the research on the effects of pornography.

References

Baron, Larry, and Murray A. Straus. 1987. Four theories of rape: A macrosociological analysis. *Social Problems,* 34 (December): 467–488.

Baron, Larry, and Murray A. Straus. 1989. *Four Theories of Rape in American Society: A State-Level Analysis.* New Haven, Conn.: Yale University Press.

Donnerstein, Edward, Daniel Linz, and Steven Penrod. 1987. *The Question of Pornography: Research Findings and Policy Implications.* New York: Free Press.

Dworkin, Andrea. 1981. *Pornography: Men Possessing Women.* New York: Perigee.

Ellis, Kate, et al. (eds.). 1988. *Caught Looking: Feminism, Pornography, and Censorship.* Seattle: Real Comet Press.

Gentry, Cynthia S. 1991. Pornography and rape: An empirical analysis. *Deviant Behavior,* 12 (July–September): 277–288.

Gibson, Pamela Church, and Roma Gibson (eds.). 1993. *Dirty Looks: Women, Pornography, Power.* London: British Film Institute.

Griffin, Susan. 1981. *Pornography and Silence: Culture's Revenge Against Nature.* New York: Harper Colophon.

Heins, Marjorie. 1993. *Sex, Sin, and Blasphemy: A Guide to America's Censorship Wars.* New York: The New Press.

Lederer, Laura (ed.). 1982. *Take Back the Night: Women on Pornography.* New York: Bantam Books.

MacKinnon, Catherine A. 1993. *Only Words.* Cambridge, Mass.: Harvard University Press.

Russell, Diana E. H. (ed.). 1993. *Making Violence Sexy: Feminist Views on Pornography.* New York: Teacher's College Press.

Segal, Lynne, and Mary McIntosh (eds.). 1992. *Sex Exposed: Sexuality and the Pornography Debate.* London: Virago Press, New Brunswick, N.J.: Rutgers University Press.

Troutman, Philip. 1965. *Velasquez.* London: Spring Books.

Erotica and Pornography: A Clear and Present Difference

GLORIA STEINEM

Human beings are the only animals that experience the same sex drive at times when we can and cannot conceive.

Just as we developed uniquely human capacities for language, planning, memory, and invention along our evolutionary path, we also developed sexuality as a form of expression; a way of communicating that is separable from our need for sex as a way of perpetuating ourselves. For humans alone, sexuality can be and often is primarily a way of bonding, of giving and receiving pleasure, bridging differences, discovering sameness, and communicating emotion.

We developed this and other human gifts through our ability to change our environment, adapt physically, and, in the long run, affect our own evolution. But as an emotional result of this spiraling path away from other animals, we seem to alternate between periods of exploring our unique abilities to forge new boundaries, and feelings of loneliness in the unknown that we ourselves have created; a fear that sometimes sends us back to the comfort of the animal world by encouraging us to exaggerate our sameness with it.

The separation of "play" from "work," for instance, is a problem only in the human world. So is the difference between art and nature, or an intellectual accomplishment and a physical one. As a result, we celebrate play, art, and invention as leaps into the unknown; but any imbalance can send us back to nostalgia for our primate past and the conviction that the basics of work, nature, and physical labor are somehow more worthwhile or even more moral.

In the same way, we have explored our sexuality as separable from conception: a pleasurable, empathetic bridge to strangers of the same species. We have even invented contraception—a skill that has probably existed in some form since our ancestors figured out the process of birth—in order to extend this uniquely human difference. Yet we also have times of atavistic suspicion that sex is not complete—or even legal or intended-by-god—if it cannot end in conception.

No wonder the concepts of "erotica" and "pornography" can be so crucially different, and yet so confused. Both assume that sexuality can be separated from conception, and therefore can be used to carry a personal message. That's a major reason why, even in our current culture, both may be called equally "shocking" or legally "obscene," a word whose Latin derivative means "dirty, containing filth." This gross condemnation of all sexuality that isn't harnessed to childbirth and marriage has been increased by the current backlash against women's progress. Out of fear

From Gloria Steinem, "Erotica and Pornography: A Clear and Present Difference." In Laura Lederer, ed., *Take Back the Night: Women on Pornography* (New York: Bantam Books, 1982), pp. 21–25. Reprinted by permission of the author.

that the whole patriarchal structure might be upset if women really had the autonomous power to decide our reproductive futures (that is, if we controlled the most basic means of production—the production of human beings), right-wing groups are not only denouncing pro-choice abortion literature as "pornographic," but are trying to stop the sending of all contraceptive information through the mails by invoking obscenity laws. In fact, Phyllis Schlafly recently denounced the entire Women's Movement as "obscene."

Not surprisingly, this religious, visceral backlash has a secular, intellectual counterpart that relies heavily on applying the "natural" behavior of the animal world to humans. That application is questionable in itself, but these Lionel Tiger-ish studies make their political purpose even more clear in the particular animals they select and the habits they choose to emphasize. For example, some male primates (marmosets, titi monkeys, night monkeys) carry and/or generally "mother" their infants. Tiger types prefer to discuss chimps and baboons, whose behavior is very "male chauvinist." The message is that females should accept their "destiny" of being sexually dependent and devote themselves to bearing and rearing their young.

Defending against such reaction in turn leads to another temptation: merely to reverse the terms, and declare that all nonprocreative sex is good. In fact, this human activity can be as constructive or destructive, moral or immoral, as any other. Sex as communication can send messages as different as life and death; even the origins of "erotica" and "pornography" reflect that fact. After all, "erotica" is rooted in "eros" or passionate love, and thus in the idea of positive choice, free will, the yearning for a particular person. (Interestingly, the definition of erotica leaves open the question of gender.) "Pornography" begins with a root "porno," meaning "prostitution" or "female captives," thus letting us know that the subject is not mutual love, or love at all, but domination and violence against women. (Though, of course, homosexual pornography may imitate this violence by putting a man in the "feminine" role of victim.) It ends with a root "graphos," meaning "writing about" or "description of," which puts still more distance between subject and object, and replaces a spontaneous yearning for closeness with objectification and voyeurism. The difference is clear in the words. It becomes even more so by example.

Look at any photo or film of people making love; really making love. The images may be diverse, but there is usually a sensuality and touch and warmth, an acceptance of bodies and nerve endings. There is always a spontaneous sense of people who are there because they want to be, out of shared pleasure.

Now look at any depiction of sex in which there is clear force, or an unequal power that spells coercion. It may be very blatant, with weapons of torture or bondage, wounds and bruises, some clear humiliation, or an adult's sexual power being used over a child. It may be much more subtle: a physical attitude of conqueror and victim, the use of race or class difference to imply the same thing, perhaps a very unequal nudity, with one person exposed and vulnerable while the other is clothed. In either case, there is no sense of equal choice or equal power.

The first is erotic: a mutually pleasurable, sexual expression between people who have enough power to be there by positive choice. It may or may not strike a sense-memory in the viewer, or be creative enough to make the unknown seem real;

but it doesn't require us to identify with a conqueror or a victim. It is truly sensuous, and may give us a contagion of pleasure.

The second is pornographic: its message is violence, dominance, and conquest. It is sex being used to reinforce some inequality, or to create one, or to tell us that pain and humiliation (ours or someone else's) are really the same as pleasure. If we are to feel anything, we must identify with conqueror or victim. That means we can only experience pleasure through the adoption of some degree of sadism or masochism. It also means that we may feel diminished by the role of conqueror, or enraged, humiliated, and vengeful by sharing identity with the victim.

Perhaps one could simply say that erotica is about sexuality, but pornography is about power and sex-as-weapon—in the same way we have come to understand that rape is about violence, and not really about sexuality at all.

Yes, it's true that there are women who have been forced by violent families and dominating men to confuse love with pain; so much so that they have become masochists. (A fact that in no way excuses those who administer such pain.) But the truth is that, for most women—and for men with enough humanity to imagine themselves in the predicament of women—pornography could serve as aversion-conditioning toward sex.

Of course, there will always be personal differences about what is and is not erotic, and there may be cultural differences for a long time to come. Many women feel that sex makes them vulnerable and therefore may continue to need more sense of personal connection and safety than men do before allowing any erotic feelings. Men, on the other hand, may continue to feel less vulnerable, and therefore more open to such potential danger as sex with strangers. Women now frequently find competence and expertise erotic in men, but that may pass as we develop those qualities in ourselves. As some men replace the need for submission from childlike women with the pleasure of cooperation from equals, they may find a partner's competence to be erotic, too.

Such group changes plus individual differences will continue to be reflected in sexual love between people of the same gender, as well as between women and men. The point is not to dictate sameness, but to discover ourselves and each other through a sexuality that is an exploring, pleasurable, empathetic part of our lives; a human sexuality that is unchained both from unwanted pregnancies and from violence.

But that is a hope, not a reality. At the moment, fear of change is increasing both the indiscriminate repression of all nonprocreative sex in the religious and "conservative" male-dominated world, and the pornographic vengeance against women's sexuality in the secular world of "liberal" or "radical" men. It's almost futuristic to debate what is and is not truly erotic, when many women are again being forced into compulsory motherhood, and the number of pornographic murders, tortures, and women-hating images are on the increase in both popular culture and real life.

Together, both of the above forms of repression perpetuate that familiar division: wife or whore; "good" woman who is constantly vulnerable to pregnancy or "bad" woman who is unprotected from violence. Both roles would be upset if we were to control our own sexuality. And that's exactly what we must do.

In spite of all our atavistic suspicions and training for the "natural" role of motherhood, we took up the complicated battle for reproductive freedom. Our bodies had borne the health burden of endless births and poor abortions, and we had a greater motive than men for separating sexuality and conception.

Now we have to take up the equally complex burden of explaining that all non-procreative sex is not alike. We have a motive: our right to a uniquely human sexuality, and sometimes even to survival. As it is, our bodies have too rarely been enough our own to develop erotica in our own lives, much less in art and literature. And our bodies have too often been the objects of pornography and the woman-hating, violent practice that it preaches. Consider also our spirits that break a little each time we see ourselves in chains or full labial display for the conquering male viewer, bruised or on our knees, screaming a real or pretended pain to delight the sadist, pretending to enjoy what we don't enjoy, to be blind to the images of our sisters that really haunt us—humiliated often enough ourselves by the truly obscene idea that sex and the domination of women must be combined.

Sexuality is human, free, separate—and so are we.

But until we untangle the lethal confusion of sex with violence, there will be more pornography and less erotica. There will be little murders in our beds—and very little love.

Feminism, Moralism, and Pornography

ELLEN WILLIS

For women, life is an ongoing good cop–bad cop routine. The good cops are marriage, motherhood, and that courtly old gentleman, chivalry. Just cooperate, they say (crossing their fingers), and we'll go easy on you. You'll never have to earn a living or open a door. We'll even get you some romantic love. But you'd better not get stubborn, or you'll have to deal with our friend rape, and he's a real terror; we just can't control him.

Pornography often functions as a bad cop. If rape warns that without the protection of one man we are fair game for all, the hard-core pornographic image suggests that the alternative to being a wife is being a whore. As women become more "criminal," the cops call for nastier reinforcements; the proliferation of lurid, violent porn (symbolic rape) is a form of backlash. But one can be a solid citizen and still be shocked (naively or hypocritically) by police brutality. However widely condoned, rape is illegal. However loudly people proclaim that porn is as wholesome as granola, the essence of its appeal is that emotionally it remains taboo. It is from their very contempt for the rules that bad cops derive their power to terrorize (and the covert approbation of solid citizens who would love to break the rules themselves.) The line between bad cop and outlaw is tenuous. Both rape and pornography reflect a male outlaw mentality that rejects the conventions of romance and insists, bluntly, that women are cunts. The crucial difference between the conservative's moral indignation at rape, or at *Hustler,* and the feminist's political outrage is the latter's understanding that the problem is not bad cops or outlaws but cops and the law.

Unfortunately, the current women's campaign against pornography seems determined to blur this difference. Feminist criticism of sexist and misogynist pornography is nothing new; porn is an obvious target insofar as it contributes to larger patterns of oppression—the reduction of the female body to a commodity (the paradigm being prostitution), the sexual intimidation that makes women regard the public streets as enemy territory (the paradigm being rape), sexist images, and propaganda in general. But what is happening now is different. By playing games with the English language, anti-porn activists are managing to rationalize as feminism a single-issue movement divorced from any larger political context and rooted in conservative moral assumptions that are all the more dangerous for being unacknowledged.

When I first heard there was a group called Women Against Pornography, I twitched. Could I define myself as Against Pornography? Not really. In itself, pornography—which, my dictionary and I agree, means any image or description intended or used to arouse sexual desire—does not strike me as the proper object of a political crusade. As the most cursory observation suggests, there are many varieties of porn, some pernicious, some more or less benign. About the only generalization one can make is that pornography is the return of the repressed, of feelings and fantasies driven underground by a culture that atomizes sexuality, defining love as a noble affair of the heart and mind, lust as a base animal urge centered in unmentionable organs. Prurience—the state of mind I associate with pornography—implies a sense of sex as forbidden, secretive pleasure, isolated from any emotional or social context. I imagine that in utopia, porn would wither away along with the state, heroin, and Coca-Cola. At present, however, the sexual impulses that pornography appeals to are part of virtually everyone's psychology. For obvious political and cultural reasons nearly all porn is sexist in that it is the product of a male imagination and aimed at a male market: women are less likely to be consciously interested in pornography, or to indulge that interest, or to find porn that turns them on. But anyone who thinks women are simply indifferent to pornography has never watched a bunch of adolescent girls pass around a trashy novel. Over the years I've enjoyed various pieces of pornography—some of them of the sleazy Forty-second Street paperback sort—and so have most women I know. Fantasy, after all, is more flexible than reality, and women have learned, as a matter of survival, to be adept at shaping male fantasies to their own purposes. If feminists define pornography, per se, as the enemy, the result will be to make a lot of women ashamed of their sexual feelings and afraid to be honest about them. And the last thing women need is more sexual shame, guilt, and hypocrisy—this time served up as feminism.

So why ignore qualitative distinctions and in effect condemn all pornography as equally bad? WAP organizers answer—or finesse—this question by redefining pornography. They maintain that pornography is not really about sex but about violence against women. Or, in a more colorful formulation, "Pornography is the theory, rape is the practice." Part of the argument is that pornography causes violence: much is made of the fact that Charles Manson and David Berkowitz had porn collections. This is the sort of inverted logic that presumes marijuana to be dangerous because most heroin addicts started with it. It is men's hostility toward women—combined with their power to express that hostility and for the most part get away with it—that causes sexual violence. Pornography that gives sadistic fantasies concrete shape—and, in today's atmosphere, social legitimacy—may well encourage suggestible men to act them out. But if *Hustler* were to vanish from the shelves tomorrow, I doubt that rape or wife-beating statistics would decline.

Even more problematic is the idea that pornography depicts violence rather than sex. Since porn is by definition overtly sexual, while most of it is not overtly violent, this equation requires some fancy explaining. The conference WAP held in September was in part devoted to this task. Robin Morgan and Gloria Steinem addressed it by attempting to distinguish pornography from erotica. According to this argument, erotica (whose etymological root is "eros," or sexual love) expresses an integrated sexuality based on mutual affection and desire between equals; pornography (which comes from another Greek root—"porne," meaning prostitute) reflects a dehumanized sexuality based on male domination and exploitation of women. The distinction sounds promising, but it doesn't hold up. The accepted meaning of erotica is literature or pictures with sexual themes; it may or may not serve the essentially utilitarian function of pornography. Because it is less specific, less suggestive of actual sexual activity, "erotica" is regularly used as a euphemism for "classy porn." Pornography expressed in literary language or expensive photography and consumed by the upper middle class is "erotica"; the cheap stuff, which can't pretend to any purpose but getting people off, is smut. The erotica-versus-porn approach evades the (embarrassing?) question of how porn is *used*. It endorses the portrayal of sex as we might like it to be and condemns the portrayal of sex as it too often is, whether in action or only in fantasy. But if pornography is to arouse, it must appeal to the feelings we have, not those that by some utopian standard we ought to have. Sex in this culture has been so deeply politicized that it is impossible to make clear-cut distinctions between "authentic" sexual impulses and those conditioned by patriarchy. Between, say, *Ulysses* at one end and *Snuff* at the other, erotica/pornography conveys all sorts of mixed messages that elicit complicated and private responses. In practice, attempts to sort out good erotica from bad porn inevitably come down to "What turns me on is erotic; what turns you on is pornographic."

It would be clearer and more logical simply to acknowledge that some sexual images are offensive and some are not. But logic and clarity are irrelevant—or rather, inimical—to the underlying aim of the anti-porners, which is to vent the emotions traditionally associated with the word "pornography." As I've suggested, there is a social and psychic link between pornography and rape. In terms of patriarchal morality both are expressions of male lust, which is presumed to be innately vicious, and offenses to the putative sexual innocence of "good" women. But feminists supposedly begin with different assumptions—that men's confusion of sexual desire with predatory aggression reflects a sexist system, not male biology; that there are no good (chaste) or bad (lustful) women, just women who are, like men, sexual beings. From this standpoint, to lump pornography with rape is dangerously simplistic. Rape is a violent physical assault. Pornography can be a psychic assault, both in its content and in its public intrusions on our attention, but for women as for men it can also be a source of erotic pleasure. A woman who is raped is a victim: a woman who enjoys pornography (even if that means enjoying a rape fantasy) is in a sense a rebel, insisting on an aspect of her sexuality that has been defined as a male preserve. Insofar as pornography glorifies male supremacy and sexual alienation, it is deeply reactionary. But in rejecting sexual repression and hypocrisy—which have inflicted even more damage on women than on men—it expresses a radical impulse.

That this impulse still needs defending, even among feminists, is evident from the sexual attitudes that have surfaced in the anti-porn movement. In the movement's rhetoric pornography is a code word for vicious male lust. To the objection that some women get off on porn, the standard reply is that this only shows how thoroughly women have been brainwashed by male values—though a WAP leaflet goes so far as to suggest that women who claim to like pornography are lying to avoid male opprobrium. (Note the good-girl-versus-bad-girl theme, reappearing as health-versus-sick, or honest-versus-devious; for "brainwashed" read "seduced.") And the view of sex that most often emerges from talk about "erotica" is as sentimental and euphemistic as the word itself: lovemaking should be beautiful, romantic, soft, nice, and devoid of messiness, vulgarity, impulses to power, or indeed aggression of any sort. Above all, the emphasis should be on *relationships,* not (yuck) *organs.* This goody-goody concept of eroticism is not feminist but feminine. It is precisely sex as an aggressive, unladylike activity, an expression of violent and unpretty emotion, an exercise of erotic power, and a specifically genital experience that has been taboo for women. Nor are we supposed to admit that we, too, have sadistic impulses, that our sexual fantasies may reflect forbidden urges to turn the tables and get revenge on men. (When a woman is aroused by a rape fantasy, is she perhaps identifying with the rapist as well as the victim?)

At the WAP conference lesbian separatists argued that pornography reflects patriarchal sexual relations: patriarchal sexual relations are based on male power backed by force: ergo, pornography is violent. This dubious syllogism, which could as easily be applied to romantic novels, reduces the whole issue to hopeless mush. If all manifestations of patriarchal sexuality are violent, then opposition to violence cannot explain why pornography (rather than romantic novels) should be singled out as a target. Besides, such reductionism allows women no basis for distinguishing between consensual heterosexuality and rape. But this is precisely its point; as a number of women at the conference put it, "In a patriarchy, all sex with men is pornographic." Of course, to attack pornography, and at the same time equate it with heterosexual sex, is implicitly to condemn not only women who like pornography, but women who sleep with men. This is familiar ground. The argument that straight women collaborate with the enemy has often been, among other things, a relatively polite way of saying that they consort with the beast. At the conference I couldn't help feeling that proponents of the separatist line were talking like the modern equivalents of women who, in an era when straightforward prudery was socially acceptable, joined convents to escape men's rude sexual demands. It seemed to me that their revulsion against heterosexuality was serving as the thinnest of covers for disgust with sex itself. In any case, sanitized feminine sexuality, whether straight or gay, is as limited as the predatory masculine kind and as central to women's oppression; a major function of misogynist pornography is to scare us into embracing it. As a further incentive, the good cops stand ready to assure us that we are indeed morally superior to men, that in our sweetness and nonviolence (read passivity and powerlessness) is our strength.

Women are understandably tempted to believe this comforting myth. Self-righteousness has always been a feminine weapon, a permissible way to make men feel bad. Ironically, it is socially acceptable for women to display fierce aggression in their crusades against male vice, which serve as an outlet for female anger without threatening male power. The temperance movement, which made alcohol the symbol of male violence, did not improve the position of women; substituting porn for demon rum won't work either. One reason it won't is that it bolsters the good girl-bad girl split. Overtly or by implication it isolates women who like porn or "pornographic" sex or who work in the sex industry. WAP has refused to take a position on prostitution, yet its activities—particularly its support for cleaning up Times

Square—will affect prostitutes' lives. Prostitution raises its own set of complicated questions. But it is clearly not in women's interest to pit "good" feminists against "bad" whores (or topless dancers, or models for skin magazines).

So far, the issue that has dominated public debate on the anti-porn campaign is its potential threat to free speech. Here too the movement's arguments have been full of contradictions. Susan Brownmiller and other WAP organizers claim not to advocate censorship and dismiss the civil liberties issue as a red herring dragged in by men who don't want to face the fact that pornography oppresses women. Yet at the same time, WAP endorses the Supreme Court's contention that obscenity is not protected speech, a doctrine I—and most civil libertarians—regard as a clear infringement of First Amendment rights. Brownmiller insists that the First Amendment was designed to protect political dissent, not expressions of woman-hating violence. But to make such a distinction is to defeat the amendment's purpose, since it implicitly cedes to the government the right to define "political." (Has there ever been a government willing to admit that its opponents are anything more than anti-social troublemakers?) Anyway, it makes no sense to oppose pornography on the grounds that it's sexist propaganda, then turn around and argue that it's not political. Nor will libertarians be reassured by WAP's statement that "We want to change the definition of obscenity so that it focuses on violence, not sex." Whatever their focus, obscenity laws deny the right of free expression to those who transgress official standards of propriety—and personally, I don't find WAP's standards significantly less oppressive than Warren Burger's. Not that it matters, since WAP's fantasies about influencing the definition of obscenity are appallingly naive. The basic purpose of obscenity laws is and always has been to reinforce cultural taboos on sexuality and suppress feminism, homosexuality, and other forms of sexual dissidence. No pornographer has ever been punished for being a woman-hater, but not too long ago information about female sexuality, contraception, and abortion was assumed to be obscene. In a male supremacist society the only obscenity law that will not be used against women is no law at all.

As an alternative to an outright ban on pornography, Brownmiller and others have advocated restricting its display. There is a plausible case to be made for the idea that anti-woman images displayed so prominently that they are impossible to avoid are coercive, a form of active harassment that oversteps the bounds of free speech. But aside from the evasion involved in simply equating pornography with misogyny or sexual sadism, there are no legal or logical grounds for treating sexist material any differently from (for example) racist or anti-Semitic propaganda: an equitable law would have to prohibit any kind of public defamation. And the very thought of such a sweeping law has to make anyone with an imagination nervous. Could Catholics claim they were being harassed by nasty depictions of the pope? Could Russian refugees argue that the display of Communist literature was a form of psychological torture? Would pro-abortion material be taken off the shelves on the grounds that it defamed the unborn? I'd rather not find out.

At the moment the First Amendment issue remains hypothetical: the movement has concentrated on raising the issue of pornography through demonstrations and other public actions. This is certainly a legitimate strategy. Still, I find myself more and more disturbed by the tenor of anti-pornography actions and the sort of consciousness they promote; increasingly their focus has shifted from rational feminist criticism of specific targets to generalized, demagogic moral outrage. Picketing an anti-woman movie, defacing an exploitative billboard, or boycotting a record company to protest its misogynist album covers conveys one kind of message, mass marches Against Pornography quite another. Similarly, there is a difference between telling the neighborhood news dealer why it pisses us off to have *Penthouse* shoved in our faces and choosing as a prime target every right-thinking politician's symbol of big-city sin, Times Square.

In contrast to the abortion rights movement, which is struggling against a tidal wave of energy from the other direction, the anti-porn campaign is respectable. It gets approving press and cooperation from the New York City government, which has its own stake (promoting tourism, making the Clinton area safe for gentrification) in cleaning up Times Square. It has begun to attract women whose perspective on other matters is in no way feminist ("I'm anti-abortion," a participant in WAP's march on Times Square told a reporter, "but this is something I can get into"). Despite the insistence of WAP organizers that they support sexual freedom, their line appeals to the anti-sexual emotions that feed the backlash. Whether they know it or not, they are doing the good cops' dirty work.

Does Pornography Cause Rape?

MICHAEL S. KIMMEL

Does pornography cause rape? This question has polarized academic researchers and feminist activists for more than a decade. What have we learned? What does the social science research tell us about the relationship between pornography and rape?

Historically, the debate pitted conservatives, who claimed that all sexual representation harmed community morality, against civil libertarians, who supported sexual openness and decriminalization of specific behaviors. To conservatives, pornography was of a piece with sex education, birth control, and abortion—all contravened the procreative function of sexual conduct within the marital relation. The opposition was concerned with the authoritarian implications of community control of sexual materials.

Since 1979 when Susan Brownmiller and others founded Women Against Pornography to expose women's subordination in the sex industry, feminists have recast the debate away from censorship versus free speech. If pornographic representation was a form of sex education, they argued, then it was information that reproduced men's power over women. In her book *Against Our Will,* Brownmiller wrote that pornography is "not a celebration of sexual freedom but a cynical exploitation of female sexual activity through the device of making all such activity, and consequently, all females, 'dirty.'" She claimed pornography is designed to "dehumanize women, to reduce the female to the object of sexual access, not to free sensuality from moralistic or parental inhibition."[1] Pornography is not free speech; it is censorship.

According to antipornography feminists, pornography injures women in three ways:

1. Pornography *is* violence against women: The unseen or offscreen activities within the production of pornography involve the coercion of women in scenes of humiliation, rape, and degradation. Linda Marchiano claims that she was forced, often at gunpoint, to perform the sexual acts filmed for *Deep Throat,* and that this was not a work of fiction but a documentary of sexual assault. "Every time someone watches that film, they are watching me being raped."[2]

2. Pornography causes violence against women, providing a "how-to" manual for rape and violence. As Robin Morgan's epigram puts it, "Pornography is the theory, rape is the practice." In their book *Stopping Rape,* Bart and O'Brien write, "Men are not born thinking women enjoy rape and torture—it's not carried on the Y chromosome. They learn it from pornography."[3]

3. Pornography inures consumers to the culture of violence that surrounds us. In a 1986 interview in the Chicago *Tribune,* Catharine MacKinnon commented that

From Michael S. Kimmel, "Does Pornography Cause Rape?" *Violence Update,* vol. 3 (June 1993), pp. 1, 2, 4, 8.

repeated exposure "desensitizes people to the abuse of women," with viewers becoming "numb to abuse when it is done through sex." MacKinnon and writer Andrea Dworkin developed an antipornography ordinance that could be adopted by city and state governments to provide civil redress to women who believe they've been harmed by pornography. Although the ordinance was passed by several city councils, it is yet to be enacted into law.

Other feminists disagreed. For them, feminism meant sexual freedom for women; pornography may or may not play some part in that liberation. The Feminist Anti-Censorship Taskforce (FACT) challenged the antipornography feminist position. Feminism can be an empowering vehicle to affirm women's sexuality, to claim appetite; pornography can be appropriated for those purposes. Anticensorship feminists dispute the crude behaviorism that is used in the arguments that pornography causes rape; they worry that censoring pornography can lead to the censorship of many other progressive forms of expression.

Recently, men have entered the debate. In *Men Confront Pornography,* I collected a group of essays by "profeminist" men—men who are sympathetic with feminist goals—who explore the meaning of pornography in the construction of male sexuality and the impact of pornography on men's attitudes, fantasies, and real relationships with women.

These debates have fueled a significant increase in empirical research on the effects of pornography. Studies fall into three categories, based on the method and research questions posed.

Studies of Sex Offenders

Some researchers have found a correlation between pornography and rape, measured by the percentage of admitted rapists who also admitted that they used pornography. A 1973 study found that 55% of the rapists surveyed admitted to being "excited to sex relations by pornography," while a study 15 years later found that 83% of rapists admitted regular use of pornography.

But such studies assume a causation that cannot be demonstrated from the evidence. It is also possible that a high percentage of rapists also had copies of the Bible in their homes and that they watched television police dramas like *Hunter.* Would we make similar causal arguments about those media?

Researcher Edward Donnerstein argued in a 1986 interview that "even if every violent rapist we could find had a history of exposure to violent pornography, we would never be justified in assuming that these materials 'caused' their violent behavior."

The simple correlation between pornography and sex crimes is contradicted by empirical evidence that reveals few differences in exposure to erotic materials between sex offenders, prisoners convicted of nonsex-related offenses (murder, robbery, and so on) and a control sample of "normal" male volunteers. Many researchers conclude that pornography is not a factor in motivating rape and other sexual crimes.

In his study of rapists, homosexuals, transsexuals, heavy users of pornography, and a control sample from the community, Goldstein found that "the control groups sampled had significantly greater exposure to erotic materials during adolescence than the deviants, convicted sex offenders, or heavy users of pornography."[4] In other words, the relationship turned out to be exactly the opposite of what antipornography campaigners might have predicted.

Experimental Laboratory Research

The greatest amount of research has attempted to study the effects of pornography on male viewers under laboratory conditions. These studies usually involve repeated exposures to a variety of materials, including consensual, nonviolent sexual images, aggressive pornography (such as rape scenes), and aggressive nonsexual images. Researchers have studied both the impact of pornography on behavior—does viewing pornography lead to an increase in aggression under laboratory conditions?—and attitudes, such as whether or not repeated viewing leads to an increased adherence to rape myths.

The meaning of the empirical results from such studies is hotly debated. For example, Russell argues that pornography provides the grounds for fantasy that, once planted, will eventually be acted out by male viewers; it "predisposes some men to want to rape women or intensifies the predisposition in other men already so predisposed... undermines some men's internal inhibitions against acting out their rape desires... and undermines some men's social inhibitions against the acting out."[5]

Others contest this, based on studies that have found

- Nonviolent, mildly arousing pornography (such as *Playboy* photographs) actually reduced aggressive tendencies in previously angered males.
- Nonviolent sexual images increase aggression at roughly the same level as nonsexual, arousing images (such as explicit films of eye operations), and thus the films' sexual content alone cannot be said to have caused the increased aggression.
- Arousing, nonviolent sexual images do not cause any increase in aggression against women.
- Violent, nonsexual images do lead to some increase in aggression, at roughly the same rate as violent, aggressive pornographic images.

In one study, researchers showed men films with violence against women but no sex, one with only sex but no violence, and one with neither violence nor sex. The aggression-only film produced far more aggressive behaviors from the men than the sex-only film, and the sex-only film produced no more aggression than the neutral film. The researchers then showed violence only, sex only, or sexual violence to the viewers. Men who saw the violence-only film expressed the most callous attitudes toward women and highest level of belief of rape myths, leading the researchers to conclude that the increase in aggressive behaviors is more the result of violence than explicit sexual images. The researchers wrote, "We find it curious that under the present system, the whole genre of slasher films, which graphically depict mutilation of women and which may be desensitizing viewers, falls into the same rating category as films that may contain no sex or violence but have two or more instances of the 'harsher sexually derived words.'"[6]

Men's Attitudes Toward Women

Research on the effect of pornography on men's attitudes toward women yields mixed findings. Some studies find that repeated massive exposure to pornographic films increases men's callousness toward women and their acceptance of rape myths, as well as a greater acceptance of premarital or extramarital sex and greater tolerance of nonexclusive and nonmonogamous relationships and a decrease in the importance of marriage, having children, and marital fidelity. Others find little or no change in attitudes after exposure to nonviolent pornography. Longer-term exposure to entire X-rated movies (instead of explicit snippets) produced no changes in attitudes toward rape and no increased tendency to report likelihood of committing rape.

Violent Pornography

Violent pornography has been found to produce more calloused attitudes toward women and an increased acceptance of rape myths. After exposure, men were more likely to trivialize women's post-rape trauma, believe that women secretly want to be raped, sentence convicted rapists to shorter prison terms in mock trials, and assume that the rape victim enjoyed it. These findings are similar to the effect of nonsexual slasher films.

The Problem with Laboratory Studies

Laboratory studies are vulnerable to the criticism that experimental conditions do not reproduce real world conditions and significantly distort the experience of pornography consumption, making any generalizations difficult.

In these studies, the pornography is decontextualized, taken out of its original context (the privacy of one's home, the movie theater or the pornographic bookstore) and removed from its original function (sexual arousal and, most often, masturbation). In one study, for example, pornography was further decontextualized by showing only those scenes in X-rated movies that were sexually explicit, thus removing any semblance of narrative. In later studies, this was corrected, but controlled laboratory experiments may produce an artificial range of available responses to the exposure (precluding, for example, masturbation), forcing the subjects to respond in ways they would not have chosen in more natural settings.

At least two field studies seem to bear this out. Smith and Hand surveyed women whose male companions either did or did not view pornographic films. Compared with the weeks prior and subsequent to the films, the women reported no significant difference in aggression from males. Similarly, those women whose companions did view the films reported no significant differences in aggression than those women whose companions did not see the films. In the same vein, Padgett, Brislin-Slutz, and Neal compared the results of a questionnaire administered to both psychology students and patrons at a pornographic theater and found no significant changes in attitudes or behaviors among either group, even when the patrons of the adult theater had watched significantly more pornography. Patrons had more favorable attitudes toward women than did male or female college students.

Aggregate Social Studies of Pornography

A third group of research studies uses aggregate statistical analyses to assess the relationship between pornography and violence against women. These studies often compare the circulation rates of various magazines or the number of adult theaters with the rates of rape and other sex crimes.

One study found no relationship between rape rates and the number of adult theaters and bookstores but did find a correlation with the circulation of outdoor magazines such as *Field and Stream* or *American Rifleman*. Another found a high correlation between the circulation rates of certain soft-core pornographic magazines (*Playboy, Penthouse, Hustler, Gallery,* and others) and rape rates, and later research also found a positive correlation between rape rates and sales of *Playgirl.*

Sales of the eight major men's magazines were five times higher per capita in Alaska and Nevada than in other states, and were lowest in North Dakota. Rape rates in those states were six times higher per capita in Nevada and Alaska than in North Dakota. Positive correlations, however, were also found between rape rates and gender inequality, social disorganization, urbanization, economic inequality, and unemployment, prompting the researchers to conclude that "a macho culture pattern independently influences men to purchase more pornography and commit more rapes."[7]

The most famous aggregate social analysis is Kutchinsky's Danish studies, which measured the aggregate effects of Denmark's legalization of pornography in the 1960s. Compared with the United States, crime rates in Denmark have always been relatively low. Following pornography's legalization, the general rate of sex crimes in Denmark declined, but the decline is due to different factors relating to different offenses. The rate of child molestation declined about 80%. There was a reduction in exhibitionism—perhaps because women are less often reporting it to the police. And finally, there were fewer reports of indecent assaults (which include all forcible physical approaches to women, including rape), with the largest reduction in reports of the less serious offenses. Young women, especially, are less likely to report minor annoyances; more serious offenses are still being reported. Kutchinsky concluded that legalizing pornography led to a decrease in sex crimes rather than an increase.

Recent research by myself and a colleague measured the inverse proposition from Kutchinsky: If legalizing pornography did not lead to an increase in sex crimes, would banning pornography lead to a decrease in sex crimes, specifically rape? Our comparison of six matched cities, two of which had banned the sale of pornography, yielded no relationship whatever between rape rates and sales of pornographic magazines. We concluded that, just as legalizing pornography has not led to an increase in rape, banning pornography will not lead to a reduction in rape rates.

Does Pornography Cause Rape?

The results of research are inconclusive. In aggregate studies and in the laboratories, researchers have not been able to isolate pornography as the cause of violence against women. The pervasiveness of rape and violence, even in the absence of a single causal mechanism, means that we have a larger and more diffuse constellation of masculine attitudes to confront.

Notes

1. Brownmiller, S. (1975). Against our will: Men, women, and rape. New York: Simon & Schuster.
2. Cited in Stoltenberg, J. (1990). Refusing to be a man. New York: Penguin.
3. Bart, P. B., & O'Brien, P. H. (1985). Stopping rape: Successful survival strategies. New York: Pergamon.
4. Goldstein, M. J. (1973). Exposure to erotic stimuli and sexual deviance. *Journal of Social Issues, 29*(3), 197–219.
5. Russell, D. (1988). Pornography and rape: A causal model. *Political Psychology, 9,* 41–73.
6. Linz, D., Donnerstein, E., & Penrod, S. (1988). Effects of long-term exposure to violent and sexually degrading depictions of women. *Journal of Personality and Social Psychology, 55,* 758–768.
7. Baron, L. (1990). Pornography and gender equality: An empirical analysis. *Journal of Sex Research, 27,* 363–380.

Chapter 12

Rape

The issue of *how rape is defined* imposes itself on any systematic discussion of the subject. Most observers would agree that certain concrete, specific, externally definable *essentialistic* qualities define rape and that nearly all of us know it when we see or read or hear about it. At the same time, by now all of us are sufficiently versed in the fact that *how actions are seen and evaluated* by different audiences varies enough for us to recognize that *our* definition of rape may not be shared by everyone. Rape is not only a set of identifiable concrete actions, but it is also a definition—a construction, if you will—that varies somewhat from one observer, audience, or party to another, from one subculture and society to another, and from one historical time period to another. In short, different audiences define rape in different ways.

There exists a spectrum or continuum with a highly "exclusive" definition—that is, a narrow, restricted definition—at one end, which sees very *few* acts of forced intercourse inflicted on women by men as rape. Some rapists, for instance, practically define rape out of existence. At the other end of the spectrum, we find a broader, more "inclusive" definition of rape, which interprets *many* instances of sex between men and women as forced and therefore as rape; some radical feminist separatists, for instance, believe that in a sexist society, *all* instances of heterosexual intercourse are rape, since men hold power over women and hence, women cannot choose to have sex in a free and open way. In between, we find the moderately exclusive and moderately inclusive definitions of rape, which is where most of the public would fall.

The legal or legalistic definition holds that rape takes place whenever a man engages in intercourse with a woman that is forced and against her will. But, as Estrich points out in her selection, "Is It Rape?," in the real world—in the society at large and in the criminal justice system (the police, prosecutors, judges, juries, and so on)—this definition is not necessarily adhered to. A variety of *extra-legal* factors come into play to influence audiences in deciding what they regard as their working definition of rape. In other words, many people decide that a given action is not rape, even though it is a case of forced intercourse, because of factors that should have nothing to do with this judgment. For instance, if a couple has been dating or having sex prior to the assault, many observers decide that this means that no rape has taken place. Or if a woman agrees to ride with a man in his car, or to accompany him to his apartment, she is somehow responsible for the sexual assault he inflicts on her. In possibly no other area of life aside from rape does the constructionist perspective have so much real-life relevance.

In one form or another, essentialism is the guiding principle underlying how most people think about rape. Most people believe that rape "is" a distinct, concrete phenomenon and that no other view or definition can be correct. Consequently, it is crucial to spell out the constructionist approach to rape.

First, let's be clear about this: By definition, rape *is* a violent act. It entails force or violence or the threat of violence. Rape, therefore, is *always and by definition* a violent act; it is *never* free of its violent character. What defines a specific action as rape is that by its very nature, it is coercive and is inflicted against the victim's will.

Given that, does this mean that the essentialistic position is correct—that if rape is by definition a violent act, then it follows that no specific instance of rape can contain any quality *other* than violence? For instance, if rape is an instance of "violence," does it therefore follow that it cannot be "sex" as well; are violence and sex mutually exclusive? Does one preclude the other? As Diana Scully says (1990), the assertion that rape isn't "about" sex, it's "about" violence argues that sex doesn't play any part in any rapes at all. This sets up a false—and essentialistic—dichotomy that assumes that rape is about *either* violence *or* sex—it can't be about both. This formulation assumes that there is one and only one way of looking at rape, that there is an inherent, intrinsic, concrete, objective, or "essence" contained by rape—violence—and that it manifests itself under any and all circumstances. And that this essence precludes other, different, and seemingly contradictory essences, such as sex, whose essence is mutual consent. Since rape lacks the essence of mutual consent, it therefore cannot be "true" or "real" sex.

According to Scully and other feminists, there are at least three ways that rape can be sex in addition to being violence. Saying that rape can be sex *in addition to* being violence does not make it any the less violent; what such a statement does is to admit the possibility, as Scully and Marolla show, that some men—rapists—engage in an extremely oppressive and coercive variety of sexual expression.

First, for some men, violence and sex are fused; for these men, the experience of forcing women to have sex is itself erotic. To these men, violence is sexy. For the women who are raped, of course, the experience is anything but erotic, but that only underscores the constructed nature of the phenomenon of rape. To some men, violence against women has become sexualized; to them, rape is sexual *because* it is a form of violence, because they are inflicting violence upon women. To these men, sex and violence do not exist in separate worlds; to the contrary, they are fused.

A second problem with the "rape isn't about sex, it's about violence" formulation is that, for many men, rape represents a means of sexual access. Rape is instrumental; it gets the offender what he wants—sexual intercourse with women, or a woman, who would otherwise be unattainable; as Scully says, some men "can use rape to seize what is not offered" (1990, p. 143).

And the last problem with the either-or, "rape isn't about sex, it's about violence" formulation is that, for some men, rape is an adventure; for some men, rape is "recreation and adventure" (Scully, 1990, p. 155). The "element of danger" makes rape "all the more exciting" (p. 157). For these men, rape is "more exiting" than "a normal sexual encounter" because it involves "forcing a stranger." Said one convicted rapist: "After rape, I always felt like I had just conquered something, like I had just ridden the bull at Gilley's" (p. 158). (Gilley's was a cowboy bar in Houston, Texas; the bull at Gilley's was a mechanical device that bucked and lurched, much like a bull at a rodeo; to ride—and stay on—such a device represented something of an accomplishment—and an adventure.) These men do not necessarily seek the humiliation of women but the thrill of doing something illegal, out of the ordinary, something that possesses "the element of danger" (p. 157).

Once again: A given act may be sex—and violence—for the perpetrator, and only violence for the victim. Adhering to a constructionist paradigm means that a given act is likely to be conceptualized, defined, seen, and judged differently by different parties or audiences. This does not deny that the humiliation of women is not a primary motive in a substantial proportion of cases of rape; it is even possible that this motive is present in a majority of cases. Nor does it deny that most or even all women who are raped do in fact feel humiliated. But it does emphasize that the motives for doing almost anything tend to be mixed, both in a specific individual and for acts generally. The infliction of violence on women is not necessarily the primary motive for all rapists—*even though they always engage in a violent act when they rape* (Goode, 1994, pp. 290–292).

In "Is It Rape?" Susan Estrich makes an extremely important point about how the criminal justice system views the crime of rape. According to the law, only one kind of rape exists: when a man forces a woman to have sex against her will, that is, without her consent. However, in practice, two kinds of rape exist: "aggravated" and "simple" rape. They are viewed quite differently by victims, by the public, and by agents of the criminal justice system. And the prosecution of these two kinds of rape is quite different as well.

Aggravated rape entails one or more of the following elements: the absence of any relationship between the perpetrator and the victim, the use of a weapon by the perpetrator, more than one assailant, or some physical harm inflicted on the victim. Cases of aggravated rape tend to be prosecuted vigorously by the criminal justice system; if the victim reports the crime and the evidence is sound, there is a good chance that the case will be pursued, the perpetrator will be arrested, charged with the crime, convicted, and will receive a substantial sentence.

In contrast, simple rape entails *all* of the following elements: a prior relationship between the perpetrator and the victim, the absence of a weapon, a single assailant, and no physical harm inflicted on the victim. Cases of simple rape (also referred to as date or acquaintance rape) tend not to be pursued vigorously by the criminal justice system. Even if the victim steps forward and reports the rape and the evidence is sound, the perpetrator is unlikely to be prosecuted; even if prosecution takes place, he is unlikely to be convicted; even if a conviction is obtained, he is unlikely to receive a substantial jail or prison sentence. Estrich argues that simple rape is real rape and that, in the prosecution of criminal cases, the justice system should recognize one and only one type of rape—*real* rape. Instead—even though, technically and legally, they are the same—the criminal justice system "constructs" two very different kinds of rape with two very different outcomes. Clearly, then, the constructionist perspective has practical, real-life implications. It is impossible to understand rape as a sociological phenomenon without grasping social constructionism.

References

Goode, Erich. 1994. *Deviant Behavior* (4th ed.). Englewood Cliffs, N.J.: Prentice-Hall.

Scully, Diana. 1990. *Understanding Sexual Violence: A Study of Convicted Rapists.* Boston: Unwin Hyman.

Riding the Bull at Gilley's: Convicted Rapists Describe the Rewards of Rape[1]

DIANA SCULLY and JOSEPH MAROLLA

Over the past several decades, rape has become a "medicalized" social problem. That is to say, the theories used to explain rape are predicated on psychopathological models. They have been generated from clinical experiences with small samples of rapists, often the therapists' own clients. Although these psychiatric explanations are most appropriately applied to the atypical rapist, they have been generalized to all men who rape and have come to inform the public's view on the topic.

Two assumptions are at the core of the psychopathological model; that rape is the result of idiosyncratic mental disease and that it often includes an uncontrollable sexual impulse (Scully and Marolla, 1985). For example, the presumption of psychopathology is evident in the often cited work of Nicholas Groth (1979). While Groth emphasizes the nonsexual nature of rape (power, anger, sadism), he also concludes, "Rape is always a symptom of some psychological dysfunction, either temporary and transient or chronic and repetitive" (Groth, 1979:5). Thus, in the psychopathological view, rapists lack the ability to control their behavior; they are "sick" individuals from the "lunatic fringe" of society.

In contradiction to this model, empirical research has repeatedly failed to find a consistent pattern of personality type or character disorder that reliably discriminates rapists from other groups of men (Fisher and Rivlin, 1971; Hammer and Jacks, 1955; Rada, 1978). Indeed, other research has found that fewer than 5 percent of men were psychotic when they raped (Abel et al., 1980).

Evidence indicates that rape is not a behavior confined to a few "sick" men but many men have the attitudes and beliefs necessary to commit a sexually aggressive act. In research conducted at a midwestern university, Koss and her coworkers reported that 85 percent of men defined as highly sexually aggressive had victimized women with whom they were romantically involved (Koss and Leonard, 1984). A recent survey quoted in *The Chronicle of Higher Education* estimates that more than 20 percent of college women are the victims of rape and attempted rape (Meyer, 1984). These findings mirror research published several decades earlier which also concluded that sexual aggression was commonplace in dating relationships (Kanin, 1957, 1965, 1967, 1969; Kirkpatrick and Kanin, 1957).[2] In their study of 53 college males, Malamuth, Haber and Feshback (1980) found that 51 percent indicated a likelihood that they, themselves, would rape if assured of not being punished.

In addition, the frequency of rape in the United States makes it unlikely that responsibility rests solely with a small lunatic fringe of psychopathic men. Johnson (1980), calculating the lifetime risk of rape to girls and women aged twelve and over,

From Diana Scully and Joseph Marolla, "Riding the Bull at Gilley's: Convicted Rapists Describe the Rewards of Rape." © 1985 by the Society for the Study of Social Problems. Reprinted from *Social Problems*, vol. 32 (February 1985), pp. 251–263 by permission.

makes a similar observation. Using Law Enforcement Assistance Association and Bureau of Census Crime Victimization Studies, he calculated that, excluding sexual abuse in marriage and assuming equal risk to all women, 20 to 30 percent of girls now 12 years old will suffer a violent sexual attack during the remainder of their lives. Interestingly, the lack of empirical support for the psychopathological model has not resulted in the de-medicalization of rape, nor does it appear to have diminished the belief that rapists are "sick" aberrations in their own culture. This is significant because of the implications and consequences of the model.

A central assumption in the psychopathological model is that the male sexual aggression is unusual or strange. This assumption removes rape from the realm of the everyday or "normal" world and places it in the category of "special" or "sick" behavior. As a consequence, men who rape are cast in the role of outsider and a connection with normative male behavior is avoided. Since, in this view, the source of the behavior is thought to be within the psychology of the individual, attention is diverted away from culture of social structure as contributing factors. Thus, the psychopathological model ignores evidence which links sexual aggression to environmental variables and which suggests that rape, like all behavior, is learned.

Cultural Factors in Rape

Culture is a factor in rape, but the precise nature of the relationship between culture and sexual violence remains a topic of discussion. Ethnographic data from pre-industrial societies show the existence of rape-free cultures (Broude and Green, 1976; Sanday, 1979), though explanations for the phenomena differ.[3] Sanday (1979) relates sexual violence to contempt for female qualities and suggests that rape is a part of a culture of violence and an expression of male dominance. In contrast, Blumberg (1979) argues that in pre-industrial societies women are more likely to lack important life options and to be physically and politically oppressed where they lack economic power relative to men. That is, in pre-industrial societies relative economic power enables women to win some immunity from men's use of force against them.

Among modern societies, the frequency of rape varies dramatically, and the United States is among the most rape-prone of all. In 1980, for example, the rate of reported rape and attempted rape for the United States was eighteen times higher than the corresponding rate for England and Wales (West, 1983). Spurred by the Women's Movement, feminists have generated an impressive body of theory regarding the cultural etiology of rape in the United States. Representative of the feminist view, Griffin (1971) called rape "The All American Crime."

The feminist perspective views rape as an act of violence and social control which functions to "keep women in their place" (Brownmiller, 1975; Kasinsky, 1975; Russell, 1975). Feminists see rape as an extension of normative male behavior, the result of conformity or overconformity to the values and prerogatives which define the traditional male sex role. That is, traditional socialization encourages males to associate power, dominance, strength, virility and superiority with masculinity, and submissiveness, passivity, weakness, and inferiority with femininity. Furthermore, males are taught to have expectations about their level of sexual needs and expectations for corresponding female accessibility which function to justify forcing sexual access. The justification for forced sexual access is buttressed by legal, social, and religious definitions of women as male property and sex as an exchange of goods (Bart, 1979). Socialization prepares women to be "legitimate" victims and men to be potential offenders (Weis and Borges, 1973). Herman (1984) concludes that the United States is a rape culture because both genders are socialized to regard male aggression as a natural and normal part of sexual intercourse.

Feminists view pornography as an important element in a larger system of sexual violence; they see pornography as an expression of a rape-prone culture where women are seen as objects available for use by men (Morgan, 1980; Wheeler, 1985). Based on his content analysis of 428 "adults only" books, Smith (1976) makes a similar observation. He notes that, not only is rape presented as part of normal male/female sexual relations, but the woman, despite her terror, is always depicted as sexually aroused to the point of cooperation. In the end, she is ashamed but physically gratified. The message—women desire and enjoy rape—has more potential for damage than the image of the violence *per se*.[4]

The fusion of these themes—sex as an impersonal act, the victim's uncontrollable orgasm, and the violent infliction of pain—is commonplace in the actual accounts of rapists. Scully and Marolla (1984) demonstrated that many convicted rapists denied their crime and attempted to justify their rapes by arguing that their victim had enjoyed herself despite the use of a weapon and the infliction of serious injuries, or even death. In fact, many argued, they had been instrumental in making *her* fantasy come true.

The images projected in pornography contribute to a vocabulary of motive which trivializes and neutralizes rape and which might lessen the internal controls that otherwise would prevent sexually aggressive behavior. Men who rape use this culturally acquired vocabulary to justify their sexual violence.

Another consequence of the application of psychopathology to rape is it leads one to view sexual violence as a special type of crime in which the motivations are subconscious and uncontrollable rather than overt and deliberate as with other criminal behavior. Black (1983) offers an approach to the analysis of criminal and/or violent behavior which, when applied to rape, avoids this bias.

Black (1983) suggests that it is theoretically useful to ignore that crime is criminal in order to discover what such behavior has in common with other kinds of conduct. From his perspective, much of the crime in modern societies, as in pre-industrial societies, can be interpreted as a form of "self-help" in which the actor is expressing a grievance through aggression and violence. From the actor's perspective, the victim is deviant and his own behavior is a form of social control in which the objective may be conflict management, punishment, or revenge. For example, in societies where women are considered the property of men, rape is sometimes used as a means of avenging the victim's husband or father (Black, 1983). In some cultures rape is used as a form of punishment. Such was the tradition among the puritanical, patriarchal Cheyenne where men were valued for their ability as warriors. It was Cheyenne custom that a wife suspected of being unfaithful could be "put on the prairie" by her husband. Military confreres then were invited to "feast" on the prairie (Hoebel, 1954; Llewellyn and Hoebel, 1941). The ensuing mass rape was a husband's method of punishing his wife.

Black's (1983) approach is helpful in understanding rape because it forces one to examine the goals that some men have learned to achieve through sexually violent means. Thus, one approach to understanding why some men rape is to shift attention from individual psychopathology to the important question of what rapists gain from sexual aggression and violence in a culture seemingly prone to rape.

In this paper, we address this question using data from interviews conducted with 114 convicted, incarcerated rapists. Elsewhere, we discussed the vocabulary of motive, consisting of excuses and justifications, that these convicted rapists used to explain themselves and their crime (Scully and Marolla, 1984).[5] The use of these culturally derived excuses and justifications allowed them to view their behavior as either idiosyncratic or situationally appropriate and thus it reduced their sense of moral responsibility for their actions. Having disavowed deviance, these men revealed how they had used rape to achieve a number of objectives. We find that some men used rape for revenge or punishment while, for others, it was an "added bonus"—a last minute decision made while committing another crime. In still other cases, rape was used to gain sexual access to women who were unwilling or unavailable, and for some it was a source of power and sex without any personal feelings. Rape was also a form of recreation, a diversion or an adventure and, finally, it was something that made these men "feel good."

Methods[6]

Sample

During 1980 and 1981 we interviewed 114 convicted rapists. All of the men had been convicted of the rape or attempted rape (n=8) of an adult woman and subsequently incarcerated in a Virginia prison. Men convicted of other types of sexual offense were omitted from the sample.

In addition to their convictions for rape, 39 percent of the men also had convictions for burglary or robbery, 29 percent for abduction, 25 percent for sodomy, 11 percent for first or second degree murder and 12 percent had been convicted of more than one rape. The majority of the men had previous criminal histories but only 23 percent had a record of past sex offenses and only 26 percent had a history of emotional problems. Their sentences for rape and accompanying crimes ranged from ten years to seven life sentences plus 380 years for one man. Twenty-two percent of the rapists were serving at least one life sentence. Forty-six percent of the rapists were white, 54 percent black. In age, they ranged from 18 to 60 years but the majority were between 18 and 35 years. Based on a statistical profile of felons in all Virginia prisons prepared by the Virginia Department of Corrections, it appears that this sample of rapists was disproportionately white and, at the time of the research, somewhat better educated and younger than the average inmate.

All participants in this research were volunteers. In constructing the sample, age, education, race, severity of current offense and past criminal record were balanced within the limitations imposed by the characteristics of the volunteer pool. Obviously the sample was not random and thus may not be typical of all rapists, imprisoned or otherwise.

All interviews were hand recorded using an 89-page instrument which included a general back-ground, psychological, criminal, and sexual history, attitude scales and 30 pages of open-ended questions intended to explore rapists' own perceptions of their crime and themselves. Each author interviewed half of the sample in sessions that ranged from three to seven hours depending on the desire or willingness of the participant to talk.

Validity

In all prison research, validity is a special methodological concern because of the reputation inmates have for "conning." Although one goal of this research was to understand rape from the perspective of men who have raped, it was also necessary to establish the extent to which rapists' perceptions deviated from other descriptions of their crime. The technique we used was the same others have used in prison research; comparing factual information obtained in the interviews, including details of the crime, with reports on file at the prison (Athens, 1977; Luckenbill, 1977; Queen's Bench Foundation, 1976). In general, we found that rapists' accounts of their crime had changed very little since their trials. However, there was a tendency to understate the amount of violence they had used and, especially among certain rapists, to place blame on their victims.

How Offenders View the Rewards of Rape

Revenge and Punishment

As noted earlier, Black's (1983) perspective suggests that a rapist might see his act as a legitimized form of revenge or punishment. Additionally, he asserts that the idea of "collective liability" accounts for much seemingly random violence. "Collective liability" suggests that all people in a particular category are held accountable for the conduct of each of their counterparts. Thus, the victim of a violent act may merely represent the category of individual being punished.

These factors—revenge, punishment, and the collective liability of women—can be used to explain a number of rapes in our research. Several cases will illustrate the ways in which these factors combined in various types of rape. Revenge-rapes were among the most brutal and often included beatings, serious injuries and, even murder.

Typically, revenge-rapes included the element of collective liability. This is, from the rapist's perspective, the victim was a substitute for the woman they wanted to avenge. As explained elsewhere, (Scully and Marolla, 1984), an upsetting event, involving a woman, preceded a significant number of rapes. When they raped, these men were angry because of a perceived indiscretion, typically related to a rigid, moralistic standard of sexual conduct, which they required from "their woman" but, in most cases, did not abide by themselves. Over and over these rapists talked about using rape "to get even" with their wives or other significant woman.[7] Typical is a young man who, prior to the rape, had a violent argument with his wife over what eventually proved to be her misdiagnosed case of venereal disease. She assumed the disease had been contracted through him, an accusation that infuriated him. After fighting with his wife, he explained that he drove around "thinking about hurting someone." He encountered his victim, a stranger, on the road where her car had broken down. It appears she accepted his offered ride because her car was out of commission. When she realized that rape was pending, she called him "a son of a bitch," and attempted to resist. He reported flying into a rage and beating her, and he confided,

> I have never felt that much anger before. If she had resisted, I would have killed her.... The rape was for revenge. I didn't have an orgasm. She was there to get my hostile feelings off on.

Although not the most common form of revenge rape, sexual assault continues to be used in retaliation against the victim's male partner. In one such case, the offender, angry because the victim's husband owed him money, went to the victim's home to collect. He confided, "I was going to get it one way or another." Finding the victim alone, he explained, they started to argue about the money and,

> I grabbed her and started beating the hell out of her. Then I committed the act,[8] I knew what I was doing. I was mad. I could have stopped but I didn't. I did it to get even with her and her husband.

Griffin (1971:33) points out that when women are viewed as commodities, "In raping another man's woman, a man may aggrandize his own manhood and concurrently reduce that of another man."

Revenge rapes often contained an element of punishment. In some cases, while the victim was not the initial object of the revenge, the intent was to punish her because of something that transpired after the decision to rape had been made or during the course of the rape itself. This was the case with a young man whose wife had recently left him. Although they were in the process of reconciliation, he remained angry and upset over the separation. The night of the rape, he met the victim and her friend in a bar where he had gone to watch a fight on TV. The two women apparently accepted a ride from him but, after taking her friend home, he drove the victim to his apartment. At his apartment, he found a note from his wife indicating she had stopped by to watch the fight with him. This increased his anger because he preferred his wife's company. Inside his apartment, the victim allegedly remarked that she was sexually interested in his dog, which he reported, put him in a rage. In the ensuing attack, he raped and pistol-whipped the victim. Then he forced a vacuum cleaner hose, switched on suction, into her vagina and bit her breast, severing the nipple. He stated:

> I hated at the time, but I don't know if it was her (the victim). (Who could it have been?) My wife? Even though we were getting back together, I still didn't trust her.

During his interview, it became clear that this offender, like many of the men, believed men have the right to discipline and punish women. In fact, he argued that most of the men he knew would also have beaten the victim because "that kind of thing (referring to the dog) is not acceptable among my friends."

Finally, in some rapes, both revenge and punishment were directed at victims because they represented women whom these offenders perceived as collectively responsible and liable for their problems. Rape was used "to put women in their place" and as a method of proving their "manhood" by displaying dominance over a female. For example, one multiple rapist believed his actions were related to the feeling that women thought they were better than he was.

> Rape was a feeling of total dominance. Before the rapes, I would always get a feeling of power and anger. I would degrade women so I could feel there was a person of less worth than me.

Another, especially brutal, case involved a young man from an upper middle class background, who spilled out his story in a seven-hour interview conducted in his solitary confinement cell. He described himself as tremendously angry, at the time, with his girlfriend whom he believed was involved with him in a "storybook romance," and from whom he expected complete fidelity. When she went away to college and became involved with another man, his revenge lasted eighteen months and involved the rape and murder of five women, all strangers who lived in his community. Explaining his rape-murders, he stated:

> I wanted to take my anger and frustration out on a stranger, to be in control, to do what I wanted to do. I wanted to use and abuse someone as I felt used and abused. I was killing my girlfriend. During the rapes and murders, I would think about my girlfriend. I hated the victims because they probably messed men over. I hated women because they were deceitful and I was getting revenge for what happened to me.

An Added Bonus

Burglary and robbery commonly accompany rape. Among our sample, 39 percent of rapists had also been convicted of one or the other of these crimes committed in connection with rape. In some cases, the original intent was rape and robbery was an afterthought. However, a number of the men indicated that the reverse was true in their situation. That is, the decision to rape was made subsequent to their original intent which was burglary or robbery.

This was the case with a young offender who stated that he originally intended only to rob the store in which the victim happened to be working. He explained that when he found the victim alone,

> I decided to rape her to prove I had guts. She was just there. It could have been anybody.

Similarly, another offender indicated that he initially broke into his victim's home to burglarize it. When he discovered the victim asleep, he decided to seize the opportunity "to satisfy an urge to go to bed with a white woman, to see if it was different." Indeed, a number of men indicated that the decision to rape had been made after they realized they were in control of the situation. This was also true of an unemployed offender who confided that his practice was to steal whenever he needed money. On the day of the rape, he drove to a local supermarket and paced the parking lot, "staking out the situation." His pregnant victim was the first person to come along alone and "she was an easy target." Threatening her with a knife, he reported the victim as saying she would do anything if he didn't harm her. At that point, he decided to force her to drive to a deserted area where he raped her. He explained:

> I wasn't thinking about sex. But when she said she would do anything not to get hurt, probably because she was pregnant, I thought, 'why not.'

The attitude of these men toward rape was similar to their attitude toward burglary and robbery. Quite simply, if the situation is right, "why not." From the perspective of these rapists, rape was just another part of the crime—an added bonus.

Sexual Access

In an effort to change public attitudes that are damaging to the victims of rape and to reform laws seemingly premised on the assumption that women both ask for and enjoy rape, many writers emphasize the violent and aggressive character of rape. Often such arguments appear to discount the part that sex plays in the crime. The data clearly indicate that from the rapists' point of view rape is in part sexually motivated. Indeed, it is the sexual aspect of rape that distinguishes it from other forms of assault.

Groth (1979) emphasizes the psychodynamic function of sex in rape arguing that rapists' aggressive needs are expressed through sexuality. In other words, rape is a means to an end. We argue, however, that rapists view the act as an end in itself and that sexual access most obviously demonstrates the link between sex and rape. Rape as a means of sexual access also shows the deliberate nature of this crime. When a woman is unwilling or seems unavailable for sex, the rapist can seize what isn't volunteered. In discussing his decision to rape, one man made this clear.

> All the guys wanted to fuck her... a real fox, beautiful shape. She was a beautiful woman and I wanted to see what she had.

The attitude that sex is a male entitlement suggests that when a woman says "no," rape is a suitable method of conquering the "offending" object. If, for example, a woman is picked up at a party or in a bar or while hitchhiking (behavior which a number of the rapists saw as a signal of sexual availability), and the woman later resists sexual advances, rape is presumed to be justified. The same justification operates in what is popularly called "date rape." The belief that sex was their just compensation compelled a number of rapists to insist they had not raped. Such was the case of an offender who raped and seriously beat his victim when, on their second date, she refused his sexual advances.

> I think I was really pissed off at her because it didn't go as planned. I could have been with someone else. She led me on but wouldn't deliver... I have a male ego that must be fed.

The purpose of such rapes was conquest, to seize what was not offered.

Despite the cultural belief that young women are the most sexually desirable, several rapes involved the deliberate choice of a victim relatively older than the assailant.[9] Since the rapists were themselves rather young (26 to 30 years of age on the average), they were expressing a preference for sexually experienced, rather than elderly, women. Men who chose victims older than themselves often said they did so because they believed that sexually experienced women were more desirable partners. They raped because they also believed that these women would not be sexually attracted to them.

Finally, sexual access emerged as a factor in the accounts of black men who consciously chose to rape white women.[10] The majority of rapes in the United States today are intraracial. However, for the past 20 years, according to national data based on reported rapes as well as victimization studies, which include unreported rapes, the rate of black on white (B/W) rape has significantly exceeded the rate of white on black (W/B) rape (La Free, 1982).[11] Indeed, we may be experiencing a historical anomaly, since, as Brownmiller (1975) has documented, white men have freely raped women of color in the past. The current structure of interracial rape, however, reflects contemporary racism and race relations in several ways.

First, the status of black women in the United States today is relatively lower than the status of white women. Further, prejudice, segregation and other factors continue to militate against interracial coupling. Thus, the desire for sexual access to higher status, unavailable women, an important function in B/W rape, does not motivate white men to rape black women. Equally important, demographic and geographic barriers interact to lower the incidence of W/B rape. Segregation as well as the poverty expected in black neighborhoods undoubtedly discourages many whites from choosing such areas as a target for house-breaking or robbery. Thus, the number of rapes that would occur in conjunction with these crimes is reduced.

Reflecting in part the standards of sexual desirability set by the dominant white society, a number of black rapists indicated they had been curious about white women. Blocked by racial barriers from legitimate sexual relations with white women, they raped to gain access to them. They described raping white women as "the ultimate experience" and "high status among my friends. It gave me a feeling of status, power, macho." For another man, raping a white woman had a special appeal because it violated a "known taboo," making it more dangerous and thus more exciting to him than raping a black woman.

Impersonal Sex and Power

The idea that rape is an impersonal rather than an intimate or mutual experience appealed to a number of rapists, some of whom suggested it was their preferred form of sex. The fact that rape allowed them to control rather than care encouraged some to act on this preference. For example, one man explained,

> Rape gave me the power to do what I wanted to do without feeling I had to please a partner or respond to a partner. I felt in control, dominant. Rape was the ability to have sex without caring about the woman's response. I was totally dominant.

Another rapist commented:

> Seeing them laying there helpless gave me the confidence that I could do it.... With rape, I felt totally in charge. I'm bashful, timid. When a woman wanted to give in normal sex, I was intimidated. In the rapes, I was totally in command, she totally submissive.

During this interview, another rapist confided that he had been fantasizing about rape for several weeks before committing his offense. His belief was that it would be "an exciting experience—a new high." Most appealing to him was the idea that he could make his victim "do it all for him" and that he would be in control. He fantasized that she "would submit totally and that I could have anything I wanted." Eventually, he decided to act because his older brother told him, "forced sex is great, I wouldn't get caught and, besides, women love it." Though now he admits to his crime, he continues to believe his victim "enjoyed it." Perhaps we should note here that the appeal of impersonal sex is not limited to convicted rapists. The amount of male sexual activity that occurs in homosexual meeting places as well as the widespread use of prostitutes suggests that avoidance of intimacy appeals to a large segment of the male population. Through rape men can experience power and avoid the emotions related to intimacy and tenderness. Further, the popularity of violent pornography suggests that a wide variety of men in this culture have learned to be aroused by sex fused with violence (Smith, 1976). Consistent with this observation, recent experimental research conducted by Malamuth et al., (1980) demonstrates that men are aroused by images that depict women as orgasmic under conditions of violence and pain. They found that for female students, arousal was high when the victim experienced an orgasm and *no* pain, whereas male students were highly aroused when the victim experienced an orgasm and pain. On the basis of their results, Malamuth et al., (1980) suggest that forcing a woman to climax despite her pain and abhorrence of the assailant makes the rapist feel powerful, he has gained control over the only source of power historically associated with women, their bodies. In the final analysis, dominance was the objective of most rapists.

Recreation and Adventure

Among gang rapists, most of whom were in their late teens or early twenties when convicted, rape represented recreation and adventure, another form of delinquent activity. Part of rape's appeal was the sense of male camaraderie engendered by participating collectively in a dangerous activity. To prove one's self capable of "performing" under these circumstances was a substantial challenge and also a source of reward. One gang rapist articulated this feeling very clearly,

> We felt powerful, we were in control. I wanted sex and there was peer pressure. She wasn't like a person, no personality, just domination on my part. Just to show I could do it—you know, macho.

Our research revealed several forms of gang rape. A common pattern was hitchhike-abduction rape. In these cases, the gang, cruising an area, "looking for girls," picked up a female hitchhiker for the purpose of having sex. Though the intent was rape, a number of men did not view it as such because they were convinced that women hitchhiked primarily to signal sexual availability and only secondarily as a form of transportation. In these cases, the unsuspecting victim was driven to a deserted area, raped, and in the majority of cases physically injured. Sometimes, the victim was not hitchhiking; she was abducted at knife or gun point from the street usually at night. Some of these men did not view this type of attack as rape either because they believed a woman walking alone at night to be a prostitute. In addition, they were often convinced "she enjoyed it."

"Gang date" rape was another popular variation. In this pattern, one member of the gang would make a date with the victim. Then, without her knowledge or consent, she would be driven to a predetermined location and forcibly raped by each member of the group. One young man revealed this practice was so much a part of his group's recreational routine, they had rented a house for the purpose. From his perspective, the rape was justified because "usually the girl had a bad reputation, or we knew it was what she liked."

During his interview, another offender confessed to participating in twenty or thirty such "gang date" rapes because his driver's license had been revoked making it difficult for him to "get girls." Sixty percent of the time, he claimed, "they were girls known to do this kind of thing," but "frequently, the girls didn't want to have sex with all of us." In such cases, he said, "It might start out as rape but, then, they (the women) would quiet down and none ever reported it to the police." He was convicted for a gang rape, which he described as "the ultimate thing I ever did," because unlike his other rapes, the victim, in this case, was a stranger whom the group abducted as she walked home from the library. He felt the group's past experience with "gang date" rape had prepared them for this crime in which the victim was blindfolded and driven to the mountains where, though it was winter, she was forced to remove her clothing. Lying on the snow, she was raped by each of the four men several times before being abandoned near a farm house. This young man continued to believe that if he had spent the night with her, rather than abandoning her, she would not have reported to the police.[12]

Solitary rapists also used terms like "exciting," "a challenge," "an adventure," to describe their feelings about rape. Like the gang rapists, these men found the element of danger made rape all the more exciting. Typifying this attitude was one man who described his rape as intentional. He reported:

> It was exciting to get away with it (rape), just being able to beat the system, not women. It was like doing something illegal and getting away with it.

Another rapist confided that for him "rape was just more exciting and compelling" than a normal sexual encounter because it involved forcing a stranger. A multiple rapist asserted, "it was the excitement and fear and the drama that made rape a big kick."

Feeling Good

At the time of their interviews, many of the rapists expressed regret for their crime and had empirically low self-esteem ratings. The experience of being convicted, sentenced, and incarcerated for rape undoubtedly produced many, if not most, of these feelings. What is clear is that, in contrast to the well-documented severity of the immediate impact, and in some cases, the long-term trauma experienced by the victims of sexual violence, the immediate emotional impact on the rapists is slight.

When the men were asked to recall their feelings immediately following the rape, only eight percent indicated that guilt or feeling bad was part of their emotional response. The majority said they felt good, relieved or simply nothing at all. Some indicated they had been afraid of being caught or felt sorry for themselves. Only two men out of 114 expressed any concern or feeling for the victim. Feeling good or nothing at all about raping women is not an aberration limited to men in prison. Smithyman (1978), in his study of "undetected rapists"—rapists outside of prison—found that raping women had no impact on their lives nor did it have a negative effect on their self-image.

Significantly a number of men volunteered the information that raping had a positive impact on their feelings. For some the satisfaction was in revenge. For example, the man who had raped and murdered five women:

> It seems like so much bitterness and tension had built up and this released it. I felt like I had just climbed a mountain and now I could look back.

Another offender characterized rape as habit forming: "Rape is like smoking. You can't stop once you start." Finally one man expressed the sentiments of many rapists when he stated,

> After rape, I always felt like I had just conquered something, like I had just ridden the bull at Gilley's

Conclusions

This paper has explored rape from the perspective of a group of convicted, incarcerated rapists. The purpose was to discover how these men viewed sexual violence and what they gained from their behavior.

We found that rape was frequently a means of revenge and punishment. Implicit in revenge rapes was the notion that women were collectively liable for the rapists' problems. In some cases, victims were substitutes for significant women on whom the men desired to take revenge. In other cases, victims were thought to represent all women, and rape was used to punish, humiliate, and "put them in their place." In both cases women were seen as a class, a category, not as individuals. For some men, rape was almost an afterthought, a bonus added to burglary or robbery. Other men gained access to sexually unavailable or unwilling women through rape. For this group of men, rape was a fantasy come true, a particularly exciting form of impersonal sex which enabled them to dominate and control women, by exercising a singularly male form of power. These rapists talked of the pleasures of raping—how for them it was a challenge, an adventure, a dangerous and "ultimate" experience. Rape made them feel good and, in some cases, even elevated their self image.

The pleasure these men derived from raping reveals the extreme to which they objectified women. Women were seen as sexual commodities to be used or conquered rather than as human beings with rights and feelings. One young man expressed the extreme of the contemptful view of women when he confided to the female researcher.

> Rape is a man's right. If a women doesn't want to give it, the man should take it. Women have no right to say no. Women are made to have sex. It's all they are good for. Some women would rather take a beating, but they always give in; it's what they are for.

This man murdered his victim because she wouldn't "give in."

Undoubtedly, some rapes, like some of all crimes, are idiopathic. However, it is not necessary to resort to pathological motives to account for all rape or other acts of sexual violence. Indeed, we find that men who rape have something to teach us about the cultural roots of sexual aggression. They force us to acknowledge that rape is more than an idiosyncratic act committed by a few "sick" men. Rather, rape can be viewed as the end point in a continuum of sexually aggressive behaviors that reward men and victimize women.[13] In the way that the motives for committing any criminal act can be rationally determined, reasons for rape can also be determined. Our data demonstrate that some men rape because they have learned that in this culture sexual violence is rewarding. Significantly, the overwhelming majority of these rapists indicated they never thought they would go to prison for what they did. Some did not fear imprisonment because they did not define their behavior as rape. Others knew that women frequently do not report rape and of those cases that are reported, conviction rates are low, and therefore they felt secure. These men perceived rape as a rewarding, low risk act. Understanding that otherwise normal men can and do rape is critical to the development of strategies for prevention.

We are left with the fact that all men do not rape. In view of the apparent rewards and cultural supports for rape, it is important to ask why some men do not rape. Hirschi (1969) makes a similar observation about delinquency. He argues that the key question is not "Why do they do it?" but rather "Why don't we do it?" (Hirschi, 1969:34). Likewise, we may be seeking an answer to the wrong question about sexual assault of women. Instead of asking men who rape "Why?", perhaps we should be asking men who don't "Why not?"

References

Abel, Gene, Judith Becker, and Linda Skinner. 1980. "Aggressive behavior and sex." Psychiatric Clinics of North America 3:133–51.

Athens, Lonnie. 1977. "Violent crime: a symbolic interactionist study." Symbolic Interaction 1:56–71.

Bart, Pauline. 1979. "Rape as a paradigm of sexism in society—victimization and its discontents." Women's Studies International Quarterly 2:347–57.

Benard, Cheryl and Edit Schlaffer. 1984. "The man in the street: why he harasses." Pp. 70–73 in Alison M. Jaggar and Paula S. Rothenberg (eds.), Feminist Frameworks. New York: McGraw-Hill.

Black, Donald. 1983. "Crime as social control." American Sociological Review 48:34–45.

Blumberg, Rae Lesser. 1979. "A paradigm for predicting the position of women: policy implications and problems." Pp. 113–42 in Jean Lipman-Blumen and Jessie Bernard (eds.), Sex Roles and Social Policy. London: Sage Studies in International Sociology.

Broude, Gwen and Sarah Greene. 1976. "Cross-cultural codes on twenty sexual attitudes and practices." Ethnology 15:409–28.

Brownmiller, Susan. 1975. Against Our Will. New York: Simon and Schuster.

Davis, Angela. 1981. Women, Race and Class. New York: Random House.

Fisher, Gary and E. Rivlin. 1971. "Psychological needs of rapists." British Journal of Criminology 11:182–85.

Griffin, Susan. 1971. "Rape: the all American crime." Ramparts, September 10:26–35.

Groth, Nicholas. 1971. Men Who Rape. New York: Plenum Press.

Hammer, Emanuel and Irving Jacks. 1955. "A study of Rorschack flexnor and extensor human movements." Journal of Clinical Psychology 11:63–67.

Herman, Dianne. 1984. "The rape culture." Pp. 20–39 in Jo Freeman (ed.), Women: A Feminist Perspective. Palo Alto: Mayfield.

Hirschi, Travis. 1969. Causes of Delinquency. Berkely: University of California Press.

Hoebel, E. Adamson. 1954. The Law of Primitive Man. Boston: Harvard University Press.

Johnson, Allan Griswold. 1980. "On the prevalence of rape in the United States." Signs 6:136–46.

Kanin, Eugene. 1957. "Male aggression in dating-courtship relations." American Journal of Sociology 63:197–204.

———.1965. "Male sex aggression and three psychiatric hypotheses." Journal of Sex Research 1:227–29.

———.1967. "Reference groups and sex conduct norm violation." Sociological Quarterly 8:495–504.

———.1969. "Selected dyadic aspects of male sex aggression." Journal of Sex Research 5:12–28.

Kasinsky, Renee. 1975. "Rape: a normal act?" Canadian Forum, September:18–22.

Kirkpatrick, Clifford and Eugene Kanin. 1957. "Male sex aggression on a university campus." American Sociological Review 22:52–58.

Koss, Mary P. and Kenneth E. Leonard. 1984. "Sexually aggressive men: empirical findings and theoretical implications." Pp. 213–32 in Neil M. Malamuth and Edward Donnerstein (eds.), Pornography and Sexual Aggression. New York: Academic Press.

LaFree, Gary. 1980. "The effect of sexual stratification by race on official reactions to rape." American Sociological Review 45:824–54.

———.1982. "Male power and female victimization: towards a theory of interracial rape." American Journal of Sociology 88:311–28.

Llewellyn, Karl N., and E. Adamson Hoebel. 1941. The Cheyenne Way: Conflict and Case Law in Primitive Jurisprudence. Norman: University of Oklahoma Press.

Luckenbill, David. 1977. "Criminal homicide as a situated transaction." Social Problems 25:176–87.

Malamuth, Neil, Scott Haber and Seymour Feshback. 1980. "Testing hypotheses regarding rape: exposure to sexual violence, sex difference, and the 'normality' of rapists." Journal of Research in Personality 14:121–37.

Malamuth, Neil, Maggie Heim, and Seymour Feshback. 1980. "Sexual responsiveness of college students to rape depictions: inhibitory and disinhibitory effects." Social Psychology 38:399–408.

Meyer, Thomas J. 1984. "'Date rape': a serious problem that few talk about." Chronicle of Higher Education, December 5.

Morgan, Robin. 1980. "Theory and practice: pornography and rape." Pp. 134–40 in Laura Lederer (ed.), Take Back the Night: Women on Pornography. New York: William Morrow.

Queen's Bench Foundation. 1976. Rape: Prevention and Resistance. San Francisco: Queen's Bench Foundation.

Rada, Richard. 1978. Clinical Aspects of Rape. New York: Grune and Stratton.

Russell, Diana. 1975. The Politics of Rape. New York: Stein and Day.

Sanday, Peggy Reeves. 1979. The Socio-Cultural Context of Rape. Washington, DC: United States Department of Commerce, National Technical Information Service.

Scully, Diana and Joseph Marolla. 1984. "Convicted rapists' vocabulary of motive: excuses and justifications." Social Problems 31:530–44.

———.1985. "Rape and psychiatric vocabulary of motive: alternative perspectives." Pp. 294–312 in Ann Wolbert Burgess (ed.), Rape and Sexual Assault: A Research Handbook. New York: Garland Publishing.

Smith, Don. 1976. "The social context of pornography." Journal of Communications 26:16–24.

Smithyman, Samuel. 1978. The Undetected Rapist. Unpublished Dissertation: Claremont Graduate School.

Weis, Kurt and Sandra Borges. 1973. "Victimology and rape: the case of the legitimate victim." Issues in Criminology 8:71–115.

West, Donald J. 1983. "Sex offenses and offending." Pp. 1–30 in Michael Tonry and Norval Morris (eds.), Crime and Justice: An Annual Review of Research. Chicago: University of Chicago Press.

Wheeler, Hollis. 1985. "Pornography and rape: a feminist perspective." Pp. 374–91 in Ann Wolbert Burgess (ed.), Rape and Sexual Assault: A Research Handbook. New York: Garland Publishing.

Notes

1. This research was supported by a grant (R01 MH33013) from the National Center for the Prevention and Control of Rape, National Institute of Mental Health. We are indebted to the Virginia Department of Corrections for their cooperation and assistance in this research. Correspondence to: Scully, Department of Sociology/Anthropology, Virginia Commonwealth University, 312 Shafer Street, Richmond, Virginia 23284.

2. Despite the fact that these data have been in circulation for some time, prevention strategies continue to reflect the "lunatic fringe" image of rape. For example, security on college campuses, such as bright lighting and escort service, is designed to protect women against stranger rape while little or no attention is paid to the more frequent crime—acquaintance or date rape.

3. Broude and Green (1976) list a number of factors which limit the quantity and quality of cross-cultural data on rape. They point out that it was not customary in traditional ethnography to collect data on sexual attitudes and behavior. Further, where data do exist, they are often sketchy and vague. Despite this, the existence of rape-free societies has been established.

4. This factor distinguishes rape from other fictional depictions of violence. That is, in fictional murder, bombings, robberies, etc., victims are never portrayed as enjoying themselves. Such exhibits are reserved for pornographic displays of rape.

5. We also introduced a typology consisting of "admitters" (men who defined their behavior as rape) and "deniers" (men who admitted to sexual contact with the victim but did not define it as rape). In this paper we drop the distinction between admitters and deniers because it is not relevant to most of the discussion.

6. For a full discussion of the research methodology, sample, and validity, see Scully and Marolla (1984).

7. It should be noted that significant women, like rape victims, were also sometimes the targets of abuse and violence and possibly rape as well, although spousal rape is not recognized in Virginia law. In fact, these men were abusers. Fifty-five percent of rapists acknowledged that they hit their significant woman "at least once," and 20 percent admitted to inflicting physical injury. Given the tendency of these men to under-report the amount of violence in their crime, it is probably accurate to say, they under-reported their abuse of their significant women as well.

8. This man, as well as a number of others, either would not or could not, bring himself to say the word "rape." Similarly, we also attempted to avoid using the word, a technique which seemed to facilitate communication.

9. When asked towards whom their sexual interests were primarily directed, 43 percent of rapists indicated a preference for women "significantly older than themselves." When those who responded, "women of any age" are added, 65 percent of rapists expressed sexual interest in women older than themselves.

10. Feminists as well as sociologists have tended to avoid the topic of interracial rape. Contributing to the avoidance is an awareness of historical and contemporary social injustice. For example, Davis (1981) points out that fictional rape of white women was used in the South as a post-slavery justification to lynch black men. And LaFree (1980) has demonstrated that black men who assault white women continue to receive more serious sanctions within the criminal justice system when compared to other racial combinations of victim and assailant. While the silence has been defensible in light of historical racism, continued avoidance of the topic discriminates against victims by eliminating the opportunity to investigate the impact of social factors on rape.

11. In our sample, 66 percent of black rapists reported their victim(s) were white, compared to two white rapists who reported raping black women. It is important to emphasize that because of the biases inherent in rape reporting and processing, and because of the limitations of our sample, these figures do not accurately reflect the actual racial composition of rapes committed in Virginia or elsewhere. Furthermore, since black men who assault white women receive more serious sanctions within the criminal justice system when compared to other racial combinations of victim and assailant (LaFree, 1980), B/W rapists will be overrepresented within prison populations as well as overrepresented in any sample drawn from the population.

12. It is important to note that the gang rapes in this study were especially violent, resulting in physical injury, even death. One can only guess at the amount of hitchhike-abduction and "gang date" rapes that are never reported or, if reported, are not processed because of the tendency to disbelieve the victims of such rapes unless extensive physical injury accompanies the crime.

13. It is interesting that men who verbally harass women on the street say they do so to alleviate boredom, to gain a sense of youthful camaraderie, and because it's fun (Bernard and Schlaffer, 1984)—the same reason men who rape give for their behavior.

Is it Rape?

SUSAN ESTRICH

A man commits rape when he engages in intercourse (in the old statutes, carnal knowledge) with a woman not his wife; by force or threat of force; against her will and without her consent. That is the traditional, common law definition of rape, and it remains the essence of even the most radical reform statutes.

But many cases that fit this definition of "rape" are not treated as criminal by the criminal justice system, or even considered rape by their women victims. In the cases on which this book focuses, the man is not the armed stranger jumping from the bushes—nor yet the black man jumping the white woman, the case that was most likely to result in the death penalty prior to 1977, and the stereotype that may explain in part the seriousness with which a white male criminal justice system has addressed "stranger" rape. Instead the man is a neighbor, an acquaintance, or a date. The man and the woman are both white, or both black, or both Hispanic. He is a respected bachelor, a student, a businessman, or a professional. He may have been offered a ride home or invited in. He does not have a weapon. He acted alone. It is, in short, a simple rape.

The man telling me this particular story is an assistant district attorney in a large Western city. He is in his thirties, an Ivy League law school graduate, a liberal, married to a feminist. He's about as good as you're going to get making decisions like this. This is a case he did not prosecute. He considers it rape—but only "technically." This is why.

The victim came to his office for the meeting dressed in a pair of tight blue jeans. Very tight. With a see-through blouse on top. Very revealing. That's how she was dressed. It was, he tells me, really something. Something else. Did it matter? Are you kidding!

The man involved was her ex-boyfriend. And lover; well, ex-lover. They ran into each other on the street. He asked her to come up and see *Splash* on his new VCR. She did. It was not the Disney version—of *Splash,* that is. It was porno. They sat in the living room watching. Like they used to. He said, lets go in the bedroom where we'll be more comfortable. He moved the VCR. They watched from the bed. Like they used to. He began rubbing her foot. Like he used to. Then he kissed her. She said no, she didn't want this, and got up to leave. He pulled her back on the bed and forced himself on her. He did not beat her. She had no bruises. Afterward, she ran out. The first thing she did was flag a police car. That, the prosecutor tells us, was the first smart thing she did.

The prosecutor pointed out to her that she was not hurt, that she had no bruises, that she did not fight. She pointed out to the prosecutor that her ex-boyfriend was

Reprinted by permission of the publishers from *Real Rape,* by Susan Estrich (Cambridge, Mass.: Harvard University Press, 1987), pp. 8–26 (references deleted).

a weightlifter. He told her it would be nearly impossible to get a conviction. She could accept that, she said: even if he didn't get convicted, at least he should be forced to go through the time and the expense of defending himself. That clinched it, said the D.A. She was just trying to use the system to harass her ex-boyfriend. He had no criminal record. He was not a "bad guy." No charges were filed.

Someone walked over and asked what we were talking about. About rape, I replied; no, actually about cases that aren't really rape. The D.A. looked puzzled. That was rape, he said. Technically. She was forced to have sex without consent. It just wasn't a case you prosecute.

This case is unusual in only one respect: that the victim perceived herself to be a victim of rape and was determined to prosecute. That is unusual. The prosecutor's response was not.

The Response of Victims

Much has been written about the incidence of rape and of rape reporting today. Some feminists have claimed that rape is at near epidemic levels, and that if the official statistics do not reflect this, it is because rape is the single most underreported major crime. Defenders of the system claim that rape is relatively uncommon and that reporting rates are not atypical and are relatively high. In a sense everyone is right, since no one is defining terms.

The dimensions of the problem of rape in the United States depend on whether you count the simple, "technical" rapes. If only the aggravated cases are considered rape—if we limit our practical definition to cases involving more than one man, or strangers, or weapons and beatings—then "rape" is a relatively rare event, is reported to the police more often than most crimes, and is addressed aggressively by the system. If the simple cases are considered—the cases where a woman is forced to have sex without consent by only one man, whom she knows, who does not beat her or attack her with a gun—then rape emerges as a far more common, vastly underreported, and dramatically ignored problem.

The Uniform Crime Reports are the official FBI tabulation of reported crime. Released annually, they are based on actual statistics contributed by state and local agencies. For purposes of the Uniform Crime Reports, forcible rape is "the carnal knowledge of a female forcibly and against her will." Assaults or attempts to commit rape by force or threat of force are also included. An estimated 69 of every 100,000 females in the nation were reported rape victims in 1984, a slight decrease since 1980, but an increase from the preceding year. Forcible rape was much more common than murder, but many times rarer than robbery, aggravated assault, and motor vehicle theft, and tens of times rarer than burglary and larceny.

Even the Uniform Crime Reports acknowledge that rape is underreported. By how much is another question. The government's answer to underreporting is found in the official victimization surveys compiled by the Department of Justice's Bureau of Justice Statistics. These surveys consist of a random sample of individuals interviewed in their homes about their experiences of victimization. According to the victimization surveys, between 1973 and 1982, for every 100,000 women in this country, 165 each year were victims of an attempted or completed rape. In 1983 the victimization surveys reported 1 rape for every 600 women—nearly twice as many as the official police reports—and, as would be expected, found that just over half of the women victims reported to the police. Reporting rates of over 50 percent make rape one of the *most* reported crimes covered by victimization surveys.

Rape, according to the official crime reports and even the victimization surveys, is committed less frequently and reported more often than most crimes. That is because rape, as the victimization surveys present it, is a crime committed by strangers. When individuals are surveyed, no definition of rape is given. Over two-thirds of those who volunteer that they were raped were raped by strangers. The survey writers conclude: "The most frightening form of rape, an assault by a total stranger, is also the most common. A woman is twice as likely to be attacked by a stranger as by someone she knows."

Perhaps. Or perhaps she is simply twice as likely to talk about it—to police or to survey interviewers. Studies of women who contact rape crisis centers have consistently found that those most likely to report to police are those raped by strangers. A recent study in Seattle found that prior relationship was the single most important factor in the underreporting of rape to the police. The author found a positive correlation between prior relationship and other variables (force, injury, circumstances of initial contact) that were positively related to reporting. But notably, even those women raped by friends or relatives, who did experience serious threats, force, or injury, were less likely to report. Similarly, a study of women who contacted rape crisis centers in Massachusetts found that nearly two-thirds knew their attackers and that the majority did not report the victimization to the police. The closer the relationship between victim and assailant, the less likely the woman was to report.

What is most noteworthy about such studies is not the reporting rates themselves but the extent to which, contrary to the picture of the official victimization surveys, nonstranger rapes outnumber assaults by strangers. In both Massachusetts and Seattle the overwhelming majority of women who contacted rape centers had been attacked by men they knew. And women who contact these centers are women who at least perceive themselves to be "rape" victims, even if they do not report to the police. It appears that most women forced to have sex by men they know see themselves as victims, but not as legitimate crime victims.

The most striking findings of this sort are based on Diana Russell's survey of 930 adult women in the San Francisco area in 1978. Some 22 percent of those surveyed responded that they had been the victims of "an attempted or completed rape" in their lives, a figure substantially higher than the victimization surveys would ever produce. Even so, when the questions were rephrased to inquire about forced intercourse or intercourse obtained by threat (rather than "rape"), the number climbed to 56 percent (of which 24 percent were completed). Eighty-two percent of Russell's total rapes involved nonstrangers—and less than 10 percent of them were reported to the police.

Russell's findings as to the prevalence of forced sex among dates, acquaintances, and friends, are not unique. In a 1977 study over half of the female college students interviewed reported having experienced offensive male sexual aggression during the previous year. A 1983 nationwide study of adolescents conservatively estimated that from 5 to 16 percent of adolescent males "sexually assault" each year, and that most of these assaults are "spontaneous events that occur in the context of a date." Yet only 5 percent of the female victims of these sexual assaults report them to the police as rape. In three separate studies of college students released in 1985, one in five women in each study reported being "physically forced" to have sexual intercourse by her date. Yet the majority of these women did not think they had been raped; as one newspaper put it in reporting the results: "Rape not rape to some victims."

The reasons given in these studies for the failure to perceive forced sex as rape, let alone report it as such, reflect an understanding of rape that discounts the "simple" case. Some women do not report because they were "successful" in resisting the actual penetration, suggesting an erroneous belief that sexual aggression is a crime only when it ends in unwanted intercourse. Other women do not report because they ended up "giving in" to the sexual pressure without a "fight," suggesting the equation of nonconsent with utmost or at least reasonable physical resistance. And many young women believe that sexual pressure, including physical pressure, is simply not aberrant or illegal behavior if it takes place in a dating situation. Thus, one study concluded that most adolescent victims do not perceive their experience of victimization "as legitimate," meaning that "they do not involve strangers or substantial violence." Forced sex does not amount to criminal victimization "unless it occurs outside a dating situation or becomes especially violent."

These findings confirm what has been learned through tests posing hypothetical examples. In those tests almost no one has any difficulty recognizing the classic, traditional rape—the stranger with a gun at the throat of his victim forcing intercourse on pain of death—as just that. When the man in the hypothetical (even a stranger) "warns her to do as he said" and "tells her to lie down" instead of "slashing her with a knife" or at least "waving" it in the air and shoving her down, those who are certain that a "rape" has taken place decrease significantly in every category except women who generally held "pro-feminist" views. In situations where a woman is presented as being forced to engage in sex after a "date with a respected bachelor" or with a man she met in a bar who takes her to a deserted road (instead of home) or with her boss after working late, less than half of the female respondents in another survey were certain that a "rape" had occurred. Notably, where the two were strangers and the circumstances of the initial contact were involuntary—accosted in parking lots, house break-ins—nearly everyone was certain that a rape had occurred. Adolescents in one survey were least likely to label clearly forced sex as "rape" when the couple was presented as dating. According to that study, "teenagers of both genders are quite accepting of forced sex between acquaintances and often don't view it as rape."

When we walk out of our house and don't see our car we know (unless we've parked illegally) that we are the victims of car theft. This is not true of women who say no, but are forced to have sex. We know that we have been abused. But many of us do not think that we have been really "raped"—unless we happen to be women who are more "pro-feminist" than most. And even if we do, we think twice—or twenty times—about reporting. With reason.

In 1971 the Bureau of the Census, in an attempt to examine the accuracy of the criminal victimization surveys, conducted what is known as a reverse record check, interviewing 620 persons who had reported to the police that they were victims of specific crimes. In the report of the San Jose Methods Test of Known Crime Victims the authors found that over 80 percent of those raped by strangers disclosed the victimization to the interviewer, while only about half of those raped by someone they knew disclosed the victimization. Rape was both more and less likely to be disclosed than other crimes—depending entirely on the circumstances. Rape committed by a stranger was the crime most likely to be reported to survey interviewers. Rape committed by a nonstranger, second to aggravated assault, was the crime least likely to be reported to the interviewers.

Why would fully half of the women who not only perceived themselves to be the victims of nonstranger rape but also went so far as to report it to the police remain silent when asked about criminal victimization by a survey interviewer? One possibility is that they were simply tired of talking about it and considered it too private or too painful to discuss with a stranger who wanted the information for a survey. But that possibility would seem to apply equally to all rape victims, not only to those raped by nonstrangers; it does not explain why the stranger victims were so willing to disclose and the nonstranger victims so unwilling. A second possibility does: that the victims who did not disclose were those who had in effect been told that they were not legitimate victims by the police and the criminal justice system.

The woman raped by her ex-boyfriend the weightlifter, in the "technical" rape my acquaintance so easily dismissed, clearly thought she had been raped. She flagged down a police car; she went to meet with the prosecutor; she was willing to persist, regardless of the odds. The response from the system was negative. I wonder what she would say if a survey interviewer came to her house one day and asked if she had been victimized in the last year. I would not be surprised if she said nothing at all.

The Response of the System

Deciding to report a simple rape is a step most victims never take. If they do, it is only the first step. The road to conviction and sentencing is long. Simple rapes are not only far less likely to be reported than aggravated rapes; if they are reported, they are less likely to result in convictions.

The initial decisions are made by the police, in many cases without any review by prosecutors. Police exercise substantial discretion, and they do so almost invisibly. Judges sometimes are attacked publicly when a convicted defendant receives what appears to be an unduly lenient sentence, but police decide to abandon cases every day and no one knows. Police decide whether a woman's complaint is "founded" or "unfounded"; only "founded" complaints are forwarded for possible prosecution. They also decide whether and how much to investigate, a decision which affects the quality of evidence available for trial, or at least for plea bargaining with the defendant's lawyers.

Most jurisdictions do collect "unfounding" statistics for crimes, but numbers can be deceptive. What appear as "high" unfounding rates for rape are invoked by some as proof that police are unfairly skeptical of rape complainants, and by others as proof that rape complainants disproportionately lie. The problem with both approaches is that cases may be "unfounded" for reasons that have nothing to do with the merits of the complaint. Some complaints are unfounded because the police, rightly or wrongly, do not believe the victim. But some are unfounded because it emerges that the alleged offense took place outside the jurisdiction. And some are unfounded because the victim missed a subsequent appointment with the police. Different jurisdictions follow different policies in marking complaints as "founded" or "unfounded," and those differences make the national statistics almost meaningless. For example, in 1973 the FBI reported that nationally 15 percent of all rape complaints were unfounded by police. This number has been termed "undeniably high" by Susan Brownmiller. To be sure. But that 15 percent includes city statistics ranging from 1.3 percent in Detroit to 54.1 percent in Chicago, with everything in between, making comparisons between cities, let alone serious reliance on the national numbers, virtually impossible.

If the numbers themselves tell us little, individual studies of jurisdictions do shed light on some of the factors that lead police to decline certain complaints. Part of the problem, it appears, comes from a male evaluation of a woman's account: in New York and Philadelphia adding a woman to the police investigative team had the effect of substantially reducing the percentage of cases considered to be without merit. But even in those jurisdictions, not all women rape victims are equally suspect: discretion to "unfound" is used more often in simple rape. In New York, for example, researchers studying police files found that 24 percent of the rape complaints in nonstranger cases were judged by the police to be without merit, compared with less than 5 percent in the stranger cases. In Philadelphia a study of police files in the mid-1970s led researchers to conclude that "the police appear to endorse an extralegal victim precipitation logic, declaring unfounded those cases in which the circumstances of the victim-offender relationship are not wholly uncompromising." An earlier study in Philadelphia pointed to race as well, along with the victim's "assumption of risk" (getting into a car, for example) and the promptness of her complaint, as factors influencing the exercise of police discretion.

Even if the police do not unfound the complaint, and even if an arrest is made, conviction is not guaranteed. Arrests are certainly easiest where the victim knows the offender; convictions are another matter. Studies of individual jurisdictions have found that only 20 percent (Washington, D.C.) or 25 percent (New York City) or 34 percent (California) or 32 percent (Indiana) of felony arrests for rape result in convictions.

Attrition of felony arrests, as it is called, is a seemingly unchangeable characteristic of the criminal justice system, and studies of different cities in the U.S. and in Europe in the 1920s and the 1970s have consistently found that from 40 to 60 percent of all felony arrests result in dismissal and acquittal. Moreover, national statistics and statistics from some individual jurisdictions suggest that rape may be more typical than is sometimes claimed in the level of felony attrition compared to other crimes of violence. In California, between 1975 and 1981, rape ranked second (behind homicide) in the percentage of felony filings of all complaints, third (behind homicide and assault) in the average percentages of offenses cleared (solved) by arrest, and third (behind homicide and robbery) in the percentages of arrests resulting in the filing of a felony complaint, felony convictions of all felony complaints filed, and felony arrests resulting in institutional sentences.

To the extent that "rapes" are screened more strictly by their victims and unfounded more often by police than other crimes, similar conviction rates are not proof of equally vigorous prosecution. And, even if the conviction rates for rape are not atypical in some jurisdictions, the question remains whether the factors relied upon to produce them are.

Like police, prosecutors are not required to state reasons when they decide to dismiss or downgrade a case. In some district attorneys' offices, there may be internal guidelines for such decisions, but they tend to be jealously guarded so that defense attorneys cannot insist that they be applied to their clients. Still, studies have been done in a number of jurisdictions of the factors that determine which rape arrests result in felony convictions and which result in dismissal or acquittal. The findings of these studies suggest that my acquaintance's refusal to charge the "technical rape" is typical. The crime-related factors which influence the disposition of rape cases are those which distinguish the jump-from-the-bushes rape from the simple and suspect rape: a prior relationship between victim and offender; lack of force and resistance; and the absence of evidence corroborating the victim's account.

The relationship of victim and offender and the circumstances of their initial encounter appear key to determining the outcome of rape cases in virtually every study. A review of the case files in New York City's district attorney's office disclosed that one-third of the cases involving strangers, and only 7 percent of the nonstranger cases led to indictments; half the nonstranger cases were dismissed outright, compared to a third of the stranger cases. These numbers are consistent with an almost systematic downgrading or dismissing of cases involving nonstrangers, a policy confirmed and defended in newspaper accounts for all crimes in that office.

New York is not unique in this regard. A national survey of prosecutors conducted by the Battelle Memorial Institute found both the relationship of the victim to the suspect and the circumstances of their initial contact to be among the ten factors considered most important in screening rape cases and obtaining convictions. In the state of Washington a 1980 study found the social interaction of victim and defendant to be the second most important factor, behind only the amount of force used, in predicting outcome. In the District of Columbia researchers found that the relationship between victim and accused was substantially more important than the seriousness of the incident in explaining conviction rates: the closer the relationship, the lower the conviction rate. In Austin, Texas, a researcher found that 58 percent of all stranger cases resulted in indictments, compared to 29 percent of the cases among acquaintances and 47 percent among friends. Even more revealing, where the initial encounter between the victim and the defendant was voluntary, only one-third of the cases resulted in indictment; where it was involuntary, the indictment rate was 62 percent.

The second set of factors critical to conviction or dismissal relates to the amount of force used by the defendant and the level of resistance offered by the victim. In the Battelle survey use of physical force was rated by prosecutors as the single most important factor in screening and securing convictions; other key factors were injury to the victim, use of a weapon, and resistance by the victim. In Washington force was the most important factor. Similarly, in Texas both great force by the defendant and substantial resistance by the victim were among the five significant predictors of indictments. The existence of resistance was particularly critical in determining the outcome of cases where the initial encounter between the victim and her assailant was voluntary (she got into the car willingly, or invited him in). In voluntary encounter cases, the probability of indictment was only 13 percent where little victim resistance was used; it jumped to 53 percent where resistance was substantial. Where the initial encounter was involuntary, resistance was far less significant.

The final set of factors predicting outcome relates to the quality of the evidence itself: whether the prosecutor finds the victim's testimony plausible and whether her account can be corroborated. In Texas, where there was no medical corroboration (at least of penetration) only 12 percent of the arrests resulted in indictment. Proof of penetration, certainly of victim identification, and the availability of witnesses were cited as among the ten most important factors in the Battelle study. Corroborative evidence was the third most important factor in the state of Washington study. In Indiana researchers found that, despite the formal change in the law eliminating its necessity, corroboration remained an informal requirement, a conclusion reached as well by researchers who conducted interviews in Michigan.

The factors emphasized by prosecutors are also considered significant by juries in the few cases that go to trial. In their landmark study of jury trials, Kalven and Zeisel found not only that juries tend to be prejudiced against the prosecution in rape cases, but that they will go to great lengths to be lenient with defendants if there is any suggestion of "contributory behavior" on the part of the victim. "Contributory behavior" warranting leniency includes the victim's hitchhiking, dating, and talking with men at parties.

Kalven and Zeisel divided their rape cases into two categories, aggravated and simple, as I have in this book. "Aggravated" rape, according to them, includes cases with extrinsic violence, multiple assailants, or no prior relationship between victim and offender (strangers). "Simple" rape includes cases in which none of these "aggravating circumstances" is present. Jury conviction rates were nearly four times as high in the aggravated cases. Kalven and Zeisel asked judges if they agreed or disagreed with the jury's verdict in particular cases. The percentage of judges in disagreement with the jury jumped from 12 percent in the aggravated cases to 60 percent in the simple cases, with the bulk of the disagreement explained by the jury's absolute determination not to convict of rape if there was any sign of contributory fault by the woman, despite enough evidence of guilt to satisfy the judge.

The fact that juries distinguish among rape cases based on prior relationship and force and resistance provides a powerful defense for the reliance on these factors by police and prosecutors. But it is not necessarily determinative, if the factors are unjustifiable in their own right: that juries may consider race and class is no excuse for prosecutors to discriminate.

When I questioned (my word; he would doubtless describe it as a bit stronger) my acquaintance about his refusal to prosecute the "technical" rape, he barely paused in mounting his defense. He was smart enough not to mention the see-through blouse or the tight jeans. He did mention the likely response of juries. And he leaned heavily on the "neutrality" of his decision. In considering force and resistance and prior relationship and lack of corroboration, factors he termed critical, he was, he claimed, treating this case just like the assaults and robberies and drug deals that he screens and dismisses every day. Feminists might claim that rape is treated uniquely, but not by him. He, and most prosecutors, consider the same factors every day in every crime. Therefore, he concluded, he was beyond reproach. He was neutral.

Not by my standards. Because of the nature of the crime, rape is less likely to be supported by corroboration than these other crimes. Because of the sex and socialization of the victim, it may require less force and generate less resistance. To take into account prior relationship in rape in the same way as in other crimes communicates the message that women victims, particularly of simple rapes, are to blame for their victimization—precisely the sort of judgment that leads them to remain silent. Rape is different from assault or robbery or burglary. Ignoring these differences allows the exclusion of the simple "technical" rape from the working definition of the crime to appear neutral, when it is not.

Consider corroboration. Without question, rape victims, particularly in the nonstranger context, initially confront substantial skepticism from police and prosecutors. Corroboration is therefore that much more important to begin with. But corroborative evidence of rape is more difficult to secure than for many other crimes. In a street theft the requirement of corroboration may be easily met: the defendant is arrested with the stolen goods in his possession. In corruption it is routine to secure needed corroboration by sending in an informant with a tape recorder (if not the video cameras of Abscam) or by wiretapping telephone lines. In drug cases there is both physical evidence and, often, tape recordings.

These procedures cannot be applied to a rape. In most cases there are no witnesses. The event cannot be reenacted for the tape recorder, as bribes or drug sales are. There is no contraband—no drugs, no marked money, no stolen goods. Unless the victim actively resists, her clothes may be untorn and her body unmarked. Medical corroboration may establish the fact of penetration, but that proves only that the victim engaged in intercourse—not that it was nonconsensual or that this defendant was the man involved. Moreover, the availability of medical corroboration turns not only on prompt and appropriate treatment by police and medical personnel but also on the victims *not* doing what interviews have found to be the most common immediate response of the rape victim, particularly in the nonstranger context: bathing, douching, brushing her teeth, gargling, let alone taking time to decide whether to report. In short, rape is a crime in which corroboration may be uniquely absent.

The same is true of force and resistance. In most crimes of violence the demographics of victim and offender tend to be nearly identical: young, male, center-city residents. Rape is different; its victims, even in jurisdictions with gender-neutral laws, are overwhelmingly female. The reality of our existence is that it takes less force to overcome most women than most men.

Nor is it "neutral" to demand that women resist, as men might resist an assault. To expect a woman to resist an attacker who is likely to be larger and stronger than she is to expect her to do what she has probably been brought up and conditioned (and, if she has read some manuals, instructed) not to do. Women understand this. Many men do not. In one study where respondents were asked to evaluate the seriousness of a rape, the male subjects overwhelmingly concluded that the rape was less serious where there was little resistance, but the female subjects had the exact opposite reaction. Seeking to explain this "startling finding," the author concluded that most of the female subjects "identified with the victim... that the rapist in the no resistance case so terrified his victim that she dared not resist apparently aroused more sympathy for her plight among female subjects. Perhaps they could more readily imagine themselves acting in a similar fashion."

Corroboration and force and resistance are not necessarily "neutral" factors equally likely to be found in rape and assault cases and therefore entitled to equal weight in both. Professor Susan Caringella-MacDonald's study of the treatment of sexual and nonsexual assault cases (including robbery) in Kalamazoo County, Michigan, between 1981 and 1983 provides empirical evidence of the differences. Caringella-MacDonald found that the mean number of witnesses was more than twice as high in the nonsexual cases and that victim credibility problems, including implausible account, inconsistent statements, and suspected ulterior motives, were noted by prosecutors in over a third of the sexual and only 15 percent of the nonsexual assault cases. She also found that the sexual assault victims, who were overwhelmingly female, offered less resistance and sustained fewer injuries (apart from the sexual attack) than the nonsexual assault victims, who were predominantly male. The overall conviction probability as rated by prosecutors was, not surprisingly, statistically higher for the nonsexual than for the sexual assault cases.

Consideration of the prior relationship between the victim and the accused and the circumstances of their initial contact presents the greatest problem. Prior relationship cases often result in dismissal because of the withdrawal of the complaining witness. The reasons victims withdraw range from intimidation by the defendant to the private resolution of their dispute to the inadequacy of either imprisonment or probation (which is all the criminal justice system can offer) as a remedy for an individual who is dependent on her attacker (a battered wife, for example). Vulnerability and dependence are not necessarily "neutral" factors, equally applicable to all victims regardless of gender or age. Rape victims are disproportionately young women, and, though they may enjoy the support of family in stranger cases, support may be less forthcoming—and pressure from the defendant far greater—when he is someone the victim knows.

Victim withdrawal in prior relationship cases is something of a self-fulfilling prophecy; if that is so generally, it would seem particularly true in rape cases. If the prosecutor believes the victim should withdraw—or that this is not a very serious case in any event—that message is unlikely to be lost on the victim. Pursuing a rape complaint under the best of circumstances has unique costs; pursuing it where the prosecutor seems to think that the crime is not serious or will not result in serious punishment or does not deserve his attention may be more than most women can endure.

But lack of victim cooperation is not the only reason, or even the most important one, for downgrading or dismissing prior relationship cases. Apart from murder, prior relationship cases are simply viewed as less serious and less deserving of the attention of the system and of punishments. At least four reasons are generally offered to support this systemic bias. Each, when applied to rape, incorporates the very notions of male power and entitlement and female contributory fault which make the exclusion of simple rape from prosecution damning for women victims.

First, prior relationship cases are described as truly "private" disputes which are not the business of the public prosecution system. I have no particular problem with this explanation when it is applied to two friends of relatively equal size and strength fighting over a bet or a baseball game. Leaving the two to their own devices is leaving them in a situation of rough equality. But if that is the case, it is unlikely that either will be pressing charges. It is quite a different matter when—and this is when one more often hears the explanation—the two are an estranged husband and wife or ex-boyfriend and girlfriend. To treat this relationship as private is to maintain the privilege of the more powerful (man) to rape or batter the less powerful (woman). The law claims to respect the privacy of a relationship by denying the request of one of the parties (the complaining witness) that it not treat the relationship as private and that it intervene to save her. To respect privacy in this context is to respect not voluntary relationships, but the abuse of greater power.

Second, prior relationship cases are said to be less serious (and the defendants less blameworthy) because they often involve a claim of right where attacks by strangers do not. The paradigmatic nonstranger theft, for example, is a case where underlying the taking of fifty dollars is a claim of right: the defendant asserts that he was legitimately owed the money and that when the victim refused to pay, he simply took it. If prosecutors want to view this case as less serious than a stranger theft or robbery, fine. But the same reasoning applied to rape cases is wholly unacceptable. The claim of right argument in this context means that if a woman has consented to sex in the past, as the victim of the "technical" rape did, then the man has a continuing right to sexual satisfaction; that her body might be his just entitlement in the same way the fifty dollars might.

Third, prior relationship cases often involve contributory fault by the complainant, while offenses by strangers do not. The paradigmatic nonstranger assault is the barroom fight. Both parties claim the other started it; both may even file complaints; and both will be dismissed. The same inquiry in the rape context conveys a very different message. There when we ask "who started it?" we imply that if the woman agreed to give the man a ride home, or to go to his office or apartment, she is to blame for her subsequent rape and should not complain. Indeed, Menachem Amir, a sociologist who studied Philadelphia rape cases in 1958 and 1960, adapted the concept of the "victim-precipitated" rape to describe, and implicitly ascribe blame for, just such cases. Amir considered rapes to be "victim precipitated" where the victim acted in a way that "could be taken as an invitation to sexual relations"—agreed to drinks, rides, or dates or failed to react strongly enough to sexual suggestions and overtures.

Finally, it is said that an attack by a nonstranger—whether a rape or assault—is less terrifying, and therefore deserving of lesser (or no) punishment. As often as I have seen and heard this explanation, it continues to confound me. People are more afraid of stranger crime because they assume, often wrongly, that no one they know would victimize them. But once it happens, betrayal by someone you know may be every bit as terrifying, or more so, than random violence. That you know your attacker is no guarantee of better treatment: for robbery and assault (no equivalent figures are presented for rape) the most recent victimization survey finds a greater likelihood of physical injury from attacks by nonstrangers than by strangers.

I would not be surprised if, someday, some study or studies definitively prove that there are substantial differences, more subtle than the categorization of factors or review of overall statistics suggest, in the way prosecutors treat rape cases. But we need not await that day to argue for change in the system. Sometimes the failure to discriminate is discriminatory; where there are real differences, failure to recognize and take account of them is the proof of unfairness. If the defenders of the system are right in saying rape cases are treated just like assault, and just like robbery and burglary, they are surely wrong in taking this as evidence of a fair and just system. The weight given to prior relationship, force and resistance, and corroboration effectively allows prosecutors to define real rape so as to exclude the simple case, and then to justify that decision as neutral, indeed inevitable, when it is neither.

Not long ago a young woman called me on the phone for advice. She had heard that I was an "expert" on rape. She had been raped by the man she used to date. The relationship had gone sour. This did not turn her into the vengeful female whom the law has so long feared. But it did, apparently, turn him into a vengeful attacker. He followed her and raped her brutally. She felt violated and betrayed. At first she did not know what to do. She talked to friends and relatives. She decided to report it to the police. She talked to the police and the assistant district attorney. She talked to the new victim-witness advocate. No one said that she was a liar, exactly. No one laughed at her, or abused her. They just said that they would not arrest him, would not file charges. It was all explained thoroughly, the way things are done these days by good district attorneys. She had not gone immediately to the doctor. By the time she did, some of the bruises had healed and the evidence of sperm had not been preserved. She had not complained to the police right away. She knew the man. They'd had a prior relationship of intimacy. He was a respected businessman. He had no criminal record. She couldn't believe their response. She had been raped. She called to ask me what she could do to make the prosecutors do something. Nothing, said I, the supposed expert. But I didn't tell her that it was all "neutral" and therefore fair. She knew better.

Chapter 13

Physical Characteristics

"Belief in a just world" or the "just world hypothesis" is the view that people get pretty much what they deserve, that justice is "immanent" or contained within actions themselves. The Swiss psychologist, Jean Piaget, demonstrated that children hold a belief in immanent justice: that knives will cut little boys who play with them or green apples that are stolen and eaten will make them sick. The punishment is immanent or dwells within the immoral or wrong actions themselves. Piaget argued that by age 12 or so, children abandon the idea of immanent justice since they see many immoral actions go unpunished (1948). In contrast, a number of psychologists believe that many adolescents and adults retain the idea of immanent justice or belief in a just world. They present evidence that argues convincingly that many adults believe that most of us get pretty much what we deserve, that the wicked are eventually punished and the virtuous are eventually rewarded. Melvin Lerner, a psychologist, refers to this belief as "a fundamental delusion" (1980).

I suspect that this naive, commonsense—and delusional—belief is responsible for a substantial portion of negative, rejecting behavior toward the possessors of certain physical characteristics. That is, that if something bad happened to people to cause an incapacitation of an organ or limb, or they are disfigured in some way, it's possible that they did something to *deserve* it. Maybe they really do deserve the misfortune they suffer. Maybe they did something bad we don't know about. There must be a *reason* why bad things happen to certain individuals. Many of us want to be convinced that the same thing couldn't have happened to *us*. We shun the handicapped because we don't want to accept the randomness and cruelty of fate; we don't want to be reminded that the same thing could happen to us. Of course, some of us are more strongly gripped by the belief in a just world than others. And some reject the handicapped more than others do. But I would maintain that this delusional way of thinking is a major factor behind the rejection of individuals who possess undesirable physical traits.

As a general rule, certain physical characteristics are stigmatizing. They result in a "spoiled identity," to use Goffman's phrase (1963). Over the years, from time to time, when I have mentioned physical traits as a form of deviance to my students, some have objected. They question whether we can properly refer to traits that are acquired involuntarily as "deviant." Are they a form of deviance? Can we refer to them in the same breath as robbery, rape, transvestism, child molestation, and so on? Let's look at a few negatively valued, involuntarily acquired characteristics to determine whether we can, in fact, refer to them as deviance. Robert Scott argues that blindness is a form of deviance in that relations between the blind and the sighted tend to be strained, awkward, and tainted; the sighted often have a condescending attitude toward the blind and attempt to force them into a narrow, demeaning stereotype (1969). Talcott Parsons described physical illness as a form of deviance, that is, as a violation of the norm of capacity, of being well and being able to perform certain basic functions (1951, pp. 428–479). Involuntary childlessness has been mentioned as a form of deviance (Miall, 1986), a condition that brings a degree of shame and stigma to its possessors. Physical, especially facial, disfigurement, such as burns and scars, extreme ugliness, albinism, a woman with no hair, a woman with a beard, being extremely short, dwarfism, obesity—all have been described as a form of involuntarily acquired undesirable physical characteristics, traits that generate a measure of condemnation, punishment, and stigma in audiences (Jones et al., 1984; Beuf, 1990; Martel and Biller, 1987; Allon, 1982; Herman et al., 1986; Maddox et al., 1968).

Perhaps involuntarily acquired undesirable physical characteristics could be divided into two main categories: First, *aesthetic violations,* traits that violate certain audiences' sense of how people ought to look; and second, *physical incapacity,* the inability to perform certain crucial activities or functions (Goffman, 1963, p. 4). Goffman mentions a third form that is, for some who are subject to it, voluntary and for others, involuntary; this is *associating* with involuntary deviants. That is, there are those who have either chosen to associate with them or who, by the hand of fate, end up with them in one way or another. This category entails what Goffman (1963, pp. 28, 30, 31) refers to as a "courtesy stigma," the stigma that is attracted to the person who associates with the disabled or in some other way physically deviant. For instance: The parents of physically disabled children; men or women who date or who are married to the obese; friends, relatives, or neighbors of those who are disabled.

Is the possession of undesirable physical characteristics a form of deviance? Should it be regarded as deviant in the same basic sense that actions that, one assumes, are chosen are? Or ideology, beliefs, political or religious views that might be seen as bizarre or that are widely condemned? After all, we do not *choose* to be short or blind or ugly or an albino. Nonetheless, people are *punished* for possessing certain physical characteristics. One might say, that isn't fair! Well, of course it isn't fair, but much of life isn't fair. It is the sociologist's job to find out what's going on in social life, whether it is fair or unfair. Possessors of undesirable traits are often made fun of; they are excluded, labeled, stigmatized, condemned, humiliated, reviled, gossiped about. Many so-called normals (as Goffman refers to those who do not possess such characteristics) find it difficult to interact with them. Clearly, in terms of motivation, these are not forms of deviance. We do not regard them, in the ordinary sense, freely chosen. But in terms of social reactions, they *are* a form of deviance. In the sense that they attract negative reactions for their possessors, clearly, they *do* represent a form of deviance.

As Sagarin says in the selection that follows, none of the positivistic causal theories—anomie, learning theory, control theory, and so on—apply to physical traits. (One causal theory does apply, however: demonology, or retaliation by spiritual forces for a past transgression. In the Middle Ages—and in some social circles, even today—individuals regarded physical disability as a punishment from God. And, of course, the "just world" hypothesis would argue that, yes, a lot of people do suspect that such traits are a sign or indication that they have not been very virtuous.) But for the most part, all etiological or causal theories are either inadequate or irrelevant. We clearly cannot explain involuntary deviance with the aid of any theory that assumes some measure of motivation. But all the theories of social control, in varying degrees, *do* apply—the theories that attempt to understand the dynamics of punishment, condemnation, social reactions, stigma, and so on. As Sagarin says, labeling theory is *centrally* relevant here. I would add, probably functionalism, probably the new sociology of social control, probably conflict theory, probably feminism, possibly, to some extent, Marxism. Consequently, the remarks that follow look at physical characteristics from the perspective of discourse rather than etiology or causality. As we've seen, constructionism focuses on how deviants are conceptualized, talked about, written about, reacted to, judged, dealt with, and treated.

However, one qualification at this point is in order: The issue of how voluntarily or involuntarily a given trait was acquired is in part a cultural concept; the notion of *agency* and *responsibility* vary from one society to another. In Western society, compared with other societies of the world, we have a fairly strict notion of who did what, responsibility for one's actions, and so on. (I have to add, of course, that the belief in a just world is always dancing around in the background somewhere, complicating the picture.) We normally do not assume that a person has *chosen* to be blind, that we are *responsible* for our blindness. In some cultures, however, there is a very different notion of responsibility. As we just saw, in some societies or even in some segments of Western society, certain physical traits are seen as a retribution from God, punishment for what one did in a former life, perhaps punishment for what one's parents did, a consequence of a moral failing in some way. For instance, many ultra-Orthodox, or haredim, believe that if a woman doesn't perform her Mikveh or ritual bath regularly, she may bear children with birth defects.

It is necessary to register a second qualification: Voluntariness and involuntariness are matters of degree. Some traits or characteristics are not entirely involuntarily acquired. Certain audiences may see physical traits in a certain light, depending on exactly *how* they were acquired. *Some* physical characteristics may in fact be a consequence of what one actually did. An example: Venereal diseases, such as AIDS, may have been acquired as a consequence of the intravenous injection of a drug or having engaged in unprotected intercourse. Those who see things this way will deny that they are "blaming the victim" in ascribing agency to the AIDS sufferer. They will argue that there *is* some causal relationship between what the victim did—and chose to do—and acquiring the disease. And for that, these observers will say, AIDS sufferers are not entirely blameless. (But notice: The idea of *cause* and the idea of *blame* are distinct and separate notions; see Felson, 1991.) Someone may have broken his or her leg as a result of a skiing or a motorcycle accident, that is, because of engaging in certain actions that bring a measure of risk; in such cases, breaking a leg should not have been altogether unexpected. Richard Pryor, a comedian, burned himself as a result of smoking freebase cocaine; his injury was related in some way to his freely chosen behavior.

In sum, then, four points must be stressed: First, voluntariness versus involuntariness is a cultural construct, not a simple matter of fact. And second, the involuntariness of physical characteristics is also a matter of degree, a continuum, not an either-or proposition.

A third point: At least one physical trait—obesity—is seen in our culture both as a physical trait and as chosen or voluntary. To audiences who condemn the obese, what are the voluntary features of obesity? What did the obese *do* to get fat? The presumption is that they were gluttonous and ate too much, and they were lazy and self-indulgent. They lacked the virtues of moderation that the rest of us possess. The obese in our society are judged to be largely, perhaps completely, responsible for their fate—being overweight. Hence, little sympathy is given to them. Instead, they are greeted with scorn and condemnation. In fact, scorn and condemnation, in the words of comedian, Joan Rivers, who at one time told antifat jokes, should be regarded by the fat as a favor to them because it reminds them that they can do something to become thin again. The obese can be openly and publicly insulted. Consequently, many obese people will internalize society's negative attitudes toward them. Many will come to see themselves as *worthy* of being reviled and humiliated. The vast majority of them will say that, if they could be of average weight, they would do so. (As opposed to homosexuals, who almost always will say, no, I *prefer* to be homosexual, thank you.) In a very puritanical society, one that distrusts sensuality and self-indulgence, fat people will be seriously looked down upon. There is something of a mania in some quarters in this society (though it has certainly abated in the past decade or so) for working out, exercising, jogging, eating and drinking moderately, avoiding fatty foods, sugar, salt, and developing a lean, hard body, curbing one's physical pleasures, playing hard, and working hard. In such a culture, it is inevitable that the fat will be despised. There is the unalterable belief that the obese could *do* something to make themselves thin. Hence, they are responsible for and *deserve* their own condemnation. Hence, it's acceptable to condemn and humiliate the obese; it's all for their own good.

A fourth point: There is a *degree of disablement* among physical conditions. As Robert Scott (1969) says, being visually impaired is a matter of degree, not an either-or proposition. Legal blindness does not necessarily entail total blindness. Most legally blind people can actually see, although extremely poorly. Obesity, too, is a matter of degree. Some people are merely twenty or thirty pounds over some ideal weight, or over the average for their height and age. Others are two or three times as heavy as most people their height. And of course there's everything in between. And just as the degree of a given condition is a matter of degree, likewise degree of rejection is a matter of degree. The possession of some traits is savagely condemned, and possessors are extremely humiliated, rejected totally and utterly. Others are only mildly rejected or shunned. As with most things in life, the deviant quality attendant upon certain physical characteristics is a matter of degree.

What the sociologist of deviance is interested in is how the disabled and unesthetic are treated by the so-called normal (again, Goffman's term) members of the society—and mistreated. Possessing certain undesirable physical characteristics (as with other forms of deviance) can be looked upon as a *master status* (Becker, 1963, pp. 33–34). It overwhelms or dominates other statuses, traits, or characteristics. It is extremely difficult for many so-called normals to overlook the fact that someone one is interacting with is a dwarf, or extremely ugly, blind, or is in a wheelchair. To many normals, the fact that someone is disabled or looks different is the only really important aspect or feature about that person. Nothing else matters. It doesn't matter if he or she is brilliant or has a Ph.D. in nuclear physics or is a brain surgeon or a gifted artist—what counts is the disability. In interaction after interaction, normals treat the disabled person *as* a disabled person, first and foremost, primarily and above all. All other things about that person fade into the background.

In short, involuntarily acquired physical characteristics qualify as a form of deviance. Though not motivated behavior as we generally understand the concept, and therefore not caused by the etiological forces that were discussed in Part II, they are subject to the processes of stigma, labeling, negative judgments, social control—in short, all the talk, thinking, and action Foucault refers to as *discourse,* or "discursive formations" (1972). Involuntarily acquired negatively viewed physical characteristics cannot be ignored as a form of deviance.

References

Allon, Natalie. 1982. The stigma of overweight in everyday life. In Benjamin B. Wolman (ed.), *Psychological Aspects of Obesity: A Handbook.* New York: Van Nostrand & Reinhold, pp. 130–174.

Becker, Howard S. 1963. *Outsiders: Studies in the Sociology of Deviance.* New York: Free Press.

Beuf, Ann Hill. 1990. *Beauty Is the Beast: Appearance-Impaired Children in America.* Philadelphia: University of Pennsylvania Press.

Cahnman, Werner J. 1968. The stigma of obesity. *The Sociological Quarterly,* 9 (Summer): 283–299.

Felson, Richard B. 1991. Blame analysis: Accounting for the behavior of protected groups. *The American Sociologist,* 22 (Spring): 5–23.

Foucault, Michel. 1972. *The Archaeology of Knowledge and the Discourse on Language* (trans. A. M. Sheridan Smith). New York: Pantheon.

Goffman, Erving. 1963. *Stigma.* Englewood Cliffs, N.J.: Prentice-Hall/Spectrum.

Herman, C. Peter, Mark P. Zanna, and E. Tory Higgins (eds.). 1986. *Physical Appearance, Stigma and Social Behavior.* Hillsdale, N.J.: Lawrence Erlbaum.

Jones, Edward E., et al. 1984. *Social Stigma: The Psychology of Marked Relationships.* New York: W. H. Freeman.

Lerner, Melvin J. 1980. *The Belief in a Just World: A Fundamental Delusion.* New York: Plenum Press.

Maddox, George L., Kurt W. Back, and Veronica Liederman. 1968. Overweight as social deviance and disability. *Journal of Health and Social Behavior,* 9 (December): 287–298.

Martel, Leslie, and Henry B. Biller. 1987. *Stature and Stigma: The Biopsychosocial Development of Short Males.* Lexington, Mass.: Lexington Books.

Miall, Charlene E. 1986. The stigma of involuntary childlessness. *Social Problems,* 33 (April): 268–282.

Parsons, Talcott. 1951. *The Social System.* New York: Free Press.

Piaget, Jean. 1948. *The Moral Judgment of the Child.* New York: Free Press.

Scott, Robert A. 1969. *The Making of Blind Men: A Study of Adult Socialization.* New York: Russell Sage Foundation.

The Disabled as Involuntary Deviants [1]

EDWARD SAGARIN

Deviance runs the gamut from voluntarism to involuntarism, from responsibility to its total absence ("nonresponsibility"). At the former extreme one might place the political deviant, at the latter the disabled, and somewhere in between people who have any number of obsessions and compulsions that they find difficult to control and that bring them into sharp conflict with society.

Merely to group the involuntary deviant with others raises conceptual and normative problems. The moment the crippled and other physically disabled are categorized in this manner, all etiological theories appear inadequate. Inasmuch as these people did not "decide" to take on the deviant status, the personal and social conditions conducive to becoming deviant are irrelevant. In the capacity of sociologist, therefore, one is no longer concerned with how people got that way, but with how and why they are defined in a disvalued manner and with what consequences for all parties. In that sense, only labeling theory is able to encompass this area of deviance, for it focuses on societal reaction as crucial and notes the similarity of treatment accorded to the actor, and of defenses created by him, whether the person labeled deviant is defined in that manner on the basis of behavior or of being.

The study of disability in relation to deviant behavior is of intrinsic interest to sociologists because it reveals much about the importance of the unspoken rules that govern our everyday behavior and their use by competent members of society. Moreover, the complex process of developing deviant roles, engaged in by the people who either desire or are condemned to play them as well as by others (the normative or the "normals"), can be examined in the area of disability and in the study of those who seek to provide rehabilitation facilities and programs for people who become handicapped. Anyone who acquires a disability, or is born with one, finds himself facing more than just adjustment to a physical impairment or long-term illness that prevents him from walking as fast as other people, riding horses, or holding a job in competitive employment. He is regarded by others and even by himself as "different," and this difference is considered an undesirable one, creating a sense of awkwardness, embarrassment, and confusion in one's social interaction with others.

The difficulty of maintaining comfortable face-to-face interaction between disabled and conventional members of society results first of all from uncertainty about the kinds of claims the disabled and the conventional person will make upon each other in social situations. If, for example, there is a crippled young man at a party, will he ask one of the young ladies present to dance? In turn, will one of the young ladies present ask that crippled young man to dance, hoping to compensate for his "natural" shyness? This type of encounter has almost no analogue in the world of

From Edward Sagarin, "The Disabled as Involuntary Deviants." In *Deviants and Deviance: An Introduction to Disvalued People and Behavior* (New York: Praeger, 1975), pp. 201–213 (references deleted).

"ordinary deviants"—ex-convicts, alcoholics, prostitutes, and so on. Secrecy is more easily maintained in "ordinary deviance," only to be dropped when it is unnecessary. The undesirable or "disabling" traits of voluntary deviants are more easily ignored if they are not openly avowed; and the conflict between the deviant and the world around him is not a collision in which there is inability to work through a given scene or a given setting.

A second source of confusion and uncertainty on the part of the disabled, and even more those who must interact with them, stems from the fact that disability is rarely acquired in a conscious way, from intentional misapplication of the designs for living that constitute the culture of the society. Rather, disability is acquired because the culture could not predict a fortuitous or accidental event or the onset of an illness so that it could be avoided; or it came at birth, an unfortunate disaster. Thus, those who are or become disabled cannot be said to have violated the rules deliberately; in fact, in many cases they were let down by those very rules. Acquiring a handicapping condition rarely involves intentional choice. Except for the born handicapped, it can be thought of as the crystallization of involuntary deviance into roles performed by previously voluntary conformists. When a once-competent person becomes disabled, the very rules that define competency are called into question. Moreover, inasmuch as this disabled person is still psychologically competent, he may start to question these rules because they proved to be unreliable.

Physically handicapped people illustrate how rules operate in a self-correcting and self-fulfilling way. Being a fully competent member of society includes recognition of the meaning of membership and competency. This reflexiveness takes the form of knowing what characteristics a member must possess and who is to be allowed to participate in particular situations. Alternatively, knowledge of what it means to be a nonmember is part of the general role of a member. These rules of identity, or constitutive norms of social life, are acquired relatively early in life. Children will observe out loud that "the man sitting in the next seat has no arm in his sleeve" and their parents will reward them for being so observant, even while admonishing them for being overly vocal in public.

Yet, what makes the entire matter of rules, behavior, presence, and identity as moral beings questionable is the fact that the physically handicapped are the purest of victims. They have committed no "immoral" act in being the way they are. Save for instances in which a disability is relevant to a particular task (for example, a person with impaired sight seeking a license to drive a car), there is no inherent logic in excluding the involuntary deviant from the world of normals, or even in categorizing him as a deviant. That this is the case seems indisputable.

Although at one time simply denounced and reviled, the physically disabled came later to be pitied. Only in the twentieth century has there been a considerable diminution in the contumely heaped upon epileptics, dwarfs, and mental retardates. Even as they ceased to be reviled, however, they continued to be avoided.

Violations of the norms of social identity are events that those who are disabled have to deal with, particularly in the company of conventional people who are strangers to the handicapped person. Every transgression of these norms in the form of a discrediting discrepancy between an actor's virtual (or expected) and actual identity calls into question the validity of these rules, since those who cannot sustain competency may still seek to do so. Then, the everyday grounds for judging others and oneself are made problematic, since actors are uncertain about the kinds of claims that might be made by either the discrepant or the conventional individuals. Thus, such encounters threaten the beliefs of all present in the culture in two ways: (1) The one-to-one correspondence of the social and the natural order—that is, the correspondence between the way things are anticipated and the way they actually turn out—is called into question. (2) Then, if either or both fail to take the discrepancy from cultural expectations into account in their relationship, they call into question the conventional character of that person or their relationship, suggesting to others a kind of joint or dual madness.

While disability may be unpredictable according to the formulas used in everyday life, every culture provides the members of society with a general idea of what it must be like to possess a handicap and even provides a rank-ordering of various impairments. This uniformity in response to disability provides a third source of uncertainty in relations between those with handicaps and others, since the latter do not want to reveal the negative attitudes they hold toward the disability. Unlike situations involving attitudes toward voluntary deviants, those who share the negativism that identifies a societal reaction feel considerable ambivalence. By condemning a victim, they condemn themselves and often feel guilty about this, if they give it any thought at all. But rather than be forced to face the inner difficulties of their own moral dilemmas, they prefer to avoid the situation altogether, but something not always possible to do.

The pervasiveness of the cultural conceptions of disability is so great that even people who were born with physical disabilities share these negative values. The amount of self-deprecation and self-hatred experienced by such people should not be underestimated as an important source of keeping them in line, particularly when the same people in many respects are voluntary conformists in society. The disabled adapt to the stigma of physical disability in several ways: Some people make a definition of self and seek to work within the framework of that definition; they project themselves as physically different but not socially deviant. This is what Fred Davis (1961) described under the heading of "deviance disavowal," in which the persons did not deny or try to conceal the handicap but sought to normalize relationships and to deny the awkward, embarrassing, or negative aspects of social interaction. Others who bear a stigma do not attempt to convey an image of normality but embrace their role, seeking to make the impairment the central focus of their lives. Ralph Turner (1972) sees this as the reverse of disavowal and has termed it "deviance avowal." Others try to conceal all information about their stigma and seek to convey the impression of being physically normal, a strategy that is available only for certain types of impairment.

There are handicapped persons who utilize combinations or modifications of these strategies. Some seek to perform conventional social roles, occasionally manifesting their differentness by their association with others like themselves. They make an effort, one might say, to "normalize" their deviance so that it does not become obtrusive in all social situations but is taken into account in all ongoing social relations. The handicapped may use one mechanism for handling the social strains with some people and quite easily switch to a different method with others. The same person can be at times secretive and blatant, self-effacing and exploitative.

"Deviance avowal" is less likely to occur in the case of physical disability than in the case of other deviant minorities, because rarely does a counterculture exist that insists that a stigma is a badge of honor rather than a discrediting discrepancy. While many homosexuals claim that "gay is good" and that one ought to be proud of one's sexual tastes, those with physical handicaps do not make similar assertions about themselves or their handicaps. They may seek to get normals to regard them in a more accepting way by insisting on the use of certain labels for their condition, but the basis of their problem and of their plea for acceptance is still the unintentionally acquired character of the impairment. Thus, there is a strain toward "normalization" among the disabled, since this is one way of diminishing the magnitude, obviousness, and obtrusiveness of their deviance.

Yet, both denial and avowal may be regarded by others as signs of severe psychological disturbance, perhaps brought on or precipitated by the acquisition of physical disability, but something that prevents the person from recognizing either his physical limitations or his other capacities; from becoming aware of the obtrusiveness or lack of it produced by the disability in the course of social interaction; from neglecting or paying an inordinate amount of attention to his other responsibilities. Conventional members of society question the competence of a person who fails to deal with "reality" or who denies what everyone else "knows" are the disadvantages of being disabled. The middle road is regarded as the wisest course because it confirms conventional ideas about disability widely accepted in the culture. As stated by Goffman (1963:122):

> The general formula is apparent. The stigmatized individual is asked to act so as to imply neither that his burden is heavy nor that bearing it has made him different from us; at the same time he must keep himself at that remove from us which ensures our painlessly being able to confirm this belief about him. Put differently, he is advised to reciprocate naturally with an acceptance of himself and us, an acceptance of him that we have not quite extended him in the first place.

In following this formula, the disabled person, either consciously or unwittingly, takes part in a process of restoration of belief in those cultural formulas that he followed and that failed him. This process begins with recognition and acceptance of the stigma by the disabled person, promoting the routinization of deviance into what has been identified as a normal-appearing round of life. In so doing, the disabled person not only removes uncertainty and strain from his life but restores his own and others' belief in the cultural formulas.

There may be less of a difference between the disabled and the nonhandicapped person than we imagine, for the self that can perform as a conventional person can often perform when afflicted by some long-term illness or impairment to physical functioning. Nevertheless, this is not always the case, and realization of one's inability to perform, the loss of hope that the performing ability will return, and the resignation to a state of permanence of the impaired self may constitute a severe shock. The bulk of findings would indicate that the objective criteria for performance of most roles in a competent manner are present, but that they are frequently misunderstood by the afflicted (who is demoralized and discouraged), by his family (overanxious yet impatient, and sometimes overindulgent), and by social agencies (especially when they fit the handicapped into preconceived stereotypes of deviance).

This is not to advocate the view that differences in personality and role performance do not arise as a result of possessing a disability. They do, but they are not inevitable, and they arise out of the social interaction more than out of the disabling characteristics. Furthermore, certain kinds of affiliations and agencies devoted to helping persons have great impact on the lives of the handicapped. Just as there is some institutional support for voluntary deviance, as in the case of professionals whose task is to prevent, study, pursue, contain, and rehabilitate in the area of crime, so there are professionals who "need" the disabled. Similarly, courts and prisons have considerable influence over the life chances of the criminal, while hospitals and rehabilitation programs have a similar effect on many of the important career choices made by their clients.

Life-Styles and Life Chances

Disability may be acquired in early childhood, even at birth, and the parents' response to a disabled child may be quite different from their response to a normal child. Moreover, it is very rare that a parent will have had any experience at all with disability when the child is born (except in the case of hereditary defects, as, for example, dwarfs), and hence he cannot be a very good model of how to adapt to it for the child. Often the parents feel very guilty, at least during the first few months after becoming aware of the child's condition. The presence of a handicapped child in the family may lead to a redefinition of the child as one who is constantly "sick," requiring a certain kind of care and attention. This perspective often has a correlate to it: that the child does not require other kinds of social and intellectual stimulation that one would give to a nonhandicapped child. In such cases, fewer demands are placed on children with disabilities, while other children in the family are expected to perform at a very unrealistic level of competency. Frequently, the unaffected developmental capacities of the handicapped child remain overlooked in order that he may be treated as a sick child. Such overcompensating efforts may also involve endless searches for cures or at least a more favorable diagnosis. As a result, the child develops a sense of self that may indeed be based on an appropriate response, but to a set of unusual expectations.

Except perhaps for the severely retarded, children with physical disabilities inevitably learn how the culture evaluates the handicap, no matter how protective parents might be. Self-deprecation or low self-esteem seems to be common in these cases, exacerbated when there are no alternative sources of support or claims of competency that can be made by the child. A child who is treated as sick may never be given the opportunity to prove himself, and his impairment may become the central focus in his life, resulting in an avowal of the role rather than a normalization.

The manner in which one learns that he is seen, not as a whole person, but in terms of the handicap, is illustrated in an autobiographical account by Leonard Kriegel (1969):

> What the cripple must face is being pigeonholed by the smug. Once his behavior is assumed from the fact that he is a cripple, it doesn't matter whether he is viewed as holy or damned. Either assumption is made at the expense of his individuality, his ability to say "I." He is expected to behave in such-and-such a way; he is expected to react in the following manner to the following stimulus. And since that which expects such behavior is that which provides the stimulus, his behavior is all too often Pavlovian. He reacts as he is expected to react because he does not really accept the idea that he can react in any other way. Once he accepts, however unconsciously, the images of self that his society presents him, then the guidelines for his behavior are clear-cut and consistent.

While most physical disability does not involve actual disfigurement, it alters the person's body sufficiently to present a discrepancy between what is expected and the image the person presents. Physical appearance seems to be a very important aspect of face-to-face interaction at all times in the life cycle. It is particularly important during adolescence as a way of classifying and rating others and oneself. It is likely, therefore, that toleration of such differences would be lowest among this age group and that consequently the physically disabled teenager would suffer a substantial reduction in self-esteem.

Physical appearance is a basic source of information about others, especially during first encounters between people. A person with a disability would need to have a wide array of social skills available in order to offset the uncertainty and potential derogation during such an encounter. Even when such a repertoire of social skills exists, the tendency among the nonhandicapped to avoid interaction with the handicapped is very great. Thus, the lack of social skills possessed by a disabled person may result from a lack of opportunity to develop them, rather than an unwillingness or an incapacity to do so. Often, those who seek out contact with the handicapped are social isolates themselves and hardly make good models for disabled children or adolescents.

One of the factors that sets the involuntary deviant apart from all others is the disvaluation that he himself places upon his condition and, frequently though not necessarily, upon himself. This protects the society from people who would "recruit" and "proselytize" others into socially undesired roles. The suggestion is not being made that a disabled or handicapped person could engage in spreading his disability but rather that, if not for his self-denigration, the diminished ability for normal interaction could well be put forth as an equally good or even preferable way of life. The loss of self-esteem, psychologically damaging as it probably is, may well serve society as a protection against cultural transmission, which some people have postulated as a major cause of the perpetuation of delinquency, or of learning to become a certain kind of disvalued individual, as has been described for marijuana users, or "bringing out," a term that apparently has its origins in the subculture of homosexuality. But all of this means, in addition, that for the "hopelessly afflicted," whose injury or condition is such that there are limits to goals of recovery and rehabilitation beyond which one should not fantasize, the development of an ideology that the condition is just as good as that of normals, or even better, is excluded as one of the forms of adaptation.

One adjustment to the presence of disability may be a kind of overconformity to other rules concerning identity, as a way of giving the impression to others that one's handicap has not led to a general neglect of personal appearance. The disabled person may appear less "interesting" to others, dress in less flamboyant colors, avoid long hair, beads, beards, and such accoutrements, as a way of saying that he can uphold some rules if not all rules of conventional identity. Accordingly, less visible aspects of identity may also take on a conforming quality. Political and religious attitudes may be very orthodox, lest they frighten away a potential friend. Overconformity is a frequent though by no means an inevitable response of those who must work hard to be regarded as acceptable in various social situations. Like the immigrant who becomes a superpatriot, the disabled may become supercritical of individual differences and, in so doing, demonstrate loyalty to a code of demeanor that few pay such strict attention to and hardly any live and die by any more. Formalization of relationships on the part of the physically disabled may be a way not only of dealing with uncertainty but also of receiving support for claims to be treated with respect.

A person with a physical disability lives a life as a deviant to the extent that he belongs both to collectivities made up exclusively of those who are similarly situated and also to others made up predominantly of nonhandicapped persons. This dual membership among one's own kind and among the others enables him to lead a "normal-appearing round of life," receiving support from each collectivity for the particular kinds of claims that he seeks to make in each world. The person who is successful in this adaptation seeks a careful balance between the world of the stigmatized and the world of the normal. Partially, at least, this balance is predicated on the person's participation in the social organizations and culture of the world of disability. The orderliness found in this culture creates a useful parallel of conventionality from which one can convey impressions of managing an intolerable situation, thereby helping to reduce the now often unpredictable nature of the conventional social order. Moreover, when accepting the primacy of socially expected roles, those with stigmas assiduously avoid over-involvement in the world of the stigmatized, thereby minimizing the extent to which normals will regard them as deviant, even in the presence of other disabled individuals.

Involvement with others in social groups of people like themselves and in organizations devoted to helping the disabled is usually greater when the disability is first acquired than later on. This is due not only to the newness of the deviant role being performed but also to the relief from uncertainty provided by organizations of others who have gone through the same social transformation. Indeed, it is at this point that one is likely to encounter "deviance avowal" as a way of dealing with the problem of uncertainty and also as a way of explaining what has happened to produce an unexpected and undesired condition. New explanations help to reduce the sense of self-blame when the newly disabled recognizes the discrepancy of his condition from that of conventional persons; and social mingling with similarly situated others reduces the despair. Some disabled persons who continue to embrace the deviant role will become formal leaders of these organizations, leading a life devoted to influencing nonhandicapped persons to be more sympathetic to the handicapped, getting greater subsidization from the government for retraining and rehabilitation, and improving their situations in numerous other ways. By performing conventional lobbying activities for unusual organizations, they demonstrate a "normal-appearing round of life," not in spite of their handicap, but rather because of it. In a personal sense, those who perform these leadership roles represent a continuous round of impression management, as they move from "deviance avowal" to normalization to denial of the impact of the disability on their competency, all in a single day, all in a single effort to increase the effectiveness of their organizations.

Not all the people who man the major posts of these organizations are themselves handicapped. From about 1960 on, mainly through the innovative programs of the various branches of the Department of Health, Education and Welfare, there was a vast expansion of rehabilitation and physical medicine services in the United States. Amid the branches and institutes of this federal agency, and with the advent of the antipoverty program and its incorporation under the Office of Economic Opportunity, there came into being a vast organizational network of "caretaker" agencies to perform the social-control functions associated with disabilities. Voluntary conformists who followed all the conventional social formulas of the culture and were rewarded with suffering, disappointment, and derogation remain a potential threat to that culture and a source of discontent in the society. This has been offset by creating a new set of careers for those in the areas of psychology, social work, prosthetics, and physical medicine, among others, based upon the belief that they can help the adjustment and rehabilitation of those Americans who fall into the general category of involuntary deviants.

The early 1960s saw a rapid increase in funds available for research and for the development of "pilot" programs in many areas of disability, including mental illness and mental retardation. These agencies both supported innovative programs and provided capital grants to establish new diagnostic clinics, rehabilitation centers, sheltered workshops for vocational rehabilitation, and the creation of permanent opportunities for noncompetitive employment in voluntary organizations. Many of these programs were modeled after efforts for the blind, particularly in the area of vocational rehabilitation and workshops, which had been established in the 1930s, with federal subsidization in the form of exclusive contracts with these facilities to supply mops and brooms assembled by the blind. Similar efforts gained acceptance after World War II as a way of aiding returning disabled veterans.

To a large extent, the proliferation of these programs and facilities was significantly retarded, after an enormous growth, by the diversion of funds to the war in Southeast Asia. At the same time, that war likewise provided a justification for increased support for programs to aid returning disabled and disfigured veterans.

Rehabilitation is a process that does not begin and end when the disabled person has developed some way of managing the problems associated with functioning with a physical handicap or even with its stigma. Organizations and their agents seek to impose their view of the particular handicap upon the person who possesses it, so that, in the words of Robert Scott (1966:138) the person "is socialized to play the kind of deviant role traditionally reserved" for those similarly handicapped. Organizations and agencies possess a perspective on disability that in no small way affects the possible adaptations available to the handicapped and the extent to which they can lead independent lives. These agencies carry on the following activities, as enumerated by Eliot Freidson (1966:71):

> First, they specify what personal attributes shall be called handicaps. Second, they seek to identify who conforms to their gratifications. Third, they attempt to gain access to those whom they call handicapped. And fourth, they try to get those to whom they gain access to change their behavior so as to conform more closely to what the institutions believe are their potentialities.

Since many of these agencies provide important services to their clients and thus make available a great deal in the way of resources, they are able to get the disabled person to accept a certain definition of himself (or at least to say so in the presence of rehabilitation workers). Attitudes of the disabled are of central importance to such workers, for continued use of the agency for services by the disabled person requires that he will not question his fate or be socially disruptive. The segregated character of these agencies—the fact that they are specialized by disability even when the help that is sought may have little to do directly with the nature of the physical impairment—promotes the development of a sense of performing a deviant role. In turn, lack of contact with those who are not handicapped, or who have nothing to do with the organized world of rehabilitation, reinforces this sense of differentness since one is judged and judges oneself by the company one keeps.

The handicapped may, as Fred Davis (1961) points out, reject the concept that he is deviant (but he is placing a different meaning on the term than do sociologists) and yet find it difficult to say that he is normal like everyone else. Davis shows how he must constantly cope with difficulties of social interaction. (This of course depends on the nature of the disability.) He was dealing with crippled persons, victims of polio, whose walking and seeing handicaps made interaction with others difficult. But the stickiness comes from two directions: that normals will aggravate the difficulties, treating the handicapped as if the situation were even worse than it is; or that normals will seek to avoid embarrassment by ignoring the difficulties, creating problems that would otherwise be more easily handled. In the words of Davis:

> Achieving ease and naturalness of interaction with normals serves naturally as an important index to the handicapped person of the extent to which the preferred definition of self—i.e., that of someone who is merely different physically but not socially deviant—has been accepted. Symbolically, as long as the interaction remains stiff, strained, or otherwise mired in inhibition, he has good rea-

son to believe that he is in effect being denied the status of social normalcy he aspires to or regards as his due.

The process of transformation from a voluntary conformist to an involuntary deviant reveals a profound underlying concern: the need for continuous restoration of the cultural and social order when threatened by anomalous situations, when things do not go according to the way they are supposed to go. Conventional actors reaffirm their belief in the conventional cultural formulas by preferring a stigma that redefines those discrepant individuals' past and future performances as no longer accountable to that set of rules. The stigmatized are "removed" from the conventional social order; in so doing, the conventional members re-establish the primacy of such cultural directives as "competent people avoid accidents."

Disability in itself, so long as it is recognized as being outside the conventional social order, does not threaten the belief systems of normal members of society. In fact, it confirms those systems as valid criteria for judging normality; failure to do so would call into question their own normality. Conventional members of society are not the only ones interested in reaffirming the validity of the cultural order. A stigma not only offers the handicapped a new identification, albeit a deviant one; he accepts it because *his* belief in the cultural formulas has been threatened, too. Thus, both the social and the cultural orders are maintained in spite of unanticipated events. Better as it undoubtedly would be if one were not handicapped, for some people the handicap offers a new label by which they can identify themselves.

Note

1. This section is based on a study conducted by Arnold Birenbaum.

The Stigma of Obesity

ERICH GOODE

Bertha was a massive woman. She weighed well over 400 pounds. Still, people enjoyed her company, and she had an active social life. One Friday night, Bertha and several of her friends stopped in a local Burger and Shake for a quick snack. Bertha disliked fast-food restaurants with good reason: Their seats were inadequate for her size. But, she was a good sport and wanted to be agreeable, so she raised no objection to the choice of an eating establishment. Bertha squeezed her huge body into the booth and enjoyed a shake and burger. A typical Friday night crowd stood waiting for tables, so Bertha and her companions finished their snack and began to vacate the booth so that others could dine. But Bertha's worst fears were realized: She was so tightly jammed in between the table and the chair that she was stuck.

Bertha began struggling to get out of the booth, without success. Her friends pulled her, pushed her, and twisted her—all to no avail. She was trapped. Soon, all eyes in the Burger and Shake were focused on the hapless Bertha and her plight. Onlookers began laughing at her. Snickers escalated to belly laughs, and the restaurant fairly rocked with raucous laughter and cruel, taunting remarks. "Christ, is she fat!" "What's the matter, honey—one burger too many?" "Look at the trapped whale!" "How could anyone get that fat!" Bertha's struggles became frenzied; she began sweating profusely. Every movement became an act of desperation to free herself from her deeply humiliating situation. Finally, in a mighty heave, Bertha tore the entire booth from its bolts and she stood in the middle of the floor of the Burger and Shake, locked into the booth as if it had been a barrel. The crowd loved it, and shrieked with laughter that intensified in volume and stridency, as Bertha staggered helplessly, squatting in the center of the room.

One of Bertha's friends ran to his car, grabbed a hammer and a wrench, came back in, and began smashing at the booth. He broke it into pieces that fell to the floor, freeing the woman from her torture chamber. Bertha lumbered and pushed her way through the laughing, leering crowd, and ran to her car, hot tears in her eyes and burning shame in her throat. The friend who freed her limply placed the pieces of the chair and table onto the counter. The employees, now irritated, demanded that he pay for the damaged booth, but he and Bertha's other companions simply left the restaurant.

After that incident, Bertha rarely left her house. Two months later, she died of heart failure. She was 31 years old.

In contemporary America, obesity is stigmatized. Fat people are considered less worthy human beings than thin people are. They receive less of the good things that life has to offer, and more of the bad. Men and women of average weight tend to look down on the obese, feel superior to them, reward them less, punish them, make

Previously unpublished.

fun of them. The obese are often an object of derision and harassment for their weight. What is more, thin people will feel that this treatment is just, that the obese deserve it, indeed, that it is even something of a humanitarian gesture, since such humiliation will supposedly inspire them to lose weight. The stigma of obesity is so intense and so pervasive that eventually the obese will come to see themselves as deserving of it, too.

The obese, in the words of one observer, "are a genuine minority, with all the attributes that a corrosive social atmosphere lends to such groups: poor self-image, heightened sensitivity, passivity, and withdrawal, a sense of isolation and rejection." They are subject to relentless discrimination, they are the butt of denigrating jokes, they suffer from persecution; it would not be an exaggeration to say that they attract cruelty from the thin majority. Moreover, their friends and family rarely give the kind of support and understanding they need to deal with this cruelty; in fact, it is often friends and family who are themselves meting out the cruel treatment. The social climate has become "so completely permeated with anti-fat prejudice that the fat themselves have been infected by it. They hate other fat people, hate themselves when they are fat, and will risk anything—even their lives—in an attempt to get thin.... Anti-fat bigotry... is a psychic net in which the overweight are entangled every moment of their lives" (Louderback, 1970, pp. v, vi, vii). The obese typically accept the denigration thin society dishes out to them because they feel, for the most part, that they deserve it. And they do not defend other fat people who are being criticized because they are a mirror of themselves; they mirror their own defects—the very defects that are so repugnant to them. Unlike the members of most other minorities, they don't fight back; in fact, they feel that they can't fight back. Racial, ethnic, and religious minorities can isolate themselves to a degree from majority prejudices; the obese cannot. The chances are, most of the people they meet will be average size, and they live in a physical world built for individuals with much smaller bodies. The only possibilities seem to be to brace themselves—to cower under the onslaught of abuse—or to retreat and attempt to minimize the day-to-day disgrace.

Our hostility toward overweight runs up and down the scale, from the grossly obese to men and women of average weight. If the hugely obese are persecuted mightily for their weight, the slightly overweight are simply persecuted proportionally less—they are not exempt. We live in a weight-obsessed society. It is impossible to escape nagging reminders of our ideal weight. Standing at the checkout counter in a supermarket, we are confronted by an array of magazines, each with its own special diet designed to eliminate those flabby pounds. Television programs and even more so, advertising, display actresses and models who are considerably slimmer than average, setting up an almost impossibly thin ideal for the viewing public. If we were to gain ten pounds, our friends would all notice it, view the gain with negative feelings, and only the most tactful would not comment on it.

These exacting weight standards not surprisingly fall more severely on the shoulders of women than on men's. In a survey of the 33,000 readers of *Glamour* who responded to a questionnaire placed in the August 1983 issue of the magazine, 75 percent said that they were "too fat," even though only one-quarter were overweight according to the stringent 1959 Metropolitan Life Insurance Company's height-weight tables. (According to Metropolitan's current standards, even fewer of *Glamour*'s readers are deemed overweight.) Still more surprising, 45 percent who were *under*weight according to Metropolitan's figures felt that they were "too fat." Only 6 percent of the respondents felt "very happy" about their bodies; only 15 percent described their bodies as "just right." When looking at their nude bodies in the mirror, 32 percent said that they felt "anxious," 12 percent felt "depressed," and 5 percent felt "repulsed."

Commenting on the *Glamour* survey, one of the researchers who analyzed its results, Susan Wooley, professor of psychiatry at the University of Cincinnati's medical school, stated, "What we see is a steadily growing cultural bias—almost no woman of whatever size feels she's thin enough" (*Glamour,* 1984, p. 199). When asked of the following, which would make them happiest, 22 percent chose success at work, 21 percent said having a date with a man they admired, 13 percent said hearing from an old friend. However, the alternative that attracted the highest proportion of the sample was losing weight—42 percent. The overwhelming majority (80 percent) said that they have to be slim to be attractive to men. A substantial proportion had "sometimes" or "often" used the potentially dangerous weight loss methods of diet pills (50 percent), liquid formula diets (27 percent), duretics (18 percent), laxatives (18 percent), fasting or starving (45 percent), and self-induced vomiting (15 percent). Judging from the results of this survey, it is safe to say that the readers of *Glamour* who responded to it are obsessed about being thin.

Evidence suggests that the standards for the ideal female form have gotten slimmer over the years. Women whose figures would have been comfortably embraced by the norm a generation or more ago are now regarded as overweight, even fat. The model for the White Rock Girl, inspired by the ancient Greek goddess Psyche, was 5'4" tall in 1894 and she weighed 140; her measurements were 37"-27"-38". Over the years, the woman who was selected to depict the "White Rock Girl" has gotten taller, slimmer, and she has weighed less. In 1947, she was 5'6", weighed 125 pounds, and measured 35"-25"-35". And today, she's 5'8", weighs 118, and measures 35"-24"-34". Commenting on this trend, in an advertising flyer the executives of White Rock explain: "Over the years the Psyche image has become longer legged, slimmer hipped, and streamlined. Today—when purity is so important—she continues to symbolize the purity of all White Rock products." The equation of slenderness with purity is a revealing comment on today's obsession with thinness: Weighing a few pounds over some mythical ideal is to live in an "impure" condition. Interestingly, today's American woman averages 5'4" and weighs 140 pounds, the same size as 1894's White Rock Girl.

Advertising models represent one kind of ideal; they tend to be extremely thin. They are not, however, the only representation of the ideal female form depicted by the media. There are, it may be said, several ideals, not only one. Photographs appear to add between five and ten pounds to the subject; clothes add a few more in seeming bulk. (White Rock's Psyche, however, wears very little in the way of clothes.) Consequently, fashion models typically border on the anorexic, and women who take them as role models to be emulated are subjecting themselves to an almost unattainable standard. It would be inaccurate to argue that all American women aspire to look like a fashion model, and it would be inaccurate to assert that women in all media are emaciated. Still, it is entirely accurate to say that the ideal woman's figure as depicted in the media is growing slimmer over the years. Even in settings where women were once fairly voluptuous, today's version has slimmed down significantly.

Prior to 1970, contestants in Miss America pageants weighed 88 percent of the average for American women their age; after 1970 this declined somewhat to 85 percent. More important, before 1970 pageant *winners* weighed the same as the other contestants; after 1970, however, winners weighed significantly *less* than the contestants who didn't win—82.5 percent of the average for American women as a whole. Similarly, the weight of women who posed for *Playboy* centerfolds also declined between 1959 and 1978. Centerfolds for 1959 were 91 percent of the weight for an average American woman in her 20s; this declined to 84 percent in 1978. The measurements of the 1959 *Playboy* were 37"-22"-36". In 1978, they were 35"-24"-34½ ", indicating a growing preference for a less voluptuous, and a slimmer and more angular, or "tubular" ideal appearance. Interestingly, during this same period, the American woman under 30 *gained* an average of five pounds (which was entirely due to an increase in height during this time, not an increase in bulk). The number of diet articles published in six popular women's magazines nearly doubled between 1959 and 1979 (Garner et al., 1980). Thus, American women suffer from what might be described as a triple whammy—they are evaluated more severely on the basis of looks than is true of men, the standards of ideal weight for them falls within a far narrower range than it does for men, and these standards are becoming more rigid over time.

The increasingly slim standards of feminine beauty represent the most desirable point on a scale. The opposite end of this scale represents undesirable territory—obesity. If American women have been evaluated by standards of physical desirability that have shifted from slim to slimmer over the years, it is reasonable to assume that during this same period it has become less and less socially acceptable to be fat. In tribal and peasant societies, corpulence was associated with affluence. An abundant body represented a corresponding material abundance. In a society in which having enough to eat is a mark of distinction, heaviness will draw a measure of respect. This is true not only for oneself but also for one's spouse or spouses, and one's children as well. With the coming of mature industrialization, however, nutritional adequacy becomes sufficiently widespread as to cease being a sign of distinction; slenderness rather than corpulence comes to be adopted as the prevailing esthetic standard among the affluent (Powdermaker, 1960; Cahnman, 1968, pp. 287–288). In fact, what we have seen is a gradual adoption of the slim standard of attractiveness in all economic classes for both men and women, but much more strongly and stringently for women. And while more firmly entrenched in the upper socioeconomic classes, the slim ideal has permeated all levels of society.

Not only is obesity unfashionable and considered unesthetic to the thin majority, it is also regarded as "morally reprehensible," a "social disgrace" (Cahnman, 1968, p. 283). Fat people are *set apart* from men and women of average size; they are isolated from "normal" society (Millman, 1980). Today, being obese bears something of a *stigma*. In the words of sociologist Erving Goffman, the stigmatized are "disqualified from full social acceptance." They have been reduced "from a whole and usual person to a tainted, discounted one." The bearer of stigma is a "blemished person... to be avoided, especially in public places." The individual with a stigma is seen as "not quite human" (Goffman, 1963, pp. i, 1, 3, 5).

Over the centuries, the word *stigma* has had two meanings—one good and the second, very bad. Among the ancient Greeks, a stigma was a brand on the body of a person, symbolizing that the bearer was in the service of the temple. In medieval Christianity, *stigmata* were marks resembling the wounds and scars on the body of Jesus, indicating that the bearer was an especially holy individual. It is, however, the negative meaning of the word that is dominant today. In ancient times criminals and slaves were branded to identify their inferior status; the brand was a stigma. Lepers were said to bear the stigma of their loathsome disease. As it is currently used, stigma refers to a stain or reproach on one's character or reputation, or a symbol or sign of this inferiority or defect. Anything that causes someone to look down upon, condemn, denigrate or ignore another can be said to be *stigmatizing*.

A stigmatizing trait is rarely isolated. Hardly anyone who possesses one such characteristic is thought to have only one. A single sin will be regarded as housing a multitude of others as well, to be the "tip of the iceberg." The one stigmatizing trait is presumed to hide "a wide range of imperfections" (Goffman, 1963, p. 5). To be guilty of one sin automatically means to be thought of as being guilty of a host of others along with it. The one negative trait is a *master status*—everything about the individual is interpreted in light of the single trait. "Possession of one deviant trait may have a generalized symbolic value, so that people automatically assume that its bearer possesses other undesirable traits allegedly associated with it." Thus, the question is raised when confronting someone with a stigma: "What kind of person would break such an important rule?" The answer that is offered is typically: "One who is different from the rest of us, who cannot or will not act as a moral human being and therefore might break other important rules." In short, the stigmatizing chracteristic "becomes the controlling one" (Becker, 1963, pp. 33, 34).

To be stigmatized is to possess a *contaminated* identity. Interaction with non-stigmatized individuals will be strained, tainted, awkward, inhibited. While the non-stigmatized may, because of the dictates of polite sociability, attempt to hide their negative feelings toward the stigmatized trait specifically, or the stigmatized individual as a whole, and act normally, they are, nontheless, intensely *aware* of the other's blemish. Likewise, the stigmatized individual remains self-conscious about his or her relations with "normals," believing (often correctly) that the stigma is the exclusive focus of the interaction.

> I am always worried about how Jane judges me because she is the real beauty queen and the main gang leader. When I am with her, I hold my breath hard so my tummy doesn't bulge and I pull my skirt down so my fat thighs don't show. I tuck in my rear end. I try to look as thin as possible for her. I get so preoccupied with looking good enough to get into her gang that I forget what she's talking to me about.... I am so worried about how my body is going over that I can

hardly concentrate on what she's saying. She asks me about math and all I am thinking about is how fat I am (Allon, 1976, p. 18).

Highly stigmatized individuals, in the face of hostility on the part of the majority to their traits and to themselves as bearers of those traits, walk along one of two paths in reacting to stigma. One is to fight back by forming subcultures or groups of individuals who share the characteristics the majority rejects, and to treat this difference from the majority as a badge of honor—or at least, as no cause for shame. Clearly, the homosexual subculture provides an example of the tendency to ward off majority prejudices and oppression. This path is trod by those who feel that the majority's opinion of them and of the characteristic the majority disvalues is illegitimate or invalid—just plain wrong. Here, the legitimacy of the stigma is rejected. A trait, characteristic, a form of behavior that others look down upon, they say, is no cause for invidiousness. You may put us down, those who travel this path say, but you have no right to do so. What we are or do is every bit as blameless, indeed, honorable, as what you are or do.

The second path the stigmatized take in reacting to stigma from the majority is *internalization*. Here, stigmatized individuals hold the same negative attitudes toward themselves as the majority does. The stigmatized individual is dominated by feelings of self-hatred and self-derogation. Thus, those who are discriminated against are made to understand that they *deserve* it; they come to accept their negative treatment as *just* (Cahnman, 1968, p. 294). They feel that the majority has a *right* to stigmatize them. They may despise themselves for being who or what they are, for doing what they do or have done. As we see in testimony from fat people themselves, there is a great deal of evidence to suggest that the obese are more likely to follow the second path than the first. In fact, it might be said that in comparison with the possessors of all stigmatized characteristics or behavior, the obese most strongly agree with the majority's negative judgment of who they are.

Negative feelings on the part of the majority have been directed at a wide range of different groups and categories. Prejudice and racism against minority groups—what Goffman calls "the tribal stigma of race, nation, and religion" (1963, p. 4)—is one type of stigma. In some all-white settings, Blacks will be stigmatized if they enter them. Likewise, in certain all-black settings, it is the reverse. Anti-Semitism is rife in some social contexts; in them, to be Jewish is to suffer discrimination. At the same time, gentiles will find themselves shunned and ostracized in specific Jewish settings or contexts. For racial, national, and religious groups, stigma may work both ways; what counts is which group has the most power and resources. Although racism, ethnic hostility, and prejudice are fascinating topics, they are not what we are concerned about here.

A second type of trait or characteristic that tends to attract stigma from the majority who does not share it is made up of individuals who possess those "blemishes of individual character," which include having a "weak will, domineering or unnatural passions, treacherous and rigid beliefs, and dishonesty." Behavior or tendencies that, to the majority, manifest these and other "blemishes of individual character" include "mental disorder, imprisonment, addiction, alcoholism, homosexuality, unemployment, suicidal attempts, and radical political behavior" (Goffman, 1963, p. 4). Sociologists commonly refer to these forms of behavior as behavioral deviance, deviant behavior, or simply deviance. The archaic notion that deviant behavior is abnormal, a product of a disordered, pathological personality, has been abandoned long ago within sociology. People who engage in disapproved behavior tend to be perfectly normal; psychological abnormality has nothing to do with the concept of deviance. In sociology, deviance simply means a departure from an approved norm, especially where this departure tends to be punished, condemned, or stigmatized. Behavioral deviance, then, is a type of stigma.

The third type of trait or characteristic that commonly attracts stigma from the majority includes what Goffman calls "abominations of the body—the various physical deformities" (1963, p. 4). While not as thoroughly or as strongly rejected or stigmatized as behavioral deviants, possessors of certain physical characteristics are not completely accepted by the majority, either. Many individuals without a physical handicap feel uncomfortable relating to or interacting with someone who has an obvious disability or disfigurement, and this feeling is translated into real-life behavior—most commonly, avoiding contact, especially if it is intimate, with the disabled. While most nondisabled individuals would state that they would or do treat those with a disability "the same" as those without one, the disabled report that their treatment at the hands of the majority shows this claim to be fictional. In one study, only a small minority of the sample said that they would marry an amputee (18 percent), someone in a wheelchair (7 percent), a blind person (16 percent), or a stutterer (7 percent). While some might object and argue that marriage is a highly individual matter, having little to do with stigma, the same pattern prevailed in other areas of life. Only a shade over half said that they would have a deaf person as a *friend* (53 percent), and for the cerebral palsied, this was under four respondents in ten (38 percent)! Barely half (54 percent) said that they would live in the same *neighborhood* as a retardate (Shears and Jensema, 1969). Clearly, stigma is alive and well for the possessors of undesirable physical characteristics. The fact that they are involuntarily acquired is no protection against their stigmatization. Stigma is ubiquitous; no society exists in which all members are free of invidious feelings toward individuals with certain physical traits.

It is clear that much the same process of stigma occurs with the obese as with other traits, characteristics, and behavior that are regarded by the majority as undesirable. In fact, obesity is unique in at least one respect: It is considered by the "thin" majority as both a physical characteristic, like blindness and disabilities, and a form of behavioral deviance, like prostitution and alcoholism. The obese, unlike the physically disabled, are held *responsible* for their physical condition. Fatness, in the eyes of the nonobese majority, is viewed as both a physical deformity and as a behavioral aberration (Cahnman, 1968, p. 293; Allon, 1982, p. 130). Being fat is regarded as a matter of choice; the obese have gotten the way they are because of something they have done.

Overweight individuals "are stigmatized because they are held responsible for their deviant status, presumably lacking self-control and will-power. They are not merely physically deviant as are physically disabled or disfigured persons, but they [also] seem to possess characterological stigma. Fat people are viewed as 'bad' or 'immoral'; supposedly, they do not want to change the error of their ways" (Allon, 1982, p. 131). Contrary to the strictly disabled, and contrary to individuals belonging to a race different from our own,

> the obese are presumed to hold their fate in their own hands; if they were only a little less greedy or lazy or yielding to impulse or oblivious of advice, they would restrict excessive food intake, resort to strenuous exercise, and as a consequence of such deliberate action, they would reduce.... While blindness is considered a misfortune, obesity is branded as a defect.... A blind girl will be helped by her agemates, but a heavy girl will be derided. A paraplegic boy will be supported by other boys, but a fat boy will be pushed around. The embarrassing and not infrequently harassing treatment which is meted out to obese teenagers by those around them will not elicit sympathy from onlookers, but a sense of gratification; the idea is that they have got what was coming to them (Cahnman, 1968, p. 294).

The obese are overweight, according to the popular view, because they eat immodestly and to excess. They have succumbed to temptation and hedonistic pleasure-seeking, where other, more virtuous and less self-indulgent individuals have resisted. It is, as with behavioral deviance, a matter of a struggle between vice and virtue. The obese must therefore pay for the sin of overindulgence by attracting well-deserved stigma (Cahnman, 1968; Maddox et al., 1968). The obese suffer from what the public sees as "self-inflicted damnation" (Allon, 1973; Allon, 1982). In one study of the public's rejection of individuals with certain traits and characteristics, it was found that the stigma of obesity was in between that of physical handicaps, such as blindness, and behavioral deviance, such as homosexuality (Hiller, 1981, 1982). In other words, the public stigmatized the obese *more* than possessors of involuntarily acquired undesirable traits, but *less* than individuals who engage in unpopular, unconventional behavior.

This introduces a *moral* dimension to obesity that is lacking in other physical characteristics. The stigma of obesity entails three elements or aspects: (1) The overweight attract public scorn; (2) they are told that this scorn is deserved; (3) they come to accept this negative treatment as just (Cahnman, 1968, p. 293). A clear-cut indication that the obese are derogated because of their presumed character defects can be seen in the fact that if obesity is seen to be caused strictly by a physical abnormality, such as hormonal imbalance, the individual is condemned by the public almost not at all, whereas if the etiology of the obesity is left unexplained (and therefore is presumed to be a result of a lack of self-control, resulting in over-eating), the individual is, indeed, severely stigmatized (DeJong, 1980). A trait that is seen as beyond the individual's control, for which he or she is held to be not responsible, is seen as a misfortune. In contrast, character flaws are regarded in a much harsher light. Obesity is seen as the outward manifestation of an undesirable character; it therefore invites retribution, in much of the public's eyes.

So powerfully stigmatized has obesity become that, in a *New York Times* editorial (Rosenthal, 1981), one observer argues that obesity has replaced sex and death as our "Contemporary pornography." We attach some degree of shame and guilt to eating. Our society is made up of "modern puritans" who tell one another "how *repugnant* it is to be fat"; "what's really disgusting," we feel, "is not sex, but fat." We are all so humorless, "so relentless, so determined to punish the overweight.... Not only are the overweight the most stigmatized group in the United States, but fat people are expected to participate in their own degradation by agreeing with others who taunt them."

References

Allon, Natalie. 1973. The stigma of overweight in everyday life. In G. A. Bray (ed.), *Obesity in Perspective*. Washington, D.C.: U.S. Government Printing Office, pp. 83–102.

Allon, Natalie. 1976. *Urban Life Styles*. Dubuque, Iowa: W. C. Brown.

Allon, Natalie. 1982. The stigma of overweight in everyday life. In Benjamin B. Wolman (ed.), *Psychological Aspects of Obesity: A Handbook*. New York: Van Nostrand Reinhold, pp. 130–174.

Becker, Howard S. 1963. *Outsiders: Studies in the Sociology of Deviance*. New York: Free Press.

Cahnman, Werner J. 1968. The stigma of obesity. *The Sociological Quarterly*, 9 (Summer), 283–299.

DeJong, William. 1980. The stigma of obesity: The consequences of naive assumptions concerning the causes of physical deviance. *Journal of Health and Social Behavior*, 21, 75–87.

Garner, David M., Paul E. Garfinkel, D. Schwartz, and M. Thompson. 1980. Cultural expectations of thinness in women. *Psychological Reports*, 47, 483–491.

Goffman, Erving. 1963. *Stigma: Notes on the Management of Spoiled Identity*. Englewood Cliffs, N.J.: Prentice-Hall/Spectrum.

Hiller, Dana V. 1981. The salience of overweight in personality characterization. *Journal of Psychology*, 108, 233–240.

Hiller, Dana V. 1982. Overweight as master status: A replication. *Journal of Psychology*, 110, 107–113.

Louderback, Llewellyn. 1970. *Fat Power: Whatever You Weigh Is Right*. New York: Hawthorn Books.

Maddox, George L., Kurt W. Back, and Veronica Liederman. 1968. Overweight as social deviance and disability. *Journal of Health and Social Behavior*, 9 (December 1968), 287–298.

Millman, Marxia. 1980. *Such a Pretty Face: Being Fat in America*. New York: W. W. Norton.

Powdermaker, Hortense. 1960. An anthropological approach to the problem of obesity. *Bulletin of the New York Academy of Medicine*, 36, 286–295.

Shears, L. M., and C. J. Jensma. 1969. Social acceptability of anomalous persons. *Exceptional Children*, 35 (1):91–96.

Chapter 14

Mental Disorder

Mental disorder or mental illness represents or results in departures from shared expectations concerning appropriate ways of thinking, feeling, and acting. It is a form of deviance because it almost always results in punishment, condemnation, humiliation, social isolation, and other forms of social control of the persons who are designated as mentally disordered or ill. There exists a mental disorder *enterprise* or, in Michel Foucault's words, a mental illness *discourse:* The psychiatric, legal, and social machinery designed to deal with the mentally ill, the writing, the research, the diagnostic manuals, the mental health industry, and the drug industry built around administering medication for the mentally ill, not to mention public attitudes focusing on mental illness, the popular beliefs, stereotypes, prejudices, legend and folklore, media attention, and so on. Thus, as with all types and forms of deviance, mental disorder can be approached from the *constructionist* or the *essentialist* perspective.

The essentialist approach is usually referred to as the *medical* model. It argues that mental disorder is very much like a medical disease; a disease of the mind is very much like or analogous to a disease of the body. The bizarre and inappropriate behaviors exhibited by mentally disordered persons are symptoms of an underlying or internal pathology of some kind. In the words of David Rosenhan, author of "On Being Sane in Insane Places," the medical model is based on the view that "patients present symptoms," that "those symptoms can be categorized," and that "the sane are distinguishable from the insane" (a view, as we'll read, that Rosenhan rejects). To put the matter more colloquially, the medical model says: "Some people are more crazy than others [and] we can tell the difference" (Nettler, 1974, p. 894). Essentialists are concerned with *epidemiology* and *etiology:* That is, first, how mental disorder or mental illness is distributed in the population and second, how this distribution of the disease provides evidence to build a theory of what causes or explains it. There is, essentialists would say, a "true" rate or incidence of mental illness in a given population, and in different societies around the world, as well as in designated groups or categories in a given population. Essentialists would ask questions such as: Are men more likely to be or become mentally disordered than women? And does this vary by specific *type* of mental disorder—for instance, schizophrenia, depression, "antisocial" tendencies, and so on? Does marital status covary with mental disorder? And is this different for men versus women? Does marriage impart some sort of immunity on men and women with respect to becoming mentally ill? Or is it that the mentally ill find it difficult to locate a willing marital partner? Is socioeconomic status correlated with mental illness? Is it that being poor in a stratified society causes people to go crazy? Or is it that the crazy can't become successful in a competitive economy and "drift" to the bottom of the socioeconomic ladder? Is *stress* an intervening link between some of these social categories and mental disorder? Could stress be a "triggering" factor that causes some predisposed persons to "go crazy"?

These and other questions have been asked by sociologists who regard mental disorder as a concretely real phenomenon with essentialistic qualities. Essentialists hold that there exists a pregiven entity or syndrome that the researcher can locate, lay his or her hands on, identify and, eventually explain or account for. The American expatriate poet and writer Gertrude Stein once said, about Oakland, California: "There is no *there* there." She meant, in contrast to cities like Paris and New York, Oakland isn't a very interesting or exciting city. Putting aside her judgment about Oakland, the same idea can be used to tell us about the essentialist view of mental disorder. The essentialist approach says, about the label, "mental disorder," there *is* a "there there." There's something concretely *there* in the material world that all reasonably informed observers can agree *is* mental disorder. It's not just a label. It's a concretely real, materially existent condition. The application of the label is *not* the most interesting thing about it or even *an* interesting phenomenon to investigate. The most interesting things about the "there"—that is, mental disorder—is what it *is,* its dynamics, how it works, and, above all, what causes it. As I said, etiology is *the* central task of the essentialist approach: What causes it? Epidemiology is also important, but epidemiology is in the service of etiology; the main question is still why people are mentally disordered. What *makes* them that way? Studying the distribution of mental disorder in the population, from one category to another, or from one society to another, is conducted so that causality may be located and explicated.

A number of different theories are used to explain the cause of mental illness. Some of them are sociological. A sociologist would argue that mental disorder is caused mainly by social factors. Most sociologists will argue that social factors combine with genetic, neurological, hormonal, and/or psychological factors. Certain persons may be genetically predisposed to mental illness and stressful socially caused experiences could push them over the edge. Still, these sociological essentialists would say, social factors are crucial in mental illness. The point is, as we saw with homosexuality, simply because a theory is sociological does not mean that it is any the less essentialistic: Even sociological theories of mental disorder hold that mental illness is an identifiable clinical entity. It is real, it is there—there *is* a there there. What counts is how that condition came about, what caused it. And what does *not* count—or at least is of secondary importance—is the importance of studying the creation and application of the label. The enterprise of mental health diagnosis and treatment is only crucial insofar as it relates specifically to the success of treatment outcomes. It's important to know which treatments work and which ones don't, but it isn't important to study treatment as a problematic factor or dynamic in its own right, as a phenomenon to be explained and understood for its own sake.

Biological and genetic theories of mental illness, which hold that sociological factors are of secondary importance, could be seen as "hard" essentialistic theories, while sociological theories could be seen as "soft" essentialistic theories. Both agree that the clinical entity is concretely real, that diagnoses tap or measure something in the real world. But they do differ on the mutability or changeability of the cause. Physical and congenital theories posit causes that are more indwelling, more inherent, more fixed than sociological theories do. (Therapeutic drugs can, of course, modify indwelling states and bring about successful treatment of these biophysically caused conditions, but the states themselves are said to have fixed causes.) Still, both social and biophysical approaches or theories agree that, because the condition is concretely real, researchers can identify and explain it and, possibly, eventually, treat it. The sociological theory of mental disorder is that certain experiences exist in some individuals' lives that cause or influence them to "go crazy." And being crazy can be readily located; the state referred to as mental disorder can be measured by certain indwelling, concrete, objectively real criteria or indicators. So the sociological essentialists don't differ on that particular point with the biological essentialists: Mental illness is concretely real, and is not simply a label. But these two approaches do disagree on the issue of degree of inherency or congenitality.

All essentialists, then, argue that mental disorder is objectively, concretely real. At the same time, all would agree that there exists some culture-to-culture and group-to-group variation with respect to definitions of mental disorder. They would also agree that some categories in the population are more likely to be diagnosed as mentally disordered than others, independent of mental condition. For instance, what is judged to be crazy in England may not be so judged in the United States. American psychiatrists are far, far more likely to diagnose schizophrenia than their British counterparts are (Kendall et al., 1971). Lower-socioeconomic patients are more likely to be diagnosed as mentally disordered *by* middle-class psychiatrists than middle-class patients are; this is not *solely* due to objective psychiatric condition. Essentialists would say, of course, this happens.

However, they do not agree that this variation refutes their position. They would say, first, these variations are fairly small; second, they would say that these variations are not theoretically crucial or important. They insist that the reality of mental disorder lies in the mind somewhere, and it is concretely real regardless of how diagnoses are made. The fact that there is some variation in how mental illness is diagnosed from one psychiatrist or one society or patient to another does not refute its essentialistic reality. They would say that this variation is due largely to ignorance, error, inevitable differences in styles of diagnosis. And they are due as well to the *inherent complexity* of mental conditions. But this is not an especially interesting issue, they would say. What's important is why people go crazy. The fact that there is ambiguity in telling the difference between day and night during the in-between condition of dawn or dusk does not deny that the difference between day and night when comparing noon and midnight is clear-cut. Of course there are ambiguities around the edges. But the condition remains concretely real regardless of how it is diagnosed, just as cancer indwells in the body regardless of how it is diagnosed. Moreover, the medical and psychiatric sciences are getting more accurate over time, thus cutting down on misdiagnoses and ambiguities. Why some psychiatrists diagnose a condition one way and others diagnose it another way is simply not worth studying.

For instance, psychiatric essentialists would say that Rosenhan's experiment, in which normal people gained admission to mental hospitals and were never discovered by the psychiatric staff to be normal, does not show that there's no scientific basis to psychiatric diagnosis. They would say that the psychiatric staff in mental hospitals are overwhelmed with cases, and have little time to spend on individual, case-by-case diagnoses. Moreover, these patients *did* get admitted to mental hospitals as a result of claiming to have classic schizophrenic symptomology. Rosenhan's experiment doesn't demonstrate much of anything, essentialists would say.

Who's right, who's wrong?

It is clear that there is some extrapsychiatric variation in diagnosis. By "extrapsychiatric" I mean independent of mental condition. As I said, English psychiatrists are much, much less likely to diagnose schizophrenia than American psychiatrists, even for the same symptomology, that is, holding symptoms constant. The difference is on the order of ten times. One study (Simon and Zussman, 1983) examined a legal case involving the victims of a flood who were suing a coal company that was responsible for the conditions that made it possible for the flood to ravage the community. The defense's psychiatrists found no psychic damage in the plaintiffs' mental condition, the plaintiff's psychiatrists found considerable psychic damage. Would this be possible with a strictly medical condition, such as cancer? It would certainly be a great deal less likely.

The fact is, the medical approach is correct when it comes to cases involving classic or "archetypical" or extreme symptomology. Persons who are severely and chronically psychotic are regarded as crazy pretty much elsewhere. In clear-cut, full-blown cases, psychiatric diagnosis is fairly accurate. There is considerable consensus in such cases. Where symptoms are less clear-cut, less classic, disagreement among psychiatrists is high (Townsend, 1978, 1980; Edgerton, 1969). In fact, most persons with whom the mental health profession has to deal do not display clear-cut or classic symptoms. Being labeled for such people is a more complex and problematic affair, and it is likely to be influenced by a variety of contingencies. Thus, to answer the question, with respect to condition versus contingencies, which influences mental health diagnoses more, the answer is it depends on how extreme the symptomology is. The medical or essentialistic model is correct in emphasizing psychiatric condition for patients displaying classic symptomatology, while the labeling or constructionist approach is correct in emphasizing contingency for patients displaying less classic symptomology. Not a very satisfying answer, but the world as a general rule tends to be a very complex place.

The constructionist approach does not necessarily *deny* the validity of the etiological question. It is not entirely or necessarily contradictory with the essentialistic approach (although many constructionists do incidentally *also* refuse to believe that we can ever locate a "cause" of mental illness, and certainly most would question that its cause is biophysical). But regardless of whether mental disorder is a concrete entity in the real world, and independent of whether it has a specific set of causes, individuals who are referred to as mentally disordered are treated in a certain way in this and in any society. They are seen, conceptualized, judged, reacted to, and dealt with—both by mental health professionals and by the general public. And this vast construction process is *not* a given, not a simple product of the nature of the condition itself. The way it is here, there, or elsewhere, is not an inevitable or a necessary outgrowth of what mental illness is in the material world, what sort of condition the mentally ill "have," and how they became mentally disordered. This treatment process is a sociological phenomenon in its own right. It is problematic, as the theorists say—it has to be explained; it can't be assumed.

The constructionist approach to mental disorder does not argue—as some of its critics have claimed—that labels are applied randomly, capriciously, arbitrarily, independent of the mental condition of the diagnosee (Turner and Edgley, 1983, come very close to this position, however). This would be truly remarkable if that were so, that diagnosis and mental condition are randomly related; even Rosenhan's pseudopatients presented with classic schizophrenic symptomatology. They were not singled out randomly; they described classic sensations that schizophrenic persons are said to have. The constructionist position does, however, say that *contingencies* are crucial in diagnosis and that variations in diagnosis, based on social factors and variables, are not only considerable, they are worth investigating, they are of theoretical interest.

The constructionist position has been associated with what has been referred to as the labeling theory of mental illness. It is associated with the work of Thomas Scheff, who published a book titled *Being Mental Ill* in 1966, a second edition of which was released in 1984. Scheff argued that people who are labeled as mentally ill engage in "residual rule-breaking," that is, behavior for which there is no handy social category. If they had not been labeled, this unusual, bizarre behavior would be transitory; in the absence of the label, it would eventually simply dissipate. The stigmatizing label reinforces a commitment to the condition of craziness. Individuals who label such behavior as a sign of mental illness are influenced by the stereotyped imagery about the mentally ill that are dominant in a society's culture at a given time. Psychiatric diagnosis and treatment actually reinforce the condition of those who are labeled, Scheff argues, because they provide a definitive, expert label of craziness. In short, if others call one crazy, one will continue to act crazy, and this label will intensify one's commitment to crazy behavior and a crazy role (Scheff, 1966, 1984).

The labeling approach holds that the label of mental disorder is applied in part as a consequence of extrapsychiatric factors, that is, factors other than mental condition. And that the application of the label, both professionally and informally, by laypersons has a profound impact on the diagnosee's behavior. If others one is close to or who have a measure of power—friends, relatives, the general public, psychiatrists, psychologists—call one crazy, one will, in all likelihood, continue to act crazy, and this label will intensify one's commitment to crazy behavior and a crazy role.

Scheff argues that psychiatric hospitalization and treatment makes people worse, not better. This view has been attacked by numerous observers. To some extent, the argument has degenerated into an either-or proposition: Either the labeling approach is right or the medical model is right. There can't be any in-between position. However, recently, some observers have argued for a "soft," or "modified," labeling approach. Bruce Link's work is a good example of this position. Link does not accept Scheff's extreme, "hard," or "strict," labeling approach by insisting that psychiatric treatment produces an intensification of commitment of persons so treated to mentally ill–associated behavior or the mentally ill role. Link is emphatic in insisting on the potentially curative role of psychiatric treatment. Consistently, he says, treated patients show better long-term outcomes than untreated persons with the same condition. On that point, the hard or extreme labeling position is simply in error (Link et al., 1989).

But, contrary to the medical model, which downplays or dismisses the importance of stigmatizing the mentally ill, Bruce Link and his colleagues find that stigma is a crucial aspect of the lives of mental patients and ex-mental patients, and influences and colors what they do and why they do it, the adaptations and strategies they use to maintain dignity and self-respect. They suffer serious debilitation and demoralization as a consequence of stigma and labeling. It is something they have to struggle against and overcome (Link et al., 1989).

Thus, we end up with a mixed scorecard for both approaches. On the one hand, it is likely that there *is* a "there" there. That is, in all likelihood, psychiatric diagnoses *do* tap or indicate something concretely real, at least for more classic cases. For the less extreme cases, the labeling approach may be correct, as psychiatric diagnoses are heavily influenced by extrapsychiatric factors, and for many, possibly most, cases (which tend to be less extreme) it is difficult if not impossible to distinguish between the sane and the insane. But the labeling approach is flat-out wrong in insisting on the harmful effects of psychiatric intervention. And the medical approach is flat-out wrong in dismissing or underplaying the damaging role of stigma in the lives of patients and ex-patients.

Goffman's essay, "The Moral Career of the Mental Patient," which later became incorporated into his book, *Asylums: Essays on the Social Situation of Mental Patients and Other Inmates* (1961), is a classic in the field of the sociology of mental illness and in the deviance literature as well. In this essay, Goffman argues against the medical model, which holds that diagnosis and treatment are largely or exclusively a result of mental condition. Instead, what we see, Goffman says, is a variety of contingencies at work, seemingly secondary, accidental or incidental factors that shouldn't play a major role in diagnosis and treatment, but which actually do: for instance, socioeconomic status, visibility of the offense, proximity to the mental hospital, the availability of treatment facilities, and community attitudes toward available treatment modalities.

Moreover, Goffman says, patients do not experience institutionalization in anything like the way mental health professionals describe it. Instead of patients seeing the efforts of others to treat them as a favor, they are likely to see it as betrayal, abandonment, and disloyalty. They experience the efforts of others to institutionalize them as a kind of coalition arrayed against them, a "betrayal funnel" that pushes them step by step into a confinement that they did not choose and do not want. Rather than experiencing treatment as liberating, they are likely to feel it as confining and alienating. They are stripped of rights and humanity; they experience "blatant attacks" on their own view of themselves. And these feelings, interpreted by the mental health profession as signs of mental disorder, are likely to be shared by anyone going through the same experiences.

There has been a huge rise in the use of psychotropic drugs in mental hospitals over the past four decades, and as a result the length of hospitalization has declined from an average of six months when Goffman wrote to two weeks today. In addition, Goffman did not consider the fact that many mental patients are self-referrals rather than involuntary admissions. Still, being exposed to Goffman's penetrating view of the experience of the mental patient is likely to be enlightening.

David Rosenhan got normal people admitted to mental hospitals by claiming to have classic schizophrenic symptoms. Once admitted, these pseudopatients then acted normally. Was their ruse detected? Were they discovered to be sane people faking the symptoms of mental illness? Rosenhan found that psychiatric labels are extremely sticky; once applied, they are rarely removed or reevaluated on the basis of new, contrary evidence. All the pseudopatients in Rosenhan's experiment continued to be dealt with by all the mental health professionals they encountered *as* mentally ill, in spite of the fact that they acted in a completely normal fashion. Any and all aspects of their behavior, however common or normal, were interpreted as a sign or manifestation of mental disorder. And, like Goffman, Rosenhan found that all patients experienced depersonalization, dehumanization, and mortification in the mental institutions in which they stayed. Rosenhan's work argues forcefully for the relevance of the constructionist approach to the study of mental disorder.

References

Edgerton, Robert B. 1969. On the recognition of mental illness. In Robert B. Edgerton (ed.), *Perspectives in Mental Illness*. New York: Holt, Rinehart & Winston, pp. 49–72.

Goffman, Erving. 1961. *Asylums*. Garden City, N.Y.: Doubleday-Anchor.

Kendall, R. E., et al. 1971. Diagnostic criteria of American and British psychiatrists. *Archives of General Psychiatry,* 25 (August): 123–130.

Link, Bruce G., et al. 1989. A modified labeling theory approach to mental disorders: An empirical assessment. *American Sociological Review,* 54 (June): 400–423.

Nettler, Gwynn. 1974. On telling who's crazy. *American Sociological Review,* 39 (December): 893–894.

Scheff, Thomas J. 1966. *Being Mentally Ill: A Sociological Theory*. New York: Aldine.

Scheff, Thomas J. 1984. *Being Mentally Ill: A Sociological Theory* (2nd ed.). New York: Aldine.

Simon, Jesse, and Jack Zussman. 1983. The effect of contextual factors on psychiatrists' perception of illness: A case study. *Journal of Health and Social Behavior,* 24 (2):186–198.

Townsend, John Marshall. 1978. *Cultural Conceptions of Mental Illness*. New York: University of Chicago Press.

Townsend, John Marshall. 1980. Psychiatry versus social reaction: A critical analysis. *Journal of Health and Social Behavior,* 21 (September): 268–278.

Turner, Ronny E., and Charles Edgley. 1983. From witchcraft to drugcraft: Biochemistry as mythology. *Social Science Journal,* 20 (4):1–12.

The Moral Career of the Mental Patient

ERVING GOFFMAN

Traditionally the term *career* has been reserved for those who expect to enjoy the rises laid out within a respectable profession. The term is coming to be used, however, in a broadened sense to refer to any social strand of any person's course through life. The perspective of natural history is taken: unique outcomes are neglected in favor of such changes over time as are basic and common to the members of a social category, although occurring independently to each of them. Such a career is not a thing that can be brilliant or disappointing; it can no more be a success than a failure. In this light, I want to consider the mental patient, drawing mainly upon data collected during a year's participant observation of patient social life in a public mental hospital,[1] wherein an attempt was made to take the patient's point of view.

One value of the concept of career is its two-sidedness. One side is linked to internal matters held dearly and closely, such as image of self and felt identity; the other side concerns official position, jural relations, and style of life, and is part of a publicly accessible institutional complex. The concept of career, then, allows one to move back and forth between the personal and the public, between the self and its significant society, without having overly to rely for data upon what the person says he thinks he imagines himself to be.

This paper, then, is an exercise in the institutional approach to the study of self. The main concern will be with the *moral* aspects of career—that is, the regular sequence of changes that career entails in the person's self and in his framework of imagery for judging himself and others.[2]

The category "mental patient" itself will be understood in one strictly sociological sense. In this perspective, the psychiatric view of a person becomes significant only in so far as this view itself alters his social fate—an alteration which seems to become fundamental in our society when, and only when, the person is put through the process of hospitalization.[3] I therefore exclude certain neighboring categories: the undiscovered candidates who would be judged "sick" by psychiatric standards but who never come to be viewed as such by themselves or others, although they may cause everyone a great deal of trouble:[4] the office patient whom a psychiatrist feels he can handle with drugs or shock on the outside; the mental client who engages in psychotherapeutic relationships. And I include anyone, however robust in temperament, who somehow gets caught up in the heavy machinery of mental hospital servicing. In this way the effects of being treated as a mental patient can be kept quite distinct from the effects upon a person's life of traits a clinician would view as psychopathological.[5] Persons who become mental hospital patients vary widely in the kind and degree of illness that a psychiatrist would impute to them,

From Erving Goffman, "The Moral Career of the Mental Patient," *Psychiatry,* vol. 22 (May 1959), pp. 123–142.

and in the attributes by which laymen would describe them. But once started on the way, they are confronted by some importantly similar circumstances and respond to these in some importantly similar ways. Since these similarities do not come from mental illness, they would seem to occur in spite of it. It is thus a tribute to the power of social forces that the uniform status of mental patient cannot only assure an aggregate of persons a common fate and eventually, because of this, a common character, but that this social reworking can be done upon what is perhaps the most obstinate diversity of human materials that can be brought together by society. Here there lacks only the frequent forming of a protective group-life by ex-patients to illustrate in full the classic cycle of response by which deviant subgroupings are psychodynamically formed in society.

This general sociological perspective is heavily reinforced by one key finding of sociologically oriented students in mental hospital research. As has been repeatedly shown in the study of nonliterate societies, the awesomeness, distastefulness, and barbarity of a foreign culture can decrease in the degree that the student becomes familiar with the point of view to life that is taken by his subjects. Similarly, the student of mental hospitals can discover that the craziness or "sick behavior" claimed for the mental patient is by and large a product of the claimant's social distance from the situation that the patient is in, and is not primarily a product of mental illness. Whatever the refinements of the various patients' psychiatric diagnoses, and whatever the special ways in which social life on the "inside" is unique, the researcher can find that he is participating in a community not significantly different from any other he has studied.[6] Of course, while restricting himself to the off-ward grounds community of paroled patients, he may feel, as some patients do, that life in the locked wards is bizarre; and while on a locked admissions or convalescent ward, he may feel chronic "back" wards are socially crazy places. But he need only move his sphere of sympathetic participation to the "worst" ward in the hospital, and this too can come into social focus as a place with a livable and continuously meaningful social world. This in no way denies that he will find a minority in any ward or patient group that continues to seem quite beyond the capacity to follow rules of social organization, or that the orderly fulfillment of normative expectations in patient society is partly made possible by strategic measures that have somehow come to be institutionalized in mental hospitals.

The career of the mental patient falls popularly and naturalistically into three main phases: the period prior to entering the hospital, which I shall call the *prepatient phase;* the period in the hospital, the *inpatient phase;* the period after discharge from the hospital, should this occur, namely, the *expatient phase*.[7] This paper will deal only with the first two phases.

The Prepatient Phase

A relatively small group of prepatients come into the mental hospital willingly, because of their own idea of what will be good for them, or because of wholehearted agreement with the relevant members of their family. Presumably these recruits have found themselves acting in a way which is evidence to them that they are losing their minds or losing control of themselves. This view of oneself would seem to be one of the most pervasively threatening things that can happen to the self in our society, especially since it is likely to occur at a time when the person is in any case sufficiently troubled to exhibit the kind of symptom which he himself can see. As Sullivan described it,

> What we discover in the self-system of a person undergoing schizophrenic changes or schizophrenic processes, is then, in its simplest form, an extremely fear-marked puzzlement, consisting of the use of rather generalized and anything but exquisitely refined referential processes in an attempt to cope with what is essentially a failure at being human—a failure at being anything that one could respect as worth being.[8]

Coupled with the person's disintegrative re-evaluation of himself will be the new, almost equally pervasive circumstance of attempting to conceal from others what he takes to be the new fundamental facts about himself, and attempting to discover whether others too have discovered them.[9] Here I want to stress that perception of losing one's mind is based on culturally derived and socially engrained stereotypes as to the significance of symptoms such as hearing voices, losing temporal and spatial orientation, and sensing that one is being followed, and that many of the most spectacular and convincing of these symptoms in some instances psychiatrically signify merely a temporary emotional upset in a stressful situation, however terrifying to the person at the time. Similarly, the anxiety consequent upon this perception of oneself, and the strategies devised to reduce this anxiety, are not a product of abnormal psychology, but would be exhibited by any person socialized into our culture who came to conceive of himself as someone losing his mind. Interestingly, subcultures in American society apparently differ in the amount of ready imagery and encouragement they supply for such self-views, leading to differential rates of *self*-referral; the capacity to take this disintegrative view of oneself without psychiatric prompting seems to be one of the questionable cultural privileges of the upper classes.[10]

For the person who has come to see himself—with whatever justification—as mentally unbalanced, entrance to the mental hospital can sometimes bring relief, perhaps in part because of the sudden transformation in the structure of his basic social situations; instead of being to himself a questionable person trying to maintain a role as a full one, he can become an officially questioned person known to himself to be not so questionable as that. In other cases, hospitalization can make matters worse for the willing patient, confirming by the objective situation what has theretofore been a matter of the private experience of self.

Once the willing prepatient enters the hospital, he may go through the same routine of experiences as do those who enter unwillingly. In any case, it is the latter that I mainly want to consider, since in America at present these are by far the more numerous kind.[11] Their approach to the institution takes one of three classic forms: they come because they have been implored by their family or threatened with the abrogation of family ties unless they go "willingly"; they come by force under police escort; they come under misapprehension purposely induced by others, this last restricted mainly to youthful prepatients.

The prepatient's career may be seen in terms of an extrusory model; he starts out with relationships and rights, and ends up, at the beginning of his hospital stay, with hardly any of either. The moral aspects of this career, then, typically begin with the experience of abandonment, disloyalty, and embitterment. This is the case even though to others it may be obvious that he was in need of treatment, and even though in the hospital he may soon come to agree.

The case histories of most mental patients document offense against some arrangement for face-to-face living—a domestic establishment, a work place, a semipublic organization such as a church or store, a public region such as a street or park. Often there is also a record of some *complainant*, some figure who takes that action against the offender which eventually leads to his hospitalization. This may not be the person who makes the first move, but it is the person who makes what turns out to be the first effective move. Here is the *social* beginning of the patient's career, regardless of where one might locate the psychological beginning of his mental illness.

The kinds of offenses which lead to hospitalization are felt to differ in nature from those which lead to other extrusory consequences—to imprisonment, divorce, loss of job, disownment, regional exile, noninstitutional psychiatric treatment, and so forth. But little seems known about these differentiating factors; and when one studies actual commitments, alternate outcomes frequently appear to have been possible. It seems true, moreover, that for every offense that leads to an effective complaint, there are many psychiatrically similar ones that never do. No action is taken; or action is taken which leads to other extrusory outcomes; or ineffective action is taken, leading to the mere pacifying or putting off of the person who complains. Thus, as Clausen and Yarrow have nicely shown, even offenders who are eventually hospitalized are likely to have had a long series of ineffective actions taken against them.[12]

Separating those offenses which could have been used as grounds for hospitalizing the offender from those that are so used, one finds a vast number of what students of occupation call career contingencies.[13] Some of these contingencies in the mental patient's career have been suggested, if not explored, such as socio-economic status, visibility of the offense, proximity to a mental hospital, amount of treatment facilities available, community regard for the type of treatment given in available hospitals, and so on.[14] For information about other contingencies one must rely on atrocity tales: a psychotic man is tolerated by his wife until she finds herself a boyfriend, or by his adult children until they move from a house to an apartment; an alcoholic is sent to a mental hospital because the jail is full, and a drug addict because he declines to avail himself of psychiatric treatment on the outside; a rebellious adolescent daughter can no longer be managed at home because she now threatens to have an open affair with an unsuitable companion; and so on. Correspondingly there is an equally important set of contingencies causing the person to bypass this fate. And should the person enter the hospital, still another set of contingencies will help determine when he is to obtain a discharge—such as the desire of his family for his return, the availability of a "manageable" job, and so on. The society's official view is that inmates of mental hospitals are there primarily because they are suffering from mental illness. However, in the degree that the "mentally ill" outside hospitals numerically approach or surpass those inside hospitals, one could say that mental patients *distinctively* suffer not from mental illness, but from contingencies.

Career contingencies occur in conjunction with a second feature of the prepatient's career—the *circuit of agents*—and agencies—that participate fatefully in his passage from civilian to patient status.[15] Here is an instance of that increasingly important class of social system whose elements are agents and agencies, which are brought into systemic connection through having to take up and send on the same persons. Some of these agent-roles will be cited now, with the understanding that in any concrete circuit a role may be filled more than once, and a single person may fill more than one of them.

First is the *next-of-relation*—the person whom the prepatient sees as the most available of those upon whom he should be able to most depend in times of trouble; in this instance the last to doubt his sanity and the first to have done everything to save him from the fate which, it transpires, he has been approaching. The patient's next-of-relation is usually his next of kin; the special term is introduced because he need not be. Second is the *complainant,* the person who retrospectively appears to have started the person on his way to the hospital. Third are the *mediators*—the sequence of agents and agencies to which the prepatient is referred and through which he is relayed and processed on his way to the hospital. Here are included police, clergy, general medical practitioners, office psychiatrists, personnel in public clinics, lawyers, social service workers, school teachers, and so on. One of these agents will have the legal mandate to sanction commitment and will exercise it, and so those agents who precede him in the process will be involved in something whose outcome is not yet settled. When the mediators retire from the scene, the prepatient has become an inpatient, and the significant agent has become the hospital administrator.

While the complainant usually takes action in a lay capacity as a citizen, an employer, a neighbor, or a kinsman, mediators tend to be specialists and differ from those they serve in significant ways. They have experience in handling trouble, and some professional distance from what they handle. Except in the case of policemen, and perhaps some clergy, they tend to be more psychiatrically oriented than the lay public, and will see the need for treatment at times when the public does not.[16]

An interesting feature of these roles is the functional effects of their interdigitation. For example, the feelings of the patient will be influenced by whether or not the person who fills the role of complainant also has the role of next-of-relation—an embarrassing combination more prevalent, apparently, in the higher classes than in the lower.[17] Some of these emergent effects will be considered now.[18]

In the prepatient's progress from home to the hospital he may participate as a third person in what he may come to experience as a kind of *alienative coalition.* His next-of-relation presses him into coming to "talk things over" with a medical practitioner, an office psychiatrist, or some other counselor. Disinclination on his part may be met by threatening him with desertion, disownment, or other legal action, or by stressing the joint and explorative nature of the interview. But typically the next-of-relation will have set the interview up, in the sense of selecting the professional, arranging for time, telling the professional something about the case, and so on. This move effectively tends to establish the next-of-relation as the responsible person to whom pertinent findings can be divulged, while effectively establishing the other as the patient. The prepatient often goes to the interview with the understanding that he is going as an equal of someone who is so bound together with him that a third person could not come between them in fundamental matters; this, after all, is one way in which close relationships are defined in our society. Upon arrival at the office the prepatient suddenly finds that he and his next-of-relation have not been accorded the same roles, and apparently that a prior understanding between the professional and the next-of-relation has been put in operation against him. In the extreme but common case the professional first sees the prepatient alone, in the role of examiner and diagnostician, and then sees the next-of-relation alone, in the role of advisor, while carefully avoiding talking things over seriously with them both together.[19] And even in those nonconsultative cases where public officials must forcibly extract a person from a family that wants to tolerate him, the next-of-relation is likely to be induced to "go along" with the official action, so that even here the prepatient may feel that an alienative coalition has been formed against him.

The moral experience of being third man in such a coalition is likely to embitter the prepatient, especially since his troubles have already probably led to some estrangement from his next-of-relation. After he enters the hospital, continued visits by his next-of-relation can give the patient the "insight" that his own best interests were being served. But the initial visits may temporarily strengthen his feeling of abandonment: he is likely to beg his visitor to get him out or at least to get him more privileges and to sympathize with the monstrousness of his plight—to which the visitor ordinarily can respond only by trying to maintain a hopeful note, by not "hearing" the requests, or by assuring the patient that the medical authorities know about these things and are doing what is medically best. The visitor then nonchalantly goes back into a world that the patient has learned is incredibly thick with freedom and privileges, causing the patient to feel that his next-of-relation is merely adding a pious gloss to a clear case of traitorous desertion.

The depth to which the patient may feel betrayed by his next-of-relation seems to be increased by the fact that another witnesses his betrayal—a factor which is apparently significant in many three-party situations. An offended person may well act forbearantly and accommodatively toward an offender when the two are alone, choosing peace ahead of justice. The presence of a witness, however, seems to add something to the implications of the offense. For then it is beyond the power of the offended and offender to forget about, erase, or suppress what has happened; the offense has become a public social fact.[20] When the witness is a mental health commission, as is sometimes the case, the witnessed betrayal can verge on a "degradation ceremony."[21] In such circumstances, the offended patient may feel that some kind of extensively reparative action is required before witnesses, if his honor and social weight are to be restored.

Two other aspects of sensed betrayal should be mentioned. First, those who suggest the possibility of another's entering a mental hospital are not likely to provide a realistic picture of how in fact it may strike him when he arrives. Often he is told that he will get required medical treatment and a rest, and may well be out in a few months or so. In some cases they may thus be concealing what they know, but I think, in general, they will be telling what they see as the truth. For here there is a quite relevant difference between patients and mediating professionals; mediators, more so than the public at large, may conceive of mental hospitals as short-term medical establishments where required rest and attention can be voluntarily obtained, and not as places of coerced exile. When the prepatient finally arrives he is likely to learn quite quickly, quite differently. He then finds that the information given him about life in the hospital has had the effect of his having put up less resistance to entering than he now sees he would have put up had he known the facts. Whatever the intentions of those who participated in his transition from person to patient, he may sense they have in effect "conned" him into his present predicament.

I am suggesting that the prepatient starts out with at least a portion of the rights, liberties, and satisfactions of the civilian and ends up on a psychiatric ward stripped of almost everything. The question here is *how* this stripping is managed. This is the second aspect of betrayal I want to consider.

As the prepatient may see it, the circuit of significant figures can function as a kind of *betrayal funnel.* Passage from person to patient may be effected through a series of linked stages, each managed by a different agent. While each stage tends to bring a sharp decrease in adult free status, each agent may try to maintain the fiction that no further decrease will occur. He may even manage to turn the prepatient over to the next agent while sustaining this note. Further, through words, cues, and gestures, the prepatient is implicitly asked by the current agent to join with him in sustaining a running line of polite small talk that tactfully avoids the administrative facts of the situation, becoming, with each stage, progressively more at odds with these facts. The spouse would rather not have to cry to get the prepatient to visit a psychiatrist; psychiatrists would rather not have a scene when the prepatient learns that he and his spouse are being seen separately and in different ways; the police infrequently bring a prepatient to the hospital in a strait jacket, finding it much easier all around to give him a cigarette, some kindly words, and freedom to relax in the back seat of the patrol car; and finally, the admitting psychiatrist finds he can do his work better in the relative quiet and luxury of the "admission suite" where, as an incidental consequence, the notion can survive that a mental hospital is indeed a comforting place. If the prepatient heeds all of these implied requests and is reasonably decent about the whole thing, he can travel the whole circuit from home to hospital without forcing anyone to look directly at what is happening or to deal with the raw emotion that his situation might well cause him to express. His showing consideration for those who are moving him toward the hospital allows them to show consideration for him, with the joint result that these interactions can be sustained with some of the protective harmony characteristic of ordinary face-to-face dealings. But should the new patient cast his mind back over the sequence of steps leading to hospitalization, he may feel that everyone's *current* comfort was being busily sustained while his long-range welfare was being undermined. This realization may constitute a moral experience that further separates him for the time from the people on the outside.[22]

I would now like to look at the circuit of career agents from the point of view of the agents themselves. Mediators in the person's transition from civil to patient status—as well as his keepers, once he is in the hospital—have an interest in establishing a responsible next-of-relation as the patient's deputy or *guardian;* should there be no obvious candidate for the role, someone may be sought out and pressed into it. Thus while a person is gradually being transformed into a patient, a next-of-relation is gradually being transformed into a guardian. With a guardian on the scene, the whole transition process can be kept tidy. He is likely to be familiar with the prepatient's civil involvements and business, and can tie up loose ends that might otherwise be left to entangle the hospital. Some of the prepatient's abrogated civil rights can be transferred to him, thus helping to sustain the legal fiction that while the prepatient does not actually have his rights he somehow actually has not lost them.

Inpatients commonly sense, at least for a time, that hospitalization is a massive unjust deprivation, and sometimes succeed in convincing a few persons on the outside that this is the case. It often turns out to be useful, then, for those identified with inflicting these deprivations, however justifiably, to be able to point to the cooperation and agreement of someone whose relationship to the patient places him above suspicion, firmly defining him as the person most likely to have the patient's personal interest at heart. If the guardian is satisfied with what is happening to the new inpatient, the world ought to be.[23]

Now it would seem that the greater the legitimate personal stake one party has in another, the better he can take the role of guardian to the other. But the structural arrangements in society which lead to the acknowledged merging of two persons' interests lead to additional consequences. For the person to whom the patient turns for help—for protection against such threats as involuntary commitment—is just the person to whom the mediators and hospital administrators logically turn for authorization. It is understandable, then, that some patients will come to sense, at least for a time, that the closeness of a relationship tells nothing of its trustworthiness.

There are still other functional effects emerging from this complement of roles. If and when the next-of-relation appeals to mediators for help in the trouble he is having with the prepatient, hospitalization may not, in fact, be in his mind. He may not even perceive the prepatient as mentally sick, or, if he does, he may not consistently hold to this view.[24] It is the circuit of mediators, with their greater psychiatric sophistication and their belief in the medical character of mental hospitals, that will often define the situation for the next-of-relation, assuring him that hospitalization is a possible solution and a good one, that it involves no betrayal, but is rather a medical action taken in the best interests of the prepatient. Here the next-of-relation may learn that doing his duty to the prepatient may cause the prepatient to distrust and even hate him for the time. But the fact that this course of action may have had to be pointed out and prescribed by professionals, and be defined by them as a moral duty, relieves the next-of-relation of some of the guilt he may feel.[25] It is a poignant fact that an adult son or daughter may be pressed into the role of mediator, so that the hostility that might otherwise be directed against the spouse is passed on to the child.[26]

Once the prepatient is in the hospital, the same guilt-carrying function may become a significant part of the staff's job in regard to the next-of-relation.[27] These reasons for feeling that he himself has not betrayed the patient, even though the patient may then think so, can later provide the next-of-relation with a defensible line to take when visiting the patient in the hospital and a basis for hoping that the relationship can be reestablished after its hospital moratorium. And of course this position, when sensed by the patient, can provide him with excuses for the next-of-relation, when and if he comes to look for them.[28]

Thus while the next-of-relation can perform important functions for the mediators and hospital administrators, they in turn can perform important functions for him. One finds, then, an emergent unintended exchange or reciprocation of functions, these functions themselves being often unintended.

The final point I want to consider about the prepatient's moral career is its peculiarly *retroactive* character. Until a person actually arrives at the hospital there usually seems no way of knowing for sure that he is destined to do so, given the determinative role of career contingencies. And until the point of hospitalization is reached, he or others may not conceive of him as a person who is becoming a mental patient. However, since he will be held against his will in the hospital, his next-of-relation and the hospital staff will be in great need of a rationale for the hardships they are sponsoring. The medical elements of the staff will also need evidence that they are still in the trade they were trained for. These problems are eased, no doubt unintentionally, by the case-history construction that is placed on the patient's past life, this having the effect of demonstrating that all along he had been becoming sick, that he finally became very sick, and that if he had not been hospitalized much worse things would have happened to him—all of which, of course, may be true. Incidentally, if the patient wants to make sense out of his stay in the hospital, and, as already suggested, keep alive the possibility of once again conceiving of his next-of-relation as a decent, well-meaning person, then he too will have reason to believe some of this psychiatric work-up of his past.

Here is a very ticklish point for the sociology of careers. An important aspect of every career is the view the person constructs when he looks backward over his progress; in a sense, however, the whole of the prepatient career derives from this reconstruction. The fact of having had a prepatient career, starting with an effective complaint, becomes an important part of the mental patient's orientation, but this part can begin to be played only after hospitalization proves that what he had been having, but no longer has, is a career as a prepatient.

The Inpatient Phase

The last step in the prepatient's career can involve his realization—justified or not—that he has been deserted by society and turned out of relationships by those closest to him. Interestingly enough, the patient, especially a first admission, may manage to keep himself from coming to the end of this trail, even though in fact he is now in a locked mental hospital ward. On entering the hospital, he may very strongly feel the desire not to be known to anyone as a person who could possibly be reduced to these present circumstances, or as a person who conducted himself in the way he did prior to commitment. Consequently, he may avoid talking to anyone, may stay by himself when possible, and may even be "out of contact" or "manic" so as to avoid ratifying any interaction that presses a politely reciprocal role upon him and opens him up to what he has become in the eyes of others. When the next-of-relation makes an effort to visit, he may be rejected by mutism, or by the patient's refusal to enter the visiting room, these strategies sometimes suggesting that the patient still clings to a remnant of relatedness to those who made up his past, and is protecting this remnant from the final destructiveness of dealing with the new people that they have become.[29]

Usually the patient comes to give up his taxing effort at anonymity, at not-hereness, and begins to present himself for conventional social interaction to the hospital community. Thereafter he withdraws only in special ways—by always using his nickname, by signing his contribution to the patient weekly with his initial only, or by using the innocuous "cover" address tactfully provided by some hospitals; or he withdraws only at special times, when, say, a flock of nursing students makes a passing tour of the ward, or when, paroled to the hospital grounds, he suddenly sees he is about to cross the path of a civilian he happens to know from home. Sometimes this making of oneself available is called "settling down" by the attendants. It marks a new stand openly taken and supported by the patient, and resembles the "coming out" process that occurs in other groupings.[30]

Once the prepatient begins to settle down, the main outlines of his fate tend to follow those of a whole class of segregated establishments—jails, concentration camps, monasteries, work camps, and so on—in which the inmate spends the whole round of life on the grounds, and marches through his regimented day in the immediate company of a group of persons of his own institutional status.[31]

Like the neophyte in many of these "total institutions," the new inpatient finds himself cleanly stripped of many of his accustomed affirmations, satisfactions, and defenses, and is subjected to a rather full set of mortifying experiences: restriction of free movement; communal living; diffuse authority of a whole echelon of people; and so on. Here one begins to learn about the limited extent to which a conception of oneself can be sustained when the usual setting of supports for it are suddenly removed.

While undergoing these humbling moral experiences, the inpatient learns to orient himself in terms of the "ward system."[32] In public mental hospitals this usually consists of a series of graded living arrangements built around wards, administrative units called services, and parole statuses. The "worst" level involves often nothing but wooden benches to sit on, some quite indifferent food, and a small piece of room to sleep in. The "best" level may involve a room of one's own, ground and town privileges, contacts with staff that are relatively undamaging, and what is seen as good food and ample recreational facilities. For disobeying the pervasive house rules, the inmate will receive stringent punishments expressed in terms of loss of privileges; for obedience he will eventually be allowed to reacquire some of the minor satisfactions he took for granted on the outside.

The institutionalization of these radically different levels of living throws light on the implications for self of social settings. And this in turn affirms that the self arises not merely out of its possessor's interactions with significant others, but also out of the arrangements that are evolved in an organization for its members.

There are some settings which the person easily discounts as an expression or extension of him. When a tourist goes slumming, he may take pleasure in the situation not because it is a reflection of him but because it so assuredly is not. There are other settings, such as living rooms, which the person manages on his own and employs to influence in a favorable direction other persons' views of him. And there are still other settings, such as a work place, which express the employee's occupational status, but over which he has no final control, this being exerted, however tactfully, by his employer. Mental hospitals provide an extreme instance of this latter possibility. And this is due not merely to their uniquely degraded living levels, but also to the unique way in which significance for self is made explicit to the patient, piercingly, persistently, and thoroughly. Once lodged on a given ward, the patient is firmly instructed that the restrictions and deprivations he encounters are not due to such things as tradition or economy—and hence dissociable from self—but are intentional parts of his treatment, part of his need at the time, and therefore an expression of the state that his self has fallen to. Having every reason to initiate requests for better conditions, he is told that when the staff feels he is "able to manage" or will be "comfortable with" a higher ward level, then appropriate action will be taken. In short, assignment to a given ward is presented not as a reward or punishment, but as an expression of his general level of social functioning, his status as a person. Given the fact that the worst ward levels provide a round of life that inpatients with organic brain damage can easily manage, and that these quite limited human beings are present to prove it, one can appreciate some of the mirroring effects of the hospital.[33]

The ward system, then, is an extreme instance of how the physical facts of an establishment can be explicitly employed to frame the conception a person takes of himself. In addition, the official psychiatric mandate of mental hospitals gives rise to even more direct, even more blatant, attacks upon the inmate's view of himself. The more "medical" and the more progressive a mental hospital is—the more it attempts to be therapeutic and not merely custodial—the more he may be confronted by high-ranking staff arguing that his past has been a failure, that the cause of this has been within himself, that his attitude to life is wrong, and that if he wants to be a person he will have to change his way of dealing with people and his conceptions of himself. Often the moral value of these verbal assaults will be brought home to him by requiring him to practice taking this psychiatric view of himself in arranged confessional periods, whether in private sessions or group psychotherapy.

Now a general point may be made about the moral career of inpatients which has bearing on many moral careers. Given the stage that any person has reached in a career, one typically finds that he constructs an image of his life course—past, present, and future—which selects, abstracts, and distorts in such a way as to provide him with a view of himself that he can usefully expound in current situations.

Quite generally, the person's line concerning self defensively brings him into appropriate alignment with the basic values of his society, and so may be called an *apologia*. If the person can manage to present a view of his current situation which shows the operation of favorable personal qualities in the past and a favorable destiny awaiting him, it may be called a *success story*. If the facts of a person's past and present are extremely dismal, then about the best he can do is to show that he is not responsible for what has become of him, and the term *sad tale* is appropriate. Interestingly enough, the more the person's past forces him out of apparent alignment with central moral values, the more often he seems compelled to tell his sad tale in any company in which he finds himself. Perhaps he partly responds to the need he feels in others of not having their sense of proper life courses affronted. In any case, it is among convicts, "wino's," and prostitutes that one seems to obtain sad tales the most readily.[34] It is the vicissitudes of the mental patient's sad tale that I want to consider now.

In the mental hospital, the setting and the house rules press home to the patient that he is, after all, a mental case who has suffered some kind of social collapse on the outside, having failed in some over-all way, and that here he is of little social weight, being hardly capable of acting like a full-fledged person at all. These humiliations are likely to be most keenly felt by middle-class patients, since their previous condition of life little immunizes them against such affronts; but all patients feel some downgrading. Just as any normal member of his outside subculture would do, the patient often responds to this situation by attempting to assert a sad tale proving that he is not "sick," that the "little trouble" he did get into was really somebody else's fault, that his past life course had some honor and rectitude, and that the hospital is therefore unjust in forcing the status of mental patient upon him. This self-respecting tendency is heavily institutionalized within the patient society where opening social contacts typically involve the participants' volunteering information about their current ward location and length of stay so far, but not the reasons for their stay—such interaction being conducted in the manner of small talk on the outside.[35] With greater familiarity, each patient usually volunteers relatively acceptable reasons for his hospitalization, at the same time accepting without open immediate question the lines offered by other patients. Such stories as the following are given and overtly accepted.

> I was going to night school to get an M.A. degree, and holding down a job in addition, and the load got too much for me.
>
> The others here are sick mentally but I'm suffering from a bad nervous system and that is what is giving me these phobias.
>
> I got here by mistake because of a diabetes diagnosis, and I'll leave in a couple of days. [The patient had been in seven weeks.]
>
> I failed as a child, and later with my wife I reached out for dependency.

> My trouble is that I can't work. That's what I'm in for. I had two jobs with a good home and all the money I wanted.[36]

The patient sometimes reinforces these stories by an optimistic definition of his occupational status: A man who managed to obtain an audition as a radio announcer styles himself a radio announcer; another who worked for some months as a copy boy and was then given a job as a reporter on a large trade journal, but fired after three weeks, defines himself as a reporter.

A whole social role in the patient community may be constructed on the basis of these reciprocally sustained fictions. For these face-to-face niceties tend to be qualified by behind-the-back gossip that comes only a degree closer to the "objective" facts. Here, of course, one can see a classic social function of informal networks of equals: they serve as one another's audience for self-supporting tales—tales that are somewhat more solid than pure fantasy and somewhat thinner than the facts.

But the patient's *apologia* is called forth in a unique setting, for few settings could be so destructive of self-stories except, of course, those stories already constructed along psychiatric lines. And this destructiveness rests on more than the official sheet of paper which attests that the patient is of unsound mind, a danger to himself and others—an attestation, incidentally, which seems to cut deeply into the patient's pride, and into the possibility of having any.

Certainly the degrading conditions of the hospital setting belie many of the self-stories that are presented by patients; and the very fact of being in the mental hospital is evidence against these tales. And of course, there is not always sufficient patient solidarity to prevent patient discrediting patient, just as there is not always a sufficient number of "professionalized" attendants to prevent attendant discrediting patient. As one patient informant repeatedly suggested to a fellow patient:

> If you're so smart, how come you got your ass in here?

The mental hospital setting, however, is more treacherous still. Staff has much to gain through discreditings of the patient's story—whatever the felt reason for such discreditings. If the custodial faction in the hospital is to succeed in managing his daily round without complaint or trouble from him, then it will prove useful to be able to point out to him that the claims about himself upon which he rationalizes his demands are false, that he is not what he is claiming to be, and that in fact he is a failure as a person. If the psychiatric faction is to impress upon him its views about his personal make-up, then they must be able to show in detail how their version of his past and their version of his character hold up much better than his own.[37] If both the custodial and psychiatric factions are to get him to cooperate in the various psychiatric treatments, then it will prove useful to disabuse him of *his* view of their purposes, and cause him to appreciate that they know what they are doing, and are doing what is best for him. In brief, the difficulties caused by a patient are closely tied to his version of what has been happening to him, and if cooperation is to be secured, it helps if this version is discredited. The patient must "insightfully" come to take, or affect to take, the hospital's view of himself.

Notes

1. The study was conducted during 1955–56 under the auspices of the Laboratory of Socio-environmental Studies of the National Institute of Mental Health. I am grateful to the Laboratory Chief, John A. Clausen, and to Dr. Winfred Overholser, Superintendent, and the late Dr. Jay Hoffman, then First Assistant Physician of Saint Elizabeths Hospital, Washington, D.C., for the ideal cooperation they freely provided. A preliminary report is contained in Goffman, "Interpersonal Persuasion," pp. 117–193; in *Group Processes: Transactions of the Third Conference,* edited by Bertram Schaffner: New York, Josiah Macy, Jr. Foundation, 1957. A shorter version of this paper was presented at the Annual Meeting of the American Sociological Society, Washington, D.C., August 1957.

2. Material on moral career can be found in early social anthropological work on ceremonies of status transition, and in classic social psychological descriptions of those spectacular changes in one's view of self that can accompany participation in social movements and sects. Recently new kinds of relevant data have been suggested by psychiatric interest in the problem of "identity" and sociological studies of work careers and "adult socialization."

3. This point has recently been made by Elaine and John Cumming, *Closed Ranks;* Cambridge, Commonwealth Fund, Harvard Univ. Press, 1957; pp. 101–102. "Clinical experience supports the impression that many people define mental illness as 'That condition for which a person is treated in a mental hospital.'... Mental illness, it seems, is a condition which afflicts people who must go to a mental institution, but until they do almost anything they do is normal." Leila Deasy has pointed out to me the correspondence here with the situation in white collar crime. Of those who are detected in this activity, only the ones who do not manage to avoid going to prison find themselves accorded the social role of the criminal.

4. Case records in mental hospitals are just now coming to be exploited to show the incredible amount of trouble a person may cause for himself and others before anyone begins to think about him psychiatrically, let alone take psychiatric action against him. See John A. Clausen and Marian Radke Yarrow, "Paths to the Mental Hospital," *J. Social Issues* (1955) 11:25–32; August B. Hollingshead and Fredrick C. Redlich, *Social Class and Mental Illness;* New York, Wiley, 1958: pp. 173–174.

5. An illustration of how this perspective may be taken to all forms of deviancy may be found in Edwin Lemert, *Social Pathology;* New York, McGraw-Hill, 1951; see especially pp. 74–76. A specific application to mental defectives may be found in Stewart E. Perry, "Some Theoretic Problems of Mental Deficiency and Their Action Implications," *Psychiatry* (1954) 17:45–73; see especially p. 68.

6. Conscientious objectors who voluntarily went to jail sometimes arrived at the same conclusion regarding criminal inmates. See, for example, Alfred Hassler, *Diary of a Self-made Convict;* Chicago, Regnery, 1954; p. 74.

7. This simple picture is complicated by the somewhat special experience of roughly a third of ex-patients—namely, readmission to the hospital, this being the recidivist or "repatient" phase.

8. Harry Stack Sullivan, *Clinical Studies in Psychiatry;* edited by Helen Swick Perry, Mary Ladd Gawel, and Martha Gibbon; New York, Norton, 1956; pp. 184–185.

9. This moral experience can be contrasted with that of a person learning to become a marihuana addict, whose discovery that he can be "high" and still "op" effectively without being detected apparently leads to a new level of use. See Howard S. Becker, "Marihuana Use and Social Control." *Social Problems* (1955) 3:35–44; see especially pp. 40–41.

10. See footnote 4: Hollingshead and Redlich, p. 187, Table 6, where relative frequency is given of self-referral by social class grouping.

11. The distinction employed here between willing and unwilling patients cuts across the legal one, of voluntary and committed, since some persons who are glad to come to the mental hospital may be legally committed, and of those who come only because of strong familial pressure, some may sign themselves in as voluntary patients.

12. Clausen and Yarrow; see footnote 4.

13. An explicit application of this notion to the field of mental health may be found in Edwin M. Lemert, "Legal Commitment and Social Control," *Sociology and Social Research* (1946) 30:370–378.

14. For example, Jerome K. Myers and Leslie Schaffer, "Social Stratification and Psychiatric Practice: A Study of an Outpatient Clinic," *Amer. Sociological Rev.* (1954) 19:307–310. Lemert, see footnote 5; pp. 402–403. *Patients in Mental Institutions,* 1941; Washington, D.C., Department of Commerce, Bureau of Census, 1941; p. 2.

15. For one circuit of agents and its bearing on career contingencies, see Oswald Hall, "The Stages of a Medical Career," *Amer. J. Sociology* (1948) 53:227–336.

16. See Cumming, footnote 3; p. 92.

17. Hollingshead and Redlich, footnote 4; p. 187.

18. For an analysis of some of these circuit implications for the inpatient, see Leila C. Deasy and Olive W. Quinn, "The Wife of the Mental Patient and the Hospital Psychiatrist." *J. Social Issues* (1955) 11:49–60. An interesting illustration of this kind of analysis may also be found in Alan G. Gowman, "Blindness and the Role of Companion," *Social Problems* (1956) 4:68–75. A general statement may be found in Robert Merton, "The Role Set: Problems in Sociological Theory," *British J. Sociology* (1957) 8:106–120.

19. I have one case record of a man who claims he thought *he* was taking his wife to see the psychiatrist, not realizing until too late that his wife had made the arrangements.

20. A paraphrase from Kurt Riezler, "The Social Psychology of Shame" *Amer. J. Sociology* (1943) 48:458.

21. See Harold Garfinkel, "Conditions of Successful Degradation Ceremonies," *Amer. J. Sociology* (1956) 61:420–424.

22. Concentration camp practices provide a good example of the function of the betrayal funnel in inducing cooperation and reducing struggle and fuss, although here the mediators could not be said to be acting in the best interests of the inmates. Police picking up persons from their homes would sometimes joke good-naturedly and offer to wait while coffee was being served. Gas chambers were fitted out like delousing rooms, and victims taking off their clothes were told to note where they were leaving them. The sick, aged, weak, or insane who were selected for extermination were sometimes driven away in Red Cross ambulances to camps referred to by terms such as "observation hospital." See David Boder, *I Did Not Interview the Dead;* Urbana, Univ. of Illinois Press, 1949; p. 81; and Elie A. Cohen, *Human Behavior in the Concentration Camp;* London, Cape, 1954; pp. 32, 37, 107.

23. Interviews collected by the Clausen group at NIMH suggest that when a wife comes to be a guardian, the responsibility may disrupt previous distance from in-laws, leading either to a new supportive coalition with them or to a marked withdrawal from them.

24. For an analysis of these nonpsychiatric kinds of perception, see Marian Radke Yarrow, Charlotte Green Schwartz, Harriet S. Murphy, and Leila Calhoun Deasy, "The Psychological Meaning of Mental Illness in the Family," *J. Social Issues* (1955) 11:12–24; Charlotte Green Schwartz, "Perspectives on Deviance: Wives' Definitions of their Husbands' Mental Illness," *Psychiatry* (1957) 20:275–291.

25. This guilt-carrying function is found, of course, in other role-complexes. Thus, when a middle-class couple engages in the process of legal separation or divorce, each of their lawyers usually takes the position that his job is to acquaint his client with all of the potential claims and rights, pressing his client into demanding these, in spite of any nicety of feelings about the rights and honorableness of the ex-partner. The client, in all good faith, can then say to self and to the ex-partner that the demands are being made only because the lawyer insists it is best to do so.

26. Recorded in the Clausen data.

27. This point is made by Cumming , see footnote 3; p. 129.

28. There is an interesting contrast here with the moral career of the tuberculosis patient. I am told by Julius Roth that tuberculosis patients are likely to come to the hospital willingly, agreeing with their next-of-relation about treatment. Later in their hospital career, when they learn how long they yet have to stay and how depriving and irrational some of the hospital rulings are, they may seek to leave, be advised against this by the staff and by relatives, and only then begin to feel betrayed.

29. The inmate's initial strategy of holding himself aloof from ratifying contact may partly account for the relative lack of group-formation among inmates in public mental hospitals, a connection that has been suggested to me by William R. Smith. The desire to avoid personal bonds that would give license to the asking of biographical

questions could also be a factor. In mental hospitals, of course, as in prisoner camps, the staff may consciously break up incipient group-information in order to avoid collective rebellious action and other ward disturbances.

30. A comparable coming out occurs in the homosexual world, when a person finally comes frankly to present himself to a "gay" gathering not as a tourist but as someone who is "available." See Evelyn Hooker, "A Preliminary Examination of Group Behavior of Homosexuals," *J. Psychology* (1956) 42:217–225; especially p. 221. A good fictionalized treatment may be found in James Baldwin's *Giovanni's Room;* New York, Dial, 1956; pp. 41–63. A familiar instance of the coming out process is no doubt to be found among prepubertal children at the moment one of these actors sidles *back* into a room that had been left in an angered huff and injured *amour-propre*. The phrase itself presumably derives from a *rite-de-passage* ceremony once arranged by upper-class mothers for their daughters. Interestingly enough, in large mental hospitals the patient sometimes symbolizes a complete coming out by his first active participation in the hospital wide patient dance.

31. See Goffman, "Characteristics of Total Institutions," pp. 43–84; in *Proceedings of the Symposium of Preventive and Social Psychiatry;* Washington, D.C., Walter Reed Army Institute of Research, 1958.

32. A good description of the ward system may be found in Ivan Belknap, *Human Problems of a State Mental Hospital;* New York, McGraw-Hill, 1956; see especially p. 164.

33. Here is one way in which mental hospitals can be worse than concentration camps and prisons as places in which to "do" time; in the latter, self-insulation from the symbolic implications of the settings may be easier. In fact, self-insulation from hospital settings may be so difficult that patients have to employ devices for this which staff interpret as psychotic symptoms.

34. In regard to convicts, see Anthony Heckstall-Smith, *Eighteen Months;* London, Wingate, 1954; pp. 52–53. For "wino's" see the discussion in Howard G. Bain, "A Sociological Analysis of the Chicago Skid-Row Lifeway" unpublished M.A. thesis, Dept. of Sociology, Univ. of Chicago, Sept., 1950; especially "The Rationale of the Skid-Row Drinking Group," pp. 141–146. Bain's neglected thesis is a useful source of material on moral careers.

Apparently one of the occupational hazards of prostitution is that clients and other professional contacts sometimes persist in expressing sympathy by asking for a defensible dramatic explanation for the fall from grace. In having to bother to have a sad tale ready, perhaps the prostitute is more to be pitied than damned. Good examples of prostitute sad tales may be found in Sir Henry Mayhew, "Those that Will Not Work," pp. 210–272; in his *London Labour and the London Poor,* Vol. 4; London, Griffin, Bohn, and Cox, 1862. For a contemporary source, see *Women of the Streets,* edited by C. H. Rolph; London, Zecker and Warburg, 1955; especially p. 6. "Almost always, however, after a few comments on the police, the girl would begin to explain how it was that she was in the life, usually in terms of self-justification." Lately, of course, the psychological expert has helped out the profession in the construction of wholly remarkable sad tales. See, for example, Harold Greenwald, *Call Girl;* New York, Ballantine, 1958.

35. A similar self-protecting rule has been observed in prisons. Thus, Hassler, see footnote 6, in describing a conversation with a fellow-prisoner; "He didn't say much about why he was sentenced, and I didn't ask him, that being the accepted behavior in prison" (p. 76). A novelistic version for the mental hospital may be found in J. Kerkhoff, *How Thin the Veil; A Newspaperman's Story of His Own Mental Crack-up and Recovery;* New York, Greenberg, 1952; p. 27.

36. From the writer's field notes of informal interaction with patients, transcribed as near verbatim as he was able.

37. The process of examining a person psychiatrically and then altering or reducing his status in consequence is known in hospital and prison parlance as *bugging,* the assumption being that once you come to the attention of the testers you either will automatically be labeled crazy or the process of testing itself will make you crazy. Thus psychiatric staff are sometimes seen not as *discovering* whether you are sick, but as *making* you sick; and "Don't bug me, man," can mean, "Don't pester me to the point where I'll get upset." Sheldom Messenger has suggested to me that this meaning of bugging is related to the other colloquial meaning, of wiring a room with a secret microphone to collect information usable for discrediting the speaker.

On Being Sane in Insane Places[1]

DAVID L. ROSENHAN

If sanity and insanity exist, how shall we know them?

The question is neither capricious nor itself insane. However much we may be personally convinced that we can tell the normal from the abnormal, the evidence is simply not compelling. It is commonplace, for example, to read about murder trials wherein eminent psychiatrists for the defense are contradicted by equally eminent psychiatrists for the prosecution on the matter of the defendant's sanity. More generally, there are a great deal of conflicting data on the reliability, utility, and meaning of such terms as "sanity," "insanity," "mental illness," and "schizophrenia."[2] Finally, as early as 1934, Benedict suggested that normality and abnormality are not universal.[3] What is viewed as normal in one culture may be seen as quite aberrant in another. Thus, notions of normality and abnormality may not be quite as accurate as people believe they are.

To raise questions regarding normality and abnormality is in no way to question the fact that some behaviors are deviant or odd. Murder is deviant. So, too, are hallucinations. Nor does raising such questions deny the existence of the personal anguish that is often associated with "mental illness." Anxiety and depression exist. Psychological suffering exists. But normality and abnormality, sanity and insanity, and the diagnoses that flow from them may be less substantive than many believe them to be.

At its heart, the question of whether the sane can be distinguished from the insane (and whether degrees of insanity can be distinguished from each other) is a simple matter: Do the salient characteristics that lead to diagnoses reside in the patients themselves or in the environments and contexts in which observers find them? From Bleuler, through Kretchmer, through the formulators of the recently revised *Diagnostic and Statistical Manual* of the American Psychiatric Association, the belief has been strong that patients present symptoms, that those symptoms can be categorized, and, implicitly, that the sane are distinguishable from the insane. More recently, however, this belief has been questioned. Based in part on theoretical and anthropological considerations, but also on philosophical, legal, and therapeutic ones, the view has grown that psychological categorization of mental illness is useless at best and downright harmful, misleading, and pejorative at worst. Psychiatric diagnoses, in this view, are in the minds of the observers and are not valid summaries of characteristics displayed by the observed.[4-6]

Gains can be made in deciding which of these is more nearly accurate by getting normal people (that is, people who do not have, and have never suffered, symptoms of serious psychiatric disorders) admitted to psychiatric hospitals and then determining whether they were discovered to be sane and, if so, how. If the sanity of such

From David L. Rosenhan, "On Being Sane in Insane Places," *Science,* vol. 179 (January 19, 1973), pp. 250–258.

pseudopatients were always detected, there would be prima facie evidence that a sane individual can be distinguished from the insane context in which he is found. Normality (and presumably abnormality) is distinct enough that it can be recognized wherever it occurs, for it is carried within the person. If, on the other hand, the sanity of the pseudopatients were never discovered, serious difficulties would arise for those who support traditional modes of psychiatric diagnosis. Given that the hospital staff was not incompetent, that the pseudopatient had been behaving as sanely as he had been outside of the hospital, and that it had never been previously suggested that he belonged in a psychiatric hospital, such an unlikely outcome would support the view that psychiatric diagnosis betrays little about the patient but much about the environment in which an observer finds him.

This article describes such an experiment. Eight sane people gained secret admission to 12 different hospitals.[7] Their diagnostic experiences constitute the data of the first part of this article; the remainder is devoted to a description of their experiences in psychiatric institutions. Too few psychiatrists and psychologists, even those who have worked in such hospitals, know what the experience is like. They rarely talk about it with former patients, perhaps because they distrust information coming from the previously insane. Those who have worked in psychiatric hospitals are likely to have adapted so thoroughly to the settings that they are insensitive to the impact of that experience. And while there have been occasional reports of researchers who submitted themselves to psychiatric hospitalization,[8] these researchers have commonly remained in the hospitals for short periods of time, often with the knowledge of the hospital staff. It is difficult to know the extent to which they were treated like patients or like research colleagues. Nevertheless, their reports about the inside of the psychiatric hospital have been valuable. This article extends those efforts.

Pseudopatients and Their Settings

The eight pseudopatients were a varied group. One was a psychology graduate student in his 20's. The remaining seven were older and "established." Among them were three psychologists, a pediatrician, a psychiatrist, a painter, and a housewife. Three pseudopatients were women, five were men. All of them employed pseudonyms, lest their alleged diagnoses embarrass them later. Those who were in mental health professions alleged another occupation in order to avoid the special attentions that might be accorded by staff, as a matter of courtesy or caution, to ailing colleagues.[9] With the exception of myself (I was the first pseudopatient and my presence was know to the hospital administrator and chief psychologist and, so far as I can tell, to them alone), the presence of pseudopatients and the nature of the research program was not known to the hospital staffs.[10]

The settings were similarly varied. In order to generalize the findings, admission into a variety of hospitals was sought. The 12 hospitals in the sample were located in five different states on the East and West coasts. Some were old and shabby, some were quite new. Some were research-oriented, others not. Some had good staff-patient ratios, others were quite understaffed. Only one was a strictly private hospital. All of the others were supported by state or federal funds or, in one instance, by university funds.

After calling the hospital for an appointment, the pseudopatient arrived at the admissions office complaining that he had been hearing voices. Asked what the voices said, he replied that they were often unclear, but as far as he could tell they said "empty," "hollow," and "thud." The voices were unfamiliar and were of the same sex as the pseudopatient. The choice of these symptoms was occasioned by their apparent similarity to existential symptoms. Such symptoms are alleged to arise from painful concerns about the perceived meaninglessness of one's life. It is as if the hallucinating person were saying, "My life is empty and hollow." The choice of these symptoms was also determined by the *absence* of a single report of existential psychoses in the literature.

Beyond alleging the symptoms and falsifying name, vocation, and employment, no further alterations of person, history, or circumstances were made. The significant events of the pseudopatient's life history were presented as they had actually occurred. Relationships with parents and siblings, with spouse and children, with people at work and in school, consistent with the aforementioned exceptions, were described as they were or had been. Frustrations and upsets were described along with joys and satisfactions. These facts are important to remember. If anything, they strongly biased the subsequent results in favor of detecting sanity, since none of their histories or current behaviors were seriously pathological in any way.

Immediately upon admission to the psychiatric ward, the pseudopatient ceased simulating *any* symptoms of abnormality. In some cases, there was a brief period of mild nervousness and anxiety, since none of the pseudopatients really believed that they would be admitted so easily. Indeed, their shared fear was that they would be immediately exposed as frauds and greatly embarrassed. Moreover, many of them had never visited a psychiatric ward; even those who had, nevertheless had some genuine fears about what might happen to them. Their nervousness, then, was quite appropriate to the novelty of the hospital setting, and it abated rapidly.

Apart from that short-lived nervousness, the pseudopatient behaved on the ward as he "normally" behaved. The pseudopatient spoke to patients and staff as he might ordinarily. Because there is uncommonly little to do on a psychiatric ward, he attempted to engage others in conversation. When asked by staff how he was feeling, he indicated that he was fine, that he no longer experienced symptoms. He responded to instructions from attendants, to calls for medication (which was not swallowed), and to dining hall instructions. Beyond such activities as were available to him on the admissions ward, he spent his time writing down his observations about the ward, its patients, and the staff. Initially these notes were written "secretly," but as it soon became clear that no one much cared, they were subsequently written on standard tablets of paper in such public places as the dayroom. No secret was made of these activities.

The pseudopatient, very much as a true psychiatric patient, entered a hospital with no foreknowledge of when he would be discharged. Each was told that he would have to get out by his own devices, essentially by convincing the staff that he was sane. The psychological stresses associated with hospitalization were considerable, and all but one of the pseudopatients desired to be discharged almost immediately after being admitted. They were, therefore, motivated not only to behave sanely, but to be paragons of cooperation. That their behavior was in no way disruptive is confirmed by nursing reports, which have been obtained on most of the patients. These reports uniformly indicate that the patients were "friendly," "cooperative," and "exhibited no abnormal indications."

The Normal Are Not Detectably Sane

Despite their public "show" of sanity, the pseudopatients were never detected. Admitted, except in one case, with a diagnosis of schizophrenia,[11] each was discharged with a diagnosis of schizophrenia "in remission." The label "in remission" should in no way be dismissed as a formality, for at no time during any hospitalization had any question been raised about any pseudopatient's simulation. Nor are there any indications in the hospital records that the pseudopatient's status was suspect. Rather the evidence is strong that, once labeled schizophrenic, the pseudopatient was stuck with that label. If the pseudopatient was to be discharged, he must naturally be "in remission"; but he was not sane, nor, in the institution's view, had he ever been sane.

The uniform failure to recognize sanity cannot be attributed to the quality of the hospitals, for, although there were considerable variations among them, several are considered excellent. Nor can it be alleged that there was simply not enough time to observe the pseudopatients. Length of hospitalization ranged from 7 to 52 days, with an average of 19 days. The pseudopatients were not, in fact, carefully observed, but this failure clearly speaks more to traditions within psychiatric hospitals than to lack of opportunity.

Finally, it cannot be said that the failure to recognize the pseudopatients' sanity was due to the fact that they were not behaving sanely. While there was clearly some tension present in all of them, their daily visitors could detect no serious behavioral consequences—nor, indeed, could other patients. It was quite common for the patients to "detect" the pseudopatients' sanity. During the first three hospitalizations, when accurate counts were kept, 35 of a total of 118 patients on the admissions ward voiced their suspicions, some vigorously. "You're not crazy. You're a journalist, or a professor [referring to the continual note-taking]. You're checking up on the hospital." While most of the patients were reassured by the pseudopatient's insistence that he had been sick before he came in but was fine now, some continued to believe that the pseudopatient was sane throughout his hospitalization.[12] The fact that the patients often recognized normality when staff did not raises important questions.

Failure to detect sanity during the course of hospitalization may be due to the fact that physicians operate with a strong bias toward what statisticians call the type 2 error.[6] This is to say that physicians are more inclined to call a healthy person sick (a false positive, type 2) than a sick person healthy (a false negative, type 1). The reasons for this are not hard to find; it is clearly more dangerous to misdiagnose illness than health. Better to err on the side of caution, to suspect illness even among the healthy.

But what holds for medicine does not hold equally well for psychiatry. Medical illnesses, while unfortunate, are not commonly pejorative. Psychiatric diagnoses, on the contrary, carry with them personal, legal, and social stigmas.[13] It was therefore important to see whether the tendency toward diagnosing the sane insane could be reversed. The following experiment was arranged at a research and teaching hospital whose staff had heard these findings but doubted that such an error could occur in their hospital. The staff was informed that at some time during the following 3 months one or more pseudopatients would attempt to be admitted into the psychiatric hospital. Each staff member was asked to rate each patient who presented himself at admissions or on the ward according to the likelihood that the patient was a pseudopatient. A 10-point scale was used, with a 1 and 2 reflecting high confidence that the patient was a pseudopatient.

Judgments were obtained on 193 patients who were admitted for psychiatric treatment. All staff who had had sustained contact with or primary responsibility for the patient—attendants, nurses, psychiatrists, physicians, and psychologists—were asked to make judgments. Forty-one patients were alleged, with high confidence, to be pseudopatients by at least one member of the staff. Twenty-three were considered suspect by at least one psychiatrist. Nineteen were suspected by one psychiatrist *and* one other staff member. Actually, no genuine pseudopatient (at least from my group) presented himself during this period.

The experiment is instructive. It indicates that the tendency to designate sane people as insane can be reversed when the stakes (in this case, prestige and diagnostic acumen) are high. But what can be said of the 19 people who were suspected of being "sane" by one psychiatrist and another staff member? Were these people truly "sane," or was it rather the case that in the course of avoiding the type 2 error the staff tended to make more errors of the first sort—calling the crazy "sane"? There is no way of knowing. But one thing is certain: any diagnostic process that lends itself so readily to massive errors of this sort cannot be a very reliable one.

The Stickiness of Psychodiagnostic Labels

Beyond the tendency to call the healthy sick—a tendency that accounts better for diagnostic behavior on admission than it does for such behavior after a lengthy period of exposure—the data speak to the massive role of labeling in psychiatric assessment. Having once been labeled schizophrenic, there is nothing the pseudopatient can do to overcome the tag. The tag profoundly colors others' perceptions of him and his behavior.

From one viewpoint, these data are hardly surprising, for it has long been known that elements are given meaning by the context in which they occur. Gestalt psychology made this point vigorously, and Asch[14] demonstrated that there are "central" personality traits (such as "warm" versus "cold") which are so powerful that they markedly color the meaning of other information in forming an impression of a given personality.[15] "Insane," "schizophrenic," "manic-depressive," and "crazy" are probably among the most powerful of such central traits. Once a person is designated abnormal, all of his other behaviors and characteristics are colored by that label. Indeed, that label is so powerful that many of the pseudopatients' normal behaviors were overlooked entirely or profoundly misinterpreted. Some examples may clarify this issue.

Earlier I indicated that there were no changes in the pseudopatient's personal history and current status beyond those of name, employment, and, where necessary, vocation. Otherwise, a veridical description of personal history and circumstances was offered. Those circumstances were not psychotic. How were they made consonant with the diagnosis of psychosis? Or were those diagnoses modified in such a way as to bring them into accord with the circumstances of the pseudopatient's life, as described by him?

As far as I can determine, diagnoses were in no way affected by the relative health of the circumstances of a pseudopatient's life. Rather, the reverse occurred: the perception of his circumstances was shaped entirely by the diagnosis. A clear example of such translation is found in the case of a pseudopatient who had had a close relationship with his mother but was rather remote from his father during his early childhood. During adolescence and beyond, however, his father became a close friend, while his relationship with his mother cooled. His present relationship with his wife was characteristically close and warm. Apart from occasional angry exchanges, friction was minimal. The children had rarely been spanked. Surely there is nothing especially pathological about such a history. Indeed, many readers may see a similar pattern in their own experiences, with no markedly deleterious consequences. Observe, however, how such a history was translated in the psychopathological context, this from the case summary prepared after the patient was discharged.

> This white 39-year-old male...manifests a long history of considerable ambivalence in close relationships, which begins in early childhood. A warm relationship with his mother cools during his adolescence. A distant relationship to his father is described as becoming very intense. Affective stability is absent. His attempts to control emotionality with his wife and children are punctuated by angry outbursts and, in the case of the children, spankings. And while he says that he has several good friends, one senses considerable ambivalence embedded in those relationships also....

The facts of the case were unintentionally distorted by the staff to achieve consistency with a popular theory of the dynamics of a schizophrenic reaction.[16] Nothing of an ambivalent nature had been described in relations with parents, spouse, or friends. To the extent that ambivalence could be inferred, it was probably not greater than is found in all human relationships. It is true the pseudopatient's relationships with his parents changed over time, but in the ordinary context that would hardly be remarkable—indeed, it might very well be expected. Clearly, the meaning ascribed to his verbalizations (that is, ambivalence, affective instability) was determined by the diagnosis: schizophrenia. An entirely different meaning would have been ascribed if it were known that the man was "normal."

All pseudopatients took extensive notes publicly. Under ordinary circumstances, such behavior would have raised questions in the minds of observers, as, in fact, it did among patients. Indeed, it seemed so certain that the notes would elicit suspicion that elaborate precautions were taken to remove them from the ward each day. But the precautions proved needless. The closest any staff member came to questioning these notes occurred when one pseudopatient asked his physician what kind of medication he was receiving and began to write down the response. "You needn't write it," he was told gently. "If you have trouble remembering, just ask me again."

If no questions were asked of the pseudopatients, how was their writing interpreted? Nursing records for three patients indicate that the writing was seen as an aspect of their pathological behavior. "Patient engages in writing behavior" was the daily nursing comment on one of the pseudopatients who was never questioned about his writing. Given that the patient is in the hospital, he must be psychologically disturbed. And given that he is disturbed, continuous writing must be a behavioral manifestation of that disturbance, perhaps a subset of the compulsive behaviors that are sometimes correlated with schizophrenia.

One tacit characteristic of psychiatric diagnosis is that it locates the sources of aberration within the individual and only rarely within the complex of stimuli that surrounds him. Consequently, behaviors that are stimulated by the environment are commonly misattributed to the patient's disorder. For example, one kindly nurse found a pseudopatient pacing the long hospital corridors. "Nervous, Mr. X?" she asked. "No, bored," he said.

The notes kept by pseudopatients are full of patient behaviors that were misinterpreted by well-intentioned staff. Often enough, a patient would go "berserk" because he had, wittingly or unwittingly, been mistreated by, say, an attendant. A nurse coming upon the scene would rarely inquire even cursorily into the environmental stimuli of the patient's behavior. Rather, she assumed that his upset derived from his pathology, not from his present interactions with other staff members. Occasionally, the staff might assume that the patient's family (especially when they had recently visited) or other patients had stimulated the outburst. But never were the staff found to assume that one of themselves or the structure of the hospital had anything to do with a patient's behavior. One psychiatrist pointed to a group of patients who were sitting outside the cafeteria entrance half an hour before lunchtime. To a group of young residents he indicated that such behavior was characteristic of the oral-acquisitive nature of the syndrome. It seemed not to occur to him that there were very few things to anticipate in a psychiatric hospital besides eating.

A psychiatric label has a life and an influence of its own. Once the impression has been formed that the patient is schizophrenic, the expectation is that he will continue to be schizophrenic. When a sufficient amount of time has passed, during which the patient has done nothing bizarre, he is considered to be in remission and available for discharge. But the label endures beyond discharge, with the unconfirmed expectation that he will behave as a schizophrenic again. Such labels, conferred by mental health professionals, are as influential on the patient as they are on his relatives and friends, and it should not surprise anyone that the diagnosis acts on all of them as a self-fulfilling prophecy. Eventually, the patient himself accepts the diagnosis, with all of its surplus meanings and expectations, and behaves accordingly.[6]

The inferences to be made from these matters are quite simple. Much as Zigler and Phillips have demonstrated that there is enormous overlap in the symptoms presented by patients who have been variously diagnosed,[17] so there is enormous overlap in the behaviors of the sane and the insane. The sane are not "sane" all of the time. We lose our tempers "for no good reason." We are occasionally depressed or anxious, again for no good reason. And we may find it difficult to get along with one or another person—again for no reason that we can specify. Similarly, the insane are not always insane. Indeed, it was the impression of the pseudopatients while living with them that they were sane for long periods of time—that the bizarre behaviors upon which their diagnoses were allegedly predicated constituted only a small fraction of their total behavior. If it makes no sense to label ourselves permanently depressed on the basis of an occasional depression, then it takes better evidence than is presently available to label all patients insane or schizophrenic on the basis of bizarre behaviors or cognitions. It seems more useful, as Mischel[18] has pointed out, to limit our discussion to *behaviors,* the stimuli that provoke them, and their correlates.

It is not known why powerful impressions of personality traits, such as "crazy" or "insane," arise. Conceivably, when the origins of the stimuli that give rise to a behavior are remote or unknown, or when the behavior strikes us as immutable, trait labels regarding the *behaver* arise. When, on the other hand, the origins and stimuli are known and available, discourse is limited to the behavior itself. Thus, I may hallucinate because I am sleeping, or I may hallucinate because I have ingested a peculiar drug. These are termed sleep-induced hallucinations, or dreams, and drug-induced hallucinations, respectively. But when the stimuli to my hallucinations are unknown, that is called craziness, or schizophrenia—as if that inference were somehow as illuminating as the others.

The Experience of Psychiatric Hospitalization

The term "mental illness" is of recent origin. It was coined by people who were humane in their inclinations and who wanted very much to raise the station of (and the public's sympathies toward) the psychologically disturbed from that of witches and "crazies" to one that was akin to the physically ill. And they were at least partially successful, for the treatment of the mentally ill *has* improved considerably over the years. But while treatment has improved, it is doubtful that people really regard the mentally ill in the same way that they view the physically ill. A broken leg is something one recovers from, but mental illness allegedly endures forever.[19] A broken leg does not threaten the observer, but a crazy schizophrenic? There is by now a host of evidence that attitudes toward the mentally ill are characterized by fear, hostility, aloofness, suspicion, and dread.[20] The mentally ill are society's lepers.

That such attitudes infect the general population is perhaps not surprising, only upsetting. But that they affect the professionals—attendants, nurses, physicians, psychologists, and social workers—who treat and deal with the mentally ill is more disconcerting, both because such attitudes are self-evidently pernicious and because they are unwitting. Most mental health professionals would insist that they are sympathetic toward the mentally ill, that they are neither avoidant nor hostile. But it is more likely that an exquisite ambivalence characterizes their relations with psychiatric patients, such that their avowed impulses are only part of their entire attitude. Negative attitudes are there too and can easily be detected. Such attitudes should not surprise us. They are the natural offspring of the labels patients wear and the places in which they are found.

Consider the structure of the typical psychiatric hospital. Staff and patients are strictly segregated. Staff have their own living space, including their dining facilities, bathrooms, and assembly places. The glassed quarters that contain the professional staff, which the pseudopatients came to call "the cage," sit out on every dayroom. The staff emerge primarily for caretaking purposes—to give medication, to conduct a therapy or group meeting, to instruct or reprimand a patient. Otherwise, staff keep to themselves, almost as if the disorder that afflicts their charges is somehow catching.

So much is patient-staff segregation the rule that, for four public hospitals in which an attempt was made to measure the degree to which staff and patients mingle, it was necessary to use "time out of the staff cage" as the operational measure. While it was not the case that all time spent out of the cage was spent mingling with patients (attendants, for example, would occasionally emerge to watch television in the dayroom), it was the only way in which one could gather reliable data on time for measuring.

The average amount of time spent by attendants outside of the cage was 11.3 percent (range 3 to 52 percent). This figure does not represent only time spent mingling with patients, but also includes time spent on such chores as folding laundry, supervising patients while they shave, directing ward clean-up, and sending patients to off-ward activities. It was the relatively rare attendant who spent time talking with patients or playing games with them. It proved impossible to obtain a "percent mingling time" for nurses, since the amount of time they spent out of the cage was too brief. Rather, we counted instances of emergence from the cage. On the average daytime nurses emerged from the cage 11.5 times per shift, including instances when they left the ward entirely (range, 4 to 39 times). Late afternoon and night nurses were even less available, emerging on the average 9.4 times per shift (range, 4 to 41 times). Data on early morning nurses, who arrived usually after midnight and departed at 8 a.m., are not available because patients were asleep during most of this period.

Physicians, especially psychiatrists, were even less available. They were rarely seen on the wards. Quite commonly, they would be seen only when they arrived and departed, with the remaining time being spent in their offices or in the cage. On the average, physicians emerged on the ward 6.7 times per day (range, 1 to 17 times). It proved difficult to make an accurate estimate in this regard, since physicians often maintained hours that allowed them to come and go at different times.

The hierarchical organization of the psychiatric hospital has been commented on before,[21] but the latent meaning of that kind of organization is worth noting again. Those with the most power have least to do with patients, and those with the least power are most involved with them. Recall, however, that the acquisition of role-appropriate behaviors occurs mainly through the observation of others, with the most powerful having the most influence. Consequently, it is understandable that attendants not only spend more time with patients than do any other members of the staff—that is required by their station in the hierarchy—but also, insofar as they learn from their superiors' behavior, spend as little time with patients as they can. Attendants are seen mainly in the cage, which is where the models, the action, and the power are.

I turn now to a different set of studies, these dealing with staff response to patient-initiated contact. It has long been known that the amount of time a person spends with you can be an index of your significance to him. If he initiates and maintains eye contact, there is reason to believe that he is considering your requests and needs. If he pauses to chat or actually stops and talks, there is added reason to infer that he is individuating you. In four hospitals, the pseudopatient approached the staff member with a request which took the following form: "Pardon me, Mr. [or Dr. or Mrs.] X, could you tell me when I will be eligible for grounds privileges?" (or "... when I will be presented at the staff meeting?" or "... when I am likely to be discharged?"). While the content of the question varied according to the appropriateness of the target and the pseudopatient's (apparent) current needs, the form was always a courteous and relevant request for information. Care was taken never to approach a particular member of the staff more than once a day, lest the staff member become suspicious or irritated. In examining these data, remember that the behavior of the pseudopatients was neither bizarre nor disruptive. One could indeed engage in good conversation with them.

The data for these experiments are shown in Table 1, separately for physicians (column 1) and for nurses and attendants (column 2). Minor differences between these four institutions were overwhelmed by the degree to which staff avoided continuing contacts that patients had initiated. By far, their most common response consisted of either a brief response to the question, offered while they were "on the move" and with head averted, or no response at all.

The encounter frequently took the following bizarre form: (pseudopatient) "Pardon me, Dr. X. Could you tell me when I am eligible for ground privileges?" (physician) "Good morning, Dave. How are you today?" (Moves off without waiting for a response.)

It is instructive to compare these data with data recently obtained at Stanford University. It has been alleged that large and eminent universities are characterized by faculty who are so busy that the have no time for students. For this comparison, a young lady approached individual faculty members who seemed to be walking purposefully to some meeting or teaching engagement and asked them the following six questions.

1) "Pardon me, could you direct me to Encina Hall?" (at the medical school: "...to the Clinical Research Center?").

TABLE 14.1 Self-initiated Contact by Pseudopatients with Psychiatrists and Nurses and Attendants, Compared to Contact with other Groups

	Psychiatric Hospitals		University Campus (non-medical)	University Medical Center Physicians		
Contact	**(1) Psychiatrists**	**(2) Nurses and Attendants**	**(3) Faculty**	**(4) "Looking for a Psychiatrist"**	**(5) "Looking for an Internist"**	**(6) No Additional Comment**
Responses						
Moves on, head averted (0%)	71	88	0	0	0	0
Makes eye contact (0%)	23	10	0	11	0	0
Pauses and chats (0%)	2	2	0	11	0	10
Stops and talks (0%)	4	0.5	100	78	100	90
Mean number of questions answered (out of 6)	*	*	6	3.8	4.8	4.5
Respondents (No.)	13	47	14	18	15	10
Attempts (No.)	185	1283	14	18	15	10

*Not applicable

2) "Do you know where Fish Annex is?" (there is no Fish Annex at Stanford).
3) "Do you teach here?"
4) "How does one apply for admission to the college?" (at the medical school: "... to the medical school?").
5) "Is it difficult to get in?"
6) "Is there financial aid?"

Without exception, as can be seen in Table 1 (column 3), all of the questions were answered. No matter how rushed they were, all respondents not only maintained eye contact, but stopped to talk. Indeed, many of the respondents went out of their way to direct or take the questioner to the office she was seeking, to try to locate "Fish Annex," or to discuss with her the possibilities of being admitted to the university.

Similar data, also shown in Table 1 (columns 4, 5, and 6), were obtained in the hospital. Here too, the young lady came prepared with six questions. After the first question, however, she remarked to 18 of her respondents (column 4), "I'm looking for a psychiatrist," and to 15 others (column 5), "I'm looking for an internist." Ten other respondents received no inserted comment (column 6). The general degree of cooperative responses is considerably higher for these university groups that it was for pseudopatients in psychiatric hospitals. Even so, differences are apparent within the medical school setting. Once having indicated that she was looking for a psychiatrist, the degree of cooperation elicited was less than when she sought an internist.

Powerlessness and Depersonalization

Eye contact and verbal contact reflect concern and individuation; their absence, avoidance and depersonalization. The data I have presented do not do justice to the rich daily encounters that grew up around matters of depersonalization and avoidance. I have records of patients who were beaten by staff for the sin of having initiated verbal contact. During my own experience, for example, one patient was beaten in the presence of other patients for having approached an attendant and told him, "I like you." Occasionally, punishment meted out to patients for misdemeanors seemed so excessive that it could not be justified by the most radical interpretations of psychiatric canon. Nevertheless, they appeared to go unquestioned. Tempers were often short. A patient who had not heard a call for medication would be roundly excoriated, and the morning attendants would often wake patients with, "Come on, you m——f——s, out of bed!"

Neither anecdotal nor "hard" data can convey the overwhelming sense of powerlessness which invades the individual as he is continually exposed to the depersonalization of the psychiatric hospital. It hardly matters *which* psychiatric hospital— the excellent public ones and the very plush private hospital were better than the rural and shabby ones in this regard, but, again, the features that psychiatric hospitals had in common overwhelmed by far their apparent differences.

Powerlessness was evident everywhere. The patient is deprived of many of his legal rights by dint of his psychiatric commitment.[22] He is shorn of credibility by virtue of his psychiatric label. His freedom of movement is restricted. He cannot initiate contact with the staff, but may only respond to such overtures as they make. Personal privacy is minimal. Patient quarters and possessions can be entered and examined by any staff member, for whatever reason. His personal history and anguish is available to any staff member (often including the "grey lady" and "candy striper" volunteer) who chooses to read his folder, regardless of their therapeutic relationship to him. His personal hygiene and waste evacuation are often monitored. The water closets may have no doors.

At times, depersonalization reached such proportions that pseudopatients had the sense that they were invisible, or at least unworthy of account. Upon being admitted, I and other pseudopatients took the initial physical examinations in a semipublic room, where staff members went about their own business as if we were not there.

On the ward, attendants delivered verbal and occasionally serious physical abuse to patients in the presence of other observing patients, some of whom (the pseudopatients) were writing it all down. Abusive behavior, on the other hand, terminated quite abruptly when other staff members were known to be coming. Staff are credible witnesses. Patients are not.

A nurse unbuttoned her uniform to adjust her brassiere in the presence of an entire ward of viewing men. One did not have the sense that she was being seductive. Rather, she didn't notice us. A group of staff persons might point to a patient in the dayroom and discuss him animatedly, as if he were not there.

One illuminating instance of depersonalization and invisibility occurred with regard to medications. All told, the pseudopatients were administered nearly 2100 pills, including Elavil, Stelazine, Compazine, and Thorazine to name but a few. (That such a variety of medications should have been administered to patients presenting identical symptoms is itself worthy of note.) Only two were swallowed. The rest were either pocketed or deposited in the toilet. The pseudopatients were not alone in this. Although I have no precise records on how many patients rejected their medications, the pseudopatients frequently found the medications of other patients in the toilet before they deposited their own. As long as they were cooperative, their behavior and the pseudopatients' own in this matter, as in other important matters, went unnoticed throughout.

Reactions to such depersonalization among pseudopatients were intense. Although they had come to the hospital as participant observers and were fully aware that they did not "belong," they nevertheless found themselves caught up in and fighting the process of depersonalization. Some examples: a graduate student in psychology asked his wife to bring his textbooks to the hospital so he could "catch up on his homework"—this despite the elaborate precautions taken to conceal his professional association. The same student, who had trained for quite some time to get into the hospital, and who had looked forward to the experience, "remembered" some drag races that he had wanted to see on the weekend and insisted that he be discharged by that time. Another pseudopatient attempted a romance with a nurse. Subsequently, he informed the staff that he was applying for admission to graduate school in psychology and was very likely to be admitted, since a graduate professor was one of his regular hospital visitors. The same person began to engage in psychotherapy with other patients—all of this as a way of becoming a person in an impersonal environment.

The Sources of Depersonalization

What are the origins of depersonalization? I have already mentioned two. First are attitudes held by all of us toward the mentally ill—including those who treat them—attitudes characterized by fear, distrust, and horrible expectations on the one hand, and benevolent intentions on the other. Our ambivalence leads, in this instance as in others, to avoidance.

Second, and not entirely separate, the hierarchical structure of the psychiatric hospital facilitates depersonalization. Those who are at the top have least to do with patients, and their behavior inspires the rest of the staff. Average daily contact with psychiatrists, psychologists, residents, and physicians combined ranged from 3.9 to 25.1 minutes, with an overall mean of 6.8 (six pseudopatients over a total of 129 days of hospitalization). Included in this average are time spent in the admissions interview, ward meetings in the presence of a senior staff member, group and individual psychotherapy contacts, case presentation conferences, and discharge meetings. Clearly, patients do not spend much time in interpersonal contact with doctoral staff. And doctoral staff serve as models for nurses and attendants.

There are probably other sources. Psychiatric installations are presently in serious financial straits. Staff shortages are pervasive, staff time at a premium. Something has to give, and that something is patient contact. Yet, while financial stresses are realities, too much can be made of them. I have the impression that the psychological forces that result in depersonalization are much stronger than the fiscal ones and that the addition of more staff would not correspondingly improve patient care in this regard. The incidence of staff meetings and the enormous amount of record-keeping on patients, for example, have not been as substantially reduced as has patient contact. Priorities exist, even during hard times. Patient contact is not a significant priority in the traditional psychiatric hospital, and fiscal pressures do not account for this. Avoidance and depersonalization may.

Heavy reliance upon psychotropic medication tacitly contributes to depersonalization by convincing staff that treatment is indeed being conducted and that further patient contact may not be necessary. Even here, however, caution needs to be exercised in understanding the role of psychotropic drugs. If patients were powerful rather than powerless, if they were viewed as interesting individuals rather than diagnostic entities, if they were socially significant rather than social lepers, if their anguish truly and wholly compelled our sympathies and concerns, would we not *seek* contact with them, despite the availability of medications? Perhaps for the pleasure of it all?

The Consequences of Labeling and Depersonalization

Whenever the ratio of what is known to what needs to be known approaches zero, we tend to invent "knowledge" and assume that we understand more than we actually do. We seem unable to acknowledge that we simply don't know. The needs for diagnosis and remediation of behavioral and emotional problems are enormous. But rather than acknowledge that we are just embarking on understanding, we continue to label patients "schizophrenic," "manic-depressive," and "insane," as if in those words we had captured the essence of understanding. The facts of the matter are that we have known for a long time that diagnoses are often not useful or reliable, but we have nevertheless continued to use them. We now know that we cannot distinguish insanity from sanity. It is depressing to consider how that information will be used.

Not merely depressing, but frightening. How many people, one wonders, are sane but not recognized as such in our psychiatric institutions? How many have been needlessly stripped of their privileges of citizenship, from the right to vote and drive to that of handling their own accounts? How many have feigned insanity in order to avoid the criminal consequences of their behavior, and, conversely, how many would rather stand trial than live interminably in a psychiatric hospital—but wrongly thought to be mentally ill? How many have been stigmatized by well-intentioned, but nevertheless erroneous, diagnoses? On the last point, recall again that a "type 2 error" in psychiatric diagnosis does not have the same consequences it does in medical diagnosis. A diagnosis of cancer that has been found to be in error is cause for celebration. But psychiatric diagnoses are rarely found to be in error. The label sticks, a mark of inadequacy forever.

Finally, how many patients might be "sane" outside the psychiatric hospitals but seem insane in it—not because craziness resides in them, as it were, but because they are responding to a bizarre setting, one that may be unique to institutions which harbor neither people? Goffman[5] calls the process of socialization to such institutions "mortification"—an apt metaphor that includes the processes of depersonalization that have been described here. And while it is impossible to know whether the pseudopatient's responses to these processes are characteristic of all inmates—they were, after all, not real patients—it is difficult to believe that these processes of socialization to a psychiatric hospital provide useful attitudes or habits of response for living in the "real world."

Summary and Conclusions

It is clear that we cannot distinguish the sane from the insane in psychiatric hospitals. The hospital itself imposes a special environment in which the meanings of behavior can easily be misunderstood. The consequences to patients hospitalized in such an environment—the powerlessness, depersonalization, segregation, mortification, and self-labeling—seem undoubtedly counter-therapeutic.

I do not, even now, understand this problem well enough to perceive solutions. But two matters seem to have some promise. The first concerns the proliferation of community mental health facilities, of crisis intervention centers, of the human potential movement, and of behavior therapies that, for all of their own problems, tend to avoid psychiatric labels, to focus on specific problems and behaviors, and to retain the individual in a relatively non-pejorative environment. Clearly, to the extent that we refrain from sending the distressed to insane places, our impressions of them are less likely to be distorted. (The risk of distorted perceptions, it seems to me, is always present, since we are much more sensitive to an individual's behaviors and verbalizations than we are to the subtle contextual stimuli that often promote them. At issue here is a matter of magnitude. And, as I have shown, the magnitude of distortion is exceedingly high in the extreme context that is a psychiatric hospital.)

The second matter that might prove promising speaks to the need to increase the sensitivity of mental health workers and researchers to the *Catch 22* position of psychiatric patients. Simply reading materials in this area will be of help to some such workers and researchers. For others, directly experiencing the impact of psychiatric hospitalization will be of enormous use. Clearly, further research into the social psychology of such total institutions will both facilitate treatment and deepen understanding.

I and the other pseudopatients in the psychiatric setting had distinctly negative reactions. We do not pretend to describe the subjective experiences of true patients. Theirs may be different from ours, particularly with the passage of time and the necessary process of adaptation to one's environment. But we can and do speak to the relatively more objective indices of treatment within the hospital. It could be a mistake, and a very unfortunate one, to consider that what happened to us derived from malice or stupidity on the part of the staff. Quite the contrary, our overwhelming impression of them was of people who really cared, who were committed and who were uncommonly intelligent. Where they failed, as they sometimes did painfully, it would be more accurate to attribute those failures to the environment in which they, too, found themselves than to personal callousness. Their perceptions and behavior were controlled by the situation, rather than being motivated by a malicious disposition. In a more benign environment, one that was less attached to global diagnosis, their behaviors and judgments might have been more benign and effective.

Notes

1. I thank W. Mischel, E. Orne, and M. S. Rosenhan for comments on an earlier draft of this manuscript.

2. P. Ash, *J. Abnorm. Soc. Psychol.* 44, 272 (1949); A. T. Beck, *Amer. J. Psychiat.* 119, 210 (1962); A. T. Boisen, *Psychiatry* 2, 233 (1938); N. Kreitman, *J. Ment. Sci.* 107, 876 (1961); N. Kreitman, P. Sainsbury, J. Morrisey, J. Towers, J. Scrivener, *ibid.*, p. 887; H. O. Schmitt and C. P. Fonda, *J. Abnorm. Soc. Psychol.* 52, 262 (1956); W. Seeman, *J. Nerv. Dis.* 118, 541 (1953). For an analysis of these artifacts and summaries of the disputes, see J. Zubin. *Annu. Rev. Psychol.* 18, 373 (1967); L. Phillips and J. G. Draguns, *ibid.* 22, 447 (1971).

3. R. Benedict. *J. Gen. Psychol.* 10, 59 (1934).

4. See in this regard H. Becker, *Outsiders: Studies in the Sociology of Deviance* (Free Press, New York, 1963); B. M. Braginsky, D. D. Braginsky, K. Ring, *Methods of Madness: The Mental Hospital as a Last Resort* (Holt, Rinehart & Winston, New York, 1969); G. M. Crocetti and P. V. Lemkau, *Amer. Sociol. Rev.* 30, 577 (1965); E. Goffman, *Behavior in Public Places* (Free Press, New York, 1964); R. D. Laing, *The Divided Self: A Study of Sanity and Madness* (Quadrangle, Chicago, 1960); D. L. Phillips, *Amer. Sociol. Rev.* 28. (1963); T. R. Sarbin, *Psychol. Today* 6, 18 (1972); E. Schur. *Amer. J. Sociol.* 75, 309 (1969); T. Szasz, *Law, Liberty and Psychiatry* (Macmillan, New York, 1963); *The Myth of Mental Illness: Foundations of a Theory of Mental Illness* (Hoeber-Harper, New York, 1963). For a critique of some of these views, see W. R. Gove, *Amer. Sociol. Rev.* 35, 873 (1970).

5. E. Goffman, *Asylums* (Doubleday, Garden City, N.Y., 1961).

6. T. J. Scheff, *Being Mentally Ill: A Sociological Theory* (Aldine, Chicago, 1966).

7. Data from a ninth pseudopatient are not incorporated in this report because, although his sanity went undetected, he falsified aspects of his personal history, including his marital status and parental relationships. His experimental behaviors therefore were not identical to those of the other pseudopatients.

8. A. Barry, *Bellevue Is a State of Mind* (Harcourt Brace Jovanovich, New York, 1971); I. Belknap, *Human Problems of a State Mental Hospital* (McGraw-Hill, New York, 1956); W. Caudill, F. C. Redlich, H. R. Gilmore, E. B. Brody, *Amer. J. Orthopsychiat.* 22, 314 (1952); A. R. Goldman, R. H. Bohr, T. A. Steinberg, *Prof. Psychol.* 1, 427 (1970); unauthored, *Roche Report* 1 (No. 13), 8 (1971).

9. Beyond the personal difficulties that the pseudopatient is likely to experience in the hospital, there are legal and social ones that, combined, require considerable attention before entry. For example, once admitted to a psychiatric institution, it is difficult, if not impossible, to be discharged on short notice, state law to the contrary notwithstanding. I was not sensitive to these difficulties at the outset of the project, nor to the personal and situational emergencies that can arise, but later a writ of habeas corpus was prepared for each of the entering pseudopatients and an attorney was kept "on call" during every hospitalization. I am grateful to

John Kaplan and Robert Bartels for legal advice and assistance in these matters.

10. However distasteful such concealment is, it was a necessary first step to examining these questions. Without concealment, there would have been no way to know how valid these experiences were; nor was there any way of knowing whether whatever detections occurred were a tribute to the diagnostic acumen of the staff or the hospital's rumor network. Obviously, since my concerns are general ones that cut across individual hospitals and staffs, I have respected their anonymity and have eliminated clues that might lead to their identification.

11. Interestingly, of the 12 admissions, 11 were diagnosed as schizophrenic and one, with the identical symptomatology, as manic-depressive psychosis. This diagnosis has a more favorable prognosis, and it was given by the only private hospital in our sample. On the relations between social class and psychiatric diagnosis, see A. deB. Hollingshead and F. C. Redlich, *Social Class and Mental Illness: A Community Study* (Wiley, New York, 1958).

12. It is possible, of course, that patients have quite broad latitudes in diagnosis and therefore are inclined to call many people sane, even those whose behavior is patently aberrant. However, although we have no hard data on this matter, it was our distinct impression that this was not the case. In many instances, patients not only singled us out for attention, but came to imitate our behaviors and styles.

13. J. Cumming and E. Cumming, *Community Ment. Health* 1, 135 (1965); A. Farina and K. Ring, *J. Abnorm. Psychol.* 70, 47 (1965); H. E. Freeman and O. G. Simmons, *The Mental Patient Comes Home* (Wiley, New York, 1963); W. J. Johannsen, *Ment. Hygiene.* 53, 218 (1969); A. S. Linsky, *Soc. Psychiat.* 5, 166 (1970).

14. S. E. Asch, *J. Abnorm. Soc. Psychol.* 41, 258 (1946); *Social Psychology* (Prentice-Hall, New York, 1952).

15. See also I. N. Mensh and J. Wishner, *J. Personality* 16, 188 (1947); J. Wishner, *Psychol. Rev.* 67, 96 (1960); J. S. Bruner and R. Tagiuri, in *Handbook of Social Psychology,* G. Lindzey, Ed. (Addison-Wesley, Cambridge, Mass., 1954), vol. 2, pp. 634–654; J. S. Bruner, D. Shapiro, R. Tagiuri, in *Person Perception and Interpersonal Behavior,* R. Tagiuri and L. Petrullo, Eds. (Stanford Univ. Press, Stanford, Calif., 1958), pp. 277–288.

16. For an example of a similar self-fulfilling prophecy, in this instance dealing with the "central" trait of intelligence, see R. Rosenthal and L. Jacobson, *Pygmalion in the Classroom* (Holt, Rinehart & Winston, New York, 1968).

17. E. Zigler and L. Phillips, *J. Abnorm. Soc. Psychol.* 63, 69 (1961). See also R. K. Freudenberg and J. P. Robertson, *American Medical Association Arch. Neurol. Psychiat.* 76, 14 (1956).

18. W. Mischel, *Personality and Assessment* (Wiley, New York, 1968).

19. The most recent and unfortunate instance of this tenet is that of Senator Thomas Eagleton.

20. T. R. Sarbin and J. C. Mancuso, *J. Clin. Consult. Psychol.* 35, 159 (1970); T. R. Sarbin, *ibid.* 31, 447 (1967); J. C. Nunnally, Jr., *Popular Conceptions of Mental Health* (Holt, Rinehart & Winston, New York, 1961).

21. A. H. Stanton and M. S. Schwartz, *The Mental Hospital: A Study of Institutional Participation in Psychiatric Illness and Treatment* (Basic, New York, 1954).

22. D. B. Wexler and S. E. Scoville, *Ariz. Law Rev.* 13, 1 (1971).

Chapter 15

White-Collar Crime

The constructionist approach is useful for pointing out that what white-collar crime is, is a social construct. It is not an action that exists in a state of nature. I do not mean simply that laws have been written by legislatures that designate or stipulate which business-related actions are white-collar or corporate crimes. I mean that what is seen and regarded as a crime—by agents of the criminal justice system, by the public at large, and by criminologists—does not simply follow the guidelines laid down by the criminal law. In general, white-collar crime is "real" crime according to the law, but it may not be so regarded by these audiences I just mentioned. At least it is not so regarded to the same degree as with street crime, "ordinary" crime, "traditional" crime—what the Federal Bureau of Investigation (FBI) refers to as Index Crimes. This is what I mean when I say that it is a social construct.

Most of us, both inside and outside the criminal justice system, have a stereotypical notion of what a crime is. And it most emphatically does *not* include the majority of white-collar or corporate crimes. It does not generate the same degree of outrage as serious street crimes, as Edwin Sutherland, author of "Is 'White Collar Crime' Crime?", our first selection in this section, points out. A convicted white-collar criminal is not seen by the general public as being tainted by the same stigma or shame as a street criminal is. Corporate and white-collar crime are also less likely to lead to arrest, on a crime-for-crime basis (although this varies by the *kind* of street crime we are discussing and, my guess is, the kind of white-collar crime as well). Conviction is certainly less likely to lead to a lengthy prison sentence. And criminologists and sociologists of crime are less likely to study and write about it (although there has been far more attention to white-collar crime over the past generation than was true in previous decades). There is a selective or biased attention paid to white-collar crime *as* crime. The question is, why?

Two possibilities present themselves. One possible explanation for this selective perception has to do with factors that are extraneous or extrinsic to the nature of the offense, some sort of contingency that is external to the offense itself. This is the sort of explanation the constructionist would favor. Socioeconomic status is one possible contingency. The reason why corporate and white-collar crime is not regarded or treated as real crime has to do with, let's say, the respectability of the offender. Or perhaps power is the explanation; for instance, the explanation might lie in the ties between the offender and various crucial social actors that could mitigate or soften the criminal nature of the offense, such as connections with politicians or executives in the media.

A second possibility would be the explanation favored by the essentialist: that this discrepancy is related to the features that are intrinsic or essential to or indwelling within the nature of white-collar crime itself. Perhaps white-collar and corporate crime is not regarded as real crime because *in fact* it is not like real crimes in its impact: It doesn't harm the public to the same degree, or not as much is stolen from the public. Unfortunately for this argument, in terms of overall or gross impact, white-collar crime *is* real crime. If, for instance, we are talking about the total amount of money that is stolen from the public pocket, white-collar crime has *more* impact than ordinary street crime. One crook like Michael Milken or Ivan Boesky, convicted Wall Street swindlers, can steal more money than an entire *category* of thieves. Officially, according to the Federal Bureau of Investigation, ordinary, run-of-the-mill robbers on the street stole roughly half a billion dollars in the United States in 1994. Half a billion, while far from a small sum, is vastly less than what our two big-time crooks stole in a single year when they were in their heyday. Another example: The American public will be paying for the savings and loan collapse—caused in part by a variety of illegal and unethical banking practices—for well into the twenty-first century. It will represent a loss that the taxpayer will have to pay to the tune of at least $1,500 for every man, woman, and child (Pizzo et al., 1992). Now, that's a substantial sum of money! Next to that, the half billion stolen by robbers each year, which averages out to roughly $12 for every man, woman, and child in the country, seems mighty small.

There is also a stereotype of white-collar crime as not being physically harmful. This is not entirely true. White-collar and corporate crime can kill. They can kill consumers, workers, and the general public. Illegal pollution is certainly responsible for uncounted (and possibly uncountable) deaths every year. The failure to install required safety features in the work setting kills thousands of workers every year in the United States. The manufacture and sale of illegal and unsafe products likewise kills hundreds, possibly thousands of Americans each year; worldwide, the number is certainly incalculable. So, the loss of human life is there. Both monetary loss and loss of life and limb are substantial with white-collar and corporate crime. Why aren't white-collar and corporate crime regarded as real crime by most of us?

Sutherland certainly makes a persuasive case that white-collar crime should be regarded as real crime. It contains all the necessary defining qualities (though it does not, as Sutherland points out, contain any of the ancillary or secondary qualities, such as lower socioeconomic status of offenders). Insofar as white-collar crime is included as a chapter in all criminology textbooks, it is a real crime in the field of criminology. Insofar as it is seen as a legitimate subject for a criminologist to study, again, it can be seen as a real crime. (However, in the 1930s and 1940s, when Sutherland was writing, this was not as true as it is today. In this sense, things have changed in the past couple of generations.) Still, white-collar crime does not fit many—possibly most—people's notion of a crime. Sutherland discusses the various factors that help explain this puzzle. Some of them are extraneous or extrinsic to the nature of the crime. The status of the executive is one factor that mitigates against many of us seeing white-collar crime as real crime. Legislators and executives are part of the same social circles, Sutherland argues. Politicians and legislators do not criminalize the activities of their friends, colleagues, and associates.

Sutherland also believed that penal sanctions were becoming less severe over time, which leads us to enforce offenses less strictly than was true previously. The overall decline in penal sanction Sutherland discusses may have been taking place in the 1930s and 1940s, but it is not true today, in the punitive 1990s. Today, with a tougher, more conservative mood gripping the country, lengthier, not more lenient, sentences will increasingly be the rule. But especially telling in our inquiry as to whether white-collar and corporate crime is real crime is the degree of public outrage or resentment against white-collar criminals as opposed to that generated by other, traditional, or ordinary street crimes. This is itself a factor that needs explaining. Why the disparity? Why is the public so much more tolerant and lenient toward business crimes?

Some of the reasons are related specifically to the nature of the offense (though, as we saw, not to the nature of the harm supposedly caused by the offense, because many corporate crimes can harm consumers, workers, and the general public). The complexity of the offense is a major factor in this equation. Who did it? Who is responsible for committing the offense? This isn't always clear. A given white-collar or corporate crime could have been committed by dozens of people, by the members of a committee. Each member of a committee may be responsible for one tiny piece of the overall action. Or the decision may be a collective decision, made as a result of interaction and negotiation among many people. The act or decision may be spatially and temporally diffuse. It may be "intermingled with legitimate behavior," to quote Michael Benson, author of "Denying the Guilty Mind," our second reading in this section. This is an intrinsic feature of white-collar crime, and it does contrast sharply with ordinary run-of-the-mill street crimes. With street crime, if we have enough evidence, we can almost always point to a specific person or set of persons who committed the illegal actions. The criminal act is more straightforward, more clear-cut; agency or authorship is almost always obvious, that is, the question of who did it is not nearly so ambiguous as with corporate crime.

In addition, victimization is likely to be diffuse, spread out over time and in portions of the population. Harm is not always easily conceptualized or identifiable. In contrast, street crime is not only generally the work of one or several individuals offending against one or several victims and the act is temporally and physically specific and concrete but also the nature of the victimization is likely to be more specific and concrete. The impact of street crime is direct and typically unambiguous. Person A hits person B over the head with a baseball bat. Person X holds a gun on person Y and demands and takes his wallet. Though some street crimes are not so concrete, street crime tends to be much more direct in its nature and its impact than white-collar crime. This makes outrage and resentment, as Sutherland says, less likely and less intense for white-collar and corporate crime.

The media do not focus on white-collar crime in so dramatic a fashion as they do with street crime. There have been some noticeable exceptions in recent years; after all, it's hard to ignore cases involving billions of dollars. Still, white-collar crimes are typically complex, often difficult to understand, and technical in nature. They do not make good copy, as members of the media say. They do not usually make for juicy, sensationalistic stories that get page one coverage and a prominent place on TV news. When they do get space in newspapers, they are usually reported only in *The Wall Street Journal* or the financial section of *The New York Times*. Such stories, while there are exceptions, tend not to be reported in the hard news section of the newspaper. They rarely break into television news unless, again, the sums involved are huge. Most of us—and this is a fact that all criminologists have to acknowledge—are bored by stories of corporate misdeeds. It is rare that we have the economic and financial training to understand the nature of the offenses; for the so-called man and woman in the street, there is usually little intrinsic drama in these stories. The shotgun robbery of a downtown bank of $100,000—now *that's* a story! The gangland execution of a mob figure while he's eating a plate of linguine—that grabs our attention! The rape of a woman jogging through a park is regarded as news. A daring jewel heist from a famous jewelry store, again, captures the attention and fancy of the public. But most white-collar crimes don't make it as news to most of us. Most of the public would turn the channel or the page if they were confronted with such a story. With rare exceptions, we are just not as interested in such stories as we are in the meat-and-potatoes serious street crime.

I'm not convinced that Sutherland's second argument, that less attention is paid to white-collar crime as a result of the fact that media executives are involved in the same activities and social circles as white-collar criminals are. To me, that sounds too conspiratorial. The media *do* sometimes report these crimes (though not, as we saw, to the same degree). The fact is, when they do report illegal corporate doings, the public is not stirred by these stories. There is something in most of us that generates less interest and less outrage by the vast majority of white-collar crimes. Most of us are part of this crime-construction process that says that white-collar and corporate crime are not real crimes to the same degree that street crime is. And this is not likely to change very much in the years and decades to come.

In addition to the general public, the criminal justice system, and criminologists, white-collar and corporate criminals have another audience who evaluate their actions and what their actions mean for who they are—themselves. For the most part, corporate criminals are respectable men and women. (The vast majority are men.) They have an extremely difficult time thinking of themselves as ordinary criminals, even after a criminal conviction. Hence, they must engage in various explanations and justifications—some observers would refer to them as "rationalizations"—so that they can feel better about themselves, especially after conviction. They must engage in "denying the guilty mind," in Michael Benson's phraseology. They make some of the following statements: Everyone has to do what I did to survive in business. It's routine business practice. Everybody does it. I just happened to get caught. I'm basically honest. I'm a scapegoat for all the other crooks. I don't *feel* like a criminal. And so on. We encountered deviant justifiers in the study of rapists by Diana Scully and Joseph Marolla, in Chapter 12. When we encounter justifications such as these, we know we have an example of deviance on our hands and that the constructionist enterprise taps a crucial dimension in the drama of deviance.

Reference

Pizzo, Stephen, Mary Fricker, and Paul Muolo. 1992. *Inside Job: The Looting of America's Savings and Loans*. New York: McGraw-Hill.

Is "White Collar Crime" Crime?

EDWIN H. SUTHERLAND

The argument has been made that business and professional men commit crimes which should be brought within the scope of the theories of criminal behavior.[1] In order to secure evidence as to the prevalence of such white collar crimes an analysis was made of the decisions by courts and commissions against the seventy largest industrial and mercantile corporations in the United States under four types of laws, namely, antitrust, false advertising, National Labor Relations, and infringement of patents, copyrights, and trademarks. This resulted in the finding that 547 such adverse decisions had been made, with an average of 7.8 decisions per corporation and with each corporation having at least 1.[2] Although all of these were decisions that the behavior was unlawful, only 49 or 9 per cent of the total were made by criminal courts and were *ipso facto* decisions that the behavior was criminal. Since not all unlawful behavior is criminal behavior, these decisions can be used as a measure of criminal behavior only if the other 498 decisions can be shown to be decisions that the behavior of the corporations was criminal.

This is a problem in the legal definition of crime and involves two types of questions: May the word "crime" be applied to the behavior regarding which these decisions were made? If so, why is it not generally applied and why have not the criminologists regarded white collar crime as cognate with other crime? The first question involves semantics, the second interpretation or explanation.

A combination of two abstract criteria is generally regarded by legal scholars as necessary to define crime, namely: legal description of an act as socially injurious, and legal provision of a penalty for the act.[3]

When the criterion of legally defined social injury is applied to these 547 decisions the conclusion is reached that all of the classes of behaviors regarding which the decisions were made are legally defined as socially injurious. This can be readily determined by the words in the statutes—"crime" or "misdemeanor" in some, and "unfair," "discrimination," or "infringement" in all the others. The persons injured may be divided into two groups: first, a relatively small number of persons engaged in the same occupation as the offenders or in related occupations, and, second, the general public either as consumers or as constituents of the general social institutions which are affected by the violations of the laws. The antitrust laws are designed to protect competitors and also to protect the institution of free competition as the regulator of the economic system and thereby to protect consumers against arbitrary prices, and to protect the institution of democracy against the dangers of great concentration of wealth in the hands of monopolies. Laws against false advertising are designed to protect competitors against unfair competition and also to protect consumers against fraud. The National Labor Relations Law is designed to protect employees against coercion by employers and also to protect the general public against interferences with commerce due to strikes and lockouts. The laws against infringe-

From Edwin H. Sutherland, "Is 'White Collar Crime' Crime?" *American Sociological Review,* vol. 10 (April 1945), pp. 132–139.

ments are designed to protect the owners of patents, copyrights, and trademarks against deprivation of their property and against unfair competition, and also to protect the institution of patents and copyrights which was established in order to "promote the progress of science and the useful arts." Violations of these laws are legally defined as injuries to the parties specified.

Each of these laws has a logical basis in the common law and is an adaptation of the common law to modern social organization. False advertising is related to common law fraud, and infringement to larceny. The National Labor Relations Law, as an attempt to prevent coercion, is related to the common law prohibition of restrictions on freedom in the form of assault, false imprisonment, and extortion. For at least two centuries prior to the enactment of the modern antitrust laws the common law was moving against restraint of trade, monopoly, and unfair competition.

Each of the four laws provides a penal sanction and thus meets the second criterion in the definition of crime, and each of the adverse decisions under these four laws, except certain decisions under the infringement laws to be discussed later, is a decision that a crime was committed. This conclusion will be made more specific by analysis of the penal sanctions provided in the four laws.

The Sherman antitrust law states explicitly that a violation of the law is a misdemeanor. Three methods of enforcement of this law are provided, each of them involving procedures regarding misdemeanors. First, it may be enforced by the usual criminal prosecution, resulting in the imposition of fine or imprisonment. Second, the attorney general of the United States and the several district attorneys are given the "duty" of "repressing and preventing" violations of the law by petitions for injunctions, and violations of the injunctions are punishable as contempt of court. This method of enforcing a criminal law was an invention and, as will be described later, is the key to the interpretation of the differential implementation of the criminal law as applied to white collar criminals. Third, parties who are injured by violations of the law are authorized to sue for damages, with a mandatory provision that the damages awarded be three times the damages suffered. These damages in excess of reparation are penalties for violation of the law. They are payable to the injured party in order to induce him to take the initiative in the enforcement of the criminal law and in this respect are similar to the earlier methods of private prosecutions under the criminal law. All three of these methods of enforcement are based on decisions that a criminal law was violated and therefore that a crime was committed; the decisions of a civil court or a court of equity as to these violations are as good evidence of criminal behavior as is the decision of a criminal court.

The Sherman antitrust law has been amended by the Federal Trade Commission Law, the Clayton Law, and several other laws. Some of these amendments define violations as crimes and provide the conventional penalties, but most of the amendments do not make the criminality explicit. A large proportion of the cases which are dealt with under these amendments could be dealt with, instead, under the original Sherman Law, which is explicitly a criminal law. In practice, the amendments are under the jurisdiction of the Federal Trade Commission, which has authority to make official decisions as to violations. The Commission has two principal sanctions under its control, namely: the stipulation and the cease and desist order. The Commission may, after the violation of the law has been proved, accept a stipulation from the corporation that it will not violate the law in the future. Such stipulations are customarily restricted to the minor or technical violations. If a stipulation is violated or if no stipulation is accepted, the Commission may issue a cease and desist order; this is equivalent to a court's injunction except that violation is not punishable as contempt. If the Commission's desist order is violated, the Commission may apply to the court for an injunction, the violation of which is punishable as contempt. By an amendment to the Federal Trade Commission Law in the Wheeler-Lea Act of 1938 an order of the Commission becomes "final" if not officially questioned within a specified time and thereafter its violation is punishable by a civil fine. Thus, although certain interim procedures may be used in the enforcement of the amendments to the antitrust law, fines or imprisonment for contempt are available if the interim procedures fail. In this respect the interim procedures are similar to probation in ordinary criminal cases. An unlawful act is not defined as criminal by the fact that it is punished, but by the fact that it is punishable. Larceny is as truly a crime when the thief is placed on probation as when he is committed to prison. The argument may be made that punishment for contempt of court is not punishment for violation of the original law and that, therefore, the original law does not contain a penal sanction. This reasoning is specious since the original law provides the injunction with its penalty as a part of the procedure for enforcement. Consequently all of the decisions made under the amendments to the antitrust law are decisions that the corporations committed crimes.[4]

The laws regarding false advertising, as included in the decisions under consideration, are of two types. First, false advertising in the form of false labels is defined in the Pure Food and Drug Law as a misdemeanor and is punishable by a fine. Second, false advertising generally is defined in the Federal Trade Commission Act as unfair competition. Cases of the second type are under the jurisdiction of the Federal Trade Commission, which uses the same procedures as in antitrust cases. Penal sanctions are available in antitrust cases, as previously described, and are similarly available in these cases of false advertising. Thus, all of the decisions in false advertising cases are decisions that the corporations committed crimes.

The National Labor Relations Law of 1935 defines a violation as "unfair labor practice." The National Labor Relations Board is authorized to make official decisions as to violations of the law and, in case of violation, to issue desist orders and also to make certain remedial orders, such as reimbursement of employees who have been dismissed or demoted because of activities in collective bargaining. If an order is violated, the Board may apply to the court for enforcement and a violation of the order of the court is punishable as contempt. Thus, all of the decisions under this law, which is enforceable by penal sanctions, are decisions that crimes were committed.

The methods for the repression of infringements vary. Infringements of a copyright or a patented design are defined as misdemeanors, punishable by fines. No case of this type has been discovered against the seventy corporations. Other infringements are not explicitly defined in the statutes on patents, copyrights, and trademarks as crimes and agents of the state are not authorized by these statutes to initiate actions against violators of the law. Nevertheless, infringements may be punished in either of two ways: First, agents of the State may initiate action against infringers under the Federal Trade Commission Law as unfair competition and they do so, especially against infringers of copyrights and trademarks; these infringements are then punishable in the same sense as violations of the amendments to the antitrust laws. Second, the patent, copyright, and trade mark statutes provide that the damages awarded to injured owners of those rights may be greater than (in one statute as much as threefold) the damages actually suffered. These additional damages are not mandatory, as in the Sherman antitrust law, but on the other hand they are not explicitly limited to wanton and malicious infringements. Three decisions against the seventy corporations under the patent law and one under the copyright law included awards of such additional damages and on that account were classified in the tabulation of decisions as evidence of criminal behavior of the corporations. The other decisions, 74 in number, in regard in infringements were classified as not conclusive evidence of criminal behavior and were discarded. However, in 20 of these 74 cases the decisions of the court contain evidence which would be sufficient to make a *prima facie* case in a criminal prosecution; evidence outside these decisions which may be found in the general descriptions of practices regarding patents, copyrights, and trademarks, justifies a belief that a very large proportion of the 74 cases did, in fact, involve willful infringement of property rights and might well have resulted in the imposition of a penalty if the injured party and the court had approached the behavior from the point of view of crime.

In the preceding discussion the penalties which are definitive of crime have been limited to fine, imprisonment, and punitive damages. In addition, the stipulation, the desist order, and the injunction, without reference to punishment for contempt, have the attributes of punishment. This is evident both in that they result in some suffering on the part of the corporation against which they are issued and also in that they are designed by legislators and administrators to produce suffering. The suffering is in the form of public shame, as illustrated in more extreme form in the colonial penalty of sewing the letter "T" on the clothing of the thief. The design is shown in the sequence of sanctions used by the Federal Trade Commission. The stipulation involves the least publicity and the least discomfort, and it is used for minor and technical violations. The desist order is used if the stipulation is violated and also if the violation of the law is appraised by the Commission as willful and major. This involves more public shame; this shame is somewhat mitigated by the statements made by corporations, in exculpation, that such orders are merely the acts of bureaucrats. Still more shameful to the corporation is an injunction issued by a court. The shame resulting from this order is sometimes mitigated and the corporation's face saved by taking a consent decree.[5] The corporation may insist that the consent decree is not an admission that it violated the law. For instance, the meat packers took a consent decree in an antitrust case in 1921, with the explanation that they had not knowingly violated any law and were consenting to the decree without attempting to defend themselves because they wished to co-operate with the government in every possible way. This patriotic motivation appeared questionable, however, after the packers fought during almost all of the next ten years for a modification of the decree. Although the sequence of stipulation, desist order, and injunction indicates that the variations in public shame are designed, these orders have other functions, as well, especially a remedial function and the clarification of the law in a particular complex situation.

The conclusion in this semantic portion of the discussion is that 473 of the 547 decisions are decisions that crimes were committed.

This conclusion may be questioned on the ground that the rules of proof and evidence used in reaching these decisions are not the same as those used in decisions regarding other crimes, especially that some of the agencies which rendered the decisions did not require proof of criminal intent and did not presume the accused to be innocent. These rules of criminal intent and presumption of innocence, however, are not required in all prosecutions under the regular penal code and the number of exceptions is increasing. In many states a person may be committed to prison without protection of one or both of these rules on charges of statutory rape, bigamy, adultery, passing bad checks, selling mortgaged property, defrauding a hotel keeper, and other offenses.[6] Consequently the criteria which have been used in defining white collar crimes are not categorically different from the criteria used in defining other crimes, for these rules are abrogated both in regard to white collar crimes and other crimes, including some felonies. The proportion of decisions rendered against corporations without the protection of these rules is probably greater than the proportion rendered against other criminals, but a difference in proportions does not make the violations of law by corporations categorically different from the violations of laws by other criminals. Moreover, the difference in proportion, as the procedures actually operate is, not great. On the one side, many of the defendants in usual criminal cases, being in relative poverty, do not get good defense and consequently secure little benefit from these rules; on the other hand, the Commissions come close to observing these rules of proof and evidence although they are not required to do so. This is illustrated by the procedure of the Federal Trade Commission in regard to advertisements. Each year it examines several hundred thousand advertisements and appraises about 50,000 of them as probably false. From the 50,000 it selects about 1,500 as patently false. For instance, an advertisement of gumwood furniture as "mahogany" would seldom be an accidental error and would generally result from a state of mind which deviated from honesty by more than the natural tendency of human beings to feel proud of their handiwork.

The preceding discussion has shown that these seventy corporations committed crimes according to 473 adverse decisions, and also has shown that the criminality of their behavior was not made obvious by the conventional procedures of the criminal law but was blurred and concealed by special procedures. This differential implementation of the law as applied to the crimes of corporations eliminates or at least minimizes the stigma of crime. This differential implementation of the law began with the Sherman antitrust law of 1890. As previously described, this law is explicitly a criminal law and a violation of the law is a misdemeanor no matter what procedure is used. The customary policy would have been to rely entirely on criminal prosecution as the method of enforcement. But a clever invention was made in the provision of an injunction to enforce a criminal law; this was not only an invention but was a direct reversal of previous case law. Also, private parties were encouraged by treble damages to enforce a criminal law by suits in civil courts. In either case, the defendant did not appear in the criminal court and the fact that he had committed a crime did not appear in the face of the proceedings.

The Sherman antitrust law, in this respect, became the model in practically all the subsequent procedures authorized to deal with the crimes of corporations. When the Federal Trade Commission bill and the Clayton bill were introduced in Congress, they contained the conventional criminal procedures; these were eliminated in committee discussions, and other procedures which did not carry the external symbols of criminal process were substituted. The violations of these laws are crimes, as has been shown above, but they are treated as though they were not crimes, with the effect and probably the intention of eliminating the stigma of crime.

This policy of eliminating the stigma of crime is illustrated in the following statement by Wendell Berge, at the time assistant to the head of the antitrust division of the Department of Justice, in a plea for abandonment of the criminal prosecution under the Sherman antitrust law and the authorization of civil procedures with civil fines as a substitute.

> While civil penalties may be as severe in their financial effects as criminal penalties, yet they do not involve the stigma that attends indictment and conviction. Most of the defendants in antitrust cases are not criminals in the usual sense. There is not inherent reason why antitrust enforcement requires branding them as such.[7]

If a civil fine were substituted for a criminal fine, a violation of the antitrust law would be as truly a crime as it is now. The thing which would be eliminated would be the stigma of crime. Consequently, the stigma of crime has become a penalty in itself, which may be imposed in connection with other penalties or withheld, just as it is possible to combine imprisonment with a fine or have a fine without imprisonment. A civil fine is a financial penalty without the additional penalty of stigma, while a criminal fine is a financial penalty with the additional penalty of stigma.

When the stigma of crime is imposed as a penalty it places the defendant in the category of criminals and he becomes a criminal according to the popular stereotype of "the criminal." In primitive society "the criminal" was substantially the same as "the stranger,"[8] while in modern society "the criminal" is a person of less esteemed cultural attainments. Seventy-five per cent of the persons committed to state prisons are probably not, aside from their unesteemed cultural attainments, "criminals in the usual sense of the word." It may be excellent policy to eliminate the stigma of crime in a large proportion of cases, but the question at hand is why the law has a different implementation for white collar criminals than for others.

Three factors assist in explaining this differential implementation of the law, namely, the status of the business man, the trend away from punishment, and the relatively unorganized resentment of the public against white collar criminals. Each of these will be described.

First, the methods used in the enforcement of any law are an adaption to the characteristics of the prospective violators of the law, as appraised by the legislators and the judicial and administrative personnel. The appraisals regarding business men, who are the prospective violators of the four laws under consideration, include a combination of fear and admiration. Those who are responsible for the system of criminal justice are afraid to antagonize business men; among other consequences, such antagonism may result in a reduction in contributions to the campaign funds needed to win the next election. Probably much more important is the cultural homogeneity of legislators, judges, and administrators with business men. Legislators admire and respect business men and cannot conceive of them as criminals, that is, business men do not conform to the popular stereotype of "the criminal." The legislators are confident that these business men will conform as a result of very mild pressures.

This interpretation meets with considerable opposition from persons who insist that this is an egalitarian society in which all men are equal in the eyes of the law. It is not possible to give a complete demonstration of the validity of this interpretation but four types of evidence are presented in the following paragraphs as partial demonstration.

The Department of Justice is authorized to use both criminal prosecutions and petitions in equity to enforce the Sherman antitrust law. The Department has selected the method of criminal prosecution in a larger proportion of cases against trade unions than of cases against corporations, although the law was enacted primarily because of fear of the corporations. From 1890 to 1929 the Department of Justice initiated 438 actions under this law with decisions favorable to the United States. Of the actions against business firms and associations of business firms, 27 per cent were criminal prosecutions, while of the actions against trade unions 71 per cent were criminal prosecutions.[9] This shows that the Department of Justice has been comparatively reluctant to use a method against business firms which carries with it the stigma of crime.

The method of criminal prosecution in enforcement of the Sherman antitrust law has varied from one presidential administration to another. It has seldom been used in the administrations of the presidents who are popularly appraised as friendly toward business, namely, McKinley, Harding, Coolidge, and Hoover.

Business men suffered their greatest loss of prestige in the depression which began in 1929. It was precisely in this period of low status of business men that the most strenuous efforts were made to enforce the old laws and enact new laws for the regulation of business men. The appropriations for this purpose were multiplied several times and persons were selected for their vigor in administration of the laws. Of the 547 decisions against the seventy corporations during their life careers, which have averaged about forty years, 63 per cent were rendered in the period 1935–43, that is, during the period of the low status of business men.

The Federal Trade Commission Law states that a violation of the antitrust laws by a corporation shall be deemed to be, also, a violation by the officers and directors of the corporation. However, business men are practically never convicted as persons and several cases have been reported, like the six per cent case against the automobile manufacturers, in which the corporation was convicted and the persons who direct the corporation were all acquitted.[10]

A second factor in the explanation of the differential implementation of the law as applied to white collar criminals is the trend away from reliance on penal methods. This trend advanced more rapidly in the area of white collar crimes than of other crimes because this area, due to the recency of the statutes, is least bound by precedents and also because of the status of business men. This trend is seen in the almost complete abandonment of the most extreme penalties of death and physical torture; in the supplanting of conventional penal methods by non-penal methods such as probation and the case work methods which accompany probation; and in the supplementing of penal methods by non-penal methods, as in the development of case work and educational policies in prisons. These decreases in penal methods are explained by a series of social changes: the increased power of the lower socioeconomic class upon which previously most of the penalties were inflicted; the inclusion within the scope of the penal laws of a large part of the upper socioeconomic class as illustrated by traffic regulations; the increased social interaction among the classes, which has resulted in increased understanding and sympathy; the failure of penal methods to make substantial reductions in crime rates; and the weakening hold on the legal profession and others of the individualistic and hedonistic psychology which had placed great emphasis on pain in the control of behavior. To some extent overlapping those just mentioned is the fact that punishment, which was previously the chief reliance for control in the home, the school, and the church, has tended to disappear from those institutions, leaving the State without cultural support for its own penal methods.[11]

White collar crime is similar to juvenile delinquency in respect to the differential implementation of the law. In both cases, the procedures of the criminal law are modified so that the stigma of crime will not attach to the offenders. The stigma of crime has been less completely eliminated from juvenile delinquents than from white collar criminals because the procedures for the former are a less complete departure from conventional criminal procedures, because most juvenile delinquents come from a class with low social status, and because the juveniles have not organized to protect their good names. Because the juveniles have not been successfully freed from the stigma of crime they have been generally held to be within the scope of the theories of criminology and in fact provide a large part of the data for criminology; because the external symbols have been more successfully eliminated from white collar crimes, white collar crimes have generally not been included within these theories.

A third factor in the differential implementation of the law is the difference in the relation between the law and the mores in the area of white collar crime. The laws under consideration are recent and do not have a firm foundation in public ethics or business ethics; in fact certain rules of business ethics, such as the contempt for the "price chiseler," are generally in conflict with the law. These crimes are not obvious, as is assault and battery, and can be appreciated readily only by persons who are expert in the occupations in which they occur. A corporation often violates a law for a decade or longer before the administrative agency becomes aware of the violation, and in the meantime the violation may have become accepted practice in the industry. The effects of a white collar crime upon the public are diffused over a long period of time and perhaps over millions of people, with no person suffering much at a particular time. The public agencies of communication do not express and organize the moral sentiments of the community as to white collar crimes in part because the crimes are complicated and not easily presented as news, but probably in greater part because these agencies of communication are owned or controlled by the business men who violate the laws and because these agencies are themselves frequently charged with violations of the same laws. Public opinion in regard to picking pockets would not be well organized if most of the information regarding this crime came to the public directly from the pick-pockets themselves.

This third factor, if properly limited, is a valid part of the explanation of the differential implementation of the law. It tends to be exaggerated and become the complete explanation in the form of a denial that white collar crimes involve any moral culpability whatever. On that account it is desirable to state a few reasons why this factor is not the complete explanation.

The assertion is sometimes made that white collar crimes are merely technical violations and involve no moral culpability, i.e., violation of the mores, whatever. In fact, these white collar crimes, like other crimes, are distributed along a continuum in which the *mala in se* are at one extreme and the *mala prohibita* at the other.[12] None of the white collar crimes is purely arbitrary, as is the regulation that one must drive on the right side of the street, which might equally well be that he must drive on the left side.

The Sherman antitrust law, for instance, is regarded by many persons as an unwise law and it may well be that some other policy would be preferable. It is questioned principally by persons who believe in a more collectivistic economic system, namely, the communists and the leaders of big business, while its support comes largely from an emotional ideology in favor of free enterprise which is held by farmers, wage-earners, small business men, and professional men. Therefore, as appraised by the majority of the population it is necessary for the preservation of American institutions and its violation is a violation of strongly entrenched moral sentiments.

The sentimental reaction toward a particular white collar crime is certainly different from that toward some other crimes. This difference is often exaggerated, especially as the reaction occurs in urban society. The characteristic reaction of the average citizen in the modern city toward burglary is apathy unless he or his immediate friends are victims or unless the case is very spectacular. The average citizen, reading in his morning paper that the home of an unknown person has been burglarized by another unknown person, has no appreciable increase in blood pressure. Fear and resentment develop in modern society primarily as the result of the accumulation of crimes as depicted in crime rates or in general descriptions, and this develops both as to white collar crimes and other crimes.

Finally, although many laws have been enacted for the regulation of occupations other than business, such as agriculture or plumbing, the procedures used in the enforcement of those other laws are more nearly the same as the conventional criminal procedures, and law-violators in these other occupations are not so completely protected against the stigma of crime as are business men. The relation between the law and the mores tends to be circular. The mores are crystallized in the law and each act of enforcement of the laws tends to re-enforce the mores. The laws regarding white collar crime, which conceal the criminality of the behavior, have been less effective than other laws in re-enforcement of the mores.

Notes

1. Edwin H. Sutherland, "White Collar Criminality," *American Sociological Review*. 5:1–12, February, 1940; Edwin H. Sutherland, "Crime and Business," *Annals of the American Academy of Political and Social Science*. 217:112–18, September, 1941.

2. Paper on "Illegal Behavior of Seventy Corporations," to be published later.

3. The most satisfactory analysis of the criteria of crime from the legal point of view may be found in the following papers by Jerome Hall: "Prolegomena to a Science of Criminal Law," *University of Pennsylvania Law Review*. 89:549–80, March, 1941; "Interrelations of Criminal Law and Torts," *Columbia Law Review*. 43:735–79, 967–1001, September–November, 1943; "Criminal Attempts—A Study of the Foundations of Criminal Liability," *Yale Law Review*. 49:789–840, March, 1940.

4. Some of the antitrust decisions were made against meat packers under the Packers and Stockyards Act. The penal sanctions in this act are essentially the same as in the Federal Trade Commission Act.

5. The consent decree may be taken for other reasons, especially because it cannot be used as evidence in other suits.

6. Livingston Hall, "Statutory Law of Crimes, 1887–1936," *Harvard Law Review*. 50:616–53, February, 1937.

7. Wendell Berge, "Remedies Available to the Government under the Sherman Act," *Law and Contemporary Problems*. 7:111. January, 1940.

8. On the role of the stranger in punitive justice, see Ellsworth Faris, "The Origin of Punishment," *International Journal of Ethics*. 25:54–67, October, 1914; George H. Mead, "The Psychology of Punitive Justice," *American Journal of Sociology*. 23:577–602, March, 1918.

9. Percentages compiled from cases listed in the report of the Department of Justice "Federal Antitrust Laws, 1938."

10. The question may be asked, "If business men are so influential, why did they not retain the protection of the rules of the criminal procedure?" The answer is that they lost this protection, despite their status, on the principle "You can't eat your cake and have it, too."

11. The trend away from penal methods suggests that the penal sanction may not be a completely adequate criterion in the definition of crime.

12. An excellent discussion of this continuum is presented by Jerome Hall, "Prolegomena to a Science of Criminal Law," *University of Pennsylvania Law Review*. 89:563–69, March, 1941.

Denying the Guilty Mind: Accounting for Involvement in a White-Collar Crime

MICHAEL L. BENSON

Adjudication as a criminal is, to use Garfinkel's (1956) classic term, a degradation ceremony. The focus of this article is on how offenders attempt to defeat the success of this ceremony and deny their own criminality through the use of accounts. However, in the interest of showing in as much detail as possible all sides of the experience undergone by these offenders, it is necessary to treat first the guilt and inner anguish that is felt by many white-collar offenders even though they deny being criminals. This is best accomplished by beginning with a description of a unique feature of the prosecution of white-collar crimes.

In white-collar criminal cases, the issue is likely to be *why* something was done, rather than *who* did it (Edelhertz, 1970:47). There is often relatively little disagreement as to what happened. In the words of one Assistant U.S. Attorney interviewed for the study:

> If you actually had a movie playing, neither side would dispute that a person moved in this way and handled this piece of paper, etc. What it comes down to is, did they have the criminal intent?

If the prosecution is to proceed past the investigatory stages, the prosecutor must infer from the pattern of events that conscious criminal intent was present and believe that sufficient evidence exists to convince a jury of this interpretation of the situation. As Katz (1979:445–446) has noted, making this inference can be difficult because of the way in which white-collar illegalities are integrated into ordinary occupational routines. Thus, prosecutors in conducting trials, grand jury hearings, or plea negotiations spend a great deal of effort establishing that the defendant did indeed have the necessary criminal intent. By concentrating on the offender's motives, the prosecutor attacks the very essence of the white-collar offender's public and personal image as an upstanding member of the community. The offender is portrayed as someone with a guilty mind.

Not surprisingly, therefore, the most consistent and recurrent pattern in the interviews, though not present in all of them, was denial of criminal intent, as opposed to the outright denial of any criminal behavior whatsoever. Most offenders acknowledged that their behavior probably could be construed as falling within the conduct proscribed by stature, but they uniformly denied that their actions were motivated by a guilty mind. This is not to say, however, that offenders *felt* no guilt or shame as a result of conviction. On the contrary, indictment, prosecution, and conviction provoke a variety of emotions among offenders.

From Michael L. Benson, "Denying the Guilty Mind: Accounting for Involvement in a White-Collar Crime," *Criminology*, vol. 23 (November 1985), pp. 589–599.

The enormous reality of the offender's lived emotion (Denzin, 1984) in admitting guilt is perhaps best illustrated by one offender's description of his feelings during the hearing at which he plead guilty.

> You know (the plea's) what really hurt. I didn't even know I had feet. I felt numb. My head was just floating. There was no feeling, except a state of suspended animation.... For a brief moment, I almost hesitated. I almost said not guilty. If I had been alone, I would have fought, but my family....

The traumatic nature of this moment lies, in part, in the offender's feeling that only one aspect of his life is being considered. From the offender's point of view his crime represents only one small part of his life. It does not typify his inner self, and to judge him solely on the basis of this one event seems an atrocious injustice to the offender.

For some the memory of the event is so painful that they want to obliterate it entirely, as the two following quotations illustrate.

> I want quiet. I want to forget. I want to cut with the past.

> I've already divorced myself from the problem. I don't even want to hear the names of certain people ever again. It brings me pain.

For others, rage rather than embarrassment seemed to be the dominant emotion.

> I never really felt any embarrassment over the whole thing. I felt rage and it wasn't false or self-serving. It was really (something) to see this thing in action and recognize what the whole legal system has come to through its development, and the abuse of the grand jury system and the abuse of the indictment system....

The role of the news media in the process of punishment and stigmatization should not be overlooked. All offenders whose cases were reported on by the news media were either embarrassed or embittered or both by the public exposure.

> The only one I am bitter at is the newspapers, as many people are. They are unfair because you can't get even. They can say things that are untrue, and let me say this to you. They wrote an article on me that was so blasphemous, that was so horrible. They painted me as an insidious, miserable creature, wringing out the last penny....

Offenders whose cases were not reported on by the news media expressed relief at having avoided that kind of embarrassment, sometimes saying that greater publicity would have been worse than any sentence they could have received.

In court, defense lawyers are fond of presenting white-collar offenders as having suffered enough by virtue of the humiliation of public adjudication as criminals. On the other hand, prosecutors present them as cavalier individuals who arrogantly ignore the law and brush off its weak efforts to stigmatize them as criminals. Neither of these stereotypes is entirely accurate. The subjective effects of conviction on white-collar offenders are varied and complex. One suspects that this is true of all offenders, not only white-collar offenders.

The emotional responses of offenders to conviction have not been the subject of extensive research. However, insofar as an individual's emotional response to adjudication may influence the deterrent or crime-reinforcing impact of punishment on him or her, further study might reveal why some offenders stop their criminal behavior while others go on to careers in crime (Casper, 1978:80).

Although the offenders displayed a variety of different emotions with respect to their experiences, they were nearly unanimous in denying basic criminality. To see how white-collar offenders justify and excuse their crimes, we turn to their accounts. The small number of cases rules out the use of any elaborate classification techniques. Nonetheless, it is useful to group offenders by offense when presenting their interpretations.

Antitrust Violators

Four of the offenders have been convicted of antitrust violations, all in the same case involving the building and contracting industry. Four major themes characterized their accounts. First, antitrust offenders focused on the everyday character and historical continuity of their offenses.

> It was a way of doing business before we even got into the business. So it was like why do you brush your teeth in the morning or something.... It was part of the everyday.... It was a method of survival.

The offenders argued that they were merely following established and necessary industry practices. These practices were presented as being necessary for the well-being of the industry as a whole, not to mention their own companies. Further, they argued that cooperation among competitors was either allowed or actively promoted by the government in other industries and professions.

The second theme emphasized by the offenders was the characterization of their actions as blameless. They admitted talking to competitors and admitted submitting intentionally noncompetitive bids. However, they presented these practices as being done not for the purpose of rigging prices nor to make exorbitant profits. Rather, the everyday practices of the industry required them to occasionally submit bids on projects they really did not want to have. To avoid the effort and expense of preparing full-fledged bids, they would call a competitor to get a price to use. Such a situation might arise, for example, when a company already had enough work for the time being, but was asked by a valued customer to submit a bid anyway.

> All you want to do is show a bid, so that in some cases it was for as small a reason as getting your deposit back on the plans and specs. So you just simply

> have no interest in getting the job and just call to see if you can find someone to give you a price to use, so that you didn't have to go through the expense of an entire bid preparation. Now that is looked on very unfavorably, and it is a technical violation, but it was strictly an opportunity to keep you name in front of a desired customer. Or you may find yourself in a situation where somebody is doing work for a customer, has done work for many, many years and is totally acceptable, totally fair. There is no problem. But suddenly they (the customer) get an idea that they ought to have a few tentative figures, and you're called in, and you are in a moral dilemma. There's really no reason for you to attempt to compete in the circumstance. And so there was a way to back out.

Managed in this way, an action that appears on the surface to be a straightforward and conscious violation of antitrust regulations becomes merely a harmless business practice that happens to be a "technical violation." The offender can then refer to his personal history to verify his claim that, despite technical violations, he is in reality a law-abiding person. In the words of one offender, "Having been in the business for 33 years, you don't just automatically become a criminal overnight."

Third, offenders were very critical of the motives and tactics of prosecutors. Prosecutors were accused of being motivated solely by the opportunity for personal advancement presented by winning a big case. Further, they were accused of employing prosecution selectively and using tactics that allowed the most culpable offenders to go free. The Department of Justice was painted as using antitrust prosecutions for political purposes.

The fourth theme emphasized by the antitrust offenders involved a comparison between their crimes and the crimes of street criminals. Antitrust offenses differ in their mechanics from street crimes in that they are not committed in one place and at one time. Rather, they are spatially and temporally diffuse and are intermingled with legitimate behavior. In addition, the victims of antitrust offenses tend not to be identifiable individuals, as is the case with most street crimes. These characteristics are used by antitrust violators to contrast their own behavior with that of common stereotypes of criminality. Real crimes are pictured as discrete events that have beginnings and ends and involve individuals who directly and purposely victimize someone else in a particular place and a particular time.

> It certainly wasn't a premeditated type of thing in our cases as far as I can see.... To me it's different than ________ and I sitting down and we plan, well, we're going to rob this bank tomorrow and premeditatedly go in there.... That wasn't the case at all.... It wasn't like sitting down and planning I'm going to rob this bank type of thing.... It was just a common everyday way of doing business and surviving.

A consistent thread running through all of the interviews was the necessity for antitrust-like practices, given the realities of the business world. Offenders seemed to define the situation in such a manner that two sets of rules could be seen to apply. On the one hand, there are the legislatively determined rules—laws—which govern how one is to conduct one's business affairs. On the other hand, there is a higher set of rules based on the concepts of profit and survival, which are taken to define what it means to be in business in a capitalistic society. These rules do not just regulate behavior; rather, they constitute or create the behavior in question. If one is not trying to make a profit or tying to keep one's business going, then one is not really "in business." Following Searle (1969:33–41), the former type of rule can be called a regulative rule and the latter type a constitutive rule. In certain situations, one may have to violate a regulative rule in order to conform to the more basic constitutive rule of the activity in which one is engaged.

This point can best be illustrated through the use of an analogy involving competitive games. Trying to win is a constitutive rule of competitive games in the sense that if one is not trying to win, one is not really playing the game. In competitive games, situations may arise where a player deliberately breaks the rules even though he knows or expects he will be caught. In the game of basketball, for example, a player may deliberately foul an opponent to prevent him from making a sure basket. In this instance, one would understand that the fouler was trying to win by gambling that the opponent would not make the free throws. The player violates the rule against fouling in order to follow the higher rule of trying to win.

Trying to make a profit or survive in business can be thought of as a constitutive rule of capitalist economies. The laws that govern *how* one is allowed to make a profit are regulative rules, which can understandably be subordinated to the rules of trying to survive and profit. From the offender's point of view, he is doing what businessmen in our society are supposed to do—that is, stay in business and make a profit. Thus, an individual who violates society's laws or regulations in certain situations may actually conceive of himself as thereby acting more in accord with the central ethos of his society than if he had been a strict observer of its law. One might suggest, following Denzin (1977), that for businessmen in the building and contracting industry, and informal structure exists below the articulated legal structure, one which frequently supersedes the legal structure. The informal structure may define as moral and "legal" certain actions that the formal legal structure defines as immoral and "illegal."

Tax Violators

Six of the offenders interviewed were convicted of income tax violations. Like antitrust violators, tax violators can rely upon the complexity of the tax laws and an historical tradition in which cheating on taxes is not really criminal. Tax offenders would claim that everybody cheats somehow on their taxes and present themselves as victims of an unlucky break, because they got caught.

> Everybody cheats on their income tax, 95% of the people. Even if it's for ten dollars it's the same principle. I didn't cheat. I just didn't know how to report it.

The widespread belief that cheating on taxes is endemic helps to lend credence to the offender's claim to have been singled out and to be no more guilty than most people.

Tax offenders were more likely to have acted as individuals rather than as part of a group and, as a result, were more prone to account for their offenses by referring to them as either mistakes or the product of special circumstances. Violations were presented as simple errors which resulted from ignorance and poor recordkeeping. Deliberate intention to steal from the government for personal benefit was denied.

> I didn't take the money. I have no bank account to show for all this money, where all this money is at that I was supposed to have. They never found the money, ever. There is no Swiss bank account, believe me.
>
> My records were strictly one big mess. That's all it was. If only I had an accountant, this wouldn't even of happened. No way in God's creation would this ever have happened.

Other offenders would justify their actions by admitting that they were wrong while painting their motives as altruistic rather than criminal. Criminality was denied because they did not set out to deliberately cheat the government for their own personal gain. Like the antitrust offenders discussed above, one tax violator distinguished between his own crime and the crimes of real criminals.

> I'm not a criminal. That is, I'm not a criminal from the standpoint of taking a gun and doing this and that. I'm a criminal from the standpoint of making a mistake, a serious mistake.... The thing that really got me involved in it is my feeling for the employees here, certain employees that are my right hand. In order to save them a certain amount of taxes and things like that, I'd extend money to them in cash, and the money came from these sources that I took it from. You know, cash sales and things of that nature, but practically all of it was turned over to the employees, because of my feeling for them.

All of the tax violators pointed out that they had no intention of deliberately victimizing the government. None of them denied the legitimacy of the tax laws, nor did they claim that they cheated because the government is not representative of the people (Conklin, 1977:99). Rather, as a result of ignorance or for altruistic reasons, they made decisions which turned out to be criminal when viewed from the perspective of the law. While they acknowledged the technical criminality of their actions, they tried to show that what they did was not criminally motivated.

Violations of Financial Trust

Four offenders were involved in violations of financial trust. Three were bank officers who embezzled or misapplied funds, and the fourth was a union official who embezzled from a union pension fund. Perhaps because embezzlement is one crime in this sample that can be considered *mala in se,* these offenders were much more forthright about their crimes. Like the other offenders, the embezzlers would not go so far as to say "I am a criminal," but they did say "What I did was wrong, was criminal, and I knew it was." Thus, the embezzlers were unusual in that they explicitly admitted responsibility for their crimes. Two of the offenders clearly fit Cressey's scheme as persons with financial problems who used their positions to convert other people's money to their own use.

Unlike tax evasion, which can be excused by reference to the complex nature of tax regulations or antitrust violations, which can be justified as for the good of the organization as a whole, embezzlement requires deliberate action on the part of the offender and is almost inevitably committed for personal reasons. The crime of embezzlement, therefore, cannot be accounted for by using the same techniques that tax violators or antitrust violators do. The act itself can only be explained by showing that one was under extraordinary circumstances which explain one's uncharacteristic behavior. Three of the offenders referred explicitly to extraordinary circumstances and presented the offense as an aberration in their life history. For example, one offender described his situation in this manner:

> As a kid, I never even—you know kids will sometimes shoplift from the dime store—I never even did that. I had never stolen a thing in my life and that was what was so unbelievable about the whole thing, but there were some psychological and personal questions that I wasn't dealing with very well. I wasn't terribly happily married. I was married to a very strong-willed woman and it just wasn't working out.

The offender in this instance goes on to explain how, in an effort to impress his wife, he lived beyond his means and fell into debt.

A structural characteristic of embezzlement also helps the offender demonstrate his essential lack of criminality. Embezzlement is integrated into ordinary occupational routines. The illegal action does not stand out clearly against the surrounding set of legal actions. Rather, there is a high degree of surface correspondence between legal and illegal behavior. To maintain this correspondence, the offender must exercise some restraint when committing his crime. The embezzler must be discrete in his stealing; he cannot take all of the money available to him without at the same time revealing the crime. Once expose, the offender can point to this restraint on his part as evidence that he is not really a criminal. That is, he can compare what happened with what could have happened in order to show how much more serious the offense could have been if he was really a criminal at heart.

> What I could have done if I had truly had a devious criminal mind and perhaps if I had been a little smarter—and I am not saying that with any degree of pride or any degree of modesty whatever, [as] it's being smarter in a bad, an evil way—I could have pulled this off on a grander scale and I might still be doing it.

Even though the offender is forthright about admitting his guilt, he makes a distinction between himself and someone with a truly "devious criminal mind."

Contrary to Cressey's (1953:57–66) findings, none of the embezzlers claimed that their offenses were justified because they were underpaid or badly treated by their employers. Rather, attention was focused on the unusual circumstances surrounding the offense and its atypical character when compared to the rest of the offender's life. This strategy is for the most part determined by the mechanics and organizational format of the offense itself. Embezzlement occurs within the organization but not for the organization. It cannot be committed accidentally or out of ignorance. It can be accounted for only by showing that the actor "was not himself" at the time of the offense or was under such extraordinary circumstances that embezzlement was an understandable response to an unfortunate situation. This may explain the finding that embezzlers tend to produce accounts that are viewed as more sufficient by the justice system than those produced by other offenders (Rothman and Gandossy, 1982). The only plausible option open to a convicted embezzler trying to explain his offense is to admit responsibility while justifying the action, an approach that apparently strikes a responsive chord with judges.

Fraud and False Statements

Ten offenders were convicted of some form of fraud or false statements charge. Unlike embezzlers, tax violators, or antitrust violators, these offenders were much more likely to deny committing any crime at all. Seven of the ten claimed that they, personally, were innocent of any crime, although each admitted that fraud had occurred. Typically, they claimed to have been set up by associates and to have been wrongfully convicted by the U.S. Attorney handling the case. One might call this the scapegoat strategy. Rather than admitting technical wrongdoing and then justifying or excusing it, the offender attempts to paint himself as a victim by shifting the blame entirely to another party. Prosecutors were presented as being either ignorant or politically motivated.

The outright denial of any crime whatsoever is unusual compared to the other types of offenders studied here. It may result from the nature of the crime of fraud. By definition, fraud involves a conscious attempt on the part of one or more persons to mislead others. While it is theoretically possible to accidentally violate the antitrust and tax laws, or to violate them for altruistic reasons, it is difficult to imagine how one could accidentally mislead someone else for his or her own good. Furthermore, in many instances, fraud is an aggressively acquisitive crime. The offender develops a scheme to bilk other people out of money or property, and does this not because of some personal problem but because the scheme is an easy way to get rich. Stock swindles, fraudulent loan scams, and so on are often so large and complicated that they cannot possibly be excused as foolish and desperate solutions to personal problems. Thus, those involved in large-scale frauds do not have the option open to most embezzlers of presenting themselves as persons responding defensively to difficult personal circumstances.

Furthermore, because fraud involves a deliberate attempt to mislead another, the offender who fails to remove himself from the scheme runs the risk of being shown to have a guilty mind. That is, he is shown to possess the most essential element of modern conceptions of criminality: an intent to harm another. His inner self would in this case be exposed as something other than what it has been presented as, and all of his previous actions would be subject to reinterpretation in light of this new perspective. For this reason, defrauders are most prone to denying any crime at all. The cooperative and conspiratorial nature of many fraudulent schemes makes it possible to put the blame on someone else and to present oneself as a scapegoat. Typically, this is done by claiming to have been duped by others.

Two illustrations of this strategy are presented below.

> I figured I wasn't guilty, so it wouldn't be that hard to disprove it, until, as I say, I went to court and all of a sudden they start bringing in these guys out of the woodwork implicating me that I never saw. Lot of it could be proved that I never saw.

> Inwardly, I personally felt that the only crime that I committed was not telling on these guys. Not that I deliberately, intentionally committed a crime against the system. My only crime was that I should have had the guts to tell on these guys, what they were doing, rather than putting up with it and then trying to gradually get out of the system without hurting them or without them thinking I was going to snitch on them.

Of the three offenders who admitted committing crimes, two acted alone and the third acted with only one other person. Their accounts were similar to others presented earlier and tended to focus on either the harmless nature of their violations or on the unusual circumstances that drove them to commit their crimes. One claimed that his violations were only technical and that no one besides himself had been harmed.

> First of all, no money was stolen or anything of that nature. The bank didn't lose any money.... What I did was a technical violation. I made a mistake. There's no question about that, but the bank lost no money.

Another offender who directly admitted his guilt was involved in a check-kiting scheme. In a manner similar to embezzlers, he argued that his actions were motivated by exceptional circumstances.

> I was faced with the choice of all of a sudden, and I mean now, closing the doors or doing something else to keep that business open.... I'm not going to tell you that this wouldn't have happened if I'd had time to think it over, because I think it probably would have. You're sitting there with a dying patient. You are going to try to keep him alive.

In the other fraud cases more individuals were involved, and it was possible and perhaps necessary for each offender to claim that he was not really the culprit.

Discussion: Offenses, Accounts, and Degradation Ceremonies

The investigation, prosecution, and conviction of a white-collar offender involves him in a very undesirable status passage (Glaser and Strauss, 1971). The entire process can be viewed as a long and drawn-out degradation ceremony with the prosecutor as the chief denouncer and the offender's family and friends as the chief witnesses. The offender is moved from the status of law-abiding citizen to that of convicted felon. Accounts are developed to defeat the process of identity transformation that is the object of a degradation ceremony. They represent the offender's attempt to diminish the effect of his legal transformation and to prevent its becoming a publicly validated label. It can be suggested that the accounts developed by white-collar offenders take the forms that they do for two reasons: (1) the forms are required to defeat the success of the degradation ceremony, and (2) the specific forms used are the ones available given the mechanics, history, and organizational context of the offenses.

Three general patterns in accounting strategies stand out in the data. Each can be characterized by the subject matter on which it focuses: the event (offense), the perpetrator (offender), or the denouncer (prosecutor). These are the natural subjects of accounts in that to be successful, a degradation ceremony requires each of these elements to be presented in a particular manner (Garfinkel, 1956). If an account giver can undermine the presentation of one or more of the elements, then the effect of the ceremony can be reduced. Although there are overlaps in the accounting strategies used by the various types of offenders, and while any given offender may use more than one strategy, it appears that accounting strategies and offenses correlate.

References

Casper, Jonathan D. 1978. Criminal Courts: The Defendant's Perspective. Washington, D.C.: U.S. Department of Justice.

Conklin, John E. 1977. Illegal But Not Criminal: Business Crime in America. Englewood Cliffs, N.J.: Prentice-Hall.

Cressey, Donald. 1953. Other People's Money. New York: Free Press.

Denzin, Norman K. 1977. Notes on the criminogenic hypothesis: A case study of the American liquor industry. American Sociological Review 42:905–920.

———. 1984. On Understanding Emotion. San Francisco: Jossey-Bass.

Edelhertz, Herbert. 1970. The Nature, Impact, and Prosecution of White Collar Crime. Washington, D.C.: U.S. Government Printing Office.

Garfinkel, Harold, 1956. Conditions of successful degradation ceremonies. American Journal of Sociology 61:420–424.

Glaser, Barney G. and Anselm L. Strauss. 1971. Status Passage. Chicago: Aldine.

Katz, Jack. 1979. Legality and equality: Plea bargaining in the prosecution of white-collar crimes. Law and Society Review 13:431–460.

Rothman, Martin and Robert F. Gandossy. 1982. Sad tales: The accounts of white-collar defendants and the decision to sanction. Pacific Sociological Review 4:449–473.

Searle, John R. 1969. Speech Acts. Cambridge: Cambridge University Press.